Handbook to The Mennonite Hymnary

Handbook to
The Mennonite Hymnary

By

Lester Hostetler, B. D.

Coeditor, *The Mennonite Hymnary*

General Conference of the Mennonite Church of North America
Board of Publications
Newton, Kansas
1949

Printed by the Brethren Publishing House, Elgin, Illinois

10397

TO

ALL WHO LOVE THE HYMNS OF THE CHURCH

AND

DESIRE TO SING THEM

WITH

THE SPIRIT AND THE UNDERSTANDING

THIS BOOK

IS DEDICATED

IN

GRATITUDE AND LOVE

CONTENTS

NOTES ON THE WORDS AND MUSIC OF THE HYMNS

vii

CONTENTS

BOOK TWO

BOOK THREE

BOOK FOUR

BOOK FIVE

BOOK SIX

INDEXES

PREFACE

The aim of this book is to serve as a companion to the *Mennonite Hymnary*. It seeks to explain, as far as possible, the origin of the words and music of every hymn in the *Hymnary*.

The great lyrics of the church, contributed by every age since the days of the apostles, are a precious heritage, and a source of inspiration and power. This work is intended to foster an understanding of and love for our hymns, new and old, and to stimulate the time-honored and blessed practice of congregational singing in the church today.

The *Handbook* may be found useful as an aid (1) in the private study of hymns or their use in family devotions; (2) in selecting suitable hymns for the many and varied services of public worship; (3) in preparing special music services or hymn sings where such occasions are planned to improve the singing in the church; (4) for study groups in hymnology in churches and schools. The historical development of hymnology may be followed in the brief "Introduction to Our Hymns and Tunes."

The author has endeavored to make the work as comprehensive as possible without overburdening the reader with too many details. Many hymns have interesting stories connected with their origin and use while others, equally valuable, were just written, without drama or incident, the poet scarcely knowing how or why, except that the Inner Voice spoke. The apocryphal tales which have been circulated concerning some hymns have been studiously avoided. The aim has been to include only such material as seems to bear genuine marks of authenticity. The bibliography of "Principal Works Consulted," found elsewhere in the book, indicates the main sources.

The original versions of translated hymns are not always readily available and for that reason they are reproduced in the *Handbook*. Translated hymns are usually selections from a much larger number of stanzas and it is often instructive to be able to study the whole structure of the original work.

Acknowledgements. I wish to acknowledge valuable help received from the following and to express hereby my gratitude to them: to Dr. Robert McCutchan, author of *Our Hymnody*, who generously responded to my request for information on a dozen or more hymns on which I had no data; to Dr. Henry Wilder Foote, of Harvard University, author of *Three Centuries of American Hymnody,* for biographical material on several hymn writers, and the use of books from his private library; to

PREFACE

Dr. Reginald McAll, Executive Secretary of the Hymn Society of America for helpful material; to Dr. Ruth Messenger, Archivist for the Hymn Society of America, who furnished nearly all the Latin originals, and the Italian original of Savonarola's hymn, and information concerning these hymns; to Dr. Armin Heussler, author of a forth-coming handbook to the *Evangelical hymnal,* for material on several of the chorales; to Wm. Runyan of the Hope Publishing Company, and to Dr. John Trowbridge of the Bible Institute of Los Angeles, for information concerning several of the gospel songs; to Dr. Cornelius Krahn who made the rich hymnic treasures of the Mennonite Historical Library at Bethel College available to me; to the late Rev. C. E. Krehbiel who loaned me material from his private library for this work but did not live to see its completion; to B. Bargen for help in preparing the manuscript for publication; to Mrs. Beatrice Buller for reading the manuscripts and proofs of the German chorales; to my wife, Charity Steiner Hostetler, who read all the manuscripts and proofs and whose constant interest and assistance were indispensable; and to others, too numerous to mention, who in any way facilitated the completion of the work.

The book, written during spare moments of a busy pastorate, is sent forth with the prayer that, in spite of errors and imperfections, it may inspire all who use it to sing with greater devotion the praises of Him who loved us and redeemed us.

Lester Hostetler

The Parsonage
Bethel College Mennonite Church
North Newton, Kansas
January 20, 1949

x

EXPLANATORY NOTES

In the interest of brevity and to avoid repetition, certain recurring words are abbreviated:

Hymnary is used for *Mennonite Hymnary.*

c. (circa) means approximate date.

Tr. is prefixed to the names of all translators.

Anon. (anonymous) means without any name acknowledged, as that of author or composer.

The word "Number" has been omitted: thus Hymn 22 means Hymn No. 22.

Cf. means compare. (Latin: confer).

The original texts of German hymns found throughout the *Handbook,* especially in the section of Chorales, Book IV, are the versions used in one or more of the following works: *Gesangbuch mit Noten,* (Berne, Ind., 1890); *Gesangbuch der Mennoniten,* (Canadian, 1942); *The Handbook to the Lutheran Hymnal,* (Concordia Pub. House, 1942); *Gesangbuch zum gottesdienstlichen und häuslichen Gebrauch in Evangelischen Mennoniten-Gemeinden,* (Konferenz der süddeutschen Mennoniten zu Ludwigshafen a. Rh. 1910); and Knapp, *Evangelischer Liederschatz.* Many variations occur in the texts as found in these versions, the explanation of which would require a much greater knowledge of German hymnody than the author possesses. An effort has been made to bring the spelling into conformity with the modern German practice of omitting the "h" where it was formerly used with the "th"; the use of "ss" instead of "sz"; and printing the initial letter of the pronouns referring to Deity, in lower case rather than with capitals.

AN INTRODUCTION TO OUR HYMNS AND TUNES

With Illustrations From the *Hymnary*

1. Definition of a Hymn. St. Augustine, 354-430, gave a definition of a hymn, which has been widely accepted:

A hymn is the praise of God by singing. A hymn is a song embodying the praise of God. If there is merely praise but not praise of God it is not a hymn. If there be praise, and praise of God, but not sung, it is not a hymn. For it to be a hymn, it is needful, therefore, for it to have three things—praise, praise of God, and these sung.

A recent definition, accepted by the Hymn Society of America, is that of the late Carl F. Price:

A Christian hymn is a lyric poem, reverently and devotionally conceived, which is designed to be sung and which expresses the worshiper's attitude toward God, or God's purposes, in human life.

L. F. Benson, America's foremost hymnologist, defines a hymn in these simple words:

The Christian hymn . . . is a form of words appropriate to be sung or chanted in public devotions.

A hymn is to be sung *by a congregation*. Its message must be simple, not subtle. It must read well and sing well. In modern usage, the hymn is not limited to the praise of God but includes other moods of worship such as resignation and consecration.

2. The Beginnings of Christian Song. Hymn singing has always been associated with Christian worship. Jesus and the Twelve sang a hymn, presumably a portion of the *Hallel* (Ps. 115-118), after the Supper was ended. Paul and Silas sang hymns, "songs of the night," during the midnight hours of their imprisonment in Philippi. The great Apostle recognized the value of song when he exhorted the churches thus:

> Be filled with the Spirit; speaking to yourselves in psalms and hymns and spiritual songs, singing and making melody in your heart to the Lord. Eph. 5:18, 19.
>
> Let the word of Christ dwell in you richly in all wisdom; teaching and admonishing one another in psalms and hymns and spiritual songs, singing with grace in your hearts to the Lord. Col. 3:16.
>
> I will sing with the spirit, and I will sing with the understanding also. I Cor. 14:15.

The Jewish converts who at first composed the church had a rich heritage of song in the Book of Psalms. This was their hymnbook, used in the Temple worship and in the home and probably also in the synagogue services. The use of the Psalms, carried over from the Jewish service, forms to this day an important element in Christian worship.

Besides the Psalms, the early church sang the nativity lyrics that adorn the first two chapters of the Gospel of Luke. It also made extensive use of *Hallelujah* as a part of the people's praise, adding, in the course of time, the *Gloria Patri,* the *Sanctus,* the *Te Deum,* and other canticles.

The nativity hymns in Luke, five in all, are extensively used in Roman Catholic and Anglican services.

Ave Maria (Hail Mary). 1:28-29, 42-45. The salutation of Gabriel and of Elizabeth.

Magnificat. "My soul doth magnify the Lord . ." 1:46-55. Hymn of the Virgin Mary.

Benedictus. "Blessed be the Lord God of Israel . . ." 1:68-79. Song of Zacharias.

Nunc Dimittis. "Lord, now lettest Thou thy servant depart in peace." 2:29-32. Song of Simeon.

Gloria in excelsis. "Glory to God in the highest . . ." 2:14. Song of the Angels. Used as a part of the Roman mass and often found in Protestant hymns, e.g., "Angels we have heard on high" (82).

Beginnings of Christian Song in the Hymnary

Psalms. Book Five. (575-600).

Gloria Patri (606-7).

Ter Sanctus (Trisagion) "Holy, holy, holy" (601-2).

Te Deum. "Holy God we praise Thy name" (519). A metrical translation of an ancient version.

3. Hymns of the Eastern Church: Greek and Syriac. The ancient Eastern Church developed a rich hymnody, rising steadily in the fourth century until it reached its culmination in the eighth and ninth centuries. Since it employed the Greek and Syriac languages, its hymnic treasures remained almost completely hidden and unknown to the English speaking churches for many centuries. It is only in recent years, through the efforts of scholars like John Mason Neale and Edward Caswall that some of the Eastern hymns have been translated and made available for modern use. Eastern hymns are characterized by an objective, dignified, contemplation of God. Except when confessing sin and unworthiness, they contain nothing of the subjective feelings of the worshipper such as is found in many modern hymns. Though there is very little in the *Hymnary* from the Eastern Church, our collection is enriched by the inclusion of a small number of hymns from this source.

Greek Hymns in the Hymnary

Clement of Alexandria, 170-220, "Shepherd of tender youth" (398)
Candle Lighting Hymn, "O gladsome light" (34)
Synesius, c. 375-430, "Lord Jesus, think on me" (196)
St. Germanus, 634-734, "A great and mighty wonder" (526)
St. John of Damascus, 8th century, "The day of resurrection" (115)
    "Come, ye faithful, raise the strain" (113)
St. Stephen the Sabaite, 725-94, "Art thou weary, heavy-laden" (143)
Candle Lighting Hynm, "Darkening night, the land doth" (32)

4. Hymns of the Western Church: Latin. Two great names are associated with the music of the Western Church: Ambrose, c. 340-97, known as the "Father of Hymnody in the Western Church;" and Gregory the Great, 540-604, the missionary-minded pope, and reformer of church music.

Ambrose, Bishop of Milan, not only composed hymns and music but stimulated others to do the same. Under his leadership there developed a large body of church music based upon four scales, which came to be known as Ambrosian Chant. Although widely known as a scholar, theologian, and preacher, Ambrose's most lasting influence was upon the music of the church. None of his hymns are found in our collection.

Gregory the Great, two centuries later, carried forward the work of Ambrose. He added four more scales or modes to the Ambrosian system, thus giving to the repertory of church music more definiteness and variety. The music that developed during the papacy of Gregory came to be known as Gregorian Chant, or plainsong, or plainchant. It is "plain" because unadorned, unharmonized and unmeasured. Its rhythm is the free rhythm of speech, the beats falling irregularly. The Gregorian Chant remained the music of the church for a thousand years and forms the basis of all Roman Catholic music today. Some of these chants were adapted by Luther for congregational singing, and set to words in the vernacular of the people. A few of the tunes, usually in a form scarcely recognizable from the original, are used today in Protestant hymnals, as for instance, the tune "Hamburg." Some of the music in the Amish church services is traceable to the Gregorian Chant.

The singing in the medieval church was liturgical in character and confined to the clergy and trained choirs. This was its weakness. The laity was not expected to sing, neither were they able to do so. Congregational singing, so important in our worship today, had for centuries been unknown in the Roman Catholic Church. Reform was inevitable and it came in due time.

While only remnants of the music survive, many hymns from the Western Church have been translated from the Latin and a few choice ones have found their way into the *Hymnary*.

Latin Hymns in the Hymnary

Prudentius, 348-c. 413, "Bethlehem, of noblest cities" (88)
Gregory the Great, 540-604, "Father, we praise Thee" (24)
Anonymous, 6th or 7th century, "Christ is made the sure" (277)
 "Joy dawned again on Easterday" (415)
Theodulph of Orleans, 9th century, "All glory, laud" (100)
Bernard of Clairvaux, 1091-1153, "Jesus the very thought" (155)
 "O sacred Head, now wounded" (539)
Bernard of Cluny, 12th century, "Jerusalem, the golden" (262-3)
Anonymous, 12th century, "O come, O come, Emmanuel" (67)
Savonarola, 1452-98 (Italian), "Jesus, Refuge of the weary" (536)
Anonymous, 17th-18th centuries, "O come, all ye faithful" (80)
 "The year is gone beyond recall" (382)

5. Hymns of the Bohemian Brethren. The followers of John Hus who came to be known as the Bohemian Brethren, and later as the Moravians, were the first Protestant group to introduce congregational singing into their worship. They also published the first Protestant hymnbooks, one in 1501 and another in 1505, containing 89 and 400 hymns, respectively, in their native Bohemian tongue. Their efforts to introduce congregational singing were sternly opposed by the Roman hierarchy. The Council of Constance condemned Hus to be burned at the stake and warned his successor, Jacob of Misi, to cease the singing of hymns in the churches. It decreed:

> If laymen are forbidden to preach and interpret the Scriptures, much more are they forbidden to sing publicly in the churches.

As a result of their persecution, the Brethren in 1508 sent out messengers to search for true Christian people into whose communion they might apply for admission—one to Russia, one to Greece, one to Bulgaria, and one to Palestine and Egypt. All returned unsuccessful. No such Christians had been found. They therefore remained in their own country, giving themselves assiduously to the translation and printing of the Bible.

In 1522 the Brethren sent two messengers to Luther to greet him and ask his advice. Luther became interested in them and welcomed their fellowship. He was impressed with the hymnbook the Brethren had published, and later used some of the hymns in his own work.

Two centuries later, the Brethren, known now as the Moravians, settled on Count Zinzendorf's estates in Saxony, spreading rapidly from thence into other countries in Europe and to the United States. One of England's foremost hymn writers and hymnologists, James Montgomery, was an adherent to their faith.

Bohemian Brethren and Moravian Hymns in the Hymnary

Michael Weisse, 1480-1534, "Christ, the Lord, is ris'n again" (544)
Tunes: "Mit Freuden Zart" (512), "Ravenshaw" (292)
von Zinzendorf, Nickolaus L., 1700-60, "Jesus, still lead on" (574)
von Zinzendorf, Christian R., 1724-62, "Man of sorrows" (537)
Henriette Luise von Hayn, 1724-82, "I am Jesus' little lamb" (430)
James Montgomery, 1771-1854, "Hail to the Lord's Anointed" (65)
       "Angels from the realms of glory" (81)
       "Go to dark Gethsemane" (107) and many others

6. Hymns of the Reformation: the German Chorales. The movement toward congregational singing, inaugurated by the Bohemian Brethren, was soon to be merged into the greater Reformation movement. Luther's influence on the worship and music of the church was revolutionary. For a thousand years the laymen had had no part in church song. Congregational singing was unknown. Ambrosian music had at first been introduced for congregational use but it became more and more liturgical, thrusting the laity into the background. The Gregorian Chant which followed was never intended for use except by the priests and trained choirs. The followers of Hus pioneered in congregational singing; but it was Luther and his followers who brought it into full fruition.

Luther was a born music lover and a musician of adequate training. Moreover he possessed a remarkable gift for writing hymns in clear thought to bring the Word of God home to the hearts of the common people. He and his followers put songs on the lips of the German people and they sang themselves into the Reformation. So effective were these songs that his enemies in the Roman church declared that "Luther's songs have damned more souls than all his books and speeches."

INTRODUCTION

Chorales. The word "chorale" ("choral" in German) refers to the hymn tunes of Lutheran Protestantism, though in common usage the term includes the words associated with the tunes. The melodies had much to do with the popularity of the songs. They came from various sources. Many of them were original compositions by Luther and others; some were borrowed from the hymn books of the Bohemian Brethren; a considerable number were adaptations of plainsongs used in the Catholic Church; still others were adopted from beloved folksongs. Luther was an eclectic in his choice of music. He used any tune from any source that suited his purpose. Many thousands of chorales came into existence in Germany during his time and the two centuries that followed. The hundreds still in use represent the best in church music today. They are characterized by a plain melody, a strong harmony, and a stately rhythm; all of which adapts them well for effective congregational singing.

The chorales at first did not have the regular rhythms that they later took on. The steady progression of even notes, invariable in Bach's day, had come only gradually into use. Some of the recent hymnbooks, in the interest of greater variety of rhythm, are returning to the original "rhythmic chorales."

Though *unison* singing has been widely practiced and is advocated today by some good authorities in church music, Luther encouraged *part* singing. In his first Preface to the *Geystliches Gesangbücklin,* 1525, he wrote:

> These songs have been set in four parts, for no other reason than because I wished to provide our young people (who both will and ought to be instructed in music and other sciences) with something whereby they might rid themselves of amorous and carnal songs, and in their stead learn something wholesome, and so apply themselves to what is good with pleasure, as becometh the young.

The period of the German chorales may be said to have begun with Luther, 1483-1546, and ended two centuries later with J. S. Bach, 1685-1750. Bach brought the chorale tunes to their highest perfection, using many of them in his larger choral works. He composed about 30 original chorale melodies, wrote reharmonizations for approximately 400, and composed many chorale preludes for the organ which are in wide use today.

The German hymns and chorale tunes, used constantly in the home and school, as well as in the church, have been of great importance in our Mennonite worship in the past. They constitute the main body of material in all our German collections of hymns. In an effort to preserve and emphasize this rich heritage, there was incorporated into the *Hymnary,* a special section, Book III, made up exclusively of chorales.

German Chorales in the Hymnary

16th Century

Martin Luther, 1483-1546, "A mighty fortress is our God" (549)
    "From heaven above to earth I come" (527)
    "Out of the depths I cry to Thee" (531-2)
Nicolaus Selnecker, 1532-92, "Now cheer our hearts" (557)
Philipp Nicolai, 1556-1608, "Wake, awake, for night is flying" (522)
    "How brightly shines the Morning Star" (529)

17th Century

(1)—Period of The Thirty Years War—1618-48
Johann Heerman, 1585-1647, "Ah, dearest Jesus" (534)
Josua Stegman, 1588-1632, "Abide with us, our Savior" (559)
Matthäus von Löwenstern, 1594-1648, "Lord of our life" (278)
Georg Weissel, 1590-1635, "Lift up your heads" (523)
Heinrich Albert, 1604-51, "God who madest earth" (573)
Ernst Homburg, 1605-81, "Christ, the life of all the living" (535)
Michael Schirmer, 1606-73, "O Holy Spirit, enter in" (546)
Paul Gerhardt, 1607-76, "O sacred Head, now wounded" (539)
    and others
Gerhard Tersteegen, 1697-1769, "God reveals His presence" (506)
    "O power of love, all else transcending" (517)
(2)—Later 17th Century
Johann Franck, 1618-77, "Deck thyself, my soul," (552)
Tobias Clausnitzer, 1619-84, "Liebster Jesu, wir sind hier" (553)
Georg Neumark, 1621-81, "He who would be in God" (571)
Johann Scheffler, 1624-77, "I am the Lord, O hear my voice" (565)
Joachim Neander, 1650-80, "Heaven and earth, the sea" (510)

18th Century

Johann Mentzer, 1658-1734, "O that I had a thousand voices" (509)
Erdmann Neumeister, 1671-1756, "Sinners Jesus will receive" (466)
Benjamin Schmolck, 1672-1737, "My Jesus, as Thou wilt" (250)
Philipp F. Hiller, 1699-1769, "O Son of God, we wait for" (524)
    "What mercy and divine compassion" (562)
Christian F. Gellert, 1715-69, "How great, almighty is Thy" (516)
Johann Sebastian Bach, 1685-1750. The life of the great musician
    marks the close of the German Chorale period and
    for that reason his name is placed here. None of
    Bach's original chorale melodies are found in the
    Hymnary but use is made of a number of his har-
    monizations. See 539, 545, 556, 557, 564, 566.

7. Hymns of the Reformation: The Metrical Psalms. While
the German people, under the leadership of Luther, were singing chorales set to original religious poems, a large section of Protestantism,
under the influence of John Calvin, confined itself to the singing of

Psalms. To the French reformer, now preaching at Geneva, hymns were "man-made," whereas the psalms were the inspired word of God and the only proper vehicle for the praise of God. Calvin, unlike Luther, was not a musician, and at first permitted only unison singing, unaccompanied. Part singing and instrumental accompaniment seemed to savor of the frivolous and worldly, an opinion which Calvin, however, was soon to modify. For two hundred years the Calvinistic churches on the Continent and in Britain were influenced in their worship song by the strict views of Calvin, limiting themselves to the metrical psalms and scriptural paraphrases. The German people in the meantime produced a rich treasury of original religious lyrics, contributed by some of their best poets.

Psalter Tunes and Metrical Psalms in the Hymnary

Genevan Psalter Tunes, 1551.
        O Seigneur (19)
        Old 134th (128, 132, 616)
        Rendez À Dieu (306)
        Old 124th (354)
        Old 100th (594))
Scottish Psalter, 1650.
        Book Five (575 to 600) with a few exceptions
New Version, 1696, Tate and Brady.
        "Through all the changing scenes of life" (583)
        "As pants the hart for cooling streams" (586)
        "O come, loud anthems let us sing" (18)
        "While shepherds watched their flocks by night" (73-4)

8. Psalm Versions. The use of the psalms in singing, first on the Continent, then in England and Scotland, and later in America, brought forth many metrical versions of the psalter, the principal ones being the following:

a. *The Genevan Psalter,* begun 1539, published complete in 1562. It was made at the request of John Calvin by Clément Morot, court poet of France, and Theodore Beza, a French scholar. It became the psalm book for the Reformation churches on the continent, and is spoken of as the most famous book of praise the Christian Church ever produced. It was issued in at least one thousand editions and translated into a number of tongues. Some of the original tunes are still in use, e.g., "Old Hundredth."

b. *The Anglo-Genevan Psalter,* Geneva, 1556. This was used by John Knox, the Scottish reformer, and his followers who fled the persecutions of "Bloody Mary," and formed a congregation at Geneva. The book incorporated some of the Sternhold and Hopkins versions which were in use in England, and added others.

c. *The Old Version*, Sternhold and Hopkins, completed in 1562. Used in England for 134 years. It is entitled, *The Whole Book of Psalmes*, but came to be known as the "Old Version."

d. *The Bay Psalm Book*, Boston, 1640. This was the first book printed in English-speaking America. It was made to obtain greater literalness to the Hebrew orginal than was found in the versions then in use. The book reigned supreme among the English churches in New England for over a century. Seventy editions of it were printed in America, the last in 1773. Eighteen editions appeared in England, and twenty-two in Scotland. There were no tunes given it until 1698, then only 13, with the air in the bass.

e. *The Scottish Psalter*, completed 1650. Special mention is made of this version of the Psalms because it is the source of nearly all the selections of metrical psalms which constitute Book Five of the *Hymnary*. The number of versions and editions of psalms which appeared on the Continent and in England were numerous and confusing, each claiming its own special merits. Finally, in the interests of better literary diction and greater unity in singing in the Scottish Presbyterian churches, the General Assembly authorized a new version. The result, after many years work, was the famous *Scottish Psalter* of 1650 which remains the standard work in Scotland today.

There is a certain "dignified crudeness" in some of the literary expressions but the psalms have long been learned in this version and have become an important part of the religious training and experience of millions of English speaking people, especially in Scotland.

The Scottish Psalter first appeared with words only. There were no notes and no suggestions for melodies. The succeeding one hundred years were a time of confusion. The tunes used were few in number, such as the leaders had learned from various sources, and passed on to succeeding generations by rote. The time came when better singing and better tunes were demanded and gradually the psalter appeared with tunes. Early tune versions put the melody invariably in the tenor. The latest edition, printed in 1929, by the Oxford Press, contains the best Psalm tunes which had gradually come into use, many of them arranged with "Faux-bourdon" (wherein the congregation sings one or more verses to the melody while the choir supplies the harmony), and "Descant" (a second melody over that of the tune).

f. *The New Version*, Tate and Brady, London, 1696. This version gradually supplanted the *Old Version* of Sternhold and Hopkins, and held its place in the worship of the church for 150 years. It was adopted, in 1789, by the Protestant Episcopal Church in the United States and bound with the prayer book of that Communion.

The above versions are only a few of the large number of psalters that were published by the Calvinistic churches on the Continent, in

Great Britain, and in America. The metrical psalms were designed for the singing church. They were intended to restore song to the people in their worship, serving in this respect a similar purpose to the chorales in Germany.

Some of the psalm books were published without music, some with the melody only, and others in four-part harmony. The statement is frequently made that Calvinistic Protestantism approved only unison singing. The appearance of numerous books, complete with four voice parts, points to the contrary. It is true that Calvin at first encouraged unison singing only, regarding harmony more in the nature of amusement than the worship of God; but upon observing the effectiveness of singing in Germany, he soon changed his views and became more liberal in this respect.

9. English Hymnody. The youthful, courageous Isaac Watts, 1674-1748, an ardent dissenter, pioneered the movement which resulted in a flood of hymns and hymnbooks in the English churches. Watts was not satisfied with the psalm singing of his time, which by now had become formal and lifeless. Parts of the psalter, he pointed out, were obviously not written in the spirit of the Gospel. "By keeping too close to David," he wrote in one of his Prefaces, "the vail of Moses is thrown over our hearts." Watts removed that "vail," Christianizing the psalms and composing during his lifetime more than 600 original hymns, expressing in the language of the time, the thoughts of the worshippers. Through his influence, his age, the 18th century, became the first age of hymn singing in England.

John and Charles Wesley, following Watts, made enormous use of hymn singing in their evangelistic work, giving the movement for congregational singing a powerful impetus. Charles is said to have composed over 6,000 hymns.

From the Wesleys onward through the 19th century, the hymn writers in England became numerous. The restrictive shackles of psalm singing had been broken and the creative urge to worship in new forms resulted in a vast number of original religious lyrics and the publication of hundreds of hymnbooks. The development can be summarized here only in outline form.

English Hymnody in the Hymnary

Early—17th Century

Henry Wotton, 1568-1639, "How happy is he" (208)
George Herbert, 1593-1633, "Teach me, my God and King" (226)
John Milton, 1608-74, "Let us with a gladsome mind" (64)
"How lovely are Thy dwellings fair" (592)

INTRODUCTION

Thomas Ken, 1637-1711, "Awake, my soul, and with the sun" (25)
"All praise to Thee, my God, this night" (33)
"Praise God, from whom all blessings flow" (618)

Joseph Addison, 1672-1719, "The spacious firmament on high" (50)
"How are Thy servants blest" (338)

18th Century

1. Two Independents:

Isaac Watts, 1674-1748, "Father of English Hymnody"
"When I survey the wondrous cross" (105-6)
"Joy to the world! the Lord is come" (70)
"God is the refuge of His saints" (257)
and many others

Philip Doddridge, 1702-51, "How gentle God's commands" (56)
(and 128, 167, 218, 383, 465)

2. The Wesleys and their Associates:

John Wesley, 1703-91, translations (170, 226, 246, 508, 558)

Charles Wesley, 1707-88, "Bard of Methodism"
"Come, Thou long-expected Jesus" (69)
"Jesus, Lover of my soul" (158-9)
"Love divine, all loves excelling" (178-9)
and many others

William Williams, 1717-91, "Sweet Singer of Wales"
"Guide me, O Thou great Jehovah" (160)

John Cennick, 1718-55, "Lo, He comes, with clouds" (130)
"Jesus, my all, to heav'n is gone" (468)

- Thomas Olivers, 1725-99, "The God of Abraham praise" (14)

Edward Perronet, 1726-92, "All hail the power of Jesus" (3, 4, 5)

3. A Calvinistic Antagonist of Wesley

Augustus Toplady, 1740-78, "Rock of Ages, cleft for me" (148)

4. The Olney Hymnists:

John Newton, 1725-1807, "Glorious things of thee" (274)
"Safely through another week" (284)
"Amazing grace! how sweet the sound" (463)

William Cowper, 1731-1800, "God moves in a mysterious way" (60)
"O for a closer walk with God" (197)
"There is a fountain filled with blood" (492)

5. Others—18th Century:

Anne Steele, 1716-78, "Father, whate'er of earthly bliss" (251)

Joseph Grigg, c. 1720-68, "Behold a Stranger at the door" (141)
"Jesus, and shall it ever be" (192)

Robert Robinson, 1735-90, "Mighty God, while angels bless" (46)
"Come, Thou fount of every blessing" (189)

John Fawcett, 1740-1817, "Blest be the tie that binds" (41)
"Lord, dismiss us with Thy blessing" (45)

xxii

INTRODUCTION

Modern English—19th Century

1. Earliest:

Thomas Kelly, 1769-1854, "Look, ye saints, the sight" (119)
"Hark, ten thousand harps and voices" (123)
"On the mountain top appearing" (336)
James Montgomery, 1771-1854, "Prayer is the soul's sincere" (184)
"Angels, from the realms of glory" (81)
"In the hour of trial" (195) and many others
Robert Grant, 1779-1838, "O worship the King" (7)
"Savior, when, in dust to Thee" (145)
Reginald Heber, 1783-1826, "Holy, holy, holy" (1)
"Bread of the world in mercy broken" (304)
"From Greenland's icy mountains" (333)
Charlotte Elliott, 1789-1871, "Just as I am, without one plea" (458)
"O holy Savior, Friend unseen" (233)
"My God and Father, while I stray" (245)
Henry Milman, 1791-1868, "Ride on, ride on in majesty" (101)
John Bowring, 1792-1872, "In the Cross of Christ I glory" (110)
"Watchman, tell us of the night" (66)
"God is love; His mercy brightens" (55)
Henry F. Lyte, 1793-1847, "Abide with me" (40)

2. The Oxford Group:

John Keble, 1792-1866, "New every morning is the love" (22)
"Sun of my soul, Thou Savior dear" (30)
Matthew Bridges, 1800-94, "Crown Him with many crowns" (118)
John Henry Newman, 1801-90, "Lead, kindly light" (162-3)
Richard Trench, 1807-86, "Lord, what a change within" (183)
Frederick Faber, 1814-63, "There's a wideness in God's mercy" (58)
"Faith of our fathers" (154)
Mrs. Cecil Frances Alexander, 1823-95, "There is a green hill" (104)
(Translators of Latin and Greek Hymns)
John Chandler, 1806-76, "Christ is our Cornerstone" (9)
"What star is this" (87)
Edward Caswall, 1814-78, "Bethlehem, of noblest cities" (88)
"Jesus, the very thought of Thee" (155)
John M. Neale, 1818-66, "O come, O come Emmanuel" (67)
"All glory, laud, and honor" (100)

3. Translators of German Hymns:

Catherine Winkworth, 1829-78, "Wake, awake for night" (522)
and 24 others
Frances E. Cox, 1812-97, "Sing praise to God" (512)
"Jesus lives" (543)
Jane L. Borthwick, 1813-97, "Be still, my soul" (54)
"My Jesus, as Thou wilt" (250)
"Jesus, still lead on" (574)
Sarah Borthwick Findlater, 1823-1907, "O happy home" (358)

4. Other Hymnists—19th Century:

Christopher Wordsworth, 1807-85, "Gracious Spirit," (174)
    "O day of rest and gladness" (285)
Horatius Bonar, 1808-89, "I heard the voice of Jesus say" (142)
    "I lay my sins on Jesus" (444)
    "When the weary, seeking rest" (203) and others
Alfred Tennyson, 1809-92, "Strong Son of God" (149)
    "Sunset and evening star" (265)
    "Ring out, wild bells" (379)
Henry Alford, 1810-71, "We walk by faith, and not by sight" (152)
    "Come, ye thankful people, come" (377)
W. W. How, 1823-97, "O Jesus, Thou art standing" (144)
    "For all the saints who from their labor rest" (317)
    "O Word of God Incarnate" (289) and others
Godfrey Thring, 1823-1903, "From the Eastern mountains" (89)
    "Thou to whom the sick and dying" (370)
Adelaide Proctor, 1825-64, "My God, I thank Thee" (177)
    "I do not ask, O Lord" (471)
Edward H. Bickersteth, 1825-1906, "Peace, perfect peace" (256)
John Ellerton, 1826-93, "Savior, again to Thy dear name" (43)
    "Now the laborer's task is o'er" (315)
    "Throned upon the awful tree" (109) and others
S. Baring-Gould, 1834-1924, "Now the day is over" (29)
    "Onward, Christian soldiers" (225)
Edwin Hatch, 1835-89, "Breathe on me, breath of God" (135)
Frances R. Havergal, 1836-79, "Take my life, and let it be" (215)
    "Lord, speak to me, that I may speak" (296)
    "Thou art coming, O my Savior" (126) and others
Samuel Stone, 1839-1900, "The Church's one foundation" (273)
George Matheson, 1842-1906, "O love that wilt not let me go" (175)

Recent English Hymns

Rudyard Kipling, 1865-1936, "Father in heav'n" (401)
Stopford A. Brooke, 1832-1916, "Let the whole creation cry" (49)
John Oxenham, 1852-1941, "In Christ there is no East" (320)
    "Peace in our time, O Lord" (357)
Percy Dearmer, 1867-1936, "Remember all God's children" (436)
Richard Roberts, 1874–, "For them whose ways" (166)
Laurence Housman, 1865–, "Father Eternal" (354)

10. American Hymns. The English speaking colonists who settled in America during the 17th century continued the psalm singing traditions of their forebears in England. The practice prevailed in their churches for two hundred years. The first book printed by them was the *Bay Psalm Book*, in 1640, at Cambridge, Massachusetts. It contained no original hymns. The singing of psalms, and later of hymns borrowed from England made up nearly the entire repertory of church music until the middle of the 19th century.

On the other hand, the German speaking colonists, including the Mennonites, had brought with them the hymn books of the Lutheran tradition and continued the use of the German chorales in their worship. The two streams of hymnody, English psalms and German chorales, went their independent courses for two centuries, scarcely influencing each other.

In the meantime there was very little original hymnody produced in America, with the exception of the work of the Wesleys during their brief experiment in Georgia, and the composition of certain hymns and tunes by the German people of Pennsylvania, which have remained, until recently, in manuscript form. Timothy Dwight's hymn on the church, "I love Thy Kingdom, Lord" (275) is probably the earliest American hymn still in use.

After the middle of the 19th century the number of hymn writers became large and their works came into increasing use, some choice examples finding their way into English hymnbooks. America's original contribution to Christian hymnody has not been only the Gospel Songs represented by the writings of Fanny Crosby, but the more permanent works of Whittier, George W. Doane, Hosmer, Samuel Longfellow, Washington Gladden, S. F. Smith, and many others. Our musical contributions have been less conspicuous, but the tunes of Mason are coming into their own again and many of them will doubtless survive for a long time, as will also those of Bradbury, Hastings, and others.

The tendency today in American hymnbooks is to unite the best in English and German traditions. The *Hymnary* illustrates this trend. It makes large use of the English hymns while at the same time preserving a considerable body of the German chorales. In keeping with this trend, the recent hymnbooks of the Episcopal, Presbyterian, Methodist and other churches of English origin, incorporate some of the German chorale tunes and in some cases the translations of the words. The hymn books of our time have become the channels through which flow the rich contributions to the stream of Christian hymnody from Christian people of all times and places.

American Hymns in the Hymnary

Early American

Timothy Dwight, 1752-1817, "I love Thy kingdom, Lord" (275)
Thomas Hastings, 1784-1872, "Hail to the brightness" (332)
Henry Ware, Jr., 1794-1843, "Happy the home when God" (361)
Wm. B. Tappan, 1794-1849, " 'Tis midnight; and on Olive's (103)
Francis Scott Key, 1779-1843, "Lord, with glowing heart" (511)
George W. Doane, 1799-1859, "Softly now the light of day" (36)

INTRODUCTION

19th Century

Leonard Bacon, 1802-81, "O God, beneath Thy guiding hand" (367)
John G. Whittier, 1807-92, "Dear Lord and Father" (181)
Ray Palmer, 1808-87, "My faith looks up to Thee" (150)
S. F. Smith, 1808-95, "The morning light is breaking" (324)
Oliver W. Holmes, 1809-94, "Lord of all being, throned afar" (53)
E. H. Sears, 1810-76, "It came upon the midnight clear" (75)
W. H. Burleigh, 1812-71, "Lead us, O Father, in the paths" (164)
Harriet Beecher Stowe, 1811-96, "Still, still with Thee" (23)
Sylvanus Phelps, 1816-95, "Savior, Thy dying love" (220)
Arthur C. Coxe, 1818-96, "O where are kings and empires" (276)
Elizabeth Payson Prentiss, 1818-78, "More love to Thee" (472)
Edward Hopper, 1818-88, "Jesus, Savior, pilot me" (161)
George Duffield, Jr., 1818-88, "Stand up, stand up for Jesus" (193)
Samuel Longfellow, 1819-92, "Holy Spirit, Truth divine" (136)
James Russell Lowell, 1819-91, "Once to every man" (346)
Anna Warner, 1820-1915, "We would see Jesus" (201)
John H. Hopkins, 1820-91, "We three kings of Orient are" (90)
Eliza Scudder, 1821-96, "Thou Grace Divine, encircling all" (57)
Samuel Johnson, 1822-82, "Father, in Thy mysterious" (188)
Jeremiah E. Rankin, 1828-1904, "God be with you" (365)
Joseph H. Gilmore, 1834-1918, "He leadeth me" (478)
Phillips Brooks, 1835-93, "O little town of Bethlehem" (84)

Recent American Hymns

Washington Gladden, 1836-1918, "O Master, let me walk" (223)
Frederick L. Hosmer, 1840-1929, "Not always on the mount" (98)
Mary Lathbury, 1841-1913, "Day is dying in the west" (31)
       "Break Thou the bread of Life" (288)
Frank Mason North, 1850-1936, "Where cross the crowded" (222)
M. Woolsey Stryker, 1851-1929, "Almighty Lord, with one" (390)
Henry van Dyke, 1852-1933, "Joyful, joyful, we adore Thee" (10)
Louis F. Benson, 1855-1930, "O sing a song of Bethlehem" (92)
Maltbie D. Babcock, 1858-1901, "This is my Father's world" (48)
Katherine Lee Bates, 1859-1929, "O beautiful for spacious" (343)
Milton S. Littlefield, 1864-1934, "O Son of man, thou" (373)
Jay T. Stocking, 1870-1936, "O Master Workman" (93)
Wm. M. Vories, 1880–, "Let there be light, Lord God" (353)
Harry Webb Farrington, 1880-1931, "I know not how that" (99)
W. Russel Bowie, 1882–, "Lord, through changing days" (402)
Howard Arnold Walter, 1884-1918, "I would be true" (207)
Earl Marlatt, 1892–, " 'Are ye able,' said the Master" (392)

11. Gospel Songs. During the latter part of the 19th century there came into use, both in the United States and in England, a type of religious song known as the Gospel Song. Less dignified than the chorales or the English hymns, these songs made a popular appeal and were widely used in prayer meetings and revivals.

The words of the typical Gospel Song are usually simple and easily remembered and concern themselves largely with the individual's salvation. The personal pronouns "I" and "my" predominate. The tunes are rhythmic and catchy and always have a refrain added. Their harmonies are largely built on the simple tonic, dominant, and subdominant chords. The masses of the people readily learned to sing these tunes and experienced a thrill in singing them which the use of the more stately and solid hymns failed to effect.

The great bulk of these songs were produced in America during the latter half of the 19th century and were found extremely useful in large mass meetings. The evangelistic work of Moody and Sankey during the 1870's, 1880's, and 1890's brought the Gospel Songs into special prominence and the Salvation Army has made them known in nearly every country in the world. Collections of Gospel Songs sold by the millions of copies and every denomination was affected, to a greater or lesser extent, by this type of singing.

Since the standard of music and words in the Gospel Songs is considerably below that which prevails in our best hymnals as well as in secular music and literature taught in the public schools, churches should seriously consider the ultimate effect of their too frequent use. It is a fallacy to assert that the people will respond to nothing better. Gospel Songs have a legitimate place, particularly in special services and revivals, but they leave much to be desired in the total work and worship of the church. Neither the music nor the words possess the strength and dignity entirely adequate for the worshipful praise of the Eternal.

The principal names associated with Gospel Songs are the following:

Authors. Fanny J. Crosby, Philip P. Bliss, Robert Lowry, Katherine Hankey, E. A. Hoffman, and many others. Most of the words, though not all, were written by Americans during the latter part of the nineteenth century. Miss Crosby was by far the most prolific of them all and many of her works are found in all modern hymnals of denominations that use this type of music. In Germany, Ernst Gebhardt became the leader of the gospel song movement, composing words and music, publishing numerous song books, and serving as song leader in great revival meetings.

Music. William B. Bradbury, Robert Lowry, W. H. Doane, Philip Philips, James McGranahan, George C. Stebbins, P. P. Bliss, D. W. Towner, Wm. J. Kirkpatrick, and others.

Song Leaders. P. P. Bliss, Ira Sankey, James McGranahan, George C. Stebbins, Charles Alexander, Homer Rodeheaver.

It should be noted that there is no absolute line of demarcation between hymns and some of the Gospel Songs. Some of the numbers in the Gospel Songs section of the *Hymnary* might well be classified as hymns, e.g., Nos. 441, 444, 447, 458, 463, 468, 470, 471, 472, and 492. Either words or music meet the generally accepted standards of a hymn.

12. Women Hymn Writers.

There have been no outstanding women composers of church tunes but some of our finest lyrics have been contributed by women, as the following list from the *Hymnary* will show:

German

Katharina von Schlegel, b. 1697, "Be still, my soul" (54)
Henriette Luise von Hayn, 1724-82, "Weil ich Jesu" (430)

English

Anne Steele, 1716-78, "Father, whate'er of earthly bliss" (251)
Marianne Nunn, 1778-1847, "One is kind above all others" (447)
Harriet Auber, 1773-1862, "Our blest Redeemer" (138)
Dorothy Ann Thrupp, 1779-1847, "Saviour, like a gentle (395)
Charlotte Elliott, 1789-1871, "Just as I am, without one plea" (458)
Margaret Mackay, 1802-87, "Asleep in Jesus" (314)
Sarah Flower Adams, 1805-48, "Nearer my God, to Thee" (202)
Jemima Luke, 1813-1906, "I think when I read that sweet" (427)
Anne Brontë, 1820-49, "Believe not those who say" (210)
Cecil Frances Alexander, 1823-95, "There is a green hill" (104)
Adelaide Proctor, 1825-64, "My God, I thank Thee" (177)
Elizabeth Clephane, 1830-69, "Beneath the Cross of Jesus" (112)
Anna L. Coghill, 1836-1907, "Work, for the night is coming" (221)
Frances R. Havergal, 1836-79, "Take my life and let it be" (215)
Dorothy Blomfield, 1858-1932, "O perfect love, all human" (312)
Jessie Adams, 1863—, "I feel the winds of God today" (391)

(Translators)

Frances Cox, 1812-97, "Sing praise to God" (512)
Jane L. Borthwick, 1813-97, "Be still my soul" (54)
Sarah Borthwick Findlater, 1823-1907, "O happy home" (358)
Catherine Winkworth, 1829-78. Numerous hymns. Foremost translator of German chorales.

American

Harriet Beecher Stowe, 1811-96, "Still, still with Thee" (23)
Elizabeth Prentiss, 1818-78, "More love to Thee, O Christ" (472)
Susan Warner, 1819-85, "Jesus bids us shine" (420)
Anna B. Warner, 1820-1915, "Jesus loves me! this I know" (428)
Fanny Crosby, 1820-1915, "Rescue the perishing" (497)
  and many others
Eliza Scudder, 1821-96, "Thou Grace Divine, encircling all" (57)

Phoebe Cary, 1824-71, "One sweetly solemn thought" (264)
Katherine Hankey, 1834-1911, "I love to tell the story" (493)
Mary Ann Thomson, 1834-1923, "O Zion, haste" (328)
Annie Sherwood Hawks, 1835-1918, "I need Thee every hour" (187)
Mary Lathbury, 1841-1913, "Day is dying in the west" (31)
"Break Thou the bread of life" (288)
Katherine Lee Bates, 1859-1929, "O beautiful for spacious" (343)

13. Mennonite Hymnody. Mennonites have made many contributions to society through their religious life and practices, but we have produced no important hymnody of our own. Throughout the four hundred years of our existence as a church, we have been a singing people, in times of persecution as well as in times of peace. Great emphasis has always been laid upon the importance of congregational singing in our worship services. Since the beginning of the 19th century the Mennonites of various branches, in America alone, have published over fifty hymnbooks. But an examination of these hymnbooks shows that we are heavily indebted to others. Instead of producing original hymns and tunes, we have borrowed, with minor exceptions, our entire repertory from other denominations. The wealth of verse and music produced by German and English writers throughout the centuries has been found to serve our needs adequately and well.

The churches in Europe used hymnbooks compiled from Lutheran and Reformed sources. Upon coming to the United States and Canada, they gradually adopted English and American hymns and in some sections of the church, the Gospel Songs came into wide use.

Our German collections of hymns have, until recently, been uniformly on a higher level, both as to music and poetry, than the collections used after the change was made to the English language. During the transition from the German to the English language, many churches, in their choice of their hymnbooks, sacrificed the fine chorales which had been a part of their religious heritage. This was due partly to the revivalistic influences of the times and partly to the fact that there were no good translations available of the German hymns which earlier were in use. The situation is gradually correcting itself. We are re-evaluating our hymnody, sifting the wheat from the chaff, and bringing back into our worship the rich treasure of song which had been used in the past. The *Mennonite Hymnary* is an effort in this direction.

14. The Antecedents of the Mennonite Hymnary. The story of the hymn books antedating the *Hymnary* may be briefly summarized by listing the following books:

1565. The first German Mennonite hymn book was published

in 1565 or 1566 (date omitted from title), entitled, *Ein schön Gesangbüchlein Geistlicher Lieder, zusammengetragen aus dem A. und N. Testament durch fromme Christen und Liebhaber Gottes, welcher hiefür etliche getrucht sei gewesen, aber noch viel dazu gethan, welche nie im Truck aussgangen seindt, in welchen auch ein recht Leben und Fundament dez rechten Christlichen Glaubens gelehrt wirdt. Coloss. 3.*

A second edition, 1570-1583, (date not given), adds to the above title the following:

Jetzo von neuem widerum übersehn, an vielen Orten gebessert und mit etlichen newen Liedern vermehret. Coloss. 3.

Of the 133 hymns in the book, 9 had been in use among other churches. Many of the others were by Mennonite authors, among them Johann Schütz, Thomas Ducker, Gerhard Siebenakker von Sttart, and Heinrich Krenen von Breidtbock. Many of the hymns are of a controversial nature and have no literary value; for example, this on infant baptism:

Die Schrift sagt nicht von Kindertaufe
Davon hab ich nicht gelesen.
Wer noch Gottes Wort getauft soll sein
Der musz glaubig wesen.

Es ist ein Bad der Wiedergeburt,
Ein Bund eines guten Gewissens
Ein' Verneurung des heiliges Geistes
Davon keine Kinder wissen.

Most of the hymns were set to secular melodies popular at the time. Very little of this first hymnal survives.

1570—*Ausbund, Das ist: Etliche schöne Christliche Lieder, wie sie in dem Gefängnis zu Passau in dem Schlosz von den Schweizer—Brüdern und von andern rechtglaubigen Christen hin und her gedichtet worden.*

At least twelve editions have been printed in Europe, the last one in Basel, 1838. Its use was confined to the South Germans and Swiss Mennonites. Reprinted in America and still in use by the Amish, the *Ausbund* has the distinction of being the oldest hymn book officially in use by any church in America.

1780—*Geistreiches Gesangbuch zur öffentlichen und besonderen Erbauung der Mennonitischen Gemeinde in und vor der Stadt Danzig.*

The book has had long use in Danzig. A revised edition appeared in 1908.

1803—*Das Kleine Geistliche Harfe der Kinder Zions.* Germantown, Pa. The first Mennonite hymnbook printed in America. It was the official hymnbook of the Franconia Conference of Mennonites of which John H. Oberholzer, founder of the General Conference of Mennonites, was a member. Seven editions were printed, the last in Elkhart, Ind., 1904.

1804—*Unpartheyisches Gesangbuch,* Lancaster, Pa. The official hymnbook of the Lancaster Mennonite Conference for almost a century. Fourteen reprints were made, the last in 1923 for the Amish.

1843—*Gesangbuch in welchem eine Sammlung geistreiche Lieder befindlich.* 9th ed. Elbing. The hymnbook of the Prussian Mennonites. It was taken by the Prussians to Russia where it was republished in Odessa, 1844.

1856—*Gesangbuch zum Gottesdienstlichen und haeuslichen Gebrauch in Evangelischen Mennoniten Gemeinden.* Worms.
Published by the churches of Baden and the Palatinate. The hymnal committee was fortunate in securing the assistance of the eminent German hymnologist, Albert Knapp. The book contains 600 hymns and an appendix of prayers. A book of melodies was also provided. This collection holds an important place in Mennonite hymnody. It was reprinted in Danzig, 1873, for use by the Danzig Mennonites, and in Philadelphia, 1873, for use in the General Conference of Mennonites. The excellent qualities of the more recent *Gesangbuch mit Noten* may be traced, in considerable measure, to this work.

1869—*Gesangbuch in Mennoniten Gemeinden für Kirche und Haus.* Published for the churches of West Prussia, this work went through at least four editions, the fourth in 1901. The book was republished in Danzig, 1873.

1873—*Gesangbuch zum Gottesdienstlichen und häuslichen Gebrauch in Mennoniten Gemeinden.* Philadelphia. Ordered by the sixth General Conference of Mennonites held at Wadsworth, Ohio. The main body of the book is the same as that published in Worms, 1856, but with the appendix of prayers omitted, and an appendix of 22 hymns added, the latter the contribution of the Mennonites in Pennsylvania. The book was intended to form a closer bond of union between the Mennonites in the East and those west of the Mississippi.

1890—*Gesangbuch mit Noten. Herausgegeben von der allgemeinen Conferenz der Mennoniten von Nord America.* Berne, Ind. The book passed through 15 editions, the last in 1936. A noteworthy collection of hymns and tunes that met with wide approval in the General Conference churches.

1894—*Mennonite Hymnal, A Blending of Many Voices.* Berne, Ind. An A. S. Barnes publication adopted, practically unchanged, by the General Conference of Mennonites. Our first official English hymnal, though many collections from other sources were finding wide use in our churches. The book has nothing of distinctiveness or distinction.

1927—*The Mennonite Hymn Book.* Berne, Ind. Published by the General Conference of Mennonites. Compiled and edited by a committee appointed by the Conference. The book was more satisfactory than the *Mennonite Hymnal* of 1894, but never became very popular. Total sales of three editions were less than 5,000 copies.

1940—*The Mennonite Hymnary.* Published by the General Conference of Mennonites of North America, Board of Publication, Mennonite Publication Office, Newton, Kansas, 1940. Now in its sixth edition.

15. The Translation of Hymns. A word may be in order concerning the translation of hymns. It is difficult to transfer the color and feeling of one language to another. For this reason many people who know the German hymns by heart have a sense of disappointment when they read them in an English version. In some instances a translation is inferior to the original but this is not necessarily the case. It is well to remember that nearly all of us read the Bible only in a translation, yet never doubt the literary quality of the English King James Version or the German Version of Luther. The hymn, "Ich weiss einen Strom," is superior as poetry, and in its religious feeling, to the English original, "O have you not heard of that beautiful stream," though the former is a translation of the latter. The reason is that Gebhardt, the translator, was a poet in his own right. Good translations are possible if the translator has poetic ability of a high order, and if he translates into his native tongue. Catherine Winkworth was the foremost translator of German hymns into English and Ernst Gebhardt performed a similar role in translating English and American hymns into German. Had either tried to do the work of the other, the results would in all probability have lacked true color and correct idiomatic and poetic expression.

16. Church Unity in the Hymnbook. The unity of the Christian Church is expressed nowhere more eloquently than in the hymns we sing. Every modern hymnal, regardless of the denominational interest it represents, reaches across the ages to gather its treasures from sources new and old; it knows nothing of the external barriers which divide Christians into denominations, but makes use of the hymns of widely divergent Christian groups. The *Mennonite Hymnary* is no exception. Here are found hymns from the early church, East and West, translated from the Greek and Latin fathers. Others, like Savonarola's hymn, come from the Middle Ages. Many are chorales from the land of Luther, or metrical psalms from the Calvinistic reformers. A substantial body of our hymnody stems from the Anglican Church, while some of our best hymns are from sturdy independents like Watts and Doddridge, and still others breathe the evangelistic fervor of Wesley, Cowper, and Newton. The Quakers too have made their contribution as well as certain Roman Catholics and Unitarians. In no aspect of our church life do we attain so nearly to ecumenicity as in our worship in song. Christians may differ widely in their religious views but they are able to unite as one body in singing their songs of praise.

The following classification of hymns by denominations is far from exhaustive. It is intended merely to suggest the wealth of material drawn from many denominations, listing only representative writers together with a representative hymn. The index of authors may be consulted for a complete list of hymns written by each author.

a. *Anglican (Church of England)*
   Addison, Joseph, "The spacious firmament on high" (50)
   Alexander, Mrs. Cecil (Irish), "Jesus calls us, o'er the tumult" (140)
   Baring-Gould, Sabine, "Onward, Christian soldiers" (225)
   Bode, John E., "O Jesus, I have promised" (212)
   Croly, George (Irish), "Spirit of God, descend" (133)
   Dix, William C., "As with gladness men of old" (530)
   Ellerton, John, "Savior, again to Thy dear name we raise" (43)
   Elliott, Charlotte, "Just as I am, without one plea" (458)
   Grant, Robert (Scotch), "O worship the King" (7)
   Hankey, Katherine, "I love to tell the story" (493)
   Havergal, Frances, "Take my life, and let it be" (215)
   Heber, Reginald, "Holy, holy, holy" (1)
   How, W. W., "O Jesus, Thou art standing" (144)
   Lyte, Henry F., "Abide with me" (40)
   Newton, John, "Glorious things of thee are spoken" (274)
   Pierpoint, Folliott S., "For the beauty of the earth" (51)
   Stone, Samuel, "The Church's one foundation" (273)
   Toplady, Augustus, "Rock of ages" (148)
   Wordsworth, Christopher, "O day of rest and gladness" (285)
b. *Baptist*
   Fawcett, John (Eng.), "Blest be the tie that binds" (41)
   Gilmore, Henry, "He leadeth me" (478)
   Hearn, Marianne (Eng.), "Just as I am, thine own to be" (393)
   Hawks, Annie S., "I need Thee every hour" (187)

Gerhardt, Paul, "Commit thou all thy griefs" (558)
Luther, Martin, "A mighty fortress is our God" (549)
Nicolai, Philipp, "Wake, awake for night is flying" (522)
Rinkart, M. Martin, "Now thank we all our God" (514)
Schmolck, Benjamin, "My Jesus, as Thou wilt" (250)
Spitta, Karl Johann Philipp, "O happy home, where Thou" (358)

i. *Methodist*

Crosby, Fanny, "Jesus, keep me near the cross" (490)
Farrington, Harry Webb, "I know not how that Bethlehem's" (99)
Gebhardt, Ernst (German), "Ich weiss einen Strom" (232)
Lathbury, Mary, "Break Thou the bread of life" (288)
Marlatt, Earl, "Are ye able, said the Master" (392)
Nicholson, James, "Lord Jesus, I long to be perfectly whole" (469)
North, Frank Mason, "Where cross the crowded ways of life" (222)
Owens, Priscilla, "We have heard the joyful sound" (334)
Wesley, Charles, "Jesus, lover of my soul" (158-9)
Williams, William (Welsh), "Guide me, O Thou great" (160)

j. *Presbyterian*

Babcock, Maltbie, "This is my Father's world" (48)
Benson, Louis, "O sing a song of Bethlehem" (92)
Clephane, Elizabeth (Scotch)), "Beneath the cross of Jesus" (112)
Duffield, George, "Stand up, stand up for Jesus" (193)
Hastings, Thomas, "Hail to the brightness" (332)
Hopper, Edward, "Jesus, Savior, pilot me" (161)
Mackay, Wm. P., "We praise Thee, O God" (437)
Merrill, Wm. P., "Rise up, O men of God" (230)
Matheson, George (Scotch), "O Love that wilt not let me go" (175)
Prentiss, Elizabeth, "More love to Thee, O Christ" (472)
Small, James G. (Scotch), "I've found a Friend" (445)
Van Dyke, Henry, "Joyful, joyful, we adore Thee" (10)

k. *Quaker*

Adams, Jessie, "I feel the winds of God today" (391)
Barton, Bernard, "Walk in the light" (209)
Whittier, John G., "Dear Lord and Father of mankind" (181)

l. *Unitarian*

Adams, Sarah F., "Nearer, my God, to Thee" (202)
Bennett, S. F., "In the sweet bye and bye" (504)
Bowring, John, "In the cross of Christ I glory" (110)
Holmes, Oliver W., "Lord of all being, throned afar" (53)
Hosmer, Frederick L., "Father, to Thee we look in all our" (249)
Johnson, Samuel, "Father, in Thy mysterious presence" (188)
Longfellow, Samuel, "I look to Thee in every need" (244)
Martineau, James, "Thy way is in the deep, O Lord" (242)
Parker, Theodore, "O Thou great Friend to all the sons" (224)
Sears, Edmund, "It came upon a midnight clear" (75)
Ware, Henry, Jr., "Great God, the followers of Thy Son" (13)

INTRODUCTION

m. *No Church Affiliation*

Bates, Katherine Lee, "O beautiful, for spacious skies" (343)

Vories, Wm. M., "Let there be light, Lord God of hosts" (353)

17. Hymn Meters. Meter (English, *Metre*) refers to the rhythmic element in poetry:

a. the number of lines in a stanza.
b. the number of syllables in a line.
c. the arrangement of accented and unaccented syllables.

The figures attached to the tune names in the *Hymnary* indicate the number of lines in a stanza and the number of syllables in a line, e. g., 8.7.8.7. means that the hymn has four lines in each stanza, the first line being made up of 8 syllables, the second of 7 syllables, the third of 8 syllables, and the last of 7 syllables. The figures are placed there to facilitate the fitting of tunes to hymns, a responsibility which is left now-a-days largely to hymnbook editors.

A given tune may be used with any variety of hymns provided the latter have the same meter as the tune. Likewise a given hymn may be sung to any tune that fits its meter, e.g., "Come, Thou Almighty King," set to the tune, "Italian Hymn," as both have the meter pattern 6.6.4.6.6.6.4. This is also the meter of "My country 'tis of thee" set to "America." Hence the words and tunes of these hymns may be interchanged. As a matter of fact, "Come Thou Almighty King" was originally used with the tune "America." The practice of using alternate tunes is less common now than formerly and must be done with care for while the meters may be suited, the words and tune may be incompatible otherwise.

Meter Names

A few meters have specific names. These, with their abbreviations are as follows:

Short Meter (S.M.) 6.6.8.6

e.g.	Blest be the tie that binds	(6)
	Our hearts in Christian love:	(6)
	The fellowship of kindred minds	(8)
	Is like to that above.	(6)

Short Meter Double (S.M.D.) is used for a tune in which the quatrain is repeated, e.g. "Terra Beata" (48), set to the words "This is my Father's world."

Common Meter (C. M.), also called Ballad Meter, consists of four lines of 8.6.8.6. syllables, e.g.

In Christ there is no East or West	(8)
In Him no South or North;	(6)
But one great fellowship of love	(8)
Throughout the whole wide earth.	(6)

Nearly all the metrical psalms appeared in this meter.

Common Meter Double (C.M.D.) is employed when two Common Meter quatrains are used to form one stanza, e.g.,

"It came upon a midnight clear." (75)

Long Meter (L.M.) consists of a four line stanza in which each line is of eight syllables, e.g.,

Praise God, from whom all blessings flow; (8)
Praise Him, all creatures here below; (8)
Praise Him above, ye heavenly host; (8)
Praise Father, Son, and Holy Ghost. (8)

Long Meter Double (L.M.D.), not often used, consists of a stanza of eight lines, each line of eight syllables, e.g.,

"The spacious firmament on high." (50)

Accentuation

In setting a hymn to music it is important that the accented syllables of the poetry fall on the accented beats of the musical bars. Try singing "Softly and tenderly Jesus is calling" (456) to the tune "Ich weiss einen Strom" (232). The meter is the same in each case—11.7.11.7.—with refrain—but the words and tune are obviously not suited to each other because of differences in accentuation.

18. Hymn Tunes. a. What is a good tune? b. Importance of tunes. c. Composers of tunes. d. Sources of tunes. e. Tune names.

a. What is a good tune? The quality of a tune must be judged by its definite and restricted use. It is to be sung by a congregation of people, the majority of whom have had only limited musical training, and without benefit of rehearsal. The tune must therefore be judged by such questions as these: Is it singable? Are the parts within easy pitch range of the voices? Is it free from difficult intervals or modulations into other keys? Is it interesting? Does it create a worshipful atmosphere? Does the mood of the tune fit the mood and thought of the words?

b. The importance of tunes. The tune is of great importance to the success of the hymn. Our "best hymns" owe their popularity in many instances, to the tune with which they are associated. On the other hand many excellent hymns remain unused because the tunes given them are too difficult or too uninteresting. It is the tune that creates the mood of worship and charges the words with emotion so that their message is carried forth with feeling and power.

c. Composers of tunes. The story of the development of the hymn tune begins with the worship song in the Temple at Jerusalem where the psalms were sung antiphonally by priests and people accompanied

by harps and trumpets. Little is known of these tunes or their composers. This early Christian music would doubtless sound strange to
modern ears.

The important names in the roll of church musicians, from the early
centuries to the present time, include the following:

Italian—Ambrose, 4th century
Gregory the Great, 6th century
Palestrina, 1525-94
French—Louis Bourgeois, *c.* 1510-?
German—Luther, 1483-1546; Nicolai, 1556-1608; Hassler, 1564-1612;
Praetorius, 1571-1621; Crüger, 1598-1662; Bach, 1685-1750.
English—Tallis, 1510-85; Gibbons, 1583-1625; Croft, 1678-1727;
Gauntlett, 1805-76; Monk, 1823-99; Dykes, 1823-76; S. Wesley,
1810-76; Barnby, 1838-96; Stainer, 1840-1901; Sullivan, 1842-
1900.
American—L. Mason, 1792-1872; Bradbury, 1816-68; Hastings, 1784-
1872; Stebbins, 1846-1945.

The great composers, besides Bach, whose names are found in church
hymnals are: Haydn, Beethoven, Handel, Mozart, Mendelssohn, Gounod, and Sibelius.

The above is only a partial list of composers of good church music.
Among their works is a corpus of fine hymn tunes far greater than has
been utilized by the church so far. For years to come, compilers of hymn
books will have a vast reservoir of excellent tunes, old yet new, to draw
from.

d. Sources of tunes. An examination of the origin of church tunes
shows a variety of sources. Many tunes were especially written for
the words to which they are set; others are adaptations from early
medieval chants; still others, as for example, the "Passion Chorale" and
"Londonderry Air", were folk tunes originally used with secular words.
Some of our best tunes are adaptations of melodies from larger musical
works, as for example, "Hymn to Joy" (10) from Beethoven's *Ninth
Symphony;* "Finlandia" (54), from a tone poem by Sibelius; and
"Seymour" (36), from Weber's opera, *Oberon.*

e. Tune names. Composers usually name their tunes in order to facilitate their identification. The names given them are selected quite
arbitrarily. W. H. Havergal, prolific composer of church music, named
his tunes after the rivers, mountains, valleys, etc., of Palestine, e.g.
"Abana," "Ahava," "Ararat," "Baca," etc. Other tunes have been named
for the composer, e.g., "Bradbury" (395); the name of a friend, e.g.,
"Rockingham" (105); name of a city or village, e.g., "Boylston" (214);
a street, "Federal Street" (192); a cottage, "Hollingside" (159); an
event in history, "Nicaea" (1); or the central idea in the words, "Pilot"
(161).

In Germany, the usual practice has been to name the tune after the first line of the hymn to which it was originally set.

Some tunes, unfortunately, are known by more than one name, e.g., "St. Michel's" (93) and "Jerusalem, Jerusalem" (125). In a few cases the same name is given to several tunes, e.g., "Wesley" (309 and 332). This is confusing and it is highly desirable that hymnbook editors strive toward uniformity of nomenclature.

19. John Wesley's Rules for Singing. In one of John Wesley's compilations of tunes, *Sacred Melody,* the great preacher and founder of Methodism gives the following rules for singing. Some of the expressions used may provoke a smile but, as Lightwood suggests, "it would be a very good thing if these were read aloud from time to time in all churches and chapels where good congregational singing is aimed at."

   a. Learn these tunes before you learn any others; afterwards learn as many as you please.

   b. Sing them exactly as they are printed here, without altering or mending them at all; and if you have learned to sing them otherwise, unlearn it as soon as you can.

   c. Sing ALL. See that you join with the congregation as frequently as you can. Let not a slight degree of weakness or weariness hinder you. If it is a cross to you, take it up, and you will find it a blessing.

   d. Sing lustily and with a good courage. Beware of singing as if you were half dead, or half asleep; but lift up your voice with strength. Be no more afraid of your voice now, nor more ashamed of its being heard, than when you sang the songs of Satan.

   e. Sing modestly. Do not bawl, so as to be heard above or distinct from the rest of the congregation, that you may not destroy the harmony; but strive to unite your voices together, so as to make one clear melodious sound.

   f. Sing in tune. Whatever time is sung be sure to keep with it. Do not run before nor stay behind it; but attend close to the leading voices, and move therewith exactly as you can; and take care not to sing too low. This drawling way naturally steals on all who are lazy: and it is high time to drive it out from among us, and sing all our tunes just as quick as we did at first.

   g. Above all sing spiritually. Have an eye to God in every word you sing. Aim at pleasing Him more than yourself, or any other creature. In order to do this attend strictly to the sense of what you sing, and see that your heart is not carried away with the sound, but offered to God continually; so shall our singing be such as the Lord will approve of here, and regard you when He cometh in the clouds of Heaven.

BOOK I

Hymns for Worship and Praise

1. Holy, holy, holy   *Reginald Heber, 1783-1826*

A metrical paraphrase of Revelation 4:8-11. The hymn was written for use on Trinity Sunday of the Church Year but has found a wide general use as a morning hymn. It ranks high in any list of "best hymns." Some give it first place.

The author, Reginald Heber, was educated at Oxford, England, for the Anglican ministry. For sixteen years he served as rector at Hodnet, Shropshire, where most of his hymns were written. He became an eminent churchman, as well as hymn-writer, and was made bishop of Calcutta in 1822. After four years, his life came to an end suddenly at the close of a day in which he had baptized forty-two native converts. He is the author of the popular missionary hymn, "From Greenland's icy mountains" (333).

"Holy, holy, holy," was one of Alfred Tennyson's favorite hymns, and it was sung at his funeral service in Westminster Abbey, April 12, 1892.

MUSIC. The tune, NICAEA, was composed for this hymn and was so named because the text deals with the doctrine of the Trinity as expounded in the Council of Nicaea which met in the city of Nicaea in Asia Minor, 325 A.D., the first ecumenical council of the Christian Church. It convened at the call of the Emperor, Constantine, to settle the so-called "Arian controversy" concerning the nature of Christ. Arius, a presbyter of Alexandria, taught that Christ was neither divine nor human, but superangelic. After sitting from May 20 to August 25, to hear all sides of the heated debate, the council decided in favor of Athanasius, a deacon of Alexandria and chief opponent of Arius. The result was incorporated in the Nicene creed which declares that Christ

1

is "the same substance with the Father." Our hymn asserts the same doctrine: "God in Three Persons, blessed Trinity."

J. B. Dykes, 1823-76, composer of the tune, was born in Hull, England, the son of a banker. He was educated at Cambridge for the ministry but had also received a thorough training in music and became one of England's leading hymn-tune writers. For a score of years he was vicar of the Anglican church, St. Oswald's, in the city of Durham. He published sermons and other writings but is best known for his 300 hymn tunes, many of which are still in wide use. One of his most popular tunes is "Lux Benigna" which is always associated with John Henry Newman's hymn, "Lead kindly light" (162).

2. God is in His holy temple   *Anonymous*

Based on Hab. 2:20: "The Lord is in his holy temple: let all the earth keep silence before him." The hymn, whose authorship is anonymous, is a call to silence and reverence as the worshipper bows in the presence of God.

MUSIC. The origin of the popular and useful tune, AUTUMN, has been in dispute. Some books refer to it as a Spanish melody, and others have seen in the tune a reminiscence of a psalm-tune found in the *Genevan Psalter* of 1551. It is ascribed here to one, Louis von Esch, but Dr. Robert McCutchan, editor of the *Methodist Hymnal* and author of *Our Hymnody,* says: "There is no basis whatever for ascribing it to any other than Barthélémon."

Francois H. Barthélémon was born in Bordeaux, July 27, 1741, and died in London, July 20, 1808. He gave up his position as an officer in the French army to make music his profession and became a composer and distinguished violinist and conductor in England. Most of his compositions were of a secular nature. His other church pieces are "Morning Hymn" (25) and "Ballerma" (146, 585). Late in life Barthélémon joined the Swedenborgian Church. He died of paralysis at the age of 67.

3, 4, 5. All hail the power of Jesus' name
Edward Perronet, 1726-92

The original version of this hymn contained eight stanzas and first appeared in the *Gospel Magazine,* Augustus Toplady's journal, the first stanza together with the tune "Miles Lane," in November, 1779, and the remaining stanzas in April, 1780. It is one of the popular, stirring hymns of the English language, sung in England almost invariably to the tune "Miles Lane" and in America more generally to "Coronation."

2

PRAISE AND ADORATION

Edward Perronet was born in 1726 and became a vicar in the Church of England in Shoreham. Later, under the influence of John Wesley, he left the established church to become an itinerant Methodist preacher. After some years he left the Methodists and ministered to a small dissenting congregation in Canterbury, where he died in 1792.

The fourth stanza is attributed by some authorities to the Rev. John Rippon, a Baptist minister.

A missionary in India, E. P. Scott, went to visit a mountain tribe when one day he found himself surrounded with a number of wild, ferocious tribesmen, pointing their spears at him. Expecting death, he closed his eyes and sang this hymn, "All hail the power of Jesus' name," playing the tune "Miles Lane" on his violin. The music and words produced such a profound effect upon these wild tribesmen that they spared Scott's life and invited him to settle among them. For over two years, until his health failed, he worked with great success among them, and when he was compelled to return to America, they accompanied him thirty or forty miles and begged him to return. Upon regaining his health, he did return and labored with them until his death.

MUSIC. MILES LANE (No. 3) was composed by William Shrubsole, 1760-1806, especially for this hymn. He was an intimate friend of the author of the hymn. Most of his life was spent as music teacher and organist in various English churches. The tune is very effective, especially in its thrilling climax in the fourfold repetition of "Crown Him." However, due to its wide melodic range, its sustained notes, and interrupted pace, it is more difficult to sing than "Coronation."

CORONATION (No. 4) was composed by Oliver Holden. He had little formal training in music and was a carpenter by trade. He was born in Shirley, Mass., Sept. 18, 1765. After the English burned Charlestown, across the river from Boston, Holden helped in the task of rebuilding and made considerable money. Later he engaged in the real estate business, owned a music store, and all the while led choirs and singing schools. He was elected representative to the Congress. He was an influential citizen and a prominent member of the Baptist Church. However, he is remembered by posterity as the composer of this much-loved tune.

DIADEM (No. 5) is an effective tune widely used on anniversary occasions. The composer, James Ellor, an English Methodist, was born in Lancashire in 1819. He was not a professional musician, but a hatter by trade. For a time he worked as a railway employee. While still a young man, he came to America, where he worked at the hatmaking trade. For some years before his death in 1899, he was nearly blind. This tune was composed when Ellor was only 19 years old. It was written especially for this hymn and has had wide use as a choir number.

6. Ye servants of God, your Master proclaim

Charles Wesley, 1707-88

This hymn by Charles Wesley, perhaps the greatest hymnist of all ages, was No. 1 in a collection published in 1774 and entitled, *Hymns for Times of Trouble and Persecution.* The original had six stanzas and was marked, "To be sung in a tumult." The Wesleys knew the meaning of persecution and tumults. They were often attacked by godless men who used physical violence. Hoodlums were known to try to break up their meetings by blowing horns, ringing bells, or barking in front of the preacher. Sometimes cattle were driven into the congregation. The Wesleys were also opposed by the clergy and people of the established church who hated the upheavals and disturbances these men caused in the staid and stolid church life of the times. Nothing could stop the Wesleys or repress their enthusiasm. John, who once thanked God for getting together such a "congregation of drunkards, swearers, and Sabbath breakers," continued his preaching; and Charles his hymn writing. With the early apostles, the Wesleys could say, "We cannot but speak the things which we have seen and heard."

Charles Wesley, John's youngest brother, graduated from Oxford in 1729 and became a devout priest in the Anglican Church. He came to Georgia in 1735 as secretary to General Oglethorpe but after one year, he returned to England on account of failing health. The years from 1738 to 1756 were devoted whole heartedly to assisting his brother John in the great revivalistic work among the masses of the common people in England, Scotland, and Ireland. He was a prolific writer, being the author of about 6,500 hymns. Of these only a few score survive, so difficult is it to write hymns that stand the test of time. Twenty-three of his hymns, more than of any other author, are included in the *Hymnary.* Wesley, being Arminian in his theology (as opposed to the predestinarian views of Calvinism) emphasizes in his hymns the power of Christ to save to the uttermost. Others of his hymns surpass this one from the standpoint of good literature, but very few equal its spirit of adoring praise and fervid enthusiasm.

MUSIC. HANOVER is a vigorous, singable, hymn-tune which has long been associated with these words, although the tune "Lyons" (7), too, is frequently set to this hymn. It is one of the earliest examples of the English psalm-tune, as distinguished from the Genevan. The triple measure was novel and met with objection when it first appeared.

The composer, William Croft, 1678-1727, had a doctor's degree in music and was organist, for a time, in Westminster Abbey, London, where his remains lie buried. He labored hard, amidst many discouragements, to improve the music in the Church of England, and made for himself in the field of sacred music, one of the greatest names in English musical history. His tunes and anthems are widely used.

4

7. O worship the King, all glorious above

Robert Grant, 1779-1838

A simple, yet majestic hymn, based on the magnificent 104th Psalm. A careful reading of the Psalm will result in a new appreciation of this free paraphrase by Grant.

Robert Grant was born in Bombay, India. When six years old, his parents moved to London. He received his education in Oxford, was admitted to the bar, elected to Parliament in 1808, and then held various responsible government positions, climaxed in 1834 by his appointment as Governor of Bombay. He died at Delpoonie, India, where a medical school, bearing his name, was erected in his memory. Though a prominent man and active in public affairs, Grant will be remembered principally as the author of this, his most important hymn. He wrote a number of other hymns but only this one and "Savior, when, in dust, to Thee" (145) have survived.

MUSIC. The tune LYONS is by Haydn, not the famous "Papa" Haydn who wrote symphonies, string quartets, and *The Creation,* but J. Michael Haydn, 1737-1806, a younger brother. He was born in Austria. Though self-taught in music (like his famous brother Franz), he became the teacher of many eminent musicians of his time, including Carl von Weber. Haydn was a warm-hearted, devout, and gifted man, and might have become famous except for two things—his life was lived in the shadow of his more illustrious brother, and he was too modest to permit most of his works to be published.

LYONS is a singable tune with a fine melodic curve and is strikingly similar to "Hanover" (6) with which it may be interchanged with good effect.

8. Come Thou Almighty King

Charles Wesley, 1707-88

This hymn of praise and prayer is widely used in all branches of the Christian church in the English speaking world and has been translated into many foreign languages. It has been generally attributed to Charles Wesley, the great "Bard of Methodism," but the authorship is uncertain. The hymn appeared as the first of only two selections in a small booklet published by John Wesley about 1757. The second hymn was by Charles Wesley and was entitled, "The Backslider." "Come, Thou Almighty King," with the title, "An Hymn to the Trinity," did not bear the name of Charles Wesley, and it appears nowhere in his collected works. No one can be certain, therefore, of the authorship or date of its writing. Like all good hymns, it rises above time or personal circumstance and expresses for all Christians their feeling of praise and adoration of God. It was originally sung to the tune, "God Save the

5

King," the hymn following the same metrical pattern as the British National Anthem and our own "America."

MUSIC. ITALIAN HYMN, also called "Trinity," and "Moscow," is one of our most famous hymn tunes and deserves its renown. It was composed for this hymn by Felice de Giardini, 1716-1796, an Italian violinist, who spent many years in England and ranked among the top-notch artists and teachers of violin in Europe. Though a great artist, he was a capricious and peevish personality, had few friends and many enemies, was a poor business manager, and died in poverty and distress in the city of Moscow where he had gone to better his fortune and failed.

9. Christ is our Cornerstone
Latin, 8th century, Tr. John Chandler, 1806-76

This is a translation of a mediaeval Latin hymn. At the beginning of the Christian era, the prevailing language was Greek. With the dominance of Rome over the empire of Alexander the Great, Greek gradually gave way to the Latin tongue, and from the fourth century to the dawn of the Reformation, a rich treasury of Latin hymns came into existence in the church. Many of these have now been translated for use in modern English speaking churches. They are stately, reverent, devout pieces of devotional literature which have been the joy and consolation of countless saintly souls down through the centuries. Other examples of hymns from Latin sources are found at Nos. 67, 80, 87, 114, 116, 171, 277, 382, and 415.

"Christ is our Cornerstone" is based on *"Angularis fundamentum,"* a dedication hymn of anonymous authorship, attributed here to the 8th century, but it may be of much earlier origin. Hymn No. 277, "Christ is made the sure foundation," is another rendering of the same Latin poem, by a different translator and into a different meter, and is there dated "6th or 7th century."

John Chandler, the translator, was one of a group of Anglican clergymen belonging to what was known in England as the Oxford Group (not to be confused with the recent Oxford group movement headed by John Buchman). They were interested in restoring to the church a dignified service of worship. These Latin hymns contributed to this purpose. Chandler was a scholar as well as preacher, author of several books and many printed sermons and tracts, and was one of the first and best translators of Latin hymns. This, of course, is not a literal translation, for consideration had to be given to poetic and doctrinal fitness for modern use.

MUSIC. The tune DARWALL was composed by John Darwall, 1731-89,

6

an Anglican clergyman and also an enthusiastic amateur musician. He composed a tune for each of the 150 metrical Psalms, each written in two parts only, treble and bass. DARWALL was set to Psalm 148. His tunes, for the most part, have not been published and have passed into oblivion.

10. Joyful, joyful, we adore Thee   *Henry van Dyke, 1852-1933*

A nature hymn of the first order, written by one who himself had a profound appreciation and love of the out-of-doors. The words from beginning to end are an expression of the beauty in nature and the resulting joy and spirit of praise it brings to the worshipper. The hymn was written in 1907 while the author was on a preaching visit to Williams College; it was designated to be sung to the "Hymn to Joy" in the last movement of Beethoven's *Ninth Symphony*. The words fit the music perfectly. It is one of the most joyful hymns in the English language.

Henry van Dyke was born in Germantown, Pa.; received his education in Princeton University and Theological Seminary; and began his work as pastor of the United Congregational Church in Newport, R. I. After four years he was called to the pulpit of the Brick Presbyterian Church in New York where he became a widely known figure. In 1900 he was called to the chair of English Literature in Princeton. He was a friend of President Woodrow Wilson who appointed van Dyke as minister to the Netherlands and Luxemburg, which post he held from 1913 to 1917. He is the author of many books, including the beautiful story entitled, *The Other Wise Man*.

MUSIC. HYMN TO JOY is a hymn tune arrangement from the fourth movement of Beethoven's *Ninth Symphony*, probably the greatest symphony ever penned, even though the composer was stone-deaf when he wrote it.

Ludwig von Beethoven was born at Bonn, Germany, in 1770 and died in Vienna in 1827. During his tempestuous life, he composed many compositions for piano, violin, orchestra, and string quartet. His nine symphonies are on the repertoire of all the great modern symphony orchestras.

11. Give to our God immortal praise   *Isaac Watts, 1674-1748*

Recognized as the best of three versions which Watts made of Psalm 136. The hymn expresses with dignity and fervor the high praise of God.

Isaac Watts, scholar, poet, and pastor of the Independent Church in Mark Lane, London, ranks among the greatest of English hymn writers.

7

He is the author of about 600 hymns and versions, many of which are still in common use. The *Hymnary* contains 19 of his works. Watts is often referred to as the "father of English hymnody." Though suffering from bodily ailments during the greater part of his adult life, he was robust in his thinking and became a bold and sturdy fighter for the cause of intellectual and religious freedom. Watts was one of the gentlest and kindest of men and a friend of the young. His wide intellectual interests enabled him to write textbooks on logic, geography, and astronomy, which were used in the universities of England as well as Harvard and Yale. Though he was never married and had no children of his own, Watts was a lover of children and wrote one of the world's most beautiful cradle songs—"Hush, my dear, lie still and slumber." In 1715, he issued a notable book of verse for children. One of the poems, entitled, "Against Quarrelling and Fighting," runs as follows:

> Let dogs delight to bark and bite
> For God hath made them so;
> Let bears and lions growl and fight
> For 'tis their nature to.

> But children, you should never let
> Such angry passions rise;
> Your little hands were never made
> To tear each other's eyes.

Let grown-ups in our day grasp the idea in this simple poem!

MUSIC. The tune, LASST UNS ERFREUEN, one of the most famous in any hymn book, was published in *Geistliche Kirchengesäng*, Cologne, 1623. It was set to an Easter hymn beginning, *"Lasst uns erfreuen herzlich sehr,"* from whence it derives its name. The tune is unusual for its simplicity of structure and its invariable repetition of phrases throughout. Usually the alleluias in lines 3 and 6 are sung in harmony, the rest of the song in unison. The tune lends itself well to antiphonal or echo singing on the rare occasions when such varied effects are desired. The composer is not known.

12. O for a thousand tongues to sing *Charles Wesley, 1707-88*

From a poem of 18 stanzas, written by Wesley to celebrate the first anniversary of his great spiritual change, a conversion experience in which he felt the clear light of the Gospel possessing his soul. The poem was entitled, "For the Anniversary Day of One's Conversion." Wesley was greatly influenced by the Moravian missionary Peter Bohler who once said to him: "Had I a thousand tongues, I would praise Him with them all." The incident, lingering in Wesley's mind, was turned into a song which expresses the joy and confidence of the redeemed.

For 150 years, and until recently, this hymn appeared as No. 1 in Methodist hymnbooks on both sides of the Atlantic.

For further comments on Charles Wesley see Hymn 6.

MUSIC. AZMON was introduced into this country from Germany where it was a favorite school song. Carl G. Gläser, the composer, was born at Weissenfels, Germany, 1784, and died at Barmen, 1829. He was a teacher of piano, violin, and voice, and director of choruses. He also owned and managed a music store.

Lowell Mason, the arranger of the tune, was one of America's earliest exponents and teachers of public school music and did much to bring worthy popular hymn tunes into the churches. He was born January 8, 1792, at Orange, N. J. At the age of 16, he was a choir leader and teacher of singing classes. At 23, he went to Savannah, Ga., as a bank clerk, returning to Boston in 1827 to become president and conductor of the Handel and Haydn Society. He wrote a large number of singable hymn tunes which have had wide use in the hymn books of all denominations. More of his compositions are found in the *Hymnary* than of any other composer. He died at Orange, N. J., August 11, 1872.

13. Great God, the followers of Thy Son

Henry Ware, Jr., 1794-1843

Written for an ordination service which took place in Baltimore in 1819, William E. Channing preaching the sermon.

The author, Henry Ware, Jr., was born at Hingham, Mass., April 21, 1794; died September 25, 1843, at Framingham, Mass. He was educated at Harvard, and served as minister of the Second Unitarian Church, Boston, 1817 to 1829, with Ralph Waldo Emerson as assistant for a time. From 1829 to 1842, he was Professor of Pulpit Eloquence and Pastoral Care in the Harvard Divinity School. He was editor of the *Christian Disciple* and later of the *Christian Register*.

MUSIC. For comments on Lowell Mason, composer of HEBRON, see Hymn 12.

14. The God of Abraham praise

Daniel Ben Judah, 14th century
Revised version by Thomas Olivers, 1725-99

This praise hymn, with its magnificent tune, had its origin in a Jewish synagogue in London. Thomas Olivers, a Welshman and follower of John Wesley, spent fifty years of his life as a Methodist minister, during which time he travelled more than 100,000 miles on horseback in his evangelistic work. His fame, however, rests upon this hymn. While

9

visiting in London, he went to the Great Synagogue in Duke's Place and heard the cantor sing the Hebrew *Yigdal* or doxology, in which the articles of the Jewish faith are recited. Upon hearing this, Oliver wrote "The God of Abraham praise," a Christian version of the *Yigdal*. The original is by Daniel Ben Judah of the 14th century. Oliver then called on the Cantor, Meyer Leoni, who gave him this melody to suit the hymn he had written.

MUSIC. LEONI, according to Winfield Douglas, is probably not older than the 17th century and is not related to ancient Jewish music. Although written in a minor key, it strikes the note of praise. Its rhythm and vigor of movement adapts it well for use as a processional or recessional hymn.

15. We praise Thee, O God, our Redeemer

Julia Bulkley Cady Cory

A notable hymn of praise written by Mrs. Julia Cady Cory, who was born and reared in what was reputed to be one of the happiest Christian homes in New York City. Her father, J. Cleveland Cady, was a nationally known architect. A devout Christian, he had a genuine love for boys and girls and was superintendent of the same Sunday school for fifty-two years. Concerning the origin of this hymn, Mrs. Cory has written:

> Years before I was married (in 1902), the organist of the Brick Presbyterian Church of New York City, knowing of my interest in hymnology, came to me and told me that he had a very fine Netherlands melody associated with most militaristic and unchristian words. He lamented the fact, and re- quested me to write more suitable words, which could be used for the Thanksgiving service at the Brick Church. The hymn as you see it today, was the result.

MUSIC. KREMSER is named after Edward Kremser, 1838-1914, a Viennese musician who arranged the tune from a Netherlands melody dating to 1625. The composer is not known. It is a stirring piece of music, simple in style, and easy to sing. It is equally impressive, whether sung in measured, stately tones like a chorale, or in the gayer festive mood in which young people like to sing. Children and young people usually respond to this hymn with enthusiasm.

16. Praise the Lord: ye heavens adore Him

Foundling Hospital Collection
Stanza 3 by Edward Osler, 1798-1863

A free rendering of some lines of Psalm 148 in which all the hosts of heaven and earth join in a magnificent chorus of praise to God.

The first two stanzas are anonymous. They were first published in the *Foundling Hospital Collection,* a book of hymns and anthems compiled by Thomas Coram, an English seaman, merchant captain and philanthropist. In later life, Mr. Coram devoted his time and fortune to the support of a children's hospital in which a chapel was also maintained and the children trained in singing.

Edward Osler, author of the third stanza, was an English surgeon and author of books on scientific as well as religious subjects. He was also a distinguished hymnologist and wrote a number of versions of the Psalms and hymns for use in the Church of England.

MUSIC. FABEN was composed by John Henry Wilcox, 1827-75, Boston organist and expert in organ construction. The tune should not be taken too fast; otherwise the short notes become choppy and the effect is spoiled. Singers should avoid slurring the intervals of the melody, especially the descending fourth at the end of the first, third and seventh lines.

17. Come, let us join our cheerful songs   *Isaac Watts, 1674-1748*

A paraphrase of Revelation 5:11-13. It is one of the most widely esteemed of Watts' poems and one of the classics of English hymnody.

The basses and tenors would be less likely to sing the wrong words at the beginning of the third score if the lines of all four stanzas had been printed. Let the song leader remind them to look ahead for the proper lines of each stanza before singing their solo part, and so avoid some incongruities of thought!

For comments on Isaac Watts see Hymn 11.

MUSIC. CAMBRIDGE is an effective tune but with most congregations it needs some rehearsal before it is usable in a worship service. The composer, John Randall, 1715-99, was an organist and Professor of Music in Cambridge University. He was a friend of the poet Thomas Gray.

18. O come, loud anthems let us sing   *Tate and Brady*

A metrical version of Psalm 95, by Tate and Brady, two Irishmen who collaborated in producing, in 1696, the *New Version* of the Psalms. Their work partly supplanted the older version by Sternhold and Hopkins, then in use.

Nahum Tate, 1652-1715, was the son of an Irish clergyman, and, like Brady, received his education at Trinity College, Dublin. He was only a second-rate poet but managed to receive appointment as Poet Laureate of England in 1690.

11

Nicholas Brady, 1659-1726, was granted the honorary degree of Doctor of Divinity from Dublin University for services rendered to the Protestant cause. Among his many appointments were the chaplaincy to the king of England and incumbency of Stratford-on-Avon. Tate and Brady recast all of the Psalms into metrical verse in an attempt to improve on the old version then in use in the churches. Their work was done in a day when only the psalms were permitted to be sung in worship services in England. The writing of hymns was still in the future. Only a few of their renderings still find a place among our modern English hymns. The *Hymnary* includes two besides this one, Nos. 583 and 586.

MUSIC. The tune was found in *St. Basil's Hymn Book* where it is credited to Haydn, but we are not told which Haydn. No further information concerning its origin has been traced. It is especially effective when sung by a large congregation.

19. When morning gilds the skies

19th century, Tr. E. Caswall, 1814-78

A radiant morning hymn of adoration. It comes from the German song, "Bei frühem Morgenlicht," of unknown authorship, which first appeared in print in the *Katholisches Gesangbuch,* 1828, bearing the title, "A Christian Greeting."

> Bei frühem Morgenlicht
> Erwacht mein Herz und spricht.
> Gelobt sei Jesus Christus!
> So sing ich früh and spät,
> Bei Arbeit und Gebet,
> Gelobt sei Jesus Christus!

The translator, Edward Caswall, was an English scholar and clergyman, educated at Oxford. He left the Church of England to become a Roman Catholic priest. Caswall did much for the sick poor and the poor children in Birmingham, England, where he lived. He wrote excellent original hymns and made many translations from German and Latin sources. (See Nos. 88 and 155.)

MUSIC. O SEIGNEUR was composed or arranged by the Frenchman L. Bourgeois, *c.* 1500- *c.* 1561, who was an adherent of Calvin and followed him to Geneva in 1541. He was assigned by Calvin the task of providing music for the metrical psalter, but his work was attended with troubles and difficulties. Once he was thrown in prison for making unauthorized alterations in certain well-known tunes. He tried hard to introduce part-singing in a day when only unison singing was permitted by Calvin. Not succeeding in this, he left Geneva and returned to Paris, his birthplace. O SEIGNEUR is a superb tune. It gathers interest and force throughout its considerable length. The tune, which also may be used as a choir anthem, should be sung in fairly lively tempo to bring out its extraordinary power.

20. Lord, in the morning
Isaac Watts, 1674-1748

Based on Psalm 5:3: "My voice shalt thou hear in the morning, O Lord; in the morning will I direct my prayer to thee, and will look up." Watts did not hesitate to change the wording of the Psalms, when necessary, to "Christianize" them. In the preface to his book of *Psalms,* he states his method and purpose in these words:

> It is necessary that I should inform my readers that they are not to expect in this book an exact translation of the Psalms of David. My design is to accommodate the Book of Psalms to Christian Worship.

For further comments on Watts see Hymn 11.

MUSIC. WARWICK, a psalm-tune of somewhat ornamental style, was composed by Samuel Stanley, 1767-1822, who for thirty-three years was the leader of singing in Carr's Lane Meeting House, Birmingham, England, where he made its music famous. He was a noted violincellist and an authority on the music of Handel. His position in the church was not then considered inconsistent with his being, for a time, keeper of the town tavern.

21. When morning gilds the skies
19th century, Tr. E. Caswall, 1814-78

For comments on the words see Hymn 19.

MUSIC. LAUDES DOMINI was composed by Joseph Barnby, 1838-96, an English organist and one of the most prolific hymn-tune writers of his time. He was conductor of the Royal Choral Society in London, which presented many splendid performances of the great oratorios. It is a reverent and vigorous tune, written especially for this hymn, and makes a good processional.

22. New every morning is the love
John Keble, 1792-1866

Taken from John Keble's *Christian Year,* a book of devotional poetry, one of the great religious classics in the English language. The original poem of sixteen stanzas is based on Lamentations 3:22b, 23a: "His compassions fail not. They are new every morning." The hymn shows a deep appreciation of the beauties of the natural world, linking them with the worship of God.

John Keble was educated at Oxford where he was an outstandingly

13

brilliant student. Later he taught at Oxford for nine years and then spent thirteen years as curate in his father's church in Gloucestershire. Following that he became vicar of Hursley where he rebuilt the parish church with profits from his book, *The Christian Year,* which passed through 90 editions during the author's lifetime. Keble was one of the influential leaders in the so-called Oxford or Tractarian Movement in England, an effort to emphasize worthier ideas of the church and a greater dignity and beauty in worship.

MUSIC. MELCOMBE, a melody of fine balance and great dignity, was composed by Samuel Webbe, 1740-1816, son of an English government official in Minorca. He spent his early life as a cabinetmaker but later turned to music, becoming a noted organist and composer of a large quantity of secular and sacred music.

23. Still, still with Thee   *Harriet Beecher Stowe, 1811-96*

Based on Psalm 139:18: "When I awake I am still with Thee." It is a beautiful, personal, morning hymn, expressing the soul's adoration upon waking to find itself in the glad consciousness of the divine presence.

Harriet Beecher Stowe belonged to a famous American family. Her father, Lyman Beecher, and her brother, Henry Ward Beecher, were eloquent and influential preachers in the Presbyterian and Congregational churches, respectively. Harriet's girlhood was spent in Cincinnati, Ohio, where her father was president of Lane Theological Seminary. She married Calvin Ellis Stowe, of the Lane faculty. In 1852, she published *Uncle Tom's Cabin,* a story which became immensely popular and made a notable contribution to the cause of freedom for the slaves.

MUSIC. CONSOLATION is No. 9 of the 48 pieces, all of distinctive lyric quality, composed by Felix Mendelssohn-Bartholdy, and known as *Songs without Words.* The tune appears here in slightly modified form. It is well adapted for the hymn but suffers frequently from dragging. It should be sung with a steady pace and clearly defined rhythm.

Felix Mendelssohn-Bartholdy was born in Hamburg, Germany, 1809, the son of a Jewish banker. His father, Abraham Mendelssohn, wished the children to be brought up as Protestant Christians and added the name "Bartholdy" to distinguish them from the Jewish members of the family. "Bartholdy" was the name of the proprietor of the garden belonging to the family. Mendelssohn composed extensively for the piano and wrote symphonies for the orchestra. Among his choral works are the great oratorios, *Elijah* and *St. Paul.* A man of culture and wealth, he travelled extensively and was popular wherever he went, especially in England. He died in Leipzig in 1847.

14

24. Father, we praise Thee

Gregory the Great, 540-604
Tr. Percy Dearmer, 1867-1936

The original of this morning hymn is attributed to Gregory the Great, Pope Gregory I, a sincere man, devoted to missions and reforms within the church, and one of the greatest of the line of Popes. The date of his election to the papacy, A.D. 590, is usually given by church historians as the end of the period of the Ancient Church and the beginning of the period of the Middle Ages—a witness to the importance of Gregory. A man of unblemished character and statesmanlike wisdom, he had a noble vision and ambition for Christianity and took a keen interest in the ritual and music of the church. Though not original or scholarly, he was a voluminous writer and had much influence in his time. He sent out missionaries, such as Augustine to England, and labored incessantly to purify and strengthen the church, care for its poor, and bring Christianity to the heathen. Gregory was particularly interested in the music of the church; and the "Gregorian Chants," many of them composed by him, became the basis of cathedral music for a thousand years. He did away with certain embellishments which had crept in through the influence of Ambrose, and inaugurated the use of the solemn, stately chants which bear his name.

The translation of this hymn is by Percy Dearmer, an English hymnologist and clergyman who became Canon of Westminster, London, in 1931. He edited *Songs of Praise,* adopted widely in England for use in churches and public schools.

MUSIC. CHRISTI SANCTORUM is a tune of uncertain origin taken from a book by Francois de la Feillée, entitled *Methode du Plain Chant,* published in 1782. The melody, easily within range of all voices, is well adapted for unison singing. It is most effective when sung somewhat slowly. Though the tune appears in a book of plainsong, the melody has rhythm and is measured, and has none of the characteristics of a plainsong.

25. Awake, my soul, and with the sun   *Thomas Ken, 1637-1711*

Taken from a *Manual of Prayers,* which Bishop Ken wrote for Winchester College students in 1674. It appeared as the "Morning Hymn." The preface of the book admonished the boys "to be sure to sing the Morning and Evening Hymn in your chamber devoutly." Both the Morning and Evening Hymn (33) had for the closing stanza the famous doxology, "Praise God from whom all blessings flow," now sung by the whole Christian church. The original poem had fourteen stanzas. According to Julian, this hymn is one of four at the head of all hymns in the English language.

Thomas Ken was an English poet and clergyman and had considerable musical talent. He was a man unafraid to declare his convictions. He once refused to read, at the king's command, a certain document to his parishioners, and was imprisoned for his defiance. He finally lost his bishopric because he refused to swear allegiance to Mary and William of Orange when they became rulers of England. Ken was known for his saintly character, his great ability and eloquence as a preacher, and his pioneering in the art of hymn writing.

That all hymns must be written in the third person, as is sometimes asserted, is disproved by this great hymn in its use of "I" and "my."

MUSIC. For comments on Francois H. Barthélémon, composer of the tune, MORNING HYMN, see Hymn 2.

26. Christ, whose glory fills the skies   *Charles Wesley, 1707-88*

One of the greatest morning hymns in the English language, based on Mal. 4:2: "But unto you that fear my name shall the sun of righteousness arise with healing in his wings." James Montgomery called it "one of Charles Wesley's loveliest progeny." It pictures Christ as the true Light and the Sun of Righteousness triumphing over the darkness of sin and grief.

Charles Wesley was the second youngest in a family of nineteen children and became the "sweet singer of Methodism." He and Isaac Watts were the most important hymnists of the 18th century in England.

For further comments on Wesley see Hymn 6.

MUSIC. LUX PRIMA is by the French composer, Charles F. Gounod, 1818-93, a musician of a deeply religious nature. Gounod had taken two years of theology with the expectation of becoming ordained, but later decided that his greatest contribution to religion would be through music. His outstanding religious work is the oratorio, *The Redemption.* While composing it, he used to spend hours in Notre Dame Cathedral in prayer and meditation. LUX PRIMA is a stirring tune, building up to a climax at "Day-star," and is widely used as a processional.

27. Come, my soul, thou must be waking

F. R. von Canitz, 1654-99
Tr. H. J. Buckoll, 1803-71

From a book of German lyrics, translated by H. J. Buckoll. The original poem of 13 stanzas begins with the words, *"Seele, du muszt munter werden."* The hymn, expressing the glories of a new day, is especially suitable for use in schools and colleges. It is a translation of stanzas 1, 6, 8, 10, and 11 of the original:

16

MORNING

Seele, du musst munter werden!
  Denn der Erden
Blickt hervor ein neuer Tag.
Komm, dem Schöpfer dieser Strah-
  len
  Zu bezahlen,
Was dein schwacher Trieb vermag.

Bitte, dass er dir Gedeihen
  Mag verleihen,
Wenn du auf was Gutes zielst;
Aber dass er dich mag stören
  Und bekehren
Wenn du böse Regung fühlst.

Denk, dass er auf deinen Wegen
  Ist zugegen,
Und erkennet, was du tust;
Dass er auch verborgne Flecken
  Kann entdecken,
Und die tiefste Sündenlust.

Drum so seufze, dass dein Schei-
  den
  Nicht ein Leiden,
Sondern sanftes Schlafen sei—
Dass ich seh' mit ew'ger Wonne
  Jene Sonne,
Wann des Todes Nacht vorbei.

Treib' nur Gottes Gnadenblicke
  Nicht zurücke
Fasse treulich ihren Schein;
Dann wird deiner Seele Frieden
  Schon hienieden
Süsser als die Sonne sein.

Friedrich Rudolph Ludwig, Freiherr von Canitz, was born in Berlin in 1654. He was a distinguished diplomat, a philanthropist, and a devout Christian. In the early morning of his last day on earth, August 11, 1699, ill with dropsy, he gazed at the rising sun and exclaimed, "Oh, if the sight of this created sun is so charming and beautiful, what will be the sight of the unspeakable glory of the Creator himself!" He was *Staatrath* (State Counsellor) at the time of his death.

The translator, Rev. Henry J. Buckoll, was educated at Oxford and spent most of his life teaching. He edited several collections of songs for schools and in 1842 published *Hymns Translated from the German.*

MUSIC. HAYDN comes from a tune in one of the movements of a string quartet by Franz Joseph Haydn, 1732-1809, the great Austrian composer, and important figure in the history of music. He was affectionately named "Papa Haydn" by Mozart. He wrote church music, song, opera, and oratorio, over 100 symphonies and 83 string quartets. His *Creation*, a sacred oratorio, is widely known. He was devoutly religious and did not hesitate to ascribe his musical scores to God's glory. He gave as one of his reasons for writing music: "that the weary and worn or the man burdened with affairs might enjoy something of solace and refreshment." There is a cheerfulness and optimism about his music which appeals to amateur and professional alike. Haydn was a teacher as well as composer and numbered among his pupils Mozart and Beethoven.

17

28. Now on land and sea descending

Samuel Longfellow, 1819-92

Written for use in a series of vesper services the author was conducting in his church. It was published, with other hymns, in a small book called *Vespers*. This hymn and "Again as evening's shadow falls" (No. 280), also by Longfellow, have become two of the most-loved evening hymns in the English language.

Samuel Longfellow, younger brother of the poet, Henry Wadsworth Longfellow, was born and died in Portland, Maine. He was educated at Harvard for the ministry and served congregations in Fall River, Mass.; Brooklyn; and Germantown, Pa., resigning the last charge to write his brother's *Life*, 1886. Though a Unitarian, he speaks of Christ as Lord and Saviour and accepted the miracles of the New Testament. He edited several important hymn books and wrote a number of hymns of excellent quality. Thirteen of his compositions are included in the *Hymnary*.

MUSIC. VESPERS is by the Russian composer Dimitri Stephanovitch Bortniansky who was born at Gloukoff, in the Ukraine, 1752, and died at St. Petersburg, 1825. He studied music at Moscow, St. Petersburg, and Venice, Italy, the Empress Catherine of Russia supplying the necessary funds. (It was this Empress Catherine who extended an in vitation in 1786 to Prussian Mennonites to settle in South Russia, promising religious toleration, military exemption, and other special privileges.) Bortniansky became Director of the Imperial Kapelle, the Empress' Church Choir. He was a distinguished composer of sacred music and has had a great and lasting influence on Russian church music. From his pen came the well-known chorale tune, *"Ich bete an die Macht der Liebe"* (No. 517).

The word "Jubilate" means "to shout for joy." It comes from the same Latin root as "jubilee" and "jubilant." Its English pronunciation in singing is Jōō-bǐ-lä-tǐ. If you prefer the Latin, sing it Yōō-bā-lä-tǐ.

29. Now the day is over

Sabine Baring-Gould, 1834-1924

Based on Proverbs 3:24:

"When thou liest down, thou shalt not be afraid;
Yea, thou shalt lie down, and thy sleep shall be sweet."

The hymn was written for children, but is suitable for worshippers of all ages.

Sabine Baring-Gould was educated at Cambridge and became a clergyman of the Church of England. He was a man of great industry and versatility, and possessed a wide range of interests. He wrote books on travel, biography, history, and is the author of several novels. He also edited several collections of folk songs. Baring-Gould is the author of "Onward Christian soldiers," another hymn written for children, which has received a much wider use than originally intended.

MUSIC. MERRIAL is a favorite tune for choir use in evening services. The average congregation can learn to sing it without difficulty, and when sung slowly and thoughtfully, it constitutes a deeply moving evening prayer.

For comments on the composer, Joseph Barnby, see Hymn 21.

30. Sun of my soul, Thou Savior dear   *John Keble,* 1792-1866

Another evening hymn, widely used, and destined to live as long as English hymns are sung. It is taken from the author's *Christian Year,* a book of devotional poetry which sold 305,500 copies in forty-six years. The original poem of fourteen stanzas, composed November 25, 1820, appeared with the title, " 'Tis Gone, that Bright and Orbèd Blaze," and was headed with the text, "Abide with us" (Luke 24:29). The hymn represents a lone traveller pressing on his way after the sun has set, but trusting in Christ, the "Sun of the soul," for guidance and protection, and lifting a prayer for the sick and poor and the helpless. Tennyson, too, likened Christ to the sun. Asked what Christ meant to him he paused beside a flower in the garden and answered: "What the sun is to that flower, Jesus Christ is to my soul. He is the Sun of my soul."

For further comments on John Keble see Hymn 22.

MUSIC. HURSLEY is a good tune but not as good as the original, *"Grosser Gott, wir loben Dich"* (No. 519), from which some unknown person adapted it. The melody and harmonization have been changed, not for the better, to suit the English words. "Hursley" was the name of the parish of which Keble was vicar, and the tune was doubtless given this name when it came to be associated with Keble's hymn.

31. Day is dying in the west   *Mary Lathbury,* 1841-1913

An evening hymn of high rank which has been used widely in American churches during the past half century.

Mary A. Lathbury, daughter of a Methodist minister, was a successful art teacher but is remembered chiefly for her work with the Methodist Sunday School Union and her literary contributions to periodicals for young people. The "Look Up" Legion which she founded had for its motto, Edward Everett Hale's four rules of good conduct:

Look up, not down;   Look out, not in,
Look forward, not back;   And lend a hand.

Miss Lathbury wrote this hymn for use at the vesper services at Lake Chautauqua, in western New York, where hundreds of young people, eager to deepen their spiritual life, have met every year since 1873 for Bible study and prayer. This hymn and "Break Thou the Bread of Life" give the author a permanent place in American hymnody.

MUSIC. CHAUTAUQUA was written especially for Miss Lathbury's hymn. William F. Sherwin, 1826-88, studied music under Lowell Mason and later became a teacher of vocal music. He was unusually successful in leading choral groups and was appointed music director at Lake Chautauqua. The tune is dignified and stately, yet simple. The refrain should be sung softly at the beginning and rise gradually to a climax.

32. Darkening night the land doth cover
Anon. Greek
Tr. Robert Bridges, 1844-1930

From an anonymous 8th-century or earlier Greek hymn. Some authorities believe it to be an expansion of the Greek candle lighting hymn (No. 34), also translated by Robert Bridges. The editors of the *Hymnary,* in search of a poem to fit the well-known UNTER LILIEN JENER FREUDEN tune in the *Gesangbuch mit Noten,* found for it this beautiful evening hymn published in the *American Oxford Hymnal.*

The translator, Robert Bridges, was one of England's great literary scholars who gave serious attention to hymnology. After graduating from Eton and Oxford, he turned his attention to medicine and became a distinguished surgeon. At the early age of 38, however, he retired from medicine to give himself to literature and music. In 1913, he was made Poet Laureate of England. His most significant work in hymnology was the famous *Yattendon Hymnal,* which he published in 1899 while living in the village of Yattendon. It consisted of 100 hymns, 44 of which were from his own pen, either as author or translator. The hymns were set to music derived largely from the *Genevan Psalter.* The hymnal represented an extraordinarily high standard, both as to words and music, but it never became popular, and copies of it are nearly impossible to find.

MUSIC. The tune, UNTER LILIEN JENER FREUDEN, is found at No. 546 of the *Gesangbuch mit Noten* where it is set to a poem by J. Allendorf. No information has been traced concerning the composer, J. Voigtländer.

33. All praise to Thee, my God this night
Thomas Ken, 1637-1711

Based on Psalm 91:4: "He shall cover thee with his feathers; and under his wings shalt thou trust."

This is the "Evening Hymn," whereas No. 25 is the "Morning

Hymn" which Bishop Ken wrote for the devotional use of students at Winchester College. His endeavor was to express in simple, fitting words the thoughts that ought to be in the minds of the boys of the school "and all other devout Christians" in the evening. The two hymns were published in 1695 and have been growing in fame and power these two and one-half centuries. Both concluded with the doxology, "Praise God from whom all blessings flow," now known and sung throughout Christendom.

MUSIC. The tune, EVENING HYMN, was originally in canon form, i.e., a form in which one voice begins the melody which is then imitated note for note by some other voice, as in a "round." Tallis, as was customary at the time, started the melody in the tenor, imitated by the soprano. The tune used here is a later and altered form which, in the judgment of this writer, is less interesting than the canonic form used in many hymnbooks. Its choice was an editorial inadvertence.

Thomas Tallis, composer of the tune, died in 1585. The exact date of his birth, probably before 1520, remains uncertain. Styled the "Father of English Cathedral Music," he was chorister at St. Paul's Cathedral, London, and later held important posts as organist. He was indisputably the greatest English musician of his age, and EVENING HYMN is his most famous tune.

34. O Gladsome Light, O Grace

Greek 1st or 2d Century
Tr. Robert Bridges, 1844-1930

This is the oldest Christian hymn in common use, belonging to the first or second century. It was sung by the early Christians as a hymn of thanksgiving at the lighting of the candles at the vesper services in the church and probably also in the home. It is still so used in the Eastern churches. St. Basil wrote c. 370 regarding this hymn: "We cannot say who is the father of this expression at the Thanksgiving of the Lighting of the Lamps; but it is an *ancient* formula which the people repeat." So in A.D. 370 the hymn was already ancient!

For comments on the translator, Robert Bridges, see Hymn 32.

MUSIC. The tune NUNC DIMITTIS is by the French musician, Louis Bourgeois, c. 1510-61, the best melodist of his day, and composer of most of the music for the *Genevan Psalter,* a French metrical version of the Psalms published in 1549. Many of his melodies have been altered, as for example, "Old Hundredth," but this one has come to us unchanged. It is a glorious melody which needs to be listened to repeatedly to be appreciated. The harmonization is by Claude Goudimel, c. 1505/10-72, another eminent Protestant musician, who provided harmonies for many of the Genevan psalm tunes. Goudimel's life came to an end in the massacre of St. Bartholomew in 1572, one of those

21

tragedies during the counter-reformation in which the Protestants suffered at the hands of the Jesuits.

35. God that madest earth and heaven

Stanza 1, Reginald Heber, 1783-1826
Stanza 2, William Mercer, 1811-73
Stanza 3, Richard Whateley, 1787-1863

The original hymn consisted of the first stanza only which was written by Reginald Heber after hearing the tune used here played by a Welch harpist in a home where Heber was visiting. Retiring to a quiet place, he promptly wrote the stanza to suit the melody.

For comments on Reginald Heber see Hymn 1.

William Mercer, author of the second stanza, was a clergyman in the Church of England in Sheffield. In 1857, he issued *The Church Psalter and Hymn Book,* the most important Church of England book of its time. His aim was to promote greater participation by the congregation in the hymn singing.

Richard Whately was archbishop of Dublin. He was a man of great brilliance of mind, though, it is said, he had no ear for music and no eye for natural beauty.

MUSIC. The tune AR HYD Y NOS is a Welsh traditional melody commonly associated with the words "All through the night." It appears in many modern hymnals. A growing number of folk tunes are being used for hymn tunes.

36. Softly now the light of day

George Washington Doane, 1799-1859

An American hymn characterized by simplicity and grace, and sung the world over wherever the English language is spoken. It appeared in 1824 in a collection of poems, *Songs by the Way,* with the heading "Evening." It is based on Psalm 141:2, "Let my prayer be set forth before Thee as incense; and the lifting up of my hands as the evening sacrifice."

George Washington Doane was born in Trenton, New Jersey, in 1799, the year that the "Father of our Country" died; hence his name. He was educated at Union College, Schenectady, New York, and ordained, at the age of 22, in the Episcopal Church. At the early age of 33 he was made bishop of New Jersey. A pioneer in education, and ahead of his time in many things, his life was full of trials. But his exceptional talents, learning and force of character made him one of the great church leaders of his time.

MUSIC. SEYMOUR is by the eminent German composer of opera,

Carl M. von Weber, 1786-1826. This tune, a great favorite, is from the opening chorus of his opera, *Oberon*, which is sung while fairies "trip it lightly" on the stage. When contributions towards the musical edition of the famous English book, *Hymns Ancient and Modern*, London, 1861, were invited by advertisement, the editor, W. H. Monk, received more requests for the insertion of this tune than any other, despite its secular origin.

37. At even, when the sun was set   *Henry Twells*, 1823-1900

This evening hymn, a prayer for the healing of our bodily as well as spiritual ills, has been translated into many foreign tongues, and is found in nearly all standard hymn books both in America and abroad. The original has eight stanzas. It is based on the touching evening scene described in Mark 1:32, "At even, when the sun was set, they brought unto him all that were sick."

Henry Twells was ordained in 1849 in the Church of England. Among the parishes he served was Stratford-on-Avon, the birthplace of Shakespeare. At the time he wrote this hymn, he was headmaster of a large grammar school and penned the verses one afternoon while the boys were writing an examination.

MUSIC. The tune, ANGELUS, appeared in somewhat different form in *Heilige Seelenlust,* one of a series of Catholic collections of hymns in Germany, written in the vernacular, and edited by Johann Scheffler. The tune is credited to Georg Josephi, a German musician of whom little is known except that he was the musical editor of *Heilige Seelenlust.* It is a tune of rare beauty though its modulations into several different keys makes it more difficult to sing than some and gives it a sense of restlessness not found in other popular tunes.

38. Savior, breathe an evening blessing

James Edmeston, 1791-1867

This hymn ranks with the best of the evening hymns of the English language though it is practically all that survives of the more than two thousand hymns that came from the too prolific pen of the author.

James Edmeston, a member of the Church of England, was an eminent London architect and surveyor who had a great love for and interest in children and possessed a gift for writing sacred poetry. He had the habit of writing a hymn every Sunday and reading it at family worship.

During the Boxer uprising in China in 1900, in which many Americans lost their lives, a group of missionaries, beleaguered outside of Shanghai, found in this hymn the expression of their feelings, as well as a great source of comfort. One of them wrote:

23

Separated from home and friends, facing death in a far-off land, and full of tenderest feelings, we lifted our hearts in song:

"Though destruction walk around us,
"Though the arrows past us fly:
"Angel guards from Thee surround us;
"We are safe if Thou art nigh."

Out of the storm each soul, renewing its strength, mounted up with wings as eagles and found peace in the secret of His presence. Our Saviour breathed, in very deed, "an evening blessing," the fragrance of which remains even unto this day. The last verse of the hymn, "Should swift death this night o'ertake us," was omitted. It seemed too probable that it might. We wanted only to think of the safe-keeping, and such, thank God, it proved to be.

MUSIC. The tune EVENING PRAYER was written by Stebbins while music director at Tremont Temple, Boston, as a response to be sung after the morning prayer. Two years later it was set to this evening hymn by the composer himself, for use in an evangelistic campaign in Providence, R. I. Stebbins writes, "I arranged to have a male choir of 20 voices sing the music as set to the beautiful hymn, and to my gratification found they were admirably suited to each other. Since then the hymn has been used in many gospel hymn books and church hymnals, both here and abroad. It has been used also in St. Paul's Cathedral, in London."

George C. Stebbins, 1846-1945, was born and reared on a farm in New York. He became interested in music through the country singing school. After serving as music director at the First Baptist Church, Chicago, and Tremont Temple, Boston, he became associated with D. L. Moody and helped organize choruses for many of Moody's evangelistic campaigns both here and abroad. He was co-editor with Ira Sankey and James McGranahan of various editions of *Gospel Hymns* and was himself one of the best composers of gospel hymn tunes. He lived to be nearly 100 years old.

The hymn is also set to the tune "Ringe Recht" (147) in some hymnals.

39. Unheard the dews around me fall   *Anonymous*

This hymn, emphasizing the silences of God as manifested in the world without and within, is of anonymous authorship. It is found in *Hymns of the Spirit* but most of the other modern hymnals have overlooked it.

MUSIC. WINDSOR is an English tune of unknown origin. It was

24

set to Psalm 116 in a book of Psalm tunes by M. William Damon, published in 1591. It is one of a number of tunes written in the minor mode which appear in the *Hymnary*. Note that the "Amen" closes with the chord in F major, in keeping with the general practice of following a minor tune with an "Amen" in which the last chord is in the major mode.

In *Songs of Praise*, London, 1931, this tune is set to the hymn "Jesus, the very thought of Thee" (155).

40. Abide with me: fast falls the eventide

Henry F. Lyte, 1793-1847

One of the great consolation songs of Christianity. It is really not an evening hymn, but for a person in his last illness, when the thought of passing through the gateway of death, and the glory of the great beyond are the soul's vital concern. It has long been sung at evening services because, presumably, the end of the natural day suggests the evening of life, and the mood of the tune is so well suited to the pensive quietness of the close of day.

Henry F. Lyte, a Scotsman, was a young clergyman in the Church of England when he wrote this hymn. There is a popular tradition that he wrote it near the end of his life when ill health compelled him to resign his parish and after he held his last communion on September 4, 1847. But James Moffatt, the distinguished historian and translator of the Bible, gives a different account of its origin. He says the hymn was inspired during the fatal illness of an intimate friend of the author, Rev. William A. Le Hunte. Dr. Lyte was constantly at the side of his dying friend who, in his closing hours, repeatedly said these words, "Abide with me," which moved Dr. Lyte to write the hymn. Twenty-seven years later, 1847, when he felt his own end approaching, he recalled the hymn.

MUSIC. EVENTIDE is Monk's best known tune. In a letter to J. C. Hadden, Mrs. Monk wrote: "This tune was written at a time of great sorrow—when together we watched, as we did daily, the glories of the setting sun. As the golden rays faded, he took up some paper and pencilled that tune which has gone over all the world." The composition is said to have been completed in ten minutes. It was the last hymn sung by the Canadian nurse Edith Cavell before she suffered martyrdom in Belgium, October 12, 1915.

Wm. H. Monk, 1823-89, English organist and composer, devoted his life to the service of church music. For forty years he held the post of organist at King's College, London, and St. Matthias, Stoke Newington, devoting himself to the advancement of good congregational singing. "He taught many to praise God who had never praised Him before; he

25

taught others to praise Him more worthily than hitherto." He was the music editor of the famous *Hymns Ancient and Modern,* published in England, 1861.

CLOSE OF WORSHIP

41. Blest be the tie that binds   *John Fawcett, 1740-1817*

This hymn is often sung at the close of church meetings. Sometimes the custom of the people joining hands while singing is observed.

John Fawcett, an English Baptist minister, was serving a small country church in Yorkshire when he received and accepted a call to a large city church in London, which paid a salary more suited to the needs of his big family. His farewell sermon had been preached, six or seven wagons stood loaded with his furniture and books, and all was ready for his departure. But when the members of his humble flock turned out to bid farewell, many of them in tears, and imploring him to stay, it was more than he or Mrs. Fawcett could stand. He ordered the wagons unloaded and the furniture put back in its place, and sent a message to the London church that he was not coming. Afterwards he wrote this hymn which was to become one of the most famous in the English language.

MUSIC. DENNIS is simple and easy of performance, yet pleasing and effective. The tune was composed by Hans Georg Nägeli, 1768-1836, a Swiss, who was born near Zurich where he spent most of his life as music publisher, composer, and teacher. He was a prominent figure in public school music and was greatly interested in church music.

Lowell Mason found this melody in manuscript form and arranged it for use as a church tune.

For comments on Lowell Mason see Hymn 12. The tune "Boylston" (214) is also used with this hymn.

42. The Lord be with us as we bend   *John Ellerton, 1826-93*

The hymn is particularly appropriate for the close of an evening service.

John Ellerton was a minister of the Church of England, a teacher, author, and one of England's most distinguished hymnists. He assisted in editing the famous *Hymns Ancient and Modern,* London, 1861. He was early surrounded with religious influences and had a happy childhood life. Of his parents he wrote, "I used to feel how happy my father and mother were, even more than how good they were." He composed about fifty hymns and made about ten translations, a large proportion of which have found their way into church hymnals. He refused to take out a copyright for any of his hymns,

26

saying that "if any are counted worthy to contribute to Christ's praise in the congregation, one ought to feel very thankful and humble." His hymns, of which there are eight in the *Hymnary*, are elevated in tone and devotional spirit.

MUSIC. BEATITUDO was written for the Revised Edition of *Hymns Ancient and Modern*, 1875, and was set to the words, "How bright these glorious spirits shine."

For comments on the composer, J. B. Dykes, see Hymn 1.

43. Savior, again to Thy dear Name we raise

John Ellerton, 1826-93

This, the most popular of Ellerton's hymns, was originally written in 1866 for a choir festival. It was revised and condensed to these four verses, rich in poetic beauty and spiritual power, to take a high place among our evening hymns. The first stanza may be used with good effect as a choral benediction. The last stanza was sung at Ellerton's funeral on June 20, 1893.

For comments on John Ellerton see Hymn 42.

MUSIC. ELLERS was composed for this hymn in 1869.

Edward John Hopkins, 1818-1901, was a distinguished English church musician who served as organist in several important London churches, including Westminster Abbey. He was a prolific composer of church music of fine quality—services, hymn-tunes, anthems, organ pieces— and enjoyed a great reputation as editor of hymn books.

44. O Savior, bless us ere we go *Frederick W. Faber, 1814-63*

A hymn for the close of evening worship.

Frederick W. Faber was educated at Oxford and became a minister in the Church of England. He began his parish work at Elton where he became a forceful preacher and was known for his fine Christian character and lovely spirit. Church attendance increased, the parish grew, and the people who had been known for their intemperance and immorality were now reputed for their thrift and good behavior.

Under the influence of John Henry Newman, Faber changed his views and joined the Roman Catholic Church. After a trip to Rome, he lived at Birmingham where he formed, with eight others, a community called "Brothers of the Will of God." Later he moved to London where he continued his service in the Catholic Church until his death at the age of forty-nine. He wrote many theological and devotional books but is best known for his hymns of which he wrote 150, among which are such favorites as "There's a wideness in God's mercy" (58) and "Faith of our fathers" (154). His hymns are numbered among the treasures of English hymnody. They are devotional in spirit and with slight alterations appropriate for use in all Christian churches.

MUSIC. SURREY is a beautiful tune which became immediately popular and has remained so, especially in England. The composer, Henry Carey, 1692-1743, was a teacher in boarding schools and private families in England. He composed a large number of secular songs and was only incidentally a writer of church music.

45. Lord, dismiss us with Thy blessing *John Fawcett, 1740-1817*

This popular dismission hymn is ascribed to the English Baptist minister, John Fawcett, who is best known as the author of "Blest be the tie that binds." The hymn has undergone some alteration with the passing of the years. The third stanza originally read:

> "So whene'er the signal's given
> "Us from earth to call away,
> "Borne on angels' wings to heaven
> "Glad the summons to obey,
> "May we ever
> "Reign with Christ in endless day."

For comments on John Fawcett see Hymn 41.

MUSIC. SICILIAN MARINERS is a familiar tune of unknown origin which has been set to various hymns, including the Latin *"O Sanctissima, O Purissima,"* and the German *"O du fröliche, o du selige."* The tune, sometimes called "Sicily," is not known in Sicily today.

GOD THE FATHER

46. Mighty God, while angels bless Thee

Robert Robinson, 1735-90

The author of this hymn had a unique career. Robert Robinson, born in Norfolk, England, of lowly parentage, was left fatherless at eight to be the sole support of his widowed mother. At fourteen he was apprenticed to a barber in London who frequently reprimanded him for giving too much time to the reading of books and too little to business. At seventeen he heard the great evangelist Whitefield preach a sermon on Matthew 3:7 and decided to dedicate his life to God. His complete conversion he dates a few years later, 1755. He began preaching under the Methodists but soon developed independent views and in 1759 he received adult baptism and united with the Baptists. Shortly afterwards he became the pastor of a small Baptist church in the university town of Cambridge. He was a gifted scholar, and though he had little formal education, he held the respect of Cambridge students, notwithstanding the taunts of university professors. Serving a small and poor congregation and being without finances to support his large family, he helped himself by engaging in farming and carrying on business as a coal and corn merchant while preaching twice a Sunday and holding evangelistic meetings during the week. In this he succeeded in a very remarkable measure, aided by the fact that he knew the soil and the tillers of the soil and was gifted with the sense of humor and a Spurgeon-like wit. Besides this hymn, he also wrote the well-known hymn, "Come, Thou fount of every blessing" (189).

MUSIC. CRUCIFER, originally known as "Bethany," was composed by Henry Smart for "Jesus, I my cross have taken." The composer favored unison singing of this melody, at moderate tempo. Most congregations will find the pitch range in the melody too wide for best results in unison singing.

Henry Smart, 1813-1879, turned from the legal profession to devote his life to music. Though largely self-taught, he became one of England's distinguished organists and builder of organs. He suffered from poor eyesight and the last fourteen years of his life he was totally blind, but he kept on playing and composing for he had a very retentive memory and possessed a rare skill in extempore playing. Smart was a strong advocate of congregational singing, but favored the unison singing of melodies, and had a decided prejudice against what he considered unduly fast congregational singing.

47. I sing the mighty power of God   Isaac Watts, 1674-1748

A hymn of praise, magnifying the power, wisdom, goodness, and omnipresence of God as revealed in creation. It appeared first in Watt's *Divine and Moral Songs for the Use of Children* where it was entitled, "Praise for Creation and Providence." The original has eight stanzas. For comments on Watts see No. 11.

MUSIC. ELLACOMBE is a cheerful, unpretentious tune that deserves to be better known. The source designated is *Gesangbuch der Herzogl* published in 1784, but some of our best authorities are content to leave its exact origin in doubt. It found its way into English hymnals soon after it was published in *Vollständige Sammlung der gewöhnlichen Melodien zum Mainzer Gesangbuche,* by X. L. Hartig, in 1833.

MAKER OF HEAVEN AND EARTH

48. This is my Father's world   Maltbie D. Babcock, 1858-1901

The original has sixteen stanzas, each beginning with the words "This is my Father's world," a good slogan to begin and end the day. It appeared in the author's *Thoughts for Every Day Living,* a book of religious verse. The hymn expresses a confident attitude toward life and a buoyant faith in God.

Maltbie D. Babcock, prominent Presbyterian minister, was born in Syracuse, New York, graduated from Syracuse University and Auburn Seminary and then began his first pastorate at the First Presbyterian Church, Lockport, N. Y. His second pastorate was at Brown Memorial Church, Baltimore, where he was popular with the students at Johns Hopkins University. He then received a call to the Brick Church, New York City, where he became the successor of Henry van Dyke. In his student days he was known as a fine student, a great athlete, a good musician, and a friend to all. He loved young people and during his ministry they turned to him for counsel.

MUSIC. The tune TERRA BEATA is simple, light in movement, and easy to sing. It was composed by Franklin Sheppard, 1852-1930, a Philadelphia business man, Presbyterian layman, and friend of Dr. Babcock. Sheppard was also an accomplished musician. He modestly attributed the tune to an old English folk melody, but it is known now that he himself was the composer. He named the tune "Terra Beata," happy or blessed earth.

The arrangement in the *Hymnary,* known as "Terra Patris," is by Edward Shippen Barnes, a contemporary American organist and composer. His harmonization is a little more difficult to sing but also more interesting than the original by Sheppard.

49. Let the whole creation cry   *Stopford A. Brooke, 1832-1916*

The hymn is an imitation of Psalm 148. It is a universal call to praise rather than an expression of praise, hence it is addressed not to God but to his creation everywhere, as a call to worship God. The hymn is characterized by literary grace, simplicity, and tenderness, and is included in many modern hymnals.

Stopford A. Brooke, born in Ireland, was educated at Dublin, then became a clergyman in the Anglican Church. For a time he was one of the most popular preachers in London. In 1880, being restive under the doctrinal standards of the church, he severed his relation with the Anglicans and continued a ministry of preaching and lecturing and writing as an independent, not associated with any denomination. His *Life and Letters of F. W. Robertson* ranks among the classic biographies. In 1881, he compiled *Christian Hymns* for use in his own congregation, in which this hymn is found, the original having ten stanzas.

MUSIC. ROLAND is an easy, flowing tune which congregations love to sing after learning it well. It is suitable for use as a processional. The composer, Caleb Simmer, born 1856, was an American musician. His sacred pieces, include anthems, quartets, cantatas, and organ music.

50. The spacious firmament on high   *Joseph Addison, 1672-1719*

This hymn was praised by Lord Selbourne as "a very perfect and finished composition, taking rank among the best hymns of the English language." The author, Joseph Addison, was an eminent Englishman of letters. Dr. Samuel Johnson said of him, "Whoever wishes to attain an English style, familiar, but not coarse, elegant but not ostentatious, must give his days and nights to the volumes of Addison." In 1712, Addison wrote a series of essays in the *Spectator,* concluding each essay with a hymn. In the issue of August 23, this hymn, a free rendering of Psalm 19, formed the conclusion to an essay on "The Proper Means of Strengthening and Confirming Faith in the Mind of Man."

MUSIC. CREATION is an adaptation of a part of the magnificent chorus (No. 14) in Haydn's oratorio, *The Creation.* For comments on Haydn, see Hymn No. 27.

51. For the beauty of the earth   *Folliott S. Pierpoint, 1835-1917*

This delightful hymn of thanksgiving was originally written for the communion service to bring the note of joy into the solemn sacrament, making it truly an "eucharist." It is now used frequently at Thanksgiving and children's services. It names many causes for praise and thanksgiving, from the "beauty of the earth" to the "church that lifteth holy hands."

The author, Folliott S. Pierpoint, was born at Bath, England, and educated at Cambridge. He was a teacher of the classics, published several books of poems, and made notable contributions to the hymnody of the church.

MUSIC. DIX appeared first in a collection of chorales edited and published by Kocher in Stuttgart in 1838, set to the hymn *"Treuer Heiland, wir sind hier."* It has long been used with the words, "As with gladness men of old" (530), by W. C. Dix, hence the name "Dix." It has a strong, joyous tune which marches with stately tread and is a favorite processional.

Conrad Kocher, 1786-1872, was a German student of church music, a composer and teacher. He studied at St. Petersburg and in Rome. He founded the School of Sacred Song in Stuttgart, which did much to improve German church music and popularize four-part singing in Germany.

52. God of the earth, the sky, the sea

Samuel Longfellow, 1819-92

A hymn which finds God in every aspect of nature. For comments on the author, Samuel Longfellow, see Hymn 28.

MUSIC. SHELTERING WING, a long-meter melody admirably suited to these words, is by the English church musician, Joseph Barnby, 1838-96. For comments on him see Hymn 19.

53. Lord of all being, throned afar *Oliver W. Holmes, 1809-94*

A hymn difficult to praise too highly, probably the greatest penned on the omnipresence of God. Its first appearance was in the *Atlantic Monthly* as the final installment of the series of articles later collected into book form and entitled *The Professor at the Breakfast Table.* The work closed with the following lines and the hymn:

> Peace to all such as may have been vexed in spirit by any utterances these pages may have repeated! They will, doubtless, forget for the moment the differences in the hues of truth we look at through our human prisms and join in singing (inwardly) this hymn to the Source of the light we all need to lead us, and the warmth which alone can make us brothers:
> Lord of all being! throned afar,
> Thy glory flames from sun and star;
> Centre and soul of every sphere,
> Yet to each loving heart how near.

Oliver Wendell Holmes was the son of a Congregational minister in Cambridge, Massachusetts, although later when he became established as a physician in Boston, he united with the Unitarians. His writings are nevertheless permeated by an evangelical warmth which has made his hymns acceptable to all denominations. Holmes was a distinguished graduate of Harvard University in Arts and Medicine and spent most of his years teaching anatomy at Harvard. But he is best known to us as a man of letters. None of his writings is so widely known as the two hymns, "Lord of all being" and "O Love divine, that stooped to share" (172), both of them found in the author's, *The Professor at the Breakfast Table.*

MUSIC. LOUVAN is by an American musician, Virgil C. Taylor, 1817-91, organist and editor of song books. This is the only one of his tunes now in common use. An alternative tune that fits the hymn very well is "St. Crispin" found at No. 149.

HIS LOVE AND MERCY

54. Be still, my soul, the Lord is on thy side

Katharina von Schlegel, born c. 1697
Tr. Jane L. Borthwick, 1813-97

The hymn is a translation of a poem by Katharina von Schlegel. She was born in Germany, 1697. No one seems to have found anything definite concerning her life, except that she wrote some hymns, one of which passed into the English language. The original, based on Psalm 46:10, "Be still and know that I am God," had four stanzas, as follows:

> Stille, mein Wille! Dein Jesus hilft siegen;
> Trage geduldig das Leiden, die Not;
> Gott ist's, der alles zum besten will fügen,
> Der dir getreu bleibt in Schmerzen und Tod.
> Stille, mein Wille! Dein Jesus wird machen
> Glücklichen Ausgang bedenklicher Sachen.
>
> Stille, mein Wille! Der Herr hat's in Händen;
> Hält sich dein Herz nur im Glauben an ihn,
> Wird er den Kummer bald wenden und enden
> Herrlich wird endlich, was wunderbar schien.
> Stille, mein Wille! Dein Heiland wird zeigen,
> Wie vor ihm Meer und Gewitter muss schweigen.
>
> Stille, mein Wille! Wenn Freunde sich trennen,
> Die du so zärtlich und innig geliebt,
> Wirst du die Freundschaft des Höchsten erkennen,
> Der sich zum Eigentum treulich dir gibt.
> Stille, mein Wille! Dein Jesus ersetzet,
> Was dich beim Sterben der Liebsten verletzet.
>
> Stille, mein Wille! Es kommen die Stunden,
> Dass wir beim Herrn sind ohn' Wechsel der Zeit;
> Dann ist das Scheiden, der Kummer verschwunden.
> Ewige Freundschaft vergütet das Leid.
> Stille, mein Wille! Nach zeitlichem Scheiden
> Sehn wir uns wieder ohn' Schmerzen und Leiden.

The words, both in the original and in the English translation, are of great beauty and their message has brought real comfort to many a burdened and disquieted soul.

The translation is by Jane Borthwick, born in Edinburgh, who, with her sister, Sarah B. Findlater, did outstanding work as a translator of German hymns. Only Catherine Winkworth surpassed her. Miss Borthwick, a member of the Free Church of Scotland, was a devout Christian character, especially interested in the mission work of the church, both home and foreign. Another of her well-known translations is "My Jesus, as Thou wilt" (250) from the original by Benjamin Schmolke.

MUSIC. FINLANDIA is from the pen of Jean Sibelius, born December 8, 1865, in Finland, and undoubtedly the greatest living composer. At this writing, 1948, he is still living, but, through the misfortunes of war, reduced to penury and poverty. Besides seven symphonies, he wrote many smaller orchestral works. This tune is from the tone poem "Finlandia," the arrangement having been made for the *Hymnal of the Presbyterian Church* in 1932. It is included in a number of recent

33

hymn books and has become a favorite with worshipping congregations wherever introduced.

55. God is love; His mercy brightens   *John Bowring, 1792-1872*

A bright, joyful hymn which we owe to a layman, Sir John Bowring, born at Exeter, England, 1792. Though a member of the Unitarian Church, his faith was apparently that of an evangelical. On his tombstone are engraved the words of another great hymn which he himself wrote, "In the Cross of Christ I glory" (See 110). Bowring was the son of a manufacturer of woolen goods and he spent his early years travelling in all parts of the world in the interest of his father's business. Though he left school at the age of 14, he became an outstanding linguist and scholar and writer. At the age of 16, he had acquired five languages and late in life he is said to have known 200 languages and spoken 100. One of his primary interests was politics. He was elected to the British Parliament and later became the British consul at Canton and the governor of Hong Kong. He published a book of *Hymns* with the desire that they might be useful in strengthening the religious faith of others who under suffering and disheartening circumstances might chance to read them.

The hymn is constructed to emphasize in each stanza the idea of God as wisdom (I Cor. 1:30) and love (I John 4:8).

MUSIC. STOCKWELL, a very useful tune, appeared in Lowell Mason's popular collection of hymns, *New Carmina Sacra,* in 1850, set to the words, "Silently the shades of evening," written by Christopher Cox.

The composer, Darius Eliot Jones, 1815-81, was born at Carroll, N. Y. His father, Abner Jones, was a well-known music teacher in New York. Darius spent twenty years of his adult life in business. He served for a time as assistant editor of the *Choral Advocate,* published by Mason Brothers, New York, and at the same time conducted the music in Plymouth Church, Brooklyn, where Henry Ward Beecher was pastor. At Beecher's suggestion, Jones prepared a new hymn book, *Temple Melodies,* 1861, for use in Plymouth Church. Feeling a call to the Christian ministry, Jones entered Iowa College, at Davenport, as a student and at the age of 43 was ordained as a Congregational minister. He served churches at Columbia City and Newton Center, Ia., until 1863, when he became treasurer of the Iowa General Association. For a year, he was agent for the American Bible Society; and for four years, 1866-70, he was agent for Iowa College, later located at Grinnell and known as Grinnell College. Here Jones published a second hymn book, *Songs for the New Life,* in 1869. From that time on, he served various churches in Iowa until his death in 1881.

56. How gentle God's commands   *Philip Doddridge, 1702-51*

This hymn, beautiful in poetic imagery, is based on I Peter 5:7, "Casting all your care upon Him: for He careth for you." When it first appeared, posthumously, in a book of hymns by the author, it bore the title, "God's care a remedy for ours."

Philip Doddridge was born in London, the youngest of a family of twenty, most of whom died in childhood. His father was an oil merchant. Before he could read, he had learned from his mother the stories of the Bible by the aid of Bible pictures on the Dutch tiles that covered a portion of the living room. Doddridge became a minister in the Congregational Church and devoted his life not only to preaching, but to writing books and teaching young men for the ministry. In 1751, he went to Lisbon to seek relief from tuberculosis but died there. He is the author of over 400 hymns, a few of which have survived, and are found in most hymn books. The *Hymnary* contains six of his compositions.

MUSIC. DENNIS. For comments on this tune see Hymn 41.

57. Thou Grace Divine, encircling all   *Eliza Scudder, 1821-96*

The hymn was written by Eliza Scudder, an American hymn writer of the middle nineteenth century. She was born in Boston, and died in Weston, Massachusetts. She was a niece of Edmund H. Sears, author of "It came upon a midnight clear" (No. 75). Miss Scudder was a person of deep religious insight and lived a quiet, retiring life. She published a book of religious verse, *Hymns and Sonnets,* in 1880. During most of her active life she was a Unitarian, but in later life joined the Episcopal Church.

MUSIC. BALLERMA (misspelled Balerma in some editions of the *Hymnary)* is a very simple tune, the second pair of lines varying only slightly from the first pair. The origin of the tune is uncertain. It is thought to be an old Spanish melody, arranged by F. H. Barthélémon.

For comments on Barthélémon see Hymn 2.

58. There's a wideness in God's mercy   *F. W. Faber, 1814-63*

The original of this poem has thirteen stanzas, the first of which reads:

> Souls of men! why will ye scatter
> Like a crowd of frightened sheep?
> Foolish hearts! why will ye wander
> From a love so true and deep?

The five stanzas selected for use here make an impressive and coherent hymn with no trace of the author's strong Roman Catholic bias which characterizes nearly all of his hymns.

For comments on F. W. Faber see Hymn 44.

MUSIC. WELLESLEY was written, by request, for the graduation hymn of the Newton (Mass.) high school class of which Miss Tourjee was then a member. The original tune had a slight fault in voice leading which was corrected, with her permission, by Dr. Hamilton C. Macdougall, then Professor of Music at Wellesley College.

Lizzie S. Tourjee, 1858-1913, was a student at Wellesley College during the year 1877-78. In 1883, she married Frank Estabrook. Her father, Dr. Eben Tourjee, encouraged her in the writing of the tune, and named it for the new college nearby where she became a student for one year.

59. Father Almighty, bless us with Thy blessing   *Anonymous*

A prayer of invocation seeking the blessing and guidance of Almighty God. The authorship is anonymous.

MUSIC. INTEGER VITAE (or FLEMMING) was composed by Flemming for a chorus of men's voices. It was set to "Integer Vitae," an ode by Horace. The tune became a great favorite with college men not only in this country but also in England and Germany. It was introduced as a hymn tune through the hymnals of Dr. Charles R. Robinson, *Songs of the Sanctuary,* and *Laudes Domine,* and has since been widely used and accepted as one of our most satisfactory hymn tunes. It is one of the favorite tunes in the *Gesangbuch mit Noten* where it is set to the words, *"Ach mein Herr Jesu."*

The composer, Frederick Ferdinand Flemming, M. D., 1778-1813, received his training in medicine and was a successful practitioner in Berlin. He is known to posterity, however, as a composer of part songs for men's choruses, and more particularly as the composer of this tune.

60. God moves in a mysterious way   *William Cowper,* 1731-1800

There is no basis, according to most hymnologists, for the story that this hymn was written after Cowper was mysteriously prevented from committing suicide by drowning. The hymn was published by John Newton in the *Olney Hymns,* 1779, and rapidly became popular. It is still found in nearly all the hymnals. Its original title was "Light shining out of darkness." Its central thought is that God is working His sovereign will even in the mystery and perplexity of human life, bringing light, not *after* darkness, but *out of* darkness.

William Cowper, 1731-1800, was the greatest English poet of his age. He had been trained for the law and was called to the bar at the age of twenty-three but had to retire on account of ill health. He lost his mental balance and became deeply melancholic, a misfortune which is attributed to cruelty received at the hands of older and stronger lads while he attended preparatory school. After treatment in a private asylum, and living for a time in the home of Rev. Morley Unwin, he moved to Olney where his devoted friend, the Rev. John Newton was curate. Here he assisted Newton in his parochial and evangelistic work and collaborated with him in the production of what became known as the *Olney Hymns*. In spite of efforts at literary work, his depression of spirit returned and never left him, except for brief intervals, until his death in 1800.

MUSIC. DUNDEE (or FRENCH) is one of the twelve Common Tunes appearing in the *Scottish Psalter, The CL Psalms of David &*, Edinburgh, 1615, where it is named "French Tune." Its first appearance in an English Psalter is in Ravencroft's *Whole Book of Psalms,* 1621, where it is called "Dundy." It is one of the best known of the psalm tunes and its smooth, flowing melody has enjoyed great popularity.

For comments on the *Scottish Psalter* see Hymn 575.

61. O God, our help in ages past *Isaac Watts, 1674-1748*

Based on Psalm 90:1-6: "Lord, thou hast been our dwelling place in all generations," etc., this is Watt's greatest hymn and one of the greatest in the English language. It is found in all English hymn books and has been translated into many languages. Its smoothness, simple dignity, and faithfulness to Scripture give it the marks of a true church hymn, and it has probably been chosen more than any other for use upon important occasions. It is an indispensable New Year's hymn.

A press dispatch related how the hymn was used during the Second World War by a group of eleven doomed Norwegians as they faced a Nazi firing squad in the village of Selbu outside of Trondheim, Norway, for "general hostility" to German occupiers. "Despite the torture to which they had been subjected to earlier," writes an eye-witness, "the group of prisoners, linked hand in hand, proudly and firmly faced their executioners. One of the men, Peter Morseth, who for years led the singing in the local church, read a short prayer and was joined by his companions in singing the hymn, 'O God our help in ages past.' Then the shots rang out."

John Wesley printed the hymn in his *Collection of Psalms and Hymns,* 1734, altering the opening line from "Our God, our help," to "O God, our help."

For comments on Isaac Watts see Hymn 11.

MUSIC. ST. ANNE appeared anonymously, in two parts—treble and bass—in *A Supplement to the New Version of Psalms by Dr. Brady and Mr. Tate. . . . the sixth edition, corrected and much enlarged,"* 1708, where it was set to Psalm 42. It is attributed upon good authority to William Croft, 1678-1727, who was interested in the production of the

Tate and Brady *New Version*. Croft is one of the greatest names in English musical history.

For further comments on Croft, see Hymn 6.

62. The Lord is my Shepherd   *James Montgomery, 1771-1854*

One of the fine metrical versions that have been made of the Twenty-third Psalm. It is found in Montgomery's *Songs of Zion, being Imitations of Psalms,* 1822. Another much-loved and widely used version of the same Psalm is that in the *Scottish Psalter* (see 579).

James Montgomery, greatest of Moravian hymn writers, was born in Ayrshire, Scotland, near the birthplace of Robert Burns. His father became a minister in the Moravian Church and finally went as a missionary to the West Indies where both he and his wife died. After spending a part of his youth in precarious and doubtful ways of living, and failing in several business ventures, James became the editor of *The Sheffield Register,* a position he held with honor and distinction for thirty-one years. He was twice imprisoned for expressing liberal political views in his paper. He is classed by the *literati* as a minor English poet, but in the writing of hymns he ranks with Wesley, Watts, and Doddridge. Of his 400 hymns, 100 are still in use. Eleven of his hymns are found in the *Hymnary,* exceeded in number only by those of Hosmer, Wesley and Watts. All of Montgomery's hymns show a marvelous knowledge of the Scriptures on the part of their author. He found in the Psalms an inexhaustible source of devotional material and made metrical versions of many of them.

MUSIC. POLAND. The tune is unique in the *Hymnary* in that the melody in the first three lines is found in the alto. To bring the melody out with sufficient clearness, the altos might well be reenforced by some sopranos, or men's voices, or both.

Thomas Koschat, 1845-1914, was an Austrian composer and singer. While a student of natural science at Vienna University he sang in the Court Opera Chorus, and soon became its leader. In 1875, Koschat organized the Kärnthner Quintet which became famous for its singing of Carinthian folk songs. He is known for his harmonization of Carinthian melodies and original songs in their style, for which he wrote the texts.

63. Father and Friend, Thy light, thy love

John Bowring, 1792-1872

A hymn on the omnipresence of God who reigns as Lord of life and cares for His children.

For comments on John Bowring see Hymn 55.

MUSIC. ILLA, a simple long-meter tune within easy compass of the voices, is by the American composer, Lowell Mason, 1792-1872, an exact contemporary of Bowring. Mason's tunes were popular at first and then for a time they were frowned upon by some of the "highbrow" musicians but in late years are returning with new favor into the hymn books. Mason's name appears 24 times in our collection.

For further comments on Mason see Hymn 12.

64. Let us with a gladsome mind   *John Milton, 1608-74*

This delightful lyric is the result of John Milton's paraphrasing of Psalm 136 when he was a boy of 15 years. The original has 26 stanzas. The Psalm tells the story of Israel's history, ending each verse with the refrain, "For his mercy endureth forever." The selections here are his renderings of verses 1, 2, 7, and 25. The closing stanza returns to verse 1.

John Milton, the poet, was born in London, the son of the John Milton, who had turned from the Roman Catholic Church to become a Protestant. The future poet went to Christ's College, Cambridge, where he received his B.A. in 1628 and M.A. in 1632. His short poems and paraphrases were written at an early age and constitute some of his best work. The second period of his literary career was given almost entirely to writings on political subjects for he lived in the day of the controversies which led to Civil War and the establishment of the Commonwealth in England. Milton joined Oliver Cromwell as his secretary for foreign tongues to the Council of State, a position he held until the eve of the Restoration, when he barely escaped the scaffold. For years he had suffered from poor eyesight and became totally blind in his forty-fourth year. The third period of his life, after the Restoration of the Monarchy, was lived in close retirement. During this time he produced his greatest writings: *Paradise Lost, Paradise Regained,* and *Samson Agonistes,* all of them dictated to others. He ranks second only to Shakespeare among English poets. He translated 19 psalms into meter. Being the scholar's rather than the people's poet, he, however, had no great influence on hymnology. His version of Psalm 84 is found at No. 592.

MUSIC. INNOCENTS appeared, anonymously, in the *Parish Choir,* 1850, a publication issued by members of the Oxford Movement in England who went by the name of "The Society for Promoting Church Music." The "Society" laid down the following principles for singing:

1. Congregational singing should be in unison.
2. The melody should be clearly marked.
3. The compass should be within the natural limits of the human voice.
4. Metrical psalmody should be confined to tunes in common time, as being more simple and solemn than triple time.

After three years of precarious existence, 1846-49, the *Parish Choir* was discontinued. INNOCENTS appeared at the end of Volume III amongst a number of old psalm tunes, appointed to be sung to a hymn for Innocents Day, hence the name. Lightwood attributes the tune to Joseph Smith, born in 1800, near Birmingham, England. Smith was not a professional musician but very fond of music, an excellent singer, and composer of many hymn tunes and other pieces. The editor of the *Parish Choir* altered the original to the present form. It made its way into *Hymns Ancient and Modern*, 1861, and is now found in many modern hymn books.

JESUS CHRIST OUR LORD

65. Hail to the Lord's Anointed   *James Montgomery, 1771-1854*

A rendering of Psalm 72, made in 1821 for the Christmas worship of a Moravian settlement. The original has eight stanzas. Montgomery was greatly interested in missions and this hymn, generally esteemed his finest composition, is a good missionary hymn as well as a splendid one for the Advent season. Dr. Adam Clarke gave it wide publicity by publishing it in his famous *Bible Commentary*, 1822, at the end of his exposition of Psalm 72, adding this note:

> I need not tell the intelligent reader that he has seized the spirit, and exhibited some of the principal beauties, of the Hebrew bard; though (to use his own words in a letter to me) his "hand trembled to touch the harp of Zion." I take the liberty here to register a wish, which I have strongly expressed to himself, that he would favor the Church of God with a metrical version of the whole book.

It is interesting to compare this hymn with Isaac Watts' rendering of the same psalm (341).

For comments on James Montgomery see Hymn 62.

MUSIC. WEBB, also known as "Morning Light," was composed for a secular song, " 'Tis dawn, the lark is singing," and first published in *Odeon: A Collection of Secular Melodies,* by G. J. Webb and Lowell Mason, 1837. It first appeared as a hymn tune in *The Wesleyan Psalmist,* 1842, and later it was used for the hymn "The morning Light is breaking," in books by Mason and Webb.

The composer, George James Webb, 1803-87, a member of the Swedenborgian Church, was born near Salisbury, England; studied theology and music; came to the United States and became associated with Lowell Mason in editing and publishing music books. He was married to Mason's daughter, Mary. He played the organ at Old South Church, Boston, and was Professor of Secular Music in the Boston Academy of Music.

40

66. Watchman, tell us of the night   *John Bowring, 1792-1872*

An Advent and missionary hymn, unique in that it consists of a dialog (between a watchman and a traveller). The hymn is based on Isaiah 21:11, 12: "Watchman, what of the night? watchman, what of the night? The watchman said, The morning cometh, and also the night: if ye will enquire, enquire ye: return, come." The meaning of the passage is not evident from the context. Dr. C. S. Robinson describes the setting as follows:

> The image it presents is singularly dramatic and picturesque. The scene is laid in the midst of the Babylonian Captivity. A lonely watchman is represented as standing on the ramparts of some tower along the defenses of the citadel. He seems to be anxiously looking for the issues of the siege leveled against it. The time is midnight. Calamity is over the land. The people are afflicted. Their enemies are pressing them hard. That solitary sentinel sadly remains at his post, peering into the unlit gloom, trying to discern signs of deliverance. But the heavens are starless, and the impenetrable clouds keep rolling on. Suddenly an unknown voice pierces the air. Whether in wailing sorrow or in bitter taunt, is not evident; but out of the stillness already grown oppressive breaks the question with repetitious pertinacity: "Watchman, what of the night? Watchman, what of the night?" The sentinel waits through a moment of surprised meditation and then tranquilly answers: "The morning cometh and also the night; if ye will inquire, inquire ye: return, come." Then the dialog lapses into silence again, and the night gathers its unbroken shadows deeper than ever.

For comments on John Bowring see Hymn 55.

MUSIC. WATCHMAN is by Lowell Mason who wrote the tune in 1830 in 3-4 time. He intended it as a duet between soprano and tenor, with the congregation repeating the last line of each stanza (the reply of the watchman). The tune also lends itself well to antiphonal singing.

For comments on Mason see Hymn 12.

67. O come, O come, Emmanuel   *From the Latin, 12th Century*
Stanza 1, Tr. John M. Neale, 1818-66
Stanzas 2, 3, Henry Sloan Coffin, 1877—

> Veni, veni, Emmanuel
> captivum solve Israel,
> qui gemit in exilio,
> privatus Dei Filio.
>
> > Gaude, gaude; Emmanuel
> > nascetur pro te, Israel.

The hymn comes from the Latin, being a translation of the first of the seven greater *Antiphons* (short anthems-verses) sung in the Roman

41

Church at Vespers on the seven days before Christmas. The refrain, "Rejoice, rejoice," etc., added to the hymn during the 13th century, is the answer to the longing for Christ expressed in each stanza.

The translation of Stanza 1 is by John M. Neale, 1818-66, a Cambridge scholar and the most noted hymnologist and liturgist of his time. He was a minister and author of books on biblical and historical subjects, but his fame rests chiefly on his translations of Greek and Latin hymns. The *Hymnary* contains ten of his works.

The second and third stanzas were translated in 1916 by Henry Sloan Coffin, eminent Presbyterian minister, formerly of the Madison Avenue Church in New York City, and then for many years president of Union Theological Seminary. He is a recognized leader in contemporary American church life.

MUSIC. VENI EMMANUEL, written in the first Gregorian mode, is an adaptation by Thomas Helmore, in 1856, of a melody said to have been found in a French manuscript in Lisbon, which has since disappeared. The original is believed to have been a 12th century "Kyrie." The harmony in the minor mode gives the tune its quaint flavor. It should be sung with spirit, in keeping with the joyful anticipation embodied in the words. It is effective with men's voices singing the first part in unison, then all the voices in harmony on the refrain. The tune also lends itself to interesting effects in antiphonal singing.

68. Veiled in darkness Judah lay

Douglas LeTell Rights, 1891—

Written in 1915, while World War I was raging in Europe and the clouds were gathering thick over the United States. The hymn is an appeal for the Spirit of Christ to bring peace and light to a troubled world. It was composed while the author, a Moravian, was a student at the Divinity School of Harvard University. It was the custom at that institution to have students of the School submit original compositions of hymns, one of which would be selected to be sung at the annual Christmas service of the school. This hymn was selected for the Christmas of 1915.

Douglas LeTell Rights, born in Winston-Salem, N. C., received his A. B. degree from the University of North Carolina and then prepared for the ministry at the Moravian Theological Seminary, Bethlehem, Pa., and at Harvard University. A member of the Moravian Church, anciently called the *Unitas Fratrum,* his first pastorate was at the First Moravian Church, Greensboro, N. C., 1916-18. In 1918-19, he was chaplain in the army in World War I. Since 1919, he has been pastor of Trinity Moravian Church, Winston-Salem, N. C. Rights is the author of *A Voyage Down the Yadkin-Great Peedee River,* 1928, and has written numerous articles on historical and archaeological subjects pertaining to his native state. His latest book is the *American Indian in North Carolina.*

MUSIC. EBELING. For comments on the composer of this tune, Johann Georg Ebeling, 1620-76, see Hymn 555.

69. Come, Thou long-expected Jesus   *Charles Wesley, 1707-88*

A dignified, yet stirring Advent hymn, based on Haggai 2:7: "The desire of all nations shall come." One of the first hymns of Wesley, it appeared in a small book of 24 pages, *Hymns for the Nativity of our Lord,* published in 1744. It is found in nearly all the modern hymn books in England and America.

For comments on Charles Wesley see Hymn 6.

MUSIC. HYFRYDOL is a Welsh tune composed by Rowland Hugh Prichard, 1811-87, of Bala, Wales, who was active in the church as song leader, soloist, and composer of tunes. This tune is a composition of his youth, while he was still under twenty. It is characterized by its length, smoothness, and utter simplicity, the whole melody moving throughout, except for one note, within the compass of the fifth.

HIS BIRTH

70. Joy to the world! the Lord is come   *Isaac Watts, 1674-1748*

This hymn, which has such an important place in the yearly celebration of the Nativity, is a free rendering of the latter part of Psalm 98: "Make a joyful noise unto the Lord, all the earth: make a loud noise, and rejoice, and sing praise." Watts entitled it , "Messiah's Coming and Kingdom." His effort to put the New Testament gospel into the Psalm resulted in a great hymn of the Advent and Nativity, though his free rendering nearly lost sight of the Psalm itself. He feels all nature thrilling with joy at the Saviour's birth.

For comments on Isaac Watts see Hymn 11.

MUSIC. ANTIOCH is an arrangement, credited by some authorities to Lowell Mason, from Handel's *Messiah.* The opening phrase resembles the first bar of the chorus, "Lift up your heads," and the four measures set to "and heaven and nature sing" are reminiscent of the introduction to the tenor recitative, "Comfort ye my people." It is a stirring tune well fitted to the words. It may be sung antiphonally to good effect, the congregation singing lines 1 and 2 (1st score), the choir, lines 3 and 4 (2d and 3d scores), and both choir and congregation the refrain (last score).

71. Christians, awake! salute the happy morn

John Byrom, 1692-1763

From a longer poem of 48 lines, written about 1749, by Dr. John

Byrom for his daughter Dolly who, when asked what she would like to have for a Christmas present, replied, "Please write me a poem." On Christmas morning she found on her plate at the breakfast table a sheet of paper on which was written this poem, entitled, "Christmas Day. For Dolly." It is based on Luke 2.

John Byrom was born in Manchester, England, graduated from Cambridge, studied medicine but gave up its practice in order to teach a system of shorthand he himself had invented, and which became the chief system of shorthand in his time. He was a friend of Charles and John Wesley and taught them shorthand, which Charles especially put to good use in dashing down hymns as they flashed into his mind. Byrom was a man of learning and piety and also was given to wit and humor. He coined the phrase "tweedledum and tweedledee" when the friends of Handel and Buononcini were debating the relative merits of the two composers:

> Some say, compared to Buononcini
> That Mynheer Handel is a ninny.
> Others aver that he to Handel
> Is scarcely fit to hold a candle.
> Strange all this difference should be
> Twixt tweedledum and tweedledee.

MUSIC. YORKSHIRE was composed by a musician and organist, John Wainwright, of whom little is known. He is remembered principally by this tune. Musically and emotionally, the tune is completely satisfactory and well deserves its great popularity. It has been a favorite among English speaking people for nearly a century.

72. Today be joy in every heart *Frederick L. Hosmer, 1840-1929*

A hymn of Christmas peace.

The author, Frederic L. Hosmer, one of America's foremost hymn writers, was born in Farmingham, Mass., and died in Berkeley, Calif. He was educated at Harvard University and Divinity School and served as minister of Unitarian churches in Northboro, Mass., Quincy, Ill., Cleveland, O., St. Louis, Mo., and Berkeley, Calif. At least 35 of his hymns have come into more or less use in this country and in England. The *Hymnary* includes thirteen, a larger number than of any other writer except Wesley and Watts.

MUSIC. DORKING, an English folk tune of anonymous composition, as all folk tunes are, has characteristic grace of melody and strength of rhythm.

73-74. While shepherds watched their flocks
Nahum Tate, 1652-1715

This carol is the work of Nahum Tate, poet laureate and co-author

44

with Nicholas Brady of the *New Version* of the psalms in meter, to which was added a supplement in 1770 containing this hymn. The quaint and picturesque paraphrase of Luke 2:9-11, closing with the doxology, was one of the few hymns permitted to be sung in the English churches along with the metrical psalms. It became very popular and has been translated into the Latin and nearly all the living languages. The words have been set to many tunes.

For comments on Nahum Tate, see Hymn 18.

MUSIC. CHRISTMAS is an adaptation of a melody from Handel's opera, *Siroe.* Geo. F. Handel was born in Prussia in 1685 (the same year as J. S. Bach) and died in 1759. He lived in England 50 years and became a naturalized English citizen. He wrote many forms of music but is chiefly known and loved for his oratorio, *The Messiah.*

MUSIC. ST. MARTIN'S (74), by William Tans'ur, is less joyful than "Christmas," but the tune fits the words perfectly. Its quiet, mystic melody suggests the serenity of the Judean hillside where shepherds watched their flocks.

William Tans'ur, 1706-83, was the son of a laborer, whose name is spelled "Tanzer" in the church register. He became a teacher of psalmody, moved from town to town to conduct singing classes, and did much to improve psalm-singing in the Church of England. He published a number of books on music. An eccentric man, given to self-advertisement, he described his first volume The *Harmony of Sion,* 1734, as "The most curiosest Book that ever was published."

75. It came upon a midnight clear   *Edmund H. Sears*, 1810-76

Published by the *Christian Register* in 1860, the hymn quickly attained wide popularity. Edmund H. Sears was minister of a Unitarian Church at Wayland, Mass. He wrote, "Though I was educated in the Unitarian denomination, I believe and preach the divinity of Christ." A careful reading of the hymn reveals a fine social message. The author was writing at a time of extraordinary unrest throughout the world, caused in America by the passing of the Fugitive Slave Law, the great forty-niner gold rush to California, and in Europe by the aftermath of the revolution in France and Germany. In the stillness of the first Christmas night, the author finds a message of healing for our restlessness, and with Isaiah looks forward to a golden age when peace shall reign on earth. But when will that time come? The Civil War, tragic irony, followed in ten years! The hope, however, abides and is valid, for peace is in the ultimate plan of God.

MUSIC. CAROL was composed by Richard Storrs Willis, brother of the American poet, N. P. Willis. It is a graceful, popular tune, and is often set to "While shepherds watched their flock by night," for which it is admirably adapted.

76. The first Noel the angel did say   *Traditional*

"Noel" is a French word which came to mean several things—a "song of the Birthday," or "Christmas," or "Carol." A carol is a religious song telling the story of a place or person or event. It is less formal and solemn than an ordinary church hymn and was originally intended to be sung outside rather than within the church walls. The words and music of this carol are traditional, which means that no one knows who composed them or when. They are known to have existed as early as the 17th century. It is a very popular carol even though not quite true to the gospel account in verse 2, for it was the wise men, not the shepherds, that saw the star. Since most of the words have to do with the coming of the wise men, the carol is fully as suitable for Epiphany as for Christmas.

MUSIC. The tune THE FIRST NOEL is one of the best-known of all English carol airs, especially in the west of England.

77. The stars were silent and the hills   *E. Royce*

The poem was published in the *Presbyterian* about 1939. No specific information is at hand concerning the author. Bixel, composer of the music, is under the impression that E. Royce was a missionary to China who sent this poem to her church paper for publication.

MUSIC. SILENT was composed for this carol by James W. Bixel, who was born at Bluffton, Ohio, November 7, 1913. After graduating from Bluffton College, Bixel studied music in Cincinnati Conservatory of Music, where he received his Master of Music degree in composition. He taught music in the public schools of Mt. Gilead, Ohio, and then spent nearly four years in Civilian Public Service. In the fall of 1947 he became a teacher of harmony and piano in the music department of Bethel College. The tune, begun and completed in one evening, has the distinction of being the only one in the *Hymnary* composed by a Mennonite. Which leads one to observe that our hymns and tunes, like many other elements in our culture, are "ours" by appreciation and use rather than by invention or creation. It may be the future will find us less "practical" minded than heretofore and that poetic and musical gifts will yet come to fruition to make our contribution to the stream of hymns and tunes that have enriched the worship of the Visible Church of all places and ages.

78. What child is this   *William C. Dix, 1837-98*

One of numerous carols written by William Dix about 1865.

William Chatterton Dix was the son of a Bristol surgeon. He was educated for a business career and became the manager of a marine insurance company in Glasgow. He maintained, however, his literary interests and wrote the *Life of Chatterton,* the poet; a book of *Pen Pictures of Popular English Preachers;* and other works, including several volumes of devotional poetry. He had been ill in bed on Epiphany Day, and after reading the Gospel for the day, he wrote this hymn, finishing it by evening. It became very popular and is found in nearly all English hymnals. The accuracy of the second verse may be questioned—"To that lowly manger bed." For it is not likely that the babe Jesus was still in the manger when the wise men appeared.

MUSIC. CHRIST THE KING, known in many hymnals as "Greensleeves," is an old English melody of the 17th century, mentioned somewhere by Shakespeare. It is a joyous tune which may be sung as a solo, or with the sopranos singing the words of the stanzas, while the other parts hum the accompaniment, then all parts singing the refrain in harmony or in unison.

79. Come, all ye shepherds   *Traditional*

A shepherd carol from Bohemia.
The words and music are traditional.

MUSIC. The tune was arranged by Edward Shippen Barnes, b. 1887, American organist and composer who received his musical education at Yale and in Paris. He now lives at Santa Monica, California. His personal counsel was solicited and secured in the compilation and editing of the *Hymnary.*

80. O come, all ye faithful   *Latin*

Adeste, fideles,	Deum de Deo;
Laeti triumphantes;	Lumen de Lumine,
Venite, venite in Bethlehem;	Gestant puellae viscera
Natum videte	Deum Verum,
Regem Angelorum:	Genitum, non factum:
Venite, adoremus Dominum.	Venite, adoremus Dominum.

Ergo Qui natus
• Die hodierna,
Iesu, Tibi sit gloria:
Patris Aeterni
Verbum Caro factum!
Venite, adoremus Dominum.

A priceless legacy from the Latin Church and one of the most popular of Christmas hymns. It has been translated into at least 125 languages. The origin of the text and tune is obscure. The original poem

47

may have been German or French of the 17th or 18th century.

From the lengthy (and on the whole profitless) discussions of the possible origins of the hymn, it may be concluded that the hymn and tune came into use together, in the services of the Roman Church, during the first part of the 18th century; that they were circulated first in manuscript form and later appeared in print, the earliest known book containing them being a small volume, *An Essay on the Church Plain Chant,* published in London, 1782. Nothing definite can be stated as to the authors of either words or music.

The translation was made in 1841 by Frederick Oakeley, 1802-80, Church of England minister who later joined the Roman Catholics.

MUSIC. ADESTE FIDELES belongs by long association to this hymn, its name being derived from the first words of the Latin. It is also widely used with "How firm a foundation." The present arrangement is credited to Vincent Novello, organist in the Portuguese Chapel in London about 1785.

81. Angels from the realms of glory
James Montgomery, 1771-1854

A graceful lyric presenting to the imagination a series of pictures—the Angels, the Shepherds, the Wise Men, and the Saints who like Simeon and Anna, were waiting for the consolation of Israel. The fourth verse is reminiscent of the prophetic words of Malachi: "The Lord whom ye seek shall suddenly come to his temple, even the messenger of the covenant whom ye delight in: behold he shall come, saith the Lord of Hosts" (3:1).

It is widely used for the Christmas season.

For comments on James Montgomery see Hymn 62.

MUSIC. REGENT SQUARE is a jubilant, vigorous tune, composed for the English *Presbyterian Hymnal* of 1867 in which it was set to Bonar's hymn, "Glory be to God the Father."

The composer, Henry Smart, 1813-79, studied law for four years and then decided to become a musician. Though he had little formal musical training, he became a great organist, composer, and conductor. He became totally blind by 1865, but, being a capable improviser, and possessing a keen memory, he was able to continue as an organist. He did much for the cause of good music in the church.

For further comments on Smart see Hymn 46.

82. Angels we have heard on high
Bishop Chadwick

A popular carol of French origin, sung first in England by the Westminster Abbey Choir and for that reason it is sometimes called the "Westminster Carol."

No information has been traced concerning Bishop Chadwick.

MUSIC. GLORIA is a traditional melody of anonymous composition. The tune has been variously harmonized. This version is found in the *St. Basil's Hymnal,* compiled by the Basilian Fathers, and published in Chicago, 1918 (Revised Ed.).

83. Silent night, holy night   *Joseph Mohr, 1792-1848*

The most loved and most widely used of all Christmas carols.

It was composed December 24, 1818, by Joseph Mohr, 1792-1848, assistant Catholic priest in an obscure German village, Oberndorf, near Salzburg, Austria. At a Christmas celebration in the schoolhouse Mohr withdrew for a time, then returned with a folded sheet of paper on which this carol was written. He handed it to his friend, Franz Gruber, 1787-1863, schoolmaster, song writer, and organist, as a Christmas gift. Gruber composed the tune for it the same evening. The author and composer sang it together, the latter accompanying on the guitar, and a choir of girls from the village joining in the melody. The hymn and the tune became immensely popular in Germany and Austria even before they appeared in print, through their use by wandering Tyrolese singers. Today the carol is sung in all Christian lands. It was a favorite of the great opera singer Madame Ernestine Schumann-Heink, and she sang it on many of her concert appearances.

MUSIC. STILLE NACHT. In keeping with German custom, the tune is named after the first line of the hymn for which it was written.

A plaque in the schoolhouse at Oberndorf bears the following inscription:

> Stille Nacht, heilige Nacht!
> Wer hat dich, O Lied, gemacht?
> Mohr hat dich so schoen erdacht,
> Gruber zu Gehoer gebracht,
> Priester und Lehrer vereint.

84. O little town of Bethlehem   *Phillips Brooks, 1835-93*

This carol was written for children, but it has become popular everywhere with adults as well.

Phillips Brooks, one of America's greatest preachers, grew up in a musical home where memorizing and reciting of hymns was a part of the children's education. By the time he was ready for college he had committed over 200 hymns to memory. He graduated from Harvard and from the Episcopal Theological Seminary, Alexandria, Virginia, and served as rector at the Church of the Advent, Philadelphia, and at Trinity Church, Boston, where his preaching powers came to full and fruitful fruition. In 1891, he became Bishop of Massachusetts. While in Philadelphia, he was given a year's leave of absence to travel in Europe and the Near East. In Christmas Week in 1865, he rode on horseback from Jerusalem to Bethlehem. The view of the little town is thought to have inspired this hymn which he wrote several years later for the Christmas service of the Sunday school in his church.

MUSIC. st. louis. Brooks asked his church organist, Lewis Redner, who was also Sunday school superintendent, to set the carol to music. This was done in great haste on the Saturday night before Christmas, 1868. The words and tune, printed on leaflets, were sung by six teachers and 36 Sunday school children, and then practically forgotten until 1892 when they were published in the *Hymnal of the Episcopal Church.* The hymn has become popular since, not only in America but also in England. The tune generally used in England, however, is not "St. Louis," but "Forest Green." (See 290.)

85. Hark the herald angels sing   *Charles Wesley, 1707-88*

One of the most popular English hymns. Julian listed four hymns as standing at the head of all in the English language: "When I survey" (105-6), "Rock of Ages" (148), "Awake my soul" (25), and this one.

It is taken from Wesley's *Hymns and Sacred Poems,* 1739. The original had 10 four-line stanzas and no refrain. The hymn has been altered in various ways and improved. For example, the lines,

> With the angelic host proclaim,
> Christ is born in Bethlehem,

originally read

> Universal nature say
> Christ the Lord is born today.

And for our familiar first lines,

> Hark! the herald angels sing!
> Glory to the new-born King,

Wesley had

> Hark! how all the welkin rings,
> Glory to the King of Kings.

These, and other changes, disprove the common assertion that hymns should always be sung just as the authors left them. As a rule, however, it still remains true that "the *professional* hymn mender is an odious creature."

For comments on Charles Wesley see Hymn 6.

MUSIC. MENDELSSOHN, also called "Bethlehem" and "St. Vincent," is from Mendelssohn's *Festgesang* for Male Chorus and Orchestra, composed in 1840 to celebrate the invention of printing. The tune is adapted from chorus No. 2 of that work. Dr. W. H. Cummings, organist at Waltham Abbey, set the tune to the words of this hymn and had it sung by the Abbey Choir. It was so well received that he published it in 1856 and it has since found its way into the hymn books of all denominations.

It is interesting to note Mendelssohn's own estimate of the tune, as he expressed it in a letter to his English publishers.

> I am sure that piece will be liked very much by the singers and hearers, but it will never do to sacred words. There must be a national and merry subject found out, something to which the soldier-like and buxom motion of the piece has some relation, and the words must express something gay and popular as the music tries to do.

86. O holy night

The night of the Saviour's birth is the subject of Christmas carols in every land, of which this and "Silent Night" are oustanding examples. The words are anonymous.

The omitted third stanza reads as follows:

> Truly He taught us to love one another;
> His law is love and His gospel is peace.
> Chains shall he break for the slave is our brother,
> And in His name all oppression shall cease.
> Sweet hymn of joy in grateful chorus raise we,
> Let all within us praise His holy name;
> Christ is the Lord, Oh, praise His name forever!
> His power and glory evermore proclaim.
> His power and glory evermore proclaim.

MUSIC. The tune, HOLY NIGHT, is by Adolphe Adam, 1803-56, distinguished French composer of comic operas and teacher of composition. He became a professor in the Conservatory of Music in Paris in 1849.

HIS EPIPHANY

87. What star is this   *C. Coffin,* 1676-1749

A Latin hymn, *Quae stella sole pulchrior,* was included in the *Paris Breviary,* 1736, and, again, in Coffin's *Hymni Sacri,* 1736. Charles Coffin, rector of the University of Paris, wrote a large number of hymns,

51

"not so much," he says, "to gratify the poetic Spirit as to achieve elegance and piety."

The translation is by John Chandler, 1806-76, in his *Hymns of the Primitive Church,* 1837. Chandler was educated at Oxford and became a minister in the Church of England. Besides making a collection of hymns, he is the author of several biographies and volumes of devotional literature. His translation of this hymn has passed into many English hymn books but invariably with some alterations.

MUSIC. PUER NOBIS is an arrangement of a German folk tune published by the German composer, Michael Praetorius, 1571-1621, which he wrote in 1609. It was harmonized in 1904 by G. R. Woodward, an English musician. It is a spirited tune and should be sung briskly and merrily.

88. Bethlehem, of noblest cities

Prudentius, 348-c. 413
Tr. E. Caswall, 1814-78

Based on Matt. 2:6: "And thou, Bethlehem, in the land of Judah, art not the least among the princes of Judah: for out of thee shall come a governor, that shall rule my people Israel," and the story of the three wise men bringing their gifts to Jesus.

The author, Prudentius, 348-c. 413, a Spaniard, was one of the best and most prolific of early Latin Christian poets. He received legal training and served as lawyer and judge in several cities. At the age of 57 he entered a monastery and for the rest of his life was a writer of poetry in defense of and in praise of the Christian faith. He is regarded by some as the first really great Christian poet and was widely read in Europe throughout the Middle Ages, Erasmus being one of his admirers.

The translation is by Edward Caswall who shortly before had left the Church of England to become a priest in the Roman Catholic Church. Caswall was a Latin scholar and did much translating of Latin hymns. For further comments on Caswall see Hymn 19.

MUSIC. STUTTGART is adapted from a melody by Christian F. Witt in his *Psalmodia Sacra,* published in Gotha, 1715, where it is set to the hymn, *"Sollt es gleich bisweilen scheinen."* It is a stately, straightforward tune of simple, rhythmic pattern and is singable by any average congregation.

Christian F. Witt, 1660-1716, was a court organist and later *Kapellmeister* at Gotha. He composed a number of hymn tunes.

89. From the eastern mountains

Godfrey Thring, 1823-1903

Based on Matt. 2:2: "We have seen his star in the east and are come to worship Him." Its reference to the guiding star and its missionary emphasis fit it ideally for the Epiphany season, but the hymn may be used appropriately on more general occasions.

Godfrey Thring was educated at Shrewsbury and Balliol College, Oxford, and held various positions as minister in the Church of England. In 1859, he succeeded his father as rector of Alford-with-Hornblotton and in 1876, became prebendary of East Harptree in Wells Cathedral. He published various hymn books of a high literary standard.

MUSIC. PRINCETHORPE. This tune, by William Pitts, 1824-1903, was taken from *The Hymnary* of the United Church of Canada. No information is at hand concerning the composer or the origin of the tune.

90. We three kings of Orient are   *John H. Hopkins, Jr.*, 1820-91

A popular carol giving the story of the wise men seeing the star and bringing gifts to the Christ child.

John Henry Hopkins, Jr., was born at Pittsburgh, Pa. His father was an Episcopalian minister who became the Bishop of Vermont. John was educated at the University of Vermont and later was minister at Williamsport, Pa. He is the author of several books of poems.

MUSIC. KINGS OF ORIENT was composed for this hymn by the author.

91. Brightest and best of the sons   *Reginald Heber*, 1783-1826

A lovely hymn of great beauty and simplicity of form and characterized by robust faith—"richer by far is the heart's adoration." It was written for the feast of Epiphany and was entitled, "Star of the East." The hymn was first published in the *Christian Observer*, 1811.

Heber, a hymnist of the first order, ranking with Wesley and Watts, was governed by three ideas in his hymn writing: (1) the hymn is liturgical and should follow the church year; (2) the hymn should follow and supplement the sermon; (3) the hymn should be literary art.

For further comments on Reginald Heber see Hymn 1.

MUSIC. BRIGHTEST AND BEST was composed by Rev. Joseph Francis Thrupp, 1827-67, fellow of Cambridge College and minister in the Church of England. He is the author of several books on Biblical subjects and wrote a number of hymns of merit, none of which have come into general use.

HIS LIFE AND MINISTRY

92. O sing a song of Bethlehem   *Louis F. Benson*, 1855-1930

Written as a Christmas carol but sings also of the later life of Jesus in Nazareth, Galilee, and at Calvary. It was contributed to *The School Hymnal* (Presbyterian), edited by Dr. Benson in 1899.

Louis Fitzgerald Benson was born in Philadelphia and educated for the bar. After seven years of practice, he gave up law to enter Princeton Theological Seminary and was ordained a Presbyterian minister. He became minister of the Church of the Redeemer, Germantown, Pa., but resigned his charge after six years, to begin his great work as editor of hymn books and writer and lecturer on hymnology. His book, *The English Hymn*, unfortunately out of print, has no rival as a source of accurate information about the development and use of English and American hymns. His *Studies in Familiar Hymns* (2 vols.) is unexcelled. For forty years Dr. Benson rendered outstanding service to all students of hymnology through his writings and lectures on the subject. He composed 32 original hymns and made 16 translations from the Latin which were published as *Hymns, Original and Translated*, Philadelphia, 1925, in which the present hymn appears.

MUSIC. BETHLEHEM, also called "Evangel," was composed by Gottfried W. Fink, 1783-1846, German minister, musician, music critic, and editor, who was appointed in 1842 to a Professorship of Music at Leipzig. It is a joyful tune in popular style, especially suitable for large choruses or congregations.

93. O Master Workman of the race   *Jay T. Stocking, 1870-1936*

A hymn entitled, "The Carpenter of Nazareth," written for young people while the author was watching some carpenters at work in an Adirondack Camp. It is one of a number of excellent modern hymns concerned with the earthly life of Jesus and connecting Him with our daily life and labor. Others are "O Master let me walk with Thee" (223), "Where cross the crowded ways" (222), and "O Son of Man, Thou madest known" (373).

Jay T. Stocking was educated at Amherst, Yale Divinity School, and at the University of Berlin. He was ordained in 1901, held a number of prominent pastorates in the Congregational Church, and was made moderator of the Congregational Council in 1934. He is the author of several books and was a member of the Commission on International Justice and Good Will of the Federal Council of Churches.

MUSIC. ST. MICHEL's appeared in a collection of *Psalms and Hymns*, compiled by William Gawler, and published in London around 1784 to 1789, for use of the children of an orphan asylum at Lambeth. It was set to "Creator Spirit, by whose aid," a long-meter hymn. Later the tune was changed to common meter double. It is also known by the names "St. Maria," "Beulah," and "Woolrich Common." The composer of the tune is not known. *The Hymnary* of the United Church of Canada attributes it to Haydn. At No. 125 of the *Hymnary* it appears as "Jerusalem, Jerusalem," where it is erroneously attributed, in the earlier editions, to Thomas Hastings—an error carried over from the *Gesangbuch mit Noten.* Hastings was born at about the same time the tune was already in print! It is possible, of course, that he made an arrangement of the tune, and thereby getting his name associated, inadvertently, with its composition.

Wm. Gawler, c. 1750-1809, was a London musician and music publisher. In 1785, while organist at the Lambeth "Asylum," a home, the first of its kind in England, for fatherless girls, he published the book *Psalms and Hymns,* referred to, later adding a supplement. Gawler made other compilations of music books and also did some composing.

94. Ye fair green hills of Galilee   *Eustace R. Conder,* 1820-92

A fine hymn, setting forth obedience to duty and love to God and man as the marks of Christ's followers. It was contributed by the author to the *Congregational Church Hymnal,* London, 1887.

Eustace Rogers Conder studied for the Congregational ministry in Birmingham and later graduated with high honors in philosophy at London University. For 17 years, he was minister of a Congregational Church at Poole, where he trained students for missionary work, besides attending to his regular duties as pastor. In 1873, he was elected chairman of the Congregational Union of England and Wales. He wrote several books, including *Outlines of the Life of Christ* and *Sleepy Forest,* a book of fairy tales for children.

MUSIC. STELLA is from an old English melody in 6-8 time which the children sang to "Sweet Mary, sweet Mary, my age is sixteen." About 1850, it was arranged by Henri F. Hemy, 1818-88, English organist, for use in Catholic churches as an easy choir number. In 1875, the tune appeared (almost note for note as in the *Hymnary*) in the Appendix of *St. Alban's Tune Book,* a book of pre-Reformation hymns set to plainsong melodies. The Appendix of the book is a treasure house of arrangements and adaptations of singable tunes from sacred and secular sources.

95. Thine arm, O Lord, in days of old
Edward H. Plumptre, 1821-91

A hymn on the healing ministry of Christ, written in 1864 for use in the Chapel of King's College Hospital, London. Suitable for Hospital Day and other occasions.

Edward Hayes Plumptre, an English scholar and church man, was educated at King's College, London, and at Oxford. He was minister in various churches (Anglican) and became Professor of New Testament Exegesis at King's College. He wrote many excellent books, including the standard *Life of Bishop Ken,* and several volumes of poems. He was appointed a member of the Old Testament Company of Revisers of the Bible. This hymn was included in the 2d edition of his *Lazarus, and other Poems,* from which it made its way into the hymnals.

MUSIC. st. matthew, a psalm tune, appeared in the 6th ed. (1708) of *A Supplement to the New Version of Psalms,* by Tate and Brady, where it was set, in two parts, treble and bass, to Psalm 33. In slightly altered form, it became one of the great hymn tunes but is more popular in England than in America.

For comments on William Croft, 1678-1727, an important name in English church music, see Hymn 6.

96. Who is he in yonder stall   *Benj. R. Hanby,* 1833–67

A hymn on the birth, ministry, passion, resurrection, and exaltation of Christ, the refrain answering the question asked in each stanza. It may be used effectively for antiphonal singing between choir and congregation.

The author, Benjamin Russel Hanby, was a minister in the United Brethren Church but was strongly inclined to music and decided to make that his life work. An interesting and talented man, he became associated with George F. Root in the publication of sacred and secular song books in Chicago. He was the author of a number of Sunday school songs and of "Darling Nellie Gray," "Old Shady," and other popular numbers. His untimely death ended his career almost before it was well begun. His father, the Rev. William Hanby, was a bishop in the church of the United Brethren in Christ and editor, for a number of years, of *The Telescope,* the church's official paper published at Circleville, Ohio.

MUSIC. lowliness was composed by the author of the words.

97. Fairest Lord Jesus   *Münster,* 1677
     Translated, c. 1850

Called the "Crusader's Hymn," but there is no foundation for the tradition that it was sung by the German knights of the 12th century on their way to Jerusalem. The text and tune are modern. The German text was published in *Münster Gesangbuch,* 1677 (Catholic). Our translation, the oldest English version, is by an unknown author, about 1850. A later translation, beginning "Beautiful Savior," was made by

J. A. Seiss in 1873. The original is as follows:

Schönster Herr Jesu,
Herrscher aller Herren,
Gottes und Mariä Sohn!
Dich will ich lieben,
Dich will ich ehren.
Meiner Seelen Freund' und Kron'.

Schön sind die Wälder,
Schöner die Felder
In der schönen Frühlingszeit.
Jesus ist schöner,
Jesus ist reiner,
Der unser traurigs Herz erfreut.

Schön leucht't der Monden,
Schöner die Sonne
Als die Sternlein allzumal.
Jesus leucht't schöner,
Jesus leucht't reiner,
Als all die Engel im Himmelssaal.

Alle die Schönheit
Himmels und der Erde
Ist nur gegen ihn als Schein.
Keiner soll nimmer
Lieber uns werden
Als er, der schönste Jesus mein!

MUSIC. CRUSADER'S HYMN, also known as *Schönster Herr Jesu,* appeared in a book of Silesian folk songs, *Schlesische Volkslieder,* Leipzig, 1842. The hymn with this tune was first published in America in *Church Carols and Choir Studies* by the American composer Richard Storrs Willis, 1850. F. Melius Christiansen, director of the St. Olaf Choir, has arranged an exquisite anthem on this melody with the words "Beautiful Savior."

It is a useful and charming melody. Its popularity in Germany ranks with Paul Gerhardt's *"Befiehl du deine Wege."*

98. Not always on the mount   Frederick L. Hosmer, 1840-1929

Based on the story of the transfiguration in Matthew 17, the lesson enforced by the hymn is that the mount is necessary for vision; we cannot abide there, yet our work in the valley will be nobler for the pattern shown us on the mount.

For comments on Frederick L. Hosmer see Hymn 72.

The hymn, written in 1882, was first published in *Unity,* Chicago, April 1, 1884. A year later it was included, in revised form, in the author's first series of *The Thought of God.*

MUSIC. TRANSYLVANIA is from a 16th century Hungarian chorale, arranged by Robert L. Sanders, F. A. A. R., Chicago, for *Hymns of the Spirit,* Beacon Press, 1938.

99. I know not how that Bethlehem's Babe

Harry W. Farrington, 1880-1931

A Christmas song written in 1910, while the author was a graduate student at Harvard University. It was awarded the prize which had been offered for the best Christmas hymn written by a student. Though simple and unpretentious, Professor George Herbert Palmer declared it "a perfect poem." The few lines encompass a vast body of Christian truth.

The author, Harry W. Farrington, 1880-1931 (date of death printed erroneously as 1911 in earlier editions of the *Hymnary*), was educated at Harvard and then became a Methodist minister. ¯He was greatly interested in work among children and inaugurated the Week Day Church School at Gary, Ind., in 1914. After returning from service in World War I, he became widely known as a speaker for children and it is estimated that he addressed more than two million children in the public schools of America. He is the author of several volumes of poems and has written books on Franklin, Washington, Lincoln, and Theodore Roosevelt.

MUSIC. ES IST EIN BORN, also named "I Do Believe," and "Camp-meeting," is an early American camp-meeting chorus sung to:

> I do believe, I now believe,
> I can hold out no more;
> I sink by dying love compelled
> And own Thee Conqueror.

It is used in the *Gesangbuch mit Noten* to the words *"Es ist ein Born, d'raus heil'ges Blut."*

100. All glory laud and honor   St. Theodulph of Orleans, c. 820
Tr. John M. Neale, 1854

From a long Latin hymn of 39 couplets, based on Psalm 24:7-10; Psalm 118:25-26; Matthew 21:1-17; and Luke 19:37-38.

> Gloria, laus et honor tibi sit, rex, Christe, redemptor,
>   cui puerile decus prompsit hosanna pium.
>
> Israel tu rex, Davidis et inclyta proles,
>   nomine qui in Domini, rex benedicte, venis.
>
> Coetus in excelsis te laudat caelicus omnis
>   et mortalis homo, cuncta creata simul.
>
> Plebs Hebraea tibi cum palmis obvia venit;
>   cum prece, voto, hymnis adsumus ecce tibi.
>
> Hi tibi passuro solvebant munia laudis;
>   nos tibi regnanti pangimus ecce melos.
>
> Hi placuere tibi; placeat devotio nostra,
>   rex pie, rex clemens, cui bona cuncta placent. Amen.

The hymn was used as the processional in the Palm Sunday service of the medieval church.

St. Theodulph of Orleans composed the words about A.D. 820. He was probably born in Italy, though neither the date nor place of his birth are definitely known. Theodulph became the abbot of a monastery in Florence but was later brought to France and made bishop of Orleans. Emperor Louis the Pious imprisoned him on a false charge of conspiracy in 818. There is a legend, but only a legend, that this hymn was composed during the author's confinement, and that St. Theodulph sang it at the window of his cell as the King passed the prison on the way to church and that the latter was so moved by it that he ordered the release of Theodulph and his restoration to his office as bishop.

The translation was made by the learned John M. Neale (see 67) who wrote that "another verse was usually sung, until the 17th century, at the pious quaintness of which we can scarcely avoid a smile:

> "Be thou, O Lord, the rider,
> "And we the little ass;
> "That to God's holy city
> "Together we may pass."

MUSIC. ST. THEODULPH was composed by Melchior Teschner (c. 1615), a Lutheran pastor and musician. It was originally sung to the German chorale, *Valet will ich dir geben* ("Farewell, I gladly bid thee"), a hymn for the dying. That the same tune is used to carry a cheerful, festive hymn, as well as a hymn for the dying, illustrates the plasticity of hymn tunes. Bach used the tune in his *St. John's Passion,* and it is also associated with Gerhardt's *"Wie soll ich dich empfangen."* It is widely used as a Palm Sunday processional with St. Theodulph's words. The refrain may be sung by the congregation, answering to the verses sung by the choir. Processional hymns were almost invariably sung that way in the medieval church and Canon Douglass suggests that "we should put this plan into far wider practice if we really desire to improve our congregational singing."

101. Ride on, ride on in majesty   *Henry H. Milman,* 1791-1868

A popular Palm Sunday hymn and incidentally one of the finest poems in our hymn books. It was written by Henry H. Milman at the age of 30, the year he was elected Professor of Poetry at Oxford University—1821.

Henry H. Milman was born in London, the son of Sir Francis Milman, physician to the King. After a brilliant career at Oxford, he was ordained at 25, appointed Professor of Poetry at Oxford at 30. Later he became canon of Westminster and finally dean of St. Paul's Cathedral in London, which high office he filled with distinction. He is the author of thirteen hymns. Milman was interested, too, in drama and wrote several plays and translated Greek plays. He is best known, however, as a historian, having published *The History of the Jews* in 1829, and the *History of Latin Christianity* in 1855, both of them classics.

MUSIC. ST. DROSTANE was written for the words "Ride on, ride on" for the *Congregational Hymn and Tune Book,* London, 1862. It has since come into wide use with this hymn. Other tunes also used with this text are "Winchester New" (369) and "Park Street" (272).

For comments on the composer, J. B. Dykes, see Hymn 1.

HIS PASSION

102. When my love to God grows weak

John R. Wreford, 1800-81

A useful hymn, true to the Gospel record, and free from the emotional morbidity that is found in many passion hymns.

John Wreford, an Englishman trained for the Unitarian ministry, was compelled to give up his ministry on account of a failing voice. He then opened a school at Edgbaston. The later years of his life were spent in retirement at Bristol. The original of this hymn written in 1837, received little notice until it was rewritten and improved by Samuel Longfellow, brother of the more famous Henry Wadsworth. In this revised form it has been included in a number of the best English hymnals.

MUSIC. ORIENTIS PARTIBUS, the so-called "Donkey Festival Tune," has a most peculiar origin. During the Middle Ages, the church in some parts of France celebrated January 14 as the "Feast of the Ass," to commemorate the flight into Egypt. A beautiful young woman holding a child in her arms rode a donkey through the streets of the town and then into the principal church. The donkey, with its burden, stood beside the high altar while mass was celebrated, during which the hymn beginning with the line *"Orientis partibus adventatis asinus"* was sung. The melody of this hymn is the basis for our tune which was adapted by Richard Redhead and published in his *Church Hymn Tunes,* 1853. The original was the work of Pierre De Corbeil, Archbishop of Sens, who died in 1222. It is a virile tune worthy of its increasing place in modern hymn books.

For Richard Redhead see Hymn 109.

103. 'Tis midnight and on Olive's brow

William Bingham Tappan, 1794-1849

A midnight hymn, depicting the darkness and sadness of Gethsemane.

60

It is often sung at communion services held on Thursday evening before Good Friday.

William Bingham Tappan, a clock maker, was an influential leader in Sunday school work in the Congregational Church in America. In early manhood he taught school in Philadelphia, and then from 1826 until his death he was in the employ of the American Sunday School Union as manager and superintendent at Philadelphia, Cincinnati, and Boston. He wrote and published eight or ten volumes of poetry of no special significance.

MUSIC. OLIVET'S BROW was composed for this hymn and was first published in The Shawm, 1853, by Bradbury and Root.

William Batchelder Bradbury, 1816-68, was born in York, Maine. After many struggles, due to poverty, he learned music from Lowell Mason and G. J. Webb and began conducting singing classes. He did outstanding work in New York City in teaching music to children. His Juvenile Music Festivals at the Baptist Tabernacle became an important feature of New York's musical life and gave a powerful stimulus to the introduction of music into the public schools. In 1847, he went abroad for further study in music. Upon returning to America, he became associated with Geo. F. Root, Thos. Hastings, and Lowell Mason in musical Normal Institute work. The group collaborated in the production of a new type of church music, known as gospel songs, which swept the country during the revivalistic work of Moody and Sankey.

104. There is a green hill far away

Mrs. Cecil Frances Alexander, 1823-95

A popular hymn on the atonement, written for children but appropriated for general use with all ages. It was first published in the author's Hymns for Little Children, 1848, her most famous book which ran into 100 editions. The accuracy of the first line may well be questioned for the Gospels do not state that Jesus was crucified on a hill, only that it was a place called "the skull" (Lk. 23:33). In any case, the sun-baked Judean hills are seldom green.

Cecil Frances Humphrey, daughter of Major John Humphrey, was a native of Ireland. Her father was an Englishman who, as a land-owner and government agent, went to reside in Ireland. In 1850, she married the Rev. Wm. Alexander who, after spending many years in obscure parish work, was elected Archbishop of Armagh and later Primate of all Ireland. Mrs. Alexander was preëminently a writer for little children, her verses being characterized by simplicity and tenderness and poetic beauty; but she also contributed some notable church songs, e.g., "Jesus calls us o'er the tumult" (140).

To make the truths of the church catechism interesting and intelli-

61

gible to little children, Mrs. Alexander wrote a series of poems to illustrate the Apostle's Creed. This hymn is on the clause "suffered under Pontius Pilate, was crucified, dead, and buried." "All things bright and beautiful" (410) was written for the first clause, "I believe in God the Father Almighty, maker of heaven and earth." For the second clause, "And in Jesus Christ His Son, born of the virgin Mary" she wrote "Once in royal David's city" (412).

MUSIC. MEDITATION appeared in *Original Tunes,* 1890, by John H. Gower, where it is set to "There is a land of pure delight." The tune has since become closely associated with Mrs. Alexander's hymn for which it forms an appropriate setting.

John Henry Gower, 1855-1922, English organist and concert artist, became professor of music at Trent College, Nottingham. Later he came to America on account of mining interests in Colorado but maintained his activity in music. He served as organist and choirmaster of St. John's Cathedral, Denver, and during the World's Fair in Chicago, 1893, became organist of the Church of the Epiphany in that city.

105-106. When I survey the wondrous cross

Isaac Watts, 1674-1748

One of the twenty-five hymns prepared by Watts to be sung at the Lord's Supper. Matthew Arnold, the famous literary critic, called it the "most majestic hymn in the English language." It is one of four hymns which have been printed in more collections, translated into more tongues, and used in more congregations, than any other. The three hymns classed with this in popularity are "Rock of Ages," "Jesus, Lover of my soul," and "All hail the power of Jesus' name."

Watts gave this hymn the title "Crucifixion to the World by the Cross of Christ." It is based on Galatians 6: 14: "God forbid that I should glory save in the Cross of our Lord Jesus Christ, by whom the world is crucified to me, and I unto the world." In the first stanza there is a reference to Phil. 3:7: "Howbeit what things were gain to me, these have I counted loss for Christ." The whole hymn, and especially the closing stanza, reflects the thought of Galatians 2:20: "I have been crucified with Christ . . . . who loved me and gave himself for me." The third stanza, a sublime picture of the suffering Saviour, should always be sung softly.

For comments on Isaac Watts, see Hymn 11.

MUSIC. ROCKINGHAM OLD is a famous tune always used with this hymn in England. It was named after the Marquis of Rockingham, a Whig statesman who was thrice prime minister of England, and a friend of the composer.

Edward Miller, 1731-1807, was born at Norwich, England, the son of a stone mason. He was a man of great literary attainments and considerable musical ability. For 56 years he was organist of the parish church at Doncaster, receiving the appointment in 1751 and retaining the post until his death in 1807. Miller played the flute in Handel's orchestra in London and had many a story to tell of the great composer's eccentricities. Dissatisfied with the church music of his time, he was led to publish a book, *Psalms of David,* which turned out to be a great success. The book contained such tunes as "Burford" (228), "St. Magnes" (582), "St. Anne" (61), "Surrey" (44), and others of a similar style from the early part of the 18th century. It also contained some of his original tunes, including ROCKINGHAM OLD, destined to become one of the most popular English tunes ever written. This tune was not identified at first with any particular words. Miller had set it to 9 different psalms, using 3 keys—F, E flat, and E. It became associated with Watts' "When I survey the wondrous cross," in 1854, the combination appearing in *Mercer's Church Psalter,* and again in 1861, in *Hymns Ancient and Modern.* The words and tune have now become inseparable in England.

HAMBURG (106), an arrangement by Lowell Mason from a Gregorian Chant, illustrates the greatness of simplicity. The tune employs only five tones of the scale and yet breathes the dignity and solemnity of the great hymn to which it is set.

For comments on Lowell Mason see Hymn 12.

107. Go to dark Gethsemane — *James Montgomery, 1771-1854*

A song of the sufferings and death of Christ.

Gethsemane, the Judgment Hall, and Calvary are successively brought to mind and at each stage there is found in the example of Christ a lesson for his disciples to learn.

The fourth verse in the original poem reads:

> Early hasten to the tomb
>   Where they laid his breathless clay·
> All is solitude and gloom;
>   Who hath taken him away?
> Christ is risen! he meets our eyes:
> Saviour, teach us so to rise.

For comments on James Montgomery see Hymn 62.

MUSIC. GETHSEMANE is a dignified tune in the minor mode, well adapted to carry the words of this hymn. It was composed by Christopher Tye (c. 1508-72), a musician and minister in the Anglican Church, of whom a contemporary document says that he is "a doctor

63

of music but not skilful at preaching." He has been called the "father of the anthem," having given it a model for others to follow.

For comments on W. H. Monk, who adapted the tune, see Hymn 40.

108. Alas! and did my Savior bleed   *Isaac Watts, 1674-1748*

A fine hymn of consecration, published by Watts in his *Hymns and Spiritual Songs,* 1707, under the title "Godly Sorrow Arising from the Sufferings of Christ." Dr. Charles S. Robinson states that "more conversions in Christian biography are credited to this hymn than to any other." Fanny Crosby, the blind poet, ten of whose lyrics are found in the *Hymnary,* credits this hymn with a share in her conversion. In telling the story she says that during a revival in the old Thirtieth Street Church, New York, in 1850, several times she sought the Saviour at the altar; but not until one evening, November 20, did the light come. "After a prayer was offered they began to sing the good old consecration hymn, 'Alas! and did my Saviour bleed,' and when they had reached the third line of the fourth stanza, 'Here, Lord, I give myself away,' my very soul flooded with celestial light."

For comments on Isaac Watts see Hymn 11.

MUSIC. MARTYRDOM. The original form of this melody is in common time (4/4). It appeared in triple time in R. A. Smith's *Sacred Music sung in St. George's Church,* Edinburgh, 1825, where it was designated "Old Scottish Melody." In 1827, it appeared in *The Seraph, Selection of Psalms and Hymns,* edited by J. Robertson and published at Glasgow. In a footnote to the tune it is stated that "the above tune 'Fennich,' or 'Martyrdom,' and by some called 'Drumclog,' was composed by Hugh Wilson, a native of Fennick." A legal dispute arose between Smith and Wilson over the ownership of the tune. The evidence was abundant to show that Wilson composed it. It is an effective tune. When it was first sung in St. George's, Edinburgh, the minister, Dr. Thomson, said, "O man! I could not sing for weeping."

Hugh Wilson, 1766-1824, the composer of the tune, learned his father's trade of shoemaking, studied and taught mathematics, and made sun-dials as a hobby. He then held positions of responsibility in certain mills and afterwards became a draftsman. He was interested in Sunday school work and wrote a number of psalm tunes but MARTYRDOM is the only one found in modern hymnals.

109. Throned upon the awful tree   *John Ellerton, 1826-93*

A solemn dirge of the Passion, written in 1875 in the seclusion of a quiet rural parish and regarded as the author's best composition. It appeared in *Hymns Ancient and Modern,* 1875.

For comments on John Ellerton see Hymn 43.

MUSIC. REDHEAD NO. 76, also called "Petra," and "Gethsemane," was composed by Richard Redhead, 1820-1901, English chorister and organist, and proponent of the Oxford Movement (not to be confused with the modern Oxford movement headed by Buchman). The tune, without name, appeared in his *Church Hymns and Tunes, Ancient and Modern,* 1853, as No. 76. In England it has long been sung to the hymn "Rock of Ages, cleft for me."

110. In the Cross of Christ I glory   *John Bowring, 1792-1872*

The most popular of John Bowring's *Hymns,* published in 1825, and a classic among the hymns of the cross. It is based on Gal. 6:14: "But God forbid that I should glory save in the cross of our Lord Jesus Christ, by whom the world is crucified unto me, and I unto the world." Bowring died on November 23, 1872, and the words, "In the cross of Christ I glory," were placed on his tombstone.

It is remarkable that so great a hymn on the cross should be written by a Unitarian, a communion which denies the deity of Jesus and the evangelical doctrine of the atonement. Yet the hymn can be sung whole-heartedly by every evangelical Christian for it magnifies the cross and makes it the center of the Christian faith. Bowring, in spite of his Unitarian connection, was a devout, evangelical believer.

For further comments on John Bowring see Hymn 55.

MUSIC. RATHBUN was composed by Ithamar Conkey, 1815-67, an organist and prominent bass soloist who took part in many oratorio performances in New York City. The tune was composed one Sunday afternoon after the minister, Dr. Hiscox, of the Central Baptist Church, Norwich, Conn., had preached one of a series of sermons on the "Words of the Cross." Conkey named the tune after the leading soprano in his choir, Mrs. Beriah S. Rathbun.

111. Cross of Jesus, Cross of sorrow   *William J. Sparrow Simpson*

From Stainer's oratorio, *The Crucifixion,* where it appears as No. 4 under the title, "The Mystery of Divine Humiliation." The original has 10 stanzas.

The libretto of *The Crucifixion* was written by Wm. J. Sparrow Simpson, Church of England clergyman. He was educated at Cambridge, ordained in 1882, and became chaplain of St. Mary's Hospital, Great Alford. His theological works include the *Catholic Conception of the Church* and the *History of the Anglo-Catholic Movement.*

MUSIC. CROSS OF JESUS in Stainer's *Crucifixion* is intended among other numbers in the oratorio, "to be sung by the congregation." Its depth of feeling is best realized if sung in rather slow tempo.

John Stainer, 1840-1901, began his career as a choir boy at St. Paul's Cathedral, London, at the age of seven, continuing there for nine years. He early became acquainted with Arthur Sullivan and the two remained fast friends throughout life. Stainer became one of England's greatest organists and succeeded Sir John Goss, at St. Paul's Cathedral. He was one of the most prolific and best-loved of the Victorian composers. A bronze tablet, installed in his honor in St. Paul's, was dedicated by a service in which parts of his cantatas were sung, and closed with his "sevenfold Amen" (623).

112. Beneath the Cross of Jesus

Elizabeth Cecilia Clephane, 1830-69

A hymn of Scottish origin, especially appropriate for use in Good Friday services, but it can also be used on more general occasions.

Elizabeth Cecilia Douglas Clephane, daughter of the Sheriff of Fife and Kinross, was born in Edinburgh. She was a member of the Free Church of Scotland. Her hymn, "There were ninety and nine," became widely known through its use by Moody and Sankey in their famous evangelistic meetings.

The hymn, "Beneath the Cross of Jesus," appeared in Scotland, three years after the death of Miss Clephane, in *The Family Treasure,* a home magazine, with this explanatory note by the editor:

> These lines express the experiences, the hopes, and the longings of a young Christian lately released. Written on the very edge of this life, with the better land fully in view of faith, they seem to us footsteps printed on the sands of Time, where those sands touch the ocean of Eternity. These footprints of one whom the Good Shepherd led through the wilderness into rest, may, with God's blessing, contribute to comfort and direct succeeding pilgrims.

MUSIC. ST. CHRISTOPHER was composed for this hymn by Frederick C. Maker, 1844-1927, an English organist and composer of numerous hymn tunes. Maker spent all his life in Bristol, England, thirty years of which were devoted to the position of organist at the Redland Park Congregational Church.

113. Come ye faithful, raise the strain

John of Damascus, c. 700
Tr. John M. Neale

A Greek hymn based on the Song of Moses, Exodus 15.

Αἴσωμεν, πάντες λαοί,
τῷ ἐκ πικρᾶς δουλείας
Φαραὼ τὸν Ἰσραὴλ ἀπαλλάξαντι
καὶ ἐν βυθῷ θαλάσσης
ποδὶ ἀβρόχως ὁδηγήσαντι
ᾠδὴν ἐπινίκιον,
ὅτι δεδόξασται.

Σήμερον ἔαρ ψυχῶν,
ὅτι Χριστὸς ἐκ τάφου,
ὥσπερ ἥλιος, ἐκλάμψας τριήμερος
τον ζοφερὸν χειμῶνα
ἀπήλασε τῆς ἁμαρτίας ἡμῶν,
αὐτὸν ἀνυμνήσωμεν,
ὅτι δεδόξασται.

Ἡ βασιλὶς τῶν ὡρῶν
τῇ λαμπροφόρῳ ἡμέρᾳ
ἡμερῶν τε βασιλίδι φανότατα
δωροφοροῦσα, τέρπει
τὸν ἔγκριτον τῆς ἐκκλησίας λαόν,
ἀπαύστως ἀνυμνοῦσα
τὸν ἀναστάτα Χριστόν.

Πύλαι θανάτου, Χριστέ,
οὐδὲ τοῦ τάφου σφραγῖδες,
οὐδὲ κλεῖθρα τῶν θυρῶν Σοι ἀντέστησαν,
ἀλλ' ἀναστὰς ἐπέστης
τοῖς φίλοις σου εἰρήνην, Δέσποτα,
δωρούμενος τὴν πάντα
νοῦν ὑπερέχουσαν.

It was written by John of Damascus about the middle of the 8th century.

John of Damascus, Greek theologian and distinguished hymnist, as well as the greatest scholar and poet of his time, was born in Damascus of a prominent family, about A.D. 700. He was educated by an Italian monk named Cosmas, and retired to the monastery of St. Sabas in the Holy Land. He died between 754 and 787. He wrote a number of canons. A canon in Greek hymnology was a series of odes, usually eight or nine, threaded on a acrostic. This hymn is from his canon for the Sunday after Easter.

For comments on the translator, John M. Neale, see Hymn 67.

MUSIC. ST. KEVIN. The composer, Arthur Sullivan, 1842-1900, was born in London, the son of an Irish band-master. He received a thorough musical education in London and on the continent and became a famous choir leader, hymn book editor, conductor, and composer. In collaboration with W. S. Gilbert, he composed light operas for which he is best known.

114. Jesus Christ is ris'n today

Latin
Charles Wesley, 1707-88

This hymn, which Percy Dearmer called "the Easter hymn par excellence," is based upon some Latin verses of an Easter carol of the 14th century, except verse 4, which is attributed to Charles Wesley.

It is of unknown authorship, appearing with the tune "Easter Hymn" in a now rare book, *Lyra Davidica.*

"Allelujah" is "Hallelujah" with the "H" omitted to soften it.

For comments on Wesley see Hymn 6.

MUSIC. EASTER HYMN, one of the most famous of all hymn tunes, is from *Lyra Davidica, or a Collection of Divine Songs and Hymns, partly New Composed, partly Translated from the High German and Latin Hymns; and set to easy and pleasant Tunes,* published in London, 1708. The composer is unknown. The hymn and tune were headed, "The Resurrection."

115. The day of Resurrection

John of Damascus, c. 700
Tr. John M. Neale

'Αναστάσεως ἡμέρα,
λαμπρυνθῶμεν λαοί.
Πάσχα Κυρίου, πάσχα.
'Εκ γὰρ θανάτου πρὸς ζωήν,
καὶ ἐκ γῆς πρὸς οὐρανόν,
Χριστὸς ὁ θεὸς
ἡμᾶς διεβίβασεν,
ἐπινίκιον ᾄδοντας.

Another resurrection hymn from the Eastern Church by John of Damascus. (See 113.) It is sung after midnight on Easter morning to set forth the fact of the resurrection. Julian describes the service in his *Dictionary of Hymnology* (p. 62). The people assemble in the church with unlighted tapers in their hands. While the priest chants in a half whisper, they await the signal that Easter Day has begun. A cannon is fired when the moment comes, the Cross is raised, and the people cry, *"Christos anesti"* (Christ is risen.) The tapers are lighted and the church is set ablaze with light. Outside there is the sound of drums and trumpets, the people embrace and congratulate each other, and salute one another with *"Christos anesti."*

The reference in stanza 2 is to Matt. 28:9: "Jesus met them, saying, 'All Hail!' "

For comments on the translator, John M. Neale, see Hymn 67.

MUSIC. LANCASHIRE, a thrilling tune of steady swing, was composed for "From Greenland's icy mountains," to be used at a missionary meeting at Blackburn, England. It is also, in some hymn books, used with "Lead on, O King Eternal" (399).

For comments on the composer, Henry Smart, 1813-79, see Hymn 46.

116. The strife is o'er, the battle done

Latin
Tr. Francis Pott, 1832-1909

Alleluia, Alleluia, Alleluia.
Finita iam sunt praelia,
Est parta iam victoria;
Gaudeamus et canamus:
Alleluia!

Surrexit die tertia
Caelesti clarus gratia
Insonemus et cantemus:
Alleluia!

Post fata mortis barbara
Devicit Iesus tartara;
Applaudamus et psallamus:
Alleluia!

Sunt clausa stygis ostia,
Et caeli patent atria;
Gaudeamus et canamus:
Alleluia!

Per tua, Iesu, vulnera
Nos mala morte libera,
Ut vivamus et canamus:
Alleluia! Amen.

One of the most celebrated of Easter hymns. It comes from an anonymous medieval Latin poem which appeared in the Jesuit *Symphonia Sirenum,* Cologne, 1695.

The translation is by Francis Pott, an Englishman. He was educated at Oxford University and after serving a long number of years as curate and rector in various churches, he retired on account of increasing deafness. Pott published several volumes of hymns and wrote a book on the *"Te Deum."* He was a member of the original committee which produced *Hymns Ancient and Modern.*

MUSIC. VICTORY, also called "Palestrina," is an adaptation from the "Gloria Patri" of a work called, *Magnificat Tertii Toni,* 1591, by the eminent Italian composer, Giovanni Pierluigi Sante Da Palestrina, 1525-94.

The present arrangement was made by Wm. H. Monk for this hymn.

Palestrina, foremost composer of the Roman Catholic Church and supreme master of polyphonic music, was born at Palestrina, Italy, the son of a wealthy peasant, Pierluigi Sante. He was named "Da Palestrina" after his birthplace, a common custom in his time. He received his musical training at Rome where he came under the powerful influence of Orlando di Lasso, the great master from the Netherlands. Palestrina served as chapelmaster in his home town, master of the boys in the Julian Chapel in Rome, and in 1555 was appointed one of the pontifical singers in the Sistine Chapel but was dismissed a few months later when he became guilty of the "crime" of matrimony. He then became chapelmaster at St. John Lateran and later of the Liberian Chapel of Santa Maria Maggiore, during which time he became known as "the saviour of church music." Many abuses had crept into the music of the church, particularly in the use of secular airs grafted on stately church themes, and improvizations by the singers who sometimes departed from the solemn words of the service and substituted profane and lewd words in Italian and French. To correct this scandal, the Ecumenical Council of Trent, in 1552, asked Palestrina to prepare a mass free from the admixture of alien words and secular melodies, and suitable for church use. The result was the composition of three 6-part services, one of which, *Missa Papae Marcelli,* has been regarded as one of the most sublime creations of all music and the model of what church music should be. As a reward for this service, Palestrina was granted a stipend by papal decree which was not large but gave him a sufficient income. In 1571 he was re-elected to his old post as Chapel-master of St. Peter's, where he remained for life. His fame as teacher and composer extended throughout Europe, but his happiness was clouded by the loss of two sons and the death of his wife in 1580, while the remaining son, Igino, became a source of grief to him. Palestrina's compositions were many and of great variety, including 93 masses, 179 motets, hymns, prayers, responses, madrigals, etc.

For comments on Monk see Hymn 40.

HIS ASCENSION

117. Hail the day that sees Him rise   *Charles Wesley*, 1707-88

This hymn, originally in ten stanzas, appeared in Wesley's *Hymns and Sacred Poems,* 1739, under the caption "For Ascension Day." The Hallelujah was added later in White's *Introits and Hymns,* 1852.

For comments on Charles Wesley see Hymn 6.

MUSIC. LLANFAIR, also named "Bethel," is a Welsh hymn tune by Robert Williams, c. 1781-1821, a basket maker. He was born blind, but became a skilled craftsman and a musician of considerable ability.

118. Crown Him with many crowns   *Matthew Bridges*, 1800-94

Based on Rev. 19:12: "On his head were many crowns." The hymn mentions a four-fold crowning of Christ, as: (1) Lamb upon His throne; (2) Son of God; (3) Lord of life; (4) Lord of heaven. Two omitted stanzas mention "Lord of peace," and "Lord of years."

Matthew Bridges was brought up in the church of England but became interested in the Oxford Movement and entered the Roman Catholic Church in 1848. He was a student of history and wrote *The Roman Empire under Constantine the Great.* He is also the author of several books of poems. The latter part of his life was spent in the Province of Quebec, Canada.

The hymn was recast by Godfrey Thring to eliminate several obvious Roman tendencies in it.

MUSIC. DIADEMATA, a solid, dignified tune which organists like to play and congregations enjoy singing, was written for this hymn and named after the Latin title given the hymn.

The composer, George Job Elvey, 1816-93, was a gifted organist and composer and a devout Christian. He received the Bachelor of Music and Doctorate in Music from Oxford University and was organist of St. George's Chapel, Windsor, for 47 years.

119. Look, ye saints, the sight is glorious

Thomas Kelly, 1769-1854

A majestic coronation hymn ranking with the best hymns of Watts and Wesley. It is based on Rev. 11:15: "The kingdoms of this world are become the kingdoms of our Lord and of his Christ. And he shall reign forever and ever."

Thomas Kelly was born in Dublin, the son of an Irish judge. He at first intended to follow his father into the legal profession, but his profound religious convictions led him to train for the ministry. As a young clergyman, he was summoned, with others, to appear before the Archbishop of Dublin to answer for his evangelistic zeal. He was rebuked and prohibited from preaching in Dublin pulpits. He then withdrew from the Church of England and started a number of independent churches. He was much interested in the hymnody of the church and wrote 736 hymns in all. They are characterized by loyalty to Jesus Christ and a deep evangelical glow.

MUSIC. CORONAE is a virile tune, written in 1871, and well adapted by its voice range for congregational singing.

For comments on the composer, Wm. H. Monk, see Hymn 40.

120. Majestic sweetness sits enthroned

Samuel Stennett, c. 1727-95

This hymn was published in John Rippon's *Selection,* 1787, with the title, "Chief among Ten Thousand: or the Excellencies of Christ." It is based on Song of Solomon 5:10-16. The original has 9 stanzas.

The author, Samuel Stennett, prominent non-conformist and champion of religious freedom, was a Baptist clergyman who in 1741 became his father's assistant in Little Wild Street Church, London, and then succeeded his father in 1758, continuing in the pastorate of the church until his death in 1795.

MUSIC. ORTONVILLE has been a favorite hymn tune for over a century. It is associated with these words now, but at first it was set to "O for a closer walk with God." Among Hastings' tunes, this is second in popularity to "Toplady" (148), the tune he made for "Rock of Ages."

Thos. Hastings, 1784-1872, was born in Connecticut, moved to New York state to farm but left the farm at the age of 33 to devote himself to music. In 1831 he moved to New York City to serve the musical interests of a group of churches. He wrote 600 hymns and about 1,000 hymn tunes. He published 50 books of music and collaborated with Lowell Mason in *Spiritual Songs for Social Worship.* The University of the City of New York gave him the degree of Doctor of Music in 1858.

121. Rejoice, the Lord is King   *Charles Wesley,* 1707-88

A jubilant song of Christ's exaltation and coming in power, based on Phil. 4:4: "Rejoice in the Lord alway, and again I say, rejoice."

The hymn, in seven stanzas, appeared first in John Wesley's *Sacred and Moral Poems,* 1744, and later in Wesley's *Hymns for our Lord's Resurrection,* 1746. Though the resurrection note is in the hymn, it is appropriate also for general occasions.

Charles Wesley wrote four great festival hymns: (1) "Hark! the herald angels sing" for Christmas; (2) "Christ the Lord is risen today" for Easter; (3) "Hail the day that sees Him rise" for Ascension; and (4) "Rejoice, the Lord is king" for Whitsuntide.

For comments on Charles Wesley see Hymn 6.

MUSIC. ARTHUR'S SEAT appeared in *Hymns and Songs of Praise* 1874, by John K. Paine and Uzziah C. Burnap. The tune is believed to be an arrangement by Burnap from a melody composed by Sir John Goss, 1800-80, English organist and composer of church choir music. Handel composed a tune, "Gopsal," especially for this hymn, but it is not well known and has not found its way into many of the hymn books.

For comments on Paine and Burnap see Hymn 134.

122. Hail, Thou once despisèd Jesus!   *John Bakewell,* 1721-1819

A worshipful and strongly doctrinal hymn, bringing out plainly the doctrine of the atonement as well as the Saviour's enthronement and glorification.

The authorship is traditionally assigned to John Bakewell, one of John Wesley's lay preachers. But it is not clear that he wrote all of it. It appeared in 1760 in a collection by M. Madan, and later, in 1776, it was included in *Psalms and Hymns* by Augustus M. Toplady. Both editors apparently made some changes and omissions in the hymn, resulting in our present version.

MUSIC. IN BABILONE is a Dutch traditional melody, its present arrangement having been made by Professor Julius Röntgen, 1855-1933, of Amsterdam. It appeared in *The English Hymnal* in 1906 and has since won its way into many American hymn books. It is a joyous, robust melody well suited to carry this hymn.

123. Hark, ten thousand harps and voices

Thomas Kelly, 1769-1854

Based on Heb. 1:6: "Let all the angels of God worship Him."

The original poem has 7 stanzas. Lowell Mason added the "Hallelujahs" and the "Amen" when he set the hymn to music. Some hymn books have softened the "Hallelujah" to "Allelujah." The last stanza is a prayer for the hastening of the day when heaven and earth shall pass away, which some may not be able to sing heartily and sincerely.

For comments on Thomas Kelly see Hymn 119.

MUSIC. HARWELL was written for this hymn in 1840. The original version had the men's voices introduce lines 5 and 6 with a dotted eighth and a sixteenth note, in unison, while the soprano and altos observed a quarter rest. Later editing changed the tune so all the parts observed the quarter rest.

For comments on the composer, Lowell Mason, see Hymn 12.

124. Alleluia! sing to Jesus!

William C. Dix, 1837-98

Based on Rev. 5:9: "Thou hast redeemed us to God by thy blood out of every nation."

The original poem of five stanzas appeared in Dix's *Altar Songs*, 1867, and was entitled "Redemption by the Precious Blood." The hymn was linked to the sacrament of the Lord's Supper. The third and fourth stanzas, omitted here, are as follows:

> Alleluia! Bread of Heaven,
>   Thou on earth our food, our stay!
> Alleluia! here the sinful
>   Flee to thee from day to day:
> Intercessor, friend of sinners,
>   Earth's Redeemer, plead for me,
> Where the songs of all the sinless,
>   Sweep across the crystal sea.

> Alleluia! King eternal,
>   Thee the Lord of lords we own:
> Alleluia! born of Mary,
>   Earth thy footstool, heav'n thy throne:
> Thou within the veil hast entered,
>   Robed in flesh, our great High Priest:
> Thou on earth both Priest and Victim
>   In the eucharistic feast.

73

For comments on William C. Dix see Hymn 78.

MUSIC. The tune was taken from *St. Basil's Hymnal,* Chicago, 1918, where it appears unnamed. It is a traditional Dutch melody. The present arrangement of it is anonymous.

HIS COMING AGAIN

125. The King shall come when morning dawns

From the Greek
Tr. by John Brownlie, 1859-1925

This hymn, setting forth the hope of Christ's Second Coming in triumph, comes from the Greek, but no information is at hand concerning the original poem. It is not included in Julian's *Dictionary.*

The translation is by John Brownlie, a Scottish minister, born in Glasgow. He published several books of original hymns and translations from the Greek.

MUSIC. JERUSALEM, JERUSALEM is wrongly attributed here to Thomas Hastings though it is possible that the arrangement is his. The same tune, named "St. Michel's," appears at No. 93, which see for comments. For comments on Thomas Hastings see Hymn 120.

126. Thou art coming, O my Savior

Frances R. Havergal, 1836-79

The first hymn Miss Havergal wrote after Advent Sunday, December 2, 1873, when she "first saw clearly the blessedness of true consecration."

Frances Ridley Havergal was the daughter of Rev. Wm. H. Havergal, an Anglican clergyman who was greatly interested in the hymns and music of the church and composed a number of tunes still in use. His tune, "Evan," is used in the *Hymnary* (153 and 253). Frances thus grew up in a cultured religious environment in which hymns and church music held a prominent place. She was handicapped by a frail body and died at the early age of forty-three. But throughout her short life, from the time of her confirmation at seventeen until the end, she had an unbounded joy in Christian service. No suffering could diminish her faith in the grace of God through Jesus Christ. Despite her poor health, she was a devoted student of the Bible and was able to repeat from memory the four Gospels, the Epistles, Revelations, all the Psalms, Isaiah, and the Minor Prophets. Besides writing many letters counselling those who sought her advice, she wrote devotional books and composed sacred hymns and poems, always emphasizing consecration and service. She made a considerable contribution to the hymnody of the church. Six of her compositions are to be found in the *Hymnary* (126, 190, 215, 219, 296, 380).

MUSIC. BEVERLEY was composed for this hymn for use in *Hymns Ancient and Modern*, Rev. ed., 1875.
For comments on W. H. Monk see Hymn 40.

127. Christis coming, let creation   *John R. Macduff, 1818-95*

A Scottish hymn setting forth the glowing hope and expectation of the coming of Christ in glory. It is based on Rev. 22:20: "He which testifieth these things saith, Surely, I come quickly. Amen. Even so, come, Lord Jesus."

John R. Macduff was minister of the Sandyford Parish, Glasgow. He is the author of several books of devotions and wrote numerous hymns. His ministry at Sandyford was singularly fruitful. George Mattheson, blind Scottish preacher, then a boy in Macduff's congregation, afterwards said of him: "Dr. Macduff gave me my first real conviction of the beauty of Christianity." Macduff held strongly to the premillennial view of the coming of Christ.

MUSIC. NEANDER. This famous tune has been associated with various words. The composer first published it in 1680 set to the hymn, *"Unser Herrscher, unser König."* It is also used with Schmolk's "Open now the gates of beauty" (505), and in England it is almost invariably associated with "Come, ye saints, and raise an anthem," by J. Hupton and others.

Joachim Neander, 1650-80, whose real name was Neumann, was born at Bremen, where he spent most of his life. As a youth he was somewhat wild but in time became converted and associated himself with the Pietists of Germany. He was a friend of Spener, the leader of the Pietists. His unconventional zeal brought him into conflict with the authorities of the Reformed Church of which he was a member, and he was dismissed for a time from his office as teacher in the Düsseldorf schools. Being obliged to leave town, he lived for some months in a cave in the region of the Rhine, where he composed many of his hymns. He is the foremost hymn writer of the German Reformed Church and is called "the Paul Gerhardt of the Calvinists." Neander, like Luther, was a man of scholarship and accomplishment in poetry and music, as well as theology. He wrote more than 60 hymns and composed tunes for them.

128. Ye servants of the Lord   *Philip Doddridge, 1702-51*

"The Active Christian" is the author's title of this hymn. It appeared first in Job Orton's posthumous edition of *Hymns founded on Various Texts,* 1755. It is founded on Luke 12:35-37:

> Let your loins be girded about, and your lights burning;
> And ye yourselves like unto men that wait for their lord, when he will return from the wedding; that when he cometh and knocketh, they may open unto him immediately.
> Blessed are those servants, whom the lord when he cometh shall find watching: verily I say unto you, that he shall gird himself, and make them to sit down to meat, and will come forth and serve them.

Doddridge, known for his sound learning and genuine Christian character, was a first-rate hymn writer. He taught Hebrew, Greek, algebra, trigonometry, logic, philosophy, and theology to classes of candidates for the Congregational ministry.

For further comments on Doddridge see Hymn 56.

MUSIC. OLD 134TH (ST. MICHAEL) is one of the greatest of short-meter tunes, derived from the tune composed by L. Bourgeois for Psalm 101 in the *Genevan Psalter* of 1551.

For comments on L. Bourgeois see Hymn 34.

129. Come, Lord, and tarry not   *Horatius Bonar*, 1808–89

A plaintive, sad hymn bordering almost on pessimism, by an able, pious author who held the doctrine of the premillenarian coming of Christ. All his life, Bonar's mind was occupied with the subject of the second advent, an interest which inspired much of his writing.

Horatius Bonar, born in Edinburgh, was the prince of Scottish hymn writers. Educated at the University of Edinburgh, he was ordained in 1837 and became a minister in the Established Church of Scotland at Kelso. At the Disruption in 1843, Bonar "came out" and was one of the founders of the Free Church of Scotland (Presbyterian). Leaving Kelso, he became the minister of Chalmer's Memorial Church in Edinburgh, where he served, a greatly beloved man, until his death. He was known as a man of wide scholarship and culture. His mind was saturated with Scripture and his heart possessed by a broad and generous faith.

His son, Rev. H. N. Bonar, wrote his father's *Life* which gives some interesting information concerning his hymn writing. Bonar carried notebooks with him in which he jotted thoughts, verses, and hymns as they came to his mind.

"These notebooks," writes the son, "contain most of the better-known hymns, hastily written down in pencil in his spare moments. They are full of contractions, with an occasional word or phrase in shorthand; sometimes a line is struck out and another substituted, yet in nearly every case the complete hymn, almost as it was afterwards published, can be gleaned from this rough draft."

MUSIC. SHIRLAND was composed by Samuel Stanley, 1767-1822, English composer and precentor of Carr's Lane Congregational Chapel, in Birmingham. Through his skilled leadership the music of this church became famous. The hymn singing attracted attention and resulted in a great growth in the congregation.

For further comments on Stanley see Hymn 20.

130. Lo, He comes, with clouds descending

John Cennick, 1718-55

A hymn on the Second Advent, based on Rev. 1:7: "Behold He cometh with clouds; and every eye shall see him, and they also which pierced him: and all kindreds of the earth shall wail because of him. Even so, Amen."

The author, John Cennick, came from a Quaker family though he grew up in the Church of England. For some years his religious convictions were unsettled. Then while engaged in land surveying, he came under the influence of Wesley and became one of his lay preachers. Later he became a follower of George Whitefield, and finally he joined the Moravians. While limited in culture and outlook, he possessed genuine lyric fire; and his name is of note among the hymnists, even though only a few of his many hymns survive.

This hymn has been much revised. It owes not a little to Charles Wesley who changed Cennick's first line, "Lo! he cometh; countless trumpets," to the familiar "Lo, He comes with clouds descending." Martin Madan, who issued the hymn in his *Collection of Psalms and Hymns,* also gave it certain finishing touches. The hymn possesses a scriptural vividness and impressive treatment of theme which have carried it throughout the English speaking world, despite the apocalyptic form of the description it sets forth.

MUSIC. HOLYWOOD is attributed to Samuel Webbe, probably the elder, 1740-1816, a London organist and composer and a member of the Roman Catholic Church. His son, Samuel Webbe, Jr., 1770-1843, following his father in the musical profession, likewise became an organist and composer.

Its solidity and triumphant note give this tune a worthy place in the music of the church.

131. Come, Holy Ghost, in love

Ray Palmer, 1808-87
Tr. from the Latin

Veni, Sancte Spiritus,
Et emitte caelitus
Lucis tuae radium:
Veni, Pater pauperum;
Veni, Dator munerum;
Veni, Lumen cordium.

O Lux beatissima,
Reple cordis intima
Tuorum fidelium.
Sine tuo numine
Nihil est in homine.
Nihil est innoxium.

Consolator optime,
Dulcis Hospes animae,
Duce Refrigerium,
In labore Requies,
In aestu Temperies,
In fletu Solacium.

Lava, quod est sordidum,
Riga, quod est aridum,
Rege, quod est devium,
Fove, quod est languidum,
Flecte, quod est rigidum,
Sana, quod est saucium.

Da tuis fidelibus
In te confidentibus
Sacrum septenarium;
Da virtutis meritum,
Da salutis exitum,
Da perenne gaudium. Amen.

This truly great Latin hymn, addressed to the Holy Spirit, comes from the 12th or 13th century. Its authorship is uncertain. Archbishop Trench characterized it as "the loveliest of all the hymns in the whole cycle of Sacred Latin Poetry." Many translations have been made of it, this one by Ray Palmer.

Ray Palmer, who held pastorates at Bath, Me., and Albany, N. Y., was for a time corresponding secretary for the American Congregational Union. His name remains the greatest among hymnists and translators in the American Congregational church. His hymn, "My faith looks up to Thee" (150), is known all over the world.

MUSIC. MALVERN is from *The Hallelujah,* a series of compilations of tunes, edited by J. J. Waite and H. J. Gauntlett, first published in 1842. The work was intended to encourage the congregation to sing in parts, an altogether novel principle in the English churches of that time. To make the music easy to read, the notes were numbered, the tonic sol-fa system having, as yet, not been developed. The present arrangement is by John Roberts, 1822-77, Welsh Methodist pastor and musician of extraordinary ability. He did much to improve congregational singing in the church and was an eminent conductor of school music festivals. Roberts wrote a number of tunes that are high in favor throughout Wales and was incomparable as an arranger of congregational hymn tunes.

132. Lord God, the Holy Ghost   *James Montgomery, 1771-1854*

One of the few hymns which deals distinctively with the Day of Pentecost. For this reason, as well as for its inherent quality, it is especially valuable.

For comments on James Montgomery see Hymn 62.

MUSIC. OLD 134TH. For comments on this tune see Hymn 128.

133. Spirit of God, descend upon my heart

George Croly, 1780-1860

Based on Gal. 5:25: "If we live in the Spirit, let us also walk in the Spirit."

George Croly was educated at Trinity College, Dublin. After ministering in Ireland for a number of years, he went to London to engage in literary pursuits. He had varied talents and became well known for his poetry, fiction, plays, and contributed articles to magazines. In 1835, he entered parish work in London, where he was greatly admired and loved. His outspoken utterances attracted large congregations of all ranks to his church. He prepared, at the request of his people, a collection of *Psalms and Hymns for Public Worship,* of which only one edition was printed. Dr. Croly dropped dead while walking one day on Holborn Street. A man of scholarship and culture, and author of many volumes, he is remembered chiefly through this hymn.

MUSIC. MORECAMBE, originally called "Hellespont," was written to be sung with "Abide with me," for use in the church at Mannington, England, where its composer was serving as organist.

Frederick Cook Atkinson, 1841-97, was an English organist and choirmaster, having received his musical education at Cambridge.

134. Holy Ghost, dispel our sadness   *Paul Gerhardt, 1607-76*

A hymn of entreaty for the indwelling of the Holy Spirit.
The original is as follows:

> O Du allersüsste Freude,
> O Du allerschönstes Licht,
> Der Du uns in Lieb und Leide
> Unbesuchet lässest nicht;
> Geist des Höchsten, höchster Fürst
> Der Du hältst und halten wirst
> Ohn' Aufhören alle Dinge
> Höre, höre, was ich singe.

79

Du bist ja die beste Gabe
  Die ein Mensch nur nennen kann;
Wenn ich Dich erwünsch' und habe,
  Geb' ich alles Wünschen d'ran.
Ach, ergib Dich, komm zu mir,
In mein Herze, das Du Dir,
  Eh ich in die Welt geboren
  Selbst zum Tempel auserkoren.

Sei mein Retter, führ' mich eben;
  Wenn ich sink', mein Stab sei Du;
Wenn ich sterbe, sei mein Leben;
  Wenn ich lieg', sei meine Ruh;
Wenn ich wieder aufersteh',
O so hilf mir, dass ich geh
  Hin, da Du in ew'gen Freuden
  Wirst die Auserwählten weiden.

The first translation was made by John Christian Jacobi, 1670-1750, for his *Psalmodia Germanica*. His rendering began
  "O Thou sweetest source of gladness"
which Augustus Montague Toplady recast into the familiar
  "Holy Ghost, dispel our sadness."

For comments on Toplady see Hymn 148.

Paul Gerhardt, next to Martin Luther, is the most noteworthy hymn writer of the Evangelical Church in Germany. Even the hymns of Luther are not as widely used today in the English speaking world as those of Gerhardt. He was born March 12, 1607, in Gräfenhynichen, a village near the celebrated Wittenberg. At 21 he began the study of theology in Wittenberg, but he received no church position until 45, when he was ordained and appointed provost at Mittenwalde, a small village. During his six years there, his hymns were published and he became widely known. In 1657, he was appointed third assistant pastor of the famous Church of St. Nicholas in Berlin. From this position he was deposed because he refused to sign a document promising that all clergymen would abstain from any references in their sermons to doctrinal differences between the Lutherans and Calvinists. Though he felt the blow keenly, he met it with Christian patience and fortitude. "This," he said, "is only a small Berlin affliction; but I am also willing and ready to seal with my blood the evangelical truth, and, like my namesake, St. Paul, to offer my neck to the sword." Additional sorrows came into his life with the death of his wife and four of his children. He was left with a single child, a boy of six, when he was called to the church at Lübden, where he labored faithfully and successfully until his death on June 7, 1676. Most of his life being spent in the distractions and disasters of the Thirty Years War, which left Germany in misery and ruins, Gerhardt knew the depths of human sorrow. Out of the depths came his hymns of comfort and hope which have been a source of strength to a multitude of believers.

MUSIC. INVOCATION was composed by Uzziah C. Burnap, 1834-1900, organist at the Church of the Heights, Brooklyn, and co-editor with John K. Paine, Professor of Music at Harvard, of *Hymns and Songs of Praise.*

135. Breathe on me, breath of God   *Edwin Hatch, 1835-89*

An earnest prayer for an inbreathing of the Holy Spirit and a greater consecration of life. The hymn was first published in a privately printed leaflet called, *Between Doubt and Prayer,* 1878. It is based on John 20:22: "He breathed on them and saith unto them, Receive ye the Holy Ghost."

Edwin Hatch, Church of England clergyman and University Reader of Ecclesiastical History at Oxford, was a scholar of world reputation. His Bampton Lectures, *The Organization of the Early Christian Church,* 1881, were translated into German by Prof. Adolph Harnack, who wrote of Hatch: "In his learning that of England's great old theologians, Ussher and Pearson, lived to me again. He was a glorious man, whose loss I shall never cease to mourn." Though a man of profound learning, his faith was as simple and unaffected as that of a child.

MUSIC. TRENTHAM is a tune of great beauty, well fitted for these words of devotion. The tenor part is especially melodious.

Robert Jackson, 1840-1914, English composer of many anthems, hymn tunes, songs and part songs, succeeded his father as organist and choirmaster at St. Peter's church, Oldham, the father and son together having a record of continuous service at the same church for 92 years. His whole life was devoted to music. He was a member of Sir Charles Halle's orchestra and conductor of the Oldham Musical Society.

136. Holy Spirit, Truth divine   *Samuel Longfellow 1819-92*

Entitled a "Prayer for Inspiration," this superb hymn of the Holy Spirit appeared in *Hymns of the Spirit,* 1864, edited by Samuel Johnson and the author. Stanzas 5 and 6 are omitted.

For comments on Samuel Longfellow see Hymn 28.

MUSIC. MERCY is an arrangement of a piano composition called, "The Last Hope," by Louis Gottschalk, 1829-69, American composer, conductor, and popular concert pianist. Among Gottschalk's works are two operas, two symphonies, and some piano pieces and songs—most of which are forgotten today. The arrangement of the tune is the work of Dr. Edwin P. Parker, 1836-1925, hymnologist and distinguished Congregationalist minister at Hartford, Conn.

137. Holy Spirit, faithful Guide   *Marcus M. Wells, 1815-95*

The hymn and tune were written by Marcus M. Wells, a farmer and maker of farm implements who lived all his life in New York State. Born at Otsego, N. Y., he was converted in a mission at Buffalo. Regarding the origin of the hymn and tune he wrote:

> On a Saturday afternoon, Oct. 1858, while at work in my cornfield, the sentiment of the hymn came to me. The next day, Sunday, being a very stormy day, I finished the hymn and wrote a tune for it and sent it to Prof. I. B. Woodbury.

The hymn sets forth God as a Presence, near the Christian's side, friendly and helpful and true, guiding him through the storms and floods and desert wastes of his pilgrimage from earth to his heavenly home. It was first published in the *New York Musical Pioneer,* edited by Isaac B. Woodbury.

138. Our blest Redeemer, ere He breathed
Harriet Auber, 1773-1862

One of the finest of our hymns on the Holy Spirit. It was written for Whitsunday and published in the author's *The Spirit of the Psalms,* 1829, in seven stanzas, the second and third being omitted here. The hymn appears in most modern hymnals and has been translated into several languages.

Harriet Auber, whose grandfather went from Normandy to England in 1685 as a Hugenot refugee, was born in London. She was a woman of refinement and culture who spent most of her life in the quiet villages of Broxbourne and Hoddesdon, Hertfordshire. She wrote numerous poems and hymns, but her name survives as the author of this exquisite lyric.

MUSIC. st. cuthbert was composed for these words by J. B. Dykes for the original edition of *Hymns Ancient and Modern,* 1861. For comments on Dykes see Hymn I.

139. Spirit divine, attend our prayer   *Andrew Reed, 1787-1862*
Samuel Longfellow, 1819-92

This is a revision by Samuel Longfellow of a hymn written by Andrew Reed, an English Congregational minister. Reed, a philanthropist and great organizer, and founder of six asylums and orphanages, wrote 21 hymns and published several hymn books. He was an ardent supporter of missionary work at home and abroad. **Writing to his son who suggested that the father should write his autobiography,** Dr. Reed summed up his own life in these words:

> I was born yesterday, I shall die tomorrow, and I must not spend today in telling what I have done, but in doing what I may for HIM who has done all for me. I sprang from the people, I have lived for the people—the most for the most unhappy; and the people when they know it will not suffer me to die out of loving remembrance.

MUSIC. BRECON. The origin of this tune has not been traced. It is a useful tune as a choir response after the prayer.

THE CALL OF CHRIST

140. Jesus calls us o'er the tumult

Cecil Frances Alexander, 1823-95

A hymn of consecration which has had far-reaching influence especially over young people. It is based on Matt. 4:18, 19: "And Jesus, walking by the sea of Galilee, saw two brethren, Simon, called Peter, and Andrew, his brother, casting a net into the sea: for they were fishers. And he saith unto them, Follow me, and I will make you fishers of men." There is also a reference to the incident by the lake recorded in John 21:15: "So when they had dined, Jesus saith to Simon Peter, son of Jonas, lovest thou me more than these?"

The hymn appeared first in *Hymns,* 1852, published by the Society for the Promotion of Christian Knowledge. In the Episcopal Church in the United States and Canada, it has been adopted as the hymn of the Brotherhood of St. Andrew.

Mrs. Alexander is known principally as a writer of children's hymns (410 and 412), but she also contributed excellent church songs for adults.

For comments on Mrs. Alexander see Hymn 104.

MUSIC. GALILEE was written for this hymn by William H. Jude, 1852-1922, English organist, composer, and lecturer on musical subjects. The tune becomes waltz-like when sung in quick tempo. Recognizing this danger, some hymn books are using other tunes with this hymn.

141. Behold a stranger at the door   *Joseph Grigg, 1720-68*

A lyric revealing in a remarkable manner the tenderness and love of Christ. It is based on Rev. 3:20: "Behold, I stand at the door and

83

knock." Bishop How's hymn, "O Jesus Thou art standing" (144), with which this may be compared, is based on the same passage.

Joseph Grigg, an English Presbyterian minister, began writing hymns when only ten years old. After a brief pastorate, he retired from the active ministry to devote himself to literary work. He published about 40 volumes, including several collections of hymns. Only two of his 43 hymns are found in modern hymnals, this one and "Jesus, and shall it ever be" (192), the latter written when he was only ten years of age.

MUSIC. BERA, a very useful tune, was composed by John Edgar Gould, 1822-75, an American musical editor, dealer in musical instruments, choral conductor, and publisher of music books. He was born in Maine, but spent most of his adult life in New York City and Philadelphia.

142. I heard the voice of Jesus say   *Horatius Bonar*, 1808-89

Based on John 1:16: "Of his fulness have all we received, and grace for grace," and originally published with the title, "The Voice from Galilee."

The hymn is constructed on three sayings of Jesus: (1) "Come unto me, all ye that labor and are heavy laden, and I will give you rest," Mt. 11:28; (2) "Whosoever drinketh of the water that I shall give shall never thirst," John 4:14; (3) "I am the light of the world; he that followeth me shall not walk in darkness, but shall have the light of life." John 8:12. In the hymn, these three sayings, blended into a perfect unity, have sounded down the ages by the "Voice from Galilee."

The hymn, as C. S. Robinson reminds us, employs the personal pronoun to emphasize the intimate relationship between Christ and the individual. "Christ says, 'Come to *me*,' and the Christian says, '*I* come.' Christ says, '*I* give the living water'; and the listener answers, '*My* thirst was quenched'; Christ says, 'I am the light'; and the child of God replies, 'I found in him *my* Star, *my* Sun.' "

For comments on Horatius Bonar see Hymn 129.

MUSIC. VOX DELECTI was composed by J. B. Dykes for this hymn in *Hymns Ancient and Modern,* Appendix, 1868. The musical difficulties of the tune are more apparent than real. They can be overcome and its possibilities appreciated by careful study and practice. The first half is written in the minor key to carry the quiet, invitational words of Jesus. The second part, the glad acceptance of the invitation, is written in the strongly contrasting major key.

For comments on J. B. Dykes see Hymn 1.

143. Art thou weary, heavy laden
Stephen the Sabaite, 725-94
Tr. John M. Neale, 1818-66

A restful, appealing lyric on the theme, "Come unto me, all ye that labor and are heavy laden, and I will give you rest" Matt. 11:28.

It is one of the few dialog hymns, [Others are "Watchman, tell us of the night" (66), and "Who is He in yonder stall?" (96)]. It may be sung antiphonally, the choir singing the questions and the congregation the answers.

Neale published this hymn in his *Hymns of the Eastern Church,* 1862, as a translation of a Greek hymn by Stephen the Sabaite. It is a paraphrase, however, rather than a translation.

For comments on John Neale see Hymn 67.

Hymnody in the Eastern Church reached its height in the 8th century. Stephen was a nephew of John of Damascus. At the age of 10 he was placed by his uncle in the monastery of Saint Sabas, located on a lofty cliff overhanging the ravine of the Kidron, between Jerusalem and the Dead Sea. Here he lived for more than half a century, known as Stephen the Sabaite. The monastery, many of the cells cut out of solid rock, still stands. The monks have been subjected to persecution, at various times, at the hands of Persians, Moslems, and Bedouin Arabs, and the monastery looks much like a fortress.

MUSIC. STEPHANOS was composed for this hymn by Henry W. Baker, and was first published in the appendix of the original edition of *Hymns Ancient and Modern,* 1868. The tune was harmonized by W. H. Monk (See 40).

Henry Williams Baker, 1821-77, was educated at Cambridge, ordained in 1844, and served as vicar of Monkland, Herefordshire, from 1851 till his death in 1877. He was editor-in-chief of the epoch-making book, *Hymns Ancient and Modern,* to which he contributed several of his own hymns and tunes. As a High Churchman, he held to the doctrine of the celibacy of the clergy and was never married.

144. O Jesus, Thou art standing
William W. How, 1823-97

Based on Rev. 3:20: "Behold, I stand at the door and knock: if any man hear my voice and open the door, I will come in to him, and sup with him, and he with me." It was composed after the author had been reading the beautiful poem by Jean Ingelow, entitled "Brothers and a Sermon," describing two brothers listening to an old parson in a fishing-village church. A part of the poem is as follows:

> The parson knew that he had lost the eyes
> And ears of those before him for he made
> A pause . . . .
> . . . . then with a sigh

Fronted the folk, lifted his grand gray head,
And said, as one that pondered now the words
He had been preaching on with new surprise,
And found fresh marvel in their sound, "Behold!
Behold!" saith He, "I stand at the door and knock."

Open the door with shame, if ye have sinned;
If ye be sorry, open it with sighs.
Albeit the place be bare for poverty,
And comfortless for lack of plenishing,
Be not abashed for that, but open it,
And take Him in that comes to sup with thee;
"Behold!" He saith, "I stand at the door and knock!"

Speak, then, O rich and strong:
Open, O happy young, ere yet the hand
Of Him that knocks, wearied at last, forbear;
The patient foot its thankless quest refrain.
The wounded heart forevermore withdraw.

Holman Hunt's picture, "The Light of the World," is an exquisite illustration of the spirit of this hymn.

William Walsham How was born at Shrewsbury, England, educated at Oxford, and ordained to the ministry in 1846. He served various churches as pastor and declined offers of positions of more distinction. He refused the bishopric of Durham, one of the most distinguished posts in the Anglican Church, with an income more than double what he then had. He was a man of broad sympathies and apostolical zeal, and was a master of the pastoral art. He collaborated with Thos. Baker Morrell in editing *Psalms and Hymns,* 1854, and in 1871 was joint editor of *Church Hymns,* published by the Society for the Promotion of Christian Knowledge, the latter becoming the greatest rival of *Hymns Ancient and Modern* which that book had had to date. His poems are marked by simplicity and beauty of diction and constitute some of the richest treasures of modern hymnody.

MUSIC. st. hilda, also known as "St. Edith," is an arrangement by Rev. Edward Husband of a tune published by Justin H. Knecht in *Vollständige Sammlung,* Stuttgart, 1799.

For comments on Knecht see Hymn 511.

Edward Husband, 1843-1908, was an English clergyman with a great deal of musical talent and interest and was a well-known lecturer on the subject of church music.

145. Savior, when, in dust, to Thee   *Robert Grant*, 1779-1838

A hymn of penitence which has had a wide use. It was published in the *Christian Observer,* 1815, as a Lenten "Litany." The last line of each stanza (five in the original) read, "Hear our solemn litany," here changed to "Hear thy people when they cry." Stanzas 2 and 4 have been much altered by an unknown hand. Grant's original hymn of five stanzas reads as follows:

1. Savior, when in dust to Thee
Low we bow the adoring knee,
When, repentant, to the skies
Scarce we lift our weeping eyes,
Oh, by all Thy pains and woe
Suffered once for man below,
Bending from Thy throne on high,
Hear our solemn litany!

2. By Thy helpless infant years,
By Thy life of want and tears,
By Thy days of sore distress
In the savage wilderness,
By the dread, mysterious hour
Of the insulting Tempter's power,
Turn, O turn, a favoring eye,
Hear our solemn litany!

3. By the sacred griefs that wept
O'er the grave where Lazarus slept;
By the boding tears that flowed
Over Salem's loved abode;
By the anguished sigh that told
Treachery lurked within Thy fold;
From Thy seat above the sky
Hear our solemn litany!

4. By Thine hour of dire despair,
By Thine agony of prayer,
By the cross, the nail, the thorn,
Piercing spear, and torturing scorn,
By the gloom that veiled the skies
O'er the dreadful sacrifice,
Listen to our humble cry,
Hear our solemn litany!

5. By Thy deep expiring groan,
By the sad sepulchral stone,
By the vault whose dark abode
Held in vain the rising God,
Oh, from earth to heaven restored,
Mighty, reascended Lord,
Listen, listen, to the cry
Of our solemn litany!

For comments on Robert Grant see Hymn 7.

MUSIC. SPANISH HYMN, also called "Spanish Chant," is from an old 17th century melody of unknown origin.

146. Come, let us to the Lord our God

John Morison, 1750-98
Scottish Paraphrase, 1781

A version, from the Scottish Presbyterian Church, of Hosea 6:1-4:
Come, and let us return unto the Lord: for he hath torn, and he will heal us; he hath smitten, and he will bind us up. After two days will he revive us: in the third day he will raise us up, and we shall live in his sight. Then shall we know, if we follow on to know the Lord: his going forth is prepared as the morning: and he shall come unto us as the rain, as the latter and former rain unto the earth.

O Ephraim, what shall I do unto thee? O Judah, what shall I do unto thee? for your goodness is as a morning cloud, and as the early dew it goeth away.

Our hymn is one of the 67 "Translations and Paraphrases, in Verse, of Several Passages of Sacred Scriptures," together with five hymns, that are appended to the *Scottish Psalter* for use in public worship in the Scotch Presbyterian Church.

John Morison was a Scotch scholar, teacher, and minister. He wrote a number of paraphrases of scriptural passages, seven of which were accepted into the authorized collection of *Scottish Paraphrases,* 1781.

MUSIC. BALLERMA. For comments on this tune see Hymn 57.

147. Lord, thy mercy now entreating

Mary Ann Sidebotham, 1833-1913

A hymn of penitence which was contributed to *The Children's Hymn Book,* 1881, published by the Society for the Promotion of Christian Knowledge, London.

The author, Mary Ann Sidebotham, was an accomplished musician and a lifelong friend of Henry Smart, the eminent organist and com-

88

poser. She spent much of her life in her brother's vicarage, St. Thomas-on-the-Bourne, Surrey, England, where she served as organist. She composed numerous songs for children and was the music editor of the above-mentioned *Children's Hymn Book.*

MUSIC. RINGE RECHT. For comments on this tune see Hymn 563.

FAITH AND VISION

148. Rock of Ages, cleft for me   *Augustus M. Toplady, 1740-78*

Few hymns are more generally familiar or more treasured in the affections of all ranks of people than this. It appeared first in the *Gospel Magazine,* edited by Toplady, March, 1776, at the end of an article entitled, "A remarkable calculation Introduced here for the sake of the Spiritual Improvements subjoined. Questions and answers relating to the National Debt." The article points out that the national debt is so large that the government will never be able to pay it off. The author then proceeds to calculate the number of sins each human being commits. Figuring the rate to be one per second, he arrives at this:

> Our dreadful account stands as follows: At ten years old each of us is chargeable with 315 millions and 360,000 sins. At twenty, with 630 millions and 720,000. At thirty with 946 millions and 80,000. . . . At eighty, with 2,522 millions and 880,000.

The conclusion is that the debt can only be paid by the blood of Christ. The hymn follows his "calculation," under the heading, "A living and dying Prayer for the Holiest Believer in the World."

For 45 years after its publication, the hymn had little acceptance in England. Its merits then became recognized, and it became very popular. In the last century and a quarter it has had world-wide use, in a form altered somewhat from the original. The hymn has been criticized for its mixed metaphors ("cleft rock," "riven side," "to thy cross I cling," "to the fountain fly"), for its false rhymes, and its over-emphasis upon sin obsession; but it has certain heart-piercing qualities which override all its faults. Like other hymns of the first rank (e.g., "Jesus Lover of my soul," "Lead kindly light," and "Nearer my God to Thee") it voices the universal need of divine help. Professor Saintsbury, a literary critic, says of this hymn: "Every word, every syllable, in this really great poem has its place and meaning."

The central imagery of the hymn is found in the following Scripture passages: Ex. 33:22: "While my glory passeth by, I will put thee in a cleft of the rock, and will cover thee with my hand while I pass by";

Isa. 26:4: "Trust ye in the Lord for ever: for in the Lord Jehovah is the rock of ages" (margin); I Cor. 10:4: "and that Rock was Christ."

A picturesque story, which originated about 1850, had it that Toplady composed the hymn while he was sheltering from a thunder storm in a great cleft of a limestone rock, some twelve years before the publication of the hymn. The story is without foundation. Toplady was fascinated by the thought of Christ as a rock and in a sermon on Isa. 42:11: "Let the inhabitants of the rock sing," he said: "Chiefly may they sing who inhabit Christ the spiritual Rock of Ages. He is a Rock in three ways: as a Foundation to support, a Shelter to screen, and a Fortress to protect."

The hymn has had a wide use among German speaking people in a translation made by Ernst Gebhardt, 1832-99.

> Fels des Heils, geöffnet mir,
> Birg' mich, ew'ger Hort in dir!
> Lass das Wasser und das Blut,
> Deiner Seite heil'ge Flut,
> Mir das Heil sein, das frei macht
> Von der Sünden-Schuld und-Macht!
>
> Dem, was dein Gesetze spricht,
> Kann mein Werk genügen nicht.
> Mag ich ringen wie ich will,
> Fliessen auch der Tränen viel,
> Tilgt das doch nicht meine Schuld,
> Herr, mir hilft nur deine Huld.
>
> Da ich denn nichts bringen kann,
> Schmieg' ich an dein Kreuz mich an
> Nackt und bloss—o kleid' mich doch.
> Hülflos—ach erbarm' dich noch.
> Unrein, Herr, flieh' ich zu dir.
> Wasche mich, sonst sterb' ich hier.
>
> Jetzt, da ich noch leb' im Licht,
> Wenn mein Aug' im Tode bricht,
> Wenn durch's finst're Tal ich geh',
> Wenn ich vor dem Richter steh',
> Fels des Heils, geöffnet mir,
> Birg' mich, ew'ger Hort in dir!

Augustus M. Toplady, born at Farnham, England, was educated at Trinity College, Dublin. His conversion occurred at the age of 16 while on a visit in Ireland. The service was held in a barn and the text was Eph. 2:13: "But now, in Christ Jesus, ye who sometimes were far off are made nigh by the blood of Christ." The preacher was an illiterate but warm-hearted layman named Morris. Concerning his conversion Toplady wrote:

> Strange that I, who had so long sat under the means of grace in England, should be brought nigh unto God in an obscure part of Ireland, amidst a handful of God's people met together in a barn, and under the ministry of one who could hardly spell his name. Surely this is the Lord's doing, and it is marvelous.

Toplady was ordained to the ministry of the Church of England in 1762 and in 1768 became vicar of Broadhembury. The last years of his life were passed in London preaching in a chapel of French Calvinists. He was a powerful preacher, and large congregations came to hear him. A strong Calvinist, and bitterly opposed to what he considered the reproach of Arminianism, he became involved in unfortunate controversies with John Wesley, during which neither disputant showed himself at his best. He died of consumption at the early age of 38.

MUSIC. TOPLADY was composed for this hymn by Thomas Hastings, 1784-1872. It is a popular easily sung tune, and universally used in America with this hymn. Hastings was not a great musician and this tune, with its "sentimentality and rocking-chair rhythm," can hardly be considered great music. But it has been a blessing to millions of people and will doubtless continue to be sung for years to come. In England the hymn is invariably set to other tunes and some American hymn books have introduced alternative tunes. The tune "Petra" (109) is used with this hymn, as is also *Grosser Gott wir loben Dich* (519).

For comments on Thomas Hastings see Hymn 120.

149. Strong Son of God, immortal love *Alfred Tennyson*, 1809-92

From the prologue of Tennyson's great poem, "In Memoriam," 1850, containing eleven stanzas; these are 1, 4, 5, and 7, unaltered.

The story of "In Memoriam" is familiar. At Cambridge University, Tennyson and Arthur Hallam became intimate friends. Hallam became engaged to Tennyson's sister, and, after graduating from the University, took a trip to the Continent. At Vienna, he became sick and died, which prompted Tennyson to write the following brief but beautiful words:

> "In Vienna's fatal walls,
> God's finger touched him, and he slept."

In 1850, seventeen years after Hallam's death, Tennyson published "In Memoriam," a memorial to Hallam, but also to himself as well. Among the individual verses of the poem which have become immortal are the familiar lines beginning, "Ring out, wild bells, to the wild sky" (See 379).

Alfred Tennyson was the son of Rev. George C. Tennyson. He was educated at Cambridge and wrote poetry while an undergraduate. Upon the death of Wordsworth in 1850, Tennyson was appointed Poet Laureate. He is regarded as one of England's greatest poets. He was not a hymn writer, yet several of his poems are used as hymns. Tennyson died October 6, 1892, and was buried in Westminster Abbey.

MUSIC. ST. CRISPIN was composed for the hymn "Just as I am, without one plea." The tune was used at the funeral of the composer. For comments on the composer, George Elvey, see Hymn 118.

150. My faith looks up to Thee   *Ray Palmer*, 1808-87

This hymn was written when the author had just left Yale at the age of 21 and was looking forward to his lifework in the Congregational ministry. The origin of the hymn is given in Duffield's *English Hymns*, as follows:

> The hymn was written in 1830, but not published (as a hymn) until 1832. The author was in New York City, "Between his college and theological studies," and was in poor health, and a teacher in a ladies' school. Dr. Palmer says: "I gave form to what I felt by writing, with little effort, the stanzas. I recollect I wrote them with very tender emotion, and ended the last lines with tears." The manuscript was then placed in a pocket-book, where it remainded for some time. Its true discoverer was Lowell Mason, the musician, who asked young Palmer if he had not some hymn or hymns to contribute to his new book. The pocket-book was produced and the little hymn, then between two and three years old, and never previously utilized, though it had been in print as a poem, was brought to light. Dr. Mason was attracted by it, and desired a copy. They stepped together into a store (it was in Boston), and the copy was made and taken away without further comment. On carefully reading the hymn at home, Dr. Mason was so interested that he wrote for it the tune "Olivet," to which it is usually sung. Two or three days later, he again met the author in the street, and scarcely waiting to salute him, he said, "Mr. Palmer, you may live many years, and do many good things, but I think you will be best known to posterity as the author of 'My Faith looks up to Thee.'"

The hymn appeared first in *Spiritual Songs for Social Worship*, 1831, by Thomas Hastings and Lowell Mason. It has been translated into many languages on the mission fields.

MUSIC. OLIVET. For comments on the composer, Lowell Mason, see Hymn 12.

151. How firm a foundation   *"K" in Rippon's Selection, 1787*

A great song of faith, calling to mind such scripture passages as Heb. 13:5: "I will never leave thee nor forsake thee"; Isa. 43:1, 2: "Fear not, for I have redeemed thee: I have called thee by thy name; thou art mine. When thou passest through the waters, I will be with thee; and through the rivers, they shall not overflow thee; when thou walkest through the fire, thou shalt not be burned; neither shall the flame kindle upon thee."

The authorship is uncertain. The hymn appeared in *A Selection of Hymns from the Best Authors,* 1787, edited by John Rippon, 1751-1836, pastor of the Baptist Church in Carter's Lane, London, where it was signed "K." Who "K" was remains uncertain. The best guess seems to be that it refers to Robert Keene, precentor in Dr. Rippon's church. It is one more example of a writer sending forth an immortal song to bless and strengthen the faith of millions, and then hiding himself completely from public notice.

MUSIC. ADESTE FIDELIS. For comments on this tune see Hymn 80.

152. We walk by faith, and not by sight   *Henry Alford, 1810-71*

Based on the story of the incredulity of Thomas in John 20:25-29: "Except I shall see in his hands the print of the nails, and put my finger into the print of the nails, and thrust my hand into his side, I will not believe . . . . blessed are they that have not seen, and yet have believed."

Henry Alford was educated at Cambridge for the Anglican ministry. After serving various churches, he finally, in 1857, became Dean of Canterbury, the highest post in the church. He was a renowned scholar and the author of numerous volumes. His *Greek Testament* was his greatest work and remained the standard critical commentary of the latter 19th century. He was a member of the New Testament Revision Company, whose work resulted in the revised version in 1881. Greatly interested in hymnology, he himself wrote and translated many hymns, and published several collections of hymns. Dean Alford was a strenuous worker, never idle, always broad-minded and throughout his life maintained cordial relations with non-conformists. A lifelong desire to visit the Holy Land remained unfilled; which fact suggested the beautiful inscription on his tombstone: *"Deversorium viatoris proficiscentis Hierosolymam"*—"the inn of a pilgrim travelling to Jerusalem."

MUSIC. ARLINGTON is a tune from Thos. A. Arne's opera *Arta-*

xerxes, arranged by Rev. Ralph Harrison, 1748-1810, an English Presbyterian minister who published it in his *Sacred Harmony,* 1784.

Thos. A. Arne, 1710-1778, was educated for the legal profession. He turned away from law to become the foremost English composer of the 18th century. He received his degree of Doctor of Music from Oxford in 1759. Arne wrote the patriotic air, "Rule Britannia," besides many other popular songs. His sister, a famous contralto, was chosen by Handel as one of the soloists for the first performance of *The Messiah* in Dublin, April 13, 1742.

153. O for a faith that will not shrink

Wm. Hiley Bathurst, 1796-1877

An excellent hymn on "The Power of Faith," based on I John 5:4: "And this is the victory that overcometh the world, even our faith." It appeared in the author's *Psalms and Hymns for Public and Private Use,* 1831.

William Hiley Bathurst graduated from Oxford in 1818. During 33 years of ministry at Barwick-in-Elmet, he endeared himself to his people by his "eminent piety, his great simplicity of character, his tender love, and his abundant generosity." He was a shy and reserved man "and had the peculiarity of becoming utterly silent if one asked the most trivial question." His father was Charles Bragge, a member of Parliament for Bristol. The son assumed the name of Bathurst on succeeding to the estate of his uncle, Earl Bathurst, at Lydney Park, Gloucester.

MUSIC. EVAN was originally a setting by Wm. H. Havergal for a poem by Burns, "O Thou dread power who reigns't above." Lowell Mason took a part of the melody and arranged it, as here, for a psalm tune, publishing it in *New Carmina Sacra,* 1850, under the name "Eva." It might be added that Havergal disapproved of the arrangement as a "sad estrangement." In spite of this, Mason's arrangement has remained popular.

Rev. W. H. Havergal, 1793-1870, graduated from Oxford and was ordained in the Church of England. He became the rector of a church, but due to a carriage accident which resulted in concussion of the brain and injury to his eyesight, he resigned his church and devoted himself to the study of church music. In this field, he made a significant contribution by his compositions and his efforts at purifying and elevating the music used in the church. His daughter, Frances Ridley Havergal, wrote many hymns, six of which are found in the *Hymnary.*

154. Faith of our fathers, living still   *Frederick W. Faber,* 1814-63

A stirring hymn of faith bringing to mind the story of the Christian martyrs and pledging loyalty till death to the faith of our fathers. The last stanza, suggesting the preaching of the faith through "kindly words and virtuous life," is especially fine and Christian in spirit.

By "faith of our fathers" we mean, as we sing the hymn, the truth contained in the Gospels, taught by the Apostles, and brought again into clear light at the Reformation. But the hymn originally, written by a Roman Catholic, had reference to the Roman Catholic faith. The author, an Englishman, wrote one verse as follows:

> Faith of our fathers! Mary's prayers
> Shall win our country back to Thee!
> And through the truth that comes from God
> England indeed shall then be free.

The lines have been adapted for Protestant services to read:

> Faith of our fathers! God's great power
> Shall soon all nations win for thee;
> And through the truth that comes from God
> Mankind shall then be truly free.

The stanza, somewhat over-optimistic, is omitted from the *Hymnary*. For comments on the author, F. W. Faber, see Hymn 44.

MUSIC. ST. CATHERINE is of English origin. The composer, Henry F. Hemy, 1818-88, was organist at St. Andrew's Roman Catholic Church in Newcastle-upon-Tyne, and a teacher of piano and singing. He wrote this tune for another hymn and published it in his *Crown of Jesus Music,* 1864, a popular book in Catholic churches in England. The refrain was added in an arrangement by James G. Walton, 1821-1905.

PEACE AND JOY

155. Jesus, the very thought of Thee

Ascribed to Bernard of Clairvaux, 1091-1153
Tr. Edward Caswall, 1814-78

"This may well be called the sweetest and most evangelical hymn of the Middle Ages. . . . It breathes the deepest love to Christ, as the fountain of all peace and comfort, and the sum of all that is pure and lovely"—Philip Schaff.

It is from the famous medieval hymn *"Jesu, dulcis memoria,"* which David Livingstone used to repeat as he explored Africa: "That hymn of St. Bernard, on the name of Christ, although in what might be termed dog-Latin, pleases me so: it rings in my ears as I wander across the wide, wide wilderness." Its beauty has charmed many others who are familiar with the Latin. The original poem has fifty quatrains, of which our hymn is a selection of the following five:

Iesus dulcis memoria,
Dans vera cordis gaudia;
Sed super mel et omnia
Dulcis eius praesentia.

Nil canitur suavius,
Auditur nil iucundius,
Nil cogitatur dulcius,
Quam Iesus, Dei Filius.

Iesu, spes paenitentibus,
Quem pius es pententibus,
Quam bonus te quaerentibus!
Sed quid invenientibus.

Nec lingua potest dicere,
Nec littera exprimere;
Experto potes credere,
Quid sit Iesum diligere.

Tu esto nostrum gaudium,
Qui es futurus praemium;
Sit nostra in te gloria
Per cuncta semper saecula.

It is usually attributed to Bernard of Clairvaux (See 539), but many authorities now question the authorship. Percy Dearmer says in *Songs of Praise Discussed* that "it is not by St. Bernard. . . . St. Bernard of Clairvaux was born 1091 and the poem itself has been found in a manuscript of the 11th century." In further commenting on the authorship he says, "We really know nothing and are not likely to know."

The translation here is by Edward Caswall.

For comments on Caswall see Hymn 19.

A translation of a different *cento* of the same hymn, by Ray Palmer, is found at No. 171.

MUSIC. ST. AGNES was written for this hymn in *A Hymnal for Use in the English Church,* 1866, edited by Rev. J. Grey. In England it is called "St. Agnes, Durham," to distinguish it from the tune, "Langran" (303) which is known in England as "St. Agnes."

For comments on the composer, John B. Dykes, see Hymn 1.

156. Rejoice, ye pure in heart   *Edward H. Plumptre,* 1821-91

A popular processional hymn written for that purpose in May, 1865, for a choir festival in Peterborough Cathedral, one of the most important Norman churches now standing in England. It was published in the same year in the author's *Lazarus, and Other Poems.* The refrain has been added.

For comments on Edward H. Plumptre see Hymn 95.

MUSIC. MARION was written in 1883 for this hymn. The tune is admirably adapted to the words and the combination has made this one of the choicest of processional hymns. It is also effective for antiphonal singing.

Arthur Henry Messiter, 1834-1916, born in Somersetshire, England, began the serious study of music at the age of 17. Coming to America in 1863, he sang for a time in the volunteer choir of Trinity Church, New York City. Three years later this famous church appointed him their director of music and organist, a position he held with distinction for 31 years. He is the author of several notable books on music and editor of *Episcopal Hymnal* of 1893.

157. Jesus, our Savior, grant us Thy peace

E. C. Poppe
Tr. Amanda Hostettler
and E. Shippen Barnes

A hymn of the peace of God, based on Col. 3:15: "And let the peace of God rule in your hearts, to which also ye are called"; and John 14: 27: "Peace I leave with you, my peace I give unto you."

The original poem of five stanzas appears in the *Gesangbuch mit Noten* where it is attributed to E. C. Poppe. Erhard Christoph Poppe, 1804-78, the son of a goldsmith, was born in Bremen. He was a colporteur for the Methodist church.

> Seliger Friede, köstliche Gab'
>   Meines geliebten Heilands, mich lab';
> Tief in mein Inn'res du dich ergiess',
>   Dass ich dich, wie ich wünsche geniess.
> O, wie schmeckst du dem Herzen so süss!

> Seit mir mein Jesus Frieden geschenkt,
>   Hat sich mein Alles in Ihn versenkt;
> Ach, wie war's Ihm am Kreuze so bang!
>   O, wie Ihn dort die Liebe so drang!
> Frieden zu spenden, Er für mich rang.

> Jesu, verklär Dich in mir noch mehr,
>   Dass solchen Frieden ferner nichts stör';
> Wie ja ein Vater Gutes gern giebt,
>   Schenkst Du auch Deinem Kind, das Dich liebt;
> Frieden, den keine Wolke mehr trübt.

Nimm Du allein das Herze uns ein,
  Dass wir recht mild und sanftmüthig sein,
Dass uns're Seelen, Dir nur geweiht,
  Ruhen in Deinem Blut allezeit;
Friede versüsst uns dann Kreuz und Leid.

Gieb Deinen Frieden immer mir so,
  Dass ich in Leid bleib' ruhig und froh,
Und wenn auch höher steiget die Noth,
  Ja, wenn zuletzt mir nahet der Tod,
Lass mich im Frieden eilen zu Gott.

This free translation, specially made for the *Hymnary,* is by Mrs. Amanda Hostettler, Upland, California, whose father, John Hirschler, was a prominent minister in the General Conference of Mennonites. A few changes in her work were made by E. Shippen Barnes.

For comments on Barnes see Hymn 48.

MUSIC. SELIGER FRIEDE, named after the initial words of the German text, appeared anonymously in the *Gesangbuch mit Noten.* Its quiet, pensive phrases are well adapted to the sentiment of the words.

158-9. Jesus, Lover of my soul   *Charles Wesley,* 1707-88

The greatest hymn of all time.

Many of the stories concerning the origin of this hymn, such as that of the bird flying in time of storm to Wesley, or a dove pursued by a hawk finding refuge in his room, or Wesley's own escape from a threatening mob, cannot be substantiated and must be dismissed as legendary, however plausible and fitting they may be.

The hymn first appeared in *Hymns and Sacred Poems,* 1740, with the title, "In time of Prayer and Temptation." The third stanza, omitted from all hymnals, reads:

> Wilt Thou not regard my call?
>   Wilt Thou not accept my prayer?
> Lo, I sink, I faint, I fall,
>   Lo, on Thee I cast my care.
> Reach me out Thy gracious hand,
>   While I of Thy strength receive,
> Hoping against hope I stand,
>   Dying, and behold, I live.

The simplicity and literacy art of the hymn are unsurpassed. Of the 188 words in the four stanzas of the hymn generally used, all but 31 are monosyllables. The hymn has been translated into virtually every language and uncounted millions have found it a source of help in time of need. Henry Ward Beecher once said: "I would rather have written that hymn than to have the fame of all the kings that ever sat upon the earth."

In the annotated edition of the *Book of Common Praise,* 1909, the following story is given:

A party of Northern tourists were on the deck of an excursion steamer, on the Potomac, one summer evening in 1881. One of the party, who had a remarkable voice, began to sing hymns to the others. When he had sung two verses of "Jesu, lover of my soul," a stranger made his way from the outskirts of the crowd: "Beg your pardon, sir, but were you actively engaged in the late war?" "Yes, sir, I fought under General Grant." "Well," the first speaker continued, "I did my fighting on the other side, and I think I was very near you one bright night eighteen years ago this month. It was much such a night as this. If I am not mistaken, you were on guard-duty. We of the South had sharp business on hand. I crept near your post of duty, my weapon in my hand; the shadows hid me. Your beat led you into the clear light. As you paced back and forth you were singing that same hymn. I raised my gun and aimed at your heart—and I had been selected for the work because I was a sure shot. Then out upon the night floated the words:

> Cover my defenceless head
> With the shadow of thy wing.

Your prayer was answered. I couldn't fire after that. And there was no attack made upon your camp that night. I felt sure, when I heard you singing this evening, that you were the man whose life I was spared from taking." The singer grasped the hand of the Southerner and said: "I remember the night very well, and the feeling of depression with which I went forth to my duty. I knew the post was one of great danger. I paced my lonely beat, thinking of home and friends and all that life holds dear. Then the thought of God's care came to me with peculiar force, and I sang the prayer of my heart and ceased to feel alone. How the prayer was answered I never knew until this evening."

For comments on Wesley see Hymn 6.

MUSIC. MARTYN. The composer of this tune, Simeon B. Marsh, 1798-1875, spent many years teaching singing classes in and near Albany, N. Y., travelling constantly on horseback from town to town through Albany Presbytery. It was while enroute on his weekly circuit, one day during the autumn of 1834, that the melody took form. He alighted from his horse and wrote the music which he set to a hymn by John Newton, "Mary to her Saviour's tomb." Thomas Hastings later set the tune to "Jesus, Lover of my soul," a combination now deeply imbedded in the affections of the American Church.

MUSIC. HOLLINGSIDE (159) is the tune composed by John B. Dykes, 1823-76, especially for this hymn. The tune has more of musical interest than the better known "Martyn," and many hymnals give it first place for use with this hymn. Dykes was always particular about the naming of his tunes, often some incident in his life supplying the name. "Hollingside" was the name of the cottage he lived in, while precentor at Durham, when he wrote this. Regarding its composition, one of his sisters wrote:

> Some scenes during that visit will live forever in my memory. As, for instance, one calm Sunday evening, when I sat in the verandah in the deepening twilight and heard, through the open window, my brother composing and playing over the tune "Hollingside," to the words "Jesu, Lover of my soul."

For comments on Dykes see Hymn 1.

GUIDANCE AND PROTECTION

160. Guide me, O Thou great Jehovah

William Williams, 1717-91

A superb hymn of guidance in which the analogies of the history of Israel in the wilderness appear in every stanza and almost in every line. It was written in Welsh in 1745 and translated into English in 1771 by Rev. Peter Williams, friend of the author and fellow-worker. Some think stanzas 2 and 3 were translated by the author himself or by his son, the Rev. John Williams.

The hymn in Welsh, with its unpronounceable words, is as follows:

Arglwydd, arwain trwy'r anialwch
  Fi bererin gwael ei wedd,
Nad oes ynof nerth na bywyd,
  Fel yn gorwedd yn y bedd:
    Hollalluog
  Ydyw'r un a'm cwyd i'r lan.

Agor y ffynnonau melus
  Sydd yn tarddu o'r Graig i maes;
'Rhyd yr anial mawr canlyned
  Afon iachawdwriaeth grâs:
    Rho imi hyny;
  Dim i mi ond dy fwynhau.

Ymddiriedaf yn dy allu,
  Mawr yw'r gwaith a wnest erioed:
Ti gest angau, ti gest uffern,
  Ti gest Satan dan dy droed:
    Pen Calfaria,
  Nac aed hwnw byth o'm cof.

William Williams was the chief hymn-writer of Wales and one of her greatest poets. He at first was in training for the medical profession but after attending some revival services, decided to become a minister. On account of his evangelical views (and his interest in evangelistic work), he came in conflict with church dignitaries, resulting in his withdrawal from the Established Church, and throwing himself into evangelistic work. His preaching itineraries took him throughout Wales. He travelled an average of 3,000 miles per year for 50 years. He wrote many hymns, stirring the nation, influencing its character, and deepening its faith. Williams was to Wales what Paul Gerhardt was to Germany and Isaac Watts to England.

MUSIC. DISMISSAL was composed for the hymn "Lord, dismiss us with Thy blessing" (45).

The composer, William Letton Viner, 1790-1867, was a student of Charles Wesley, Jr. He was organist at St. Michael's Church, Bath, for 18 years and at St. Mary's Penzance for 21 years. In 1859, he came to the United States. He composed organ and church music and songs, and edited several hymnals.

161. Jesus, Savior, pilot me   *Edward Hopper, 1818-88*

A beautiful hymn suggested by the seafaring life. It was published anonymously in *Sailors' Magazine,* 1871, and again in the *Baptist Praise Book,* 1871, and in C. S. Robinson's collection of *Spiritual Songs,* 1878. The author of the hymn, unknown for several years, was discovered at the anniversary of the Seamen's Friend Society, held at the Broadway Tabernacle, New York City, May 10, 1880. Dr. Edward Hopper, popular pastor of the Church of the Sea and Land in New York, having been asked to write a special hymn for the occasion, brought instead, "Jesus Savior, pilot me," not aware that the hymn had already been published in several church hymnals. The public learned then for the first time the real authorship of the hymn. The original has six stanzas, this being a selection of 1, 5, and 6.

Edward Hopper was born in New York City. He graduated from New York University and then prepared himself at Union Theological Seminary, New York, for the Presbyterian ministry. For many years he was pastor of the Church of the Sea and Land in New York, which sailors attended in large numbers.

MUSIC. PILOT, universally sung and beautifully adapted to these words, was written just before the composer sailed for Europe a short while before his death. He played the tune on the piano the night before he embarked on shipboard for his last earthly voyage.

For further comments on the composer, John E. Gould, see Hymn 141.

162-3. Lead, kindly Light   *John Henry Newman, 1801-90*

A prayer for light and guidance, written on Sunday, June 16, 1833, while the author, travelling for his health, was lying, sick in mind and body, on the deck of a sail vessel that was becalmed for a whole week in the Straits of Bonifacio, in the Mediterranean Sea. Newman was going through a period of great heart-searching because of the disturbed conditions in England, both in church and state. His depressed feelings were accentuated by the wretched state of his health. The hymn deserves its wide popularity, for it expresses the universal longing for divine help in time of deep depression. The meaning of "kindly light" was never explained by the author. To some it represents the Inward Light of conscience; to others just the divine guidance; but to most people it doubtless means Christ as the Light of the World.

John Henry Newman was born in London, the son of a banker. His parents were devout nonconformists and brought up their son in the evangelical faith. After a distinguished career at Trinity College, Oxford, Newman was ordained in the Church of England, and became the vicar of the Oxford University Church, a post he filled with distinction from 1828 to 1843. His charm of personality and pulpit eloquence made him a profound influence at the University. Newman became a leader in the Oxford Movement and finally, in 1845, after a period of much hesitation, he left Anglicanism to unite with the Roman Catholic Church. His *Apologia pro Vita Sua*, a masterpiece of autobiography, constitutes a powerful defense of the Roman system of belief. In 1879, after some years of neglect by the church, he was made a cardinal. His fine Christian character, and spiritual force, as well as his literary ability, were universally recognized. Newman was a great Englishman and a great saint though referred to by some writers as an "angel who lost his way."

MUSIC. LUX BENIGNA was written for these words by J. B. Dykes. Dykes told a friend that the tune came to him while walking through the Strand in London. The tune is also known as "St. Oswald."

A friend visiting Cardinal Newman said to him of "Lead, Kindly Light": "It must be a great pleasure to you to know that you have written a hymn treasured wherever English speaking Christians are to be found: and where are they not found?" To which Newman, after thoughtful silence, replied: "Yes, deeply thankful, and more than thankful: but you see it is not the hymn, but the tune, that has gained the popularity! The tune is Dykes', and Dr. Dykes was a great master."

For comments on J. B. Dykes see Hymn 1.

SANDON was also written for this hymn. It appeared in *The Church and Home Metrical Psalter and Hymnal*, 1860, edited by Purday himself. It is simpler in form than LUX BENIGNA and is an effective and desirable alternative tune.

Charles Purday, 1799-1885, the composer, was at one time a noted singer in London. He became a publisher of music and was a popular lecturer on musical subjects.

164. Lead us, O Father, in the paths of peace

Wm. H. Burleigh, 1812-71

A hymn on the journey of life, entitled by the author, "Prayer for Guidance."

William Henry Burleigh was brought up on a farm at Plainfield, Conn. At the age of 25, he went to Pittsburgh, Pa., and learned the printing trade and journalism. He later became editor of the *Christian Freeman,* an abolitionist journal, at Hartford, Conn. He was an ardent temperance reformer and advocate of the abolition of slavery. His last appointment was harbour master at New York, a post he held for 15 years. Burleigh belonged to a distinguished group of Unitarians who have contributed to American hymnody. His wife, Celia Burleigh, was for some time minister of the Unitarian Church at Brooklyn, Conn., and wrote the *Life* of her husband.

MUSIC. LONGWOOD was composed for John Ellerton's hymn, "Savior, again to thy dear name we raise" (43).

For comments on the composer, Joseph Barnby, see Hymn 21.

165. O'er the trackless ocean guided   *Wm. H. Adams, 1864—*

A hymn on pioneer service, written probably with the Pilgrim Fathers in mind, but equally applicable to other groups of immigrants who came "o'er the trackless ocean" to build "rude homes" in the "new land, wild and lonely."

Information concerning the author has not been traced. The hymn is not listed in *Julian's Dictionary.*

MUSIC. BEECHER. For comments on this tune and its composer see Hymn 178.

166. For them whose ways are in the height

Richard Roberts, 1874—

This hymn for travellers by air was created to meet the new day of amazing development which has taken place in modern travel. It is a welcome addition to the hymnody of travel.

Richard Roberts, born in Wales, in 1874, is an eminent preacher. Before going to Canada where he became the first Moderator of the United Church of Canada, he occupied pulpits in Wales, London, and Brooklyn. He is one of the founders of the "Fellowship of Reconciliation." His views on the relation of the church to war are well expressed in his own words:

> The world order in which war is inherent, the church exists to transform. When it supports the method of war, an end-product of the unredeemed world order, the church is not only proclaiming its own failure, but is hauling down its own flag and hoisting instead the flag of the world.

MUSIC. MORWELLHAM was composed by Charles Steggall, 1826-1905, an English musician who was educated at the Royal Academy of Music in London and then for half a century was chief professor of the organ in the same institution. He is said to have trained more organists than any teacher in England. Steggall was an enthusiast for the music of Bach and served as honorary secretary of the Bach Society. He composed anthems and church music and had a lifelong interest in hymnology. He succeeded W. H. Monk as musical editor of *Hymns Ancient and Modern.*

167. O God of Bethel, by whose hand

Philip Doddridge, 1702-51
and others

A paraphrase of Genesis 28:20-22: "And Jacob vowed a vow, saying, If God will be with me, and will keep me in this way that I go, and will give me bread to eat, and raiment to put on, so that I come again to my father's house in peace; then shall the Lord be my God: and this stone, which I have set for a pillar, shall be God's house: and of all that thou shalt give me I will surely give the tenth unto thee."

The hymn has undergone certain changes and additions so that it really is a composite production, the details of which need not be enumerated here. Ours is the Scottish version found in the *Scottish Paraphrases,* 1781. In Scotland it is the best-loved of the paraphrases as "The Lord's My Shepherd" is the best-loved of the psalms.

For comments on Philip Doddridge see Hymn 56.

MUSIC. SALZBURG is an adaptation of an air in a movement of a Mass composed by J. M. Haydn "for the use of country choirs." It was originally in 6-8 time. An entirely different tune by the same name is found at Hymn 545.

For comments on Johann Michael Haydn see Hymn 7.

168. Captain of Israel's host, and Guide   Charles Wesley, 1707-88

Based on the story of God's guidance of the Israelites during their exodus from Egypt and their journeyings in the wilderness, Exodus 13: 17-22.

For comments on Charles Wesley see Hymn 6.

MUSIC. MIDDLESEX is an anonymous tune, the origin of which has not been traced. The hymn and tune were taken from *The Hymnary,* published in Toronto, 1930, by the United Church of Canada.

169. Eternal Father! strong to save   William Whiting, 1825-78

A hymn for travellers by sea. This hymn and tune have long been used more frequently than any other for that purpose. Sir Evelyn Wood wrote regarding this hymn: "It is much used by those at sea, and, when the wind blows hard, by those on land." The words, written in 1860, have been revised several times.

It was the favorite hymn of the late Franklin D. Roosevelt and was sung at his funeral at Hyde Park, New York, April 14, 1945.

William Whiting was a native of Kensington, London, and was for over twenty years master of the Choristers' School at Winchester College.

MUSIC. MELITA was written for this hymn. For comments on the composer, J. B. Dykes, see Hymn 1.

LOVE AND GRATITUDE

170. Jesus, Thy boundless love to me   Paul Gerhardt, 1607-76
Tr. John Wesley

A hymn of the love of Christ, suited especially well for the Communion Service. This great hymn by Paul Gerhardt first appeared in Crüger's *Praxis Pietatis Melica,* Berlin, 1653, in sixteen stanzas. John Wesley, great revivalist and eminent translator of German hymns, rendered the entire hymn into English, in a different meter, and published it in *Hymns and Sacred Poems,* 1739. Our hymn consists of the first three stanzas, the original of which are as follows:

> O Jesu Christ, mein schönstes Licht,
>   Der du in deiner Seelen
> So hoch mich liebst, dass ich es nicht
>   Aussprechen kann noch zählen:
> Gib, dass mein Herz dich wiederum
>   Mit Lieben und Verlangen
>   Mög' umfangen   .

Und als dein Eigentum
Nur einzig an dir hangen!

Gib, dass sonst nichts in meiner Seel'
Als deine Liebe wohne;
Gib, dass ich deine Lieb' erwähl'
Als meinen Schatz und Krone!
Stoss alles aus, nimm alles hin,
Was dich und mich will trennen
Und nicht gönnen,
Dass all mein Mut und Sinn
In deiner Liebe brennen!

Wie freundlich, selig, süss und schön
Ist, Jesu, deine Liebe!
Wo diese steht, kann nichts bestehn,
Das meinen Geist betrübe;
Drum lass nichts andres denken mich,
Nichts sehen, fühlen, hören,
Lieben, ehren
Als deine Lieb' und dich,
Der du sie kannst vermehren!

The prayer for the realization of the love of Christ was answered abundantly in Wesley's own life. In his *Plain Account of Christian Perfection,* he wrote:

In the beginning of the year 1738, as I was returning from Savannah, the cry of my heart was

"O grant that nothing in my soul
May dwell but Thy pure love alone."

On May 24 of the same year, in the Society Meeting in Aldersgate Street, about a quarter before nine, during the reading of Luther's Preface to the Epistle to the Romans, I felt my heart strangely warmed. I felt I did trust in Christ, Christ alone, for Salvation; and an assurance was given me that He had taken away my sins, even *mine,* and saved *me* from the law of sin and death.

Wesley became interested in the German chorales through his contact with the Moravians. In 1735, he and his brother Charles Wesley set sail for Georgia. Among their fellow passengers on the boat were 26 Moravians who made much of the singing of hymns and seemed to meet every storm and trial with unfaltering faith. Wesley was so impressed that on the third day out he began the study of German and soon joined in the daily worship of the Moravians. The fervor and spontaneity of their singing made an indelible impression on his mind. He later translated a number of chorales into English. (See 246, 508, 558.)

For comments on Paul Gerhardt see Hymn 134.

MUSIC. STELLA. For comments on this tune see Hymn 94.

171. Jesus, Thou Joy of loving hearts

Latin 11th Century
Tr. Ray Palmer

A hymn of devotional meditation especially appropriate for the Communion Service.

From the same Latin hymn, *"Jesu dulcis memoria,"* as Hymn 155 (which see) but using a different set of quatrains, Nos. 4, 3, 20, 28, and 10, which appear in the Latin as follow:

Jesu, dulcedo cordium;
Fons veri, lumen mentium,
Excedit omne gaudium,
Et omne desiderium.

Qui te gustant, esuriunt;
Qui bibunt, adhuc sitiunt:
Desiderare nesciunt
Nisi Jesum, quem diligunt.

Jesus, spes poenitentibus,
Quam pius es petentibus,
Quam bonus te quaerentibus!
Sed quid invenientibus?

Quoconque loco fuero,
Mecum Jesum desidero;
Quam laetus, cum invenero!
Quam felix, cum tenuero!

Mane nobiscum, Domine,
Et nos illustra lumine,
Pulsa mentis caligine,
Mundum replens dulcedine.

For comments on the translator, Ray Palmer, see Hymn 131.

MUSIC. QUEBEC. This tune by Henry Baker was originally set to the hymn, "Sun of my soul." It is also called "Hesperus" and "Whitburn."

Henry Baker (not to be confused with Henry W. Baker), 1835-1910, son of Rev. James Baker, was educated as a civil engineer and spent many years in his profession on railroad work in India. He loved music, and, encouraged by John B. Dykes, proceeded in 1867 to his musical degree (Mus. Bac.) at Exeter College, Oxford.

172. O love divine, that stooped to share

Oliver Wendell Holmes, 1809-94

One of Holmes' best hymns to which he gave the title, "Hymn of Trust." It is found in the author's *Poems*, 1862. It was first published as one of the poems in *The Professor at the Breakfast Table*, where it was represented as having been heard by the professor as he walked by a sick room. The little refrain, "Thou art near," is based on Psalm 119:151: "Thou art near, O Lord; and all thy commandments are truth."

Oliver Wendell Holmes, American poet and man of letters, was the son of Rev. Abiel Holmes, a Congregational minister. He graduated from Harvard in 1829, studied medicine at home and abroad, and became Professor of Anatomy and Physiology at Dartmouth in 1838. He was elected to the same chair at Harvard in 1847, a position he filled with distinction for 35 years. During all his years of teaching he was also engaged in literary work and published many volumes. Holmes was chief founder of the *Atlantic Monthly.* He was a member of the Unitarian Church though in later years he fell back for spiritual comfort on the great evangelical hymns of Watts and Wesley, finding in them a source of satisfaction and power which the hymns of his own denomination failed to supply. His son, Oliver Wendell, Jr., became an eminent member of the Supreme Court of the United States.

For further comments on Holmes see Hymn 53.

MUSIC. QUEBEC. For comments on this tune see Hymn 171.

173. Immortal Love, forever full

John Greenleaf Whittier, 1807-92

One of the great hymns on the living presence and sympathy of Christ. It is taken from the poem, "Our Master," of 38 stanzas, of which this hymn is a selection of stanzas 1, 5, 13, 14, and 16 of the original.

John Greenleaf Whittier, the "Quaker Poet," was born near Haverhill, Mass., where he began life as a farm boy and village shoemaker. At the age of 20, with only a limited education, he entered the profession of journalism, largely as the result of becoming acquainted with William Lloyd Garrison. He became editor of the *American Manufacturer* in 1828, and of the *New England Review* in 1830. In 1836 he became the secretary of the American Anti-Slavery Society and editor of its official organ, the *Freeman.* Whittier was a staunch advocate of the freedom of slaves, and as a Quaker, he was just as strongly opposed to war. His poems are characterized by wide sympathy and a fervent love for God and man. Though a staunch Quaker, wearing the distinctive garb and using the Quaker mode of speech all his life, there was no narrow sectarianism in his heart. A letter written to friends in Whittier, California, a city named after the poet, for the dedication of the Protestant Episcopal Church at that place, illustrates his large-hearted religious views:

> I see the good in all denominations, and hope that all will be represented in the settlement; . . . . diligent in business and serving the Lord, not wasting strength and vitality in spasmodic emotions, not relying on creed and dogma, but upon faithful obedience to the voice of God in the soul. I see your town is spoken of as an orthodox Quaker colony. I hope

there will be no sectarian fence about "Whittier," but that good men, irrespective of their creeds, will find a home there. Nothing would be worse for it than to have the idea get abroad that anything like intolerance and self-righteousness was its foundation. I am gratified to know that the people of the town which bears my name will remember me on my birthday. I watch its growth with great interest. It has the reputation among all who have seen it that it occupies one of the loveliest sites in California, and that in a moral and religious and educational point of view it need

> Fear not the skeptic's puny hand
> While near the school the church will stand;
> Nor fear the blinded bigot's rule
> While near the church shall stand the school.

MUSIC. SERENITY is taken from a larger work entitled, *Waft ye winds.* Though the tune is named "Serenity," the composer's life was anything but serene; he was the world's most restless and most picturesque composer. William Vincent Wallace, 1812-65, son of an Irish bandmaster, became a brilliant violinist. He loved adventure and travel and made successful concert tours to Australia, the South Sea Islands, India, South America, Mexico, the United States, and elsewhere. Wallace spent 14 years in Germany composing piano music chiefly, but also writing a number of operas. On account of failing health, he abandoned writing, and went to New York where he lost all his fortune through the failure of a piano factory. Undiscouraged by this disaster, he once more resumed his career as composer, returned to London, and then on doctor's orders went to the Pyrenees where he died at the age of 51.

174. Gracious Spirit, Holy Ghost

Christopher Wordsworth, 1807-85

Written for one of the pre-Lenten Sundays *(Quinquagesima),* the lesson for the day being I Corinthians 13. It is a fine enough hymn, but no poet can render this great paean of praise of love into verse to equal in poetic beauty the English of the King James Version.

Christopher Wordsworth was a nephew of the poet William Wordsworth. He was a brilliant student and a good athlete. After graduation from Cambridge, he became Head Master of Harrow for a time, then minister of a church where he proved to be a model parish priest, and later was appointed Bishop of Lincoln. Among his writings are a *Commentary on the Bible,* and a book of devotional poetry, *The Holy Year,* prepared for use in public worship.

MUSIC. CAPETOWN is an adaptation of a melody in *"Vierstimmiges Choralbuch herausgegeben von Dr. F. Filitz,"* Berlin, 1847. It was originally set to the hymn, *"Morgenglanz der Ewigkeit"* (554).

The composer, Friedrich Filitz, 1804-76, was a musician and editor of German chorale books. He spent all his life in Munich except the years 1843-47 in Berlin.

175. O Love that wilt not let me go *George Matheson*, 1842-1906

A song of joyful resignation, love, and trust, born out of the author's experience of suffering. The story has been circulated that the hymn was written after the woman whom Matheson loved gave him up because of his becoming blind—a good story with one defect, *viz.*, that it isn't true. It could not be true because Matheson became blind at 15 and the hymn was not written until he was 40 years old.

The author's own account of the composition of the hymn is as follows:

> My hymn was composed in the manse of Innellan, on the evening of June 6, 1882. I was at that time alone. It was the day of my sister's marriage, and the rest of the family were staying over night in Glasgow. Something had happened to me, which was known only to myself, and which caused me the most severe mental suffering. The hymn was the fruit of that suffering. It was the quickest bit of work I ever did in my life. I had the impression rather of having it dictated to me by some inward voice than of working it out myself. I am quite sure that the whole work was completed in five minutes, and equally sure that it never received at my hands any retouching or correction. The Hymnal Committee of the Church of Scotland desired the change of one word. I had written originally "I climb the rainbow in the rain." They objected to the word "climb" and I put in "trace."

George W. Matheson, son of a wealthy merchant in Glasgow, was an able and greatly honored minister in the Presbyterian Church of Scotland. He was educated at Glasgow University and licensed to preach when 24 years old. During his University course, and all the rest of his life, he had to depend on the eyesight of others, which makes his accomplishments all the more remarkable. He was a brilliant student and became a distinguished preacher and pastor. At St. Bernard's Church, Edinburgh, he served a membership of over 2,000, never neglecting his duties of pastoral calling in which he was invariably accompanied by his devoted sister. He was a scholar of distinction and was the author of 25 books, including such well-known works as *Representative Men of the Bible, Representative Women of the Bible, The Spiritual Development of St. Paul,* and a book of *Sacred Songs.* Of the many hymns he wrote, several have been used in hymn books but only this one has gained universal popularity.

110

MUSIC. ST. MARGARET was written one summer day as the composer was sitting by the sea on the island of Arran and reading over Matheson's verses. The tune came to him suddenly and he hastened to the house where he was staying where (in his own words): "I wrote the music straight off, and I may say that the ink of the first note was hardly dry when I finished the tune."

The composer, Albert Lister Peace, 1844-1912, was organist at Glasgow Cathedral and at the time he wrote this tune, he was music editor of the revised *Scottish Hymnal* of 1885.

176. For common gifts we bless Thee, Lord

Charlotte M. Packard

A hymn of gratitude for the common gifts too often taken for granted—the physical senses, the air, sun, darkness and sleep, the courtesies of friendship, etc. The last stanza is a prayer for unforgetful gratitude.

Information regarding the author, Charlotte M. Packard, has not been traced. The hymn was taken from *Hymns of the Spirit,* 1937, Boston.

MUSIC. ILLSLEY appeared in *A Sett of New Psalm Tunes in Four Parts by John Bishop,* c. 1700, where it is set to Psalm 100.

John Bishop, the composer, 1665-1737, was an English musician who became organist of Winchester College in 1695 and in 1729 was appointed organist of Winchester Chapel. He is buried in the Cloisters of the College with the following epitaph:

> Vir singulari probitate, integerrima vita, moribus innocuis, musicaeque scientiae bene peritus, qui, postquam huic Collegio per XLII, annos sedulo inserviisset, ad Caelestam Choram placide migravit, decimo nono die Decembris, anno Dom. 1737, Aetat. 72. (A man of unexampled honesty, purest life, blameless morals, and of excellent skill in music, who, after serving this College diligently for 42 years, passed tranquilly to the Celestial Choir on the 19th of December A.D. 1737, aged 72.)

177. My God, I thank Thee, who hast made

Adelaide Anne Proctor, 1825-64

A hymn of pure gratitude, expressing thankfulness even for the trials of life. It is equally useful for the sick and the well.

Adelaide Anne Proctor was born in London, the daughter of Bryan W. Proctor, known in literary circles as "Barry Cornwall." She possessed extraordinary intellectual power and was specially gifted in

111

music and language. Miss Proctor contributed lyrics to *Household Verses,* edited by Chas. Dickens, who wrote with admiration of her verse making, her mental resources, humor, and works of beneficence. At 38 years of age her physical strength weakened and then followed 15 weary months of helplessness during which, however, she maintained her old cheerfulness with never a trace of depression or regret. She was brought up in the Church of England, but at the age of 26 united with the Roman Catholics. Her broad sympathies and deep religious convictions placed her above the dogmas of any one communion and enabled her to express the aspirations of all God's children. Besides her hymns, Miss Proctor is best known as the author of the popular song, "The Lost Chord," set to music by Arthur Sullivan.

MUSIC. WENTWORTH was composed for this hymn in *The Bristol Tune Book,* 2d series; 1876. The middle section of the tune, lines 3 and 4, passes from the Key of C to A minor, D major and G major, making an effective contrast to the opening and closing lines, in the key of C.

For comments on the composer, Frederick C. Maker, see Hymn 112.

178-9. Love divine, all loves excelling   *Charles Wesley, 1707–88*

The hymn appeared in the curiously named collection, *Hymns for those that seek and those that have Redemption in the Blood of Christ,* 1747, and was entitled "Jesu, show us Thy salvation." It dwells upon the thought of God as love, an idea not too common in the early hymns. The thought of the hymn is complete without stanza 2 and many hymnals omit it. Some have objected to this stanza because of the line, "Take away our power of sinning." Literally interpreted this would be a prayer to have taken away the power of free moral choice, which is hardly what Wesley intended. To obviate this difficulty, the line has been changed to "Take away the *love* of sinning."

For comments on Wesley see Hymn 6.

MUSIC. BEECHER was composed by John Zundel, 1815-82, German-American organist and composer who rendered distinguished service as minister of music in the Plymouth Congregation Church, Brooklyn, of which Henry Ward Beecher was pastor. He assisted Beecher in the production of the famous *Plymouth Collection* of hymns published in 1855. The tune, now known throughout the world, was named after the great pulpiteer.

SONATA (179) is an adaptation of the theme-melody in Mozart's piano Sonato No. 16, where it is marked, *Andantino grazioso.* Dudley Buck writes:

Wolfgang Amadeus Mozart, 1756-91, composed 972 pieces

of which we know. He is considered the greatest composer the world has ever seen, judged by the versatility and power of his genius. In every sort and kind of composition he was equally excellent. Beside being a great composer he was also a great performer, being the most accomplished pianist of his day. He was also an excellent player on the violin.

PRAYER AND COMMUNION

180. Pray when the morn is breaking

Mrs. Jane Cross Simpson, 1811–86
and others

A hymn setting forth the idea of prayer in a very simple way.

Jane Cross Simpson was the daughter of James Bell, a Glasgow attorney. In 1837, she married her cousin J. B. Simpson, of Glasgow. At the age of 20, she had written a poem, "Go when the morning shineth," which, after some revision, had become popular. When *Songs of Praise,* an important English hymbook, was in the making, this poem was again revised to make the present hymn. The "others" referred to are responsible for the revision and according to *Songs of Praise Discussed* consisted of Percy Dearmer, Stephen Gwynn, Mabel Dearmer, and Jan Struther.

MUSIC. MEIRIONYDD is a vigorous tune of easy rhythm, on the pattern of many Welsh tunes except that the last two lines, instead of being simple repeats of the first two lines, as in the majority of such melodies, are varied imitations of them.

The composer, William Lloyd, 1786-1852, a Welshman, was a self-educated man. Though a cattle-dealing farmer, he possessed an excellent voice and had a considerable knowledge of music. He held singing meetings and conducted music classes in Wales.

181. Dear Lord and Father of mankind

John Greenleaf Whittier, 1807-92

A song of quietude and peace, reflecting the inner life of the "Quaker Poet."

The verses are from a poem called, "The Brewing of Soma," in which Whittier tells of a certain sect of devotees in India who drank intoxicating liquor brewed from the Soma plant. The drinking of it brought them to a state of intoxicated excitement in which they imagined they were god-possessed. The poet then points out how among Christians emotional excitement is often mistaken for spiritual power.

"In sensual transports, wild as vain,
We brew in many a Christian fane,
The heathen Soma still."

Then follow the beautiful verses of our hymn in praise of the higher life of restfulness in God. The poem was written in 1832, after a particularly noisy and distasteful revival in Whittier's neighborhood.

For comments on John Greenleaf Whittier see Hymn 173.

MUSIC. WHITTIER, also called "Rest" and "Elton," was written for this hymn.

For comments on the composer, Frederick C. Maker, see Hymn 112.

182. Sweet hour of prayer — *William W. Walford*

One of the most popular of all modern prayer meeting hymns, sometimes erroneously ascribed to Fanny Crosby. It was composed in 1842 by Rev. William W. Walford, a blind minister of England, of whom little is known except that he recited the words of this hymn to Rev. Thos. Salmon, Congregational minister at Coleshill, England, who wrote them down and later sent them to the New York *Observer,* in which publication they were printed September 13, 1845. The original has four stanzas, the last two being omitted here.

MUSIC. CONSOLATION, a tune well suited to the words, was composed by Wm. B. Bradbury in 1859. It is also know as "Sweet Hour" and "Walford."

For comments on the composer, Wm. B. Bradbury, see Hymn 103.

183. Lord, what a change within us one short hour

Richard C. Trench, 1807-86
Arr. W. P. Merrill, 1867—

A hymn of the peace and power available through the practice of prayer. It is an arrangement of Trench's sonnet on "Prayer."

Richard Chenevix Trench was born in Dublin, educated at Twyford School, Harrow, and Trinity College, Cambridge. He was preacher, poet, professor of divinity and later the Archbishop of Dublin. Trench, a scholar of distinction, is the author of valuable books, including *Notes on the Parables, Notes on the Miracles,* and *Study of Words.*

The poem came into the hymn books through the arrangement made of it by Dr. W. P. Merrill who first became acquainted with the sonnet through hearing it read about 1907 by President Charles Cuthbert Hall, of Union Theological Seminary in the course of a lecture at the University of Chicago. As sonnets each have fourteen lines, changes were necessary to make the poem suitable for singing. Dr. Merrill omitted two lines and arranged the rest to make three symmetrical four-line stanzas.

William Pearson Merrill was born in Orange, N. J., January 10, 1867. After graduating from Rutgers College, he trained for the Presbyterian ministry at Union Theological Seminary, New York. He served churches in Philadelphia and Chicago and then went, in 1911, to the Brick Presbyterian Church in New York City to begin a long and distinguished pastorate which ended with his retirement in 1938. He was president of the Church Peace Union, was long active in The American Hymn Society, and is the author of several books. His influence as preacher and religious leader extends beyond his own denomination.

MUSIC. FFIGYSBREN, known in Wales as "Clod" (Praise), is a tune of simple construction, but when sung rather slowly it is remarkably powerful and effective. It appeared in America in *The Harvard University Hymn Book,* edited by Archibald T. Davidson in 1926. It is one of an increasing number of Welsh tunes which are becoming available to enrich our hymnody with the element of unique beauty and fervor that is so characteristic of the singing of the Welsh people.

184. Prayer is the soul's sincere desire

James Montgomery, 1771-1854

A classic poem on prayer, written in 1818 at the request of the Rev. E. Bickersteth for his *Treatise on Prayer.* In 1825 it was published in *The Christian Psalmist,* headed, "What is Prayer?" The original has eight stanzas of which our hymn is a selection of 1, 2, 4, 5. Prayer is more, to be sure, than "the soul's sincere desire," for we sincerely desire many things that are in conflict with God's will. But taken as a whole, the poem is an elaborate description of the nature of prayer and teaches its principles and practice with truth and power. The last stanza, unfortunately omitted in the *Hymnary,* is itself a beautiful, direct petition:

O Thou by whom we come to God,
The Life, the Truth, the Way,
The path of prayer Thyself hast trod,—
Lord, teach us how to pray.

For comments on James Montgomery see Hymn 62.

MUSIC. ST. AGNES. For comments on this tune see Hymn 155. In some books the hymn is set to the tune *"Es Ist Ein Born"* (241).

185. Thou art the Way, to Thee alone

George W. Doane, 1799-1859

Based on John 14:6: "I am the way, the truth, and the life; no man cometh unto the Father, but by me."

The hymn was written by one of the most able and influential men in the Episcopal Church in America. It takes high rank among all the hymns America has produced, and is one of the few hymns of American origin included in the famous English book, *Hymns Ancient and Modern*. It is written in simple style, employing only twelve words of more than one syllable.

For further comments on Bishop Doane see Hymn 36.

MUSIC. LAMBETH was composed in 1871 by Wilhelm A. M. Schulthes. No information is at hand concerning the composer. The tune was taken from *The Hymnal* (Protestant Episcopal, 1916).

186. What a friend we have in Jesus *Joseph Scriven, 1820-86*

A spiritual song of comfort and hope and the most popular Canadian contribution to the hymnody of the church.

The authorship of this hymn long remained a secret. In one publication it was erroneously attributed to Horatius Bonar. Scriven composed it for his mother to comfort her in time of special sorrow, not intending that anyone else should see it. This information was revealed to a friend who sat up with the author in his last illness.

Joseph Scriven, born in Dublin, came to Canada at the age of 25 and settled first at Rice Lake and later at Port Hope, Ontario. He was unmarried and lived with several families in succession. An eccentric person, he was always assisting others, and was known as "the man who sawed wood for widows and sick people who are unable to pay." He was found drowned in a stream near Rice Lake. A monument to his memory was erected by the people who had been helped by him, and by others in the district.

MUSIC. ERIE was composed for this hymn by Charles Crozat Converse, 1832-1918, an American, trained in Germany for the musical profession. On returning to America, he studied law, graduating from Albany Law School in 1861, and from 1875 practicing the legal profession at Erie, Pa. He maintained his interest in music and published several compositions during his career as lawyer.

187. I need Thee every hour *Annie Sherwood Hawks, 1835-1918*

A song expressing the Christian believer's ever-present sense of divine help and guidance. It first appeared in a small collection of gospel songs prepared for the National Baptist Sunday School Association which met in Cincinnati, Ohio, November, 1872, and was sung there.

Mrs. Annie Sherwood Hawks was an active member of the Baptist Church in Brooklyn of which Rev. Robert Lowry, who wrote the music to the words and added the refrain, was the pastor. Concerning the hymn, Mrs. Hawks wrote:

> Whenever my attention is called to it I am conscious of great satisfaction in the thought that I was permitted to write the hymn, "I need Thee every hour," and that it was wafted out to the world on the wings of love and joy, rather than under stress of a great personal sorrow, with which it has so often been associated in the minds of those who sing it.
>
> I remember well the morning . . . . when in the midst of the daily cares of my home . . . . I was so filled with the sense of nearness to the Master that, wondering how one could live without Him either in joy or pain, these words, "I need Thee every hour," were ushered into my mind, the thought at once taking full possession of me . . . .
>
> For myself the hymn was prophetic rather than expressive of my own experience at the time it was written, and I do not understand why it so touched the great throbbing heart of humanity. It was not until long years after, when the shadow fell over my way—the shadow of a great loss—that I understood something of the comforting in the words I had been permitted to write and give out to others in my hours of sweet security and peace.

MUSIC. NEED. The tune was written for this hymn. The composer, Rev. Robert Lowry, 1826-99, was born in Philadelphia and educated at Bucknell University. After a few years in the Baptist ministry he became Professor of Rhetoric at his alma mater. The University gave him his doctorate in 1875. He resigned his chair in 1875 and the following year resumed the work of the ministry at Plainfield, N. J., continuing until his death. Though he had no serious training in music, Lowry wrote many tunes and edited several popular collections of hymns. He did much to encourage the gospel song movement in America.

188. Father, in Thy mysterious presence kneeling

Samuel Johnson, 1822-82

A beautiful hymn of contrition, and prayer for the "Presence."

Samuel Johnson was born in Salem, Mass. After graduating from Harvard University and Harvard Divinity School, he became minister of the Independent Church at Lynn, Mass., where he served from 1853 to 1870. He was a fellow-student and close friend of Samuel Longfellow, the two "Sams" collaborating in the editing of *A Book of Hymns* which passed through twelve editions and became the source of excellent hymnic material not published before. He was a Unitarian by faith. A competent scholar, he published *Oriental Religions,* the first adequate study of comparative religions by an American.

MUSIC. HENLEY is one of Mason's most appreciated tunes. It appeared in *The Hallelujah,* 1854, by the composer, set to the hymn "Come unto me, when shadows darkly gather."

For comments on Lowell Mason see Hymn 12.

189. Come, thou Fount of every blessing
Robert Robinson, 1735-90

An old hymn that has been a "fount of blessing" itself to multitudes, written only three years after the author's conversion. It sounds a note of anxiety lest the paths of sin lure the soul away from God. The Scripture reference in the second stanza is to I Sam. 7:12: "Then Samuel took a stone and set it between Mizpeh and Shen, and called the name of it Ebenezer, saying, Hitherto hath the Lord helped me."

For comments on the author, Robert Robinson, see Hymn 46.

MUSIC. NETTLETON appeared in John Wyeth's *Repository,* 1813, arranged with the melody in the treble. The authorship of the tune is unknown. It has been attributed to Wyeth and to Asahel Nettleton, 1783-1844, a New England evangelist and compiler of *Village Hymns.* It has been suggested that a friend of Nettleton composed the tune and named it in his honor.

John Wyeth was born in Cambridge, Mass., 1770, and followed the printing and publishing business all his life. He was postmaster at Harrisburg, Pa., under President Washington but was removed by President Adams because of "incompatibility of the office of post master and editor of a newspaper." He died in Philadelphia, June 23, 1858.

LOYALTY AND STEADFASTNESS

190. Who is on the Lord's side
Frances R. Havergal, 1836-79

An impressive call to Christian service. The hymn is based on the incident in the life of David in I Chron. 12:18: "Then the spirit came upon Amasai who was the chief of the captains, and he said, 'Thine are we, David, and on thy side' . . . . Then David received them and made them captains of the band."

For comments on Frances Havergal see Hymn 126.

MUSIC. ARMAGEDDON. This stirring tune was first used to "Onward, Christian Soldiers," and later with the above hymn. It is an arrangement by John Goss of a tune by Louise Reichardt which appeared in *Kern des Deutschen Kirchengesangs,* 1853.

Louise Reichardt, 1788-1826, was a teacher of vocal music in Berlin.

For comments on John Goss see Hymn 121.

191. When courage fails, and faith burns low

Frederick L. Hosmer, 1840-1929

A triumphant song setting forth the ultimate victory of truth, and encouraging young people to stand loyally for the truth, even "though men deride."

For comments on the author, Frederick L. Hosmer, seee Hymn 72.

MUSIC. WINCHESTER OLD. For comments on this tune see Hymn 588.

192. Jesus, and shall it ever be

Joseph B. Grigg, 1720-68

Entitled by the author "Ashamed of Me." The hymn is based on Mark 8:38: "Whosoever therefore shall be ashamed of me and of my words in this adulterous and sinful generation; of him also shall the Son of man be ashamed, when he cometh in the glory of his Father with the holy angels."

The original poem, composed when the author was only ten years of age, has been altered somewhat by Benjamin Francis, an English Baptist preacher who was born in Wales in 1734. Francis was an earnest and popular minister and received flattering calls to London and elsewhere but chose to remain with his flock at the Baptist Church at Shortwood where he ministered from 1757 until his death in 1799.

For comments on Joseph B. Grigg see Hymn 141.

MUSIC. FEDERAL STREET is the name of a street in Salem, Mass., where the composer lived and where his wife was born, lived, and died. The tune was written in 1832 to a child's funeral hymn by Anne Steele, which began, "So fades the lovely, blooming flower."

Henry Kemble Oliver, 1800-85, was a great lover of music even though his father disapproved of music and forbade the son having anything to do with it. After graduating from Dartmouth, he had a varied career as teacher, manager of cotton mills, adjutant-general of his state, treasurer of the State of Massachusetts, and mayor of Salem. He had acquired some musical education and found time to compose and publish a considerable amount of sacred music.

193. Stand up, stand up for Jesus

George Duffield, Jr., 1818-88

A hymn of the Christian warfare, widely known, and found in nearly all English hymn books. The origin of it is best given in the author's own words in a leaflet printed in Detroit, 1883, and quoted by his son, Samuel Duffield, in *English Hymns,* 1886:

> "Stand up for Jesus" was the dying message of the Rev. Dudley A. Tyng, to the Young Men's Christian Association, and the ministers associated with them in the Noon-Day Prayer Meeting, during the great revival of 1858, usually known as "The Work of God in Philadelphia."

A very dear personal friend, I knew young Tyng as one of the noblest, bravest, manliest men I ever met; not inferior in eloquence to his honored father, and the acknowledged leader of a campaign for Christ that has become historical. The Sabbath before his death he preached in the immense edifice known as Jaynes' Hall, one of the most successful sermons of modern times. Of the five thousand men there assembled, at least one thousand, it was believed, were "the slain of the Lord." His text was Exodus 10:11, and hence the allusion in the third verse of the hymn.

The following Wednesday, leaving his study for a moment, he went to the barn floor, where a mule was at work on a horse-power, shelling corn. Patting him on the neck, the sleeve of his silk study gown caught in the cogs of the wheel, and his arm was torn out by the roots! His death occurred in a few hours. Never was there greater lamentation over a young man than over him, and when Gen. 50:26 was announced as the text for his funeral sermon, the place at once became a Bochim, and continued so for many minutes.

The following Sunday the author of the hymn preached from Eph. 6:14, and the above verses were written simply as the concluding exhortation. The superintendent of the Sabbath-school had a fly-leaf printed for the children—a stray copy found its way into a Baptist newspaper—and from that paper it has gone in English, and in German and Latin translations all over the world. The first time the author heard it sung outside of his own denomination, was in 1864, as the favorite song of the Christian soldiers in the Army of the James.

. . . . . . George Duffield

Detroit, May 29, 1883.

George Duffield, Jr., 1818-88, son of Rev. George Duffield, was educated at Yale and Union Theological Seminary for the Presbyterian ministry and held pastorates in Brooklyn, Philadelphia, Galesburg, Ill., Adrian and Lansing, Michigan. His son, Samuel W. Duffield, was the author of *English Hymns*.

MUSIC. WEBB. For comments on this tune see Hymn 65.

194. God's trumpet wakes the slumb'ring world

Samuel Longfellow, 1819-92

A stirring call to a loyal stand for truth and witness against wrong. The hymn first appeared in *Hymns of the Spirit*, 1864.

For comments on Samuel Longfellow see Hymn 28.

MUSIC. ALL SAINTS NEW was written for Bishop Heber's hymn, "The Son of God goes forth to war."

The composer, Henry Stephen Cutler, 1824-1902, received his education at Boston, his birthplace, and in Europe. He became a well-known organist and choir master, serving churches in Boston, New York, and other cities, and attracted attention by robing his choir members and seating them in the chancel, innovations in his day.

TRIALS AND TEMPTATIONS

195. In the hour of trial
James Montgomery, 1771-1854
Alt. Frances A. Hutton and
Godfrey Thring

The hymn is based on Luke 22:32: "I have prayed for thee, that thy faith fail not." It was written October 13, 1834, with the title, "In trial and temptation," and published in 1853 in Montgomery's *Original Hymns* under the title "Prayers on Pilgrimage." The third and fourth stanzas have been altered considerably, not entirely for the better. Montgomery began the second stanza:

> With its witching pleasures.

In the first stanza he had

> Jesus *pray* for me;

to which there was much objection on scriptural grounds, in spite of the words of Christ, "I pray for them" (John 17:9).

For comments on James Montgomery see Hymn 62.

MUSIC. PENITENCE was composed by Spencer Lane, 1843-1903, who received musical training in the Boston Conservatory of Music and became a teacher of vocal and instrumental music. He was in charge of music in various churches in Rhode Island, Massachusetts, Virginia, and Maryland. While choirmaster at St. James Church, Woonsocket, R. I., he wrote this tune one Sunday while his wife was preparing dinner. It was used at a parish choir festival on "Easter Tuesday, 1899, at 7:30 p.m." and at the suggestion of the rector of the church, it was sent to Dr. Chas. L. Hutchins, who included it in the *Episcopal Hymnal* of 1879. Of the various tunes composed by Lane, this is the only one in general use today.

196. Lord Jesus, think on me
Synesius, c. 375-430
Tr. Allen W. Chatfield, 1808-96

A subjective and meditative hymn of trust, coming to us from the ancient Eastern Church.

Synesius, a native of Cyrene, came from an illustrious family. He studied at Alexandria and became a Christian in 401. Against his own wishes, but in response to the will of the people, he was elected bishop of Ptolemais. He is described in Chas. Kingsley's *Hypatia* as a distinguished churchman, philosopher, statesman, and patriot.

The translator, Rev. A. W. Chatfield, was an Anglican clergyman who had a distinguished career at Cambridge. He translated many of the hymns of the early Greek poets into English.

The original poem, of which this is a paraphrase rather than an exact translation, is as follows:

> Μνώεο, Χριστέ,
> υἱὲ Θεοῖο
> ὑψιμέδοντος,
> οἰκέτω Σοῦ,
> Κῆρ' ἀλιτροῖο
> Τάδε γράψαντος·
> Καί μοι ὄπασσον
> λύσιν παθέων
> κηριτρεφέων
> τά μοι ἐμφυῆ
> ψυχᾷ ῥυπαρᾷ·
> δὸς δὲ ἰδέσθαι,
> Σῶτερ 'Ιησοῦ,
> ζαθέαν αἴγλαν
> Σάν, ἔνθα φανεὶς
> μέλψω ἀοιδὰν
> παίονι ψυχᾶν,
> παίονι γυίων,
> Πατρὶ σὺν μεγάλῳ
> Πνεύματί Θ' 'Αγνῷ.

MUSIC. SOUTHWELL, a characteristic psalm tune, was set to Psalm 45 in *Damon's Psalms of David,* 1579, and was named "Southwell" in Ravencroft's *Psalm Book* of 1621. It was originally written in the Dorian mode (the first "authentic" Gregorian mode, D as keynote). A fuller explanation may be found in the *History of Music in the Western Church,* by Dickinson, pp. 113 ff.

For comments on *Damon's Psalter* see Hymn 589.

197. O for a closer walk with God   *William Cowper,* 1731-1800

A tender, beautiful hymn, in use wherever English is spoken.

It was published in the *Olney Hymns* (See 60) under the title "Walking with God." It is based on Genesis 5:24: "Enoch walked with God." The hymn was written December 9, 1769, during the serious illness of the poet's dear friend, the wife of Rev. Morley Unwin, in whose home he stayed and found the tenderest of care during his own illness. Concerning her, Cowper wrote in a letter the day following the composition of this hymn:

> She is the chief of blessings I have met with in my journey since the Lord was pleased to call me. . . . Her illness has been a sharp trial to me. Oh, that it may have a sanctified effect, that I may rejoice to surrender up to the Lord my dearest comforts, the moment He may require them. . . . I began to compose the verses yesterday morning before daybreak but fell asleep at the end of the first two lines: when I awaked again, the third and fourth were whispered to my heart in a way which I have so often experienced.

For comments on William Cowper see Hymn 60.

MUSIC. BELMONT is an adaptation from a melody in *Sacred Melodies . . . . adapted to the best English poets,* Vol. I; 1812, by William Gardiner. The *Sacred Melodies* appeared in six volumes containing tunes by the best masters, adapted to English words.

The composer, William Gardiner, 1770-1853, was an English stocking manufacturer who travelled extensively at home and abroad, principally in the interests of his business, but also making acquaintance with musicians of all ranks and with their music. He published songs and duets of his own composition in his youth, over the *nom de plume* of "W. G. Leicester." His *Sacred Melodies,* referred to above, did valuable service in drawing attention to many fine compositions otherwise unknown.

198. Soldiers of Christ, arise   *Charles Wesley, 1707-88*

For comments on Charles Wesley see Hymn 6.

"The Whole Armor of God" is the title of this hymn in Wesley's *Hymns and Sacred Poems,* 1749. It is based on Ephesians 6:10-18: "Put on the whole armor of God, that ye may be able to stand against the wiles of the devil," etc. The entire poem contains 16 double stanzas, of which our hymn is a selection of the first, second, and sixteenth.

MUSIC. DIADEMATA. For comments on this tune see Hymn 118.

ASPIRATION AND HOPE

199. While Thee I seek, protecting Power
Helen M. Williams, 1762-1827

A hymn of faith and trust in God.

Helen Maria Williams, an English Unitarian, lived for some years with her sister who had married a French Protestant. It was during the period of the Revolution and the reign of terror. Being an outspoken

123

republican, she was imprisoned by Robespierre, and was released only after his death in 1794. She was a woman of extraordinary intellectual strength and published many volumes on politics, religion, and literary questions, and finally her collected poems, entitled, *Poems on Various Occasions.* She lived in England and in France, and the closing years of her life were spent in Holland in the home of a nephew who was pastor of a Reformed Church in Amsterdam.

MUSIC. BRATTLE STREET. For comments on the composer of this tune, Ignace Pleyel, see Hymn 238.

200. Rise, my soul, and stretch thy wings

Robert Seagrave, 1693-c. 1759

This hymn, entitled "The Pilgrim's Song," first appeared in *Hymns for Christian Worship,* by Robert Seagrave, London, 1742.

Robert Seagrave, son of Rev. Robert Seagrave, was educated at Cambridge and was ordained a clergyman in the Church of England. He became interested in the Wesleys and Whitefield and published pamphlets and sermons designed to reform the clergy and Church of England. He wrote 50 original hymns, of which this one is still in use. The exact year of Seagrave's death is not certain.

MUSIC. AMSTERDAM is attributed to James Nares, 1715-1783, but most authorities believe the tune to be much older. It appears in what is known as the *Foundery Collection,* the first Methodist hymnal, by John Wesley, 1742, and is said to be one of the German chorale tunes which John Wesley acquired from the Moravian Brethren.

201. We would see Jesus

Anna B. Warner, 1820-1915

Based on John 12:20-23: "There were certain Greeks among them that came up to worship at the feast: the same came therefore to Philip, which was of Bethsaida of Galilee, and desired him, saying, Sir, we would see Jesus. . . . And Jesus answered them saying, The hour is come, that the Son of man should be glorified."

The hymn first appeared in six stanzas in *Hymns of the Church Militant,* compiled by Anna Warner, New York, 1858, and published in 1861. It is another example of a fine hymn contributed by a woman.

The third and fourth stanzas, omitted here, are of the same excellent quality as the others:

> We would see Jesus: other lights are paling,
>   Which for long years we have rejoiced to see;
> The blessings of our pilgrimage are failing;
>   We would not mourn them for we go to Thee.

> We would see Jesus: yet the spirit lingers
> Round the dear objects it has loved so long,
> And earth from earth can scarce unclose its fingers;
> Our love to Thee makes not this love less strong.

Anna Bartlett Warner, lived on Constitution Island in the Hudson River, near West Point, where she and her more famous sister, Susan Warner, conducted a Bible class for nearly two generations for the cadets of the United States Military Academy. Because of this service, she was buried with military honors upon her death in 1915. Miss Warner wrote novels under the pseudonym of "Amy Lothrop," but she is best known for this hymn and the song beloved of all little children, "Jesus loves me: this I know."

MUSIC. HENLEY. For comments on this tune see Hymn 188.

202. Nearer, my God, to Thee   *Sarah Flower Adams*, 1805-48

A hymn of high poetic quality which has preserved its popularity from generation to generation. It is based on the story of Jacob at Bethel in Gen. 28:10-22:

> And Jacob went out from Beersheba, and went toward Haran. And he lighted upon a certain place, and tarried there all night, because the sun was set; and he took of the stones of that place, and put them for his pillows, and lay down in that place to sleep. And he dreamed, and behold a ladder set up on the earth, and the top of it reached to heaven: and behold the angels of God ascending and descending on it . . . . And Jacob rose up early in the morning, and took the stone that he had put for his pillows, and set it up for a pillar, and poured oil upon the top of it. And he called the name of that place Bethel.

Sarah Flower Adams was the daughter of Benjamin Flower, an editor; she married William B. Adams, an engineer and inventor, in 1834. She was a member of a Unitarian congregation in London. A woman of fine intellect, she wrote much prose and verse, and was a friend of Robert Browning. She died of tuberculosis, contracting the disease while caring for her sister, Eliza, who had fallen victim to the same disease two years earlier.

MUSIC. BETHANY was written by Lowell Mason for this hymn. Its resemblance to the tune of the well-known "Oft in the stilly night" has been noted. The tune to this hymn was played by the ship's band on board the "Titanic" as the vessel sank on its maiden voyage, Sunday, April 14, 1912, after colliding with an iceberg in the Atlantic. 1635 passengers were lost, ending life's voyage with the strains of the familiar and appropriate prayer resounding across the waters—"Nearer, my God, to Thee."

For comments on Lowell Mason see Hymn 12.

203. When the weary, seeking rest   *Horatius Bonar, 1808-89*

Entitled, "Intercession for All Conditions of Men," in Bonar's *Hymns of Faith and Hope,* 3d series, 1867.

The history of this hymn is given by the author's son, Rev. H. N. Bonar, as follows:

> My father was asked to provide words to the music, and was especially requested to furnish a fitting refrain to the two love-ly lines of Mendelssohn's with which Callcott's tune, "Interces-sion," ends. In searching for a Scripture theme containing some reiterated phrase almost of the nature of a refrain, he was struck with Solomon's prayer at the dedication of the temple (2 Chron. 6) in which every separate petition concludes with substantially the same words.
>
> This idea was taken for his starting point, and Solomon's words, "Hear thou from heaven thy dwelling place and for-give," became the familiar couplet:
>
> > "Hear then in love, O Lord, the cry
> > In heaven, thy dwelling place on high."
>
> This foundation once provided, the rest of the hymn was built upon it.

For comments on Horatius Bonar see Hymn 129.

MUSIC. INTERCESSION was composed by William H. Callcott, 1807-82, an English musician. He was organist of Ely Chapel, Holborn, and afterwards of St. Barnabas' Church, Kensington, and composed anthems and songs.

The refrain is from Mendelssohn's oratorio, *Elijah,* part of the prayer for rain by the prophet and the people. Bonar's hymn was written for this tune.

204. Lord, I hear of show'rs of blessing
Elizabeth Codner, 1824-1919

Based on Gen. 27:34: "Bless me, even me also, O my Father," and Ezek. 34:26: "There shall be showers of blessing." It is an especially useful hymn at revival meetings.

Elizabeth Codner was the wife of Rev. David Codner, a clergyman of the Church of England. She engaged in some literary work and was much interested in the Mildmay Protestant Mission in North London.

The author has given the origin of the hymn as follows:

> A party of young friends over whom I was watching with

126

anxious hope attended a meeting in which details were given of a revival work in Ireland. They came back greatly impressed. My fear was lest they should be satisfied to let their own fleece remain dry, and I pressed upon them the privilege and responsibility of getting a share in the out-poured blessing. On the Sunday following, not being well enough to get out, I had a time of quiet communion. Those children were still on my heart, and I longed to press upon them an earnest individual appeal. Without effort words seemed to be given to me, and they took the form of a hymn. I had no thought of sending it beyond the limits of my own circle, but, passing it on to one and another, it became a word of power, and I then published it as a leaflet. Of its future history I can only say the Lord took it quite out of my own hands. It was read from pulpits, circulated by tens of thousands, and blessed in a remarkable degree. Every now and then some sweet token was sent to cheer me in a somewhat isolated life, of its influence upon souls. Now it would be tidings from afar of a young officer dying in India and sending home his Bible with the hymn pasted on the flyleaf as the precious memorial of that which brought him to the Lord. Then came the story of a poor outcast gathered into the fold by the same means. Then came to me a letter given me by Mr. E. P. Hammond, which he had received, and in which were the words: "Thank you for singing that hymn 'Even Me,' for it was the singing of that hymn that saved me. I was a lost woman, a wicked mother. I have stolen and lied and been so bad to my dear, innocent children. Friendless, I attended your inquiry meeting; but no one came to me because of the crowd. But on Saturday afternoon, at the First Presbyterian Church, when they all sang that hymn together, those beautiful words, 'Let some drops now fall on me,' and also those, 'Blessing others, O bless me,' it seemed to reach my very soul. I thought, 'Jesus can accept me—"even me"' and it brought me to his feet, and I feel the burden of sin removed. Can you wonder that I love those words and I love to hear them sung?"

The original rendering has in a variety of instances been departed from. To some alterations I have consented, but always prefer that the words remain unchanged from the form in which God so richly blessed them. The point of the hymn, in its close and individual application, is in the "Even me" at the end of the verse. I thankfully commit them to whoever desires to use them in the services of our blessed Master.

MUSIC. EVEN ME. For comments on the composer, Wm. B. Bradbury, see Hymn 103.

THE CHRISTIAN LIFE

205. Blest are the pure in heart   *J. Keble, 1792-1866 and others*

A hymn of the simple, pure life. Purity of heart has a wider meaning than the specific virtue of chastity. Stanzas 1 and 3 are from Keble's, *The Christian Year*, 1827. Stanzas 2 and 4 are from the *New Mitre Hymn Book*, 1836, and their authorship is uncertain. Some think they are from the pen of the editor of the book, W. J. Hall, or of the co-editor, Edward Osler.

For comments on John Keble see Hymn 22.

MUSIC. FRANCONIA is from a book compiled by Johann Balthaser König, *Harmonischer Lieder-Schatz*, Frankfurt-am-Main, 1738, where it is set to the hymn, *Was ist, das mich betrübt?* The original melody may have been by König himself.

The present tune, arranged by Rev. W. H. Havergal, has become one of the best known Short-Meter (6.6.8.8.) tunes.

For comments on W. H. Havergal see Hymn 153.

206. How blest are they whose hearts are pure
W. H. Bathurst, 1796-1877

Based on the beatitude in Matt. 5:8: "Blessed are the pure in heart: for they shall see God."

For comments on the author, W. H. Bathurst, see Hymn 153.

MUSIC. GLENLUCE is one of the Common Tunes (see 20) in the *Scottish Psalter* of 1635.

For comments on the *Scottish Psalter* see Hymn 575.

207. I would be true   *Howard Arnold Walter, 1884-1918*

A popular hymn at young people's summer conferences and other youth gatherings. The words have often been reprinted in trade journals and newspapers and used on many a motto card. The ideals of youth—truth, purity, strength, bravery, friendship, generosity, humility, laughter, love, and helpfulness, encompassed in these few lines—were all revealed in the author's brief life.

Howard Arnold Walter was graduated *cum laude* in 1905 from Princeton University while Woodrow Wilson was president of the institution. He then entered Hartford Theological Seminary to prepare himself for the ministry, but after the first year went to Japan to teach English in Waseda University in Tokyo. After one year, he returned to Hartford where, upon graduation, he won the Two-Year Fellowship. In 1909 and 1910 he studied in Edinburgh and in German

Universities. He chose the foreign mission field for life service but, owing to a weak heart, was unable to pass the required physical examination. In spite of his handicap, he volunteered for Y.M.C.A. work and was assigned by John R. Mott to India, where he worked among the Mohammedan students in Foreman Christian College, Lahore. He died there November 1, 1918, during the influenza epidemic, leaving a devoted wife and three small children. The words, "I would be true," were inscribed on a memorial tablet erected in his home church in New Britain, Conn.

The hymn was written in 1907 in Japan when Walter was just 23 years old. Recalling the joys and friendships of his home, the words came to him on New Year's morning as he was on his knees. He mailed the poem entitled, "My Creed," to his mother who sent it to *Harper's Magazine* in order to share with others the beauty of its message. It appeared in the May, 1907, issue of that magazine and later found its way into a number of hymn books.

The third stanza, making the hymn more complete, was later written by the author and sent to Rev. Theodore A. Green, minister of the First Church of Christ, New Haven, Connecticut:

> I would be prayerful through each busy moment;
> I would be constantly in touch with God;
> I would be tuned to hear the slightest whisper;
> I would have faith to keep the path Christ trod.

MUSIC. PEEK. No one seemed to know anything of the composer of this tune until very recently when Dr. Reginald L. McAll, secretary of the Hymn Society of America, assigned to the Hon. Edgar M. Doughty, Brooklyn, an official referee of the New York State Supreme Court, an accomplished musician and active member of the Baptist Church, the task of searching out in behalf of the Society the facts concerning Mr. Peek. The Hon. Mr. Doughty completed his research just before his death in 1947, at the age of 80 and the information presented here is based on a document compiled from his papers by his secretary, Miss Mildred Taylor Denisch:

Joseph Yates Peek, 1843-1911, born in Schenectady, N. Y., had very little formal musical training, but was endowed with a love for music and considerable native musical ability and became a proficient amateur performer on the violin and piano. In early life he was a carpenter and farmer but later established a business as florist and horticulturist. A deeply religious man, always interested in the church, he retired from business in 1904, and in spite of his advanced years, became a prominent lay preacher in the Methodist Church. In 1911 he was ordained, but his career as a regular minister was cut short when a heart attack, which occurred while preaching, resulted in his death.

Peek was a humble Christian gentleman who sought no honors for himself, which may account for the fact that his identity as the composer of this tune remained hidden so long. Then, too, he may have felt that the credit for the tune did not belong entirely to himself, for he received considerable help from a friend, Dr. Tuller, an organist and composer, who jotted down the notes as Peek whistled the melody, and later added the harmonization.

Peek had received a copy of Walter's poem which was printed on a New Year's card and entitled, "My Creed." He was greatly impressed with the words, and in a moment of inspiration gave them wings of song to carry them over the wide world.

The tune has become immensely popular in spite of its weak downcurve of melody. The hymn may also be sung to Barnby's more sturdy tune, "Perfect Love" (312), which fits the words perfectly.

208. How happy is he born and taught *Henry Wotton, 1568-1639*

The original of this hymn was published in *Reliquiae Wottonianae* with a memoir by Isaac Walton, 1651. The poem was altered somewhat to make it suitable for a congregational hymn.

Henry Wotton graduated from Oxford in 1588. He had a varied career, travelling on the continent, acting as agent to the Earl of Essex for collection of foreign intelligence, and then settling in Venice where he was ambassador at the court from 1604-24, with two intervals during which he was engaged in diplomatic missions to other countries and in parliamentary work in England. From 1624 until his death he was provost of Eton. Besides the above-named book, he published *The Elements of Architecture*, 1624, and *Ad Regem e Scotia reducem* in 1633.

MUSIC. WAREHAM, by William Knapp, is from *A Sett of New Psalm Tunes and Anthems, in Four Parts by Wm. Knapp*, 1738, where it is set to Psalm 36:5-10 with the heading, "For the Holy Sacrament." It is a deservedly popular melody, remarkably smooth, moving throughout by step except the perfect fourth interval between the fifth and sixth notes.

209. Walk in the light! so shalt thou know
Bernard Barton, 1784-1849

A useful hymn, by a Quaker poet, setting forth the characteristic Quaker doctrine of the "Inner Light," based on I John 1:7: "But if we walk in the light, as he is in the light, we have fellowship one with another, and the blood of Jesus Christ his Son cleanseth us from all sin."

The hymn appeared in the author's *Devotional Verses*, London, 1826.

Bernard Barton, known in England as the "Quaker Poet" (as was Whittier in America), was born in London and educated at a Quaker school at Ipswich. When 26 years old he became a Clerk in Alexander's Bank at Woodbridge, Suffolk, and stayed there the remainder of his life. On Nov. 16, 1843, he wrote in a letter:

> I took my seat on the identical stool I now occupy at the desk to the wood of which I have now well-nigh grown, in the third month of the year 1810, and there I have sat for three and thirty years beside the odd eight months without one month's respite in all that time. I often wonder that my health has stood this sedentary probation as it has and that my mental facilities have survived three and thirty years of putting down figures in three rows, casting them up and carrying them forward, *ad infinitum*.

He might have given some of these years to literary pursuits had he not followed the good advice of Charles Lamb who wrote him:

> Throw yourself on the world, without any rational plan of support beyond what the chance employ of booksellers would afford you! Throw yourself rather, my dear sir, from the steep Tarpeian rock, slap-dash headlong upon iron spikes. If you have but five consolatory minutes between the desk and the bed, make much of them, and live a century in them, rather than turn slave to the booksellers. They are Turks and Tartars when they have poor authors at their beck. Hitherto you have been at arm's length from them—come not within their grasp. I have known many authors' want for bread—some repining, others enjoying the blessed security of a counting-house—all agreeing they had rather have been tailors, weavers, what not? rather than the things they were. I have known some starved, some go mad, one dear friend literally dying in a work-house. Oh, you know not—may you never know—the miseries of subsisting by authorship!

He published eight or ten volumes of verse. His writings show an extensive acquaintance with the Scriptures.

MUSIC. DEDHAM. For comments on the composer, William Gardiner, see Hymn 197.

210. Believe not those who say   *Anne Brontë, 1820-49*

A hymn of courage. The original is in 10 stanzas, of which this hymn is a selection of stanzas 1, 2, 8, 9, 10.

Anne Brontë, one of three illustrious sisters, the other two being Charlotte and Emily, was born near Bradford, England, the daughter of the Rev. Patrick Brontë, Vicar of Haworth, Yorkshire. She was joint author with her sisters of a book of *Poems,* 1846, and wrote other volumes under the pseudonym, "Acton Bell."

MUSIC. The tune, VIGIL, is by the Italian composer, Giovanni Paisiello, 1741-1816, whose works include 100 operas, a Passion oratorio, 30 masses, a requiem, 40 motets, and 8 symphonies. From 1776 to 1784, he was in the service of Empress Catherine of Russia, who a few years later was receiving Mennonites from Danzig and West Prussia to settle her crown lands at Chortitz. Paisiello was called to Paris to organize the music of the First Consul, meanwhile composing some church music. His last years were spent in Naples, where he was choirmaster to Joseph Bonaparte and Murat.

211. Go forth to life *Samuel Longfellow,* 1819-92

A challenge to live life bravely and true. The hymn is from *Hymns of the Spirit,* 1864, prepared by Samuel Longfellow and Samuel Johnson. It is one of the lyrics which helped establish Longfellow's reputation as a hymn-writer.

For comments on Samuel Longfellow see Hymn 28.

MUSIC. MENDON is a variation of a "German Air" introduced into American hymn books by Samuel Dyer. The original had an additional note in each line and a different last line. The change to the present form and its name is attributed to Lowell Mason.

Samuel Dyer, 1785-1835, born in England, came to America when 26 years old and became a choir leader and teacher of sacred music in New York, Philadelphia, and Baltimore. He published several collections of sacred music, one of which, *Philadelphia Collection of Sacred Music,* 1828, gives valuable sketches of composers, and information about Dyer himself.

CONSECRATION AND STEWARDSHIP

212. O Jesus, I have promised *John Ernest Bode,* 1816-74

A hymn of consecration which the author wrote on the occasion of the confirmation of his daughter and two sons as "O Jesus, *we* have promised." It is frequently, and appropriately, used at baptismal services.

John Ernest Bode graduated with high honors from Oxford, where he was a fellow and tutor for six years; then became rector of Westwall, Oxfordshire, and later of Castle Campus, Cambridgeshire. He was a man of considerable attainments and was Bampton Lecturer in

132

1855. He wrote a number of hymns and is the author of several volumes of poetry.

MUSIC. ANGEL'S STORY, also known as "Supplication" and "Water-mouth," was written for Emily H. Miller's hymn, "I love to hear the story which angel voices tell," from which it derives its name. It first appeared in the *Methodist Sunday School Hymn Book*, 1881, but has since come into wide usage set to "O Jesus, I have promised."

The composer, Arthur H. Mann, 1850-1930, was a distinguished English organist, and musical editor of *The Church of England Hymnal*. He was an authority on the music of Handel, and composed much church music. Oxford University gave him the degrees of Bachelor of Music and Doctor of Music.

213. We give Thee but thine own   *W. W. How, 1823-97*

Based on Prov. 19:17: "He that hath pity on the poor lendeth to the Lord." It is a hymn on Christian giving and liberality, sounding the real humanitarian note, a side of religion which an effective and virile hymnology cannot ignore. It may appropriately be sung by choir or congregation in the dedication of the offering. (See comments at 611.)

For comments on W. W. How see Hymn 144.

MUSIC. SCHUMANN, a fine short-meter tune, is ascribed to Robert Schumann but it seems as if no one has ever found anything among his musical writings from which the tune could have been derived. It appeared in Lowell Mason's *Cantica Laudis* in 1850.

For comments on Schumann see Hymn 296.

214. A charge to keep I have   *Charles Wesley, 1707-88*

One of the greatest of Wesley's short hymns taken from *Short Hymns on Select Passages of the Holy Scriptures,* 1762, where it is headed, "Keep the charge of the Lord, that ye die not" (Lev. 8:35).

The hymn strikes a much-needed note regarding the serious significance of this life. Thomas Carlyle expressed the same thought in his old age when he said: "The older I grow, and now I stand upon the brink of eternity, the more comes back to me the sentence in the catechism which I learned when a child, and the fuller and deeper its meaning becomes: 'What is the chief end of man? To glorify God and enjoy Him forever.'"

For comments on Charles Wesley see Hymn 6.

MUSIC. BOYLSTON was composed by Lowell Mason and named after one of the towns in his native state. It appeared in *The Choir,* 1832, set to "Our days are as the grass." The tune is widely used with "Blest be the tie that binds."

For comments on Lowell Mason, see Hymn 12.

215. Take my life and let it be   *Frances R. Havergal, 1836-79*

One of the finest hymns of consecration and service. It has been translated into many languages, including Russian, and many of Africa and Asia.

The author's own story of how this hymn was written after her visit in a certain home throws a vivid light on her evangelical zeal:

> There were ten persons in the house, some unconverted and long prayed for, some converted but not rejoicing Christians. He gave me the prayer, "Lord give me ALL in this house." And He just did. Before I left the house everyone had got a blessing. The night of my visit, after I had retired, the governess asked me to go to the two daughters. They were crying. Then and there both of them trusted and rejoiced. I was too happy to sleep, and passed most of the night in praise and renewal of my own consecration; and these little couplets formed themselves and chimed in my heart one after the other, till they finished with "Ever, ONLY, ALL for Thee!"

The hymn appears here unaltered from the original.

For further comments on Frances Havergal see Hymn 126.

MUSIC. HENDON. This tune appeared first in America in *Carmina Sacra*, 1841, edited by Lowell Mason. The composer, Henri Abraham César Malan, 1787-1864, born in Geneva, Switzerland, was a man of many interests. He was a well educated minister, a blacksmith, carpenter, printer, and artist. He had a burning zeal for the conversion of souls. Convinced that the national church stood in need of reform, he aroused much opposition. After preaching an unorthodox sermon at the College of Geneva, he was dismissed from his regentship at the college and was finally driven from the state church. He then built a chapel in his own garden and preached there for 43 years, attracting overflowing crowds and becoming widely known throughout Belgium, France, England, and Scotland for his evangelism. He wrote more than 1,000 hymns and set tunes to them, a remarkable achievement. As the originator of the modern hymn movement in the French Reformed Church, Malan has a permanent place in French Hymnody.

216. My Jesus, I love Thee   *William Rolf Featherstone, 1842-78*

The authorship of this hymn was unknown until recently when Robert McCutchan, author of *Our Hymnody*, discovered that it was written by William Rolf Featherstone, a Canadian by birth, when he was only sixteen years of age. The author sent the hymn to an aunt, Mrs. E. Featherstone Wilson, living in Los Angeles, who suggested to her nephew that it be published. No further information concerning Featherstone is at hand.

MUSIC. GORDON. The tune was written for this hymn which the composer, Dr. Gordon, found in the *London Hymn Book,* 1864. This combination of hymn and tune became popular and is widely known in America.

Adoniram Judson Gordon, 1836-1895, was born at New Hampton, New Hampshire, educated at Brown University and Newton Theological Seminary, and became the distinguished pastor of the Clarendon Street Baptist Church, Boston. He at one time was editor of *The Watchword,* and is author of a series of books called *Quiet Talks.*

217. Have Thine own way, Lord   *Adelaide Pollard, 1862-1934*

A hymn of the believer's humble resignation to God, as the clay to the potter.

The author, Adelaide Addison Pollard, was a modest poet. She signed her writings for many years with only her initials, but in recent times her publishers have used her full name. Miss Pollard was born in Iowa, but died in New York City. She was buried in the family plot at Ft. Madison, Iowa. While a teacher of elocution and expression, she became interested in deeper spiritual things through the ministry of R. A. Torrey and James M. Gray, and enrolled for further Bible training at the Moody Bible Institute, Chicago. She became a teacher in the Missionary Alliance Bible School at Nyack, N. Y., and also did missionary work in South Africa. Miss Pollard wrote numerous hymns and devotional poems. Her two best-known hymns are: "Have Thine own way, Lord," and "Shepherd of Israel." Her mother was Rebecca Pollard who wrote the song poem, "I surrender all," for which D. B. Towner wrote the music.

MUSIC. ADELAIDE. The name of the tune is obviously derived from the name of the author of the words for which it was composed. For comments on the composer, Geo. C. Stebbins, see Hymn 38.

218. Fountain of good, to own thy love

Philip Doddridge, 1702-51

An appealing hymn on fellowship and service as well as consecration.

The author entitled the hymn, "On Relieving Christ in the Poor." The original first line began "Jesus, my Lord, how rich thy grace." The hymn was rewritten by Edward Osler, 1798-1863, for Hall's *Mitre Hymn Book,* 1836, in which form it is found in modern hymnals, including the *Hymnary.*

For comments on Philip Doddridge see Hymn 56.

MUSIC. DALEHURST was composed by Arthur Cottman, 1842-79, an Englishman trained for the law but interested keenly in sacred music.

135

It was first published in Cottman's *Ten Original Tunes,* 1874, and has since been introduced into the hymnals and set to various texts. It is a tune of simple pattern, contemplative in mood, and should be sung in an even, moderate tempo.

219. Master, speak! thy servant heareth

Frances R. Havergal, 1836-79

Based on the conversation between Samuel and Eli, I Sam. 3:1-10.

Miss Havergal's favorite name for Christ was "Master," because, she said, "it implies rule and submission, and this is what love craves. Men may feel differently, but a true woman's submission is inseparable from deep love."

For comments on Frances Havergal see Hymn 126.

MUSIC. AMEN, JESUS HAN SKAL RAADE ("Amen, Jesus, He shall reign") comes from Denmark. The composer, Anton Peter Berggreen, 1801-80, was born in Copenhagen and lived there all his life. He studied music and became a composer of many works, the most popular being his *National Songs* in eleven volumes. His collection of *Psalm Tunes* are widely used in Danish churches. He was organist at Trinity Church, Copenhagen, and organized musical associations among laboring people which are still popular. For a number of years he was Professor of Singing at the Metropolitan School and inspector of the public schools in his native city.

220. Savior, thy dying love

Sylvanus D. Phelps, 1816-95

Phelps gave this hymn to be published in *Pure Gold,* a Sunday school songbook which Robert Lowry, composer of music, was then editing and of which more than a million copies were sold. The hymn was given the heading, "Lord, what wilt Thou have me to do?" (Acts 9:6.)

Sylvanus Dryden Phelps, Baptist minister, was born in Suffolk, Conn.; received his education at Brown University; and in 1846 became pastor of the First Baptist Church, New Haven, Conn., where he remained for 28 years. He published three volumes of poetry. His son, William Lyon Phelps, was the distinguished Professor of English Literature at Yale and a lay preacher.

MUSIC. SOMETHING FOR JESUS was written for this hymn. At the time he composed this tune, Lowry was pastor of a Baptist Church in Lewisburg, Pa., and Professor of Literature in Bucknell University.

For further comments on Robert Lowry see Hymn 187.

221. Work, for the night is coming

Anna Louisa Coghill, 1836-1907

Based on John 9:4: "I must work the works of him that sent me, while it is day: the night cometh, when no man can work." The hymn was written when the author, eighteen years old, lived in Canada. It was published in a Canadian newspaper and later in her small volume of poems, *Leaves from the Backwoods,* Montreal, 1864.

Anna Louisa Walker was born in England but went in her teens with her parents to Sania, Canada, where her brothers were railway engineers. Returning to England, she became a governess for a time, then she reviewed books, making her home with her second cousin, a Mrs. Oliphant, for some years. In 1883 she married Harry Coghill, a wealthy merchant. She published six novels and a book of poems, *Oak and Maple,* and edited the *Autobiography and Letters* of Mrs. Oliphant.

MUSIC. WORK SONG, known in England as "Diligence," was written for this hymn. To fit the tune it became necessary to drop a syllable in the fourth line of each verse, an alteration which the author disliked extremely and which she never sanctioned.

For comments on Lowell Mason see Hymn 12.

222. Where cross the crowded ways of life

Frank Mason North, 1850-1935

An unexcelled "Hymn for the City." The following account of it is given in *The Churchman,* July, 1938, in an article by Eloise R. Griffith, on "Our Great Hymns":

> Frank Mason North, D.D., a well-known clergyman of the Methodist Church, is the author of this well-loved hymn. It is sometimes called "A Prayer for the City," or "A Prayer for the Multitudes," and has the distinction of appearing in more standard hymnals today than any other hymn written in this century. To those of us who are concerned about "how the other half lives," and who know either from our own experiences or those of friends about the darker side of life in a great city and particularly in our own country during the last nine years,—this beautiful hymn never fails to find a heartfelt response. It paints a picture with which many city dwellers are all too familiar.

> In 1903, Dr. North was editor of *The Christian City,* the organ of the Methodist City Missionary Society. His office was in the Fifth Avenue building of the Methodist Book Concern. One day one of the professors of Wesleyan University (who was on the committee to prepare and revise the new Methodist

hymnal, and who knew North's ability to write hymns), met him in one of the halls. "Why don't you write a missionary hymn for us, Dr. North?" asked the professor. "We need more missionary hymns in our new hymnal." Dr. North modestly answered that he did not feel he would be able to write a hymn worthy of the proposed new hymnal, but that he would try.

Soon after this incident occurred, Dr. North was preaching a sermon from the text in St. Matthew 22:9: "Go ye therefore into the highways," etc. During his preparation for this sermon, he was again especially impressed by the rendering of the Greek text in the Revised Version, which reads "Go ye therefore into the partings of the highways." Dr. North thought of and described in his sermon the appealing challenge made by great crowds of people thronging the crossroads of the city— places like Madison Square and Union Square in the New York of 1903. Dr. North knew New York City very thoroughly, and his heart yearned over the sick, the lonely, the destitute, the troubled. So, while he preached, the first line of this great hymn came to him—"Where cross the crowded ways of life." It did not take him long to compose the words which followed, and after the publication of the hymn in *The Christian City*, it was at once accepted for the new Methodist hymnal of 1905. The hymn is widely used in Canada and throughout Great Britain, and has been translated into several foreign languages, including some of the Far East ones.

MUSIC. GERMANY is a fine long-meter tune found in a book, *Sacred Melodies,* in which the compiler, William Gardiner, 1770-1853, an English stocking manufacturer interested in music, collected compositions by the best foreign composers, adapting them to English words. The tune is also known by the name "Walton," especially in England. As to its origin, Gardiner says in his book, *Music and Friends,* that it "is somewhere in the works of Beethoven, but where I cannot now point out." This may be a mistake, for no one else has ever found it in a Beethoven collection.

223. O Master, let me walk with Thee

Washington Gladden, 1836-1918

A greatly loved service hymn which the author entitled, "Walking with God." In a note dated June 15, 1907, Gladden says:

This hymn was written in 1879 for a magazine, *Sunday Afternoon,* which I was then editing. There were three eight-line stanzas. Dr. Charles H. Richards found the poem, which was not intended for a hymn, and made a hymn of it by omitting the second stanza, which was not suitable for devotional purposes.

138

The omitted stanza reads as follows:

> O Master, let me walk with Thee
> Before the taunting Pharisee;
> Help me to bear the sting of spite,
> The hate of men who hide thy light,
> The sore distrust of souls sincere
> Who cannot read thy judgments clear,
> The dullness of the multitude
> Who dimly guess that thou art good.

Washington Gladden, distinguished Congregational minister and author, was reared on a farm near Oswego, N. Y., attending country school and Oswego Academy and later entering Williams College, from which he graduated in 1859. He was licensed to preach in 1860; then held pastorates in Congregational churches in New York and Massachusetts, and finally in 1882 began his widely known and influential work as pastor of the First Congregational Church in Columbus, Ohio, which was to last for 28 years. His lectures and writings on social questions were prophetic messages of the time. After 50 years in the ministry, he wrote: "If the church would dare to preach and practice the things which Jesus Christ has commanded, she would soon regain her lost power," He is the author of thirty or more volumes but is remembered best by this poem which has come into such wide use in the worship services of all the churches.

MUSIC. MARYTON was written for the words, "Sun of my soul, Thou Savior dear," in *Church Hymns and Tunes,* 1874; but it has become inseparably associated with Gladden's hymn. Permission to use this hymn was granted by the author only on condition that it be used with this tune.

The composer, Henry Percy Smith, 1825-98, was a minister in the Church of England, deeply interested in church music. After graduating from Balliol College, Oxford, he served various churches as curate and vicar and finally became chaplain at Cannes and Canon of Gibraltar.

224. O Thou great Friend to all the sons of men
Theodore Parker, 1810-60

Based on the Scriptural passages, John 15:14: "Ye are my friends if ye do the things which I command you" and John 14:6: "I am the way, the truth, and the life."

The author, Rev. Theodore Parker, an outstanding abolitionist and a leader in New England Unitarianism, was educated at Harvard and spent most of his ministry in Boston. While travelling abroad in the hope of restoring his health, he became ill and died at Florence, Italy, where he was buried.

MUSIC. FFIGYSBREN. For comments on this tune see Hymn 183.

225. Onward, Christian soldiers *S. Baring-Gould, 1834-1924*

A hymn of the Christian warfare, written by a Church of England clergyman for a children's processional, but now having a much wider use. The author gave the following account of the writing of the hymn:

> Whitmonday is a great day for school festivals in Yorkshire. One Whitmonday, thirty years ago, it was arranged that our school should join forces with a neighboring village. I wanted the children to sing when marching from one village to another; so I sat up at night, resolved that I would write something myself. "Onward, Christian soldiers" was the result. It was written in great haste, and I am afraid some of the rhymes are faulty. Certainly nothing has surprised me more than its popularity.

An omitted stanza reads:

> What the saints established,
>   That I hold for true;
> What the saints believed,
>   That believe I too.
> Long as earth endureth
>   Men that faith will hold,
> Kingdoms, nations, empires
>   In destruction rolled.

For comments on the author, S. Baring-Gould, see Hymn 29.

MUSIC. ST. GERTRUDE was written for these words by Sir Arthur Sullivan and dedicated to Mrs. Gertrude Clay-Ker-Seymer, in whose house the composer often stayed. The hymn derived a great part of its popularity from its use with this stirring tune.

For comments on Sullivan see Hymn 113.

226. Teach me, my God and King *George Herbert, 1593-1633*
Adapted by John Wesley

A hymn of consecration and heavenly-mindedness that marks the Christian life. Verses 2 and 4 are by John Wesley, and the third verse was altered by him. For comments on John Wesley see Hymn 170.

George Herbert, noted English poet and minister in the Church of England, was born in Wales; educated at Cambridge; and became a great pastor and preacher, serving, during his all too brief career,

140

churches at Layton Ecclesia in 1626, and at Bemerton from 1630 to his death in 1632. His spare moments were given to the cultivation of sacred music. His principal work is *The Temple,* a book of poems. His popularity was greatly increased through the publication of his *Life,* written by Isaak Walton.

MUSIC. MORNINGTON is an arrangement of a chant written about 1760 by the Earl of Mornington, whose name was Garret Wellesley (or Wesley), 1735-81. He was the father of the Duke of Wellington. The name was changed from Wesley to Wellesley about 1790. A composer of much secular and sacred music, he lived most of his life in Dublin, and was the first Professor of Music at Dublin University.

227. When thy heart with joy o'erflowing

Theodore C. Williams

A hymn setting forth the spirit of brotherhood in terms of sharing. Information regarding the author, Rev. Theodore C. Williams, has not been traced.

MUSIC. BULLINGER was written in 1874 by Ethelbert William Bullinger, 1837-1913, an English clergyman who made the study of music his avocation. He is remembered principally as the composer of this tune with its last phrase somewhat awkward due to the long, tied initial note.

228. Who is thy neighbor?

William Cutter, 1801-67

Based on the parable of the Good Samaritan. The hymn first appeared in *The Christian Mirror,* Portland, Me., 1838, in seven stanzas. One of the omitted stanzas reads:

> Thy neighbor? Yonder toiling slave,
> Fettered in thought and limb;
> Whose hopes are all beyond the grave,
> Go thou, and ransom him.

The author, William Cutter, was an editor and publisher, born at Yarmouth, Me., a graduate of Bowdoin College, and member of the Congregational Church. He was in business in Portland, Me., for several years and then in Brooklyn, N. Y. He has been described as "a deserving writer who has hitherto missed his due meed of acknowledgement."

MUSIC. BURFORD, a very good tune in triple time, written in the minor mode, is of uncertain authorship, though it is credited in some books to Henry Purcell, *c.* 1658-95, one of England's great composers and organists. It is set to Psalm 42 in *A Book of Psalmody,* 1718, by

141

John Chetham, and appears in a large number of other 18th century psalmodies, invariably without composer's name.

229. O brother man, fold to thy heart thy brother

John Greenleaf Whittier, 1807-92

A hymn of brotherly love and service, taken from a poem of 15 stanzas, entitled, "Worship," to which was affixed the scriptural reference, James 1:27: "Pure religion and undefiled before God the Father is this, To visit the fatherless and widows in their affliction, and to keep himself unspotted from the world." A concern for the well being of his fellow man was to Whittier a vital part of the Christian faith, as witness his championship of the cause of the slaves.

For comments on John Greenleaf Whittier see Hymn 173.

MUSIC. COMFORT. The tune appears anonymously in the "Supplement" to *Hymns of the Spirit,* 1937.

230. Rise up, O men of God   *William P. Merrill, 1867—*

A hymn challenging the *men* of the church to loyal service to Christ. It is widely used in America and has found a place in English and Canadian hymnals. Concerning the origin of the hymn, Dr. Merrill says, in a letter to the writer, dated, April 18, 1947:

> I was asked back in 1911 to write a hymn to be used in the "Brotherhood Movement," then going strong. I had come upon an article by Gerald Stanley Lee, entitled, "The Church of the Strong Men"; and that gave me a start. I can give no interesting details as to how I wrote it; I just did it.
>
> Highchurchmen have objected to the hymn, because they have said that only God can make the church great. To that I have answered that if anyone can show me a single instance in history where God has made the church great without using MEN OF GOD to do it, I should be interested. No answer has ever come. I heard that hymn sung in Europe, in India, China, and Japan.

For comments on the author, William P. Merrill, see Hymn 183.

MUSIC. LEIGHTON was composed by Henry Wellington Greatorex, 1811-58, an Englishman by birth. Coming to the United States in 1839, he served as organist at Central Congregational Church, Hartford, Conn., in St. Paul's and Calvary Churches, New York City, and finally in an Episcopal Church at Charleston, S. C. He edited the *Greatorex Collection* of 1856 and did much to improve the standards of music used in the worship service. He composed a widely used setting for the "Gloria Patri" (606). Dr. Merrill's hymn has been set to various tunes, the one generally used and preferred by the author being "Festal Song," by William H. Walter.

231. Go, labor on; spend and be spent   *Horatius Bonar, 1809-89*

A hymn to encourage Christian workers. It was published in *Songs for the Wilderness*, 1843, under the title, "Labour for Christ." In *Hymns of Faith and Hope*, 1867, it was entitled, "The Useful Life."

Regarding the origin of the hymn, Rev. H. N. Bonar, son of the author wrote:

> It was probably in the year 1836 that my father first wrote a hymn not primarily intended for the young. To encourage his faithful fellow workers in his mission district, he wrote, to the tune of the "Old Hundredth," the now-familiar hymn, "Go, labour on."

For comments on Horatius Bonar see Hymn 129.

MUSIC. ERNAN was written for *Cantica Laudis*, 1850, one of the books which Mason published with the assistance of Geo. J. Webb. For comments on the composer, Lowell Mason, see Hymn 12.

THE INNER LIFE

232. O have you not heard of that beautiful stream
R. Torrey, Jr.

Based on Rev. 22:1, 17: "And he showed me a pure river of water of life, clear as crystal, proceeding out of the throne of God and of the Lamb."

"And the Spirit and the bride say, Come. And let him that heareth say, Come. And let him that is athirst come. And whosoever will, let him take the water of life freely."

It is reminiscent also of Ezek. 47:1-12, the vision of the healing stream of water flowing from the house of God to the Dead Sea, causing new life to flourish. "Everything shall live whither the river cometh." (v. 9).

An omitted stanza reads:

> With murmuring sound doth it wander along
>   Through fields of eternal green;
> Where songs of the blest, in their haven of rest
>   Float soft on the air serene.

The poem, with the present music, appeared in Asa Hull's, *The Casket*, published in Philadelphia, 1865, where it is credited to R. Torrey, Jr. To date, no information has come to light concerning the author. He lived a generation earlier than the well known preacher and teacher, R. A. Torrey. In 1868, the hymn was published, anony-

143

mously, in *Spiritual Harp,* Boston, a book of songs for congregational use dedicated by the authors to "the Spirtualists and Reformers of the world, love of truth and progress." Two years later, in 1870, the words and music appeared in England, in the *Sunday School Hymnary,* published by the National Sunday School Union in London.

The German version is a free translation made by Ernst Heinrich Gebhardt, 1832-99, a Methodist minister and evangelist, known in Germany, the place of his birth, as the father of German revivalistic and holiness songs. It is superior, in poetic quality and evangelistic appeal, to the English original.

Gebhardt was born in Ludwigsburg, Württemberg, July 12, 1832. He prepared to be an apothecary but later decided to go to Chile, South America, to live with relatives. After spending five years on a farm in Chile, he returned to Germany to visit his mother. A shipwreck on the return voyage resulted in a deep spiritual awakening. Arriving in Ludwigsburg, he accompanied his mother to the Sylvester service on New Year's night, 1859, in the Methodist Church, where he dedicated his life to Christian work. Having decided to become an evangelist, he attended the school for ministers in the Methodist Church at Bremen where his zeal and musical gifts were quickly recognized. He was appointed *Reiseprediger* and in this capacity served in Ludwigsburg (1860-62), Heilbronn (1862-66), Pforzheim (1866-68), Bremen (1868-71), Ludwigsburg (1871-74), Zurich (1874-77), Strassburg i. E. (1877-81), Biel, Kt. Bern (1880-84), Zwickau (1884-88) and finally in Karlsruhe (1888-99). Gebhardt was married and had a family of nine children.

His activities included a trip to the United States, 1881-83, during which he travelled through 30 States. In Brighton, England, he took part in holiness meetings held there, and later travelled with R. Pearsall Smith, of Philadelphia, through Germany and Switzerland, serving as song leader in the evangelistic meetings conducted by Smith.

Gebhardt is the author of many original hymns and made over 50 translations from the English, most of them from the Moody and Sankey songs. He compiled numerous song books where his works appeared. "Ich weiss einen Strom" was published in his *Frohe Botschaft,* 1875, a popular book of gospel songs drawn mostly from English sources, both words and music. The third stanza, omitted here, reads:

> Der Strom ist gar tief und sein Wasser ist klar,
> Es schmecket so lieblich und fein;
> Es heilet die Kranken und stärkt wunderbar,
> Ja, machet die Unreinsten rein!

MUSIC. ICH WEISS EINEN STROM, originally entitled, "Beautiful Stream," and written in 6/8 time, first appeared in *Casket of Sunday*

School Melodies, 1865, published by the composer, Asa Hull, in Philadelphia. The tune is wedded inseparably to Torrey's words. It is very popular among General Conference of Mennonites churches where it is usually sung in the slow tempo and dignity of a chorale. Neither the words nor the music, with its refrain, have the characteristics of a chorale. It is a useful song, especially for evangelistic services.

Asa Hull was born January 18, 1828, in Keene, N. Y. He studied harmony and composition with B. F. Baker and Geo. J. Webb in Boston, and at the age of 20 became organist and choirmaster at Watertown, Mass. He composed many church tunes. Hull, a pioneer publisher of Sunday school and gospel song books, was also known as a shrewd business man. His publications numbered 30 books and about 100 pamphlets. *Gem of Gems,* published in 1881, sold over 300,000 copies. On the fly leaf of his *Casket of Sunday School Melodies* is found this advertisement:

> Asa Hull, Philadelphia agent for the Hallett and Cumston Piano Fortes, will keep a variety of styles and exhibits at his store, which he will sell at lower prices for cash than any other first class instrument can be bought in the city. 240 S. Eleventh Street, Philadelphia, Pa.

233. O holy Savior, Friend unseen   *Charlotte Elliott,* 1789-1871

A hymn which is best understood by those who have had experience in suffering and sorrow. Entitled, "Clinging to Christ," it was written in 1834, shortly after the death of the author's father and published in the 1834 edition of her *Invalid's Hymn Book.*

Charlotte Elliott, a member of the Church of England, was born and reared amid refined, cultured, Christian surroundings. Her grandfather, Rev. Henry Venn, was an "eminent Church of England divine of apostolic character and labors," and the author of *The Whole Duty of Man.* Charlotte was a woman of keen intellect and was gifted in music and art. Unfortunately, she became an invalid at 32 and remained so till the end of her long life, oftentimes enduring great suffering. This may account for the note of tenderness found in all her hymns. In spite of her invalidism, she did a large amount of literary work, publishing four or five volumes of poetry. She was a modest woman, publishing all her books anonymously. A large number of her 150 hymns are still in use, the most popular being "Just as I am, without one plea" (458).

MUSIC. INTEGER VITAE (FLEMMING). For comments on this tune see Hymn 59.

234. Thou true Vine, that heals the nations   *T.S.N.*

Based on John 15:1-5: "I am the true vine, and my Father is the husbandman. Every branch in me that beareth not fruit he taketh away: and every branch that beareth fruit, he purgeth it, that it may bring forth more fruit. Now are ye clean through the work which I have spoken unto you. Abide in me, and I in you. As the branch cannot bear fruit of itself, except it abide in the vine; no more can ye, except ye abide in me. I am the vine, ye are the branches; He that abideth in me and I in him, the same bringeth forth much fruit: for without me ye can do nothing."

The hymn was composed for *Songs of Praise,* 1933, London. The author is not identified except by the initials T.S.N.

MUSIC. PLEADING SAVIOUR, a folk-song type of tune, is from the *Plymouth Collection of Hymns and Tunes,* New York, 1855, which Henry Ward Beecher compiled for use in the Plymouth Congregational Church, Brooklyn, of which he was pastor. The musical editors were John Zundel (178) and the Rev. Charles Beecher.

235. God of my heart   *Anonymous*

A hymn celebrating the believer's life in God. It was taken from *St. Basil's Hymnal* compiled by the Basilian Fathers, published in 1918. The musical editors were Healey Willan and Jules Brazil. The authorship of the hymn is anonymous.

MUSIC. CARMEN NATURAE is an arrangement from a melody in Donizetti's opera, *Carmen.*

Gaetano Donizetti, 1797-1848, son of an Italian weaver, studied music in Naples. He composed 66 operas, 6 masses, 12 string quartets, a requiem, songs, and other compositions.

236. Since Jesus is my Friend   *Paul Gerhardt,* 1607-76
                                           Tr. by Catherine Winkworth, 1829-78

A hymn of consolation and joy to give strength and courage to troubled hearts. It is based on Romans 8:31: "If God be for us, who can be against us?" The original has 15 stanzas. The lines translated here are as follows:

> Hab ich das Haupt zum Freunde
> Und bin geliebt bei Gott,
> Was kann mir tun der Feinde
> Und Widersacher Rott'?

> Sein Geist spricht meinem Geiste
> Manch süsses Trostwort zu,
> Wie Gott dem Hülfe leiste
> Der bei ihm suchet Ruh.

146

Mein Herze geht in Sprüngen
Und kann nicht traurig sein,
Ist voller Freud' und Singen,
Sieht lauter Sonnenschein.

Die Sonne, die mir lachet
Ist mein Herr Jesus Christ,
Das, was mich singen machet,
Ist, was im Himmel ist.

For comments on the author, Paul Gerhardt, see Hymn 134.

The translation by Miss Winkworth appeared in her *Lyra Germanica,* first series, 1855.

Catherine Winkworth, an English poet, was the foremost translator of German chorales. She made a special study of the German hymns and hymn writers and is the author of *Lyra Germanica,* 1st. ser., 1855; 2d. ser., 1858; *The Chorale Book for England,* 1863; and *Christian Singers of Germany,* 1869. Twenty-five of her works are found in the *Hymnary.* She was a member of the Church of England.

MUSIC. GREENWOOD was composed for the hymn beginning, "We lift our hearts to Thee," in a *Collection of Church Music,* 1849, by Root and Sweetser.

The composer, Joseph Emerson Sweetser, 1825-73, was an English organist and composer of vocal music. A part of his life was spent in New York City as organist at the Church of the Puritans.

237. O heart of God! *F. Stanfield*

A hymn of confidence and trust resulting from the mystical repose in the heart of God.

The words and tune are found in *St. Basil's Hymnal,* compiled by the Basilican Fathers, and published in Chicago, 1918.

The author, Francis Stanfield, a Roman Catholic priest, was born in London, November 5, 1836, the son of Clarkson Stanfield, an artist. He was educated at St. Edmund's College, near Ware. After ordination, he spent most of his time conducting missions and retreats, though he was stationed for brief periods in several parishes. He is the author of numerous hymns which were collected and published by the Benedictine Fathers, at Ramsgate, England. The present hymn is an adaptation, made by the editors of the *Hymnary,* of his "O Sacred Heart, our home lies deep in Thee." The original is too Catholic for Protestant use.

No information is at hand concerning the composer of the tune.

238. Life of all that lives below *Charles Wesley, 1707-88*
Samuel Longfellow, 1819-92

This hymn, a prayer for a fuller life nurtured by Christ, the living Bread, is of composite authorship, but no information is at hand concerning the part which Wesley and Longfellow, respectively, had in it. It is not listed in Julian's *Dictionary of Hymnology.*
For comments on Charles Wesley see Hymn 6.
For comments on Longfellow see Hymn 28.

MUSIC. PLEYEL is taken from the *Andante* movement of the composer's *Fourth String Quartet, Op. 7.* It appeared as a long-meter tune in *Arnold and Callcott's Psalms,* 1791, set to Addison's hymn, "The spacious firmament on high."
Ignace Josef Pleyel, 1757-1831, 24th child of an Austrian schoolmaster, was a favorite pupil of Haydn and gained fame as a composer and conductor. Mozart spoke highly of his quartets. Later in life he engaged in business, publishing and selling music, and manufacturing pianos of high quality. The manufacturing house of Pleyel and Company is still well and favorably known in Europe.

239. There is a place of quiet rest *Cleland B. McAfee, 1866-1944*

The heart of the message of this popular devotional hymn, according to a statement made by the author to the present writer, is in the second stanza, "There is a place of comfort sweet, near to the heart of God." Cleland B. McAfee was a distinguished preacher, author, and teacher in the Presbyterian Church. He was accustomed to write an original hymn for the communion service in his church. It was in 1901, during his pastorate in Chicago, that a great sorrow came into his life occasioned by the death of his nephew. The communion was to be held the following Sunday and the members of the congregation came to the church tense with speculation about the service and the kind of hymn their pastor had composed for the day. These simple words and tune were offered them and seemed to fit the occasion perfectly. Since then the hymn has been translated into many languages and gone all over the world. It was not included in the new *Presbyterian Hymnal,* 1933, because the words and music were considered to be more of the nature of a gospel song than a hymn.
Cleland M. McAfee received his education at Park College and Union Theological Seminary, New York. From 1888 to 1901, he was pastor and professor at Park College; pastor of the First Presbyterian Church, Chicago, 1901-04; and of the Lafayette Avenue Presbyterian Church, Brooklyn, 1904-12. He later was connected with McCormick Theological Seminary in Chicago, first as Professor of Systematic Theology and then as president of the institution. He is the author of sev-

eral books on religious subjects, and also wrote extensively on foreign missions, a subject in which he had a keen interest.

COURAGE AND COMFORT

240. Come unto Me, ye weary
William C. Dix, 1837-98

Based on some of the precious promises of Christ, especially Matt. 11:28: "Come unto me, all ye that labor and are heavy-laden and I will give you rest." It may be compared with Bonar's hymn, "I heard the voice of Jesus say" (142) on the same text.

The author gives the story of the hymn as follows:

> I was ill and depressed at the time, and it was almost to idle away the hours that I wrote the hymn. I had been ill for many weeks, and felt weary and faint, and the hymn really expresses the languidness of body from which I was suffering at the time. Soon after its composition I recovered, and I always look back to that hymn as the turning point in my illness.

For comments on the author, William Chatterdon Dix, see Hymn 78.

MUSIC. ICH WEISS AN WEN ICH GLAUBE is taken from the *Gesangbuch mit Noten* (206) where it is used with a hymn by Ernst Moritz Arndt, beginning with these words.

241. When in the madd'ning maze of things
John Greenleaf Whittier, 1807-92

Preëminently an experienced person's meditation on trust in God. The hymn is taken from a poem of 22 stanzas entitled, "The Eternal Goodness," written apparently without any thought of their being sung. In the first line the editors substituted the initial word "when" for the original "yet."

For comments on John Greenleaf Whittier see Hymn 173.

MUSIC. ES IST EIN BORN. For comments on this tune see Hymn 99.

242. Thy way is in the deep, O Lord James Martineau, 1805-1900

Based on Psalm 77:19: "Thy way is in the sea, and thy path in the great waters."

James Martineau, English Unitarian, was a man of letters, a philosopher, a theologian, and the most eloquent and distinguished preacher of his church in his time. He served churches in Liverpool and London and was Professor of Mental and Moral Philosophy in Manchester New College. He edited *Hymns for the Christian Church and Home*, 1840, a book widely used among Unitarians in England.

MUSIC. GRÄFENBERG, sung somewhat slowly, is a tune of fine stateliness and dignity. It is from the 5th edition of Crüger's *Praxis Pietatis Melica,* Berlin, 1653. It is also known as *"Nun Danket All."*

Johann Crüger, 1598-1662, one of the most distinguished musicians of his time, was born near Brandenburg. He received a thorough musical training under Paulus Homberger in Regensburg and in 1622 he was appointed cantor of the St. Nicholas Lutheran Church, in Berlin, and one of the masters of the Greyfriars Gymnasium. He founded the noted choir of St. Nicholas Church. Crüger was a tune-writer of the first rank and composed some of the most famous and favorite chorales. He published various collections of hymns, among them the celebrated *Praxis Pietas Melica,* 1644, which passed through more than fifty editions. He died in Berlin, February 23, 1662.

243. Come, ye disconsolate

Thomas Moore, 1779-1852
Thomas Hastings, v. 3

A hymn of consolation by an author whose life was far from exemplary. It may be the hymn should on this account have been omitted; but something in his heart enabled the author, through his lyrics, to touch the heart of humanity, and his songs have been widely used and admired in spite of the strange chapters and romantic incidents in his life.

Thomas Moore, Irish poet, was born in Dublin, studied at Trinity College, and then moved to London and began the study of law. He held a government position in Bermuda for some time and during his life published many volumes of prose and poetry. He will always be remembered by his songs, "Believe me if all those endearing young charms," "The last rose of summer," and "Oft in the stilly night."

The third stanza is by Thomas Hastings, coeditor with Lowell Mason of *Spiritual Songs for Social Worship,* in which the hymn first appeared. Moore's third stanza, omitted in all hymn books, reads:

> Go ask the infidel what boon he brings us,
> What charm for aching hearts he can reveal,
> Sweet as that heavenly promise Hope sings us—
> Earth has no sorrow that God cannot heal.

It is a good stanza, but, then, good hymns do not argue.

For comments on Thomas Hastings see Hymn 120.

MUSIC. CONSOLATOR, also known as "Consolation," "Webbe," "Alma" or "Alma Redemptor," is an adaptation of a tune by Samuel Webbe.

For comments on Samuel Webbe see Hymn 22.

244. I look to Thee in every need   *Samuel Longfellow*, 1819-92

A hymn, much-needed, to express the effect of religious faith and trust upon mental and bodily health. The idea, so essential to the Gospel, has been too largely neglected in most Protestant Churches. The hymn is representative of the fine literary and devotional quality of the author's poetry. Though an American hymn, it was introduced into the church's worship in England before it was used in this country.

For comments on Samuel Longfellow see Hymn 28.

MUSIC. O JESU appeared in *J. B. Reimanns Org. v. Hirschb. alter und neuer Melodien Evangel. Lieder,* etc., 1747, where it was set to the hymn, *"O Jesu, warum legst du mir."* In the original, the first and last notes of each line were half-notes. It is a tune "of a simple, familiar pattern but with a certain quiet dignity."

The composer, Johann Balthaser Reimann, 1702-47, was a German cantor and organist in churches in Neustadt, Breslau, and Hirschberg, Schleswig.

245. My God and Father, while I stray

Charlotte Elliott, 1789-1871

A hymn written by one who had disciplined herself to accept with patience and resignation the bitter cross of ill health which was laid upon her.

She writes of her experience:

> Oh, many struggles and apparently fruitless ones it has cost me to become resigned to the appointments of my Heavenly Father. But the struggle is now over. He knows, and he alone, what it is, day after day, hour after hour, to fight against bodily feelings of almost overpowering weakness, languor, and exhaustion; to resolve not to yield to slothfulness, depression, and instability, such as the body causes me to long to indulge, but to rise every morning determined to take for my motto: "If any man will come after Me, let him deny himself, take up his cross daily and follow Me."

The hymn is based on Matt. 26:42: "O my Father, if this cup may not pass away from me, except I drink it, thy will be done." It is a hymn of humble resignation. Another hymn, setting forth the will of God as demanding active co-operation, is found at No. 342. Some fine stanzas have been omitted here:

> Though Thou hast called me to resign
> What most I prized, it ne'er was mine;
> I have but yielded what was Thine—
>   "Thy will be done."

151

Should grief or sickness waste away
My life in premature decay,
My Father, still I strive to say,
"Thy will be done."

Let but my fainting heart be blest
With Thy sweet Spirit for its Guest;
My God, to Thee I leave the rest—
"Thy will be done."

For comments on Charlotte Elliott see Hymn 233.

MUSIC. HANFORD was written for "Jesus, my Saviour, look on me," another of Miss Elliott's hymns. The composer, who often stayed in the home of Mrs. Gertrude Clay-Ker-Seymer at Hanford, in Dorsetshire, wrote the tune there, hence its name.

For comments on the composer, Arthur Sullivan, see Hymn 113.

246. Give to the winds thy fears
Paul Gerhardt, 1607-76
Tr. by John Wesley, 1703-91

A hymn of comfort to the afflicted and courage to the dying. It is a part of Paul Gerhardt's poem, *"Befiehl du deine Wege"* (558). These are stanzas 9, 10, 12, 13, unaltered, of Wesley's translation, which contains 16 four-line stanzas. Gerhardt passed through the agonies of the Thirty Years' War, and suffered, in addition, the loss of his wife and four children. He gives expression in this hymn to his own deep feelings of trust and assurance. His words have helped many anxious souls maintain faith in God who "sitteth on the throne, and ruleth all things well."

For comments on Paul Gerhardt see Hymn 134.

For comments on John Wesley, who translated the hymn, see No. 170.

MUSIC. STATE STREET is a popular tune, scarcely any hymn book missing it, but it is not wedded to any single hymn. The composer, J. C. Woodman, 1813-94, born at Newbury, Mass., became one of Lowell Mason's assistants in introducing music into the public schools of Boston. He was one of the first soloists of the Boston Academy of Music and served for a time as organist of the First Presbyterian Church of Brooklyn. In 1858, Woodman compiled *The Musical Casket,* which contained many of his songs, sacred and secular. "State Street" is the last tune in the book, set to Watts' lyric, "Blessed are the sons of peace."

247. Day by day the manna fell
Josiah Conder, 1789-1855

A hymn of confidence that God will supply daily strength for daily needs, based on Exodus 16:12-21 and the petition in the Lord's Prayer, "Give us this day our daily bread."

The hymn suggests a Jewish story quoted by W. F. Tillett in *The Hymns and Hymn Writers of the Church:*

> The pupils of Rabbi Ben Jochai once asked him with regard to the manna sent to the Israelite host in the wilderness: "Why did not the Lord furnish enough manna to Israel for a year all at one time?" "I will answer you with a parable," responded the teacher. "Once there was a king who had a son to whom he gave a yearly allowance, paying him the entire sum on a fixed day. It soon happened that the day on which the allowance was due was the only day in the year when the father ever saw the son. So the king changed his plan and gave his son day by day that which sufficed for the day. And now the son visited his father every morning. Thus God dealt with Israel."

The author, Josiah Conder, born in London, was an editor and publisher. His friends included a large number of eminent literary and church men of the early 19th century. He was a member of the Congregationalist Church. A devout and earnest believer who knew what it was to struggle for daily bread, he had the occasion to practice the gospel of daily trust. He wrote many hymns, published more than a dozen scholarly books, and edited *The Congregational Hymn Book* in 1836, a work which attained wide popularity in England.

MUSIC. SEYMOUR. For comments on this tune see Hymn No. 36.

248. One thought I have, my ample creed

Frederick L. Hosmer, 1840-1929

Several of Hosmer's hymns express his "thought of God," this being one of the finest. It relates all of life and its needs to the thought of God.

For comments on Frederick L. Hosmer see Hymn 72.

MUSIC. PRAETORIUS is from *Harmoniae Hymnorum Scholae Gorlicensis,* Görlitz, 1599. It is supposed to have been written by M. Praetorius, for it appeared in his *Musae Sionae,* Pt. VI, 1609, and hence its name.

Michael Praetorius, 1571-1621, was born in Kreuzburg, Thuringia. He was educated at the University of Frankfurt-an-der-Oder and became Kapellmeister at Lüneburg. Praetorius was a prolific composer, but his fame rests chiefly on a four-volume work on musical theory entitled, *Syntagma musicum.*

249. Father, to Thee we look in all our sorrow

Frederick L. Hosmer, 1840-1929

A hymn of comfort written in 1881 on the death of a member of the author's congregation. The hymn was published in Hosmer's *Thought of God,* 1st series, 1885. The last lines are particularly striking:

> "Yet shalt thou praise Him when these darkened furrows,
> Where now He ploweth, wave with golden grain."

MUSIC. STRENGTH AND STAY. For comments on J. B. Dykes, the composer of this tune, see Hymn 1.

250. My Jesus, as Thou wilt

Benjamin Schmolck, 1672-1737
Tr. Jane Borthwick, 1813-97

Based on Mark 14:36: "Abba, Father, all things are possible unto Thee; take away this cup from me: nevertheless not what I will, but what thou wilt." The hymn was originally published in eleven stanzas in his *Heilige Flammen,* 1704. We give here five stanzas of the original, our hymn being the usual selection of 1, 3, and 5.

Mein Jesu, wie du willt,
  So lass mich allzeit wollen;
Wenn Trübsal, Angst und Leid
  Mich hier betreffen sollen,
So gib, dass allezeit
  Dein Wille werd' erfüllt,
Ich leb' und sterbe dir;
  Mein Jesu, wie du willt!

Mein Jesu, wie du willt!
  Soll ich in Armut leben,
So mach hingegen du
  Die Seele reich, daneben
Gib, dass dein Wort mir nur
  Den Hunger allzeit stillt,
Und nimm sonst alles hin:
  Mein Jesu, wie du willt!

Mein Jesu, wie du willt!
  Soll ich in Tränen schwimmen,
So lass mein Fünklein Trost
  Nicht ganz und gar verglimmen.
Hast du doch selbst geweint;
  Drum, wenn's nicht anders gilt,
So wein' ich auch mit dir.
  Mein Jesu, wie du willt!

Mein Jesu, wie du willt!
  Soll ich denn endlich sterben,
Ich weiss, du lässt mich auch
  Im Sterben nicht verderben,
Wenn meine Seele sich
  In deine Wunden hüllt;
Drum soll's gestorben sein,
  Mein Jesu, wie du willt!

Mein Jesu, wie du willt!
  So bin ich auch zufrieden;
Hast du mir Lieb' und Leid,
  Not oder Tod beschieden,
So nehm' ich's auf dein Wort,
  Dein Wille werd' erfüllt.
Drum sag' ich noch einmal:
  Mein Jesu, wie du willt!

Schmolck was known all over Germany for his many hymns and

spiritual songs. A number of them have been translated into English. This one reflects his fervent love for Christ and bears a message of trust and comfort which grew out of his own exhausting labors and physical suffering.

For further comments on Benjamin Schmolck see Hymn 505.

The translation is by Jane Borthwick in her *Hymns from the Land of Luther,* 1854. For comments on Jane Borthwick see Hymn 54.

MUSIC. JEWETT is from a melody in Weber's opera *Der Freuschütz.* The present arrangement was made by Joseph Holbrook, in 1862. The tune has become associated almost exclusively with this hymn in America.

Joseph Holbrook, 1822-88, born near Boston, was a tune writer of the school of Mason, Hastings, and Bradbury. He compiled several hymn books and was musical editor of *Songs of the Sanctuary,* a popular Methodist book under the editorship of the eminent hymnologist, Charles S. Robinson.

251. Father, whate'er of earthly bliss   *Anne Steele,* 1716-78

Based on I Tim. 6:6-8: "But godliness with contentment is great gain. For we brought nothing into this world, and it is certain we can carry nothing out. And having food and raiment let us be therewith content."

Anne Steele was the first woman writer of English hymns. Her father was a timber merchant who for 30 years was deacon and occasional preacher in the Baptist Church in Hampshire, England, and then for 30 years more he was pastor, without salary, of the same church. On the day before Miss Steele was to be married, at the age of 21, her fiance met accidental death through drowning. Out of this bitter experience in her early life and a succession of other trials, came this lyric of resignation and hope. The original has 10 stanzas, the last three of which have been edited by Augustus Toplady to make this her best hymn. Miss Steele is the foremost of Baptist hymn writers.

MUSIC. NAOMI, a tune brought to America by Lowell Mason, was set to this hymn in his *Modern Psalmist,* 1839. It at once gained popularity and was included in many hymn books.

For comments on the composer, Hans Nägeli, see Hymn 41.

252. Thy way, not mine, O Lord   *Horatius Bonar,* 1808-89

An admirable hymn of submission, faith, and love, based on Matt. 26: 39: "Not as I will, but as Thou wilt."

It was published in 7 stanzas in the author's *Hymns of Faith and*

Hope, 1st series, 1857 under the title, "Thy way, not Mine."
The omitted stanza (No. 6) reads:

Choose Thou for me my friends,	Choose Thou my cares for me,
My sickness or my health:	My poverty or my wealth.

For comments on Horatius Bonar see Hymn 129.

MUSIC. O LEIDE, LEIDE GERN is from the *Gesangbuch mit Noten,*
where it appears anonymously set to the words, "O leide, leide, gern!
Es ist der Will' des Herrn."

253. Lord, it belongs not to my care   *Richard Baxter,* 1615-91

A hymn of love, trust, and hope, based on Phil. 1:21: "For me to
live is Christ, and to die is gain."

Richard Baxter, English Presbyterian, was born in Shropshire, England. He took holy orders in the Church of England, but withdrew
from this church to become one of the outstanding Nonconformists of
his time. Though he never attended university, he published over 250
volumes, among them several classics, *The Reformed Pastor* and *The
Saints' Everlasting Rest.* A fearless man and willing to suffer for what
he believed to be right, Baxter did not hesitate to rebuke Cromwell for
his assumption of supreme power of the State. Once, when falsely
charged of libeling the Church, Chief Justice George Jeffreys taunted
him by, "Richard, I see the rogue in thy face." Baxter replied, "I had
not known before that my face was a mirror." After an infamous trial,
Baxter was condemned and thrown into prison where he remained for
18 months.

As to music in the church, he did not share the views of the large
number of his fellow Puritan clergymen who disapproved of it. "I
have made a psalm of praise in the holy assembly the chief delightful ex-
ercise of my religion and my life, and have helped to bear down all the
objection which I have heard against church music." He also took a
stand for the use of original hymns to supplement psalm singing, and
favored the use of the organ, though he did not introduce the latter
where it led to disputes.

MUSIC. EVAN. For comments on this tune and its composer, William
H. Havergal, see Hymn 153.

254. Holy Father, cheer our way   *Richard H. Robinson,* 1842-92

Based on Zech. 14:7: "But it shall come to pass, at evening time it
shall be light." The hymn was written in 1869 for the author's congregation, to be sung at evening prayer. It appeared in *Church Hymns,*
1871, published by the Society for Propagating Christian Knowledge,
London.

Richard Hayes Robinson, a clergyman of the Church of England, was born in London. He was educated at King's College, London, and served as minister in various churches. On the day of his second wedding, he was taken ill on the train and died the next day. He published several volumes of sermons.

MUSIC. MÜDE BIN ICH, GEH ZUR RUH is a well-known German melody in the *Gesangbuch mit Noten,* where it appears anonymously, set to Louise Hensel's hymn from which the tune derives its name. The melody, in slightly different form, appeared in 1842 in *Lieder-Buch für Kleinkinder-Schulen . . . . con Theodor Fliedner.* It is used in the *Methodist Hymnal* (1935) set to the words, "Jesus, tender Shepherd, hear."

255. O Lord, how happy should we be   *Joseph Anstice, 1808-36*

Based on I Peter 5:7: "Casting all your care upon Him; for He careth for you," and on the Scripture lesson in Matthew 6:24-34. The original poem was in five stanzas. The hymn was written out of experiences of sickness, pain, and trial.

Joseph Anstice, a friend of Gladstone during student days at Oxford, was appointed Professor of Classical Literature at King's College, London, at the age of 22. Within three years his health failed, and he died at the age of 28, whereupon Gladstone, who had been deeply influenced by him at Oxford, wrote in his *Diary,* "Read to my deep sorrow of Anstice's death on Monday. His friends, his young widow, the world can spare him ill." This and 53 other hymns were dictated to his wife in the afternoons during his last illness.

MUSIC. MERIBAH. For comments on the composer, Lowell Mason, see Hymn 12.

256. Peace, perfect peace   *Edward H. Bickersteth, 1825-1906*

This hymn on perfect peace is based on Isaiah 26:3: "Thou wilt keep him in perfect peace whose mind is stayed on Thee: because he trusteth in Thee."

The origin of the hymn was furnished Dr. Julian by Rev. S. Bickersteth, a son of the author:

> This hymn was written by Bishop Edward Henry Bickersteth while he was spending his summer holiday in Harrogate in the year 1875. On a Sunday morning in August the Vicar of Harrogate, Canon Gibbon, happened to preach from the text, "Thou wilt keep him in perfect peace, whose mind is stayed on thee," and alluded to the fact that in the Hebrew the words are "peace, peace," twice repeated and happily rendered in the

1611 translations by the phrase "perfect peace." This sermon set my father's mind working on the subject. He always found it easiest to express in verse whatever subject was uppermost in his mind, so that when on the afternoon of that Sunday he visited an aged and dying relative, Archdeacon Hill, of Liverpool, and found him somewhat troubled in mind, it was natural to him to express in verse the spiritual comfort which he desired to convey. Taking up a sheet of paper, he then and there wrote down the hymn just exactly as it now stands and read it to this dying Christian.

It is not always noticed that the first line in each verse is in the form of a question referring to some one or other of the disturbing experiences of life, and the second line in each verse endeavors to give the answer. . . . The hymn has been translated into many tongues, and for years I doubt if my father went many days without receiving from different people assurances of the comfort which the words had been allowed to bring to them. The most touching occasion on which, personally, I ever heard it sung was round the grave of my eldest brother, Bishop Edward Bickersteth, of South Tokyo, at Chiselden in 1897, when my father himself was chief mourner.

MUSIC. PAX TECUM was written for this hymn by George Thomas Caldbeck, 1852-?, concerning whose life one reads contradictory statements. Some writers say he was a missionary in China when he wrote this tune; others, including James Moffatt, give the account essentially as follows: that Caldbeck, while a student in London, was compelled through ill health to give up his purpose of becoming a missionary, went to Ireland to teach school and engage in independent missionary work. Later he returned to London where he did much open-air preaching, making a meagre living by selling Scripture text-cards from door to door. For selling without a license, he was arrested one day but dismissed by the judge on being informed that the defendant was the composer of this well-known hymn tune.

The tune was arranged by Charles John Vincent, born 1852, English organist, composer and editor of much church music.

257. God is the refuge of His saints   *Isaac Watts, 1674-1748*

Based on Psalm 46:1-5: "God is our refuge and our strength; a very present help in time of trouble," etc., and was entitled by Watts, "The Church's Safety and Triumph." It is interesting to compare this free rendering of the Psalm with that of the *Scotch Psalter*, 1650, (588), where the thought of the psalm and the stately King James version combine to make up the greatest metrical form of the psalm. Martin Luther's version of the same Psalm is found in his great hymn *"Ein feste Burg ist unser Gott"* (549).

For comments on Isaac Watts see Hymn 11.

MUSIC. WARRINGTON was composed by Ralph Harrison, 1748-1810, an Englishman and son of a Presbyterian minister. Educated at Warrington Academy, he became a noted teacher of ancient languages, but maintained a keen interest in sacred music. He compiled *Sacred Harmony,* 2 vols., 1784-1791, a collection of psalm tunes, ancient and modern, in which were found some of his own compositions, including this tune.

258. Awake, our souls! away, our fears   *Isaac Watts, 1674-1748*

A free rendering of Isaiah 40:28-31.

The hymn is from Watts' *Hymns and Spiritual Songs,* 1707, where it is headed, "The Christian Race."

For comments on Isaac Watts see Hymn 11.

MUSIC. SAMSON. This tune is an adaptation, a very considerable one, from Chorus 31: "Then round about the starry throne," in Handel's oratorio, *Samson.* The tune is taken from various parts of the chorus.

For comments on Handel see Hymn 70.

259. There is no sorrow, Lord, too light   *Jane Crewdson, 1809-63*

Another of the "songs in the night," written by one who, like Charlotte Elliott (See 245), was an invalid the greater part of her life and suffered much pain.

Jane Fox was born in Cornwall, England. In 1836 she married Thomas D. Crewdson, a Manchester manufacturer. Always delicate, she became a confirmed invalid, but her sufferings served to deepen her spiritual life. She was a woman of fine intellectual power and poetic gifts and through her writings testified gloriously to the all-sufficiency of her Savior's love. Her attitude toward her suffering is well expressed in the beautiful third verse of the hymn:

> There is no secret sigh we breathe
> But meets Thine ear divine:
> And every cross grows light beneath
> The shadow, Lord, of thine.

This was the favorite hymn of Dr. John Henry Jowett, at one time minister of the Fifth Avenue Presbyterian Church, New York City.

MUSIC. COOLING first appeared in *The American Choir,* 1858. No information has been obtained concerning the composer, Alonzo Judson Abbey, 1825-87.

260. Hark, hark, my soul! angelic songs are swelling

Frederick W. Faber, 1814-63

A lovely song of the journey of life—the Christian's pilgrimage to heaven, the heart's true home. "The Pilgrims of the Night" was the title given this hymn by its author, F. W. Faber, the warm-hearted Roman Catholic hymn writer. The phrases of the poem are wrapped in mystery and loveliness. Their meaning is not always clear but the rhythm and musical ring of the hymn are effective and its popularity is genuine and wide-spread.

For comments on F. W. Faber see Hymn 44.

MUSIC. PILGRIMS was written for this hymn for the appendix to the original edition of *Hymns Ancient and Modern.*

For comments on the composer, Henry Smart, see Hymn 46.

261. Forever, with the Lord!   *James Montgomery, 1771-1854*

From Montgomery's poem of twenty-two 4-line stanzas, in two parts, published in the *Amethyst,* 1835. It is based on I Thess. 4:17: "Then we which are alive and remain shall be caught up together with them in the clouds, to meet the Lord in the air: and so shall we ever be with the Lord." Canon Farrar once said, "I can scarcely ever join in singing 'Forever with the Lord' without tears."

The hymn voices the aspirations of multitudes of Christians. In time of sorrow and death it points to the life beyond as the true goal of all our earthly striving.

For comments on James Montgomery see Hymn 62.

MUSIC. NEARER HOME, also called "Montgomery," was composed for this hymn and was published in *The Choral Advocate,* 1852. The composer, Isaac Baker Woodbury, 1819-58, was an American singer, teacher of music, composer of hymn tunes and sacred songs, and editor of *Musical Review.* His career was cut short by his death at the early age of thirty-nine.

262. Jerusalem the golden   *Bernard of Cluny, 12th century*
Tr. John M. Neale, 1818-66

"And the city was pure gold" Rev. 21:21.

This hymn is from a Latin manuscript of 3,000 lines entitled *"De Contemptu Mundi"* (On Contempt of the World), written by Bernard of Cluny while he was a monk at the famous monastery of Cluny, France, *c.* 1145. Practically nothing is known of him except his authorship of this poem. Two other hymns, "Brief life is here our portion," and "For thee, O dear, dear country," not in the *Hymnary*, are taken from the same poem. The original was not written as a hymn at all but as a "bitter satire on the fearful corruption of the age," especially of the Church of Rome, in contrast to which the author paints the joys of the new Jerusalem. The author employed throughout the unusually difficult meter known as "dactylic hexameter with tailed rhymes," of which Bernard himself says: "Unless the Spirit of wisdom and understanding had flowed in upon me, I could not have put together so long a work in so difficult a meter." The reading of the Latin stanzas best reveal the rhythm and music of the original:

1. Urbs Sion aurea, patria lactea,
     Cive decora,
   Omne cor obruis, omnibus ob-
         struis
   Et cor et ora.

2. Nescio, nescio, quae iubilatio,
     Lux tibi qualis,
   Quam socialia gaudia, gloria
     Quam specialis.

3. Sunt Sion atria coniubilantia,
     Martyre plena,
   Cive micantia, principe stantia,
     Luce serena.

4. Sunt ibi pascua mentibus afflua
     Praestita sanctis;
   Regis ibi thronus, agminis et
         sonus
     Est epulantis.

5. Gens duce splendida, contio candida
     Vestibus albis,
   Sunt sine fletibus in Sion aedibus,
     Aedibus almis. Amen.

For comments on the translator, John M. Neale, see Hymn 67.

MUSIC. EWING, composed for "For thee, O dear, dear country" (see above), was originally in triple time and named, "St. Bedes." In *Hymns Ancient and Modern,* 1861, it was set to the present words and the tune changed to common time without the consent of the composer. Ewing disliked the change and expressed himself thus: "In my opinion the alteration of the rhythm has very much vulgarized my little tune. It now seems to be a good deal like a polka. I hate to hear it." In spite of the composer's opinion, the tune is generally accepted in its revised form and considered preferable to the original.

Alexander Ewing, 1830-95, of Aberdeen, Scotland, was a skilled musician. One evening after choir practice, he modestly introduced what he called his first effort at writing a hymn tune, offering copies of the voice parts, and asking the choir to sing it over. This was done, the choir liked it, and the tune EWING was launched on its long and popular career.

161

263. Jerusalem the golden

Bernard of Cluny, 12th century
Tr. John M. Neale, 1818-66

For comments on this hymn see No. 262.

MUSIC. URBS BEATA (The City Beautiful) was composed in 1887 for these words. The composer found words for the refrain by repeating lines 1, 6, 7, and 8 of the first stanza. It makes a first-rate choir number. To keep up the proper tempo it should be sung with two beats to the measure. When the tune is used for congregational singing, the high notes in the refrain are intended to be sung by the sopranos in the choir.

The composer, George LeJeune, 1842-1904, was the son of a well-known musical family in London. He began his musical career in Canada; later he studied with Joseph Barnby. His great work was done as church organist and organ recitalist at St. John's Chapel of Trinity Parish, New York City, where he served 28 years.

264. One sweetly solemn thought

Phoebe Cary, 1824-71

A poem in contemplation of heaven, written in 1852, entitled, "Nearer Home," with no thought of its being used as a hymn. In fact its original irregular rhythm hardly permitted it to be sung. The words have been changed to fit the short-meter tune, and have become popular as a hymn. Upon reading the story of how the hymn was instrumental in the conversion of two gamblers in China, who, after betting and drinking and card playing, decided upon a change of life and consecrated themselves to Christian work, Miss Cary wrote to a friend:

> I enclose the hymn and story for you, not because I am vain of the notice, but because I thought you would feel a peculiar interest in them when you knew the hymn was written eighteen years ago (1852) in your house. I composed it in the little, back, third-story bedroom on Sunday morning after coming from church, and it makes me happy to think that any word I could say has done a little good in the world.

Phoebe Cary was born on a farm near Cincinnati, Ohio. Her early days were a struggle with hardship and poverty. "I have cried in the street because I was poor," she wrote in her later and more prosperous years, "and the poor always seem nearer to me than the rich." With her sister Alice Carey, she published a small volume of verse in 1849, then the two moved to New York City where they became quiet but influential leaders in literary society. Their friendship with Whittier was a noted factor in the lives of the Carey sisters. Phoebe was a member of the Church of the Pilgrims in New York, and later attended the Church of the Stranger in the same city.

MUSIC. DULCE DOMUM is an arrangement from the composer's popular song, "One sweetly solemn song," later published as an anthem.

Robert Steele Ambrose, 1824-1908, born in England, came with his parents to Canada in his first year. He prepared himself for the musical profession and became organist successively in churches in Guelph, Kingston, and Hamilton, Ontario. He is known best by the above-mentioned song.

265. Sunset and evening star   *Alfred Tennyson, 1809-92*

A song of immortality, written in ten minutes in the author's eighty-first year. It is always printed at the end of Tennyson's poems. Tennyson once said: "I can hardly understand how any great, imaginative man, who has lived, suffered, thought and wrought, can doubt of the soul's continuous progress in the after life."

The poem was written on an October day in 1869, as the poet was crossing from Aldworth to Farringford. Tennyson's son wrote in his *Memoir* of his father, concerning its origin:

> Before he reached Farringford he had the moaning of the bar in his mind, and after dinner he showed me this poem written out. I said: "That is the crown of your life's work." He answered: "It came in a moment." He explained the "Pilot" as "that Divine and Unseen who is always guiding us." A few days before my father's death, in 1892, he said to me: "Mind you put 'Crossing the Bar,' at the end of all editions of my poems." My father considered Edmund Lushington's translation into Greek of "Crossing the Bar" one of the finest translations he had ever read.

MUSIC. CROSSING THE BAR was composed for these words. The tune, in the nature of an unaccompanied quartet anthem, may be sung with freedom in regard to time and shading.

For comments on the composer, Joseph Barnby, see Hymn 21.

266. Blest be the everlasting God   *Isaac Watts, 1674-1748*

A paraphrase of I Peter 1:3-5.

The original by Watts was published in his *Hymns and Spiritual Songs*, 1707, from which it was taken over unchanged into the *Scottish Paraphrases* of 1745 and of 1751. In the final 1781 edition, the third stanza was omitted and the fourth altered from

> There's an inheritance divine
> Reserved against that day;
> 'Tis incorrupted, undefiled,
> And cannot waste away.

The improvements are attributed to William Cameron, 1751-1811, who, as a young licentiate, was entrusted with the final revision of the *Scottish Paraphrases.*

For comments on Isaac Watts see Hymn 11.

MUSIC. st. stephen (abridge) is described by Archibald Jacob as a "beautifully fluent and graceful melody. . . . in the best 18th-century style of this class of tune." It appeared originally in *A Collection of Psalm Tunes in Three Parts. . . .* by Isaac Smith, *c.* 1770, under the name abridge, by which it continues to be known in England. In *Sacred Harmony for Use in St. George's,* Edinburgh, 1820, it appeared under the name st. stephen, with slight modification of the last line.

Isaac Smith, *c.* 1725-*c.* 1800, was a London linen-draper with a taste for music. He composed and published a number of Psalm-tunes which long remained popular, though abridge is almost the only one now left of his compositions. Smith named his tunes after localities in and about London. abridge was the name of a small village near Epping Forest, in Essex.

THE KINGDOM OF GOD

267. Forward through the ages   *Frederick L. Hosmer,* 1840-1929

A hymn expressing the unity of God's people in their labor for the Kingdom through the ages. "The goodly fellowship of the prophets" is set forth here with power and poetic beauty.

For comments on Frederick L. Hosmer see Hymn 72.

MUSIC. onward, with its strong rhythm and moving power, lends itself well for processional use, resembling in this respect the tune "St. Gertrude" (225), for which the present hymn was written.

No information is at hand concerning the composer, J. W. Barrington.

268. Thy Kingdom come, on bended knee
Frederick L. Hosmer, 1840-1929

One of the few hymns written on the petition, "Thy Kingdom come," in the Lord's Prayer. Canon Percy Dearmer speaks of this as "one of the noblest hymns in the language." It is a fervent prayer for the day when there shall be more justice, knowledge, peace, and righteousness on the earth.

The hymn was written June 21, 1891, for the commencement of the Meadville Theological School, Pennsylvania.

For comments on Frederick L. Hosmer see Hymn 72.

MUSIC. irish, also called "Dublin," appeared first in *Hymns and*

Sacred Poems, published in Dublin in 1749. The composer is not known. It is a smooth, triple-time tune which young people love to sing. Its name is misleading, for there is no indication of an Irish origin other than, as stated, its appearance in a book published in Dublin.

269. Come, Kingdom of our God   *John Johns, 1801-47*

A prayer for the coming of the Kingdom of God on earth, based on the petition in the Lord's Prayer, "Thy Kingdom come, thy will be done."

Rev. John Johns, English Presbyterian minister, was known for many years in Liverpool as the "minister to the poor." He was a man of fine poetic gifts and published several volumes of poetry but is remembered for his life of service among the poor.

MUSIC. st. thomas is one of the oldest and best tunes of the church. It has good rhythm, graceful form, and a strong forward movement to give it unusual singing merit.

The composer, Aaron Williams, of Welsh descent, was born in London in 1731, and died there in 1776. He was composer, engineer, publisher, music teacher, and clerk of the Scotch Church, London Wall. He published a number of important collections of tunes: *The Universal Psalmodist,* 1763, and *New Universal Psalmodist,* 1770, in which the above tune appeared.

270. Thy Kingdom come, O Lord   *Frederick L. Hosmer, 1840-1929*

Another hymn on the petition, "Thy Kingdom come," in the Lord's Prayer, setting forth its coming in relation to the unity of nations. Compare Hosmer's other hymn on the Kingdom (268) where the emphasis is on righteousness and justice. This is an appropriate hymn for use in gatherings concerned with Christian unity and world friendship.

For comments on Frederick L. Hosmer see Hymn 72.

MUSIC. invitation. For comments on the composer of this tune see Hymn 112.

271. Thy Kingdom come, O God   *Lewis Hensley, 1824-1905*

Another of the few hymns that have been written on the petition in the Lord's Prayer, "Thy Kingdom come." See Hymns 268, 269, 270.

Lewis Hensley had a distinguished career at Trinity College, Cambridge, England, as student and then six years as fellow and tutor. He became a minister in the Church of England and for a time was Rural Dean.

MUSIC. ST. CECILIA was composed for Dr. Bonar's hymn, "Thy way, not mine, O Lord" (252), appearing with these words in *The Merton Tune Book,* Oxford, 1863.

The composer, Rev. Leighton George Hayne, 1836-83, was educated at Oxford, took holy orders in 1861, was appointed conductor of the chorus of the University and public examiner in the School of Music, and then served for a time as organist of Eton College. The last 12 years of his life were spent as minister in various churches. He wrote many hymn tunes and edited, with Rev. H. W. Sargeant, *The Merton Tune Book.*

272. Before Jehovah's awful throne   *Isaac Watts, 1674-1748*

A paraphrase of Psalm 100, revised by John Wesley.
The original text by Watts began:

> Sing to the Lord with joyful voice
> Let every land his name adore;
> The British Isles shall sound the noise
> Across the ocean to the shore.

Wesley, considering this an unpromising initial stanza, omitted it, and changed the second stanza, lines 1 and 2, from

> Nations attend before his throne
> With solemn fear, with sacred joy

to

> ·Before Jehovah's awful throne
> Ye nations bow with sacred joy.

Wesley severely condemned the practice of changing another's hymns, but in this case his own "transgression" resulted in a greatly improved hymn.

The word "awful" in the first line is spelled "awe-full" in some hymnals in order to convey more nearly its original meaning.

For comments on Isaac Watts, see Hymn 11.

MUSIC. PARK STREET was composed by Frederick M. A. Venua, 1788-1872, an eminent French organist, a native of Paris. It is a favorite tune in America where it is invariably associated with this hymn by Watts.

THE CHURCH

273. The Church's one foundation   *Samuel J. Stone, 1839-1900*

A truly great hymn, honoring the church of Christ and longing for its prosperity. The author, then a young curate of 27 years in the

Church of England, was so stirred by the attacks made on the church in his time that he determined to write a series of twelve hymns on the Apostles' Creed. This one is based on the article, "I believe in the holy Catholic Church, the communion of saints." The controversy which then raged in England concerning the nature of the inspiration of the Scriptures is reflected in the third stanza, the author leaning strongly on the conservative side.

Samuel J. Stone was a clergyman of the Church of England, born in Staffordshire, and educated at Oxford. He served various churches, finally succeeding his father at St. Paul's, Haggerston, London. For twenty years he had a fruitful ministry in this East End parish among the poor and depraved, before moving to another part of the city to another church. He is the author of many hymns and translations and published several volumes of poetry.

MUSIC. AURELIA (signifying "golden") one of our most stately tunes, combining ease of singing with churchly dignity, was written for the hymn, "Jerusalem the golden" (262). It was set to the present hymn in *Hymns Ancient and Modern* and did much to carry the hymn into the churches. It has become one of the great processional hymns of the church.

Samuel Sebastian Wesley, 1810-76, grandson of Charles Wesley, was like his father, Samuel Wesley, a great English composer and organist. He had a consuming love of the outdoors, as well as of music, and was passionately fond of fishing. He was outspoken in his demands for reform in the music of the church and was, consequently, frequently at odds with his superiors. Wesley received inadequate recognition for the contributions he made to the music of his time.

274. Glorious things of thee are spoken *John Newton,* 1725-1807

Based on Psalm 87:3: "Glorious things are spoken of thee, O city of God," and other passages, especially Isaiah 33:20, 21, and Exodus 13:22.

It is one of our best hymns on the Church and, says Julian, "It ranks with the first hymns in the language." In ordinary use the omission of the third stanza is desirable. Augustine Smith suggests in *Lyric Religion* that "the last score should always be repeated, the second time sung broader and fuller, building into a superb climax."

John Newton is remembered among the hymn writers because of the radical change that took place in his life at conversion. Born in London, his only schooling was from his eighth to his tenth year. He went to sea at eleven, his godly mother following the profligate youth with her prayers. As a midshipman in the navy he deserted his post, was captured, and reduced to a common seaman, and later became a servant of a slave dealer in Africa. He was converted at 23 after an awful night steering a water-logged ship in the face of death. Though converted, he retained certain blind spots in his social outlook and he continued as a slave dealer. This hymn was written when he was on a voyage from Sierra Leone, Africa, with a load of slaves shackled closely together and being taken to London or America to be sold. "I have never had such sweet communion with Jesus as I had on that voyage," he wrote. This may seem like hypocrisy, but it must be remembered that slavery was a common practice and that only a few people of the time understood clearly its complete denial of the spirit of Christ. It may be that future generations will see in our times evils that flourished unchallenged while we prayed and sang according to the light we had. In 1750, Newton married Mary Catlett, a noble and pious woman, and a godsend in his life. In 1755, he settled down as customs officer in Liverpool, becoming at the same time greatly interested in Wesley and Whitefield and other evangelical leaders. Three years later he became a minister in the Church of England, and in 1764, he began a distinguished career as curate at Olney, where he was associated with his friend, William Cowper, the poet. The two were joint authors of the *Olney Hymns,* 1779. After sixteen years in Olney, he moved to London where for 28 years he did faithful and successful work as rector of St. Mary Woolnoth. He wrote his own epitaph which is found on a plain marble tablet near the vestry door of his church in London:

John Newton, Clerk
Once an Infidel and Libertine,
A servant of slaves in Africa,
Was, by the rich mercy of our Lord and Saviour
Jesus Christ
Preserved, restored, and pardoned,
And appointed to preach the Faith
He had long labored to destroy,
Near 16 years at Olney in Bucks
And . . . years in this church
On Feb. 1, 1750, he married
Mary,
Daughter of the late George Catlett
Of Catham, Kent.
He resigned her to the Lord who gave her
On 15th of December, 1790

MUSIC. AUSTRIAN HYMN is founded on a Croatian melody. It was used in Germany as the tune of "Deutschland über alles." Joseph Haydn, 1732-1809, made a setting of it to be sung at the Emperor's birthday, Feb. 12, 1797, to the words, "Gott erhalte Franz der Kaiser."

The tune was a great favorite of Haydn and he used it as a theme in one of the movements in his famous *"Emperor Quartet,"* No. 76.

For comments on Franz Joseph Haydn, see Hymn 27.

275. I love Thy Kingdom, Lord   *Timothy Dwight*, 1752-1817

Based on Psalm 137:5, 6: "If I forget thee, O Jerusalem, let my right hand forget her cunning. If I do not remember thee, let my tongue cleave to the roof of my mouth; if I prefer not Jerusalem above my chief joy." It is rated high among all the hymns on the church and is probably the earliest American hymn in use today.

Timothy Dwight, the great president of Yale, was the grandson of Jonathan Edwards and shared in a large measure the intellectual brilliance of the Edwards family. A precocious youth, he entered Yale College at 13 and graduated at 17. An oustanding personality of his time, he was honored for his sound scholarship, elected a member of the Massachusetts legislature, and served as minister of the Congregational Church at Greenfield, Conn. From 1795 until his death in 1817, he was President of Yale, simultaneously holding the Chair of Theology. His presence at Yale changed the whole moral and religious attitude of the campus, there having been only four or five professed Christians at the college, according to Prof. W. W. Sweet, when he became president. At the request of the General Association of Congregational Churches in Connecticut and with the concurrence of the Presbyterian General Assembly, he revised *The Psalms of David*, by I. Watts, a work which was used in the Presbyterian and Congregational Churches of Connecticut for over 30 years.

Dwight did a prodigious amount of work in spite of a serious physical handicap. His eyesight, for the greater part of forty years, was so poor that his reading was done only with the greatest of difficulty and with frequent and agonizing pain behind the eyeballs.

MUSIC. STATE STREET. For comments on this tune see Hymn 246.

276. O where are kings and empires now

Arthur C. Coxe, 1818-96

From a larger poem by Coxe, entitled "Chelsea," containing ten stanzas of eight lines each. It is a hymn of confidence that the church, built on a solid foundation, will survive all earthly kings and empires and will be able to withstand every earthly foe.

Arthur Cleveland Coxe was born at Clifton Springs, N. Y.; graduated from the University of New York and General Theological Seminary; and then became the rector successively of St. John's Church, Hartford, Conn.; Grace Church, Baltimore; and Calvary Church, New

York City. In 1865, he was elected Bishop of Western New York. He was a member of the Hymnal Commission for the Protestant Episcopal Church, which compiled the *Hymnal* of 1872, but refused, out of modesty, permission to include in that work any of his own hymns.

MUSIC. ST. ANNE. For comments on this tune see Hymn 61.

277. Christ is made the sure foundation

Latin, 6th or 7th century
Tr. John M. Neale, 1818-66

From Part II of an ancient Latin hymn of the 6th or 7th century beginning: *"Urbs beata Hierusalem."* The author is not known. The first verse reflects Ephesians 2:20-21: "And are built upon the foundation of the apostles and prophets, Jesus Christ himself being the chief cornerstone; in whom all the building fitly framed together groweth unto an holy temple in the Lord."

The hymn is often used at the dedication of churches, stanzas 3 and 4 being especially appropriate for that purpose.

Dr. Neale's translation of the hymn, in nine stanzas, appeared in his *Medieval Hymns,* 1851. Our hymn is a selection of stanzas 5, 6, 7, and 8, of his translation, with some changes in the words. The Latin of our first three stanzas is as follows:

> Angularis fundamentum
>   lapis Christus missus est
> Qui conpage parietis
>   in utroque nectitur,
> Quem Sion sancta suscepit,
>   In quo credens permanet.
>
> Hoc in templo, summe Deus,
>   exoratus adveni,
> Et clementi bonitate
>   precum vota suscipe;
> Largam benedictionem
>   hic infunde iugiter.
>
> Hic promereantur omnes
>   petita adquirere
> Et adepta possidere
>   cum sanctis perenniter,
> Paradisum introire,
>   translati in requiem.

For comments on John M. Neale see Hymn 67.

MUSIC. REGENT SQUARE. For comments on this tune see Hymn 81.

278. Lord of our life, and God of our salvation

Philip Pusey, 1799-1855
Based on Matthäus von Löwenstern, 1594-1648

One of the "songs of the night," the original of which was written out of the bitter experiences of the Thirty Years' War in Germany. It tells of the peril to which the Reformed Church was then exposed but expresses confidence that the church, founded upon the Rock, will prevail against evil.

Matthäus Apelles von Löwenstern, son of a saddler, had musical and business ability which won him recognition and employment by the Duke of Münsterberg and the Emperors Ferdinand II and his son Ferdinand III. He wrote about 30 hymns and set them to melodies of his own composition. His hymn, named "Sapphic Ode. For Spiritual and Temporal Peace," in 1644, is as follows:

Christe, du Beistand deiner Kreuzgemeine,
Eile, mit Hilf' und Rettung uns erscheine;
Steure den Feinden, ihre Blutgerichte
Mache zunichte!

Streite doch selber für uns arme Kinder,
Wehre dem Teufel, seine Macht verhinder';
Alles, was kämpfet wider deine Glieder,
Stürze danieder!

Frieden bei Kirch' und Schulen uns beschere,
Frieden zugleich der Obrigkeit gewähre,
Frieden dem Herzen, Frieden dem Gewissen
Gib zu geniessen!

Also wird zeitlich deine Güt' erhoben,
Also wird ewig und ohn' Ende loben
Dich, o du Wächter deiner armen Herde,
Himmel und Erde.

The English version by Pusey is not a translation of the German but rather a free paraphrase. Philip Pusey, brother of Edward Pusey, the famous leader in the Oxford Movement, was educated at Oxford. After graduating he settled on his estate and devoted himself largely to agriculture. He wrote extensively on agricultural subjects and was one of the founders of the Royal Agriculture Society. Later he became a member of Parliament. He wrote this hymn to portray the state of the Church of England at the time, which he described as being "assailed from without, enfeebled and detracted from within, but on the eve of a great awakening."

MUSIC. INTEGER VITAE. For comments on this tune see Hymn 59.

279. Dear Shepherd of Thy people   *John Newton, 1725-1807*

A hymn composed for a prayer meeting.

John Newton and William Cowper, the English poet, instituted prayer meetings at Olney where the two labored together in a famous ministry, Newton as minister of the church, and Cowper as his voluntary assistant. The prayer meetings were attended in such large numbers that it became necessary to move the services into a large room. For the first meeting in this new room, each of the men prepared a special hymn, the one by Newton being our hymn, with his first, third, and seventh stanzas omitted.

For further comments on John Newton see Hymn 274.

MUSIC. DURHAM appeared in *Ravenscroft's Psalter,* 1621, set to Psalms 28 and 76, and marked as a "Northern Tune." The *Scottish Psalter* of 1635 includes it among the Common Tunes.

280. Again, as evening's shadow falls
Samuel Longfellow, 1819-92

"Vesper Hymn" is the title which this hymn bears in the author's volume, *Vespers,* 1859, a small book of songs prepared for use in evening services. In a letter dated Feb. 11, 1890, Longfellow wrote, "My two favorites among my hymns are the vesper hymn, 'Again, as evening's shadow falls,' and the one beginning, 'I look to Thee in every need'" (244).

For comments on Samuel Longfellow see Hymn 28.

MUSIC. GERMANY. For comments on this tune see Hymn 222.

281. We love the place, O God   *William Bullock, 1798-1874*
Henry W. Baker, 1821-77

Based on Psalm 26:8: "Lord, I have loved the habitation of thy house, and the place where thine honor dwelleth." The hymn was written by William Bullock, then a young sailor-missionary, for the dedication of a mission chapel at Trinity Bay, Newfoundland, in 1827. Seventy years later, when a new church located on the same site was dedicated, this hymn as revised by H. W. Baker, was once more sung. The sermon preached by Bullock at the opening of the chapel was read to the people.

Wm. Bullock was educated at Christ's Hospital and then entered the

Royal Navy. While on a survey of the coast of Newfoundland, he decided to devote himself to missionary work in that colony. He did this and served 32 years under the Society for Propagating the Gospel. He became Dean of Nova Scotia at Halifax. In 1854, he published *Songs of the Church* which, he said, were "written amid the various scenes of missionary life, and are intended for the private and domestic use of Christians in new countries deprived of all public worship."

For comments on Henry W. Baker, reviser of the hymn see Hymn 143.

MUSIC. QUAM DILECTA was composed for this hymn in *Hymns Ancient and Modern,* 1861.

The composer, Henry L. Jenner, 1820-98, was a curate in the Anglican Church. After serving various churches in England, he was consecrated first Bishop of Dunedin, New Zealand, 1866. He was one of the Cambridge group which revived interest in ecclesiology, ancient hymnology, plainsong, etc.

282. Unto Thy temple, Lord, we come   *Robert Collyer,* 1823-1912

A hymn describing the church as the home of "rich and poor, bond and free, great and small." It is suitable for the general worship service and especially for the dedication of a church.

Information concerning the author, Robert Collyer, has not been traced. *Julian's Dictionary* notes a William Collyer, 1782-1854, eminent English evangelical preacher who was ordained for a small church of ten communicant members. He is described as a man of "amiable disposition, polished manners, Christian courtesy, and popular with rich and poor alike; who labored in the church with great success and honor until his death." He wrote numerous hymns. Was our hymn written by a son brought up with his father's noble conception of the church?

MUSIC. MENDON. For comments on this tune see Hymn 211.

THE LORD'S DAY

283. The dawn of God's dear Sabbath   *Ada Cross,* 1844-?

A hymn on the Sabbath, picturing the day as a time when weary souls may turn from daily toil to refresh themselves with the water of life drawn from the wells of salvation.

Ada Cross was born in England, November 21, 1844, the daughter of Henry Cambridge. She married an Australian, the Rev. George F. Cross, and spent most of her life in Australia where her husband was minister of the Anglican Church in Coleraine, Victoria. She was in-

173

terested in the liturgy of the Church and issued several collections of hymns.

MUSIC. ENDSLEIGH is credited to Salvatore Ferretti, 1817-74, concerning whom no information has been traced. The arrangement was made by James Turle, 1802-82, an English teacher of music, a distinguished organist, and composer of hymn tunes, chants, and anthems. For sixty-three years he was connected with Westminster Abbey in London. He was endowed, it is said, with unusually large hands so that he could easily span an octave and a half with one hand. His sole musical interest was in serving the church.

284. Safely through another week   *John Newton, 1725-1807*

This hymn was composed by Newton for use on Saturday evening. To give it wider usefulness, the verses were slightly changed to make them suitable for the Sunday morning service.

For comments on John Newton see Hymn 274.

MUSIC. SABBATH was written for this hymn in 1824.

For comments on the composer, Lowell Mason, see Hymn 12.

285. O day of rest and gladness

Christopher Wordsworth, 1807-85

A hymn which serves to keep vividly before us the meaning and value of the Lord's Day. It appears as the opening hymn in the author's *The Holy Year,* 1862, where is is entitled "Sunday." It is based on Psalm 118:24: "This is the day which the Lord hath made; we will rejoice and be glad in it."

For comments on Christopher Wordsworth see Hymn 174.

MUSIC. MENDEBRAS was written for this hymn in 1839. It is an arrangement by Lowell Mason of a German folk song.

For comments on Lowell Mason see Hymn 12.

286. Again returns the day of holy rest   *William Mason, 1725-97*

The author of this Lord's Day hymn was the Rev. William Mason, an English Episcopalian, born at Kingston-on-Hull. He graduated with honors from St. John's College, Cambridge; received ordination, served as one of the chaplains of King George III, and at the time of death he had been for 32 years the Precentor and Canon of York. A man of high literary attainments, and a friend of Thomas Gray, he edited that poet's works in 1775 and later wrote the memoirs of Gray. The latter was done in the gossiping style, imitated later by Boswell when he wrote the *Life of Samuel Johnson.* Mason wrote four volumes of poetry and won recognition from Johnson as one of the British poets.

The present hymn, by which the author is best remembered, is found at the end of Volume I of the *Works of William Mason, M. A., Precentor of York and Rector of Aston,* 1811.

Our author is not to be confused with his contemporary of the same name, 1719-91, who succeeded Toplady in the editorship of *The Gospel Magazine* and who was also a minister and hymn writer.

MUSIC. ELLERS. For comments on this tune and its composer, Edward J. Hopkins, see Hymn 43.

287. This is the day of light · John Ellerton, 1826-93

A worshipful Sabbath day hymn, breathing the spirit of rest, light, and peace, written in 1867.

For comments on the author, John Ellerton, see Hymn 43.

MUSIC. FRANCONIA. For comments on this tune see Hymn 205.

288. Break Thou the bread of life Mary A. Lathbury, 1841-1913

This gem, entitled, "Study Song," was written for the Chautauqua Literary and Scientific Circle and for Bible Study groups, but it also has a wider use. Dr. G. Campbell Morgan used this hymn every Sunday for many years immediately before the sermon. It is not a communion hymn although it is often used for that purpose. The breaking of bread refers to the feeding of the multitude beside the Sea of Galilee and not to the Last Supper; and the "bread of life" is the teaching of Jesus.

For comments on Mary Lathbury see Hymn 31.

MUSIC. BREAD OF LIFE is a popular American tune, sincere and simple in style, written for this hymn and indissolubly associated with it.

For comments on the composer, William F. Sherwin, see Hymn 31.

THE HOLY SCRIPTURES

289. O Word of God Incarnate W. W. How, 1823-97

A hymn addressed to Christ, the Word of God Incarnate, setting forth in a succession of beautiful figures—a lantern, the golden casket, a banner, a beam, chart and compass—the value of the written word, and the duty of the Church to carry the light of God's word, both as incarnate and written, to the nations. It was written in 1867, headed by the text Prov. 6:23: "For the commandment is a lamp; and the law is light; and reproofs of instruction are the way of life." The author himself was a living witness to the power of the Word. His definition of a minister shows the high ideal he had of the preacher of the Word, and, incidentally, is an accurate description of his own life:

A man pure, holy, and spotless in his life; a man of much prayer; in character meek, lowly, and infinitely compassionate;

of tenderest love to all; full of sympathy for every pain and sorrow, and devoting his days and nights to lightening the burdens of humanity; utterly patient of insult and enmity; utterly fearless in speaking the truth and rebuking sin; ever ready to answer every call, to go wherever bidden in order to do good; wholly without thought of self; making himself the servant of all; patient, gentle, and untiring in dealing with the souls he would save; bearing with ignorance, wilfulness, slowness, cowardice in those of whom he expects most; sacrificing all, even life itself, if need be, to save some.

For further comments on W. W. How, see Hymn 144.

MUSIC. MUNICH, "one of the most beautiful and perfectly constructed of tunes," is of German origin and is known in Germany as "Königsberg Choral." It appeared first in *Lobsingende Harffe,* 1682. The composer is unknown. Mendelssohn used the tune as the basis for his fine chorale, "Cast thy burden on the Lord," in his oratorio, *Elijah.*

290. Thy Word is like a garden, Lord   *Edwin Hodder, 1837-1904*

The metaphors used in this hymn to describe the Word of God are very suggestive: "a garden," "a deep, deep mine," "a starry host."

Edwin Hodder was born in England but migrated at 19 years of age to New Zealand where he was one of a pioneer group of idealists who introduced progressive sociological ideas for which that country is noted. He returned to England where he was engaged in the civil service from 1861 until his retirement in 1897. Hodder wrote biographies and devotional works, and in 1863 issued *The New Sunday School Hymn Book* which contained twenty-seven of his own hymns, including this one.

MUSIC. FOREST GREEN is an arrangement of an English folk song called, "The Ploughboy's Dream." R. Vaughan Williams, 1872–, who arranged the tune is England's leading living composer. He has collected and edited for publication many folksongs and carols, written several symphonies for the orchestra, and has composed numerous choral works.

Some good hymnals use this tune as the setting for Phillips Brooks' popular Christmas carol, "O little town of Bethlehem."

291. The heavens declare Thy glory, Lord
Isaac Watts, 1674-1748

Here is an unusual rendering of Psalm 19, which Watts entitled, "The Books of Nature and of Scripture." In the Psalm itself we find the Book of Nature in the first half and the Book of Scripture in the second half of the psalm. Instead of following this order, Watts sets the one over in couplets against the other, so that the first two lines of each stanza have to do with nature, the last two with Scripture.

For comments on Isaac Watts, see Hymn 11.

MUSIC. UXBRIDGE. This tune is by the American composer and teacher of music, Lowell Mason. The psalm tune "Burford" (228) is also named "Uxbridge" in some books.

For comments on Mason see Hymn 12.

292. Lord, Thy word abideth   *Henry W. Baker, 1821-77*

A hymn on the Scriptures, written for *Hymns Ancient and Modern,* 1861.

For comments on Henry W. Baker see Hymn 143.

MUSIC. RAVENSHAW is from *Ein Neu Gesangbüchlein,* 1531, the earliest German hymn book of the Bohemian Brethren, edited by Michael Weisse. The melody is older and was associated with a Latin hymn, *Ave Hierarchia, coelestis et pia.* The present arrangement is by William H. Monk. For comments on Monk see Hymn 40.

For a note on the Bohemian Brethren and Michael Weisse see Hymn 544.

THE MINISTRY

293. Shine Thou upon us, Lord   *John Ellerton, 1826-93*

A hymn for teachers.
For comments on John Ellerton, see Hymn 42.

MUSIC. BROUGHTON. For comments on the composer of this melody, Thomas Hastings, see Hymn 120.

294. O still in accents sweet and strong
Samuel Longfellow, 1819-92

The author's title of this hymn is, "Behold the Fields are White." For comments on Samuel Longfellow see Hymn 28.

MUSIC. BELMONT. For comments on this tune see Hymn 197.

295. Pour out Thy Spirit from on high
James Montgomery, 1771-1854

Written in 1833 for the Rev. J. Birchell, clergyman in the Church of England, who published it in his *Selection of Hymns.* It was printed in the same year in Edward Bickersteth's *Christian Psalmody.* For comments on Bickersteth see Hymn 256. The hymn's original title was,

"For a Meeting of Clergy." It is not intended to be sung by a body of people as a prayer for ministers but as a prayer hymn to be sung by ministers themselves.

For comments on James Montgomery see Hymn 62.

MUSIC. MELCOMBE. For comments on this tune see Hymn 22.

296. Lord, speak to me, that I may speak

Frances R. Havergal, 1836-79

"A Worker's Prayer" is Miss Havergal's title of this hymn and the text associated with it is Rom. 14:7: "None of us liveth to himself and no one dieth to himself." It was composed April 28, 1872, at Winter-dyne.

For comments on Frances Havergal see Hymn 126.

MUSIC. CANONBURY, a favorite tune found in nearly all hymn books, is from Robert Schumann's *Nachtstücke*, Op. 23.

Robert Schumann, 1810-56, greatest of the early German Romantics, was born in Zwickau, Saxony. He wrote symphonies and chamber music but is known best for his amazingly fine piano works and songs. His wife, Clara Wieck Schumann, one of the greatest piano players the world has produced, was devoted to him, as were also his children. Schumann became mentally ill, attempted unsuccessfully to drown himself in the Rhine, and was cared for in a hospital for two years before his death. He had a gift for journalism and wrote books and magazine articles on music.

297. Thou who Thyself didst sanctify   George Rawson, 1807-89

An appropriate hymn for use in ordination to the Christian ministry or dedication to other forms of Christian service.

George Rawson, an English Congregational layman, was born at Leeds where he practiced law many years. He had a considerable knowledge of music and was a gifted hymn writer. He rendered valuable assistance to his own denomination as well as to the Baptists in the preparation of hymn books for use in the church. A shy, retiring man, of sincere piety, he at first published his hymns, a considerable collection, anonymously, but later had to acknowledge his identity. About 50 of his hymns are still in use.

(The name is misspelled "Dawson" in the Hymnary.)

MUSIC. DUNDEE (or FRENCH) is one of the twelve Common Tunes appearing in the *Scottish Psalter, The CL Psalms of David, &,* Edinburgh, 1615, where it is named "French Tune." Its first appearance in an English Psalter is in Ravencroft's *Whole Book of Psalms,* 1621, where it is called "Dundy." It is one of the best known of the psalm tunes

and its smooth, flowing melody has enjoyed great popularity.
For comments on the *Scottish Psalter* see Hymn 575.

CONSECRATION OF CHILDREN

298. Gracious Savior, gentle Shepherd

Jane Eliza Leeson, 1807-1882
John Keble, 1792-1866

A hymn for the children's consecration service, evolved by John
Keble from three hymns—"Shepherd in thy bosom, folded," "Loving
Shepherd of Thy sheep" (429), and "Infant sorrow, infant weakness,"
written by Jane Eliza Leeson. Keble took the main ideas of these
hymns and rewrote them into a hymn of five stanzas, two of which are
omitted here.

Jane Eliza Leeson was born in London and died there. She had
rare gifts in writing for children, and published several books of hymns
—*Infant Hymnings,* and *Hymns and Scenes of Childhood*—specially for
children. Very little is known of her life, except that she was a prominent figure in the Catholic Apostolic Church and that some of her
hymns were supposedly "prophetical utterances," prompted by the Holy
Spirit, at public services, which she "delivered slowly with short pauses
between the verses." Late in life she united with the Roman Catholic
Church.

For comments on John Keble, see Hymn 22.

MUSIC. MANNHEIM is from the source mentioned in the note on
Hymn 174. The present form of the melody is much altered from the
original.

299. All hidden lie the future ways

Frederick L. Hosmer, 1840-1929

A lyrical phrasing of the emotions that arise in the hearts of parents
as they contemplate the faring forth of little children into the hidden
future.

For comments on the author, Frederick L. Hosmer, see Hymn 72.

MUSIC. NUN SICH DER TAG GEENDET HAT is a tune set to various hymns
in the *Gesangbuch mit Noten.*

For comments on the composer, Aaron Williams, see Hymn 269.

300. A little child the Savior came   *William Robertson, 1820-64*

A Scotch Presbyterian minister, William Robertson, contributed this
hymn to the Church of Scotland's *Hymns for Public Worship* in 1861.
The author, keenly interested in hymnody and Scotch psalmody, was

a member of the Hymnal Committee of the Church of Scotland in 1851, 1853, and 1857.

MUSIC. ALSTONE was composed by C. E. Willing, 1830-1904, for the children's hymn, "We are but little children weak," in *Hymns Ancient and Modern,* Appendix, 1868. Willing was chorister of Westminster Abbey and held various responsible positions as organist and choral conductor in England.

BAPTISM

301. Come, Father, Son, and Holy Ghost

Charles Wesley, 1707-88

The original poem of six stanzas is from *Hymns and Sacred Poems,* 1749, where it was entitled, "At the Baptism of Adults."

Wesley's second line of the first stanza read

"Honor the means injoin'd by Thee,"

which was changed to "ordained by Thee" for the *Collection* of 1780. The awkward expression, "Effectuate now the sacred sign," Wesley's second line of stanza 3, was changed to "Effectual make the sacred sign," by the editors of the hymn book in 1849.

For comments on Charles Wesley see Hymn 6.

MUSIC. SO LANGE JESUS BLEIBT DER HERR is a familiar melody, of unknown origin, from the *Gesangbuch mit Noten.*

302. I'm not ashamed to own my Lord

Isaac Watts, 1674-1748

This hymn is based on II Timothy 1:8-12.

James Moffatt writes that when Henry Drummond was on his death bed, Nov. 7, 1897, his friend, Dr. Hugh Barbour, played several hymn tunes to him without gaining any response. Then he tried the Old Scots melody of "Martyrdom" to which Drummond beat time with his hand and joined in the words, "I'm not ashamed to own my Lord." When the hymn was done, he said, "There's nothing to beat that, Hugh."

For comments on Isaac Watts see Hymn 11.

MUSIC. DEDHAM. The tune is attributed to William Gardiner, 1770-1853, an Englishman of whom nothing much of importance is known except that he published *Sacred Melodies* in 1812, a collection of excellent tunes, which was expanded to six volumes published in 1815.

303. Here, O my Lord, I see Thee face to face

Horatius Bonar, 1808-89

Entitled by the author, "This Do in Remembrance of Me."

It is a famous communion hymn, emphasizing, in keeping with the Reformed tradition, the thought that Christ Himself presides at His Table. All His followers are therefore welcome.

Three members of the Bonar family became eminent ministers in the Free Church of Scotland (Presbyterian)—Andrew in Glasgow; John in Greenock; and Horatius in Edinburgh. Horatius was accustomed to visit his brother John once a year at the communion service. Hymns were still not permitted to be sung in the church, but an original poem was invariably read after the communion. This hymn was written by Horatius Bonar at the request of his brother John for the occasion of such a visit in October, 1855. It has become a widely used communion hymn in all churches.

For further comments on Horatius Bonar see Hymn 129.

MUSIC. LANGRAN, known in England as "St. Agnes," is named after the composer, James Langran, 1835-1909, London organist and composer, who wrote this music for "Abide with me" (40). It was published separately in 1861 and two years later appeared in *Psalms and Hymns adapted to the services of the Church of England, with accompanying tunes selected and revised by John Foster.*

The hymn is also sung to "Ellers" (See 43 or 286).

304. Bread of the world, in mercy broken

Reginald Heber, 1783-1826

"A quiet communion hymn full of loveliness and warm reality of faith."—Reeves.

This popular communion hymn by Bishop Heber was published posthumously with the title, "Before the Sacrifice."

For comments on Reginald Heber see Hymn 1.

MUSIC. EUCHARISTIC HYMN, a tune "beautiful in its simplicity," has always been associated with this hymn by Heber. The composer, John Sebastian Bach Hodges, 1830-1915, son of the illustrious organist, Edward Hodges, was born in Bristol, England, but came to America when eight years old. He received his education at Columbia University and General Theological Seminary, New York City, and became a noted minister in the Protestant Episcopal Church. He had excellent musical knowledge and founded in Baltimore the earliest choir school in the United States. He also did much work on the various revisions of the Episcopal hymnal.

305. According to Thy gracious word

James Montgomery, 1771-1854

One of the best-loved and most useful of communion hymns, profound, yet simple. It appeared first in Montgomery's *Christian Psalmist,* 1825, and has since passed into the hymn books of all denominations of evangelical Christians. The words of Luke 22:19 furnish the scriptural basis of the hymn: "This do in remembrance of me."

For comments on James Montgomery see Hymn 62.

MUSIC. ST. JOHN, more properly called "St. John's, Westminster," was composed by James Turle, 1802-82.

For comments on James Turle see Hymn 283.

306. Bread of the world, in mercy broken

Reginald Heber, 1783-1826

The *Church Hymnary,* London, 1927, has the following practical note at the bottom of the page where this hymn appears:

> As this hymn consists of one verse only, it is suggested that it be sung twice over: once by the choir alone, and again by choir and people in unison. It may also be used as a short motet for unaccompanied singing by the choir.

For further comments on this hymn see No. 304.

MUSIC. RENDEZ À DIEU was composed or adapted by L. Bourgeois for the *French Genevan Psalter,* where it was set to Psalm 118. In the *Scottish Psalter* of 1564, the tune was again used to John Craig's version of the same Psalm. It is described in *Songs of Praise Discussed* as being "in some ways the finest of all the early psalm tunes. . . . perfectly proportioned. . . . a tune which gives the true 'spinal thrill'; of its kind it is unsurpassed."

For comments on L. Bourgeois see Hymn 34.

307. Come, risen Lord, and deign to be our guest

George W. Briggs, 1875—

Based on the account of the supper at Emmaus, Luke 24:28-31:

> And they drew nigh unto the village, whither they went: and he made as though he would have gone further. But they constrained him saying, Abide with us: for it is toward evening, and the day is far spent. And he went in to tarry with them. And it came to pass, as he sat at meat with them, he took bread, and blessed it, and brake, and gave to them. And their eyes were opened, and they knew him; and he vanished out of their sight.

It stresses the doctrine that Christ Himself is the celebrant at the Lord's Supper.

George Wallace Briggs is a Cambridge scholar, an outstanding preacher, educator, writer, and editor in the Anglican church. He has composed a number of hymns (See 570) and hymn tunes.

MUSIC. BIRMINGHAM is from F. Cunningham's *A Selection of Psalm Tunes,* 2d ed., 1834, where it is set to the words, "Come, gracious Spirit, heavenly dove." Cunningham published an earlier collection of psalm tunes in 1826.

308. I hunger and I thirst
John S. B. Monsell, 1811-75

A simple, tender, communion hymn which ought to have a wider use.

John Samuel Bewley Monsell was educated at Trinity College, Dublin; labored for a number of years in the church in Ireland; and then became vicar of Egham in the Diocese of Worcester, England, and finally rector of St. Nicholas, Guildford. His home life at Guildford is described as having been "full of the beauty of holiness, with genial brightness and gaity playing like sunshine over all the troubles of life." His life came to a tragic end when he fell from the roof of the church while it was being rebuilt. He composed about 300 hymns and is the author of many other poetic works.

MUSIC. MAINZ (MARIA JUNG UND ZART) originally appeared in a Catholic book, *Ausserlesene Catholische, Geistliche Kirchengesänge von Pfingsten, biss zum Advent,* Cologne, 1632. It was slightly changed and printed in its present form in *Psalteriolum Harmonicum Sacrarum Cantilenarum,* 1642.

309. Author of life divine
Charles Wesley, 1707-88

This fine communion hymn is from *Hymns on the Lord's Supper,* 1745, by John and Charles Wesley. It is attributed in many hymnals to Charles, but there is no conclusive evidence to show which of the two brothers wrote it. The thought of the hymn is said to be in full accord with John's teaching concerning the Holy Communion.

For comments on Charles Wesley see Hymn 6.

MUSIC. WESLEY. The original source of this tune has not been traced. In the *English Hymnal* it is set to the words, "Behold a little child." The tune should not be confused with Lowell Mason's of the same name (See 332).

183

310. By Christ redeemed, in Christ restored

George Rawson, 1807-89

Written in 1857 and published first in a Baptist book, *Psalms and Hymns,* 1858.

Julian comments: "It is a hymn of more than usual excellence and has attained to a greater position in modern hymnals than any other of the author's numerous compositions."

The refrain, "Until He come," is reminiscent of I Cor. 11:26: "For as oft as ye eat this bread and drink this cup, ye do shew forth the Lord's death, till he come."

For comments on George Rawson see Hymn 297.

MUSIC. IN MEMORIAM. For comments on the composer of this tune, Frederick Charles Maker, 1844-1927, see Hymn 112.

311. Bread of heaven, on Thee we feed

Josiah Conder, 1789-1855

The hymn appeared in the author's *Star of the East,* 1821, as "Bread of heaven, on Thee I feed." The first person singular was altered to the plural throughout, and other changes made, improving the original.

For comments on Josiah Conder see Hymn 247.

MUSIC. ALETTA is by the American composer of popular church and Sunday school music, William B. Bradbury, 1816-68. For further comments on Bradbury see Hymn 103.

Conder's hymn may also be sung to *"Nicht so Traurig"* (538).

MARRIAGE

312. O perfect Love, all human thought transcending

Dorothy Blomfield Gurney, 1858-1932
Doxology added by John Ellerton, 1826-93

A singularly appropriate hymn for a Christian wedding. The author, Dorothy Gurney, born near London in 1858, was the daughter of Rev. Frederick Blomfield, a minister of the Anglican Church. She married a minister's son, Gerald Gurney, and with her husband, united with the Roman Catholic Church in 1919. Mrs. Gurney has given the following account of the writing of this popular hymn for holy matrimony:

> We were all singing hymns one Sunday evening and had just
> finished "O Strength and Stay," the tune to which was an es-

pecial favorite of my sister's, when someone remarked what a pity it was that the words should be unsuitable for a wedding. My sister, turning suddenly to me, said: "What is the use of a sister who composes poetry if she cannot write me new words to this tune?" I picked up a hymn-book and said: "Well, if no one will disturb me, I will go into the library and see what I can do." After about fifteen minutes I came back with the hymn, "O perfect Love," and there and then we all sang it to the tune of "Strength and Stay." It went perfectly, and my sister was delighted, saying that it must be sung at her wedding. For two or three years it was sung privately at many London weddings, and then it found its way into the hymnals. The writing of it was no effort whatever after the initial idea had come to me of the twofold aspect of perfect union, love and life; and I have always felt that God helped me to write it.

It is the most popular wedding hymn extant.

For comments on John Ellerton, who added the third stanza, see Hymn 42.

MUSIC. PERFECT LOVE is from an anthem composed by Joseph Barnby for the marriage of Princess Louise of Wales to the Duke of Fife, July 27, 1889. The anthem has been sung at many subsequent royal weddings.

For comments on Joseph Barnby see Hymn 21.

BURIAL OF THE DEAD

313. Safe in the arms of Jesus   *Fanny J. Crosby, 1820-1915*

Written April 30, 1868, at the request of W. H. Doane, composer of the tune to which it was to be sung. The hymn and tune were published first in *Songs of Devotion for Christian Associations*, 1870. It is a tender lyric which has given peace and satisfaction to many who have faced death and especially to mothers who have lost children.

Fanny Crosby, born in Putnam County, N. Y., became blind when six weeks old as the result of an application of a warm poultice to her eyes. She was educated in the New York (City) Institute for the Blind and there served as a teacher for a time. In 1858, she was married to Alexander van Alstyne, a blind musician. Miss Crosby began writing verses when a child of eight years and throughout her long life showed a marvelous facility for expression in poetry, which resulted in the writing of nearly 6,000 hymns besides many secular poems. Many of her hymns were written for W. H. Doane, Robert Lowry, Philip Phillips, Ira Sankey, and others who were editors of evangelistic song books. She is best known by her maiden name but also wrote under her married name and 216 *noms de plume*. She was a member of the Methodist Episcopal Church. Ten of her hymns are in the *Hymnary*.

MUSIC. SAFE IN THE ARMS, also known as "Refuge," was composed by William Howard Doane, 1832-1916, a manufacturer of wood-working machinery in Cincinnati, Ohio. He was a member of the Baptist Church and served many years as superintendent of the Sunday school in his church. A music enthusiast, he published 35 collections of song books and composed numerous hymn tunes, anthems, and cantatas. In 1875, Denison University, Granville, Ohio, conferred on him the degree of Doctor of Music.

314. Asleep in Jesus. . . .   *Margaret Mackay*, 1802-87

Written by Margaret Mackay, wife of a distinguished officer in the English army. She composed numerous hymns and poems, but none is so widely known as this tender lyric so often used as a funeral hymn, which she entitled, "Burial of the Dead." The hymn was suggested by an inscription she saw on a tombstone in the burying ground of Penny-cross Chapel, a rural spot in Devonshire:

"Sleeping in Jesus."

One stanza, the fifth, has been omitted. It reads:

Asleep in Jesus: time nor space
Debars this precious "hiding place."
On Indian plains or Lapland snows
Believers find the same repose.

The hymn was first published in *The Amethyst*, 1832, in Edinburgh.

MUSIC. REST. For comments on the composer, William B. Bradbury, see Hymn 103.

315. Now the laborer's task is o'er   *John Ellerton*, 1826-93

Written for *Church Hymns*, 1871, by John Ellerton, distinguished hymnist of the Church of England. His biographer has written concerning this hymn:

We now come to the loveliest and most loved of Mr. Ellerton's hymns. It has been sung and will continue to be sung at the graveside of princes, divines, statesmen, poets, artists, authors, as well as many a Christian labourer of humble life.

For comments on John Ellerton see Hymn 42.

MUSIC. REQUIESCAT was written for this hymn. It appeared first in *Hymns Ancient and Modern*, 1875. For comments on the composer, John B. Dykes, see Hymn 1.

316. O Lord of life, where'er they be
Frederick L. Hosmer, 1840-1929

This hymn, a source of comfort and courage to many mourners, was composed by Hosmer in 1888 for the Easter service in his own church in Cleveland, Ohio.

The note of triumph runs throughout the hymn, each stanza ending with a jubilant "Allelujah." It was written to be sung with Palestrina's tune, "Victory."

For comments on Frederick Hosmer see Hymn 72.

MUSIC. VICTORY. For comments on this tune see Hymn 116.

317. For all the saints
William W. How, 1823-97

The original, in eleven stanzas, was published in 1864 in *Hymns for Saints' Days,* by a layman, Lord Nelson. One of the omitted stanzas reads:

> For the Apostles' glorious company
> Who, bearing forth the Cross o'er land and sea,
> Shook all the mighty world, we sing to Thee.

For comments on William How see Hymn 144.

MUSIC. SARUM. The tune was composed for the *Sarum Hymnal,* 1869, for these words by Bishop How. It is also known as "St. Philip" and "For All the Saints."

For comments on the composer, Joseph Barnby, see Hymn 21.

318. We cannot think of them as dead
Frederick L. Hosmer, 1840-1929

Written in 1876 after the death by drowning of a young member of the church of which the author was minister.

For comments on the author, Frederick L. Hosmer, see Hymn 72.

MUSIC. ST. FLAVIAN is from the *English Psalter* of 1562 which was printed by John Day in London. The present is the first half, with some alterations, of the tune set to Psalm 132.

319. Come, let us join our friends above *Charles Wesley, 1707-88*

The first of a group of *Funeral Hymns,* published in 1759. It sets forth the assurance that friends gone before are not lost to those who mourn,

> For all the servants of the King
> In earth and heaven are one.

187

This hymn, one of Wesley's greatest, has had wide use throughout the English speaking world in times of sorrow and loss of loved ones. It is an exposition of the words of the ancient Creed, "I believe in the communion of saints."

The third and fourth verses, containing the idea of One Church, are among the finest in the whole range of hymnody.

The hymn was a great favorite of John Wesley. It so happened that he gave it out to be sung at a service he was conducting, at the very hour of the death of his brother Charles, giving the hymn a peculiarly pathetic interest.

For comments on Charles Wesley see Hymn 6.

MUSIC. DUNDEE. For comments on this tune see Hymn 297.

CHURCH UNITY

320. In Christ there is no East or West   *John Oxenham, 1852-1941*

A poem of human brotherhood, carrying a fine missionary message much needed in our day. It is written in the spirit of St. Paul— "where there is neither Greek nor Jew, circumcision nor uncircumcision, Barbarian, Scythian, bond nor free: but Christ is all and in all," Col. 3:11. It stands in striking contrast to Kipling's more narrow nationalism in his "East is East, and West is West, and never the twain shall meet."

This hymn which has now found its way into most modern hymn books was written for a missionary pageant, *The Pageant of Darkness and Light,* which the London Missionary Society asked the author to write, for use in connection with a great missionary exhibition in London, an affair which ran for a month and did much to stimulate interest in missions in all the churches. Oxenham wrote the *libretto* and planned the scenes for the pageant. The composer of the music, Hamish MacCunn, sent to him in a hurry one day for a few verses to fill in a gap. To this request Oxenham responded with the beautiful, simple lines, "No East or West."

John Oxenham, English publisher, poet, and novelist, was born in Manchester. He wrote this poem in 1908; and in 1939 sent the hymn, "Peace in our time" (357) with a personal letter to the editors of the *Hymnary.* The name John Oxenham is a *nom de plume* for William Arthur Dunkerley. For some years Dunkerley was engaged in business, in the interest of which he travelled extensively in Europe and Canada, and lived in France and the United States. He once investigated the possibilities of cotton growing and sheep raising in the Southern States but decided against the venture. He began writing as a relief from business, and then, later, dropped business in favor of writing.

MUSIC. ST. PETER, also known as "St. Peter's, Oxford," was composed for Psalm 118, by Alexander R. Reinagle, 1799-1877, distinguished organist for thirty-one years in St. Peter's-in-the-East Church, Oxford. The tune derives its name from the church which the composer served so long. It appeared in *Psalm Tunes for the Voice and the Pianoforte*, published by Reinagle in 1830. It is a majestic tune and should be sung in moderate time with strong rhythmic accent.

321. Jesus, Lord, we look to Thee   *Charles Wesley*, 1707-88

Four simple, lovely stanzas setting forth the unity of believers in Christ.

For comments on Charles Wesley see Hymn 6.

MUSIC. MÜDE BIN ICH, GEH ZUR RUH. For comments on this tune see Hymn 254.

322. All praise to our redeeming Lord   *Charles Wesley*, 1707-88

A favorite and appropriate hymn for use at religious reunions and conference gatherings. Wesley entitled it, "At meeting of Friends." For comments on Charles Wesley see Hymn 6.

MUSIC. ARMENIA was composed by Sylvanus Billings Pond, 1792-1871, Albany, N. Y., a piano manufacturer. Billings wrote many fine tunes and in 1841 issued the *United States Psalmody*, in which this tune appeared.

323. How sweet, how heavenly is the sight

Joseph Swain, 1761-96

A beautiful hymn of Christian love, suggesting lines by Alice Carey:

> He who loves best his fellowman
> Is loving God the holiest way he can.

It appeared in the author's *Walworth Hymns*, 1792, entitled, "The Grace of Christian Love."

Joseph Swain, English Baptist minister and hymn writer, lost his parents early in life and was apprenticed to an engraver. He led a careless, frivolous life until his conversion at the age of twenty-two, when he became a fervent Christian. He qualified for the Baptist ministry and began serving as minister of a congregation in East Street, Walworth, in 1791. His poetic gifts, formerly given worldly and superficial expression, were now turned with great effect to his evangelistic

189

appeals. His short ministry of five years, cut off by a lamented early death, was very successful.

MUSIC. REMEMBER ME. For comments on Asa Hull, composer of the tune, see Hymn 232.

MISSIONS

324. The morning light is breaking   *Samuel F. Smith, 1808-95*

A great missionary hymn, though a little too optimistic. It was written in 1832 while the author was a student in Andover Theological Seminary. After reading an inspiring account by Adoniram Judson of his great missionary work in Burma, Smith put his enthusiasm for missions into these verses, now sung in all the churches.

Rev. Samuel F. Smith, Harvard graduate in the class with Oliver Wendell Holmes, became the foremost American Baptist hymn writer of the 19th century. He is the author of numerous hymns but is best known by "My country, 'tis of thee" and the present hymn. His desire to be a missionary himself was never fulfilled, but his son volunteered for the service and became the successor to Judson in the great work in Burma. "The morning light is breaking" has been translated into many tongues. In a letter dated March 17, 1883, the author said of this hymn: "I have heard versions of it sung in Karen, Burman, Italian, Spanish, Portuguese, Swedish, German, and Telegu." Dr. Smith was a great linguist. He taught modern languages for a time in Colby College and had a familiarity with no less than fifteen languages. It is said that at the age of 86 he was seeking a suitable textbook to use in the study of the Russian language. He served as minister of Baptist churches at Waterville, Me., and Newton Center, Mass., and was secretary of the Baptist Missionary Union for 15 years.

MUSIC. WEBB. For comments on this tune and its composer, George J. Webb, see Hymn 65.

325. Far and near the fields are teeming   *J. O. Thompson*

A popular missionary hymn based on Luke 10:2: "The harvest truly is great, but the laborers are few: pray ye therefore the Lord of the harvest, that he would send forth laborers into his harvest."

No information has been found concerning the author, J. O. Thompson, or the composer of the tune, J. B. O. Clemm. The song appeared in *The Epworth Hymnal,* edited by John H. Vincent, afterward a Bishop, and published by Phillips and Hunt, Methodist Publishers, New York, in 1885. It was copyrighted by them as of that year.

326. Father, whose will is life and good

Hardwicke Drummond Rawnsley, 1851-1920

A prayer for the sick, and for physicians engaged in medical missionary work.

The hymn first appeared in *A Missionary Hymn Book,* 1922, published by the Society for the Promotion of Christian Knowledge, in London. The author, Rev. Hardwicke Drummond Rawnsley, was an influential minister and educator in the Church of England. He spent much of his life in the Lake District in northern England, and, being a man of public spirit and a lover of nature, he championed the rights of the people in securing for public use in perpetuity many beautiful tracts of the Lake District and other parts of the country. His friends remembered him as one "who, greatly loving the fair things of nature and of art, set all his love to the service of God and man."

MUSIC. "TALLIS," says William H. Havergal in *Notes on Certain Tunes,* is "simplicity itself. A child may sing the tune, while manly genius will admire it."

For comments on the composer, Thomas Tallis, see Hymn 33.

327. Christ for the world we sing   *Samuel Wolcott, 1813-86*

The author of this hymn, Samuel Wolcott, born at South Windsor, Conn., graduated from Yale at 20, spent two years in Syria as a missionary, and then, on account of failing health, returned to the United States where he served as pastor in various Congregational churches. The hymn was suggested to him by a motto, "Christ for the World and the World for Christ," made from branches of evergreen, in a Cleveland church where a Y.M.C.A. convention was held. One night, walking home from the convention to which he was a delegate, the words of the hymn took form. Yankton College, South Dakota, has adopted it as the opening hymn for each term of school.

MUSIC. MALVERN. For comments on this tune and its composer, John Roberts, see Hymn 131.

328. O Zion, haste, thy mission high fulfilling

Mary A. Thomson, 1834-1923

One of the strongest and most useful missionary hymns in the English language.

Mary Ann Faulkner was born in London but came to this country as a girl and became the wife of John Thomson, Librarian of the Free Library, in Philadelphia. A member of the Protestant Episcopal Church, her hymns, about forty in all, were published in *The Churchman,* New York, and in *The Living Age,* Chicago.

Of the origin of this missionary hymn, Mrs. Thomson has written:

> I wrote the greater part of the hymn, "O Zion, haste," in the year 1868. I had written many hymns before, and one night, while I was sitting up with one of my children who was ill of typhoid fever, I thought I should like to write a missionary hymn to the tune of the hymn beginning, "Hark, hark, my soul, angelic songs are swelling," as I was fond of that tune; but as I could not then get a refrain I liked, I left the hymn unfinished, and about three years later I finished it by writing the refrain which now forms part of it. By some mistake 1891 is given instead of 1871 as the date of the hymn in the (Episcopal) *Hymnal.* I do not think it is ever sung to the tune for which I wrote it. Rev. John Anketell told me, and I am sure he is right, that it is better for a hymn to have a tune of its own, and I feel much indebted to the composer of the tune TIDINGS for writing so inspiring a tune to my words.

She was mistaken in the last sentence, for Walch's tune, strangely enough, was composed for the words "Hark, hark my soul" (260).

MUSIC. TIDINGS was written, as stated above, for the hymn, "Hark, hark my soul! Angelic songs are swelling" (260), by James Walch, 1837-1901, an English composer and organist. The tune was never accepted for that hymn, because there already were several good tunes for it in use. In the providence of God, it found this hymn. The union was favored from the beginning and continues so today.

329. Word of Life, most pure, most strong

Jonathan F. Bahnmaier, 1774-1841
Tr. Catherine Winkworth, 1829-78

One of the best and most useful hymns for foreign missions.

The original poem has six stanzas, our hymn comprising the last three, translated by Catherine Winkworth. The German text is found at No. 551, the hymn there being a free translation by Percy Dearmer.

For comments on Catherine Winkworth see Hymn 236.

Jonathan F. Bahnmaier was born at Oberstenfeld where his father, J. C. Bahnmaier, was town preacher. He received his education at Tübingen and became assistant, in 1798, to his father. Later he had an appointment as Professor of Education and Homiletics at Tübingen but resigned in 1819 to become dean and town preacher at Kirchheim-unter-Teck, a post he held until his death. Bahnmaier was greatly interested in education, missions, and Bible societies and was on the committee which compiled the *Württemburg Gesangbuch,* published after his death in 1842. One other of his hymns, *"Jesu als du wiederkehrtest,"* entitled, "Prayer after School," has been translated into English.

MUSIC. MOZART is adapted from the "Kyrie" of the *Twelfth Mass* by the famous composer, Wolfgang Amadeus Mozart, 1756-91.

For comments on Mozart see Hymn 179.

330. O Spirit of the living God — James Montgomery, 1771-1854

One of the greatest missionary hymns in the English language. It was composed for a missionary service held in Leeds, England, June 4, 1823, and was entitled, "The Spirit Accompanying the Word of God." Its lyric beauty, its burning passion for the spread of the gospel, combined with its dignity and healthy-mindedness make it an extraordinarily useful hymn. Setting forth and emphasizing the relation of the Holy Spirit to the work of missions, it fills an important place in the *Hymnary.*

For comments on James Montgomery see Hymn 62.

MUSIC. ALSTONE. For comments on this tune see Hymn 300.

331. Fling out the banner! let it float

George W. Doane, 1799-1859

A stirring missionary hymn entitled, "Missions, Home and Foreign."

It is based on Psalm 60:4: "Thou hast given a banner to them that fear thee, that it may be displayed because of the truth."

The hymn was written in response to a request from the young women at St. Mary's Hall, Burlington, N. J., a girls' college founded by Bishop Doane, to be sung at a flag raising. The author, writing what has become a widely known hymn, gave the occasion a far wider significance than the girls had foreseen.

Bishop George Doane, a zealous advocate of missions, was known in his own church as "the missionary bishop of America." The modern missionary movement arose and spread in his lifetime. The hymn reflects Doane's enthusiasm and aggressive missionary leadership.

For further comments on the author see Hymn 36.

MUSIC. WALTHAM—also known as "Doane" and "Camden"—was written by John Baptiste Calkin, 1827-1905, English pianist and organist, professor of music, and composer of church music, both instrumental and vocal. The tune with its martial swing lends itself well for use as a processional.

332. Hail to the brightness of Zion's glad morning

Thomas Hastings, 1784-1872

A missionary hymn written in 1832, at the beginning of the modern missionary movement. It was first published in *Spiritual Songs for*

Social Worship, 1833, a volume compiled jointly by Hastings and Mason, set to the present tune by Lowell Mason. *Spiritual Songs* was a notable volume, publishing for the first time such well-known hymns as "The morning light is breaking," "My faith looks up to Thee," and introducing in America, Toplady's famous "Rock of Ages."

For comments on Thomas Hastings see Hymn 120.

MUSIC. WESLEY, also called "Hail to the Brightness," was written by Lowell Mason for this hymn. It is a simple, straightforward melody, whose merit as a hymn tune is unquestionable.

For comments on Lowell Mason see Hymn 12.

333. From Greenland's icy mountains

Reginald Heber, 1783-1826

One of the most famous missionary hymns ever written. An interesting story is attached to its origin, a detailed account of which was written by Thomas Edgeworth on the fly-leaf of a facsimile of the original manuscript as follows:

> On Whitsunday, 1819, the late Dr. Shipley, Dean of St. Asaph, and Vicar of Wrexham, preached a sermon in Wrexham Church in aid of the Society for the Propagation of the Gospel in Foreign Parts. That day was also fixed upon for the commencement of the Sunday evening lectures intended to be established in the church, and the late Bishop of Calcutta (Heber), then rector of Hodnet, the Dean's son-in-law being together in the vicarage, the former requested Heber to write "something for them to sing in the morning"; and he retired for that purpose from the table where the Dean and a few friends were sitting to a distant part of the room. In a short time the Dean enquired, "What have you written?" Heber having then composed the three first verses, read them over. "There, there, that will do very well," said the Dean. "No, no, the sense is not complete," replied Heber. Accordingly he added the fourth verse, and the Dean being inexorable to his repeated request of "Let me add another; oh, let me add another!" thus completed the hymn of which the annexed is a facsimile and which has since become so celebrated. It was sung the next morning in Wrexham Church the first time.

The tune to which it was sung was " 'Twas when the seas were roaring," from *The Beggar's Opera*—a fine but somewhat incongruous selection.

The words of the hymn reflect the enthusiasm and zeal of consecrated youth, eager, like Livingstone, to go out to a distant people needing help and to sacrifice life for the cause. Greatly interested in missions, Heber was offered the Bishopric of Calcutta and accepted it against the advice of his friends. After three years of strenuous, devoted labor, he was stricken with apoplexy and found dead in his bath on the evening of a busy day in which he had baptized forty-two native converts.

The much-discussed second stanza, omitted in the *Hymnary* because of its seeming low estimate of man, is as follows:

> What though the spicy breezes
> Blow soft o'er Ceylon's isle;
> Though every prospect pleases
> And only man is vile;
> In vain with lavish kindness
> The gifts of God are strown;
> The heathen in his blindness
> Bows down to wood and stone.

The hymn is widely used among German speaking people in the following translation made by Dr. Ch. G. Barth, 1799-1862:

Von Grönlands eis'gen Zinken,
　China's Korallenstrand,—
Wo Ophirs Quellen blinken,
　Fortströmend goldnen Sand,—
Von manchem alten Ufer,
　Von manchem Palmenland
Erschallt das Fleh'n der Rufer:
　"Löst unsrer Blindheit Band!"

Gewürzte Düfte weben
　Sanft über Ceylons Flur;
Es glänzt Natur und Leben
　Schlecht sind die Menschen nur.
Umsonst sind Gottes Gaben
　So reichlich ausgestreut;
Die blinden Heiden haben
　Sich Holz und Stein geweiht.

Und wir, mit Licht im Herzen,
　Mit Weisheit aus den Höh'n,
Wir könnten es verschmerzen,
　Dass sie im Finstern geh'n?
Nein, nein! das Heil im Sohne
　Sei laut und froh bezeugt,
Bis sich vor Christi Throne
　Der fernste Volkstamm beugt!

Ihr Wasser sollt es tragen,
　Ihr Winde, führt es hin,
Bis seine Strahlenwagen
　Von Pol, zu Pole ziehn;
Bis der versöhnten Erde,
　Das Lamm, der Sünderfreund,
Der Herr und Hirt' der Heerde
　In Herrlichkeit erscheint!

MUSIC. MISSIONARY HYMN, like the hymn to which it is sung, was written in a few minutes time. Miss Mary W. Howard of Savannah, Ga., read the words in the American edition of *The Christian Observer*, of February, 1823, and was so impressed with them that she requested a young bank clerk who had gone to Georgia from New England, to write a tune for them. He complied, and in a half hour handed her the tune which is now sung all over the world. The clerk was Lowell Mason. For further comments on Mason see Hymn 12.

334. We have heard the joyful sound

Priscilla Jane Owens, 1829-c. 99

A missionary hymn written for the anniversary of a Sunday school in Baltimore in which the author had been a worker for many years.

Priscilla Jane Owens, of Scottish and Welsh descent, was born and died in Baltimore where she was a public school teacher and an untiring worker in the Sunday school. Most of her hymns were written for children's services.

MUSIC. JESUS SAVES was composed by William J. Kirkpatrick, 1838-1921, a native of Duncannon, Pa. He was a regimental musician during the Civil War and was skilled as an organist, gospel singer, and composer, and was editor and publisher of gospel songs.

335. We've a story to tell to the nations   *Colin Sterne, 1862-1928*

A popular missionary hymn, breathing the spirit of Christ's great commission: "Go ye therefore, and make disciples of all nations, baptizing them into the name of the Father and of the Son and of the Holy Spirit: teaching them to observe all things whatsoever I commanded you: and lo, I am with you always, even unto the end of the world."

The message of the hymn, in which lies the hope of the nations, is summarized in the chorus.

The words and music are by the same person, Henry Ernest Nichol, who was born at Hull, England, December 10, 1862. He always signed his correct name to a tune, and the anagram "Colin Sterne," to a hymn. Oxford University gave him his degree in music. His compositions, many of them for the church, have the simplicity and directness of the folk song. The tune here forms a splendid musical setting for the words and may be sung variously, as a solo, duet, all the voices in unison, or in four parts.

336. On the mountain top appearing   *Thomas Kelly, 1769-1854*

Based on Isa. 52:7: "How beautiful upon the mountains are the feet of him that bringeth good tidings." The hymn was written after the good news came from the island of Tahiti that the first little band of mission workers sent there by the London Missionary Society, was kindly received by the natives, their message heard and welcomed, and that there was every prospect for the success of the mission. Hearing the news, Rev. Thomas Kelly wrote this hymn, entitling it, "On the Good News from Tahiti." The London Missionary Society met soon afterward for an enthusiastic gathering where this hymn was first sung.

For comments on Thomas Kelly see Hymn 119.

MUSIC. ZION. This tune is also used with the hymn, "Guide me, O Thou great Jehovah," but it is better suited to the present hymn.

For comments on the composer, Thomas Hastings, see Hymn 120.

337. Ye Christian heralds, go proclaim

Bourne H. Draper, 1775-1843

A hymn, originally of four stanzas, written as a farewell to missionaries.

The author, Rev. Bourne H. Draper, was born of a Church of England family, near Oxford, England. He joined the Baptist Church while employed as a printer's apprentice at the Clarendon Press, Oxford. He trained himself for the Baptist ministry and became pastor of the Baptist Church at Chipping-Norton. A man of great piety and poetic gift, he wrote numerous books for children as well as devotional works and volumes of sermons.

MUSIC. MISSIONARY CHANT appeared in the composer's *American Harp,* 1835, where it was identified with this hymn. Concerning the composition of the tune, Zeuner said: "I was sitting on one of those seats on Boston Commons on a most beautiful moonlight evening, all alone, with all the world moving about me, and suddenly 'Missionary Chant' was given me. I ran home as fast as ever I could and put it on paper before I should forget."

Charles Heinrich Christopher Zeuner, 1795-1857, a native of Germany, came to America at the age of 29 and settled in Boston. His musical ability was soon recognized, and he was made president of the Handel and Hadyn Society, and later its conductor. He published a book, *American Harp,* of nearly 400 pages of tunes, in 1832, mostly his own compositions. He moved to Philadelphia where he served as organist of St. Anne's Episcopal Church and later of the Arch Street Presbyterian Church. Due to harsh criticism of his playing, he became despondent and took his own life one November day at a lonely spot in the woods. Zeuner was never married and had no relatives in this country.

338. How are Thy servants blest   *Joseph Addison,* 1672-1719

A hymn of the Christian traveller, particularly descriptive of the experience of many Christian missionaries. It is known as the "Traveller's Hymn" and has been found useful as a part of the daily devotions by Christians journeying in foreign lands.

It appeared in ten stanzas in the *Spectator* for September 20, 1712, at the end of an article on "Greatness," with special reference to the greatness and awesomeness of the sea. The hymn was "made by a

197

gentleman upon the conclusion of his travels." Returning in 1700 from the terrors of a voyage on the Mediterranean Sea, Addison gives here, years afterwards, a picture of his own trying experiences. The second stanza describes some of the hardships through which he passed. The omitted stanzas (3, 4, 5, 7, 8) of the hymn picture the storm at sea, its subsidence, and the traveller's trust in God. They are as follows:

3. Thy mercy sweetened every soil,
   Made every region please:
   The hoary Alpine hills it warmed,
   And smoothed the Tyrrhene seas.

4. Think, O my soul, devoutly think
   How with affrighted eyes
   Thou sawest the wide-extended deep
   In all its horrors rise!

5. Confusion dwelt in every face,
   And fear in every heart;
   When waves on waves, and gulfs on gulfs,
   O'ercame the pilot's art.

7. When by the dreadful tempest borne
   High on the broken wave,
   They know Thou art not slow to hear,
   Nor impotent to save.

8. The storm is laid, the winds retire,
   Obedient to thy will;
   The sea, that roars at thy command,
   At thy command is still.

For comments on Joseph Addison see Hymn 50.

MUSIC. KILMARNOCK appeared in England as a Psalm tune in *Parochial Psalmody: a New Collection of the Most Approved Psalm Tunes. . . By J. P. Clark, Second Edition,* 1831.

The composer, Neil Dougall, 1776-1862, son of a shipwright, went to school until he was 15, then took to the sea. Three years later he met with an accident which resulted in the loss of his eyesight and his right arm. He then took up the study of music and for 45 years was a successful teacher of singing classes. He wrote about 100 psalm and hymn tunes.

339. See how great a flame aspires   *Charles Wesley,* 1707-88

A rousing missionary hymn which Wesley wrote after preaching to the coal miners at Newcastle. The imagery of the great flame was suggested by the night scene—the glow in the sky from the blazing fires connected with the mines. The climax of the hymn, stanza 4, was inspired by an incident in the life of Elijah. When his servant returned the seventh time from looking toward the sea from the housetop, he reported: "Behold there ariseth a little cloud out of the sea like a man's hand! . . . . And it came to pass in the meantime that the heaven was black with clouds and wind, and there was a great rain" (I Kings 18:41-45).

For comments on Charles Wesley see Hymn 6.

MUSIC. BENEVENTO is an adaptation from a motet on the words, "*Tibi omnes angeli,*" by Samuel Webbe, 1740-1816, a London organist and composer.

340. The whole wide world for Jesus

J. Dempster Hammond, 1719-83

The watchword, "the whole wide world for Jesus," brings to mind the motto, "The evangelization of the world in this generation," which served to inspire the Student Volunteer Movement in the days of John R. Mott, Robert E. Speer, and Sherwood Eddy. Two world wars have shaken the foundations of the missionary enterprise, but those closest to the movement still declare the motto to be both a possibility and an obligation. The missionary forces are making resolute plans for giving the Gospel to the entire world.

No information is at hand concerning the author, J. Dempster Hammond.

MUSIC. THE WHOLE WIDE WORLD. The composer, John H. Maunder, was born in Chelsea, England, in 1858, and died in 1920. He received his musical education at the Royal Academy of Music in London; held various musical appointments and became a well-known and popular accompanist for vocalists. As a composer, he was widely known for his anthems, cantatas, and services which have met with wide approval. His *A Song of Thanksgiving,* a cantata, has been quite popular in this country, as have several of his anthems. In the secular field he has written much excellent choral music, one of the best being his "The Song of Thor."

341. Jesus shall reign where'er the sun   *Isaac Watts, 1674-1748*

Founded on the last part of Psalm 72, this is the earliest of the great English hymns on missions. It is sung by all Christian congregations in the homelands and has probably been translated into a greater number of languages and dialects than any other English hymn.

Watts did not hesitate to use the name of Jesus in interpreting the Psalm. On this point, he wrote in the preface to his Psalms:

Where the original runs in the form of prophecy concerning Christ and his salvation, I have given an historical turn to the sense; there is no necessity that we should always sing in the obscure and doubtful style of prediction, when the things foretold are brought into the open light by a full accomplishment.

"Peculiar honors" in stanza 5 means honors appropriate to the various peoples who bring them.

For comments on Isaac Watts see Hymn 11.

MUSIC. DUKE STREET. This is a psalm tune by John Hatton (d. 1793), a native of Warrington, England, of whom little is known. The tune appeared first in *A Select Collection of Psalm and Hymn Tunes,* Glasgow, 1793. It has long been associated with this hymn, although other tunes—"Old Hundredth," "Warrington," and "Truro"—have also been used with it.

342. Lord of light, whose name outshineth

Howell Elvet Lewis, 1860—

Based on the petition, "Thy will be done on earth as it is in heaven." The hymn was written for the *Congregational Hymnary* (England), 1916. A note by the author explains his purpose in the hymn:

The hymn was written to declare that in doing God's will, active co-operation is as much needed as humble resignation. Charlotte Elliott, in her hymn, "My God and Father, while I stray," had expressed the latter thought beautifully. My hope was to supplement her hymn as best I could.

(Miss Elliott's hymn is found at No. 245).

Howell Elvet Lewis, of Welsh birth, became an influential leader in English Congregationalism. He served as minister of the Welsh Tabernacle, King's Cross, London, and was at one time chairman of the Congregational Union of England and Wales. He is the author of a number of volumes of poems and biography.

MUSIC. HAST DU JESU RUF VERNOMMEN appears anonymously in the *Gesangbuch mit Noten,* set to a missionary hymn beginning with these words. By repeating the first four lines of the first stanza of the present hymn the refrain was made possible.

The tune was written by John R. Sweney, 1837-99, a native of West Chester, Penna., who received his degrees of Mus. Bac. and Mus. Doc. at the Pennsylvania Military Academy, Chester, Penna. Sweney was a skilled choir leader, violinist, and pianist. He collaborated with Wm. J. Kirkpatrick in the production and publishing of numerous gospel hymn tunes and hymnals. After the Civil War, he taught music in the school from which he received his degrees and became well known as a song-leader at summer religious assemblies, especially at Ocean Grove, N. J.

NATIONAL AND INTERNATIONAL LIFE

343. O beautiful for spacious skies

Katharine Lee Bates, 1859-1929

A beautiful poem expressing genuine love for America and faith in human brotherhood. The historical accuracy of the second and third stanzas may be questioned. To one familiar with New England theocracy, it is clear that the Pilgrims were not, as the poet suggests, the champions of freedom of thought and religion. On the contrary, they were intolerant of any form of opposition, whether religious or political.

The hymn is less limited to the New England landscape than "My country, 'tis of thee," and probably for that reason has overshadowed the latter as a popular national hymn.

Katharine Lee Bates, born in Falmouth, Mass., was educated at Wellesley College where she later became Professor of English. She is the author of many books.

A folder published by the author, giving the exact title and words of the hymn, also contains interesting data concerning its origin and history:

> *America the Beautiful* was written in its original form, more literary and ornate than the present version, in the summer of 1893. I was making my first trip west. After visiting at Chicago the World's Fair, where I was naturally impressed by the symbolic beauty of the White City, I went on to Colorado Springs. Here I spent three weeks or so under the purple range of the Rockies, which looked down with surprise on a summer school. This had called to its faculty several instructors from the east, Dr. Rolfe coming from Cambridge to teach Shakespeare, Professor Todd from Amherst for lectures on Astronomy, Professor Katharine Coman from Wellesley for a course in Economics. My own subject, which seemed incongruous enough under that new and glowing sky, was English Religious Drama.
>
> We strangers celebrated the close of the session by a merry expedition to the top of Pike's Peak, making the ascent by the only method then available for people not vigorous enough to achieve the climb on foot nor adventurous enough for burro-riding. Prairie wagons, their tail-boards emblazoned with the traditional slogan, "Pike's Peak or Bust," were pulled by horses up to the half-way house, where the horses were relieved by mules. We were hoping for half an hour on the summit, but two of our party became so faint in the rarified air that we were bundled into the wagons again and started on our downward

plunge so speedily that our sojourn on the peak remains in memory hardly more than one ecstatic gaze. It was then and there, as I was looking out over the sea-like expanse of fertile country spreading away so far under those ample skies, that the opening lines of the hymn floated into my mind. When we left Colorado Springs the four stanzas were pencilled in my note-book, together with other memoranda, in verse and prose, of the trip. The Wellesley work soon absorbed time and attention again, the note-book was laid aside, and I do not remember paying heed to these verses until the second summer following, when I copied them out and sent them to *The Congregationalist,* where they first appeared in print July 4, 1895. The hymn attracted an unexpected amount of attention. It was almost at once set to music by that eminent composer, Silas G. Pratt, and re-published with his setting, in *Famous Songs,* issued in 1895 by the Baker and Taylor Company. Other tunes were written for the words and so many requests came to me, with still increasing frequency, to permit its use in various publications and for special services that, in 1904, I re-wrote it, trying to make the phraseology more simple and direct.

The new form first appeared in the *Evening Transcript* of Boston, November 19, 1904. After the lapse of a few years, during which the hymn had run the gauntlet of criticism, I changed the wording of the opening quatrain of the third stanza. The hymn as printed above is the final version, of which I retain the copyright, not as a matter of money-making, for I have given hundreds, perhaps thousands, of free permissions for its use, but in order to protect it from misprints and conscious alterations.

But here comes a difficulty. Over sixty original settings, some of them by distinguished musicians, have been written for the hymn, which thus suffers from an embarrassment of riches. It is associated with no one tune. The original setting which has, thus far, won widest acceptance is that of the former Municipal Organist of Portland, Will C. MacFarlane (sold by Cressey and Allen, 534 Congress Street, Portland, Maine). His tune, which is played on the city chimes of Springfield, Mass., he has made the theme of a spirited march, *America the Beautiful,* arranged for band music. In an octavo published by Oliver Ditson Company are included four settings, one by Clarence G. Hamilton, professor of music at Wellesley College, and another by W. W. Sleeper, formerly pastor of the Wellesley Congregational Church. Both these settings have found favor with choruses and made their way into various hymnals. This octavo carries, also, settings by William Arms Fisher, musical editor of the Boston house of Ditson. Other tunes that have a strong following are those of the celebrated composer, Horatio W. Parker (in the *Methodist Sunday School Hymnal*), Charles

S. Brown (in *Junior Carols*, Society of Christian Endeavor),
John Stainer (in the *Pilgrim Hymnal*), J. A. Demuth, professor
of music at Oberlin (in *Oberlin's Favorite Hymns*, published
by Arthur P. Schmidt), and Herbert G. Peabody of Fitchburg,
Mass., (published by H. W. Gray Company of New York).
Other attractive settings, published, privately printed or yet in
manuscript, have their special circles, and the words have been
fitted to various old tunes, as those of *Auld Lang Syne, The
Harp that Once through Tara's Halls, The Son of God goes
forth to War* and *O Mother Dear Jerusalem.* To this last, Materna, by S. A. Ward, in many hymnals and well known
throughout the country, *America the Beautiful* is at present
most often sung.

That the hymn has gained, in these twenty odd years, such
a hold as it has upon our people, is clearly due to the fact that
Americans are at heart idealists, with a fundamental faith in
human brotherhood.

KATHARINE LEE BATES

(Quoted by permission.)

MUSIC. MATERNA (Mother) was composed for "O mother dear,
Jerusalem." The composer, Samuel Ward, 1847-1903, resided at New-
ark, N. J., where he operated a successful music business and was for
14 years the director of the Orpheus Club. The tune has by popular
preference become inseparably associated with the words.

344. My country, 'tis of thee   *Samuel F. Smith*, 1808-95

The best loved of our patriotic hymns, widely used, and deeply imbedded in the American soul.

His Harvard classmate, Oliver Wendell Holmes, saluted Smith in a
poem written for their class reunion on the 30th anniversary of their
graduation as follows:

> And there's a nice youngster of excellent pith—
> Fate tried to conceal him by naming him Smith:
> But he shouted a song for the brave and the free—
> Just read on his medal, "My country," "of thee."

The inspiration for this hymn came from the reading of a German
patriotic poem sent him by Lowell Mason (See 348). The author, then
a young student at Andover Theological Seminary, says:

> I instantly felt the impulse to write a patriotic hymn of my
> own, adapted to the tune. Picking up a scrap of waste paper
> which lay near me, I wrote at once, probably within half an
> hour, the hymn, "America," as it is now known everywhere.
> The whole hymn stands today as it stood on the bit of waste
> paper.

203

The hymn was first sung at a children's festival in Park Street Church, Boston, July 4, 1832.

For comments on the author, Samuel F. Smith, see Hymn 324.

MUSIC. AMERICA is also the tune used with the national anthem of Britain, "God save the king." The melody is of obscure origin. It has been known in England for several centuries. In Denmark it was used toward the end of the 18th century for a national hymn, *"Heil dir dem liebenden,"* and in Germany it was widely used in Prussian and other northern states to patriotic words. In earlier days in the United States, the words, "Come Thou Almighty King," were sung to this tune. The tune has thus nearly come to be an International Anthem.

Henry Carey, 1692-1743, an English musician of considerable ability, known as the composer of the song, "Sally in Our Alley," is sometimes credited with this tune but the evidence is disputed. He wrote songs and poems for light and burlesque operas but always with regard for decency and good manners. His life was ended by suicide.

345. Judge Eternal, throned in splendor

Henry Scott Holland, 1874-1918

A prayer for the nation.

The hymn was written with the English Empire in mind, but its message and concern for the removal of national evils are such as to make it appropriate for use nearly everywhere.

Henry Scott Holland had a distinguished career at Oxford and attained to numerous positions of responsibility in the Church of England. He was Professor of Divinity at Oxford and later Canon of St. Paul's Cathedral. The two chief interests of his fruitful life were social reform and missionary work, both of which are embodied in this, his only hymn. The poem was published in July, 1902, in *The Commonwealth,* a Christian social magazine which Dr. Holland edited, and was included in the *English Hymnal* in 1906.

MUSIC. SILICIAN MARINERS. For comments on this tune see Hymn 45.

346. Once to every man and nation

James Russell Lowell, 1819-91

A powerful hymn of national righteousness, taken from Lowell's poem called "The Present Crisis," 1845, the crisis being the war with Mexico which the author held to be unjust and would only result in enlarging the area of slavery. To make the meter of the poem regular enough to be sung, some alteration was inevitable.

James Russell Lowell graduated from Harvard in 1838 and was admitted to the bar two years later. He succeeded Longfellow as Professor of Modern Languages and Literature in Harvard, in 1855. From 1857 to 1862 he edited the *Atlantic Monthly* and the nine years following that he was editor of the *North American Review*. In 1877 he was appointed minister to Spain, and in 1881, to England, remaining at the latter post four years. He wrote various volumes of poetry and was a prominent anti-slavery writer both in verse and prose.

MUSIC. TON-Y-BOTEL, also known as "Ebenezer," is a "solemn tune, of very simple structure, being formed, throughout, of imitations of the first bar." A letter from the copyright owners, W. Gwenlyn Evans and Son, Caernarvon, Wales, written by A. Vaughan Evans, throws interesting light on this tune and the origin of the fictitious story which gave rise to the name TON-Y-BOTEL. It reads, in part:

. . . We have pleasure in granting permission to use the tune Ebenezer (Ton-Y-Botel) free of charge in the Mennonite Hymn Book. . . . It is an original Welsh composition by T. J. Williams . . . and was part of a Memorial Anthem *'Goleu yn y Glyn'* (Light in the Vale) in memory of a friend of the composer. . . . .

You will have noticed above that the correct name of the tune is Ebenezer and it may be of interest to learn how it acquired the 'nickname' Ton-Y-Botel (the bottle tune). Not long after the Welsh Revival of 1904 the tune spread all over Wales and then England and Scotland 'by ear.' There were no written or printed copies of it. A crowd of young men were singing it on a hilltop just outside this town of Caernarvon and the usual questions were asked: Who was the composer, etc., when a lad for a joke said the tune had been found in a bottle washed up by the tide on the beach at Dinas Dinlle (a small bathing place in the Irish Sea near here). Ever since the tune has been called by the Welsh equivalent of "Bottle Tune." One of the young men made a written copy of the music as it was sung all over the country, and brought it to us to print. The demand was enormous and we published hundred of thousands of copies. . . . We purchased the copyright and now the tune appears in hymnals all over the world—except in Wales, the country of its origin. I do not think it is a case of the prophet being without honour in his own country, but rather that the popularity was so great that it was sung everywhere—in taverns and public houses, non-religious words were sung to it, etc.— with the result that the tune was regarded as not quite 'respectable' by the generation which produced it. No doubt it will be valued by later generations of Welsh people. This has happened with several of the best-known Welsh hymns as many of them 200 years ago were of secular origin.

I am giving the above details so that something of its history may be on record in the United States, and hope they may be of interest.

347. God of our fathers, whose Almighty hand

Daniel C. Roberts, 1841-1907

A hymn of broadminded patriotism, called forth by the "Centennial" Fourth of July celebration in 1876, held at Brandon, Vt. It was published in various papers at the time and included in the *Hymnal* of the Protestant Episcopal Church in 1894. Since then it has appeared in a number of other church hymnals.

The hymn was written by Daniel C. Roberts, a graduate of Kenyon College, and a clergyman in the Episcopal Church.

MUSIC. NATIONAL HYMN was used at the Columbian celebration service at St. Thomas' Church, New York City, Sunday morning, October 9, 1892. It is one of the finest processional tunes in the hymn book. The trumpet introduction and the interludes, making it unique among hymn tunes, gives it a quickening martial rhythm yet without losing its spirit of sanctity and reverence.

The composer, George William Warren, 1828-1902, was an American organist, born at Albany, N. Y. Though self-taught, he held responsible positions as organist in Albany and then at Holy Trinity and St. Thomas' churches in New York.

348. God bless our native land

Siegfried A. Mahlmann, 1771-1826
Stanza 3, William E. Hickson, 1803-70

The first two stanzas are a free translation of Stanzas 1 and 3 of the following patriotic song for Saxony:

1. Gott segne Sachsenland,
   Wo fest die Treue stand
     In Sturm und Nacht!
   Ew'ge Gerechtigkeit,
   Hoch überm Meer der Zeit,
   Die jedem Sturm gebeut,
     Schütz uns mit Macht!

2. Blühe, du Rautenkranz
   In schöner Tage Glanz
     Freudig empor!
   Heil, Friedrich August, dir!
   Heil, guter König, dir!
   Dich, Vater, preisen wir
     Liebend im Chor!

3. Was treue Herzen flehn
   Steigt zu des Himmels Höh'n
     Aus Nacht zum Licht.
   Der unsre Liebe sah,
   Der unsre Tränen sah,
   Er ist uns huldreich nah,
     Verlässt uns nicht.

A fourth stanza, identical with the first, follows.

It was written by the German song writer, Siegfried Augustus Mahlmann, and published in G. W. Fink's, *Musikalischer Hausschatz*, 1842.

The hymn was first sung Nov. 13, 1815, in the presence of the King of Saxony. The hymn was also the inspiration for Samuel F. Smith's, "My country 'tis of thee."

The translation was made in 1834 by Charles T. Brooks, while a student at the Divinity School at Cambridge, Mass. It was revised by John Sullivan Dwight, 1813-93, to form our version. Dwight was a graduate of Harvard Divinity School and became a Unitarian minister in Northampton, Mass., but gave up the ministry to devote himself to literature and music. For thirty years he owned and edited Dwight's *Journal of Music*.

The third stanza, raising the hymn above any narrow patriotism, was added by William E. Hickson, an English shoe manufacturer who retired from that business to pursue literary and philanthropic interests. Much interested in the musical culture of his people, he published various books on music and composed numerous musical works of merit. For a time he was editor of the *Westminster Review*.

MUSIC. DORT. For comments on the composer of this tune, Lowell Mason, see Hymn 12.

349. Great God of nations, now to Thee

Alfred A. Woodhull, 1810-36

Entitled "Thanksgiving Hymn," this poem was written in 1828 when the author was only eighteen years old. It was published in the Presbyterian *Psalms and Hymns*, 1829, Princeton, N. J. There have been many alterations of the lines.

Alfred Alexander Woodhull, son of a Presbyterian minister, graduated from Princeton at 18 years of age, and then took a medical course at the University of Pennsylvania. He began the practice of medicine at Marietta, Pennsylvania, then moved to Princeton where within a year he contracted a fever which occasioned his death. Known as a fine Christian man as well as a skilled physician, his early death was greatly lamented. He was a member of the Presbyterian Church.

MUSIC. MENDON. For comments on this tune see Hymn 211.

WORLD FRIENDSHIP AND PEACE

350. O God, we pray for all mankind

Howard J. Conover, 1850-1925

A prayer for all the nations.

The author, Howard J. Conover, was born in New Jersey, the son of devout Christian parents. He was educated at Pennington Seminary, Pennington, N. J., and Dickinson College. He took up the ministry and was known to be a studious, devout, and thoroughly faithful pastor, serving a number of churches in his native state. A nephew, Elbert M. Conover, is the director of The Interdenominational Bureau of Architecture, with offices in New York City, serving twenty-five denominations.

MUSIC. ORTONVILLE. For comments on this tune see Hymn 120.

351. God the All-Merciful   *Henry F. Chorley*, 1808-72

A touching cry for peace, based on the Russian national hymn by Chorley. This paraphrase was written by John Ellerton, in 1870, during the Franco-Prussian War. It was published in *Church Hymns* in 1871.

Henry F. Chorley, an English man of letters, received his education at the Royal Institution, Liverpool. He was a literary and music critic and a friend and great admirer of Charles Dickens. For 34 years he was on the editorial staff of the *Athenaeum,* published in London.

MUSIC. RUSSIAN HYMN was composed for the words, "God save the Czar," the national Russian anthem written in 1833. It is a stately, powerful tune which most congregations love to sing, especially after it has been used often enough to overcome certain of its difficulties. It was written at the command of the Czar who ordered it adopted for the army. But there is nothing about the tune itself to render it inappropriate for the churches. In his *Memoirs,* Lwoff says that in composing this tune he "felt and fully appreciated the necessity of accomplishing something which would be robust, stately, stirring, national in character, something worthy to reverberate either in a church, through the soldiers' ranks, or amongst a crowd of people, something which would appeal alike to the lettered and the ignorant."

The composer, Alexis T. Lwoff, 1799-1871, was an eminent Russian musician, succeeding his father in St. Petersburg as head of the imperial choir where he not only maintained the traditions of that great organization, but raised it to still greater heights of eminence. He composed violin concertos, operas, and church music. Lwoff had a thorough understanding of the canonical services of the Russian Church, and his collection of ritual chants is still considered authoritative.

352. O God of love, O King of peace   *Henry W. Baker*, 1821-77

An ardent prayer for universal peace. This noble hymn was contributed by the author to *Hymns Ancient and Modern,* London, 1861, a notable book of which Baker was chief editor.

For comments on the author, Henry W. Baker, see Hymn 143.

MUSIC. QUEBEC. For comments on this tune and its composer see Hymn 171.

353. Let there be light, Lord God of hosts

William Merrill Vories, 1880—

A good peace hymn.

The author, William Merrill Vories, was born in Leavenworth, Kansas. He is the founder of an independent mission in the province of Omi, Japan. Vories published the present poem February, 1909, in the *Advocate of Peace.* Since that time, it has found a place in a number of hymn books. The copyright, appropriately enough, is held by the American Peace Society.

MUSIC. PENTECOST, a dignified tune, simple in structure, was first used with the hymn, "Veni Creator," and appeared in *Thirty-two Hymn Tunes, Composed by Members of the University of Oxford,* 1868. It was revised by Arthur Sullivan who set it to Monsell's hymn, "Fight the good fight with all thy might," for the tune lends itself to spirited rendition as well as the more devotional and contemplative as required by the present hymn.

The composer, Rev. William Boyd, 1847-1928, was born in Jamaica and educated at Oxford where Baring-Gould was his tutor. The latter asked him to compose a tune to "Come, Holy Ghost, our souls inspire," for a meeting of Yorkshire coal miners on the Day of Pentecost. The result was this tune to which he gave the name PENTECOST. Boyd was ordained priest in 1882 and from 1893 until his retirement in 1918, he was vicar of All Saints, Norfolk Square, London.

354. Father eternal, Ruler of creation

Laurence Housman, 1865—

One of the hymns of our time in which, characteristically, the international note is struck. It was written at the request of the Rev. H. R. L. (Dick) Sheppard, minister of St. Martin's-in-the-Fields, London, for the Life and Liberty movement after World War I. The bitter experiences of that war, with the subsequent fear and distrust among the nations, had intensified the longing for the realization of the petition in the Lord's Prayer, "Thy will be done in earth, as it is in heaven." This hymn gives utterance to that longing.

Laurence Housman is an English artist known chiefly for his book illustrations, but he is also known as a writer of poetry and prose of merit. A contemporary wrote of him: "He has the heart of compassion for the little ones of the earth, the dumb and the helpless, that ought to be, but is not always, an essential part of poetry. His is the true Franciscan spirit."

MUSIC. OLD 124TH is from the *Genevan Psalter*, 1551, where it is set to Psalm 124. It is commonly attributed to L. Bourgeois (See 34). The tune has always been popular in England with the non-conformist churches and is one of the few surviving tunes from the *Old Version Psalter*.

355. Not alone for mighty empire
William Pierson Merrill, 1867—

A hymn of thanksgiving and of the higher patriotism, glorying not in empire nor in battleship and fortress but in the things of the spirit which have made America great. It was first printed in *The Continent*, a Presbyterian paper, now defunct, published in Chicago.

Concerning the origin of the hymn, Dr. Merrill wrote in a letter dated April 18, 1947:

> The occasion for the writing of this hymn was a Union Thanksgiving Service in Chicago, where Jenkin Lloyd Jones made a prayer, in which he thanked God more for spiritual values in our national life than for any temporal ones. That prayer inspired my hymn.

Howard Chandler Robbins, Professor of Pastoral Theology in the General Theological Seminary, New York City, says: "On Thanksgiving Day we all ought to be singing Dr. Merrill's great Thanksgiving hymn, one of the greatest national hymns in the English language." For comments on William Pierson Merrill see Hymn 183.

MUSIC. IN BABILONE. For comments on this tune see Hymn 122.

356. Thy Kingdom come! O Lord, we daily cry
Henry W. Hawkes, 1843-1917

One of our few hymns on the petition, "Thy Kingdom come." It is an earnest prayer for social righteousness and peace. The hymn was written by Henry Warburton Hawkes, an English Unitarian.

No further information is at hand concerning the author.

MUSIC. FFIGYSBREN. For comments on this tune see Hymn 183.

357. Peace in our time, O Lord
John Oxenham, 1852-1941

A beautiful prayer for the peace which is "based upon Thy will and built in righteousness." The author, having learned that a new hym-

210

nary was to be published, and aware of the Mennonite position on war and peace, sent this hymn from England for inclusion in this book with the request that it be used with the tune "Diademata."

For comments on the author, John Oxenham, see Hymn 320.

MUSIC. DIADEMATA. For comments on this tune and its composer, George J. Elvey, see Hymn 118.

THE CHRISTIAN HOME AND FAMILY

358. O happy home, where Thou art loved the dearest

Carl J. P. Spitta, 1801-59
Tr. Sarah L. Findlater, 1823-1907

O selig Haus, wo man dich aufgenommen,
　　Du wahrer Seelenfreund, Herr Jesu Christ;
Wo unter allen Gästen, die da kommen,
　　Du der gefeiertste und liebste bist;
Wo aller Herzen dir entgegenschlagen
　　Und aller Augen freudig auf dich sehn;
Wo aller Lippen dein Gebot erfragen
　　Und alle deines Winks gewärtig stehn!

O selig Haus, wo Mann und Weib in *einer,*
　　In deiner Liebe *eines* Geistes sind,
Als beide *eines* Heils gewürdigt, keiner
　　Im Glaubensgrunde anders ist gesinnt;
Wo beide unzertrennbar an dir hangen
　　In Lieb' und Leid, Gemach und Ungemach,
Und nur bei dir zu bleiben stets verlangen
　　An jedem guten wie am bösen Tag!

O selig Haus, wo man die lieben Kleinen
　　Mit Händen des Gebets ans Herz dir legt,
Du Freund der Kinder, der sie als die Seinen
　　Mit mehr als Mutterliebe hegt und pflegt;
Wo sie zu deinen Füssen gern sich sammeln
　　Und horchen deiner süssen Rede zu
Und lernen früh dein Lob mit Freuden stammeln,
　　Sich deiner freun du lieber Heiland, du!

O selig Haus, wo du die Freude teilest,
　　Wo man bei keiner Freude dein vergisst!
O selig Haus, wo du die Wunden heilest
　　Und aller Arzt und aller Tröster bist,
Bis jeder einst sein Tagewerk vollendet,
　　Und bis sie endlich alle ziehen aus
Dahin, woher der Vater dich gesendet,
　　Ins grosse, freie, schöne Vaterhaus!

211

Based on Luke 19:9: "This day is salvation come to this house," the poem originally bore the title, "Salvation is come to this house." It is probably the best hymn ever written on the Christian home.

The author of the hymn enjoyed a singularly happy and peaceful home life, not only under the parental roof, but also after he was married and had established his own home. Carl Spitta, Lutheran minister and greatest German hymn-writer of the nineteenth century, was born in Hannover. His father came from a Hugenot family that fled France during the Catholic persecutions and died when Carl was only four years old. His mother was a Christian Jewess whose loving care no doubt inspired the son to write this hymn on the home. After completing his theological studies in 1824, Spitta taught school for four years and then was ordained in 1828 to the Lutheran ministry. He passed through a deep spiritual experience about this time which resulted in the composition of his finest hymns. "In the manner in which I formerly sang," he wrote a friend in 1826, "I sing no more. To the Lord I dedicate my life, my love, and likewise my song. He gave to me song and melody. I give it back to Him."

His hymns were received with enthusiasm and held in the same esteem in Germany as Keble's *Christian Year* in England. His collection of hymns, *Psalter und Harfe,* first published in 1833, passed through more than 50 editions and a second collection printed in 1843 had by 1887 passed through 42 editions.

Spitta had a family of seven children, one of whom became Professor of New Testament Exegesis and Practical Theology in the University of Strassburg, and another, John August Spitta, wrote the monumental four-volume work on the life of J. S. Bach.

The translator of the hymn, Sarah Findlater, also knew the blessings of a happy home. Her daughter wrote concerning her mother:

> Her home life with my father was almost idyllically happy, in the small manse at Lochearnhead, where there never was enough of money, yet where my parents exercised unceasing hospitality—almost foolish hospitality. They were both great readers, and used to read aloud to each other for hours. My mother was an excellent linguist, and her German translations were a great pleasure to her. That simple little hymn of hers which begins "O happy home," is really an epitome of her homelife with my father—they were so single-eyed in their longing to serve God: it came first with them always.

For further comments on Sarah Findlater, see comments on her sister, Jane Borthwick, Hymn 54.

MUSIC. o selig haus is a popular German melody written in 1854 by Edward Niemeyer. Information concerning the composer has not been traced.

359. Thou gracious God, whose mercy lends

Oliver Wendell Holmes, 1809-94

Written by Oliver Wendell Holmes in 1869 to be read or sung at the annual meeting of the 1829 college class of Harvard University, of which he was a member. The famous class included in its membership J. Freeman Clarke, founder of the Disciples, and Samuel F. Smith, author of "America." The forty years of retrospect, mingled with sunshine and shadow, are touched here with tenderness and grace.

For comments on Oliver W. Holmes see Hymn 172.

MUSIC. ES KAM DIE GNADENVOLLE appears in the *Gesangbuch mit Noten* to the words, "Früh Morgens da die Sonn' Aufgeht."

The composer, Johann Heinrich Egli, 1741-1810, was born in Seegräben, Switzerland. He was a pupil of Pastor Schmiedli at Wetzikon, and became a music teacher in Zurich, where he died. His compositions for voice, both sacred and secular, won great popularity in Switzerland.

360. There is beauty all around   *John H. McNaughton, 1863*

A tender lyric in praise of the home where love dwells. Especially fine are the lines,

> All the earth is filled with love
> When there's love at home,

for it recognizes the wide influence of the home, the primary social institution where the first lessons of the Christian life are learned. A nation's peace and prosperity is rooted in the quality of life found in its homes.

The words and music are by John Hugh McNaughton, who was born 1829, in Caledonia, N. Y., of Scottish parentage. His lyrics have some literary qualities and Henry W. Longfellow once wrote to McNaughton: "Your poems have touched me very much." He composed many popular songs, including "The Blue and the Gray," and "Faded Coat of Blue," which sold by the hundreds of thousands of copies. He is the author of a *Treatise on Music* and *Onnalinda,* a metrical romance.

361. Happy the home when God is there

Henry Ware, Jr., 1794-1843

One of the strongest hymns on the Christian home. It first appeared in *Selections of Hymns and Poetry,* Boston, 1846, compiled by Mrs. Herbert Mayo, where it was entitled, "The Happy Home."

For comments on the author, Henry Ware, Jr., see Hymn 13.

MUSIC. ST. AGNES. For comments on this tune see Hymn 155.

362. Bless the four corners of this house
Arthur Guiterman, 1871-1943

A poem for use in the dedication of a Christian home, first printed in *House and Garden* magazine about thirty years ago. Since then it has become widely known both here and abroad. Its first use as a hymn was in the *Methodist Hymnal* of 1935, edited by Dr. Robert Mc-Cutchan.

The author, Arthur Guiterman, was a writer, poet, and speaker. He was born in Vienna, Austria, November 20, 1871, of American parents, his mother being a native of Ohio. Most of his education was received in New York City, his college course having been completed in the City College. Guiterman was a frequent contributor to *Harper's Magazine, The Saturday Evening Post, The Youth's Companion, Ladies Home Journal,* and other leading magazines. His poetry is written on a large variety of subjects. Joyce Kilmer characterized him as "the most American of poets."

MUSIC. ICH SINGE DIR is a familiar melody in the *Gesangbuch mit Noten* where it appears anonymously, set to the words, *"Ich singe Dir mit Herz und Mund,"* by Paul Gerhardt.

363. Lord of life and King of glory
Christian Burke, 1859—

A mother's prayer, written by Miss Burke in December, 1903, and published the following February in *The Treasury,* where it was headed, "Prize Hymn for Mothers' Union Service." It was included in *The English Hymnal,* 1906.

Miss Christian Burke was born in London. She contributed poems to various periodicals and in 1896 published a collection of her poetic writings, with the title, *The Flowering of the Almond Tree.*

MUSIC. The tune was found in *St. Basil's Hymnal,* published by the Basilian Fathers, Chicago, 1918. It bears no name and the composer is not identified. The hymn is also sung to the tune "Silician Mariners" (45).

MOTHER'S DAY

364. Motherhood, sublime, eternal
J. S. Cutler, 1856-1930

Suitable for Mother's Day.

Th hymn and tune are found in *Hymns of the Spirit,* published in Boston, 1937.

Julian Stearns Cutler, born at Thomaston, Maine, graduated from

214

Tufts Theological School, Tufts College, Mass., in 1885, and served Universalist churches in Marblehead, Melrose, and Orange, Mass., 1896-1904; in Little Falls, N. Y., 1904-10; and in Pawtucket, R. I., 1910-26. He wrote a good deal of occasional verse published in newspapers, especially in the *Boston Transcript,* and his collected poems were privately printed under the title, *Songs of Cheer,* about a year after his death. His hymn, "Motherhood, sublime, eternal," written about 1910, was adapted for use in Universalist hymn books and in slightly altered form in *Hymns of the Spirit,* 1937. It was taken from the latter for use in the *Hymnary.*

MUSIC. MOTHERHOOD. No information has been traced concerning the origin of this tune or its composer, Willis A. Moore, except that Moore was a member of the Universalists but left their fellowship some years ago. The Universalist Publishing House, Boston, from whom inquiry was made, has no further information at hand.

FAREWELL SERVICE

365. God be with you till we meet again

Jeremiah E. Rankin, 1828-1904

Written for the purpose of a Christian good-by.

The author, Jeremiah E. Rankin, was pastor of the First Congregational Church in Washington, D. C., when he wrote this hymn. Later, in 1889, he became president of Howard University, a Negro institution in the same city. He was always a friend of the colored people and did what he could for their advancement.

He has given us the origin of the hymn as follows:

> Written in 1882 as a Christian good-by, it was called forth by no person or occasion, but was deliberately composed as a Christian hymn on the basis of the etymology of "good-by," which is "God be with you." The first stanza was written and sent to two composers—one of unusual note, the other wholly unknown and not thoroughly educated in music. I selected the composition of the latter, submitted it to J. W. Bishoff (the musical director of a little book we were preparing), who approved of it but made some criticisms which were adopted. It was sung for the first time one evening in the First Congregational Church in Washington, of which I was then the pastor and Mr. Bishoff the organist. I attributed its popularity in no little part to the music to which it was set. It was a wedding of words and music, at which it was my function to preside; but Mr. Tomer should have his full share of the family honor.

MUSIC. FAREWELL was composed by William G. Tomer, 1832-96, an American journalist who made music his avocation. In early life he

215

taught school, later becoming the editor of the *Hunterdon Gazette* at High Ridge, New Jersey. The hymn he helped make famous was sung at his funeral by a large assembly of friends and neighbors.

OUR FOREFATHERS

366. Uplift the song of praise   *Frederick L. Hosmer, 1840-1929*

A hymn of praise for God's leading of our forefathers. The author traced his own descent from the Pilgrim Fathers, one of his ancestors, James Hosmer, having come to Concord in 1635. In writing the hymn, he had the Pilgrims in mind, but his words are fully as applicable to other immigrant groups such as the Mennonites who came at different times from Europe to settle here in "lands untrod."

For comments on Frederick L. Hosmer see Hymn 72.

MUSIC. LEONI (Yigdal). For comments on this tune see Hymn 14.

367. O God, beneath Thy guiding hand
Leonard Bacon, 1802-81

Written for the 200th anniversary of the founding of New Haven, Conn., celebrated April 25, 1833, in Center Church where the author was pastor. Dr. Bacon delivered the main historical address on this occasion and used the theme of the sermon for the basis of this hymn.

Leonard Bacon, son of missionaries to the Indians at the then frontier trading post of Detroit, graduated from Yale and Andover Theological Seminary. He was minister of the Center Congregational Church, New Haven, for the forty-one years from 1825 to 1866 and professor and lecturer at Yale Divinity School from 1866 till his death in 1881. Always interested in sacred music, he rendered a great service to the church by the hymns he wrote as well as his compilations of hymns.

MUSIC. DUKE STREET. For comments on this tune see Hymn 341.

368. In pleasant lands have fall'n the lines
James Flint, 1779-1855

A fine memorial hymn.

The author, James Flint, was born in Reading, Mass. After graduating from Harvard, he served as pastor of the Unitarian Church at East Bridgewater, Mass., 1806-1821, and at the East Church, Salem, Mass., from 1821 until his death in 1855. His hymns were published in his *Collection of Hymns for the Christian Church and Home,* 1840, the present being the single one which survives today.

MUSIC. WAREHAM. For comments on this tune see Hymn 208.

216

369. Eternal One, Thou living God   *Samuel Longfellow,* 1819-92

A hymn of the Church Universal, the great company of faithful souls of every age and land. The God who led our fathers, still leads His people into new truth and sets before them new goals.

For comments on Samuel Longfellow see Hymn 28.

MUSIC. WINCHESTER NEW. This tune is also used extensively with Milman's hymn, "Ride on! Ride on in majesty" (101). It was set to the hymn, *"Wer nur den lieben Gott lässt walten,"* in the *Musikalisches Handbuch,* printed in Hamburg, 1690. The earlier history of the tune is obscure, and its composer is unknown. It appeared in various collections under the name "Frankfurt" and "Crasselius." In a volume published in Glasgow, 1762, entitled, *The Psalm-Singer's Delightful Pocket Companion,* it was used in long meter and named "Winchester." It should not be confused with "Winchester Old" (191).

HOSPITAL SUNDAY

370. Thou to whom the sick and dying

Godfrey Thring, 1823-1903

A hospital hymn written in 1870 under the text, "And they brought unto Him all sick people. . . . and He healed them" (Matt. 4:24).

It was first published in *Hymns for the Church Service,* 1871, by W. H. Hutton. Later it was revised for the author's *Hymns and Sacred Lyrics,* 1874.

For comments on Godfrey Thring, see Hymn 89.

MUSIC. WALTHAM. The tune appears with its original name, "Gott des Himmels und der Erden," at Hymn 573, which see for comments on the tune and the composer. The original form of the melody is in triple time. Bach thought enough of the tune to use it in his *Christmas Oratorio.*

TEMPERANCE SUNDAY

371. Now to heav'n our pray'r ascending

William E. Hickson, 1803-70

A crusading hymn full of assurance that the cause of right, though delayed by its foes, will surely succeed in God's own time.

For comments on the author, William E. Hickson, see Hymn 348.

MUSIC. GOD SPEED THE RIGHT is attributed to Ernst Moritz Arndt, 1769-1860, a German preacher, editor, professor of history, and writer of sacred and secular songs. Julian speaks of him as a "man of learning, a true patriot, a distinguished poet. . . . a man of deep religious feeling, and a true-hearted and earnest witness of the Evangelical Faith." The *Dictionary* notes a number of his hymns but makes no mention of musical compositions.

LABOR DAY

372. Jesus, Thou divine Companion   *Henry van Dyke*, 1852-1933

A fine hymn on the dignity of labor, holding up the ideal of Christian service.

For comments on the author, Henry van Dyke, see Hymn 10.

MUSIC. HYFRYDOL. For comments on this Welsh tune see Hymn 69.

373. O Son of Man, Thou madest known
Milton S. Littlefield, 1864-1934

A hymn on the sacredness of work, connecting Jesus with the labor of mankind. The emphasis on the social aspect of religion in terms of our common life is a dominant note in twentieth-century hymnody.

The author, Milton S. Littlefield, was born in New York City; educated at Johns Hopkins and Union Theological Seminary; and became an honored and prominent Presbyterian minister. Recognized as an authority in the field of hymnology, he edited two hymn books and was elected president of the American Hymn Society, 1927-28. Besides the present hymn, he wrote another beginning with the line, "Come, O Lord, like morning sunlight." Both are serviceable hymns, and it is singular that neither found its way into the Presbyterian *Hymnal*, 1933.

MUSIC. BROOKFIELD. This tune first appeared in the *Congregational Church Hymnal*, London, 1887, edited by Dr. E. J. Hopkins (See 43). The book contained the best hymn tunes for congregational singing then available.

The composer, Thomas Bishop Southgate, 1814-68, received his musical education under Sir John Goss and Samuel S. Wesley. For many years he was organist at St. Anne's Church, London.

374. Though lowly here our lot may be *William Gaskell*, 1805-84

A hymn on the dignity of all work which is done through faith and trust in Christ.

The author, William Gaskell, studied at Glasgow University and Manchester College, York, and became a Unitarian minister. His one and only charge was Cross Street Chapel, Manchester. He became Professor of English History and Literature in Manchester New College and was an influential leader in the community in the promotion of education and culture. His denomination bestowed upon him its highest honors. Mrs. Gaskell, a woman of brilliance and unusual literary gifts was encouraged by her husband to engage in literary work to distract her mind from the grief caused by the death of their little son. She turned out to be a popular writer, publishing works of fiction and the life of Charlotte Brontë. A memorial to her bears testimony to her genius, and to the "tenderness and fidelity" with which she adorned the minister's home. Gaskell, a pioneer in social reform, wrote this hymn sometime before 1860.

MUSIC. ABRIDGE is also known as "ST. STEPHEN" (See 266 and 590). For comments on the tune see Hymn 266.

HARVEST AND THANKSGIVING

375. We plow the fields, and scatter

Matthias Claudius, 1740-1815

This is one of the finest harvest hymns.

In 1783 Claudius wrote a sketch called, "Paul Erdman's Feast," in which there is an interesting picture of a harvest thanksgiving celebration in the home of a North German farmer. The farm folk gather at the house of Erdman and as they do so they sing:

> Wir pflügen und wir streuen
> Den Samen auf das Land,
> Doch Wachstum und Gedeihen
> Steht nicht in unserer Hand.
> Alle gute Gabe
> Kommt oben her, von Gott
> Vom schönen blauen Himmel herab.

Matthias Claudius, son of a Lutheran pastor in Germany, became distinguished in journalism and literature. He studied theology with a view of entering the ministry; but through the influence of the rationalistic teachings in Germany at the time, he lost interest in religion and decided to take up journalism. Later, stricken with a critical illness, he realized the spiritual emptiness of the life he had been living, and again turned to his childhood faith. In the lyrics he wrote, though not composed as church hymns, there may be observed a transition from the spiritual impoverishment of the rationalistic period to a new type of religious poetry giving expression to a turning once more to the rugged faith of evangelicalism.

219

The hymn was translated by Jane Campbell, 1817-78, a successful teacher of music to children. She published a *Handbook for Singers* in which are found the musical exercises the author used in her work with London children. The original hymn is in 17 four-line verses.

MUSIC. WIR PFLÜGEN appeared in *Lieder für Volkschulen,* a collection of melodies for public schools, published, 1800, in Hannover. It was set to an arrangement of verses 3-10 of Claudius' song, with the chorus sung by peasants, altered to suit the melody. The hymn has ever since been extraordinarily popular throughout Germany. "The tune, in spite of its wide compass, has become one of the best known and favored of all hymn tunes, and fully deserves its popularity."

376. Thank the Lord

G. N. Fischer, 1748-1800
Tr. C. E. Krehbiel, 1869-1948

Based on Jeremiah 33:11,

> Give thanks to the Lord of hosts,
> For the Lord is good,
> For his kindness endures forever.
> (Am. Trans.)

> Dankt dem Herrn! mit frohen Gaben
> Füllet er das ganze Land!
> Alles, Alles, was wir haben,
> Kommt aus seiner Vaterhand.

> Dankt dem Herrn! er giebt uns Leben
> Giebt uns Nahrung und Gedeihn.
> O wer wollt ihn nicht erheben
> Und sich seiner Güte freun!

> Dankt dem Herrn! vergisz, O Seele,
> Deines guten Vaters nie!
> Werd ihm ähnlich und erzähle
> Seine Wunder spät und früh.

The author, Gottlob Nath. Fischer, was born at Graba, near Saalfeld. At the time of his death he was head master of the cathedral school and counselor of the consistory at Halberstadt.

The translation was made by C. E. Krehbiel, Mennonite minister and editor who was born at Summerfield, Ill., the son of Rev. Christian and Susanna Ruth Krehbiel. After completing his education at the Presbyterian Theological Seminary, Bloomfield, N. J., 1898-99, and in Berlin University, Germany, 1899-1901, Krehbiel became a member of the business firm, The Herald Publishing Co., Newton, Kansas, serving in the editorial and business offices for a period of 20 years. He served as editor of *Der Christlicher Bundesbote,* 1930-46, and as president of the General Conference of Mennonites for the two trienniums, 1935-41. Krehbiel was also a member of the committee that compiled the *Hymnary*.

MUSIC. RINGE RECHT. For comments on this tune see Hymn 563.

377. Come, ye thankful people, come   *Henry Alford, 1810-71*

A popular and widely used hymn at harvest festivals, especially in England. It was first published under the title "After Harvest," in 1844. In 1867, it was revised by the author, the form here being this revised version.

For comments on Henry Alford see Hymn 152.

MUSIC. ST. GEORGE'S WINDSOR has long been associated with these words, to which it is well suited in every way. Originally, however, the tune was set to the hymn "Hark! the song of jubilee."

For comments on the composer, George J. Elvey, see Hymn 118.

378. To Thee, O Lord, our hearts we raise
William Chatterdon Dix, 1837-98

A popular thanksgiving hymn, written in the author's most facile and musical style. The hymn was published in St. Raphael's *Hymns for the Service of the Church,* Bristol, 1864.

For comments on the author, William Chatterdon Dix, see Hymn 78.

MUSIC. ST. GALL is from *Katolisches Gesangbuch zum Gebrauch bei dem öffentlichen Gottesdienste,* 1863, the revised edition of the old hymn book used in the Benedictine Monastery founded in 614 A.D. by the Irish monk, St. Gall. It is a fine tune with a good swinging rhythm when sung at a fairly lively tempo.

NEW YEAR

379. Ring out, wild bells   *Alfred Tennyson, 1809-92*

From Sec. 106 of the poem "In Memoriam" (See 149).

After tracing his grief through successive Christmas celebrations, the poet burst into this song of confident faith in God at the opening of the new year. The poet turns from the past and rises above his private grief to sing of the future and its hopes for mankind.

For comments on Alfred Tennyson see Hymn 149.

MUSIC. WILD BELLS was written for this poem by Henry Lahee, 1826-1912, organist at the Holy Trinity Church, Brompton, England, for about 30 years. Lahee, a versatile composer, won many prizes for his glees, madrigals, and part songs.

The tune is very effective but too difficult for ordinary congregational singing. It was included in the *Hymnary* for use by singing groups preparing for special celebrations of New Year.

380. Another year is dawning   *Frances Ridley Havergal, 1836-79*

A prayer for the New Year, hailing its advent as another opportunity for progress, service, and training in close fellowship with God.

The poem was written in five stanzas of four lines each as the text of a New Year's card and distributed by Miss Havergal among friends under the title, "A Happy New Year! Ever Such May It Be!"

The omitted fifth stanza reads:

> Another year is dawning
> Dear Father, let it be
> On earth, or else in heaven
> Another year for Thee.

For comments on Frances R. Havergal see Hymn 126.

MUSIC. CRUCIFIX, of anonymous composition, was taken from the *Hymns of the Spirit,* Boston: Beacon Press, 1938, where it is used as a second tune to Miss Havergal's hymn.

381. Another year of setting suns

John W. Chadwick, 1840-1904

This poem came from the Unitarian stream of hymnody which was so strong during the middle of the nineteenth century. Chadwick, born at Marblehead, Mass., graduated from Harvard in 1864 and the following 40 years served as minister of the Second Unitarian Church in Brooklyn. He wrote biographies of Channing and Parker and is the author of considerable poetry. It has been noted that many of his hymns possess the simplicity and spirit of the writings of Whittier, the Quaker poet, and might easily pass for his.

MUSIC. HOLY CROSS. The source of this tune is not clear. It is ascribed in various hymnals to Thomas Hastings, to Mendelssohn, to John Stainer, and to Mozart. James Love, who was well informed on English hymn tunes, says that it was adapted from an anonymous organ "Andante" which was said to be based on a theme by Mozart. The tune, in 3-4 time, appears in the *Methodist Hymnal,* 1935, the arrangement credited to James C. Wade, an organist and conductor of choral groups, born in Staffordshire, England, 1847.

222

382. The year is gone beyond recall
Latin

Tr. F. Pott, 1832-1909

From a Latin hymn, *Lapsus est annus*, found in a Breviary of Meaux, 1713 and 1734. It was used for compline after the first vespers of the Festival of the Circumcision, which is the last office sung on December 31. The original reads as follows:

> Lapsus est annus: redit annus alter:
> Vita sic mutis fugit acta pennis:
> Tu, Deus, cursum moderaris, unus
> Arbiter, aevi.
>
> Gens tuis plaudit cumulata donis:
> Te simul votis Dominum precatur,
> Servet intactum fidei verendae
> Patriae munus.
>
> Supplices poscunt alimenta cives:
> Finibus morbos patriis repellas:
> Larga securae referas, benignus
> Commoda pacis.
>
> Postulant culpas venia relaxes:
> Limites arctos vitiis reponas;
> Past graves pugnas tua dat salubrem
> Dextera palmam.
>
> Noxiae vitae maculas perosi
> Cor, Deus, nostrum tibi devovemus:
> Da bonos annos, facilemque Patris
> Indue vultum.
>
> Dum dies currunt, redeunt et anni,
> Et gradu certo sibi saecla cedunt,
> Debitas laudes Triadi supremae
> Concinat orbis.

Text from Daniel, H. A., *Thesaurus hymnologicus*, 5 vols.; Lipsiae: 1855-1856, IV, 319.

The translation was made by Francis Pott, M. A., Curate of Ticehurst, Sussex, and one of the editors of *Hymns Ancient and Modern*, London, 1861. The original form of Pott's translation appeared first in a hymnal compiled by him, *Hymns Fitted to the Order of Common Prayer, etc.*, London, 1864. It reads as follows:

> The year is gone beyond recall;
> 'Tis gone—with all its hopes and fears,
> With all its joys for those new born,
> With all its troubled mourners' tears.

223

We thank Thee, Lord, for countless gifts,
For dangers we have passed unscathed;
We thank Thee for Thy Church preserved;
Oh! seal to us her ancient Faith.

Again we ask Thy goodness, Lord;
The coming year in mercy bless;
Guard Thou our land from pestilence;
And give us grace and plenteousness.

Forgive this nation's many sins;
Destroy the strength that sin has gained;
And give us grace with sin to strive;
And give us crowns through strife attained.

We hate the sins that stain the past;
We would henceforth from them be free;
O grant us peaceful years, good Lord;
And we will spend them all to Thee.

We would that our good Father's eye
Should look on us—but not in wrath;
And we, Thy children, year by year,
A purer song of praise pour forth. Amen.

When the hymn was selected for *Hymns Ancient and Modern*, the translation was altered into its present form. The last stanza is omitted in the *Hymnary*. The English and Latin are published in *Hymns, Ancient and Modern*, Historical Edition, London, Clowes, 1909.

MUSIC. TALLIS, also called "Tallis' Ordinal," is from *The Whole Psalter translated into English Metre, which contayneth an hundreth and fifty Psalmes*, a work by Matthew Parker, Archbishop of Canterbury, printed about 1561. At the end of the book are nine tunes in four parts by Thomas Tallis. This is the last of the nine and is set to the version of *Veni Creator Spiritus*, which appears in the *English Prayer Book Ordinal*. The tune was evidently derived by Tallis from a 15th-century English carol tune, "This endris Nyght"—for it is an adaptation to common time of the first two lines of this carol melody.

For comments on Thomas Tallis, see Hymn 33.

383. Great God, we sing that mighty hand

Philip Doddridge, 1702-51

A New Year's hymn from the posthumous edition of Doddridge's *Hymns founded on various texts in the Holy Scriptures*, 1745, where it is headed, "Help obtained from God. Acts 26:22. For the New Year."

It is based on Acts 26:22: "Having therefore obtained help of God, I continue unto this day, witnessing both to small and great, saying none other things than those which the prophets and Moses did say should come."

Most of Doddridge's hymns were composed for use in his own congregation in connection with his sermons. None of them were published during his life time.

For further comments on Doddridge see Hymn 56.

MUSIC. GERMANY. For this tune see Hymn 222.

WINTER

384. 'Tis winter now　　　　　　　*Samuel Longfellow, 1819-92*

A "delicately etched winter hymn" which appeared in *Hymns of the Spirit,* 1864, by Samuel Longfellow and Samuel Johnson.

For comments on the author, Samuel Longfellow, see Hymn 28.

MUSIC. MELROSE. For comments on the composer, Frederick C. Maker, see Hymn 112. This combination of hymn and tune was made by the editors of the *Hymnary.*

SPRING

385. The glory of the spring, how sweet
　　　　　　　　　　　Thomas Hornblower Gill, 1819-1906

Based on Psalm 104:30: ". . . . thou renewest the face of the earth," and Ephesians 4:23: ". . . . be renewed in the spirit of your mind."

It is an exquisite lyric, expressing not only the glory of the springtime with its newborn life, but depicting also, with rare beauty and power, the renewal of life which God works in the soul—a new birth of faith and love, prayer and song. The author himself wrote that, as a result of the study of the New Testament, "truth upon truth brake upon my gaze and God put a new song into my mouth."

Thomas Hornblower Gill, born in Birmingham, England, was brought up a Unitarian, but, unsatisfied with the Unitarian view of the person of Christ, he withdrew from that church and joined the Evangelical party in the Church of England. One of the major influences leading him to this decision was his study of the hymns of Isaac Watts. He saw "the contrast between their native force and fulness and their shrunken and dwindled presentation in the mutilated version in Unitarian hymnbooks." Gill published a number of books of poems which R. W. Dale, in compiling a hymnbook for his congregation at Carr's Lane, Birmingham, found "a very mine of wealth."

MUSIC. KING'S LANGLEY, "a delightfully gay tune," is an arrangement of a traditional English May-day carol. It appeared in the *English Hymnal* of 1906. The arrangement is by Miss L. E. Broadwood, an English lady of considerable musical talent.

SUMMER

386. Summer suns are glowing   *William W. How, 1823-97*

One of the most welcome of the hymns of the changing year. It was written for *Church Hymns,* 1871.

The author wrote a hymn for each of the four seasons, another appearing at No. 387.

For comments on W. W. How see Hymn 144.

MUSIC. RUTH, composed by Samuel Smith, privately printed in 1865, was set to the present hymn in 1874 by Arthur Sullivan when he was editing the music for *Church Hymns.*

Samuel Smith, 1821-1917 (not to be confused with the author of "My country, 'tis of thee"), was an English organist, serving Trinity Church, Windsor, for 34 years. He succeeded Sir George Elvey as conductor of the Windsor and Eton Choral Society.

AUTUMN

387. The year is swiftly waning   *Wiliam W. How, 1823-97*

A hymn for the autumn season. Like No. 386, it was written for the author's *Church Hymns,* 1871.

For comments on W. W. How see Hymn 144.

MUSIC. WAS KANN ES SCHÖN'RES GEBEN is from the *Gesangbuch mit Noten* where it appears anonymously, set to a hymn by Philipp Spitta, "Was kann es schön'res geben."

SCHOOLS AND COLLEGES

388. Father of men, in whom are one
Henry Cary Shuttleworth, 1850-1900

A deeply sympathetic Christian hymn, written for the Friendly Societies of the Church of England, but may appropriately be used for many occasions of a more general character. It is especially useful in the life of a college campus.

The author, Henry Cary Shuttleworth, was educated at Oxford for the Anglican ministry. He was a minor canon in St. Paul's Cathedral, 1876-84, and rector of St. Nicholas Cole Abbey, London, from 1883.

Concerned for the poor and down-trodden of London, Shuttleworth became a prominent member of the Christian Social movement. For a time he was Professor of Pastoral and Liturgical Theology in King's College, London. An able musician, he wrote many carols and hymns and published a book, *The Place of Music in Public Worship.* The present hymn appeared in the St. Nicholas Cole Abbey *Hymnal Appendix,* 1897, and in the *Church Monthly,* 1898, with music by the author.

MUSIC. ST. LO is a unique melody, constructed on three phrases of three measures each. It is a simple, diatonic tune, moving within the pitch range of a sixth, with the third phrase a repetition of the first. It should be sung in a quiet manner, and is well adapted for unison singing. The tune, an old Breton melody, appeared in *School Worship,* London, 1926, from whence it was introduced into the *Presbyterian Hymnal* of 1935 and from thence to the *Hymnary.*

389. O grant us light, that we may know

Lawrence Tuttiett, 1825-97

A prayer for the light from God to illuminate the mind in its search for truth.

The author wrote many of his hymns on returning from visiting the sick and bereaved, expressing in them thoughts of consolation for families in sorrow and trouble. That this hymn may have had a similar origin is indicated by the omitted Stanzas 4 and 5, which are as follows:

> O grant us light, in grief and pain,
> To lift our burdened hearts above,
> And count the very cross a gain,
> And bless our Father's hidden love.
>
> O grant us light, when, soon or late,
> All earthly scenes shall pass away,
> In Thee to find the open gate
> To deathless home and endless day.

Lawrence Tuttiett, son of a surgeon in the English Royal Navy, at first intended to follow his father into the medical profession, but, after studying at Christ's Hospital and King's College, London, he decided to become a minister. He was ordained in 1848 and devoted his life to the Episcopal Church, ministering in various parishes in England and Scotland. His publications include *Hymns for Churchmen,* 1854; *Hymns for Children of the Church,* 1862; and *Gems of Thought on the Sunday Services,* 1864. The present hymn appeared in the last-named publication.

Music. CANONBURY. For comments on this tune see Hymn 296.

390. Almighty Lord, with one accord

Melancthon Woolsey Stryker, 1851-1929

"A College Hymn" was the title given this poem, first printed in *The New York Evangelist,* February 27, 1896. It was included in *The College Hymnal,* New York, the same year and in the *Methodist Hymnal* of 1905.

The author, Melancthon Woolsey Stryker, a prominent Presbyterian minister, was educated at Hamilton College, New York, and Auburn Theological Seminary. After serving churches in Auburn and Ithaca, New York; Holyoke, Mass.; and Chicago, Ill., he became president of his Alma Mater, Hamilton College. A student of hymnology, he compiled several hymnals and books of sacred songs.

The hymn is appropriately used for commencement programs at Christian colleges. On such occasions it is often sung to the familiar tune "Azmon" (397).

MUSIC. PATTEN was written for this hymn for use in *The Methodist Hymnal,* 1905. The composer, Peter C. Lutkin, 1858-1931, the youngest of six children, was born of Danish parents, at Thompsonville, Wis., March 27, 1858. He was only a lad when both his parents died, shortly after the family had moved to Chicago. His ability at the organ and his success as boy soloist at the Protestant Episcopal Cathedral in Chicago opened to him attractive opportunities for the study of music, and he advanced rapidly. After teaching piano at Northwestern University for several years, he left for Europe to study music in Berlin, Paris, and Vienna, returning after four years to Chicago where he held various positions as organist and choirmaster. In 1896, he organized the Northwestern University School of Music and was given the title of "Dean." An authority in the field of church music and hymnology, Dean Lutkin did much through his teaching and writing to raise the standards of music throughout all the churches.

YOUTH

391. I feel the winds of God today   *Jessie Adams, 1863—*

For many years the authorship of this hymn was unknown since the writer preferred to remain anonymous. It finally came to light that the lines were penned by Miss Jessie Adams, a member of the Society of Friends in England. She was a progressive teacher and a leader of the local Adult School at Frimley, England, where she long resided. Miss Adams wrote the hymn after a long period of service as teacher in which she felt a considerable measure of disappointment and failure, as if tugging and laboring at the oars of a boat without making much headway. She wrote:

> If then, quitting the labors at the oars, we humbly believe that God's Spirit still leads us aright, we shall pass the point of danger and helplessness. Some little act of kindness may be as the upturned sail which that spirit waits to fill, in spite of past and future.

The message of the hymn is for our time. Many in our day labor at the oars, in their own strength, only to find themselves worn and discouraged. Progress comes by lifting the sails and permitting the invisible power of God to carry life forward.

MUSIC. HARDY NORSEMEN is an anonymous Norse melody, the origin of which has not been traced. It is a popular tune among the Dutch Mennonites where it is often sung at their young people's gatherings.

392. "Are ye able," said the Master   *Earl Marlatt, 1892—*

Written for a consecration service at Boston University School of Religious Education, in 1926, where the author was Professor of Religious Education.

It is based on Jesus' question of James and John, and their answer: "Are ye able to drink of the cup that I shall drink of and to be baptized with the baptism that I am baptized with? They say unto Him, Lord, we are able" (Matt. 20:22).

The second verse came to the author's mind as a result of seeing the Passion Play at Oberammergau, where he was greatly moved by the scene where the dying thief turned to Jesus and said, "Remember me when Thou comest into Thy Kingdom." "As Anton Lang, playing the part of Christ, said, 'Today, shalt thou be with me in paradise,'" the author writes, "Immortality suddenly became as real to me as the sunlight at that moment driving the clouds from the mountains, and I knew that nothing, nothing could ever shake my faith in that vision."

The hymn was written for the tune "Beacon Hill." The combination of words and tune was adopted as one of the school songs of Boston University School of Theology, whose students have carried it all over the world. It was incorporated into the *Methodist Hymnal* of 1935, from whence it came into the *Hymnary*.

Earl Bowman Marlatt, son of a Methodist minister, was born at Columbus, Indiana. He graduated from De Pauw University and then studied at Boston University, Harvard, Oxford, and the University of Berlin, becoming Professor of Philosophy at Boston University in 1923 and later Professor of Religious Education in that institution.

MUSIC. BEACON HILL received its name from Beacon Hill, Boston, where Marlatt resided when he wrote the words for this tune. The composer, Harry Silvernale Mason, born in 1881, was a student at Boston University when he wrote the tune. He is now serving as instructor in Fine Arts in Religion at Auburn Theological Seminary, Auburn, N. Y.

393. Just as I am, Thine own to be   *Marianne Hearn*, 1834-1909

A young people's consecration hymn, contributed to *The Voice of Praise*, 1887, published by the Sunday School Union of London. Verses 5 and 6, omitted here, read as follows:

> With many dreams of fame and gold,
> Success and joy to make me bold,
> But dearer still my faith to hold,
>   For my whole life I come.

> And for Thy sake to win renown,
> And then to take the victor's crown,
> And at Thy feet to cast it down,
>   O Master, Lord, I come.

It was written by an Englishwoman, Marianne Hearn (*nom de plume*, Marianne Farningham), who, in early life, was a teacher in the primary schools, and later became a successful writer of articles for various periodicals, including *The Christian Herald*, published by James Clarke and Co. For a time she edited the London *Sunday School Times*. Miss Hearn published a half dozen or more volumes of poetry and an autobiography, *A Working Woman's Life*.

MUSIC. JUST AS I AM. For comments on the composer, Joseph Barnby, see Hymn 21.

394. Savior, while my heart is tender
John Burton, the younger, 1803-77

A hymn of dedication to Christian service, suitable for use with young people's groups.

The author, John Burton, usually called "the younger" to distinguish him from another English hymn writer of the same name, was born and died in Stratford, England. From his 15th to 25th year he suffered greatly from ill health but recovered sufficiently to spend the next 50 years in business as a cooper and basket-maker in his home town. A devout Congregationalist, he served as deacon in his church and as a Sunday school teacher for 27 years. While visiting a poor chimney sweeper, he contracted small pox and died of that disease. He published several volumes of religious works, including *One Hundred Original Hymns for the Young*, 1850, in which the present hymn is found.

MUSIC. LILLE is an old French melody, the origin of which has not been traced.

(Correction: second last soprano note in the first score should be on B, not A as in the earlier editions of the *Hymnary.)*

395. Savior, like a shepherd lead us

Dorothy Ann Thrupp, 1779-1847

Published anonymously in the author's *Hymns for the Young,* 1836. Dorothy Ann Thrupp was born and reared in London where she spent all her life. She had a special gift for writing hymns suited to the worship experiences of children. A modest person, always avoiding personal publicity, Miss Thrupp did not always receive full credit for her work. This hymn is sometimes wrongly credited to H. F. Lyte.

MUSIC. BRADBURY was written for this hymn and derives its name from the composer. It first appeared in a popular Sunday school book, *Oriola,* published in 1859 by W. B. Bradbury.

For comments on the composer, W. B. Bradbury, see Hymn 103.

396. O Son of man, our hero   *Frank Fletcher,* 1870-1936

A hymn deeply sympathetic with the aspirations and needs of young Christians, and appealing to the heroism of youth.

Frank Fletcher was Head Master of Charterhouse School, Godalming, England, the first layman elected to such a position. He wrote these words in 1921, while on a motor drive between London and Charterhouse. After having been sung for some time in Charterhouse School, the poem was sent to a church newspaper, *The Challenge,* and from thence it found its way into the hymnals of England and America. The word "mate" in the last line comes from an explanation of the trinity given by a Bishop in answer to a working man's question on that subject: "God our Father, God our Brother, God our Mate." Fletcher heard the Bishop give this answer and the phrase stuck in his mind.

MUSIC. LONDONDERRY, the famous Irish traditional melody, is a tune which every congregation loves to sing. It rises gradually and skilfully to an effective climax near the end. The tune, unfortunately, has suffered at the hands of arrangers who have employed it, with various degrees of merit, for many different combinations of voices and instruments. Its appropriateness for church use is questioned only by those who have long associated it with secular words and occasions.

397. Lord in the fulness of my might

Thomas Hornblower Gill, 1819-1906

A consecration hymn for young people, much used in schools and colleges. It was written by Gill in 1855 and published in his *Golden Chain of Praise,* 1869, under the title, "Early Love. 'How good it is to close with Christ betimes!' Oliver Cromwell." The original poem has eight stanzas.

For comments on Thomas Hornblower Gill see Hymn 385.

MUSIC. AZMON. For comments on this tune see Hymn 12.

398. Shepherd of eager youth

Clement of Alexandria, c. 170–c. 220
Tr. Henry M. Dexter, 1821-90

A hymn to Christ, based on a Greek poem attributed to Clement of Alexandria, beginning with the line

Στόμιον πώλων ἀδαῶν.

The poem is one of two which Clement attached to his book, *The Tutor.* Some say it is the earliest Christian hymn extant. (But see comments on Hymn 34).

Titus Flavius Clemens, known as St. Clement of Alexandria, *c.* 170-*c.* 220, remains something of an enigmatic figure in church history. It is not known where or exactly when he was born. He was a pagan philosopher in his younger days. After his conversion to Christianity, he became head of the Cathedral School at Alexandria, then the center of Christian scholarship. Here he remained until A.D. 203 when he was driven out by persecution under Septimus Severus. Clement then became a wanderer and nothing is known of his later life.

Henry Martyn Dexter was a graduate of Yale and Andover Theological Seminary, a Congregational minister and editor. He translated the text of Clement's hymn into prose and then made a free rendering of it into verse, in 1846. The hymn was written for use in a service in Dexter's church in which he preached on the text, Deut. 32:7: "Remember the days of old," his sermon topic being, "Some Prominent Characteristics of the Early Christians."

Hymnbook editors have made a few changes in the text: "eager youth" for "tender youth" in the first stanza; and "let all the holy throng" for "infants and the glad throng" in Stanza 4. The third stanza, omitted here, reads as follows:

> Thou art the great High Priest;
> Thou hast prepared the feast
> Of holy love;
> And in our mortal pain
> None calls on Thee in vain;
> Help Thou dost not disdain.
> Help from above.

MUSIC. KIRBY BEDON was composed by Edward Bunnett, 1834-1923, a prominent English organist and composer of church music. The tune first appeared in *The Congregational Hymnary* of the Congregational Union of England and Wales.

399. Lead on, O King Eternal   *Ernest W. Shurtleff, 1862-1917*

Written upon request of the author's classmates at Andover Theological Seminary, as a hymn for their graduation in 1887. It has come into wide use as a processional and a recessional on baccalaureate and other occasions.

Ernest W. Shurtleff, graduate of Harvard University and Andover Theological Seminary, held Congregational pastorates in Massachusetts and at Minneapolis, Minn. He then went to Frankfurt, Germany, where he did his finest work as founder and pastor of the American Church at that place. He also served as spiritual counselor to a large group of American students in Paris. During the first World War, he and his wife were active in relief work in Europe. Besides his gifts as preacher, and pastor, Shurtleff also possessed ability as musician and writer, and published several volumes of poetry.

MUSIC. LANCASHIRE. For comments on this tune see Hymn 115.

400. Give of your best to the Master   *Howard B. Grose, 1851—*

A challenge to youth to give heart and strength to the service of the Master.

The author, Howard B. Grose, was born in Millerton, N. Y. After graduating from the University of Rochester, he served successively as pastor of the First Baptist Church, Poughkeepsie, N. Y., the First Baptist Church, Pittsburgh, Pa.; president of the University of South Dakota; and teacher of history in the University of Chicago. In 1910 he became editor of the Baptist magazine, *Missions.* He was a leader in the Christian Endeavor movement and wrote this hymn for a Christian Endeavor hymnal that he was then editing.

MUSIC. BARNARD was composed by Charlotte A. (Mrs. Charles C.) Barnard, 1820-69, an Englishwoman who after her marriage in 1851 began composing songs and ballads under the pseudonym of "Claribel." These were very popular in their day. She composed a hymn tune, "Brocklesbury," which is widely used with the hymn, "Jesus, tender Shepherd, hear me."

The descant was written by Professor W. H. Hohmann, head of the music department of Bethel College. The "descant" is an old variation in the use of tunes. It consists of a second melody over that of the tune and is to be sung by a few sopranos. It is only an embellishment and should be no more than audible, otherwise it will detract from the melody which should remain as the main center of interest.

401. Father in heav'n who lovest all

Rudyard Kipling, 1865-1936

"The Children's Hymn," in Kipling's *Puck of Pook's Hill,* published in 1906. It was written for boys, but is suitable also for adults. Permission to use the hymn in the *Hymnary* was granted by Mrs. Kipling on condition that all eight stanzas, unaltered, be used.

Rudyard Kipling, famous English writer, was born in Bombay, India, and died in Sussex, England. After receiving his education in England, he returned to India to engage in journalism and became widely known for his short stories, novels, children's books, histories, and books of travel. The Nobel Prize for Literature was awarded him in 1907, and he received honorary degrees from universities all over the world. His *Jungle Book, Just-So Stories, Puck of Pook's Hill, Rewards and Fairies* made him beloved of all children. His writings extol the virtues of clean living and manly duty which make a nation great. However, his passionate patriotism made him pen the unfortunate lines:

"O East is East and West is West
And ne'er the twain shall meet"

a prophecy completely discredited by the world events of recent years.

MUSIC. HEBRON. For comments on Lowell Mason, the composer of this tune, see Hymn 12.

402. Lord, through changing days, unchanging

W. Russell Bowie, 1882—

This hymn was written originally for the hymn book of the Hill School, of Pottstown, Pa., from which the author graduated as a boy in 1900, and where he afterward taught for a year. The motto of the school is "Whatsoever things are true" (Phil. 4:8). The hymn is built around that theme.

W. Russell Bowie was born in Richmond, Va. After taking an A.B. and an A.M. at Harvard and teaching for a year at the Hill School, he spent most of three years at the Theological Seminary of Virginia, near Alexandria, graduating with the B.D. degree in 1908. Part of his senior year was spent in special study at Union Theological Seminary in New York. For many years he was rector of Grace Church (Episcopal) in New York, a post he resigned in 1939 to become Jesup Graduate Professor of Practical Theology and Dean of Students at Union Seminary. He is the author of a number of books, the most widely known of which is the *Story of the Bible,* published by the Abingdon-Cokesbury Press. Among his other volumes are *The Children's Year, The Inescapable Christ, The Master: A Life of Christ* (1928) and *Which Way Ahead* (1943). In the late 1920's he was elected Bishop Coadjutor of Pennsylvania, but did not accept.

MUSIC. REGENT SQUARE. For comments on this tune see Hymn 81.

BOOK II

Hymns for Children

403. A gladsome hymn of praise we sing
Ambrose N. Blatchford, 1842-1924

Written by the pastor of the Lewin's Mead Unitarian Church, Bristol, England, for use in a Sunday school anniversary, 1876, in his church. The hymn is suitable for adults as well as for children.

Ambrose N. Blatchford, born in Devonshire, England, was educated at Tavistock Grammar School and Manchester New College, London. After serving as assistant minister at Lewin's Mead Unitarian Church for ten years, he took full charge in 1876 and continued until his retirement in 1915, an unusual record of nearly 50 years of service in one church. He was a man of sympathy with all classes of people, possessed unusual vitality, and was a trusted friend and pastor. Blatchford was interested in the life and progress of the community and became one of the most influential and most-loved men in the city.

MUSIC. CANAAN. The tune was taken from the *Hymnary* of the United Church of Canada. The composer is unknown. It is a good, fluent melody constructed on a straightforward melodic line which is repeated three times.

404. Children of Jerusalem
John Henley, 1800-42

A children's hymn of praise, based on Matthew 21:15-16:

And when the chief priests and scribes saw the wonderful things that he did, and the children crying in the temple, and saying, Hosanna to the son of David; they were sore displeased, and said unto him, Hearest thou what these say? And Jesus saith unto them, Yea: have ye not read, Out of the mouth of babes and sucklings thou hast perfected praise?

The hymn was written by Rev. John Henley, an English Methodist minister, known widely for his deep spirituality and entire consecration to Christ. Henley gave much of his time and energy in behalf of the suffering and poor in his parishes.

MUSIC. INFANT PRAISE, also known as "Children of Jerusalem," first appeared in John Curwen's *Tune Book to the Hymns and Chants for Sunday Schools,* published in 1842. The hymn and tune appeared a year later in *The Juvenile Harmonist: A Selection of Tunes and Pieces for Children,* by Thomas Clark of Canterbury.

John Curwen, 1816-80, was a minister in the Independent Church in England, and an ardent advocate of congregational singing. He developed and promoted the Tonic Sol-Fa method of teaching to sing. using it in his own church and schools, and lecturing upon it in various parts of the country. Resigning his ministry on account of ill health, in 1867, he established a printing and publishing business and assisted in the founding of a Tonic Sol-Fa Association for the promotion of that method of singing. Curwen compiled and edited popular collections of songs for use in Sunday schools.

405. Around the throne of God in heaven

Anne Shepherd, 1809-57

The author of this hymn was born on the Isle of Wight, the daughter of Rev. Edward H. Houlditch, a minister in the Church of England. In 1843 she married S. Saville Shepherd. The hymn, originally in five stanzas, is one of 64 hymns written by Mrs. Shepherd and published in 1836 under the title, *Hymns Adapted to the Comprehension of Young Minds.*

MUSIC. GLORY was published in England in Curwen's *Tune Book to the Hymns and Chants for Sunday Schools,* 1842, with these words. The combination of hymn and tune has continued to the present.

NATURE

406. A little seed lay fast asleep

Clara Writer, 1859-1915

A song of growth under God's daily care.

The lyric is a poetic description of the development of a seed from its first awakening to life under the touch of God's sunshine, to the tall, fair plant with its golden ear of corn.

No biographical information is at hand concerning the author, Clara Writer.

MUSIC. KING'S LANGLEY. For comments on this tune see Hymn 385.

238

407. See the shining dewdrops
Anonymous

No information is at hand concerning the origin of this children's poem on the theme, "God is good."

MUSIC. The melody appeared anonymously in *Kleiner Liederschatz,* a small but useful book of songs for use in German schools and homes. The book was compiled and edited by several Kansas teachers and school friends who preferred to withhold their names. It was first published in 1901, Newton, Kansas.

The arrangement was made especially for the *Hymnary,* by E. Shippen Barnes, in 1939.

For comments on Barnes see Hymn 48.

408. God sees the little sparrow fall
Maria Straub, 1838-98

A hymn of God's love, based on Jesus' teaching that God notes the fall of the sparrow and arrays the flowers in beauty and loveliness.

No information has been traced concerning the author, Maria Straub, or her contemporary, S. W. Straub, 1842-99, who composed the music.

409. Birds are singing, woods are ringing
L. F. Cole

A joyous song of praise. No information has been found concerning L. F. Cole, author of the words.

MUSIC. The tune, BIRDS ARE SINGING, is anonymous.

410. All things bright and beautiful
Cecil Frances Alexander, 1823-1895

A nature song. It was written, as were Hymns 104, "There is a green hill far away," and 412, "Once in royal David's city," to illustrate the Apostle's Creed, the present being a comment on the phrase, "Maker of heaven and earth." It is based on Gen. 1:31: "And God saw everything that He had made, and, behold, it was very good."

One of her stanzas,

> The rich man in his castle
> The poor man at his gate;
> God made them high and lowly
> And ordered their estate

is omitted in most hymn books because it is obviously not in keeping with Christian teachings concerning wealth and poverty. *(Cf.* the Parable of Dives and Lazarus). The author grew up in the wealthy atmosphere of an Irish estate where her father was a land agent.

For further comments on Mrs. Alexander see Hymn 104.

MUSIC. GREYSTONE. The first stanza, which serves as a "refrain," is to be sung after each verse. The hymn is an interesting study in metre. In the refrain, the first line is trochaic (— -), but the second changes to the more common iambic (- —). The tune is written to take care of this. It owes its unique effect to this refrain, which keeps coming in with this change of metre accompanied by a change of key from C to G. No information is at hand concerning the composer.

CHRISTMAS

411. The happy Christmas comes once more

Nikolai F. S. Grundtvig, 1783-1872

A charmingly fresh Christmas hymn written by the greatest of Danish hymn writers. An omitted stanza reads:

> O let us go with quiet mind,
> The gentle Babe with shepherds find,
> To gaze on him who gladdens them
>   * The lovliest flower of Jesse's stem.

Nikolai F. S. Grundtvig was born in Udby, Denmark, 1783, the son of a Lutheran pastor. He lived in a day when rationalistic "new theology" had dried up the stream of spirituality in the church. The church worship had lost its evangelical glow, and the sermons had deteriorated into lectures on science and domestic economy. Young Grundtvig, in the course of his studies for the ministry, had come under the influence of this rationalism and for a time lost all interest in religion. Various influences opened his eyes to the spiritual poverty existing in the church, and he became an indefatigable worker for the dawn of a new day in the life of the people. His zeal sometimes led him into extravagances which put him at odds with his fellow ministers, but his preaching and writings, nevertheless, became a powerful influence in Denmark and resulted in fresh stirring of the Spirit in the church. His poems and hymns, entitled *Hymns and Spiritual Songs,* were published in five volumes.

MUSIC. The melody is found in a book, *Children's Voices,* published by the Augsburg Press (Lutheran). No information is at hand regarding the composer, C. Belle. The arrangement was made by E. Shippen Barnes for the *Hymnary.*

For comments on Barnes see Hymn 48.

412. Once in royal David's city

Cecil Frances Alexander, 1823-95

One of a series of children's songs written by Mrs. Alexander to il-

240

CHRISTMAS

lustrate the Apostles' Creed, this being a comment on the second clause, "And in Jesus Christ his only Son, our Lord, who was conceived by the Holy Ghost, born of the Virgin Mary." Others in the series are "There is a green hill far away" (No. 104) and "All things bright and beautiful" (No. 410).

MUSIC. IRBY was written for this hymn to be sung by voices in unison, with harmonized accompaniment. It has become one of the best-known hymn tunes for children, and is always associated with these words.

Henry John Gauntlett, 1805-76, the composer, was an English musician who gave up law in 1844 to devote himself to music. He became a noted organist and prolific composer, his tunes running into thousands. He was much in demand for editing the music of hymn books and made a notable contribution to the promotion of hymnody of the church. Mendelssohn said of him: "His literary attainments, his knowledge of the history of music, his acquaintance with acoustical laws, his marvelous memory, his philosophical turn of mind, as well as his practical experience, rendered him one of the most remarkable professors of the age."

413. Come hither, ye children   *Christian Schmidt, 1768-1854*

A popular Christmas song which all children love to sing.

Christian Schmidt was born in Dinkelsbühl, the oldest son of the city clerk. In 1791, he was ordained to the ministry and given the headship of the school and made school inspector in Thannhausen at Mindel. His was a singularly fruitful ministry in which he devoted most of his talent to the benefit of the young people. He was in the habit of using the hours from four until eight in the morning in writing for young people, this being the only time of the day that he considered his own. As a child of ten years, he was greatly impressed with the nativity scenes which had been built in the corridors of the state church in Dinkelsbühl and which he saw daily during the Advent season. The vivid recollection of this childhood experience resulted in the composition of this beloved Christmas song for children:

> Ihr Kinderlein, kommet, o kommet doch all'!
> Zur Krippe her kommet, in Bethlehems Stall,
> Und seht, was in dieser hoch-heiligen Nacht
> Der Vater im Himmel für Freude uns macht.

> O seht in der Krippe, im nächtlichen Stall,
> Seht hier bei des Lichtleins hellglänzendem Strahl,
> In reinlichen Windeln das himmlische Kind,
> Viel schöner und holder als Engel es sind.

O betet: du liebes, du göttliches Kind,
  Was leidest du Alles für unsere Sünd'!
Ach, hier in der Krippe schon Armut und Not,
  Am Kreuze dort endlich den bitteren Tod!

Was geben wir Kinder, was schenken wir dir,
  Du bestes und liebstes der Kinder, dafür?
Nichts willst du von Schätzen und Reichtum der Welt;
  Ein Herz nur voll Demut allein dir gefällt.

Our translation, appearing anonymously, employs the first stanza and two others from the original not given here.

The poem first appeared in the second edition of *Christliche Gesänge zur öffentlichen Gottesverehrung*, Augsburg, 1811.

MUSIC. IHR KINDERLEIN KOMMET should be sung with lively tempo. No information is at hand concerning the composer of the tune.

414. Away in a manger *Anonymous*

A beautiful Christmas carol which has long been ascribed to Martin Luther. However, many of our best hymnologists—among them Percy Dearmer, James Moffatt, and Robert McCutchan—hold that it has never been traced to any of Luther's works, and that it does not resemble anything that Luther ever wrote. The words must, therefore, be classed "anonymous" until more information is forthcoming.

MUSIC. The music, too, is of unknown origin. The name of the composer, Carl Mueller, to whom it is attributed, is German and the tune is in the style of a German folk song. Other than this there seems to be no information regarding the composer or the tune.

EASTER

415. Joy dawned again on Easter Day *Latin*
Tr. John Mason Neale, 1818-66

The Latin original of this hymn comprises stanzas 9, 10, and 11 of *Aurora lucis rutilat,* one of the most ancient Easter hymns in existence. It is found in the earliest monastic hymnaries of the sixth to the ninth centuries with a wide diffusion in continental as well as Anglo-Saxon and Celtic sources. Its authorship is unknown.

The Latin text may be found in *Analecta Hymnica Medii Aevi,* v. 51, p. 89; A. S. Walpole, *Early Latin Hymns,* Cambridge University Press, 1922, p. 356; or *Hymns Ancient and Modern, Historical Edition,* London: Clowes, 1909, p. 199.

Aurora lucis rutilat

Stanza 9. Claro paschali gaudio
Sol mundo nitet radio,
Cun Christum iam apostoli
Visi cernunt corporeo.

10. Ostensa sibi vulnera
In Christi carne fulgida
Resurexisse Dominum
Voce fatentur publica.

11. Rex Christe clementissime,
Tu corda nostra posside,
Ut tibi laudes debitas
Reddamus omni tempore.

Doxology Quaesumus, auctor omnium,
In hoc paschali gaudio
Ab omni mortis impetu
Tuum defendas populum.

Gloria tibi, Domine,
Qui surrexisti a mortuis,
Cum Patre et sancto Spiritu
In sempiterna saecula.

The full hymn was used at first as a morning hymn throughout the Easter season. Later it was broken up into parts for various services during the day, as follows: *Aurora lucis rutilat*, stanzas 1-4; *Tristes erant apostoli*, stanzas 5-8; *Claro paschali gaudio*, stanzas 9-11. A traditional double doxology of two stanzas which varies in form but which is always present, completes the third hymn. The subject matter follows the Biblical narrative of the events of Easter morning.

The entire hymn was translated by John Mason Neale, *Collected Poems of John Mason Neale,* London: Hodder and Stoughton, 1914, pp. 121-122, and published in *The Hymnal Noted,* in 1852. The full translation which has been greatly altered may also be found in *Hymns Ancient and Modern,* pp. 198-199, in a traditional form.

Those who sing this hymn at Eastertide may be assured that it has been in unbroken use for fourteen centuries, a universal expression of the season's unchanging faith and joy.

MUSIC. PUER NOBIS. For comments on this tune see Hymn 87.

LOYALTY AND CONSECRATION

416. Hushed was the evening hymn   *James D. Burns,* 1823-64

Based on the incident of the call of Samuel in I Samuel 3. The verses were published in *The Evening Hymn,* 1857, a small volume consisting of an original hymn and an original prayer for every evening of the month, by Burns when he was minister of the Hampstead Presbyterian Church, London. The hymn lends itself well to dramatization.

James Drummond Burns received his training for the ministry at the University of Edinburgh. When the Disruption took place in the Scottish Church, he followed his teacher, Dr. Chalmers, into the Free Church in 1843. For reasons of health he went to France and some years later, his health improved, he returned to London and built up a strong congregation at Hampstead where a church had been newly organized. His winsome character and broadmindedness, together with an especially beautiful voice, made his work unusually effective. He published several books and is the author of an article on "Hymns" in the eighth edition of the *Encyclopaedia Brittanica*.

MUSIC. SAMUEL was composed for this hymn, the original arrangement, made in 1874, being for treble voices in unison, with organ accompaniment. The composer later made the present four-part arrangement in which form it has come into many church hymnals.

For comments on Arthur Sullivan see Hymn 113.

417. In our work and our play

Whitefield Glanville Wills, 1841–91

A beautiful prayer of consecration.

The author, Whitefield Glanville Wills, an Englishman, was born in Bristol. He published a small collection, *Hymns for Occasional Use* in 1881. The present hymn, entitled "Children of God," was contributed by him to *School Hymns,* England, 1891.

MUSIC. ROSSLYN is an English melody taken from the Supplement to the *Primitive Methodist Hymnal,* 1912. The composer is not known.

418. The wise may bring their learning

Anonymous

A hymn setting forth the important lesson that children, however poor, may bring useful gifts to the King. It appeared anonymously in *The Book of Praise for Children,* published in England, 1881.

MUSIC. ELLON is a perfectly adapted tune for these words, though it was written originally for another hymn. The tune is popular with children and is sung with interest also by adults.

The composer, George F. Root, 1820-95, an American musician, studied music in Boston and then became a teacher and organist. In 1841, he became associated with Lowell Mason in teaching music in the public schools of Boston. Three years later he moved to New York, where he taught in various institutions, including Union Theological Seminary and the New York Institution for the Blind. In the latter place, the blind hymn-writer, Fanny Crosby, was one of his pupils. Root organized and conducted many music institutes and joined his brother, E. T. Root, and C. M. Cady in the publishing of music in Chicago under the firm name, Root and Cady. He composed many tunes for religious and secular use, and during the Civil War wrote numerous "war songs" which became popular. He also wrote cantatas— *Under the Palms, David, the Shepherd Boy,* and others—which have been used by singing organizations all over America.

419. Tell me the stories of Jesus   *W. H. Parker,* 1845-1929

A hymn for children on the life of Christ. It first appeared in *The Sunday School Hymnary,* published in England, 1885. It was written by William Henry Parker, a member of the General Baptist Church in England, a layman, interested especially in Sunday school work. He was a machinist by trade, working nearly all his life in a large lace-making plant in Nottingham. For many years he composed hymns for anniversary festivals in the Sunday school. These were published in 1882 in a volume entitled, *The Princess Alice and Other Poems.*

MUSIC. STORIES OF JESUS was written for these words and included in a volume published by the National Sunday School Union, London.

The composer, Frederic Arthur Challinor, was born in Staffordshire, England, 1866, the son of a miner. Poverty compelled him in childhood to seek employment to supplement the family income. At the age of ten he began working in a brick yard. Two years later he found employment in a coal mine and then in a china manufacturing plant. All the while he was interested in music and spent his spare time studying harmony. By hard work and perseverance, he finally won his Mus. Bac. degree in 1903. Challinor has composed several popular cantatas and published more than four hundred compositions for voices.

420. Jesus bids us shine   *Susan Warner,* 1819-85

A hymn for small children, which first appeared, anonymously, in *The Little Corporal,* Chicago.

The author, Susan Warner, sister of Anna B. Warner (see Hymn 201), was the daughter of a reputable attorney in New York State. Her father fell into undeserved misfortune which left the daughters as the breadwinners of the household. This burden they fulfilled by writing stories and books. Susan's first book, *The Wide, Wide World,* published in 1865 under the pseudonym of "Elizabeth Wetherall," became one of the most widely read of American novels, second in popularity only to *Uncle Tom's Cabin.* It was translated into French and German and became a best-seller on both sides of the Atlantic. She also wrote a number of definitely religious books for children. Like her sister, Anna, she was buried at West Point, where the two had conducted a Bible class for many years for the cadets of the U. S. Military Academy.

MUSIC. The tune is by Edwin O. Excell, 1851-1921, an American composer of Gospel song tunes. In England, the hymn is sung to "Lumetto," a tune by Edward Arthur, composed in 1927.

421. Here we come with gladness   *Julia H. Johnston, 1852—*

Intended to be sung as a collection march.

The author, Julia Harriette Johnston, born at Salineville, Ohio, was educated at Gettysburg and Peoria, Illinois, High School. She was much interested in missions and Sunday-school work and frequently contributed articles to magazines, on those subjects. Among her publications were *The School of the Master, Bright Threads,* and the *Life of Adoniram Judson.*

MUSIC. AUS DEM HIMMEL FERNE is a traditional German melody of unknown authorship. It appeared in the *Gesangbuch mit Noten* and in *Kleiner Liederschatz,* and is a well known children's tune.

PRAYER

422. We thank Thee, O our Father   *Catherine Mary McSorley*

A prayer of thanksgiving, especially for the flowers which, growing in the most unlikely places, make the world so bright and fair and reveal the power and love of God.

Julian attributes the hymn to Catherine Mary McSorley but gives no information concerning her. The hymn appeared in the Appendix of the Irish *Church Hymnal,* 1891, and was published in *Church Hymns,* England, 1903.

MUSIC. ENDSLEIGH. For comments on this tune see Hymn 283.

423. Father, we thank Thee for the night

Rebecca J. Weston, c. 1890

A morning prayer. The words were written by Rebecca J. Weston, about 1890, but no information concerning her has been traced. This seems to be her only hymn. It appeared in a music-book, *The Tonic Sol-fa Course,* published by the Oliver Ditson Company. The editor of that book was the Rev. D. Batchellor, who composed the tune. The hymn was included in *Songs of Praise,* London, 1933.

424. Savior, teach me, day by day   *Jane Eliza Leeson, 1807-82*

"Love's sweet lesson" has never been presented more beautifully to

246

the young than in this lyric from Miss Leeson's *Hymns and Scenes of Childhood*, 1842, where it is entitled "Obedience." The Scriptural basis is I John 4:19: "We love him because he first loved us."

For comments on the author, Jane Eliza Leeson, see Hymn 298.

MUSIC. POSEN is a short, vigorous tune which children, as well as adults, love to sing. The bass is no less interesting than the melody.

The composer, George C. Strattner, 1650-1705, was an able German musician whose most important work consisted in editing the fifth edition of Joachim Neander's *Collected Hymns*, with music, published 1691, in which POSEN first appeared.

425. Jesus, tender Shepherd, hear me   *Mary L. Duncan, 1814-40*

A beautiful evening prayer, written by the author for her own children.

Mrs. Mary Duncan was the daughter of Rev. Robert Lundie, minister at Kelso, England. In 1836, she married the Rev. William Wallace Duncan, minister of the Scottish parish of Cleish. Between July and December of 1839, the year before her death, she wrote a number of hymns for her small children. These were published in a *Memoir* by her mother and later issued separately—twenty-three in all—as *Rhymes for My Children*, 1842. Mrs. Duncan, whose life ended so prematurely, was a woman of fine intellect and lovable character, the memory of whom has been described as one of the "aids to the devout life" of Scotland in the last generation. Her sister married Dr. Horatius Bonar (Hymn 129), minister and hymn writer.

MUSIC. EVENING PRAYER. For comments on the composer, John Stainer, see Hymn 111. The tune was composed for this hymn in the first edition of *The Church Hymnary*, London.

426. Praise Him! Praise Him!   *Anonymous*

A simple song, of unknown origin, which tiny tots love to sing. The truth the song enforces—"God is love"—is one the child will carry into adulthood and into eternity.

The tune is an arrangement by Hubert P. Main, 1839-1925, American composer of popular Sunday school and evangelistic music, and editor of many hymn books. For sixty years, Main was connected with the Bigelow and Main publishing house in Chicago, now out of business. His private library of song and hymn books, consisting of over 7,000 volumes, is one of the largest of its kind to be found anywhere. Nearly one-half of it is in the Chicago Public Library where it is known as the "Main Collection." Among his most popular tunes are: "We shall

Meet Beyond the River," "The Bright Forever," and "In the Fadeless Springtime."

427. I think when I read that sweet story

Jemima Luke, 1813–1906

A hymn that has gone all over the world and has been learned by a countless number of children of many nations and races. Concerning its origin, Mrs. Luke has written:

> I went one day on some missionary business to the little town of Wellington, five miles from Taunton, in a stage coach. It was a beautiful spring morning, it was an hour's ride, and there was no other inside passenger. On the back of an old envelope I wrote in pencil the first two of the verses now so well known, in order to teach the tune to the village school supported by my stepmother, and which it was my province to visit. The third verse was added afterwards to make it a missionary hymn.

Jemima Luke was the daughter of Thomas Thompson, one of the founders of the British and Foreign Sailors' Society and a "friend of every good cause." She volunteered to do missionary work in India, but ill health made that impossible. All her life, however, she maintained an active interest in foreign missions. In 1843, she married the Rev. Samuel Luke, a Congregational minister in Clifton, England.

MUSIC. SWEET STORY is an arrangement by Wm. B. Bradbury (see Hymn 103) of a Greek tune known as "Salamis" or "Athens." Mrs. Luke heard the melody (in its original form) used as a marching song by a group of children in a school near her home where she had gone to learn something of the teaching methods used. She was intrigued by the tune and wrote the words to fit it. The words and music are inseparably associated, the original form of the melody being used in England, and Bradbury's adaptation (easier but less interesting) in America.

428. Jesus loves me! this I know   *Anna B. Warner, 1820–1915*

A hymn beloved by all the children. It was composed about 1860. For comments on the author, Anna Bartlett Warner, see Hymn 201.

MUSIC. JESUS LOVES ME. Bradbury's tune was composed for this hymn in *The Golden Choir,* 1861.

For comments on William B. Bradbury, see Hymn 103.

429. Loving Shepherd of Thy sheep   *Jane Eliza Leeson, 1807–82*

From Miss Leeson's *Hymns and Scenes of Childhood,* 1842. Based

248

on John 10: 27: "My sheep hear my voice, and I know them and they follow me."

For comments on the author, Jane Eliza Leeson, see Hymn 298.

MUSIC. INNOCENTS. For comments on this tune, see Hymn 64.

430. I am Jesus' little lamb   *Henriette Luise von Hayn, 1724-82*

A song of the Good Shepherd's care of His lambs, based on Isa. 40:11: "He shall feed his flock like a shepherd: he shall gather the lambs with his arm, and carry them in his bosom."

Henriette Luise von Hayn, born in Idstein, Nassau, early in life gave her heart to Christ and often rose at night to spend hours on her knees in prayer. Influenced by the writings of Zinzendorf, she became interested in joining the "Brotherhood," against the wishes of her parents. One morning, after reading Matthew 10:37, "He that loveth father or mother more than me is not worthy of me," she decided to leave home and did so, mailing a letter in the neighboring village to her parents explaining her intention to go to Herrnhag to join the Moravian colony at that place. However, she was detained at Frankfurt and returned to her home. Her parents now granted her wish to join the Moravians and the rest of her life was spent as a useful and influential member of the Brotherhood, first at Herrnhag and later at Herrnhut, where she received spiritual instruction from Zinzendorf himself. On August 8, 1776, she wrote "Weil ich Jesu Schäflein bin," a poem of seven stanzas, in honor of Sister Christine Petersen's thirty-sixth birthday. Our hymn is a selection of three stanzas from this poem.

The German version of the poem is as follows:

> Weil ich Jesu Schäflein bin
>   Freu ich mich nur immerhin
> Ueber meinen guten Hirten
>   Der mich wohl weiss zu bewirten,
> Der mich liebet, der mich kennt
>   Und bei meinem Namen nennt.

> Unter seinem sanften Stab
>   Geh' ich aus und ein, und hab'
> Unaussprechlich süsse Weide
>   Dass ich keinen Mangel leide;
> Und so oft ich durstig bin,
>   Führt Er mich zum Brunnquell hin.

> Sollt' ich denn nicht fröhlich sein,
>   Ich beglücktes Schäfelein?
> Denn nach diesen schönen Tagen
>   Werd' ich endlich heimgetragen
> In des Hirten Arm und Schoss:
>   Amen, ja mein Glück ist gross!

No information concerning the translator, William F. Stevenson, has been traced.

MUSIC. WEIL ICH JESU SCHÄFLEIN BIN is a popular melody, from the *Gesangbuch mit Noten* where it appears anonymously. It also appears with the same words and translation in the United Lutheran *Common Service Book,* 1918, where the tune is credited to Dölker's *Geistliche Lieder,* 1876.

431. Sleep, baby, sleep Ferdinand F. Buermeyer

The author of this lullaby, Ferdinand F. Buermeyer, has not been traced. The words were written in 1876.

MUSIC. SCHLAF', KINDLEIN, SCHLAF' is a German melody composed by Louise Reichardt, 1788-1826, a German musician, born in Berlin. Her father, Johann Friedrich Reichardt, was a composer of operas and other music, and editor of a number of musical periodicals. Louise was a singing teacher in Hamburg from 1814 until her death. She composed many songs, a collection of which was published by G. Rheinhardt, Munich, 1922.

432. When He cometh, when He cometh
Wm. O. Cushing, 1823-1903

Based on Malachi 3:17: "They shall be mine, saith the Lord of hosts, in that day when I make up my jewels."

The author, William Orcutt Cushing, was a minister of the Christian Church and served congregations of that denomination in various cities in New York State. Towards the close of his life, however, he joined the Methodist church. He is the author of more than 300 hymns of the gospel song type.

MUSIC. JEWELS. For comments on the composer of this tune, George F. Root, see Hymn 418.

433. From yon distant heaven W. Hey, 1789-1854
Tr. J. R. Thierstein, 1867-1941

Aus dem Himmel ferne,
  Wo die Englein sind,
Schaut doch Gott so gerne
  Her auf jedes Kind.

Höret seine Bitte
  Treu bei Tag und Nacht,
Nimmt's bei jedem Schritte
  Väterlich in Acht.

Gibt mit Vaterhänden
  Ihm sein Täglich Brot
Hilft an allen Enden
  Ihm aus Angst und Not.

Sagt's den Kindern allen
  Dass ein Vater ist,
Dem sie wohlgefallen,
  Der sie nie vergisst.

250

A popular song for children which appeared originally in the author's *Noch 50 Fabeln für Kinder, nebst einem ernsthaften Anhang,* 1857.

Wilhelm Hey was born in Laucha, near Gotha, where he later became minister of the local parish. He received his education at Jena and Göttingen Universities and became a well-known writer, minister, and teacher. His stories for children and young people were widely read. As a minister he was especially helpful to the poor and sick in the parishes he served, and took much interest in the distribution of Bibles where needed.

The translation was made by John R. Thierstein, Ph.D., Professor of German and French, Bethel College, North Newton, Kansas. Dr. Thierstein was born in Bowil, Bern, Switzerland. In addition to his work as college professor, he served the church for a time as editor of *The Mennonite,* and at the time of his death he was chairman of the Board of Publications of the General Conference of Mennonites, a position he held for some years. In the latter capacity it became his duty to see the *Mennonite Hymnary,* 1940, through the press, a responsibility he discharged with efficiency and enthusiasm.

MUSIC. AUS DEM HIMMEL FERNE. For comments on this tune see Hymn 421.

434. Lo! the heavens are breaking   *Anonymous*

A spring song, setting forth the love and goodness of God.
Both words and melody are anonymous.

435. Can a little child like me

Ascribed to Mary Mapes Dodge, 1831-1905

A children's hymn of thanksgiving.

Mary Mapes Dodge, to whom the poem is ascribed, wrote stories and poetry for children. *Hans Brinker of the Silver Skates* is her best-known work. She was also first editor of *St. Nicholas* magazine.

No information has been traced concerning the composer of the tune, W. K. Basswood. Words and music were taken from *The Hymnary,* Toronto, 1930, published by the United Church of Canada.

MISSIONS

436. Remember all God's children   *Percy Dearmer, 1867-1936*

A missionary hymn for children, but suitable also for adults. It was written at the request of the Church Missionary Society (London) for their children's magazine, *The Round World*. A few months later, January 1, 1930, it was reprinted in *Songs of Praise for Boys and Girls*. The original is in three stanzas of eight lines each. The first stanza and the first half of the second, omitted in the *Hymnary*, are as follows:

> Remember all the people
> Who live in far-off lands
> In strange and lovely cities,
> Or roam the desert sands,
> Or farm the mountain pastures,
> Or till the endless plains
> Where children wade through rice-fields
> And watch the camel-trains:
>
> Some work in sultry forests
> Where apes swing to and fro,
> Some fish in mighty rivers,
> Some hunt across the snow.

Percy Dearmer, prominent figure in the Church of England, was educated at Oxford, served important posts as minister, and in 1919 became Professor of Ecclesiastical Art in King's College, London. He was editor of two epoch-making hymn books in England—*The English Hymnal* and *Songs of Praise*—and wrote an unexcelled handbook to the latter, entitled *Songs of Praise Discussed*. He is the author of a number of religious books.

MUSIC. EINTRACHT is a melody from the *Gesangbuch mit Noten*, arranged for unison or two-part singing by Prof. W. H. Hohmann, head of the Music Department of Bethel College.

Walter H. Hohmann, born at Halstead, Kansas, received his education at Bethel College and Bush Conservatory of Music, Chicago, the latter granting him the degree of Bachelor of Music in 1922, and Master of Music in 1928. After teaching several years at Freeman Junior College, and one year at Nebraska State Teachers College, he joined the Bethel College faculty in 1923. In recognition of his long years of service, Bethel College gave him the honorary degree of Doctor of Music, in 1947. He has composed a number of songs and served as co-editor of the *Mennonite Hymnary*, 1940. He is the author of a booklet, *Outlines in Hymnology with Emphasis on Mennonite Hymnology*, 1941.

BOOK III

Gospel Songs

437. We praise Thee, O God   *Wm. Paton Mackay, 1839-85*

A popular song in the Moody and Sankey revivals. It has few equals as a "rouser" in a revival or prayer meeting. To create interest and add variety in a special song service, Rodeheaver suggests that the leader try having the choir sing the chorus all the way through, the congreggation joining only in the "Hallelujah," and the last phrase, "Revive us again."

The author, Wm. Paton Mackay, received his education in the University of Edinburgh. For some time he was interested in medicine but gave that up to become the minister of the Prospect Street Presbyterian Church, Hull, England. He came to an untimely death through an accident. Seventeen of his hymns appeared in W. Reid's *Praise Book,* 1872. Among these was the present hymn, the author's most widely known work.

MUSIC. REVIVE US AGAIN is well suited to the text, though it is also used with Horatio Bonar's hymn:

Rejoice and be glad! for our King is on high;
He pleadeth for us on his throne in the sky.

Rejoice and be glad! for He cometh again;
He cometh in glory, the Lamb that was slain.

Refrain: Sound His praises! tell the story of Him who was slain!
Sound His praises! tell with gladness, "He liveth again."

The composer, John Jenkins Husband, 1760-1825, born in Plymouth, England, was clerk at Surrey Chapel. In 1809, he came to the United States and settled in Philadelphia, where he taught music and served as clerk of St. Paul's Protestant Episcopal Church. Husband is the composer, also, of several anthems.

438. Praise Him! Praise Him! *Fanny J. Crosby, 1820-1915*

One of the many fine lyrics by the blind poet, Fanny Crosby, first published in Bigelow and Main's *Bright Jewels,* 1869. A useful and popular praise song.

For comments on Fanny Crosby, see Hymn 313.

MUSIC. ALLEN, a favorite tune wherever gospel songs are in use, was composed by Chester Allen, 1812-77, who belongs to an American group of popular hymn-tune writers composed of Lowry, Bliss, Webb, H. P. Main, and others. No biographical information concerning him is at hand.

439. Come, let us all unite to sing *Anonymous*

A hymn built around the theme "God is love," I John 4:8, 16. The author is unknown.

MUSIC. GOD IS LOVE. This tune was composed by Rev. Edmund S. Lorenz, a prolific writer of gospel hymn-tunes, and founder and president of the Lorenz Publishing Company, Dayton, Ohio. Lorenz was born in Stark County, Ohio, July 13, 1854, and received his education at Otterbein University, Union Theological Seminary, Yale Divinity School, and the University of Leipzig. He was a pastor in the United Brethren Church for a time and then became president of Lebanon Valley College, a post he was compelled to resign on account of illness. Regaining his health, he went into the publishing business. He prepared *The Church Hymnal* for the United Brethren in Christ in 1935. His publications include *Práctical Church Music, The Singing Church,* 1937, and other volumes on sacred music.

440. There is no name so sweet on earth

George W. Bethune, 1805-62

A hymn honoring the name of Jesus. John Wesley always objected to words like "dear" and "sweet" applied to Jesus, as being too sentimental, and the terms are never so used in the New Testament. But the gospel song writers have employed them frequently and many good Christians have no heistancy in singing them.

George W. Bethune was the son of a prominent merchant, philanthropist, and churchman in New York City. On the day of his birth he was dedicated to God by his godly parents, their prayer being that the child may "be made a faithful, honored and zealous minister of the everlasting gospel." The son was given many educational advan-

254

tages and made good use of them. He was admitted to college at 14 and graduated from Princeton Theological Seminary when only 20 years of age. After serving for a year as chaplain to the seamen in the port of Savannah, he returned north to accept the pastorate of a Dutch Reformed Church and later served churches in Philadelphia, Brooklyn, and elsewhere. A man of fine literary taste and good scholarship, he was offered, but declined, the Provostship of the University of Pennsylvania and the Chancellorship of New York University. He preferred to be a preacher of the Gospel. To his son and sons-in-law, he gave this dying charge: "My sons, preach the Gospel. Tell dying sinners of a Saviour. All the rest is but folly." He went to Florence, Italy, for his health and died there on a Sunday night after having preached in the Scottish Church in the morning on the text, "Be of good cheer: thy sins be forgiven thee." The following poem, found in his portfolio, was written on the Saturday before his death:

When time seems short and death is near,
   And I am pressed by doubt and fear,
And sins, an overflowing tide,
   Assail my peace on every side,
This thought my refuge still shall be,
   I know the Saviour died for me.

His name is Jesus, and he died,
   For guilty sinners crucified;
Content to die that he might win
   Their ransom from the death of sin:
No sinner worse than I can be,
   Therefore I know he died for me.

If grace were bought, I could not buy;
   If grace were coined, no wealth have I;
By grace alone I draw my breath,
   Held up from everlasting death;
Yet, since I know his grace is free,
   I know the Saviour died for me.

I read God's holy Word, and find
   Great truths which far transcend my mind;
And little do I know beside
   Of thoughts so high, so deep, so wide:
This is my best theology,
   I know the Saviour died for me.

My faith is weak, but 'tis Thy gift;
   Thou canst my helpless soul uplift,
And say, "Thy bonds of death are riven,
   Thy sins by Me are all forgiven;
And thou shalt live from guilt set free,
   For I, thy Saviour, died for thee.

255

His body was brought to New York for burial. Among the directions he had left for his funeral was this: "Sing my own hymn, 'It is not death to die,' to a cheerful tune." The request was carried out. The hymn referred to is a translation he had made of a poem by the distinguished Swiss preacher, César Malan.

MUSIC. SWEETEST NAME. The name of the tune is obviously derived from the words for which it was composed. For comments on the composer, Wm. B. Bradbury, see Hymn 103.

441. Take my heart, O Father, take it   *Anonymous*

A simple hymn of consecration and devotion whose author evidently preferred to remain anonymous.

MUSIC. DORRNANCE. The tune is simplicity itself. Concerning his tunes, Woodbury wrote in the preface to his *New Lute of Zion*, 1856:

> The music is not designed for the fastidious and scientific musician whose highest delight, and perhaps sole worship, is music as an art, but for those who love to worship God in the simple song of praise.

For comments on the composer, Isaac B. Woodbury, 1819-58, see Hymn 261.

442. 'Tis the promise of God, full salvation to give
Philip P. Bliss, 1838-76

A hymn with a curious origin which became popular in revival meetings. It voices the spontaneous thanksgivings that break out at the announcement of a conversion. Bliss wanted to include "Hallelujah! Thine the glory" (No. 437) in his *Gospel Songs*, 1874. The owner of the copyright refused permission whereupon Bliss wrote "Hallelujah! 'tis done"—both words and music—as a substitute.

Philip P. Bliss, a Congregationalist, born in Rome, Pa., was reared in the country. He had only the meagerest early advantages for the development of his musical talents but he made the most of them and became one of the greatest leaders and writers of evangelistic songs. Combining the gift of poet and musician, he succeeded in putting gospel truths in poetic and singable form, usually writing both words and music. In his early career he conducted musical conventions throughout the Middle West, served as director of music for the First Congregational Church in Chicago, and was connected with the music publishing house of Root and Cady in Chicago. Through the influence of D. L. Moody, he gave up his business and professional pursuits and entered the evangelistic field. He assisted Sankey in the editing of the series called *Gospel Hymns*, in which some of his own celebrated hymns and songs first appeared. His rare gifts as a singer and leader, combined with an impressive personality, made him one of the outstanding leaders in the evangelistic movement. His life came to an early and tragic end December 29, 1876, in a railroad disaster near Ashtabula, Ohio, while he and Mrs. Bliss were returning to Chicago from Rome, Pa., where the two had spent Christmas. A railroad bridge gave way, resulting in a wreck which took the lives of one hundred passengers. Bliss had escaped unhurt, but going back to rescue his wife, he was evidently overcome by the flames which had spread and was not seen again. His premature death at the age of 38 was widely lamented.

443. Come, we that love the Lord   *Isaac Watts, 1674-1748*

This hymn, entitled by Watts, "Heavenly Joy on Earth," appeared in his *Hymns and Sacred Songs,* 1707.

For comments on Isaac Watts, see Hymn 11.

MUSIC. The tune is by Robert Lowry, 1826-99, a Baptist minister who held a pastorate in Brooklyn, N. Y., and did much to promote the gospel song movement. He edited a series of eight books for Bigelow and Main, with such titles as *Bright Jewels* and *Pure Gold,* to which he added a large number of tunes of his own composition. The public bought these books by the hundreds of thousands. Lowry had no serious training in music and did not take up composition until middle life. He was concerned mostly with the production of music which was popularly effective.

Watts' hymn appears in many hymn books with the more dignified tune, "St Thomas," by Williams (No. 269).

444. I lay my sins on Jesus   *Horatius Bonar, 1808-89*

The hymn, entitled "The Fulness of Jesus," was written for children in a desire to provide something which children could sing and appreciate in divine worship. It is generally supposed to be the first hymn Bonar wrote. He used to say of this hymn that it might be good gospel but that it was not good poetry. Bonar loved children and for them his first hymns were written.

For further comments on Horatius Bonar see Hymn 129.

MUSIC. PRYSGOL, composed by W. Owen, 1814-93, was taken from the *Hymnary* of the United Church of Canada. No information regarding the composer or the origin of the hymn has been traced.

445. I've found a Friend, O such a Friend

James G. Small, 1817-88

This hymn was written by a minister of the Free Church of Scotland

and appeared in *The Revival Hymn Book,* 2d series, 1863, and later in the author's *Psalms and Sacred Songs,* 1866.

James Grindlay Small was educated at Edinburgh University where Dr. Thomas Chalmers was one of his professors. He became minister of a church in 1847, but owing to peculiarities of voice and manner, he never succeeded well as a preacher. However, he was a man of fine Christian character and had the confidence of his brethren. Small was interested in hymnology and is the author of a number of hymns and poems.

MUSIC. FRIEND. The tune was written by Stebbins while he and Dr. Pentecost were conducting an evangelistic campaign in Providence, R. I. It was first published in *Gospel Hymns No. 3,* one of a series of popular books with which the composer's name was associated as co-editor.

For comments on George Stebbins see Hymn 38.

446. I have found a Friend in Jesus   *C. W. Fry*

A song of the friendship of Jesus and its meaning to one who experiences it. The words are based on Song of Songs 2:1-2:

"I am the rose of Sharon, and the lily of the valleys. As the lily among the thorns, so is my love among the daughters." Also on Revelation 22:16: "I am the root and offspring of David, and the bright and morning star."

The author, C. W. Fry, was prominent in Salvation Army circles in London.

MUSIC. LILY OF THE VALLEY is an English melody of anonymous composition.

447. One is kind above all others   *Marianne Nunn, 1778-1847*

A hymn on the love of Jesus, which has been used extensively as a song for children, especially in England. It was originally written to adapt John Newton's hymn:

> "One there is above all others,
> Well deserves the name of friend,"

to the Welsh air, "Ar hyd y nos" (No. 35), and the hymn may well be sung to this tune.

Marianne Nunn was an English woman of refinement and culture. She is the author of *The Benevolent Merchant,* and of several hymns. The latter were published in *Psalms and Hymns,* 1817, a collection

258

compiled by her brother, Rev. John Nunn, who also contributed some of his own hymns to the same volume.

MUSIC. CARITAS. No information has been traced concerning Richard W. Beaty, 1799-1883, composer of the tune. The editors of the *Hymnary* found the tune and words in the *Hymnary* of the United Church of Canada.

448. Brightly beams our Father's mercy

Philip P. Bliss, 1838-76

A song which is best understood by people living on the sea-coast or lakeshore, or whose lives are spent in work which keeps them upon the water.

The words were suggested by an illustration given by D. L. Moody in one of his sermons:

> On a dark, stormy night, when the waves rolled like mountains and not a star was to be seen, a boat, rocking and plunging, neared the Cleveland harbor. "Are you sure this is Cleveland?" asked the captain, seeing only one light from the lighthouse. "Quite sure, sir," replied the pilot. "Where are the lower lights?" "Gone out, sir." "Can you make the harbor?" "We must, or perish, sir!" With a strong hand and a brave heart the old pilot turned the wheel. But, alas, in the darkness he missed the channel, and with a crash upon the rocks the boat was shivered, and many a life lost in a watery grave. Brethren, the Master will take care of the great lighthouse; let us keep the lower lights burning.

MUSIC. LOWER LIGHTS. There is awakening power in the tune and congregations love to sing it. It is especially effective when sung by a large number of voices. The chorus lends itself to interesting antiphonal effects in a special song service. Let the whole congregation sing the first phrase, a smaller group the second; the whole congregation again the third phrase, and the smaller group the last.

For comments on the author and composer, Philip P. Bliss, see Hymn 442.

449. Lead me gently home, Father

Will L. Thompson, 1847-1909

Written by the author of "Softly and tenderly, Jesus is calling."

For comments on Will L. Thompson, who wrote both words and music, see Hymn 456.

450. I know whom I have believed

Daniel W. Whittle, 1840-1901

The hymn is built around the verse: "I know whom I have believed, and am persuaded that he is able to keep that which I have committed to him against that day" (II Tim. 1:12), which serves as a refrain. The general structure of the hymn is similar to Farrington's "I know not how that Bethlehem's Babe" (No. 99).

Daniel W. Whittle was born in Chicopee Falls, Mass. At the age of 15, he went to Chicago to work in a bank, but at the outbreak of the Civil War he became attached to the Illinois Infantry and served for the duration, going with Sherman, as a lieutenant, on his "March to the Sea." At the close of the war he was promoted to the rank of major. He was the treasurer of a business firm, when, in 1873, he heeded the call of God to enter the evangelistic field where he became associated with D. L. Moody. He was a powerful speaker and lecturer; and frequently, with the assistance of singers like P. P. Bliss, James McGranahan, and George Stebbins, continued evangelistic campaigns begun by Moody, under the latter's direction. Whittle was a great friend of children and knew how to put evangelical truth in words they understood, supplementing his talks with wall maps, illustrations, and chemical experiments. His daughter, Mary, became the wife of Will L. Moody, son of the evangelist. He was a member of the Congregational Church. His hymns, written after 1877, mostly for McGranahan, reveal true poetic talent, though he made no claim to be a poet. Among his best known hymns are: "I know whom I have believed," "Dying with Jesus," "Moment by moment," "Fierce and wild." The latter was translated into German by Ernst Gebhardt, translator of *"Ich weiss einen Strom."*

MUSIC. The tune is by James W. McGranahan, 1840-1907, who succeeded the lamented P. P. Bliss as song leader in the evangelistic campaigns conducted by Major Whittle. Between 1881 and 1885, Whittle and McGranahan made two successful tours of England, Scotland, and Ireland, and the chief cities of America. McGranahan, born at Adamsville, Pa., received only an elementary-school eduction. His native musical talent and some assistance from men like Bassini, Webb, Root, and Zerrahn enabled him to make rapid progress in music; and he soon taught music classes of his own. He was gifted with a beautiful tenor voice and an impressive personality to add to his power as a song leader.

451. O Christ, in Thee my soul hath found   *Anonymous*

The authorship of this hymn remains unknown. That "gospel songs" are often appreciated by highly educated and cultured people is illustrated by the fact that this hymn was a favorite of Professor Henry

Drummond, who used it frequently at meetings for university students in Edinburgh, 1885-89.

Music. NONE BUT CHRIST was composed for this hymn and published in McGranahan's *Sacred Songs and Solos,* 1883.

For comments on James McGranahan see Hymn 450.

452. Low in the grave He lay   *Robert Lowry, 1826-99*

The words and music of this Easter song are by Rev. Robert Lowry, written while he was pastor of a Baptist church in Brooklyn, N. Y.

Lowry was a faithful and successful minister of the Gospel, but is more widely known as a composer of sacred music. "I felt a sort of meanness when I began to be known as a composer," he said. His first love was preaching. Music was to him a "side issue," and the making and delivery of a sermon ranked far above the writing of a hymn. He is the author of the popular song, "Where is my wandering boy tonight," and wrote the tune to "I need Thee every hour," and edited many successful Sunday school and evangelistic hymn books.

For further comments on Lowry see Hymn 187.

453. I know that my Redeemer liveth

Jessie H. Brown, 1861-1921

A popular Easter song based on Job 19:25: "I know that my redeemer liveth, and that he shall stand at the latter day upon the earth."

Jessie H. Brown was born in Hiram, a college suburb of Cleveland, Ohio. Due to ill health in childhood ,she gained most of her education at home. At 15 years of age, she began to write for Cleveland newspapers and religious weeklies and for many years wrote hymns for Fillmore Bros. In 1896 she married Rev. John E. Pounds, at that time pastor of the Central Christian Church in Indianapolis, and later college pastor at Hiram. Her early poems bear her maiden name, while the later ones (No. 498, for example) are signed "Jessie B. Pounds." She is the author of 9 books, 50 librettos for cantatas and operettas, and nearly 400 hymns. Her best known song poems are "Anywhere with Jesus, I can safely go," "The way of the Cross leads home," "Beautiful Isle of Somewhere," and the present, "I know that my Redeemer liveth." The latter appeared first in an Easter cantata entitled, *Hope's Messenger.*

MUSIC. FILLMORE was composed by James H. Fillmore who was born June 1, 1849, in Cincinnati, Ohio, into a musical family. After his father's death, James headed the Fillmore music publishing business in Cincinnati for many years. His compositions include numerous popular

261

titles: "I am resolved," "I know that my Redeemer liveth," "Only wait-ing," and many more.

454. O the unsearchable riches of Christ

Fanny J. Crosby, 1820–1915

The well-known fact that Fanny Crosby was blind all her life adds pathos to the power of her songs. The hymn reveals the spiritual riches in her life nothwithstanding the cross of affliction laid on her through the loss of her eyesight. Frances Ridley Havergal (See Hymn 126), the gifted English poet and hymn writer, paid her tribute to Fanny Crosby in the following lines:

> How can she sing in the dark like this?
> What is her fountain of light and bliss?
> With never the light of a loving face
> Must not the world be a desolate place?

> O, her heart can see, her heart can see!
> And its sight is strong and swift and free.
> Never the ken of mortal eye
> Could pierce so deep and far and high
> As the eagle vision of hearts that dwell
> In that lofty, sunlit citadel.

> For the King himself, in his tender grace,
> Hath shown her the brightness of his face;
> She can read his law as a shining chart,
> For his finger hath written it on her heart;
> And she reads his love, for on all her way
> His hand is writing it every day.
> O, this is why she sings so free:
> Her heart can see, her heart can see!

MUSIC. For comments on the composer, John R. Sweney, 1837-99, see Hymn 342.

455. It may be at morn, when the day is awaking

H. L. Turner

A song of the imminent return of our Lord, based on I Thess. 5:2: "The day of the Lord so cometh as a thief in the night,"—and the lengthier passage in I Thess. 4:15-18.

Information concerning the author, H. L. Turner, has not been traced.

MUSIC. CHRIST RETURNETH. For comments on the composer, James McGranahan, see Hymn 450.

456. Softly and tenderly Jesus is calling

Will L. Thompson, 1847-1909

A song which has wide use as an invitational hymn at revival meetings.

Will Lamartine Thompson was born at East Liverpool, Ohio, and made his home there all his life. He attended Mt. Union College, Alliance, Ohio, and studied music at the Boston Conservatory of Music. His greatest interest was in sacred song, but he also wrote secular songs, among them the popular, "Come where the lilies bloom." A successful businessman and song writer, Thompson was known also as a man of beautiful and sterling Christian character. "Simplicity, sincerity, humility, and righteousness marked his life." He once called to inquire of D. L. Moody at a time when the latter lay very ill and visitors were forbidden. Moody insisted that Thompson be admitted and said to him in the course of their brief conversation: "I would rather have written 'Softly and tenderly Jesus is calling' than anything I have been able to do in my whole life."

457. Come, every soul by sin oppressed

John H. Stockton, 1813-77

An invitation hymn that has been a help and blessing to many. The original refrain:

"Come to Jesus, come to Jesus,
Come to Jesus now."

was changed by Ira Sankey to

"Only trust Him, only trust Him."

In leading this song, Sankey sometimes changed the chorus to

"I will trust Him," or "I do trust Him."

John H. Stockton, composer of words and music, was born at New Hope, Pa., and reared in a Presbyterian family. At the age of 19 he was converted in a Methodist camp meeting and became a Methodist preacher. After many years of pastoral and evangelistic work, as a member of the New Jersey Annual Conference, he retired in 1874. He had considerable musical ability and published two gospel song books, *Salvation Melodies,* 1874, and *Precious Songs,* 1875. He rendered valuable assistance in the Moody and Sankey meeting held in Philadelphia, after which Sankey wrote him:

I thank my Heavenly Father for enabling you to write so much sweet music, as well as words; and I hope you may long be spared to bless the world with your "precious songs." I wish you to accept our regards for one whose songs have been blessed to tens of thousands in the lands beyond the seas.

Stockton died suddenly while talking to friends just after having attended the morning service at Arch Street Church, Philadelphia, on March 25, 1877.

458. Just as I am, without one plea   *Charlotte Elliott, 1789-1871*

An immortal hymn expressing the feelings and needs of all penitent believers. It has been a source of comfort and help to multitudes of people.

"You must come to Christ just as you are." These words, spoken to Miss Elliott by Dr. César Malan of Geneva, at a time when she was suffering and spiritually depressed, resulted in a new birth and formed the basis of her hymn, written twelve years later, in 1834, and now known all over the world. The hymn was first published in the author's *Invalids' Hymn Book,* 1836, headed with the text, John 6:37: "All that the Father giveth me shall come to me; and him that cometh to me I shall in no wise cast out."

The words were written one day when other members of her family were busy arranging for a bazaar to be held for a school banquet. The immediate circumstances are related by Dr. Handley C. G. Moule, Bishop of Durham, as follows:

> The night before the bazaar she was kept wakeful by distressing thoughts of her apparent uselessness; and these thoughts passed into a spiritual conflict till she questioned the reality of her whole spiritual life and wondered whether it were anything better, after all, than an illusion of the emotions—an illusion ready to be sorrowfully dispelled. The next day, the busy day of the bazaar, the troubles of the night came back upon her with such force that she felt they must be met and conquered in the grace of God. She gathered up in her soul the grand certainties, not of her emotions, but of her salvation: her Lord, his power, his promise. And taking pen and paper from the table, she deliberately set down in writing for her own comfort the formulae of her faith. So in verse she restated to herself the gospel of pardon, peace, and heaven. As the day wore on, her sister-in-law, Mrs. H. V. Elliott, came in to see her and bring news of the work. She read the hymn and asked (she well might) for a copy. So it first stole out from that quiet room into the world, where now for sixty years it has been sowing and reaping till a multitude which only God can number have been blessed through its message.

Though a helpless invalid, Miss Elliott probably did more that day for her Lord and the upbuilding of His Kingdom than the rest of the family, all strong in body.

The hymn was sent to Dora Wordsworth, daughter of the poet, while she was on her death bed. Her husband, Edward Quillinan, has written of the incident in a letter to Miss Elliott, dated July 28, 1847. He tells of Dora's appreciation of the hymn and her continual use of it during her last days on earth.

After Miss Elliott died, more than a thousand letters, thanking her for this hymn, were found.

For further comments on Charlotte Elliott see Hymn 233.

A translation of this hymn has had wide use in Germany where it is sung to the tune, "Jesus, meine Zuversicht."

> Wie ich bin, komm' ich zu dir—
> Nichts hat mir die Tür erschlossen,
> Als dein Ruf: "Kommt her zu mir,"
> Und dein Blut, für mich geflossen;
> Diesz allein ermutigt mich—
>   Gotteslamm, hier komme ich!
>
> Wie ich bin, komm' ich zu dir!
> Auch nicht einen meiner Fehle
> Auszutilgen, steht bei mir;
> Meine schuldbefleckte Seele
> Wird gereinigt nur durch dich,
>   Gotteslamm, hier komme ich!
>
> Wie ich bin, komm' ich zu dir,
> Ob auch Zweifel mich umfangen;
> Umgetrieben bin ich hier
> Von so manchem Kampf und Bangen,
> Trübsal in—und äuszerlich—
>   Gotteslamm, hier komme ich!
>
> Wie ich bin, tret' ich herzu—
> Elend, arm, am Geist erblindet;
> Meinen Mangel stillest du;
> Heilung, Reichtum, der nicht schwindet,
> Alles finde ich durch dich—
>   Gotteslamm, hier komme ich!
>
> Wie ich bin, komm' ich zu dir,
> Deine Liebe sonder Gleichen
> Ist zu stark geworden mir,
> Alle Schranken müssen weichen;
> Dir, nur dir verschreib' ich mich—
>   Gotteslamm, hier komme ich!

MUSIC. WOODWORTH was first published in Hastings' and Bradbury's hymnal, *The Third Book of Psalms,* 1849, set to the words, "The

God of love will surely indulge." The tune became widely known after its association with "Just as I am, without one plea." It is the most popular of Bradbury's tunes and appears in nearly all American hymnals.

For comments on Wm. Bradbury see Hymn 103.

459. Come, ye sinners, poor and needy   Joseph Hart, 1712-68

An evangelistic song, written by a Congregational minister. Hart, born in London and brought up in a devout Christian home, was well educated and taught the classics for many years. Early in life he departed from his religious training and fell into a life of "carnal and spiritual wickedness, irreligious and profane." After continuing in this state for a long period of years, during which he exerted a pernicious influence upon all with whom he associated, Hart became deeply convicted, in his fortieth year, and betook himself to daily prayer and Bible reading. He was finally converted upon hearing a sermon on Rev. 3:10: "Because thou hast kept the word of my patience, I also will keep thee from the hour of temptation, which shall come upon all the world, to try them that dwell upon the earth"—preached in the Moravian Chapel in Fetter Lane, London. Becoming an earnest and consecrated Christian, and writer of hymns, he was importuned to become a preacher, which he did, although in his 48th year. From 1760 till his death in 1768, he preached regularly as pastor of an Independent Congregation in London, drawing large crowds. He died in the midst of labors and successes almost unprecedented, and it is said that 20,000 people came to his funeral. He is remembered chiefly, however, for his hymns, most of them of the evangelistic type.

MUSIC. GREENVILLE, a beautifully quaint and popular tune, was not written for sacred use but for a little song in the opera *Le Devin du Village,* by Rousseau. It was once popular in a piano arrangement known as "Rousseau's Dream."

Jean Jacques Rousseau, 1712-78, philosopher and musician, was born at Geneva. Though not a religious man, he greatly influenced education in Europe and became one of the great forces in modern literature. A political radical, he was forced to leave France and for a time lived in England. His opera, *Le Devin du Village,* was a success, but none of his later musical efforts came to anything. He lived an unhappy life and is thought to have committed suicide. His death occurred near Paris, July 3, 1778.

460. I have a Savior, He's pleading in glory   S. O'Maley Cluff

A favorite prayer-meeting hymn for many years, in many churches.

Sankey came across these words in a printed leaflet while he was on his first visit with D. L. Moody to Ireland in 1874. It was the second hymn to which he wrote music and was much used in later Moody-Sankey revival services.

No definite information has been traced by hymnologists concerning Samuel O'Malley Clough to whom the words are attributed. He is believed to have been an Irish clergyman who left the Established Church to unite with the Plymouth Brethren in Ireland; later (1881) seceding from that body to lead a "holiness" schism which has since become extinct. Julian and others spell the name "Clough"; Sankey spells it "Cluff."

MUSIC. CLUFF derives its name from the author of the words to which Sankey set the tune.

Ira David Sankey, 1840-1908, famous singer of "gospel songs," was born in Edinburg, Pa., and was a member of the Methodist Church. For many years he was associated with D. L. Moody in evangelistic work in America and England. He composed many gospel tunes, the most popular of which is his "Ninety and Nine," and edited numerous songbooks. Concerning his own gift of singing and songs suited to his purpose, he wrote:

> I am no musician, I am no singer; I was never taught to sing.
> . . . As to my singing there is no art or conscious design in it.
> I never touch a song that does not speak to me in every word and phrase. Before I sing I must feel, and the hymn must be of such a kind that I know I can send home what I feel into the hearts of those who listen. I find it much more difficult to get good words than good music. Our best words come from England; the music which best suits our purpose comes from America. Your composers, apparently, do not care to write simple songs such as we need. We can get plenty of the grand and solid style, but though that is useful now and again, our services could not thrive on it.

Homer Rhodeheaver has used this song with antiphonal effects by letting the choir sing the first phrase of the refrain, the audience responding with the second; or, if the audience is large, letting one side, then the other side, then the whole congregation, then the gallery sing, successively, one phrase each of the refrain.

461. A ruler once came to Jesus by night   *W. T. Sleeper*

Based on our Lord's words to Nicodemus: "Verily, verily, I say unto you, . . . ye must be born again" (John 3:3-7).

The hymn was written by Rev. W. T. Sleeper, one of the pastors in the city of Worcester, Mass., upon the request of Geo. C. Stebbins, who was assisting Dr. Pentecost in a revivalistic campaign in that city. One of the latter's sermon themes was "The New Birth." As the truth of this great theme was being enforced and illustrated, it occurred to Stebbins that a musical setting of this Scripture passage in John 3 would be an effective means of emphasizing the truth of the new birth. He asked the Rev. Sleeper to write some verses on the subject and the result was this hymn. Before the meetings closed, Stebbins had composed this tune for the words. The song was published in *Gospel Hymns, No. 3,* and has been widely used as solo, choir number, and congregational song in revival meetings and otherwise.

MUSIC. BORN AGAIN. For comments on George C. Stebbins, 1846-1945, a composer of the tune, see Hymn 38.

462. I hear the Savior say   *Elvina M. Hall,* 1818-?

A much-used and much-loved revival hymn which came into use, especially in Methodist churches, several years before Moody's great revivalistic movement.

Mrs. Elvina M. Hall (later Mrs. Myers), author of the words, was born in Alexandria, Va., in 1818. She composed this hymn, strangely enough, while sitting in the choir of the M. E. Church, Baltimore, penciling the first draft on a fly-leaf of a hymn book, *The New Lute of Zion,* during the pastor's prayer! It is the only hymn known that can be traced to such an origin. The author's mind, indeed, wandered from the immediate service of worship, but it did not stray from God and prayer.

MUSIC. ALL TO CHRIST. John T. Grape, born in Baltimore, Md., 1833, was choir director in his church when he wrote the tune, after having made it "a matter of prayer and study." He writes that "it was pronounced very poor by my choir and my friends, but my dear wife persistently declared it was a good piece of music and would live." Mrs. Grape's faith was justified by the wide reception and use the tune has enjoyed. The minister of the church, Rev. Mr. Schrick, liked the tune upon hearing it and suggested that it be used with the words written by Mrs. Elvina M. Hall. This was done, and the song started on its career. It was first published in a volume called, *Sabbath Chords.*

463. Amazing grace! how sweet the sound
                                        John Newton, 1725-1807
The original has six stanzas and is entitled, "Faith's Review and Expectation."

The hymn reminds one of Newton's words: "I can never forget two things: first, that I was a great sinner, and second, that Jesus is a great Saviour." It is based on I Chron. 17:16, 17:

Who am I, O Lord God, and what is mine house, that Thou hast brought me hitherto? And yet this was a small thing in thine eyes, O God; for thou hast also spoken of thy servants's house for a great while to come, and hast regarded me according to the estate of a man of high degree, O Lord God.

For comments on John Newton, see Hymn 274.

MUSIC. MCINTOSH, also known as "Amazing Grace," is believed to be an old Southern melody. It appeared in *Southern Harmony,* by William Walker, 1835, anonymously. Dr. Robert McCutchan thinks it may be a variant of an old tune called "Loving Lamb."

For comments on Edwin O. Excell, 1851-1921, who arranged the tune, see Hymn 420.

464. Down at the cross where my Savior died

Elisha A. Hoffman, 1839-?

The words are by the Rev. Elisha A. Hoffman who was born of Pennsylvania German parents. Hoffman became a Congregational minister and served churches of his denomination in Lebanon, Pa., and other places, and wrote a number of hymns and tunes.

MUSIC. GLORY TO HIS NAME. For comments on the composer of this tune, Rev. John H. Stockton, see Hymn 457.

465. O happy day, that fixed my choice

Philip Doddridge, 1702-51

This hymn, reflecting spiritual joy, is often used at baptismal services and is also one of the best revival hymns. It is based on II Chron. 15: 15: "And all Judah rejoiced at the oath; for they had sworn with all their heart, and sought him with their whole desire; . . . and the Lord gave them rest round about."

The original title was "Rejoicing in our covenant engagements to God." It was published in 1819, by the author's great-grandson, John Doddridge Humphreys.

The hymn was chosen by Prince Albert, the consort of Queen Victoria, to be sung always on occasions when members of the royal family were confirmed. It reflects a deep and rich experience of God. "Blessed is the man," says James Montgomery, "who can take the words of the hymn and make them his own from similar experience."

For comments on Philip Doddridge see Hymn 56.

MUSIC. HAPPY DAY is an adaptation from a work by E. F. Rimbault, 1816-76, a London scholar, musician and writer. He became organist at Swiss Church, Soho, London, and was offered, but declined, the chair of professor of music at Harvard University. The tune was originally a popular secular melody. The English *Hymnary* uses this hymn set to a tune called "Heaton Norris," with refrain omitted.

466. Sinners Jesus will receive

Arr. from Erdmann Neumeister, 1671-1756
Tr. Emma Frances Beaven, 1827-1909

An English version of a popular German hymn which appeared first in the author's *Evangelische Nachklänge*, Hamburg, 1719. The hymn is appropriate for missionary services. The original in eight stanzas, written by Neumeister as a conclusion to a sermon on Luke 15:1, "Then drew near to him all the publicans and sinners for to hear him," is as follows:

1. Jesus nimmt die Sünder an;
   Saget doch dies Trostwort allen,
   Welche von der rechten Bahn
   Auf verkehrten Weg verfallen!
   Hier ist, was sie retten kann:
   Jesus nimmt die Sünder an.

2. Keiner Gnade sind wir wert,
   Doch hat er in seinem Worte
   Eidlich sich dazu erklärt
   Sehet nur, die Gnadenpforte
   Ist hier völlig aufgetan:
   Jesus nimmt die Sünder an.

3. Wenn ein Schaf verloren ist,
   Suchet es ein treuer Hirte;
   Jesus, der uns nie vergisst,
   Suchet treulich das Verirrte,
   Dass es nicht verderben kann:
   Jesus nimmt die Sünder an.

4. Kommet alle, kommet her,
   Kommet, ihr betrübten Sünder!
   Jesus rufet euch, und er
   Macht aus Sündern Gottes Kinder.
   Glaubet's doch und denket dran:
   Jesus nimmt die Sünder an.

5. Ich Betrübter komme hier
   Und bekenne meine Sünden.
   Lass, mein Heiland, mich bei dir
   Gnade zur Vergebung finden,
   Dass dies Wort mich trösten kann:
   Jesus nimmt die Sünder an.

6. Ich bin ganz getrostes Muts.
   Ob die Sünden blutrot wären,
   Müssten sie kraft deines Bluts
   Dennoch sich in Schneeweiss kehren
   Da ich gläubig sprechen kann:
   Jesus nimmt die Sünder an.

7. Mein Gewissen beisst mich nicht,
   Moses darf mich nicht verklagen;
   Der mich frei und ledig spricht,
   Hat die Schulden abgetragen,
   Dass mich nichts verdammen kann:
   Jesus nimmt die Sünder an.

8. Jesus nimmt die Sünder an,
   Mich hat er auch angenommen
   Und den Himmel aufgetan,
   Dass ich selig zu ihm kommen
   Und auf den Trost sterben kann:
   Jesus nimmt die Sünder an.

The four stanzas of our text correspond to stanzas 1, 4, 7, and 8 of the original. The translation is by Mrs. Emma Frances Beaven, 1827-1909, concerning whom no biographical information has been traced. Her work was altered somewhat to fit McGranahan's tune.

Erdmann Neumeister was a distinguished student and afterwards lecturer at Leipsig University. Later he achieved fame as a court preacher and as pastor of St. James' Church, Hamburg. An eloquent preacher and a strong High Lutheran, he opposed the Moravians and the Pietists of his day, holding that their teachings were too subjective. Besides being a gifted preacher, he was also a musician of ability and eminence. He originated the cantata form of church music and composed a number of works in that form. He is the author of 650 hymns, many of them of the highest rank and still in general use in Germany though only a few have been translated into English.

MUSIC. NEUMEISTER. For comments on the composer of this popular gospel tune with its change of rhythm in the refrain, James McGranahan, see Hymn 450.

The German words are set to the tune, *"Grosser Gott wir loben Dich"* in the *Gesangbuch mit Noten.*

467. The whole world was lost   *Philip P. Bliss, 1838-76*

Based on the incident in John 9, in which Jesus restored the sight to the man born blind, and the saying of Jesus, "I am the light of the world" (John 9:5).

For comments on Philip P. Bliss, author and composer, see Hymn 442.

468. Jesus, my all, to heaven is gone   *John Cennick, 1718-55*

A hymn which has had wide use in prayer-meeting and camp-meeting assemblies. A hearty unison "crescendo" on the last stanza is impressive:

> "Then will I tell to sinners round
> What a dear Savior I have found;
> I'll point to His redeeming blood,
> And say, 'Behold, the way to God.' "

The author had known the joy of finding Christ and his hymn reflects his personal experience. While frequenting London, as a youth, in a vain search for employment,

> He became addicted, in consequence, to sight-seeing, song-singing, play-going, card-playing, horse-racing, ball-frequenting, and the like. But on an Easter visit to London, in 1735, he was seriously impressed as he was walking hastily in Cheapside. He became greatly distressed on account of his sins, broke off from his sinful course, and walked softly before God; but he found no peace until September 6, 1737, in his nineteenth year, when he was enabled to trust in Christ alone and find joy and peace in believing.

For further comments on John Cennick, see Hymn 130.

MUSIC. DUANE STREET, a stirring revival tune, was composed by Rev. George Coles, in 1835, for one of James Montgomery's hymns, but has been associated with this hymn for many years.

George Coles, 1792-1858, was born in Stewkley, England, and died in New York City. He came to America as a young man and spent all his life in the Methodist ministry. He was editor of the *New York Christian Advocate* and the *Sunday School Advocate,* for some years, and was a composer of ability, besides being a good singer.

469. Lord Jesus, I long to be perfectly whole
James Nicholson, 19th cent.

A hymn that has brought joy and release to many sin-burdened souls, especially encouraging with its promise in stanza 4:

> "To those who have sought Thee
> Thou never saidst, No."

It is built around the verse
> "Wash me, and I shall be whiter than snow" (Psalm 51:7).

The hymn appeared in Sankey's *Songs and Solos.*

The author, James Nicholson, was an American Methodist minister of the 19th century.

MUSIC. FISCHER. The composer, William Gustavus Fischer, 1835-1912, was born in Baltimore, Md. Moving to Philadelphia in early life, he received a good musical education and became a teacher of piano and singing, and conductor of choral groups and Welsh singing societies in that city. For ten years he was Professor of Music at Girard College, and at the same time became associated with J. E. Gould in a flourishing piano business, under the firm name of Gould and Fischer. in 1876, he led the Moody and Sankey choir in the great building at Thirteenth and Market Streets in Philadelphia.

470. O Thou, in whose presence my soul takes delight

Joseph Swain, 1761-96

Swain entitled this hymn, "A Description of Christ by His Grace and Power," which was suggested to him by the description of the "Shepherd" in Solomon's Song 1:7. The original poem has nine stanzas of eight lines each.

For comments on the author, John Swain, see Hymn 323.

MUSIC. MY BELOVED, also called "Beloved" and "Meditation," is of uncertain origin. It appeared in a book, *The Beauties of Harmony*, compiled by Freeman Lewis in 1813 and was arranged by Hubert P. Main in 1869. Lewis, 1780-1859, was by profession a surveyor at Uniontown, Pa. Music was his avocation.

For comments on Hubert P. Main see Hymn 426.

471. I do not ask, O Lord, that life may be

Adelaide A. Proctor, 1825-64

A hymn reflecting the quiet strength resulting from faith and trust in God. It is the most admired of Miss Proctor's hymns.

For comments on Adelaide Anne Proctor, see Hymn 177.

MUSIC. SUBMISSION, a tune well suited to the meaning and spirit of the poem, was composed for this hymn.

For comments on the composer, Albert L. Peace, see Hymn 175.

472. More love to Thee, O Christ   *Elizabeth Prentiss, 1818-78*

A simple prayer put into verse, written hastily, as many hymns have been, and, after some years, printed as a leaflet. It was then included by Dr. Doane in his *Songs of Devotion*, in four stanzas, the third being omitted here. In form and sentiment, the hymn is an echo of "Nearer, my God, to Thee," and is more explicitly Christian, for the latter omits the name of Christ completely.

Elizabeth Payson Prentiss was born in Portland, Maine the daughter of the famous minister, Rev. Edward Payson. After teaching school

273

for some years, she married Dr. George L. Prentiss, eminent Presbyterian clergyman, and professor at Union Theological Seminary in New York City, who published her *Life and Letters* soon after her death. Mrs. Prentiss wrote poetry and prose for the *Youths' Companion* and published several volumes of poems.

MUSIC. MORE LOVE TO THEE was written for this hymn and published in Dr. Doane's *Songs of Devotion,* 1870.

For comments on Wm. Howard Doane see Hymn 313.

473. What a wonderful Savior   *Elisha A. Hoffman*

A hymn on the atonement.

Words and music are by the Rev. Elisha A. Hoffman.

For comments on Hoffman, see Hymn 464.

474. Pass me not, O gentle Savior   *Fanny J. Crosby, 1820-1915*

One of Fanny Crosby's best and most popular songs. Ira D. Sankey says of it: "No hymn in our collection was more popular than this at our meetings in London in 1874." Miss Crosby wrote it in 1868 at the request of Dr. W. H. Doane, who gave her the first line as a theme. Doane published the hymn in his *Songs of Devotion,* 1870.

For comments on Fanny Crosby see Hymn 313.

MUSIC. PASS ME NOT was written for this hymn. For comments on the composer, W. H. Doane, see Hymn 313.

475. I am Thine, O Lord   *Fanny J. Crosby, 1820-1915*

A song of consecration, based on Heb. 10:22, "Let us draw near with a true heart." It was written one evening while Miss Crosby was visiting in the home of Dr. William H. Doane in Cincinnati, Ohio. The latter composed for it the tune by which the song has become familiar to a multitude of worshippers.

For comments on Fanny Crosby and W. H. Doane see Hymn 313.

476. Are you weary, are you heavy-hearted
         Jeremiah E. Rankin, 1828-1904

A song that has touched many a burdened heart, written by the author of "God be with you till we meet again." For comments on Jeremiah E. Rankin, see Hymn 365.

MUSIC. TELL IT TO JESUS. For comments on the composer, E. S. Lorenz, see Hymn 439.

477. Yield not to temptation
Horatio R. Palmer, 1834-1907

A song that has been a source of strength to many in time of temptation.

The words and tune are by Horatio Richmond Palmer, Mus. Doc., an American musician born at Sherburne, New York. He studied music in Berlin and Florence and became the director of the Rushford Academy of Music, New York, in 1857. In 1884, he took charge of the Church Choral Union in New York, an organization which grew to a membership of 4,000 singers devoted to the improvement of church music. He was dean, for a time, of the school of music at Chautauqua, N.Y., and compiled a number of popular choral collections. He is the author of *A Theory of Music* and *A Manual for Teachers.*

Concerning the composition of this hymn and tune, Dr. Palmer wrote:

> This song is an inspiration. I was at work on the dry subject of "Theory" when the complete idea flashed upon me, and I laid aside the theoretical work and hurriedly penned both words and music as fast as I could write them. I submitted them to the criticism of a friend afterward, and some changes were made in the third stanza, but the first two are exactly as they came to me. The music was first written in A flat; but I soon saw that B flat was better, and for many years it has appeared in that key. I am reverently thankful it has been a power for good.

MUSIC. YIELD NOT TO TEMPTATION. The tune, composed for the hymn by Dr. Palmer himself, appeared in *Sabbath School Songs* (1868). It is also named "Fortitude."

478. He leadeth me, O blessed thought
Joseph H. Gilmore, 1834-1918

A widely used hymn, based on Psalm 23:2: "He leadeth me beside the still waters." "It has the true hymn quality, combining all the simplicity of spontaneous thought and feeling with perfect accent and liquid rhythm" (Brown and Butterworth).

Joseph Henry Gilmore, a Baptist minister, was born in Boston, the son of Joseph A. Gilmore. He graduated from Brown University in 1858 and from Newton Theological Seminary in 1861. In 1863-64 he served as private secretary to his father, then governor of New Hampshire. From 1865 to 1867, he was pastor of the Second Baptist Church at Rochester, N. Y., and Acting Professor of Hebrew in Rochester Theological Seminary, 1867-68. In 1868, he became Professor of Logic, Rhetoric, and English Literature in the University of Rochester, a position he held for about forty years. One of his published volumes is *Outlines of English and American Literature,* 1905.

The hymn was written after Dr. Gilmore had conducted the Wednesday evening service at the First Baptist Church, Philadelphia, where he expounded the twenty-third Psalm. After the service, the discussion of the subject was continued in the home where he was stopping. The author says:

> During the conversation, the blessedness of God's leadership so grew upon me that I took out my pencil, wrote the hymn just as it stands today, handed it to my wife, and thought no more about it. She sent it, without my knowledge, to the *Watchman and Reflector.* Three years later, I went to Rochester to preach for the Second Baptist Church. On entering the chapel, I took up a hymn book, thinking: "I wonder what they sing." The book opened at "He Leadeth Me," and that was the first I knew my hymn had found a place among the songs of the Church.

MUSIC. HE LEADETH ME. Finding the hymn in a Christian periodical, Bradbury composed for it this popular tune with which it has since been associated. In singing the tune, holds should be observed at the end of lines 2, 3, and 4 of the stanzas, and at the end of lines 2 and 4 of the refrain. "Few composers have so exactly caught the tone and spirit of their text as Bradbury did when he vocalized the gliding measures of 'He Leadeth Me.'"

For comments on the composer, Wm. Bradbury, see Hymn 103.

479. Joys are flowing like a river   *M. P. Ferguson*

A song of comfort and joy useful for the quiet hour. The presence of Jesus brings to the trusting soul a blessed quietness as it did to the disciples on the stormy lake when He awoke and spoke the word of peace (Mark 4:37-41).

No information has been traced concerning the author of the words, M. P. Ferguson, or the composer, W. S. Marshall, from whose work the tune is an arrangement.

480. Blessed assurance, Jesus is mine

Fanny J. Crosby, 1820-1915

Another of Fanny Crosby's fine lyrics, sung the world over, in which is revealed the secret of the author's own serene trust and cheerful faith. In her *Memories of Eighty Years,* Miss Crosby makes the following reference to this hymn:

> Often I take in my mind some tune already well known as a model or, perhaps, more accurately speaking, as a guide, and work to it. This, however, does not imply that the tune will ultimately be chosen as the companion of the words; for it has probably already its own true and lawful mate, with which it

is to be happy and useful. Sometimes a tune is furnished me for which to write the words. The hymn titled "Blessed Assurance" was made in this manner. My dear friend, Mrs. Joseph F. Knapp, so well-known as a writer and singer of most excellent music and as an aid and inspiration to all who knew her, had composed the tune; and it seemed to me one of the sweetest I had heard for a long time. She asked me to write a hymn for it, and I felt while bringing the words and tones together that the air and the hymn were intended for each other. In the many hundred times that I have heard it sung, this opinion has been more and more confirmed.

For comments on Fanny Crosby, see Hymn 313.

MUSIC. ASSURANCE was written by Mrs. Joseph Fairchild Knapp, 1839-1908, the daughter of Dr. Walter and Mrs. Phoebe Palmer. Her husband was the founder of the Metropolitan Life Insurance Company in New York City. Both Mr. and Mrs. Knapp were members of the Methodist Episcopal church and gave much of their wealth to charitable and religious work. Mrs. Knapp, a close friend of Fanny Crosby, was an excellent singer, an accomplished organist, and an earnest Christian worker.

481. Sweet are the promises
Wm. A. Ogden, 1841-97

The third stanza is based on Matt. 11:28: "Come unto me, all ye that labor and are heavy laden, and I will give you rest," but the author has substituted "weary" for the word "labor."

Wm. A. Ogden, who wrote the words and music of this song, was born in Franklin County, Ohio. At the age of six, he moved with his parents to Indiana where he enlisted, at the outbreak of the Civil War, in the 13th Indiana Volunteer Infantry. After the close of the war, he resumed his musical studies under Lowell Mason, Thomas Hastings, E. E. Bailey, and B. F. Baker, President of the Boston School of Music. In 1870, he published *Silver Song* which reached the enormous sale of 500,000 copies. Ogden won distinction as a teacher and conductor of large convention choruses. For six years he was director of music at Iowa Normal School but his greatest musical work was done at Toledo, Ohio, where he moved in 1881 and served as superintendent of public school music from 1887 until his death. He loved children and enjoyed teaching them. His training of 3,000 children in 1894 was the distinct triumph of the great *Saengerfest* held that year in Toledo. Ogden wrote scores of popular songs, always composing both the words and music.

482. Will your anchor hold
Priscilla J. Owens, 1829-c. 99

A hymn setting forth life in terms of the sea and its billowing waves, and the confidence one may have if anchored to the Rock, which is Christ.

For comments on the author, Priscilla Jane Owens, and the composer of the tune, William J. Kirkpatrick, 1838-1921, see Hymn 334.

483. Hide me, O my Savior, hide me

Fanny J. Crosby, 1820-1915

For comments on Fanny Crosby and Wm. H. Doane who wrote tunes for many of Miss Crosby's hymns, see Hymn 313.

484. When peace, like a river, attendeth my way

Horatio G. Spafford, 1828-88

A hymn of resignation and submission, written out of bitter experiences of loss and suffering.

Horatio Gates Spafford, born in New York State, was a lawyer who had established himself in Chicago. He lost most of his fortune during the great fire in that city. Then on November 22, 1873, to add to his trials, he lost four of his children when the French steamer, "Villa de Havre," on which Mrs. Spafford and the children were sailing for Europe, sank in midocean, half an hour after colliding with a large sailing vessel. Mrs. Spafford was rescued and, landing at Cardiff, Wales, ten days later, cabled her husband, "Saved Alone." Spafford started immediately for Europe to bring his wife to Chicago. D. L. Moody, under whose preaching the Spafford children had been converted in North Chicago shortly before sailing, travelled from Edinburgh to Liverpool to comfort the bereaved parents and was pleased to hear them say, "It is well: the will of God be done."

Mr. and Mrs. Spafford later became much interested in the second coming of Christ, becoming so enthusiastic that in 1881 they went to Jerusalem with their remaining daughter, to witness the coming of the Lord. After seven years in Palestine, Spafford died there, September 5, 1888, his widow continuing to live there as the head of a communistic society with headquarters in a building outside of Jerusalem. The daughter, very popular among the natives, became the teacher of a large body of children, instructing them in English and in American ways.

MUSIC. IT IS WELL WITH MY SOUL. The music, "a gentle, gliding melody that suits the mood of the words," was written especially for Spafford's words and published in *Gospel Hymns No. 3.* The hymn and tune inmmediately became popular.

For comments on the composer, P. P. Bliss, see Hymn 442.

485. Take the name of Jesus with you   *Lydia Baxter, 1809-74*

A popular gospel song widely used in the Moody and Sankey revivals. Lydia Baxter, born in Petersburg, New York, was converted under the preaching of a Baptist missionary, the Rev. Eben Tucker, and, with her sister, became a leader in the organization of a Baptist Church in her native town. After her marriage she moved to New York City. Though an invalid for many years, she was known for her astonishing cheerfulness and to her home came many a Christian worker for inspiration and advice. A volume of her poems, *Gems by the Wayside*, was published in 1855.

MUSIC. PRECIOUS NAME was written for this hymn. It is inseparably associated with these words and has done much to give the hymn the widespread popularity which it enjoys.

For comments on the composer, W. H. Doane, also a Baptist, see Hymn 313.

486. When we walk with the Lord   *James H. Sammis, d. 1919*

The origin of this hymn is related in Ira Sankey's *Story of the Gospel Hymns:*

> "Some years ago," says Professor Towner, musical director of Moody Bible Institute, "Mr. Moody was conducting a series of meetings in Brockton, Mass., and I had the pleasure of singing for him there. One night a young man rose in a testimony meeting and said, 'I am not quite sure—but I am going to trust and obey.' I just jotted that sentence down, and sent it with the little story to the Rev. J. H. Sammis, a Presbyterian minister. He wrote the hymn and the tune was born. The chorus,
>
> 'Trust and obey
> For there's no other way
> To be happy in Jesus
> But to trust and obey.'
>
> was written before the hymn was."

James H. Sammis was born in Brooklyn, N. Y., and became a business man in Logansport, Indiana. As an active Christian layman, he was much interested in the Young Men's Christian Association, and finally gave up his business connections to serve as a General Secretary in the "Y". After further education at Lane and McCormick Seminaries, he entered the ministry and served as pastor of Presbyterian churches in Indiana, Michigan, and Minnesota. In 1909, he went to California as a teacher in the Bible Institute of Los Angeles, continuing there until his death, June 12, 1919.

MUSIC. TRUST AND OBEY. The composer of this tune, D. W. Towner, 1850-1919, was born in Rome, Pa., and became a member of a group of singers and evangelists associated with D. L. Moody. He was a capable leader of choirs and large assemblies. In 1893, he became director of the musical department of Moody Bible Institute in Chicago, a position he held until his death. In recognition of his services, the University of Tennessee honored him with the degree of Doctor of Music, in 1900.

487. My hope is built on nothing less   Edward Mote, 1797-1874

"A grand hymn of faith" is the characterization given by Bishop Bickersteth of this poem. Written in 1834, and printed as a leaflet, it was later included in the author's *Hymns of Praise*, 1836, entitled, "The Immutable Basis of a Sinner's Hope." The hymn is reminiscent of the words of Paul: "Other foundation can no man lay than that is laid, which is Jesus Christ" (I Cor. 3:11).

Edward Mote, born in London, worked as a cabinet-maker for some years but at length entered the ministry and from 1852 until his death in 1874 served the Baptist Church at Horsham, Essex.

The refrain of this hymn came into his mind one morning as he was walking up Holborn Hill on his way to work. Four stanzas were completed that day and two more were added the following Sunday.

MUSIC. SOLID ROCK. For comments on the composer of this tune, Wm. B. Bradbury, see Hymn 103.

488. 'Tis so sweet to trust in Jesus   Louisa M. R. Stead

A hymn of simple trust. Information concerning the author, Louisa M. R. Stead, has not been traced.

MUSIC. TRUSTING was composed for these words by the gospel singer and composer, Wm. J. Kirkpatrick, 1838-1921.

For comments on Kirkpatrick see Hymn 334.

489. What a fellowship, what a joy divine   Elisha A. Hoffman

For comments on the author, Elisha A. Hoffman, see Hymn 464.

MUSIC. LEANING ON JESUS was composed by Anthony J. Schowalter, who was born at Cherry Grove, Pa., May 1, 1858. The following from his pen tells the story of the origin of this hymn and tune:

> While I was conducting a singing-school at Hartsells, Alabama, I received a letter from two of my former pupils in South Carolina, conveying the sad intelligence that on the same day each of them had buried a wife. I tried to console them by writing a letter that might prove helpful in their hour of sadness. Among other Scriptures, I quoted this passage, "Underneath are the everlasting arms." Before completing the writing of the sentence, the thought came to me that the fact that we

may lean on these everlasting arms and find comfort and strength, ought to be put in a song; and before finishing that letter, the words and music of the refrain were written. The manuscript was sent to Elisha Hoffman. . . . in a few days his completion of the poem was received.

490. Jesus, keep me near the cross   *Fanny J. Crosby, 1820-1915*

A hymn on "the cross." The refrain suggests the words of Paul: "God forbid that I should glory save in the cross of our Lord Jesus Christ" (Gal. 6:14). This is another instance in which the words of the blind hymn-writer and the music of Mr. Doane were combined to make a popular gospel song.

For comments on Fanny Crosby and Wm. H. Doane, composer of the tune, see Hymn 313.

491. Nearer the cross   *Fanny Crosby, 1820-1915*

For comments on the author of these words, Fanny Crosby, see Hymn 313.

For Mrs. J. F. Knapp, composer of the tune, see Hymn 480.

492. There is a fountain filled with blood
William Cowper, 1731-1800

The imagery in the first verse is drawn from Zechariah 13:1: "In that day there shall be a fountain opened to the house of David and to the inhabitants of Jerusalem for sin and for uncleanness." The dislike which some have for this Old Testament phraseology has given rise to much dispute concerning the hymn, but all attempts to revise it have been without success. It is excellent poetry and should be left as Cowper wrote it.

The hymn was published in Conger's *Collection of Psalms and Hymns,* 1772, and later in the *Olney Hymns* (See Hymn 60).

For comments on William Cowper see Hymn 60.

MUSIC. CLEANSING FOUNTAIN, also called "Western Melody" in some of the older books, is a stirring tune reminiscent of the early American camp meeting songs. It is attributed here to Lowell Mason, but it is not certain whether he wrote it or whether it is an adaptation from his tune, "Cowper," which it resembles and to which the hymn is set in *The Hymnal,* 1933 (Presbyterian).

For comments on Lowell Mason see Hymn 12.

493. I love to tell the story   *Katherine Hankey, 1834-1911*

A simple song which became popular and has been translated into several different languages, because it expresses what is in the hearts of multitudes of people.

The words are from a long poem of 50 stanzas, in two parts, on the life of Jesus. Part I, dated January 29, 1866, is entitled, "The Story Wanted." Part II, dated November 18, 1866, is entitled, "The Story Told." The author composed the poem during a long period of convalescing after a serious illness. This hymn and "Tell me the old, old story" (No. 495) are selections from Part II and Part I, respectively, of the above-mentioned poem.

Katherine Hankey, born in Clapham, England, was the daughter of a banker. She was a refined, consecrated woman, a Sunday school teacher, and organizer of Bible classes among working girls. She travelled in South Africa to look after an invalid brother and became so interested in mission work that she devoted thereto the income from her writings.

MUSIC. HANKEY was composed for these words. For comments on the composer, Wm. G. Fischer, see Hymn 469. The melody, written in 1869, was harmonized by Hubert P. Main (No. 426) and became popular at revival meetings. It is one of the gospel song tunes that is included in the more dignified church hymnals.

494. Sing them over again to me   *Philip P. Bliss, 1838-76*

Written especially for use in the first issue of *Words of Life,* a Sunday school paper published by Fleming H. Revell. Two years later, George Stebbins introduced the song in an evangelistic campaign which he and Dr. Pentecost were conducting in New Haven, Conn., the two men singing the song as a duet. The song was received with enthusiasm and immediately became popular. It was published in *Gospel Hymns, No. 3* and has had a wide use in evangelistic services and in the Sunday schools throughout the country.

For comments on Philip P. Bliss, author and composer, see Hymn 442.

495. Tell me the old, old story   *Katherine Hankey, 1834-1911*

For comments on the author, Katherine Hankey, and an account of the origin of this hymn, see Hymn 493.

MUSIC. Dr. W. H. Doane heard the poem read at a Y.M.C.A. Conference at Montreal in 1867 and was so impressed by it that he copied it and later set it to music while riding on a stage coach during a vacation in the White Mountains.

For comments on W. H. Doane, see Hymn 313.

496. There is a Name I love to hear

Frederick Whitfield, 1829-1904

A hymn on the name of Jesus which was published in 1855 in hymn-sheets and leaflets in various languages. In 1861, it appeared in the author's *Sacred Poems and Prose,* a volume containing twenty-six hymns.

Frederick Whitfield, born at Threapwood, Shropshire, was a minister in the Anglican Church. Educated at Trinity College, Dublin, where he took his B.A. degree in 1859, he became, successively, curate of Otley, vicar of Kirby-Ravensworth, senior curate of Greenwich, and vicar of St. John's, Bexley. He is the author of nearly thirty volumes of prose and poetry.

MUSIC. O HOW I LOVE JESUS is a traditional melody of unknown authorship.

497. Rescue the perishing

Fanny J. Crosby, 1820-1915

A rallying song for Christian workers in all parts of the world. This is the only one of Fanny Crosby's hymns to be included in the famous English publication, *Hymns Ancient and Modern.* It was a great favorite of Frances E. Willard and Frances Murphy, temperance crusaders, and D. L. Moody was very fond of it.

The hymn had its origin in a visit which the blind poet made to one of the worst slum districts in New York City. When she addressed the men at a rescue mission, Miss Crosby heard harrowing tales of lost and perishing people. She wrote:

"While I sat there that evening the line came to me, 'Rescue the perishing, care for the dying.' I could think of nothing else that night. When I arrived at my home, I went to work at once, and before I retired the entire hymn was ready for a melody."

For comments on Fanny J. Crosby see Hymn 313.

MUSIC. RESCUE was composed by Dr. Doane for this hymn. The hymn and tune have resounded through many thousands of mission services.

For comments on Wm. H. Doane see Hymn 313.

498. O scatter seeds of loving deeds

Jessie Brown Pounds, 1861-1921

For comments on Jessie Brown Pounds, see Hymn 453.

Her song poem has gone around the world on the wings of this tune composed by Fred A. Fillmore, of the musically famous Fillmore brothers. See comments at Hymn 453. Fred A. was born May 15, 1856, at Paris, Illinois.

499. Judge me, God of my salvation

Psalm 43

A metrical version of Psalm 43 which may be compared with the version from the Scottish Psalter at No. 587. The fifth verse of the Psalm is made to serve as the refrain. The poet who made the version has not been identified. The hymn and tune were taken from the *Psalter* of the United Presbyterian Church.

MUSIC. AMARA was composed by William O. Perkins, concerning whom no information has been found.

500. I can hear my Savior calling

E. W. Blandy

An intimate hymn of personal consecration. The repetition of the phrases and the close harmony of the music have made the use of this song, even without the aid of an accompanying instrument, easy and enjoyable. No information has been found concerning the author, E. W. Blandy (misspelled Blandly in the *Hymnary*).

MUSIC. WHERE HE LEADS ME is admirably suited to the words. No information has come to light concerning the composer, J. S. Norris.

501. And must I be to judgment brought

Charles Wesley, 1707-88

The hymn, originally in eight stanzas, was entitled "A Thought on Judgment" and was written for children! Why Wesley wrote such serious-minded hymns for children is explained in his preface to *Hymns for Children,* from which this hymn is taken:

> There are two ways of writing or speaking to children. The one is to let ourselves down to them; the other, to lift them up to us. Dr. Watts wrote in the former way, and has succeeded admirably well, speaking to children as children and leaving them as he found them. The following hymns are written on the other plan. They contain strong and manly sense, yet expressed in such plain and easy language as even children may understand. But when they do understand them, they will be children no longer—only in years and in stature.

For comments on Charles Wesley, see Hymn 6.

MUSIC. MARLOW was composed by Rev. John Chetham, 1700-63, an English clergyman, curate of Skipton.

502. Savior, lead me lest I stray

Frank M. Davis, 1839-96

The words and music were written on the deck of a steamer that plied between Baltimore and Savannah.

Frank M. Davis was born on a farm near Marcellus, New York, the youngest of a family of ten children. He began composing tunes at an early age and became a teacher of vocal and instrumental music. He travelled extensively through the eastern and southern states, directing chorus choirs and teaching vocal classes. He compiled several Sunday school collections, among them *New Pearls of Song*, 1877, and *Notes of Praise*, of which more than 100,000 copies were sold. Davis is the author of over 100 vocal and instrumental compositions. He died suddenly of heart failure at Chesterfield, Indiana, where he was attending a camp meeting.

503. My days are gliding swiftly by   *David Nelson, 1793-1844*

A hymn written by a preacher while hiding from pursuing slave holders whose anger and violence were aroused by Nelson's aggressive anti-slavery views.

David Nelson, a surgeon in the U. S. Army during the war of 1812, left his profession to become a minister, meanwhile owning and operating a plantation in Missouri. After listening to an address on slavery, he declared himself in favor of freeing the slaves and advocated the plan of colonizing them in Africa. This so enraged some of the slaveholders that they drove Nelson from his home. To avoid mob violence, he escaped, reaching, after three days and nights of wandering, the Mississippi River opposite Quincy, Illinois. Hiding there in the bushes, with his pursuers near but unable to find him, the river gliding swiftly before him, he wrote this hymn on the back of old letters he had in his pocket. He was finally rescued by members of the Quincy Congregational Church who, having learned of his plight, took him on a fishing canoe and rowed him across the river, still pursued, to safety and friends, on the hospitable shore of a free state.

MUSIC. SHINING SHORE, one of the composer's most popular tunes, has been given various arrangements for voice and instruments. Root has written concerning the origin of the tune:

> One day, I remember, as I was working at a set of graded part-songs for singing classes, mother passed through the room and laid a slip from one of the religious newspapers before me, saying, "George, I think that would be good for music." I looked at the poem which began, "My days are gliding swiftly by," and a simple melody sang itself in my mind as I read. I jotted it down and went on with my work. That was the origin of the music of "The Shining Shore." Later, when I took up the melody to harmonize it, it seemed so very simple and commonplace, that I hesitated about setting the other parts to it. I finally decided that it might be useful to somebody, and I completed it, though it was not printed until some months afterward. In after years I examined it in an endeavor to

account for its great popularity—but in vain. To the musician there is not one reason in melody or harmony scientifically regarded, for such a fact. To him hundreds of others, now forgotten, were better.

For comments on George F. Root, 1820-95, see Hymn 418.

504. There's a land that is fairer than day

S. F. Bennett, 1836-98

"It'll be all right *by and by*." This trivial remark by Webster, when one morning, seemingly depressed, he was asked by his partner, Bennett, what was wrong with him, was the occasion for the writing of this hymn. The author and composer were friends and partners in the music publishing business in the village of Elkhorn, Wis. Webster, the musician of the firm, was inclined to be nervous and subject to periods of depression. His partner understood this and often effected a cure, as on this occasion, by putting him to work on a new song. Upon Bennett's suggestion, the two agreed that morning to make a hymn out of the idea, "The sweet by and by." Bennett penned the words and handed them to Webster, who promptly wrote the music. Words and music were thus produced in the incredibly short time of about thirty minutes. The song was published soon afterward in a Sunday school song book, *The Signet Ring*, which the two men were compiling. From there it found its way into numerous collections of songs until today "it is translated into various foreign languages and sung in every land under the sun."

Sanford Filmore Bennett was a native of the West. He settled in Elkhorn, Wis., in 1861, to devote himself to music but later studied medicine and practiced in Richmond, Ill.

MUSIC. SWEET BY AND BY. Joseph Philbrick Webster, 1819-75, composer of this tune, was born in New Hampshire. He was an active member of the Handel and Haydn Society and various other musical organizations. He lived in Madison, Indiana, and Racine, Wisconsin, before finally moving to Elkhorn, in 1857.

BOOK IV

The Christian Year in Chorales

CALL TO WORSHIP

505. Open now Thy gates of beauty

Benjamin Schmolck, 1672-1737
Tr. Catherine Winkworth, 1829-78

1. Tut mir auf die schöne Pforte,
   Führt in Gottes Haus mich
   ein!
   Ach, wie wird an diesem Orte
   Meine Seele fröhlich sein!
   Hier ist Gottes Angesicht,
   Hier ist lauter Trost und Licht.

2. Herr, ich bin zu dir gekom-
   men;
   Komme du nun auch zu mir!
   Wo du Wohnung hast genom-
   men
   Ist der Himmel hell vor mir.
   Zeuch in meinem Herzen ein,
   Lass es deinen Himmel sein!

3. Mache mich zum guten Lande,
   Wenn dein Saatkorn auf
   mich fällt;
   Gib mir Licht in dem Ver-
   stande,
   Und was mir wird vorgestellt,
   Präge du dem Herzen ein;
   Lass es mir zur Frucht gedeihn.

4. Stärk in mir den schwachen
   Glauben,
   Lass dein teures Kleinod mir
   Nimmer aus dem Herzen rau-
   ben,
   Halte mir dein Wort stets
   für;
   Ja, das sei mein Morgenstern,
   Der mich führet zu dem Herrn!

5. Rede, Herr, so will ich hören,
   Und dein Wille werd' erfüllt!
   Lass nichts meine Andacht stören,
   Wenn der Brunn' des Lebens quillt.
   Speise mich mit Himmelsbrot,
   Tröste mich in aller Not!

287

A beautiful worship hymn, first published in the author's *Kirchen-Gefährte*, 1732, in seven stanzas, entitled, "The First Step into the Church." Its joyous spirit is characteristic of many of Schmolck's poems.

Benjamin Schmolck, the most popular and prolific hymn writer of his time, was born in Silesia, and educated in the University of Leipzig. He was ordained to become his father's assistant in the church at Brauchitzchdorf, his birthplace. Later he became the pastor of Friedenskirche at Schweidnitz, in Silesia, where he labored patiently for a period of 35 years, beloved of his people for his understanding and sympathy. He had rare poetic gifts and published a number of volumes of devotional books in which his hymns were included. His contemporary, Johann Sebastian Bach, 1685-1750, greatest of all church musicians, helped to make the poems of Schmolck immortal.

Catherine Winkworth translated five stanzas of this hymn; three of which are used here.

For comments on Miss Winkworth see Hymn 236.

MUSIC. NEANDER. For comments on this tune, and the composer, Joachim Neander, see Hymn 127.

506. God reveals His presence

Gerhard Tersteegen, 1697-1769
Tr. Frederick W. Foster, 1760-1835
John Miller, 1756-1810
William Mercer, 1811-73

1. Gott ist gegenwärtig!
   Lasset uns anbeten,
   Und in Ehrfurcht vor ihn
   treten.
   Gott ist in der Mitte;
   Alles in uns schweige,
   Und in Ehrfurcht vor ihn
   beuge.
   Wer ihn kennt, wer ihn nennt,
   Schlagt die Augen nieder;
   Kommt, ergebt euch wieder!

2. Gott ist gegenwärtig,
   Dem die Cherubinen
   Tag und Nacht mit Ehrfurcht dienen;
   Heilig, heilig singen
   Alle Engelchören,
   Wenn sie Gott mit Jauchzen
   ehren.
   Herr, vernimm unsre Stimm',
   Da auch wir Geringen
   Unsre Opfer bringen.

4. Majestätisch Wesen!
   Möcht' ich dich recht preisen,
   Und im Geist dir Dienst erweisen
   Möcht' ich wie die Engel
   Immer vor dir stehen
   Und dich gegenwärtig sehen!
   Lass mich dir für und für
   Trachten zu gefallen,
   Liebster Gott, in Allen.

288

First published in the author's *Geistliches Blumengärtlein,* entitled "Remembrance of the glorious and delightful presence of God," 1729.

Gerhard Tersteegen, one of the greatest of German hymn writers, was born at Mörs in Westphalia, the son of a tradesman. He was educated at the grammar school of his native place, and then bound as an apprentice to an elder brother, a shop-keeper at Mülheim. When his time was out, he left his brother and moved to a little cottage near Mülheim where for some years he supported himself by weaving silk ribbons, giving his money to the poor, and living a life so simple that it brought upon him the contempt of his thriving and money-getting relatives. For a time, due to various disappointments, he lived in a "state of darkness," a five year period of spiritual depression, during which he doubted the love, if not the existence, of God. He at last, as in a moment, regained peace and joy, whereupon he signed, with his own blood, a covenant with God to devote himself to His service. Soon he was found speaking at prayer meetings and other places and became popular as a religious teacher and counsellor. From far and wide people came to him for personal interviews, and his public meetings were always crowded.

Tersteegen was never ordained. Grieved by the open sin of the church people of his time, he early dissociated himself from the organized church and absented himself from the communion service. Though he had a wide following, he never organized a sect of his own, and, after his death, most of his disciples reunited with the Reformed Church. Like all great leaders, he pled the cause of the underprivileged. He was a mystic of the purest type, yet his faith was practical. He provided food and simple medicines for the poor and became widely known as the physician to the poor and forsaken. Tersteegen had many friends among the Mennonites and often preached in their church at Krefeld.

He is the author of 111 hymns, many of which have been rendered into English.

Frederick Foster and John Miller, translators of stanzas one and two, respectively, were both members of the Moravian Church. William Mercer, translator of stanza three, was an English scholar who translated and paraphrased many of the Latin and German hymns into English, but is best known for his successful work as editor of *The Church Psalter and Hymn Book,* 1857, the most popular hymn book of the Church of England. Another translation of this hymn appears at No. 508.

MUSIC. ARNSBERG, also called "Wunderbarer König," and "Gott ist gegenwärtig," was composed by the poet and musician, Joachim Neander, 1650-80. It appeared in his collection, *Glaub-und Liebesübung,* Bremen, 1680, set to the hymn, "Wunderbarer König."

For comments on Neander see Hymn 127.

507. Jehovah! Jehovah! Jehovah!

Gottlieb Konrad Pfeffel, 1736-1809
Tr. C. Haas, 1862-1928
Stanzas 2 and 3, G. F. W. Schultz, 1774-1842
Tr. C. E. Krehbiel, 1869-1948

Jehova! Jehova! Jehova!
Deinem Namen sei Ehre, Macht, und Ruhm!
Amen. Amen.
Bis einst der Tempel dieser Welt
Auf dein Wort in Staub zerfällt,
Soll in unsern Hallen,
Das Heilig, Heilig, Heilig, erschallen.
Halleluja! Halleluja!

The original is a one-stanza hymn. The author, Gottlieb Pfeffel, was born at Colmar in Alsace. His literary work consisted primarily of the writing of fables and hymns for instruction in the Colmar schools. At the age of 21 he became totally blind, but carried on, despite the handicap, a magnificent life work as president of the schools at Colmar. He was also the founder of a nursery for Protestant children.

Christian George Haas, translator of the hymn, was a minister in the Evangelical Church. After graduating from Eden Theological Seminary, he held pastorates in St. Paul and in Buffalo, and edited the *Hymnal of the Evangelical Church,* 1898.

Two stanzas were added to Pfeffel's hymn, by G. F. W. Schultz:

Sohn Gottes! Sohn Gottes! Sohn Gottes!
Deinen Namen preist unser Lobgesang!
Amen. Amen.
Du kamst aus Lieb' zu uns herab,
Siegtest über Tod und Grab,
Alle zu erlösen,
O Heiland, Heiland, Heiland, vom Bösen!
Sei hochgelobt! Sei hochgelobt!

Geist Gottes! Geist Gottes! Geist Gottes!
Deinen Namen erhebet unser Lied!
Amen. Amen.
Du heiligst, führ'st in's Vaterland,
Bist des Gnadenerbes Pfand.
Deiner die Erlösten
Du Heil'ger, Heil'ger, Heil'ger, sich trösten!
Halleluja! Halleluja!

No information has been traced concerning the author.

For comments on C. E. Krehbiel who translated stanzas 2 and 3, see Hymn 376.

MUSIC. JEHOVAH. No information is at hand concerning Johann C. Gerold, composer of this somewhat long, but dignified and effective tune, with its peculiar meter.

290

508. Lo, God is here! let us adore *Gerhard Tersteegen, 1697-1769*

Tr. John Wesley, 1703-91

The most widely used of Tersteegen's hymns. The German version and another translation are found at No. 506.

For comments on Tersteegen see Hymn 506.

The present translation was made by John Wesley, the founder of Methodism. For comments on Wesley see Hymn 170.

MUSIC. MACH'S MIT MIR GOTT, also called "Schein," and "Eisenach," was composed by J. H. Schein, 1586-1630, for the hymn "Mach's mit mir Gott." Schein was the son of a Lutheran pastor and became one of the most distinguished musicians of his time. For a number of years he held the honored position of cantor of St. Thomas' Church and School in Leipzig, and composed many hymn tunes. He is best known by the great hymn book he edited for the Lutheran Church, *Cantional, oder Gesangbuch Augsburgischer Confession,* Leipzig, 1627.

The present form of the melody is an adaptation of the original and is the one used by J. S. Bach in his *St. John's Passion.* "The tune is not one of the 'grand' chorales, but retains, even in its later version, a suave, song-like character."

PRAISE

509. O that I had a thousand voices *Johann Mentzer, 1658-1734*

Tr. Catherine Winkworth, 1829-78

1.

O dass ich tausend Zungen hätte
Und einen tausendfachen Mund,
So stimmt' ich damit in die Wette
Vom allertiefsten Herzensgrund
Ein Loblied nach dem andern an
Von dem, was Gott an mir getan!

2.

O dass doch meine Stimme schallte
Bis dahin, wo die Sonne steht,
O dass mein Blut mit Jauchzen wallte,
So lang es noch im Laufe geht!
Ach wäre jeder Puls ein Dank,
Und jeder Odem ein Gesang!

3.

Was schweigt ihr denn, ihr meine Kräfte?
Auf, auf, braucht allen euren Fleiss

Und stehet munter im Geschäfte
Zu Gottes, meines Herren, Preis!
Mein Leib und Seele, schicke dich
Und lobe Gott herzinniglich!

4.

Ihr grünen Blätter in den Wäldern,
Bewegt und regt euch doch mit mir!
Ihr schwanken Gräschen in den Feldern,
Ihr Blumen, lasst doch eure Zier
Zu Gottes Ruhm belebet sein
Und stimmet lieblich mit mir ein!

5.

Ach alles, alles, was ein Leben
Und einen Odem in sich hat,
Soll sich mir zum Gehilfen geben,
Denn mein Vermögen ist zu matt
Die grossen Wunder zu erhöhn,
Die allenthalben um mich stehn.

6.

Dir sei, o allerliebster Vater,
Unendlich Lob für Seel und
Leib;
Lob sei dir, mildester Berater,
Für allen edlen Zeitvertreib,
Den du mir in der ganzen Welt
Zu meinem Nutzen hast bestellt.

7.

Mein treuster Jesu, sei gepriesen,
Dass dein erbarmungsvolles
Herz
Sich mir so hülfreich hat erwiesen,
Und mich durch Blut und
Todesschmerz
Von aller Teufel Grausamkeit
Zu deinem Eigentum befreit.

8.

Auch dir sei ewig Ruhm und Ehr
O heiligwerter Gottes-Geist,
Für deines Trostes süsse Lehre,
Die mich ein Kind des Lebens
heisst.
Ach wo was Gut's von mir ge-
schicht,
Das wirket nur dein göttlich Licht.

9.

Wer überströmet mich mit Segen?
Bist du es nicht, o reicher Gott?
Wer schützet mich auf meinen
Wegen?
Du, du, o starker Zebaoth.
Du trägst mit meiner Sünden-
schuld
Unsäglich gnädige Geduld.

10.

Vor andern küss ich deine Rute,
Die du mir aufgebunden hast.
Wie viel tut sie mir doch zu Gute,
Und ist mir eine sanfte Last;

Sie macht mich fromm und zeigt
dabei,
Dass ich von deinen Liebsten sei.

11.

Ich hab es ja mein Lebetage
Schon so manch liebes Mal ges-
pürt,
Dass du mich unter viele Plage
Recht wunderbarlich hast ge-
führt.
Denn in der grössesten Gefahr
Ward ich dein Trostlicht stets ge-
wahr.

12.

Wie sollt ich nun nicht voller
Freuden
In deinem steten Lobe stehn?
Wie sollt ich auch im tiefsten
Leiden
Nicht triumphierend einher-
gehn?
Und fiele auch der Himmel ein,
So will ich doch nicht traurig sein.

13.

Drum reisz ich mich jetzt aus der
Höhle
Der schnöden Eitelkeiten los,
Und rufe mit erhöhter Seele:
Mein Gott, du bist sehr hoch
und gross;
Kraft, Ruhm, Preis, Dank und
Herrlichkeit
Gehört dir jetzt und allezeit.

14.

Ich will von deiner Güte singen,
Solange sich die Zunge regt,
Ich will dir Freudenopfer bringen,
Solange sich mein Herz bewegt.
Ja, wenn der Mund wird kraftlos
sein,
So stimm' ich doch mit Seufzen
ein.

15.

Ach nimm das arme Lob auf Erden,
Mein Gott, in allen Gnaden hin!
Im Himmel soll es besser werden,
Wenn ich bei deinen Engeln bin.
Da sing' ich dir im höhern Chor
Viel tausend Halleluja vor.

A popular hymn of praise and thanksgiving, written in 1704, shortly after the author's home was destroyed by fire! Our version is a selection of stanzas 1, 4, 5, and 15, of the original 15.

The author, Johann Mentzer, was for 38 years a pastor at Kemnitz, Saxony, and belonged to the more conservative Pietistic school of hymn writers. He is the author of 34 hymns, many of them of high merit.

For comments on the translator, Catherine Winkworth, see Hymn 236.

MUSIC. O DASS ICH TAUSEND ZUNGEN HÄTTE was composed by Johann Balthasar König, 1691-1758, director of music in several churches in Frankfurt-am-Main. The tune appeared in *Harmonischer Liederschatz,* Frankfurt, 1738, where it is set to the hymn, "Ach sagt mir nichts von Gold und Schätzen." The *Harmonischer Liederschatz,* edited by König, is the most comprehensive chorale-book of the 18th century. It contains 1940 tunes, including several of König's own compositions.

510. Heav'n and earth, the sea the air

Joachim Neander, 1650-80
Tr. Catherine Winkworth, 1829-78
Frances Cox, 1812-97

1.
Himmel, Erde, Luft und Meer,
Aller Welten zahllos Heer
Jauchzen Gott, dem Schöpfer, zu;
Meine Seele, sing' auch du!

2.
Ihn erhebt das Sonnenlicht,
Wann es durch die Wolken bricht.
Mondesglanz und Sternenpracht
Loben Gott in stiller Nacht.

3.
Seht, wie er das Land erquickt
Und mit Luft und Segen schmückt!
Wälder, Flur und jedes Tier
Zeigen Gottes Finger hier.—

4.
Seht, wie fleugt der Vögel Schaar
In den Lüften frisch und klar!
Donner, Blitz, Dampf, Hagel, Wind
Seines Willens Diener sind.

5.
Seht der Wasserwellen Lauf,
Wie sie steigen ab und auf!
Von der Quelle bis zum Meer
Rauschen sie des Schöpfers Ehr'.

6.
Ach, mein Gott, wie wunderbar
Stellst du dich der Seele dar!
Drücke stets in meinen Sinn,
Was du bist, und was ich bin!

Based on Psalm 19 and Acts 14:17. The hymn sings of God's revelation to man in nature. It once had a footnote: "Is also a traveler's hymn by land and water," to which we might add, "and air." The hymn first appeared in the author's *Glaub-und Liebesübung,* Bremen, 1680.

For comments on Joachim Neander see Hymn 127.

The translation is mainly from Catherine Winkworth, but partly from Frances Cox.

For comments on Miss Winkworth see Hymn 236. For Miss Cox, Hymn 512.

MUSIC. GOTT SEI DANK, also known as "Lübeck," "Berlin," and "Carintha," is by an unknown composer. The tune, since slightly altered, first appeared in J. A. Freylinghausen's *Neues Geistreiches Gesangbuch,* Halle, 1704, an important collection described as "the only book which can, as a collection, be set alongside with *Praxis Pietatis Melica.*" It is a lively, spirited tune, its moderate range making it especially suitable for unison singing.

511. Lord, with glowing heart I'd praise Thee
Francis Scott Key, 1779-1843

The author of this hymn, Francis Scott Key, is known to every American child as the man who wrote our national anthem, "The Star Spangled Banner." Born in Frederick County, Virginia, he was educated at St. John's College, Annapolis. He practiced law in Washington, D. C., and served as United States District Attorney for three terms, till his death on January 11, 1843. As a member of the Protestant Episcopal Church, he held a lay reader's license and for many years read the service and visited the sick. He taught a Bible class and conducted family prayers twice a day, requiring all members of the household, including the servants, to be present. He did much for the negroes of the south and although he lived in a slave state, he was moved by conscientious scruples to free his own slaves. The hymn, as he wrote it, had four stanzas. The second and third stanzas, omitted here, read as follows:

> Praise, my soul, the God that sought thee,
>   Wretched wanderer, far astray;
> Found thee lost, and kindly brought thee
>   From the paths of death away;
> Praise, with love's devoutest feeling,
>   Him who saw thy guilt-born fear,
> And, the light of hope revealing,
>   Bade the blood-stained cross appear.
>
> Praise thy Saviour God that drew thee
>   To that cross, new life to give,
> Held a blood-sealed pardon to thee,
>   Bade thee look to Him and live.
> Praise the grace whose threats alarmed thee,
>   Roused thee from thy fatal ease,
> Praise the grace whose promise warmed thee,
>   Praise the grace that whispered peace.

Among his other hymns is, "Before the Lord we bow," a thanksgiving hymn written by Key in 1832 for a Fourth of July celebration.

MUSIC. WOMIT SOLL ICH DICH WOHL LOBEN is by Justin H. Knecht, 1752-1817, who was born in Biberach, Swabia. He studied music under Kramer and became one of the great organists of his time. His most valuable production was the *Württemberg Choralbuch* which he edited along with J. F. Christmann, and to which he contributed 97 tunes of his own composition.

512. Sing praise to God who reigns above

Johann J. Schütz, 1640-90
Tr. Frances E. Cox, 1812-97

1.
Sei Lob und Ehr' dem höchsten Gut,
Dem Vater aller Güte,
Dem Gott, der alle Wunder tut,
Dem Gott, der mein Gemüte
Mit seinem reichen Trost erfüllt,
Dem Gott, der allen Jammer stillt;
Gebt unsrem Gott die Ehre!

2.
Es danken dir die Himmelsheer',
O Herrscher aller Thronen;
Und die in Lüften, Land und Meer
In deinem Schatten wohnen,
Die preisen deine Schöpfersmacht,
Die Alles also wohlbedacht.
Gebt unsrem Gott die Ehre!

3.
Was unser Gott geschaffen hat,
Das will er auch erhalten,
Darüber will er früh und spat
Mit seiner Gnade walten.
In seinem ganzen Königsreich
Ist Alles recht und Alles gleich;
Gebt unsrem Gott die Ehre!

4.
Ich rief dem Herrn in meiner Not:
"Ach Gott, vernimm mein Weinen!"
Da half mein Helfer mir vom Tod
Und liess mir Trost erscheinen.
Drum dank' ich, Gott, drum dank' ich dir;
Ach danket, danket Gott mit mir,
Gebt unsrem Gott die Ehre!

5.
Der Herr ist nun und immer nicht
Von seinem Volk geschieden;
Er bleibet ihre Zuversicht,
Ihr Segen, Heil und Frieden.
Mit Mutterhänden leitet er
Die Seinen stetig hin und her.
Gebt unsrem Gott die Ehre!

6.
Wenn Trost und Hülfe mangeln muss,
Die alle Welt erzeiget,
So kommt, so hilft der Ueberfluss,
Der Schöpfer selbst, und neiget
Die Vateraugen denen zu,
Die nirgendwo sonst finden Ruh.
Gebt unsrem Gott die Ehre!

7.
Ich will dich all mein Lebenlang,
O Gott, von nun an ehren;
Man soll, Gott, meinen Lobgesang
In allen Orten hören.
Mein ganzes Herz ermuntre sich,
Mein Geist und Leib erfreue dich;
Gebt unsrem Gott die Ehre!

8.
Ihr, die ihr Christi Namen nennt,
Gebt unsrem Gott die Ehre;
Ihr, die ihr Gottes Macht bekennt,
Gebt unsrem Gott die Ehre!
Die falschen Götzen macht zu Spott;
Der Herr ist Gott, der Herr ist Gott!
Gebt unsrem Gott die Ehre!

9.

So kommet vor sein Angesicht,
Mit Jauchzen Dank zu bringen,
Bezahlet die gelobte Pflicht
Und lasst uns fröhlich singen:
Der Herr hat Alles wohl bedacht,
Und Alles, Alles recht gemacht!
Gebt unsrem Gott die Ehre!

The hymn is based on Deut. 32:3: "Because I will publish the name of the Lord: ascribe ye greatness unto our God." The original poem of nine stanzas, Schütz's only hymn, first appeared in his *Christliches Gedenkbüchlein*. Our hymn is a translation of stanzas 1, 3, 5, and 7 of the original.

The author, Johann Jakob Schütz, born at Frankfurt-am-Main, was a lawyer by profession. He was a man of deep religious convictions and a close friend of P. J. Spener and Joachim Neander, early leaders of the Pietist movement in Germany. Schütz left the Lutheran church and became a separatist. He died at Frankfurt-am-Main.

The translation is by Frances Cox, 1812-97, an English woman of culture and learning who is second only to Catherine Winkworth as a translator of German hymns.

MUSIC. MIT FREUDEN ZART, one of our finest hymn tunes, was used by the Bohemian Brethren, and is probably much older than their *Gesangbuch* of 1566 in which it first appeared. The tune is a joyous one, as the name indicates, and should not be sung too slowly. All the voices are to sing the melody, the accompanying instrument bringing out the harmonization.

513. Praise thou the Lord, O my soul

Johann D. Herrnschmidt, 1675-1723
Tr. Lester Hostetler

1.
Lobe den Herren, o meine Seele!
Ich will ihn loben bis zum Tod;
Weil ich noch Stunden auf Erden zähle,
Will ich lobsingen meinem Gott.
Der Leib und Seel' gegeben hat,
Werde gepriesen früh und spat.
Halleluja! Halleluja!

2.
Fürsten sind Menschen, vom Weib geboren,
Und kehren um zu ihrem Staub;
Ihre Anschläge sind auch verloren,
Wenn nun das Grab nimmt seinen Raub.
Weil denn kein Mensch uns helfen kann,
Rufe man Gott um Hilfe an!
Halleluja! Halleluja!

3.
Selig, ja selig ist der zu nennen,
Des Hilfe der Gott Jakobs ist.
Welcher vom Glauben sich nicht lässt trennen
Und hofft getrost auf Jesum Christ.

Wer diesen Herrn zum Beistand hat,
Findet am besten Rat und Tat.
Halleluja! Halleluja!

4.

Dieser hat Himmel, Meer und die Erden,
Und was darinnen ist, gemacht.
Alles muss pünktlich erfüllet werden,
Was er uns einmal zugedacht.
Er ist's, der Herrscher aller Welt,
Welcher uns ewig Glauben hält.
Halleluja! Halleluja!

5.

Zeigen sich welche, die Unrecht leiden,
Er ist's, der ihnen Recht verschafft.
Hungrigen will er zu Speis' bescheiden,
Was ihnen dient zur Lebenskraft.
Die hart Gebundnen macht er frei,
Seine Genad' ist mancherlei.
Halleluja! Halleluja!

6.

Sehende Augen gibt er den Blinden;

Erhebt, die tief gebeuget gehn.
Wo er kann gläubige Seelen finden,
Die lässt er seine Liebe sehn.
Sein Trostwort ist des Fremdlings Trutz
Witwen und Waisen hält er im Schutz.
Halleluja! Halleluja!

7.

Aber der Gottesvergessenen Tritte
Kehrt er mit starker Hand zurück,
Dass sie nur machen verkehrte Schritte
Und fallen selbst in ihren Strick.
Der Herr ist König ewiglich,
Zion, dein Gott sorgt stets für dich!
Halleluja! Halleluja!

8.

Rühmet, ihr Menschen, den hohen Namen
Des, der so grosse Wunder tut!
Alles, was Odem hat, rufe Amen!
Und bringe Lob mit frohem Mut.
Ihr Kinder Gottes, lobt und preist
Vater und Sohn und Heil'gen Geist!
Halleluja! Halleluja!

The hymn is a poetic version of Psalm 146. It was first published in the second part of Freylinghausen's *Gesangbuch,* Halle, 1714, the original having 8 stanzas. The translation here given is a free rendering of stanzas 1 and 8, and was made especially for the *Hymnary.*

The author of this hymn, Johann Daniel Herrnschmidt, a learned and devout man, was born in Bopfingen, in Württemberg, where his father was pastor. He was a pupil and for a time assistant of pastor August Francke in Halle. Later he became minister in Bopfingen, then superintendent and councilman at Nassau-Idstein. In 1715 he became teacher and pastor in Halle where he died 8 years later.

MUSIC. LOBE DEN HERREN, O MEINE SEELE, inseparably united with this hymn, is one of the most brilliant and striking gems in our chorale treasury. The composer is unknown. The tune first appeared in *Anhang der Seelen-Harpff,* Onolzbach, 1665, and later in Freylinghausen's *Gesangbuch,* 1714.

514. Now thank we all our God

Martin Rinkart, 1586-1649
Tr. Catherine Winkworth, 1829-78

1.

Nun danket alle Gott
Mit Herzen, Mund und Händen,
Der grosse Dinge tut
An uns und allen Enden,
Der uns von Mutterleib
Und Kindesbeinen an
Unzählig viel zugut
Und noch jetzund getan!

2.

Der ewig reiche Gott
Woll' uns bei unserm Leben
Ein immer fröhlich Herz
Und edlen Frieden geben
Und uns in seiner Gnad'
Erhalten fort und fort
Und uns aus aller Not
Erlösen hier und dort!

3.

Lob, Ehr, und Preis sei Gott,
Dem Vater und dem Sohne
Und dem, der beiden gleich
Im höchsten Himmelsthrone,
Dem dreieinigen Gott,
Als es im Anfang war
Und ist und bleiben wird
Jetzund und immerdar!

The *Te Deum* of Germany. It is the most celebrated hymn coming out of the second period (1570-1648) of German hymnody.

The first two stanzas of the hymn were composed as a *Tischlied,* a grace after meat, to be sung by the author's household. The third stanza was added as a doxology. The hymn was sung at the conclusion of the Peace of Westphalia which ended the Thirty Years' War, and has been used since on many national occasions of thanksgiving, not only in Germany but in England and America as well.

Martin Rinkart was born in Eilenburg, Saxony, the son of a cooper. After graduating from the University of Leipzig, he held appointments as Master at the Gymnasium and Cantor of St. Nicholas Church in Eisleben, then became, in 1617, Archidiaconus at Eilenburg, a position he held the rest of his life. Rinkart was poet, dramatist, and musician, as well as pastor. During the Thirty Years' War, his church at Eilenburg became an asylum for refugees from all parts. The suffering from famine and pestilence was indescribable. For some time, Rinkart was the only clergyman in the town, and he frequently conducted as many as forty funeral services in one day. A man of sympathy and generosity, he strained his own resources in his efforts to keep others from starving.

The translation is from Miss Winkworth's *Lyra Germanica,* 1858.

For comments on Catherine Winkworth see Hymn 236.

MUSIC. NUN DANKET was composed by Johann Crüger, 1598-1662. It appeared in his famous collection, *Praxis Pietatis Melica,* which was issued in more than fifty editions during the century after its first publication in 1644. Mendelssohn used the tune in his *Lobgesang,* in six-part harmony.

For comments on Crüger see Hymn 242.

515. Praise to the Lord, the Almighty
Joachim Neander, 1650-80
Tr. Catherine Winkworth, 1829-75

1.
Lobe den Herren, den mächtigen
   König der Ehren!
Meine geliebete Seele, das ist
   mein Begehren.
Kommet zuhauf!
Psalter und Harfe, wacht auf!
Lasset die Musikam hören!

2.
Lobe den Herren, der alles so
   herrlich regieret,
Der dich auf Adelers Fittichen
   sicher geführet,
Der dich erhält,
Wie es dir selber gefällt.
Hast du nicht dieses verspüret?

3.
Lobe den Herren, der künstlich
   und fein dich bereitet,
Der dir Gesundheit verliehen,
   dich freundlich geleitet!
In wie viel Not
Hat nicht der gnädige Gott
Ueber dir Flügel gebreitet!

4.
Lobe den Herren, der deinen
   Stand sichtbar gesegnet,
Der aus dem Himmel mit Strömen
   der Liebe geregnet!
Denke daran,
Was der Allmächtige kann,
Der dir mit Liebe begegnet!

5.
Lobe den Herren, was in mir ist lobe den Namen!
Alles, was Odem hat, lobe mit Abrahams Samen!
Er ist dein Licht,
Seele, vergiss es ja nicht!
Lobende, schliesse mit Amen!

The hymn is based on Psalm 103:1-6 and Psalm 150. It is "a magnificent song of praise, probably the finest there is, when we consider the tune, and certainly the finest production of Neander's."

Neander was the first prominent writer of hymns in the Reformed Church of Germany which for a long time used only metrical versions of the Psalms in public worship. After a brief and stormy ministry, he died at the age of thirty.

For further comments on Neander see Hymn 505.

For coments on Miss Winkworth see Hymn 236.

MUSIC. LOBE DEN HERREN is a tune of great vigor and strength, yet simple of structure. It is very usable in a service of praise and thanksgiving and has been sung with great effect by large chorus choirs. The origin of the tune is uncertain. It appeared anonymously in *Ander Theil des Erneuerten Gesangbuch,* Stralsund, 1665, to the words, "Hast du denn, Liebster, dein Angesicht gänzlich verborgen," by Ahasuerus Fritsch, which suggests a secular origin of the melody. It is believed, by some authorities, that Neander himself adapted it from an earlier chorale. The tune appears with many variants of melody and harmonization in different hymn books. The present form has been used since 1708.

516. How great, Almighty, is Thy kindness

Christian F. Gellert, 1715–69
Tr. Margarete Münsterburg, 1917

1.

Wie gross ist des Allmächt'gen Güte!
  Ist der ein Mensch, den sie nicht rührt,
Der mit verhärtetem Gemüte
  Den Dank erstickt, der ihm gebührt?
Nein, seine Liebe zu ermessen,
  Sei ewig meine grösste Pflicht;
Der Herr hat mein noch nie vergessen,
  Vergiss, mein Herz, auch seiner nicht!

2.

Wer hat mich wunderbar bereitet?
  Der Gott, der meiner nicht bedarf.
Wer hat mit Langmut mich geleitet?
  Er, dessen Rat ich oft verwarf.
Wer stärkt den Frieden im Gewissen?
  Wer gibt dem Geiste neue Kraft?
Wer lässt mich so viel Guts geniessen?
  Ist's nicht sein Arm, der Alles schafft?

3.

Blick', O mein Geist! in jenes Leben,
  Zu welchem du erschaffen bist,
Wo du, mit Herrlichkeit umgeben,
  Gott ewig sehn wirst, wie Er ist.
Du hast ein Recht zu diesen Freuden,
  Durch Gottes Güte sind sie dein.
Sieh, darum musste Christus leiden,
  Damit du könnest selig sein.

4.

Und diesen Gott sollt' ich nicht ehren,
  Und seine Güte nicht verstehn?
Er sollte rufen, ich nicht hören?
  Den Weg, den er mir zeigt, nicht gehn?
Sein Will' ist mir ins Herz geschrieben,
  Sein Wort bestärkt ihn ewiglich:
Gott soll ich über Alles lieben,
  Und meinen Nächsten gleich als mich.

5.

Dies ist mein Dank, dies ist sein Wille,
  Ich soll vollkommen sein, wie er.
So lang ich dies Gebot erfülle,
  Stell' ich sein Bildnis in mir her.
Lebt seine Lieb' in meiner Seele,
  So treibt sie mich zu jeder Pflicht;
Und ob ich schon aus Schwachheit fehle,
  Herrscht doch in mir die Sünde nicht.

6.

O Gott! lass deine Güt' und Liebe
  Mir immerdar vor Augen sein!
Sie stärk' in mir die guten Triebe,
  Mein ganzes Leben dir zu weihn;
Sie tröste mich zur Zeit der Schmerzen,
  Sie tröste mich zur Zeit des Glücks,
Und sie besieg' in meinem Herzen
  Die Furcht des letzten Augenblicks!

The hymn was first published in Leipzig, 1757, in six stanzas, entitled, "The Goodness of God."

Gellert was one of the most popular writers in German literature. Born in Saxony, the son of a Lutheran country preacher, he attended Fürstenschule at Meissen, and then went to the University of Leipzig where he studied philosophy and theology. Later he lectured at that university on poetry, elocution, and moral philosophy. He was beloved by all his classes, the lectures sometimes being attended by four hundred. Outside the university he was even more popular. A poor peasant once unloaded a cart full of wood before Gellert's house, begging him to accept the gift as thanks for his beautiful fables. The keynote of his popularity is expressed in one of his letters:

> Mein grösster Ehrgeiz besteht darin, dasz ich den Vernünftigen dienen und gefallen will, und nicht den Gelehrten im engen Verstande. Ein kluges Frauenzimmer gilt mir mehr als eine gelehrte Zeitung, und der niedrigste Mann von gesundem Verstande ist mir würdig genug, seine Aufmerksamkeit zu suchen, sein Vergnügen zu befördern und ihm in einem leicht zu behaltenden Ausdrucke gute Wahrheiten zu sagen und edle Empfindungen in seiner Seele rege zu machen.

Gellert's reputation rests chiefly on his fables and stories. His best religious poems are "Wie gross ist des Allmächt'gen Güte," "Dies ist der Tag, den Gott gemacht," and "Jesus lebt, mit ihm auch ich" (543).

No information is at hand concerning the translator, Margarete Münsterburg.

MUSIC. WIE GROSS IST DES ALLMÄCHT'GEN GÜTE is ascribed here to C. F. Richter. The Canadian *Gesangbuch* credits the tune to J. Freylinghausen.

Christian Friedrich Richter, 1676-1711, born at Sorau, in Niederlausitz, studied medicine and theology in Halle and became practicing physician in the Orphanage in Halle. A deeply religious man with poetic insight, he wrote 33 hymns, and is the author of a treatise on the Crucifixion of Christ.

517. O Pow'r of love, all else transcending

Gerhard Tersteegen, 1697-1769
Tr. H. Brueckner, 1883—

1.
Ich bete an die Macht der Liebe,
Die sich in Jesu offenbart;
Ich geb' mich hin dem freien Triebe,
Mit dem ich heiss geliebet ward;
Ich will, anstatt an mich zu denken,
Ins Meer der Liebe mich versenken.

2.

Wie bist du mir so hoch gewogen,
  Und wie verlangt dein Herz
    nach mir!
Durch Liebe sanft und stark ge-
    zogen,
  Neigt sich mein Alles auch zu
    dir.
Du, teure Liebe, gutes Wesen,
Du hast mich, ich hab' dich er-
    lesen!

3.

Ich fühl's, du bist's, ich muss dich
    haben;
  Ich fühl's, ich muss für dich nur
    sein;
Nicht im Geschöpf, nicht in' den
    Gaben,
  Mein Leben ist in dir allein!
Hier ist die Ruh', hier ist Ver-
    gnügen;
Drum folg' ich deinen sel'gen Zü-
    gen.

4.

Dein ewig ist mein Herz und
    Leben,
  Erlöser, du, mein einzig Gut!
Du hast für mich dich hingegeben
  Zum Heil durch dein Erlö-
    sungsblut.
Du Heil des schweren, tiefen
    Falles,
Für dich ist ewig Herz und Alles!

5.

Ich liebt' und lebte recht im
    Zwange,

Als ich mir lebte ohne dich.
  Ich wollte dich nicht, ach so lange!
Doch liebtest du und suchtest
    mich!
O wenn doch dies der Sünder
    wüsste,
Sein Herz wohl bald dich lieben
    müsste!

6.

O Jesu, dass dein Name bliebe
  Im Geist mir; drück ihn tief
    hinein!
Lass deine süsse Jesusliebe
  In Herz und Sinn gepräget sein!
In Wort and Werk, in allem We-
    sen
Sei Jesus und sonst nichts zu lesen!

7.

In deinem teuren, heil'gen Namen
  Eröffnet sich des Vaters Herz,
Da find' ich lauter Ja und Amen,
  Und Trost und Heilung für den
    Schmerz.
O dass dies jeder Sünder wüsste,
Sein Herz gar bald dich lieben
    müsste!

8.

Preis sei dem hohen Jesusnamen,
  In dem der Liebe Quell ent-
    springt,
Von dem hier alle Ströme kamen,
  Aus dem die sel'ge Schaar dort
    trinkt!
Wie beugen sie sich ohne Ende,
Wie falten sie die frohen Hände!

One of the great hymns by the German mystic, Gerhard Tersteegen.

For comments on Tersteegen see Hymn 506.

Our version is a free translation of stanzas 1, 2, and 4 of the original 8.

Herman Brueckner, translator of the hymn, was born in Eisenach, Germany, and was educated at the Universities of Leipzig, Greifswald, and Jena. The latter gave him the doctors degree in theology in 1923. Coming to America, Brueckner served a year as Lutheran Seaman's Pastor for the Port of New York. From 1915 to 1931 he was pastor of St. Matthaeus Lutheran Church, Hoboken, N. J., and since that time has served as Professor of Church History in Hartwick Seminary. He is the author of a number of volumes on ecclesiastical and historical subjects, among them, *Church and State in Germany,* published in 1934.

Brueckner's translation was slightly altered by the editors of the *Hymnary,* at two points:

Stanza 1, line 4: "And sign of thy celestial lore," to "Thy name to honor and adore."

Stanza 2, line 5: "Thy love, so tender, and caressing," to "Thy love, so tender, so possessing."

MUSIC. ST. PETERSBURG, also known as "Wells," "Wellspring," and "Shangana," is adapted from a portion of a mass by the Russian composer, Dimitri S. Bortniansky, 1752-1825.

For comments on Bortniansky see Hymn 28.

The "Don Cossacks" sing this melody with thrilling effect to "Kol slavan," a Russian folk song. The tune, slightly altered, has in recent years been introduced into a number of American hymnals.

518. Lord, who can be with Thee compared

Johann A. Cramer, 1723-88
Tr. Harriet R. Spaeth, 1913

Herr! Dir ist Niemand zu vergleichen!
   Kein Lob kann deine Gröss erreichen,
Kein noch so feuriger Verstand.
   Pracht, Majestät und Ruhm umgeben,
Dich, aller Wesen Quell' and Leben;
Licht ist dein strahlenvoll Gewand.
   In hohen, unermess 'nen Fernen,
Wohin kein sterblich Auge schaut,
   Hast du, weit über allen Sternen,
Dir deinen hohen Sitz erbaut.

   Als du allmächtig sprachst: "Es werde!"
   Da gründetest du fest die Erde,
   Vor Alters war die Tief ihr Kleid.
Auf allen Bergen standen Wasser
Du schalt'st sie, da enfloh'n die Wasser,
   Durch deines Donners Kraft zerstreut.
Der Berge Gipfel, Herr ershienen,
   Erhoben durch dein mächtig Wort,
Die Täler sanken unter ihnen
   An den für sie bestimmten Ort.

   Erheb', erheb' o meine Seele,
Gott, meinen Schöpfer, und erzähle,
   Verkündige sein Lob der Welt!
Ihm singe deine Jubellieder;

Der Fromme halle sie ihm wieder,
Dem Mächtigen, der uns erhält!
Frohlockt ihm, alle seine Heere,
Ihm weihet euren Lobgesang!
Der Herr ist würdig, Preis und Ehre
Zu nehmen, Lob und Ruhm und Dank!

A hymn in praise of God, the Creator of heaven and earth, originally in 10 stanzas. It is based on Psalm 104, one of the great nature Psalms.

Johann Andreas Cramer was the son of a Lutheran pastor. He was educated at Leipzig and became famous as a preacher and teacher, later serving as Professor of Theology and Chancellor of the University of Kiel in Germany. He wrote numerous religious lyrics and psalm versions, a number of which passed into the hymnbooks of his time, and several of which have been translated into English.

The present hymn is a translation of stanzas 1 and 10 of the German original. No information has been traced concerning Harriett R. Spaeth, the translator.

MUSIC. HERR DIR IST NIEMAND VERGLEICHEN derives its name from the first line of the hymn with which it is associated. The composer, Justin Heinrich Knecht, 1752-1817, was an eminent German organist and music director of the town of Biberach, Swabia. He edited the *Württemberg Choralbuch,* an important collection of tunes, to which he contributed 97 of his own compositions.

519. Holy God, we praise Thy name   *Ignaz Franz, 1719-90*
Tr. Clarence Walworth, 1820-1900

1.
Grosser Gott, wir loben dich!
Herr, wir preisen deine Stärke!
Vor dir neigt die Erde sich
Und bewundert deine Werke.
Wie du warst vor aller Zeit,
So bleibst du in Ewigkeit!
2.
Alles, was dich preisen kann,
Cherubim und Seraphinen,
Stimmen dir ein Loblied an;
Alle Engel, die dir dienen,
Rufen dir in selger Ruh:
Heilig, heilig, heilig zu.
3.
Heiliger Gott Zebaoth!
Heil'ger Herr der Himmelsheere!
Starker Helfer in der Not!

Himmel, Erde, Luft und Meere
Sind erfüllt mit deinem Ruhm;
Alles ist dein Eigentum!
4.
Der Apostel heilger Chor,
Der Propheten grosse Menge
Schickt zu deinem Thron empor
Neue Lob- und Dankgesänge;
Der Blutzeugen grosse Schar
Lobt und preist dich immerdar.
5.
Auf dem ganzen Erdenkreis
Loben Grosse dich und Kleine.
Dir, Gott Vater, dir zum Preis
Singt die heilige Gemeinde,
Und verehrt auf seinem Thron
Deinen eingebornen Sohn.

6.

Sie verehrt den heil'gen Geist,
Welcher uns mit seinen Lehren
Und mit Troste kräftig speist,
Dich, den Herrscher voller Ehren
Der mit dir, O Jesu Christ,
Und dem Vater Eines ist!

7.

Du, des Vaters ew'ger Sohn,
Hast die Menschheit angenommen,
Bist, O Herr, von deinem Thron
Zu uns in die Welt gekommen!
Du hast uns dein Reich gebracht:
Uns von Sünde frei gemacht!

8.

Nun kann zu der Gnade Thron
Jeder freien Zugang finden;
Wer da glaubet an den Sohn,
Hat Vergebung seiner Sünden;
Denn des Lammes teures Blut
Spricht für uns beim Vater gut.

9.

Stehe denn, O Herr, uns bei,
Die wir dich in Demut bitten:
Sprich von aller Schuld uns frei,
Da du auch für uns gelitten;
Nimm uns nach vollbrachtem Lauf
Zu dir in den Himmel auf!

10.

Alle Tage wollen wir
Deinen heil'gen Namen preisen,
Und zu allen Zeiten dir
Ehre, Lob und Dank erweisen.
Gib dass wir in allem Tun
Nur in deinem Willen ruhn!

11.

Herr, erbarm, erbarme dich!
Ueber uns, Herr, sei dein Segen!
Deine Güte zeige sich,
Dass wir lauter preisen mögen!
Auf dich hoffen wir allein,
Lass uns nicht verloren sein!

The words are a rhymed form of the *Te Deum* which Luther, in strict ecclesiastical style, translated from the Latin. The hymn is popular among Roman Catholics, Lutherans, and Anglicans, as a post-communion hymn, and is a great favorite among Mennonite churches. It sounds a universal note of praise that can be sung by Christians of all denominations. The hymn was used at the opening of the first World Assembly of Churches, held at Amsterdam, August 22 to September 4, 1948, where it was sung simultaneously in different tongues.

The author, Ignaz Franz, was born at Protzan, Kr. Frankenstein, in Silesia. He first was priest in Schlowa, and then became rector of a graduate school for priests in Breslau. In 1772, under the influence of the Enlightenment, he published a Catholic hymnbook. He is described as a man filled with zeal for the good things in religion and the church.

Note: The *Te Deum* is a long Latin hymn of uncertain origin, constituting the supreme expression of rejoicing in the Roman Catholic, Anglican, and other Christian Churches. It is sometimes called the "Canticle of Ambrose and Augustine," from the legend that at the baptism of Augustine by Ambrose it was sung antiphonally, extempore, by the two men. It dates back to the fourth or fifth century. Its contents are drawn from different sources: the Apostles' Creed, the "Gloria in Excelsis," and the Psalms (e.g. 28:9, 31:1, 33:22, 123:3, 145:2). Luther, who translated it into German, praised it as a "fine symbol or confession, not only for confessing the right faith but also for praising and thanking God withal." A real confession of faith ought to be sung, and as such the *Te Deum* has been on the lips of the Church, in one form or another, ever since it was composed.

MUSIC. GROSSER GOTT, WIR LOBEN DICH is of unknown composition. The tune first appeared in the *Katholisches Gesangbuch,* a book undated but not earlier than 1774, set to the words, "Grosser Gott." Its first appearance in a Protestant hymn book was in Schicht's *Choral-Buch,* Leipzig, 1819. It was set to English words in *Melodia Sacra,* Dublin, 1844, to the hymn, "Jesus, and shall it ever be," where the tune was modified to fit the words and named, "Stillorgan." Later, under the name, "Hursley", it became widely associated with Keble's evening hymn, "Sun of my Soul" (No. 30). *St. Basil's Hymnal* (Roman Catholic, 1918), as well as the *Gesangbuch mit Noten,* attribute the tune to Peter Ritter; *Glaubensharfe,* to J. Haydn. There seems to be no good evidence for either. The English *Church Hymnary,* London, 1935, has set the tune, naming it "Pascal", to Toplady's "Rock of Ages." In some of the books the last score is marked with a repeat sign for the sake of emphasis and climax.

520. Holy Lord, holy Lord *Anonymous*

The notes of thanksgiving and praise are dominant. The origin of the hymn has not been traced.

MUSIC. FAHRE FORT, attributed erroneously in the *Hymnary* to Johann E. Schmidt, is of anonymous origin. It appeared in Freylinghausen's *Gesangbuch,* Halle, 1704, with the well-known hymn, "Fahre fort, fahre fort," by Johann E. Schmidt, 1669-1745. The tune derived its name from this hymn.

521. All glory be to God on High Nikolaus Decius, c. 1490-1541
Tr. Catherine Winkworth, 1829-78

1.
Allein Gott in der Höh' sei Ehr'
Und Dank für seine Gnade,
Darum dass nun und nimmer-
    mehr
Uns rühren kann kein Schade.
Ein Wohlgefall'n Gott an uns hat,
Nun ist gross' Fried' ohn' Unter-
    lass,
All' Fehd' hat nun ein Ende.

2.
Wir loben, preis'n, anbeten dich
Für deine Ehr'; wir danken,
Dass du, Gott Vater, ewiglich
Regierst ohn' alles Wanken.
Ganz ungemess'n ist deine Macht,
Fort g'schieht, was dein Will' hat
    bedacht;
Wohl uns des feinen Herren!

3.

O Jesu Christ, Sohn eingebor'n
Deines himmlischen Vaters,
Versöhner der'r, die war'n ver-
lor'n,
Du Stiller unsers Haders.
Lamm Gottes, heil'ger Herr und
Gott,
Nimm an die Bitt' von unsrer Not,
Erbarm' dich unser aller!

4.

O heil'ger Geist, du höchstes Gut,
Du allerheilsamst' Tröster,
Vor's Teufels G'walt fortan be-
hüt',
Die Jesus Christ erlöset
Durch grosse Mart'r und bittern
Tod,
Abwend all unsern Jamm'r und
Not!
Darauf wir uns verlassen.

An example of what a good, popular hymn should be—"neither didactic nor introspective, but natural, strong, and churchly."

The author, Nikolaus Decius, was a contemporary of Luther. (The date, "1626," in the *Hymnary* is obviously wrong.) He was a monk in the Roman Catholic Church but became a follower of Luther, leaving the cloister at Steterburg, in 1519, to become a teacher and evangelical preacher. His work was carried on under constant opposition from the Church of Rome. He died suddenly in 1541 with some suspicion of having been poisoned by his enemies. Three hymns are ascribed to Decius: versions of the *Sanctus,* the *Gloria in excelsis,* and the *Agnus Dei* (No. 540). The present hymn is a translation of the second, the *Gloria in excelsis.* It became very popular, though Luther did not use it in any of his collections.

For comments on Catherine Winkworth see Hymn 236.

MUSIC. NUN FREUT EUCH is also attributed to Decius who was a good musician as well as a popular preacher. It is often called "Luther's Hymn" but there is no evidence that he wrote it. The tune appeared in *Geistliche Leider,* Wittenberg, 1535, where it was set to Luther's hymn, "Nun freut euch, liebe Christengemein."

ADVENT

522. Wake, awake, for night is flying Philipp Nicolai, 1556-1608
Tr. Catherine Winkworth, 1829-78 Alt.

1.

Wachet auf! ruft uns die Stimme
Der Wächter sehr hoch auf der
Zinne,
Wach auf, du Stadt Jerusalem!
Mitternacht heisst diese Stunde,
Sie rufen uns mit hellem Munde:

Wo seid ihr klugen Jungfrauen?
Wohlauf, der Bräut'gam kömmt,
Steht auf, die Lampen nehmt!
Halleluja!
Macht euch bereit zu der Hoch-
zeit,
Ihr müsset ihm entgegengehn!

CHORALES

2.

Zion hört die Wächter singen,
Das Herz tut ihr vor Freuden
  springen,
Sie wacht und stehet eilend auf.
Ihr Freund kommt vom Himmel
  prächtig,
Von Gnaden stark, von Wahrheit
  mächtig,
Ihr Licht wird hell, ihr Stern
  geht auf.
Nun komm, du werte Kron',
Herr Jesu, Gottes Sohn!
  Hosianna!
Wir folgen all' zum Freudensaal
Und halten mit das Abendmahl.

3.

Gloria sei dir gesungen
Mit Menschen- und mit Engel-
  zungen,
Mit Harfen und mit Zimbeln
  schön.
Von zwölf Perlen sind die Pforten
An deiner Stadt, wir sind Kon-
  sorten
Kein Aug, hat je gespürt,
Kein Ohr hat mehr gehört
  Solche Freude.
Das sind wir froh, i-o, i-o,
Ewig in dulci iubilo.

This hymn, with it magnificent tune, has long been known as the "King of Chorals." (For the "Queen of Chorals" see No. 529). Percy Dearmer writes of this choral: "There is no other hymn like this, surely the grandest and most thrilling, both in words and music—and both words and music by the same man." It is based on the parable of the wise and foolish virgins in Matt. 25:1-13, and on Rev. 19:6-9 (the marriage of the Lamb); 21:22; 1 Cor. 2:9; Ezek. 3:17; and Isa. 52:8.

Nicolai, an ardent Lutheran and influential preacher, was fierce in his denunciation of both Calvinism and Roman Catholicism. He held pastorates in various places. From 1601 until his death, he was chief pastor of St. Katherine's, Hamburg. It was during his five years at Unna, Westphalia, that a terrible pestilence swept through the community, claiming the lives of over 1300 people. Nicolai's parsonage overlooked the church yard where the burial of the victims was taking place continually. These scenes of sorrow and death moved him to write this great judgment hymn which he entitled, "Of the Voice at Midnight, and the Wise Virgins who meet their Heavenly Bridegroom." For comments on Miss Winkworth, translator, see Hymn 236.

MUSIC. WACHET AUF, one of the greatest and most solemn melodies of evangelical Christendom, was composed by Nicolai. The present setting is by Michael Praetorius, 1571-1621, a writer on the theory of music and a composer of note. The melody was used by Bach in one of his cantatas and Mendelssohn used it in his *St. Paul.* Handel used the seventh and eighth lines of the melody with great effect in the "Hallelujah Chorus," with the phrase, "The kingdom of this world."

308

523. Lift up your heads, ye mighty gates

Georg Weissel, 1590-1635
Tr. Catherine Winkworth, 1829-78

1.

Macht hoch die Tür, die Tor'
    macht weit,
Es kommt der Herr der Herrlich-
    keit,
Ein König aller Königreich',
Ein Heiland aller Welt zugleich,
Der Heil und Leben mit sich
    bringt;
Derhalben jauchzt, mit Freuden
    singt;
  Gelobet sei mein Gott,
  Mein Schöpfer, reich von Rat!

2.

Er ist gerecht, ein Helfer wert,
Sanftmütigkeit ist sein Gefährt,
Sein Königskron' ist Heiligkeit,
Sein Zepter ist Barmherzigkeit.
All unsre Not zum End' er bringt,
Derhalben jauchzt, mit Freuden
    singt:
  Gelobet sei mein Gott,
  Mein Heiland, gross von Tat!

3.

O wohl dem Land, o wohl der
    Stadt,
So diesen König bei sich hat!
Wohl allen Herzen insgemein,
Da dieser König ziehet ein!
Er ist die rechte Freudensonn',
Bringt mit sich lauter Freud' und
    Wonn'.
  Gelobet sei mein Gott,
  Mein Tröster, früh und spat!

4.

Macht hoch die Tür, die Tor'
    macht weit,
Eu'r Herz zum Tempel zübereit't,
Die Zweiglein der Gottseligkeit
Steckt auf mit Andacht, Lust und
    Freud'!
So kommt der König auch zu euch.
Ja Heil und Leben mit zugleich,
  Gelobet sei mein Gott,
  Voll Rat, voll Tat, voll Gnad'!

5.

Komm, o mein Heiland Jesu Christ,
Mein's Herzens Tür dir offen ist!
Ach zeuch mit deiner Gnade ein,
Dein' Freundlichkeit auch uns erschein',
Dein heil'ger Geist uns führ' und leit'
Den Weg zur ew'gen Seligkeit!
  Dem Namen dein, o Herr,
  Sei ewig Preis und Ehr'!

One of our finest German Advent hymns, based on Psalm 24. It was written for use on the first Sunday in Advent.

Georg Weissel was born at Domnau, Prussia. He was a student of theology, a teacher, and, from 1623, until his death in 1635, the pastor of Roszgärt'schen Church in Königsberg. He is the author of twenty hymns, this being probably the best and most widely used. Our version is a translation of stanzas 1, 2, 3, and 5 of the original.

For comments on Catherine Winkworth see Hymn 236.

MUSIC. MACHT HOCH DIE TÜR is one of several chorale tunes, probably the most popular, to which this hymn is set.

CHORALES

The composer, Johann Freylinghausen, 1670-1739, was born at Gandersheim, the son of the town's burgomaster. He was educated at Jena. After the death of his father-in-law, August Francke, Pietist leader, he became the latter's successor as director of the Paedagogium and the Orphanage in Halle and pastor in full charge of St. Ulrich's. Freylinghausen was a musician and wrote some 22 church melodies but his outstanding work consists of his two collections of hymns: *Geistreiches Gesangbuch*, 1704, and *Neues Geistreiches Gesangbuch*, 1714. The former contains 683 hymns and 173 melodies, and the latter, 815 hymns and 154 melodies.

524. O Son of God, we wait for Thee

Philipp F. Hiller, 1699-1769
Tr. Joseph A. Seiss, 1823-1904

1.
Wir warten dein, O Gottes Sohn,
Und lieben dein Erscheinen;
Wir wissen dich auf deinem Thron,
Und nennen uns die deinen.
Wer an dich glaubt
Erhebt sein Haupt,
Und siehet dir entgegen,
Du kommst uns ja zum Segen.
2.
Wir warten deiner mit Geduld
In unsern Leidenstagen;
Wir trösten uns, dass du die Schuld
Für uns am Kreuz getragen.
So können wir
Nun gern mit dir
Uns auch zum Kreuz bequemen,
Bis du's hinweg wirst nehmen.

3.
Wir warten dein; du hast uns ja
Das Herz schon hingenommen.
Du bist zwar unserm Geiste nah,
Doch wirst du sichtbar kommen;
Da willst uns du
Bei dir auch Ruh',
Bei dir auch Freude geben,
Bei dir ein herrlich Leben.
4.
Wir warten dein, du kommst gewiss,
Die Zeit ist bald vergangen;
Wir freuen uns schon über dies
Mit kindlichem Verlangen.
Was wird geschehn,
Wenn wir dich sehn,
Wenn du uns heim wirst bringen,
Wenn wir dir ewig singen!

In clear and concise language, the hymn voices the hope for the coming of Christ.

Phillipp Friedrich Hiller, son of a Lutheran Pastor, was born at Mühlhausen, Württemberg. To escape the French invaders, he fled with his parents, at the age of 8, to Heidenheim. In 1713, he went to the Klosterschule, Denkendorf, where Bengel had a decided influence upon him. In 1748, he became the pastor in Steinheim, where, after three years of faithful service, a throat disease afflicted him, resulting in the loss of his voice. No longer able to preach, he gave himself to Bible study and writing, composing more than 100 hymns, and publishing a volume of religious poetry, *Geistliches Liederkästlein*.

The translation is by Joseph Augustus Seiss, a Lutheran minister, born at Graceham, Md., and educated at Gettysburg College and Seminary. Seiss was a noted pulpit orator in his denomination and held pastorates in Virginia, Maryland, and, finally, in Philadelphia.

MUSIC. GASTORIUS is ascribed by some authorities to Johann Pacherbel of Nürnberg, a contemporary of Gastorius. The melody appeared in the *Auserlesenes Weimarisches Gesangbuch*, 1681. Zahn, on the basis of careful study of the sources, does not hesitate to credit its composition to Gastorius, about 1675. It was originally set to a hymn by Samuel Rodigast, "Was Gott tut, das ist wohlgetan."

Severus Gastorius, cantor in Jena, was born about 1650. Details concerning his life are not available. .

CHRISTMASTIDE

525. All my heart this night rejoices   *Paul Gerhardt, 1607-76*
Tr. Catherine Winkworth, 1829-78

1.
Fröhlich soll mein Herze springen
Dieser Zeit, da vor Freud'
Alle Engel singen.
Hört, hört, wie mit vollen Chören
Alle Luft laute ruft:
Christus ist geboren!

2.
Heute geht aus seiner Kammer
Gottes Held, der die Welt
Reisst aus allem Jammer.
Gott wird Mensch dir, Mensch, zugute.
Gottes Kind, das verbind't
Sich mit unserm Blute.

3.
Sollt' uns Gott nun können hassen,
Der uns gibt, was er liebt
Ueber alle Massen?
Gott gibt, unserm Leid zu wehren,
Seinen Sohn aus dem Thron
Seiner Macht und Ehren.

4.
Sollte von uns sein gekehret,
Der sein Reich und zugleich
Sich uns selbst verehret?
Sollt' uns Gottes Sohn nicht lieben,
Der jetzt kömmt, von uns nimmt,
Was uns will betrüben?

5.
Hätte vor der Menschen Orden
Unser Heil einen Greu'l,
Wär' er nicht Mensch worden.
Hätt' er Lust zu unserm Schaden,
Ei, so würd' unsre Bürd'
Er nicht auf sich laden.

6.
Er nimmt auf sich, was auf Erden
Wir getan, gibt sich an,
Unser Lamm zu werden,
Unser Lamm, das für uns stirbet
Und bei Gott für den Tod
Gnad' und Fried' erwirbet.

7.

Nun, er liegt in seiner Krippen,
  Ruft zu sich mich und dich,
Spricht mit süssen Lippen:
  Lasset fahr'n, o leibe Brüder,
Was euch quält, was euch fehlt,
  Ich bring' alles wieder.

8.

Ei, so kommt und lasst uns laufen!
  Stellt euch ein, gross und klein,
Eilt mit grossem Haufen!
  Liebt den, der vor Liebe bren-
  net;
Schaut den Stern, der uns gern
  Licht und Labsal gönnet.

9.

Die ihr schwebt in grossen Leiden,
  Sehet, hier ist die Tür
Zu den wahren Freuden.
  Fasst ihn wohl, er wird euch
  führen
An den Ort, da hinfort
  Euch kein Kreuz wird rühren.

10.

Wer sich fühlt beschwert im Her-
  zen,
  Wer empfind't seine Sünd'
Und Gewissensschmerzen,
  Sei getrost, hier wird gefunden,
Der in Eil' machet heil
  Die vergift'ten Wunden.

11.

Die ihr arm seid und elende,
  Kommt herbei, füllet frei
Eures Glaubens Hände!
  Hier sind alle guten Gaben
Und das Gold, da ihr sollt
  Euer Herz mit laben.

12.

Süsses Heil, lass dich umfangen,
  Lass mich dir, meine Zier,
Unverrückt anhangen!
  Du bist meines Lebens Leben;
Nun kann ich mich durch dich
  Wohl zufrieden geben.

13.

Meine Schuld kann mich nicht
  drücken,
  Denn du hast meine Last
All' auf deinem Rücken.
  Kein Fleck ist an mir zu finden,
Ich bin gar rein und klar
  Aller meiner Sünden.

14.

Ich bin rein um deinetwillen;
  Du gibst g'nug Ehr, und
  Schmuck,
Mich darein zu hüllen.
  Ich will dich ins Herze schlies-
  sen;
O mein Ruhm, edle Blum',
  Lass dich recht geniessen!

15.

Ich will dich mit Fleiss bewahren,
  Ich will dir leben hier,
Dir will ich abfahren;
  Mit dir will ich endlich schweben
Voller Freud' ohne Zeit
  Dort im andern Leben.

Paul Gerhardt's beautiful Christmas poem, in 15 stanzas, appeared
in Johann Crüger's *Praxis Pietatis Melica*, Berlin, 1653, together with
a tune composed for it by Crüger. The present hymn is a selection of
stanzas 1, 7 and 8, from Catherine Winkworth's translation. The original 15 stanzas are printed here in full for the benefit of those who may
wish to read the whole hymn and study its structure.

For comments on Paul Gerhardt see Hymn 134.

For comments on Miss Winkworth see Hymn 236.

MUSIC. WARUM SOLLT ICH MICH DENN GRÄMEN, also called, "Ebeling," and "Bonn," soon superseded Crüger's tune. It was originally set to another of Gerhardt's hymns, "Warum sollt ich mich denn grämen," from whence the tune derives its name. The composer, Johann Georg Ebeling, 1620-76, was cantor of St. Nicholas Cathedral, Berlin, and director of music at the Grayfriars Gymnasium there, succeeding Johann Crüger to these positions, in 1662. Six years later, he became Professor of Music at the Carolinen Gymnasium, Stettin.

The harmonization is by W. H. Hohmann, Professor of Music, Bethel College, and co-editor of the *Hymnary*.

526. A great and mighty wonder

St. Germanus, 634-734
Tr. John M. Neale, 1818-66

This is one of a half dozen or more hymns in our book that have come down from the ancient Eastern or Greek Church. (Other hymns from this period are Nos. 34, 113, 115, 143, and 398.)

St. Germanus was born and died in Constantinople. He lived to be a hundred years old. He became an influential leader in the church, and served, for a time, as Patriarch, or Bishop of Constantinople.

For this translation, we are indebted to John M. Neale, English hymnologist and classical scholar. Neale possessed extraordinary linguistic skill and did more than anyone else to make available to English speaking people some of the rich treasure of Greek and Latin hymnody.

MUSIC. ES IST EIN' ROS' ENTSPRUNGEN, also known as "Rosa Mystica," is a traditional German melody, originally set to a well-known carol beginning with the stanza:

Es ist ein Reis entsprungen
Aus einer Wurzel zart,
Als uns die Alten sungen,
Von Jesse kam die Art,
Und hat ein Blümlein bracht
Mitten im kalten Winter
Wohl zu der halben Nacht.

It is an attractive and interesting tune, of irregular rhythm. The present setting was made by Michael Praetorius, 1517-1621, German composer and Kapellmeister.

For comments on Praetorius see Hymn 248.

527. From heaven above to earth I come

Martin Luther, 1483-1546
Tr. Catherine Winkworth, 1829-78

1.
Vom Himmel hoch, da komm' ich her,

Ich bring' euch gute neue Mär,
Der guten Mär bring' ich so viel,
Davon ich sing'n und sagen will.

313

2.

Euch ist ein Kindlein' heut' ge-
bor'n
Von einer Jungfrau auserkor'n,
Ein Kindelein, so zart und fein,
Das soll eur, Freud', und Wonne
sein.

3.

Es ist der Herr Christ, unser Gott,
Der will euch führ'n aus aller Not,
Er will eu'r Heiland selber sein,
Von allen Sünden machen rein.

4.

Er bringt euch alle Seligkeit
Die Gott der Vater hat bereit,
Dass ihr mit uns im Himmelreich
Sollt leben nun und ewiglich.

5.

So merket nun das Zeichen recht,
D i e   Krippe,   Windelein   s o
schlecht,
Da findet ihr das Kind gelegt,
Das alle Welt erhält und trägt.

6.

Des lasst uns alle fröhlich sein
Und mit den Hirten gehn hinein,
Zu sehn, was Gott uns hat be-
schert,
Mit seinem lieben Sohn verehrt.

7.

Merk auf, mein Herz, und sieh
dorthin!
Was liegt dort in dem Krippelein?
Wer ist das schöne Kindelein?
Es ist das liebe Jesulein.

8.

Bist willekomm, du edler Gast!
Den Sünder nicht verschmähet
hast
Und kommst ins Elend her zu mir,
Wie soll ich immer danken dir?

9.

Ach Herr, du Schöpfer aller Ding',
Wie bist du worden so gering,
Dass du da liegst auf dürrem Gras,
Davon ein Rind und Esel asz!

10.

Und wär' die Welt vielmal so weit,
Von Edelstein und Gold bereit't,
So wär sie doch dir viel zu klein,
Zu sein ein enges Wiegelein.

11.

Der Sammet und die Seide dein,
Das ist grob Heu und Windelein,
Darauf du König gross und reich
Herprangst, als wär's dein Him-
melreich.

12.

Das hat also gefallen dir,
Die Wahrheit anzuzeigen mir:
Wie aller Welt Macht, Ehr' und
Gut
Vor dir nichts gilt, nichts hilft
noch tut.

13.

Ach mein herzliebes Jesulein,
Mach dir ein rein, sanft Bettelein,
Zu ruhen in mein's Herzens
Schrein,
Dass ich nimmer vergesse dein!

14.

Davon ich allzeit fröhlich sei,
Zu springen, singen immer frei
Das rechte Susaninne schon,
Mit Herzenslust den süssen Ton.

15.

Lob, Ehr' sei Gott im höchsten
Thron,
Der uns schenkt seinen ein'gen
Sohn!
Des freuen sich der Engel Schar
Und singen uns solch neues Jahr.

This children's Christmas carol, based on the second chapter of Luke,
was written by Martin Luther for his little son Hans for the Christmas
celebration in his own home, 1534. Luther's instructions were that the
first seven verses were to be sung by a man dressed as an angel, whereupon the children would greet him with the singing of verses eight to
fifteen. The present hymn is a selection of stanzas 1, 2, 3, 8, 13, and 15.

For comments on the translator, Miss Winkworth, see Hymn 236.

MUSIC. VOM HIMMEL HOCH, also by Luther, was early associated with the words of the carol and has become one of the best known chorales. J. S. Bach made several settings of the tune, one of them is his *Christmas Oratorio.*

NEW YEAR

528. For Thy mercy and Thy grace   *H. Downton, 1818-85*

Originally in seven stanzas, this hymn was first published, 1843, in the *Church of England Magazine,* under the title, "A Hymn for the Commencement of the Year." It is a first-rate quality hymn for the New Year.

The author, Henry Downton, was born in Pulverbatch, Shropshire, England. In 1840, he graduated from Cambridge where his father was sub-librarian of Trinity College. After serving as curate of St. John's Chatham, Downton became English chaplain at Geneva in 1857, returning to England in 1873 to become rector of Hopton, Suffolk. In Geneva, he had become acquainted with the hymnody of the Swiss and French Churches, and translated a number of their hymns into English. He published *Hymns and Verses, Original and Translated,* 1873.

MUSIC. CULBACH appeared in *Heilige Seelenlust,* Breslau, 1657, set to the hymn, "Ach wann kommt die Zeit heran." The melody, simple in structure and well within the pitch range of all voices, is admirably adapted to congregational singing, in unison or in parts. The composer is unknown.

EPIPHANY

529. How brightly shines the Morning Star
Philipp Nicolai, 1556–1608
Tr. Catherine Winkworth, 1829–78

1.

Wie schön leuchtet der Morgenstern
Voll Gnad' und Wahrheit von dem Herrn,
Die süsse Wurzel Jesse!
Du Sohn Davids aus Jakobs Stamm,

Mein König und mein Bräutigam,
Hast mir mein Herz besesssen,
Lieblich, freundlich,
Schön und herrlich, gross und ehrlich,
Reich von Gaben,
Hoch und sehr prächtig erhaben!

2.

Ei meine Perl', du werte Kron',
Wahr'r Gottes- und Mariensohn,
Ein hochgeborner König!
Mein Herz heisst dich ein Lilium,
Dein süsses Evangelium
Ist lauter Milch und Honig.
Ei mein Blümlein,
Hosianna, himmlisch Manna,
Das wir essen,
Deiner kann ich nicht vergessen!

3.

Geuss sehr tief in mein Herz hin-
ein,
Du heller Jaspis und Rubin,
Die Flamme deiner Liebe
Und erfreu' mich, dass ich doch
bleib'
An deinem auserwählten Leib
Ein' lebendige Rippe!
Nach dir ist mir,
Gratiosa coeli rosa,
Krank und glimmet
Mein Herz, durch Liebe verwun-
det.

4.

Von Gott kommt mir ein Freuden-
schein,
Wenn du mit deinen Aeugelein
Mich freundlich tust anblicken.
O Herr Jesu, mein trautes Gut,
Dein Wort, dein Geist, dein Leib
und Blut
Mich innerlich erquicken!
Nimm mich freundlich
In dein' Arme, dass ich warme
Werd' von Gnaden!
Auf dein Wort komm' ich geladen.

5.

Herr Gott Vater, mein starker
Held,
Du hast mich ewig vor der Welt
In deinem Sohn geliebet.
Dein Sohn hat mich ihm selbst
vertraut,
Er ist mein Schatz, ich bin sein'
Braut,
Sehr hoch in ihm erfreuet.
Eia, eia,
Himmlisch Leben wird er geben
Mir dort oben!
Ewig soll mein Herz ihn loben.

6.

Zwingt die Saiten in Zithara
Und lasst die süsse Musika
Ganz freudenreich erschallen,
Dass ich möge mit Jesulein,
Dem wunderschönen Bräut'gam
mein,
In steter Liebe wallen!
Singet, springet,
Jubilieret, triumphieret,
Dankt dem Herren!
Gross ist der König der Ehren!

7.

Wie bin ich doch so herzlich froh
Dass mein Schatz ist das A und O
Der Anfang und das Ende!
Er wird mich doch zu seinem Preis
Aufnehmen in das Paradeis,
Des klopf' ich in die Hände.
Amen! Amen!
Komm, du schöne Freudenkrone,
Bleib nicht lange,
Deiner wart' ich mit Verlangen!

Known as the "Queen of the Chorales." The words and music were
written in 1527 by the Lutheran pastor, Philipp Nicolai, during the
same pestilence that inspired "Wachet auf," the "King of Chorales"
(No. 522). Nicolai, in deep meditation concerning the suffering around
him, started writing the hymn one morning, and forgetting his noon-
day meal, worked on till he had finished it in the late afternoon. It
was first published in the author's *Freuden-Spiegel*, Frankfurt, 1599, under the title, "A Spiritual bridal song of the believing soul, concerning

her Heavenly Bridegroom, founded in the 45th Psalm of the prophet David." Catherine Winkworth wrote of the chorale:

> So popular did it soon become, that its tune was often chimed by city chimes, lines and verses from it were printed by way of ornament on the common earthenware of the country, and it was invariably used at weddings and certain festivals.

For comments on Miss Winkworth see Hymn 236.

MUSIC. NICOLAI is usually known by the first line of the words for which it was written, "Wie shön leuchtet der Morgenstern." It is a magnificent chorale tune. Mendelssohn used the tune in his *Christus,* and Bach made a harmonization of it.

530. As with gladness men of old

William Chatterdon Dix, 1837-98

A popular Epiphany hymn, written on Epiphany Day, about 1858, while the author was sick in bed. After reading the Gospel of the day, Dix started writing this hymn and finished it by evening.

For comments on William Chatterdon Dix, see Hymn 78.

MUSIC. DIX is an abridgement of a melody written by Conrad Kocher and first published in his *Stimmen aus dem Reiche Gottes,* Stuttgart, 1838.

For comments on Kocher see Hymn 51.

LENT

531. Out of the depths I cry to Thee   *Martin Luther,* 1483-1546
Tr. Catherine Winkworth, 1829-78

1.
Aus tiefer Not schrei' ich zu dir,
  Herr Gott, erhör mein Rufen;
Dein' gnädig' Ohren kehr zu mir
  Und meiner Bitt sei offen!
Denn so du willst das sehen an,
Was Sünd' und Unrecht ist getan,
  Wer kann, Herr, von dir bleiben?
2.
Bei dir gilt nichts denn Gnad' und Gunst,
  Die Sünde zu vergeben;
Es ist doch unser Tun umsonst
  Auch in dem besten Leben

Vor dir niemand sich rühmen kann,
Des muss dich fürchten jederman
  Und deiner Gnade leben.
3.
Darum auf Gott will hoffen ich,
  Auf mein Verdienst nicht bauen;
Auf ihm mein Herz soll lassen sich
  Und seiner Güte trauen,
Die mir zusagt sein wertes Wort,
Das ist mein Trost und treuer Hort,
  Des will ich allzeit harren.

317

4.

Und ob es währt bis in die Nacht
Und wieder an den Morgen,
Doch soll mein Herz an Gottes
Macht
Verzweifeln nicht noch sorgen.
So tu' Israel rechter Art,
Der aus dem Geist erzeuget ward
Und seines Gott's erharre.

5.

Ob bei uns ist der Sünden viel,
Bei Gott ist viel mehr Gnade,
Sein' Hand zu helfen hat kein
Ziel,
Wie gross auch sei der Schade.
Er ist allein der gute Hirt,
Der Israel erlösen wird
Aus seinen Sünden allen.

A metrical version of Psalm 130. It is considered by many to be Luther's best production and Julian ranks it with the finest German psalm versions. The hymn was first published in Luther's *Etlich Cristlich Lider,* Wittenberg, 1524, and in his *Eyn Enchiridion,* Erfurt, 1524, in four stanzas. It was then rewritten and expanded into five stanzas and in this form published in Johann Walther's *Geystliche Gesangk Buchleyn,* Wittenberg, 1524, and again in Luther's later work, *Christliche Geseng zum Begrebnis,* Wittenberg, 1542. It is appropriate for use at a Christian burial, as well as other occasions, and was sung at Halle, in 1546, while Luther's body was being brought from Eisleben to Wittenberg for burial.

The "depths" from which the psalmist cries to God for deliverance, are not so much physical and psychical as moral and spiritual. The writer is conscious of his sinfulness, as well as the sinfulness of his people and sees that there is no help except through penitence and acceptance of the mercy and forgiveness of God.

The first three stanzas from Catherine Winkworth's translation were selected for use here.

For comments on Miss Winkworth see Hymn 236.

MUSIC. AUS TIEFER NOT, also called "De Profundis," and "Luther's 130th," is attributed to Luther himself. J. S. Bach's cantata, *Aus tiefer Not schrei' ich zu Dir,* is built on this tune. Luther believed in the power of music to drive away the Evil One and frequently, when anxious about the fate of his cause, he would say to his companions, "Come, let us confound the devil and all his followers, by singing together the psalm, 'Aus tiefer Not.' "

532. Out of the depths I cry to Thee   *Martin Luther, 1483-1546*
Tr. Catherine Winkworth, 1829-78

For comments on this hymn see No. 531.

MUSIC. AUS TIEFER NOT became popular in our churches through its inclusion in the *Gesangbuch mit Noten.* The tune is credited to J. M. Biermann, an American writer of tunes of the gospel hymn type. He was musical editor of *Hosianna,* Cleveland, 1876, published by the

Evangelical Church. The composer seems to have borrowed from the tune "Macht Hoch die Tür," No. 523. *Hosianna* contains about 35 of his tunes and arrangements.

533. Jesus, I never can forget

Paul Gerhardt, 1607-76
Tr. J. Gambold, 1711-71

1.

Ein Lämmlein geht und trägt die Schuld
Der Welt und ihrer Kinder;
Es geht und träget in Geduld
Die Sünden aller Sünder;
Es geht dahin, wird matt und krank,
Ergibt sich auf die Würgebank,
Verzeiht sich aller Freuden;
Es nimmet an Schmach, Hohn und Spott,
Angst, Wunden, Striemen, Kreuz und Tod
Und spricht: Ich will's gern leiden.

2.

Mein Lebetage will ich dich
Aus meinem Sinn nicht lassen;
Dich will ich stets, gleich wie du mich,
Mit Liebesarmen fassen.
Du sollst sein meines Herzens Licht,
Und wenn mein Herz im Tode bricht,
Sollst du mein Herz verbleiben.
Ich will mich dir, mein höchster Ruhm,
Hiemit zu deinem Eigentum
Beständiglich verschreiben.

3.

Ich will von deiner Lieblichkeit
Bei Nacht and Tage singen,
Mich selbst auch dir zu aller Zeit
Zum Freudenopfer bringen.
Mein Born des Lebens soll sich dir
Und deinem Namen für und für
In Dankbarkeit ergiessen;
Und was du mir zu gut getan
Das will ich stets, so tief ich kann,
In mein Gedächtnis schliessen.

These are stanzas 1, 5, and 6 of the original ten. The hymn is based on John 1:29; "Behold the Lamb of God, which taketh away the sin of the world"; and Isa. 53:7: "He was oppressed, and he was afflicted, yet he opened not his mouth: he is brought as a lamb to the slaughter, and as a sheep before her shearers is dumb, so he openeth not his mouth." It was published in the third edition of Johann Crüger's *Praxis Pietatis Melica,* in 1648.

For comments on Paul Gerhardt see Hymn 134.

Our hymn consists of stanzas 5 and 6, translated by J. Gambold. Biographical data concerning Gambold has not been found.

MUSIC. EIN LAMM GEHT HIN, also called "An Wasserflüssen Babylon," first appeared in the third part of the Strassburg *Kirchenampt,* 1525, where it is set to Wolfgang Dachstein's hymn on Psalm 137, beginning with the stanza:

An Wasserflüssen Babylon,
Da sassen wir mit Schmerzen;
Als wir gedachten an Zion,

Da weinten wir von Herzen.
Wir hingen auf mit schwerem Mut
Die Orgeln und die Harfen gut
An ihren Bäum' und Weiden,
Die drinnen sind in ihrem Land,
Da mussten wir viel Schmach und Schand'
Täglich von ihnen leiden.

The tune appeared anonymously but may have been composed, as some authorities believe, by Dachstein himself.

534. Ah, dearest Jesus, how hast Thou offended

Johann Heermann, 1585-1647
Tr. Robert Bridges, 1844-1930

1. Herzliebster Jesu, was hast du verbrochen,
   Dass man ein solch scharf Urteil hat gesprochen?
   Was ist die Schuld? in was für Missentaten
   Bist du geraten?

2. Du wirst gegeisselt und mit Dorn'n gekrönet,
   Ins Angesicht geschlagen und verhöhnet,
   Du wirst mit Essig und mit Gall' getränket,
   Ans Kreuz gehenket.

3. Was ist doch wohl die Ursach' solcher Plagen?
   Ach, meine Sünden haben dich geschlagen!
   Ich, ach Herr Jesu! habe dies verschuldet,
   Was du erduldet.

4. Wie wunderbarlich ist doch diese Strafe!
   Der gute Hirte leidet für die Schafe;
   Die Schuld bezahlt der Herr selbst, der Gerechte,
   Für seine Knechte.

5. Der Fromme stirbt, der recht und richtig wandelt;
   Der Böse lebt, der wider Gott misshandelt;
   Der Mensch verwirkt den Tod und ist entgangen;
   Gott wird gefangen.

6. Ich war von Fuss auf voller Schand' und Sünden,
   Bis zu dem Scheitel war nichts Gut's zu finden;
   Dafür hätt' ich dort in der Hölle müssen
   Ewiglich büssen.

7. O grosse Lieb', o Lieb, ohn' alle Masse!
   Die dich gebracht auf diese Marterstrasse;
   Ich lebte mit der Welt in Lust und Freuden,
   Und du musst leiden!

8. Ach grosser König! gross zu allen Zeiten;
   Wie kann ich g'nugsam deine Lieb' ausbreiten?
   Kein Menschenherz vermag es auszudenken,
   Was dir zu schenken.

15. Wenn so, Herr Jesu! dort vor deinem Throne
Wird stehn auf meinem Haupt die Ehrenkrone,
Da will ich dir, wenn Alles wohl wird klingen,
Lob und Dank singen.

Based on 1 Peter 3:18: "For Christ also hath once suffered for sins, the just for the unjust, that he might bring us to God."

Robert Bridges included this hymn in his *Yattendon Hymnal*, 1899, London, and later it became known to a wider public by its appearance in the *English Hymnal*, 1906, and in *Songs of Praise*, 1933.

Johann Heermann, a distinguished scholar and one of the greatest of German hymn writers, was a Lutheran minister and pastor, in Silesia. On account of ill health, he retired and devoted himself to literary work. This hymn, written during the miseries of the Thirty Years' War, was composed for Passiontide and was entitled, "The Cause of the Bitter Sufferings of Jesus Christ and Consolations from His Love and Grace." The author experienced much suffering himself. First came the death of his wife in 1617, then the failure of his own health, and then the war. His hymns are characterized by tenderness and depth of feeling, and illustrate the truth that real poets "learn in suffering what they teach in song."

For comments on the translator, Robert Bridges, see Hymn 32. His first two stanzas are translations of 1 and 2 of the original; while stanzas 3 and 4 contain suggestions, only, of 6 and 7 and the rest of Heermann's poem.

MUSIC. HERZLIEBSTER JESU is a grandly impressive tune, composed by the distinguished musician and writer of chorales, Johann Crüger, 1598-1662. It has been observed that nearly five-sevenths of this whole melody has a downward movement, which accounts for some of its intensely solemn character. J. S. Bach used the tune in his *St. Matthew's Passion*.

For comments on the composer, Johann Crüger, see Hymn 242.

535. Christ, the Life of all the living   *Ernst C. Homburg, 1605-81*
Tr. Catherine Winkworth, 1829-78

1.

Jesu, meines Lebens Leben,
  Jesu, meines Todes Tod,
Der du dich für mich gegeben
  In die tiefste Seelennot,
In das äusserste Verderben,
Nur dass ich nicht möchte sterben;
  Tausend-, tausendmal sei dir,
  Liebster Jesu, Dank dafür!

2.

Du, ach, du hast ausgestanden
  Lästerreden, Spott und Hohn,
Speichel, Schläge, Strick' und
  Bande,
  Du gerechter Gottessohn,
Mich Elenden zu erretten
Von des Teufels Sündenketten!
  Tausend-, tausendmal sei dir,
  Liebster Jesu, Dank dafür!

3.

Du hast lassen Wunden schlagen,
Dich erbärmlich richten zu,
Um zu heilen meine Plagen
Und zu setzen mich in Ruh'!
Ach, du hast zu meinem Segen
Lassen dich mit Fluch belegen!
Tausend-, tausendmal sei dir,
Liebster Jesu, Dank dafür!

4.

Man hat dich sehr hart verhöhnet,
Dich mit grossem Schimpf belegt
Und mit Dornen gar gekrönet:
Was hat dich dazu bewegt?
Dass du möchtest mich ergötzen,
Mir die Ehrenkron' aufsetzen.
Tausend-, tausendmal sei dir,
Liebster Jesu, Dank dafür!

5.

Du hast dich hart lassen schlagen
Zur Befreiung meiner Pein,
Fälschlich lassen dich anklagen.
Dass ich könnte sicher sein;
Dass ich möchte trostreich pran-
gen,
Hast du sonder Trost gehangen.
Tausend-, tausendmal sei dir,
Liebster Jesu, Dank dafür!

6.

Du hast dich in Not gestecket,
Hast gelitten mit Geduld,
Gar den herben Tod geschmecket,
Um zu büssen meine Schuld;
Dass ich würde losgezählet,
Hast du wollen sein gequälet.
Tausend-, tausendmal sei dir,
Liebster Jesu, Dank dafür!

7.

Deine Demut hat gebüsset
Meinen Stolz und Uebermut,
Dein Tod meinen Tod versüsset,
Es kommt Alles mir zu gut;
Dein Verspotten, dein Verspeien
Muss zu Ehren mir gedeihen.
Tausend-, tausendmal sei dir,
Liebter Jesu, Dank dafür!

8.

Nun, ich danke dir von Herzen,
Jesu, für gesamte Not:
Für die Wunden, für die Schmer-
zen,
Für den herben, bittern Tod,
Für dein Zittern, für dein Zagen,
Für dein tausendfaches Plagen,
Für dein' Angst und tiefe Pein
Will ich ewig dankbar sein.

The most popular of Homburg's hymns. It was first published in his *Geistliche Lieder, Jena*, 1659, for Passiontide, entitled, "Hymn of Thanksgiving for his Redeemer and Saviour for His bitter sufferings."

Ernst Christoph Homburg, born near Eisenach, was a lawyer by profession, and a poet of high rank. His life was not without its cup of bitterness. Domestic troubles, arising from the illness of himself and of his wife, and other difficulties, bore heavily upon him and he was led, as a result, to turn to God and place all his confidence in Him. In the preface to one of his hymn collections, he wrote: "I was especially induced and compelled to their composition by the anxious and sore domestic afflictions by which God . . . has for some time laid me aside." He is the author of 148 hymns.

For comments on Miss Winkworth see Hymn 236. Her translation of stanzas 1, 2, and 8 comprises our hymn.

MUSIC. JESU MEINES LEBENS LEBEN appeared in *Kirchengesangbuch*, Darmstadt, 1687. The composer is not known.

536. Jesus, Refuge of the weary

Girolamo Savonarola, 1452-98
Tr. Jane F. Wilde, 1826-96

The original hymn is in Italian, entitled,

Laude al Crucifisso

1.

Iesù, sommo conforto,
Tu se' tutto el mio amore;
El mio beato porto,
E santo redentore.
O gran bontà,
Dolce pietà,
Felice quel che teco unito
sta!

2.

O quante volte offeso
T'ha l'alma e'l cor meschino!
E tu sei in croce esteso
Per salvar me tapino.
O gran bontà etc.

3.

Iesù, qual forza ha spinto
L'immensa tua bontade?
Dhe! qual amor t'ha vinto
Patir tal crudeltade?
O gran bontà etc.

4.

A te fui sempre ingrato,
E mai non fui fervente;
E tu per me impiagato
Sei stato crudelmente.
O gran bontà etc.

5.

Iesù, tu hai el mondo
Suavemente pieno
D' amor dolce e iocondo,
Che fa ogne cor sereno.
O gran bontà etc.

6.

Iesù, fammi morire
Del tuo amor vivace;
Iesu, fammi languire
Con te, Segnior verace.
O gran bontà etc.

7.

Iesù, fuss'io confitto
Sopra quell'alto ligno
Dove ti veggo afflitto,
Iesù, Signor benigno.
O gran bontà etc.

8.

O Croce, fammi loco,
E le mie membra prendi.
Che del tuo sancto foco
El cor e l'alma accendi.
O gran bontà etc.

9.

Infiamma el mio cor tanto
Del tuo amor divino,
Si ch'arda dentro tanto
Che paio un serafino.
O gran bontà etc.

10.

La Croce e'l Crucifisso
Sia nel mio cor scolpito;
Et io sia sempre affisso
In gloria ove egli è ito.
O gran bontà etc.

The hymn is based on Mark 15:29, 30: "And they that passed by railed on him, wagging their heads, and saying, Ah, thou that destroyest the temple, and buildest it in three days, Save thyself, and come down from the cross."

Savonarola of Florence, one of the greatest of medieval preachers and reformers in the Catholic Church, was destined by his parents to enter the medical profession, but after a careful study of the Scriptures and the writings of Thomas Aquinas, he decided to enter a Dominican monastery. Here he spent many years in further study and thinking out his preaching message. Living in a time when the moral tone of Christianity was at a very low ebb, Savonarola preached boldly and eloquently against the sins of a corrupt world and a corrupt church. His relentless denunciation of the pope and priests resulted in his excommunication by Pope Alexander VI, and on May 23, 1498, he was publicly executed on one of the streets of Florence. His death as a martyr proved to Luther, across the Alps, that it is "hopeless to hope in the purification of Rome," and gave to the reformation movement a powerful impulse.

The translation of the hymn is by Jane Elgee, daughter of Archdeacon Elgee, of Ireland. In 1851 she married Sir William Wilde, an oculist living in Dublin.

MUSIC. O DU LIEBE MEINER LIEBE comes from Johann Thommen's *Erbaulicher Musikalischer Christenschatz,* Basel, 1745, where it is set to the hymn, "O du Liebe meiner Leibe," by Johann Scheffler (See 565). The tune is also called, "Cassel," and "Lucerne." Like numerous other chorale tunes, it was originally a folk tune, and had been in use by the Moravian Brethren at Herrnhut. It is one of the well-known tunes in the *Gesangbuch mit Noten,* deserving of its popularity.

537. Man of Sorrows, now my soul shall greet Thee

Christian Renatus, Graf von Zinzendorf, 1727-52
Tr. J. C. Hansen, 1916

1.

Marter Gottes, wer kann dein vergessen
    Der in dir sein Wohlsein findt?
Unser Herze wünscht sich unterdessen
    Stets noch mehr zum Dank entzündt.
Unsre Seele soll sich daran nähren,
Unsre Ohren nie was Lieb'res hören;
    Alle Tage kommt er mir
    Schöner in dem Bilde für.

2.

Tausend Dank, du unser treues Herze!
    Leib und Geist bet' drüber an,
Dass du unter Martern, Angst und Schmerze
    Hast genug für uns getan.
Lass dich jedes um so heisser lieben,
Als es noch im Glauben sich muss üben,
    Bis es einst als deine Braut
    Dich von Angesichte schaut.

3.

Mein kranke und bedürftge Seele
  Eilt auf deine Wunden zu;
Denn sie findt in deiner Seitenhöhle
  / Trost und Labsal, Fried und Ruh.
Lass mich nur die Kreuzesluft anwehen,
Und dein Marterbild stets vor mir stehen,
  So geht mir bis in mein Grab
  Nichts an Seligkeiten ab.

4.

Die wir uns allhier beisammen finden,
  Schlagen unsre Hände ein,
Uns auf deine Marter zu verbinden,
  Dir auf ewig treu zu sein;
Und zum Zeichen, dass dies Lobgetöne,
Deinem Herzen angenehm und schöne,
  Sage Amen und zugleich:
  Friede, Friede sei mit euch!

A heart-searching passion hymn, from the pen of Christian Renatus, Graf von Zinzendorf, second son of the renowned Nikolaus Ludwig, Graf von Zinzendorf, founder of the Moravian Brüdergemeinde at Herrnhut. (See Hymn 574.) Born at Herrnhut, and educated by his parents, he became his father's assistant in 1744, continuing until 1749. Illness overtook him and he spent the last years of his life, an invalid, in London where he died at the age of 25. Zinzendorf was a young man of maturity and deep Christian convictions, and composed a number of hymns. The present hymn, probably his best production, was first published in the appendix of the *London Hymn Book*, 1755.

The translation is by J. C. Hansen, formerly Professor of Classical Languages at Eden Seminary and now of Elmhurst College, Elmhurst, Ill., and a member of the Evangelical Church.

MUSIC. MARTER CHRISTI, with its considerable length, its irregular meter, and repetition of phrases, is a typical chorale tune, deserving of its popularity. Its origin is unknown.

538. Dark the day on Calvary's Cross

Lauchlan MacLean Watt, 1867—

A Scottish hymn composed by Lauchlan MacLean Watt who was born in Scotland and educated in the Edinburgh University. Watt entered the ministry of the Scottish Presbyterian Church and attained the charge of Glasgow Cathedral in 1923, remaining until his resignation in 1934. In 1933 he was Moderator of the General Assembly of the Church of Scotland. He is the author of numerous books and served on the Committee for the Revision of the *Church Hymnary*, Edinburgh, 1927.

CHORALES

MUSIC. NICHT SO TRAURIG, also called "Pressburg," is from Freylinghausen's *Neues Geistreiches Gesangbuch*, 1714, where it is set to Gerhardt's hymn, "Nicht so traurig, nicht so sehr." The melody has been
simplified somewhat from the original to fit the English words. It was
included in the *Hymnary* for choir use during the season of Lent.

539. O sacred Head, now wounded

Bernard of Clairvaux, 1091-1153
Tr. Paul Gerhardt, 1607-76
Tr. James W. Alexander, 1804-59

1.
O Haupt voll Blut und Wunden,
  Voll Schmerz und voller Hohn,
O Haupt, zum Spott gebunden
  Mit einer Dornenkron',
O Haupt, sonst schön gezieret
  Mit höchster Ehr' und Zier,
Jetzt aber höchst schimpfieret:
  Gegrüsset sei'st du mir!
2.
Du edles Angesichte,
  Davor sonst schrickt und scheut
Das grosse Weltgewichte,
  Wie bist du so bespeit!
Wie bist du so erbleichet!
  Wer hat dein Augenlicht,
Dem sonst kein Licht nicht glei-
  chet,
  So schändlich zugericht't?
3.
Die Farbe deiner Wangen,
  Der roten Lippen Pracht
Ist hin und ganz vergangen;
  Des blassen Todes Macht
Hat alles hingenommen,
  Hat alles hingerafft,
Und daher bist du kommen
  Von deines Leibes Kraft.
4.
Nun, was du, Herr, erduldet,
  Ist alles meine Last;
Ich hab' es selbst verschuldet,
  Was du getragen hast.
Schau her, hier steh' ich Armer,
  Der Zorn verdienet hat;
Gib mir, o mein Erbarmer,
  Den Anblick deiner Gnad'!

5.
Erkenne mich, mein Hüter,
  Mein Hirte, nimm mich an!
Von dir, Quell aller Güter,
  Ist mir viel Gut's getan.
Dein Mund hat mich gelabet
  Mit Milch und süsser Kost;
Dein Geist hat mich begabet
  Mit mancher Himmelslust.
6.
Ich will hier bei dir stehen,
  Verachte mich doch nicht!
Von dir will ich nicht gehen,
  Wenn dir dein Herze bricht;
Wenn dein Haupt wird erblassen
  Im letzten Todesstoss,
Alsdann will ich dich fassen
  In meinen Arm und Schoss.
7.
Es dient zu meinen Freuden
  Und kommt mir herzlich wohl,
Wenn ich in deinem Leiden,
  Mein Heil, mich finden soll.
Ach, möcht' ich, o mein Leben,
  An deinem Kreuze hier
Mein Leben von mir geben,
  Wie wohl geschähe mir!
8.
Ich danke dir von Herzen,
  O Jesu, liebster Freund,
Für deines Todes Schmerzen,
  Da du's so gut gemeint.
Ach gib, dass ich mich halte
  Zu dir und deiner Treu'
Und, wenn ich nun erkalte,
  In dir mein Ende sei!

9.

Wenn ich einmal soll scheiden,
So scheide nicht von mir;
Wenn ich den Tod soll leiden,
So tritt du dann herfür;
Wenn mir am allerbängsten
Wird um das Herze sein,
So reiss mich aus den Aengsten
Kraft deiner Angst und Pein!

10.

Erscheine mir zum Schilde,
Zum Trost in meinem Tod,
Und lass mich sehn dein Bilde
In deiner Kreuzesnot!
Da will ich nach dir blicken,
Da will ich glaubensvoll
Dich fest an mein Herz drücken.
Wer so stirbt, der stirbt wohl.

A profound hymn coming originally out of the golden age of Latin hymnody. *Salve caput cruentatum* is the last of a series of seven poems on the crucified Savior, each poem addressing itself to a separate member of Christ's body—feet, knees, hands, side, breast, heart, and head. The work is attributed to Bernard of Clairvaux, preacher of the Second Crusade, and one of the most brilliant of Latin hymn writers. Luther wrote of him: "If there has ever been a pious monk who feared God it was St. Bernard, whom alone I hold in much higher esteem than all other monks and priests throughout the globe." Bernard founded a monastery in Wormwood, a robber-infested valley in France. He changed the name to "Clara Vallis," (Beautiful Valley), from which is derived the designation "Clairvaux."

Though composed in the twelfth century, the hymn did not achieve fame until five centuries later when it was translated into German by Paul Gerhardt, who, next to Luther, was the greatest of all German hymn writers. His translation, a free paraphrase, appeared in Crüger's *Praxis,* 1656, and is considered by Philip Schaff to be "fully equal to the original."

For comment on Gerhardt see Hymn 134.

The translation into English was made in 1849 by James W. Alexander of Princeton, a Presbyterian. Schaff wrote that "Dr. Alexander is beyond doubt one of the best translators of German hymns into idiomatic English." He also wrote concerning this hymn that it has "shown an imperishable vitality in passing from the Latin into the German and from the German into the English, and proclaiming in three tongues and in the name of three confessions—the Catholic, the Lutheran, and the Reformed—with equal effect, the dying love of our Savior, and our boundless indebtedness to Him."

Our hymn is a selection of stanzas 1, 4, 8, and 10. In the first stanza, the line, "I marvel at the story," is substituted for Alexander's original which read, "Yet though despised and gory." Stanza 10 has been frequently used as a prayer for the dying.

MUSIC. PASSION CHORALE was originally set to a love song entitled, "Mein G'müt ist mir verwirret." The tune was composed by the distinguished organist, Hans Leo Hassler, and first appeared in his *Lust-*

garten Neuer Teutscher Gesäng, 1601. In 1613 it appeared in *Harmoniæ Sacræ,* set to the hymn, "Herzlich thut mich verlangen," and later it became associated with "O Haupt voll Blut und Wunden." It was a favorite melody with Bach, who used it five times in his *St. Matthew Passion.*

Hans Leo Hassler, 1564-1612, was born at Nürnberg and died at Frankfurt at the age of 47. He was a member of a distinguished musical family. After an early career as organist, he was sent to Venice to study under Andrea Gabriele, organist of St. Mark's, becoming the earliest of important German composers to receive an Italian training. Returning to Germany, Hassler held positions in Augsburg, Nürnberg, and elsewhere. His numerous compositions for voice and organ are of such a standard as to give him a high place in German music, and most of them have been reprinted in modern times.

J. S. Bach, 1685-1750, who arranged the tune, is by far the greatest musician the Protestant Church has produced. Most of his life was spent in Leipzig where he labored from 1723 until his death in 1750, as cantor of the Thomas School and director of music at the Thomas and Nicolai churches. His genius as a master of the organ and composer of chorales and passion music has never been equaled. Though he lived in an age when opera flourished in Europe, he paid no attention to it, devoting all his talent to church music. There is something in his music that touches the deepest chords of religious emotion.

540. Lamb of God most holy
Nikolaus von Hofe (Decius), 1490?-1541

O Lamm Gottes, unschuldig
   Am Stamm des Kreuzes geschlachtet,
Allzeit funden geduldig,
   Wiewohl du warest verachtet:
All' Sünd' hast du getragen,
Sonst müssten wir verzagen.
   Erbarm dich unser, O Jesu!

O Lamm Gottes, unschuldig
   Am Stamm des Kreuzes geschlachtet,
Allzeit funden geduldig,
   Wiewohl du warest verachtet:
All' Sünd' hast du getragen,
Sonst müssten wir verzagen.
   Erbarm dich unser, O Jesu!

O Lamm Gottes, unschuldig
   Am Stamm des Kreuzes geschlachtet,
Allzeit funden geduldig,
   Wiewohl du warest verachtet:

All' Sünd' hast du getragen,
Sonst müssten wir verzagen.
Gib uns dein'n Frieden, o Jesu!

Based on John 1:29: "Behold the Lamb of God, which taketh away the sin of the world." The hymn, called the *Agnus Dei* in liturgical literature, is a prayer for God's mercy and peace, and a confession that Christ alone is able to take away the sin of the world. It is an ancient song which has been in use in the church since 701 A.D. and originally was chanted antiphonally by clergy and laity. Since the 12th century the custom has been to repeat the chant three times. In some churches it is always sung just before the communion of the Lord's Supper.

For comments on Decius see Hymn 521.

The translation is composite.

MUSIC. o LAMM GOTTES, UNSCHULDIG is based on an ancient Gregorian setting for the *Agnus Dei* and may have been arranged by Decius himself, for he was a musician as well as a preacher. The word "Gregorian" stems from Gregory the Great, who was Pope from 590 to 604 A.D. He was distinguished for his public service and his contribution to church music, developing the use of the plain chant (also called "plain song" and "Gregorian chant") which is identified with his name.

EASTERTIDE

541. Jesus Christ, my sure defense

Luise Henriette von Brandenburg, 1627-67
Tr. Catherine Winkworth, 1829-78

1.
Jesus, meine Zuversicht
 Und mein Heiland, ist im Leben;
Dieses weiss ich, sollt' ich nicht
 Darum mich zufrieden geben.
Was die lange Todesnacht
Mir auch für Gedanken macht?

2.
Jesus, er, mein Heiland, lebt;
 Ich werd' auch das Leben schauen,
Sein, wo mein Erlöser schwebt;
 Warum sollte mir denn grauen?
Lässet auch ein Haupt sein Glied,
Welches es nicht nach sich zieht?

3.
Ich bin durch der Hoffnung Band
 Zu genau mit ihm verbunden;

Meine starke Glaubenshand
 Wird in ihn gelegt befunden,
Dass mich auch kein Todesbann
Ewig von ihm trennen kann.

4.
Ich bin Fleisch und muss daher
 Auch einmal zu Asche werden;
Das gesteh' ich, doch wird er
 Mich erwecken aus der Erden,
Dass ich in der Herrlichkeit
Um ihn sein mög' allezeit.

5.
Dann wird eben diese Haut
 Mich umgeben, wie ich gläube,
Gott wird werden angeschaut
 Dann vor mir in diesem Leibe,
Und in diesem Fleisch werd' ich
Jesum sehen ewiglich.

6.

Dieser meiner Augen Licht
  Wird ihn, meinen Heiland, ken-
  nen;
Ich, ich selbst, kein Fremder nicht,
  Werd' in seiner Liebe brennen;
Nur die Schwachheit um und an
Wird von mir sein abgetan.

7.

Was hier kranket, seufzt und fleht,
  Wird dort frisch und herrlich
  gehen;
Irdisch werd' ich ausgesät,
  Himmlisch werd' ich auferste-
  hen;
Hier geh' ich natürlich ein,
Nachmals werd' ich geistlich sein.

8.

Seid getrost und hocherfreut.
  Jesus trägt euch, meine Glieder!
Gebt nicht Raum der Traurigkeit!

Sterbt ihr, Christus ruft euch
  wider,
Wenn die letzt' Drommet' er-
  klingt,
Die auch durch die Gräber dringt.

9.

Lacht der finstern Erdenkluft,
  Lacht des Todes und der
  Höllen;
Denn ihr sollt euch durch die Luft
  Eurem Heiland zugesellen!
Dann wird Schwachheit und Ver-
  druss
Liegen unter eurem Fuss.

10.

Nur dass ihr den Geist erhebt
  Von den Lüsten dieser Erden
Und euch dem schon jetzt ergebt,
  Dem ihr beigefügt wollt werden
Schickt das Herze da hinein,
Wo ihr ewig wünscht zu sein!

An Easter hymn of the first rank, an "acknowledged masterpiece of Christian poetry that will ever remain a treasure among the hallowed songs of the Evangelical Church." It is based on I Cor. 15:35ff and Job 19:25-27.

Luise Henriette, a woman of noble Christian character and a member of the Reformed Church, was born in The Hague, Holland. She was married to Elector Friedrich Wilhelm of Brandenburg. Interested in the economic as well as religious welfare of her people, she founded model farms, introduced the culture of the Irish potato, and was helpful in many ways in the restoration of the country after the ravages of the Thirty Years War. Luise Henriette is credited with numerous hymns but Julian points out that there is uncertainty whether she actually wrote all of them or selected them as her favorites. She had a great admiration for Paul Gerhardt and his poetry.

The hymn is a selection of stanzas 1, 2, 3, and 10. For comments on Catherine Winkworth, translator, see Hymn 236.

MUSIC. For comments on the tune, GROSSER GOTT WIR LOBEN DICH, see Hymn 519.

542. Welcome, Thou Victor in the strife

Benjamin Schmolck, 1672-1737
Tr. Catherine Winkworth, 1829-78

1.

Willkommen, Held im Streite,
  Aus deiner Grabes Kluft!

Wir triumphieren heute
Um deine leere Gruft!

2.

Der Feind' wird Schau getragen,
Und heisst nunmehr ein Spott;
Wir aber können sagen:
Mit uns ist unser Gott!

3.

Der Fried' ist uns erstritten,
Und jeder Schrecken flieht;
In der Gerechten Hütten
Erschallt das Siegeslied.

4.

Teil' uns des Sieges Beute,
Den Trost nun reichlich aus;
Ach komm, und bring' noch heute
Dein Heil in Herz und Haus!

5.

In deines Grabes Staube
Liegt unsre Schuld bedeckt;
Des tröstet sich der Glaube,
Dass ihn kein Feind mehr
schreckt.

6.

Du hast das Heil erworben;
Wir preisen dich dafür.
Sind wir mit dir gestorben,
So leben wir mit dir.

7.

Wir wollen ohne Grauen
Mit dir zu Grabe gehn,
Wenn wir nur dort dich schauen,
Und selig auferstehn.

8.

Schwing' deine Siegesfahnen
Auch über unser Herz,
Und zeig' uns einst die Bahnen
Vom Tode himmelwärts.

9.

Was kann uns denn noch
schaden?
Des Todes Pfeil ist stumpf!
Wir sind bei Gott in Gnaden,
Und rufen schon: Triumph!

An Easter hymn, first published in the author's *Lustiger Sabbath,*
1712, entitled, "Easter Triumphal Arch. At Midday on Easter Day."
In 1746, it was included in Burg's *Gesangbuch,* Breslau.

For comments on Benjamin Schmolck see Hymn 505.

Our hymn is composed of Miss Winkworth's translation of stanzas
1, 2, 3, and 8.

For comments on Catherine Winkworth see Hymn 236.

MUSIC. DIE HELLE SONNE IST DAHIN was composed by Sigmund Gottlieb "Theophil" Staden, 1607-1655. He was born and died in Nürnberg. Staden composed *Seelewig,* the first comic opera to be printed.
He also composed chorales and wrote an instruction book for singing.

543. Jesus lives! thy terrors now   *Christian F. Gellert,* 1715-69
                                          Tr. Frances E. Cox, 1812-97

1.

Jesus lebt, mit ihm auch ich,
    Tod, wo sind nun deine
        Schrecken?
Jesus lebt und wird auch mich
    Von den Toten auferwecken.
Er verklärt mich in sein Licht:
Dies ist meine Zuversicht.

2.

Jesus lebt. Ihm ist das Reich
    Ueber alle Welt gegeben.
Mit ihm werd' ich auch zugleich
    Ewig herrschen, ewig leben.
Gott erfüllt, was er verspricht:
Dies ist meine Zuversicht.

3.

Jesus lebt! wer nun verzagt,
  Sündigt an des Mittlers Ehre.
Gnade hat er zugesagt,
  Dass der Sünder sich bekehre.
Gott verstösst in Christo nicht;
Dies ist meine Zuversicht.

4.

Jesus lebt. Sein Heil ist mein:
  Sein sei auch mein ganzes Leben;
Reines Herzens will ich sein
  Und der Lüsten widerstreben.
Er verlässt den Schwachen nicht:
Dies ist meine Zuversicht.

5.

Jesus lebt. Ich bin gewiss;
  Nichts soll mich von Jesu scheiden,
Keine Macht der Finsternis,
  Keine Herrlichkeit, kein Leiden.
Er gibt Kraft zu jeder Pflicht:
Dies ist meine Zuversicht.

6.

Jesus lebt. Nun ist der Tod
  Mir der Eingang in das Leben.
Welchen Trost in Todesnot
  Wird er meiner Seele geben,
Wenn sie gläubig zu ihm spricht:
Herr, Herr, meine Zuversicht!

Based on John 14:19: "Yet a little while and the world seeth me no more; but ye see me: because I live, ye shall live also."

The hymn was first published in Gellert's *Geistliche Oden und Lieder,* 1757, with the title, "Easter Hymn." It soon became popular in Germany and is widely used now among English speaking people. The hymn is often used at funerals, and sometimes at the dedication of a cemetery. Gellert, a saintly Professor of Philosophy and Poetry at Leipzig, had no fear of death. In the period of the so-called Enlightenment, when religion had become cold and rationalistic, and the old hymns had been watered down, he wrote one of our best and most evangelical hymns.

For comments on the translator, Frances E. Cox, see Hymn 512.

The original poem was without the "Hallelujah."

MUSIC. CHRIST IST ERSTANDEN is a traditional German melody dating to the 13th century. It was used with words beginning, "Christ ist erstanden." Luther said of this tune: "after a time one tires of singing all other hymns, but the 'Christ ist erstanden' one can always sing again." It is within easy range of all voices and therefore well adapted for unison singing, though it need not be limited to that.

544. Christ the Lord is risen again! *Michael Weisse, c. 1480-1534*
Tr. Catherine Winkworth, 1829-78

1.

Christus ist erstanden
Von des Todes Banden,
Des freuet sich der Engel Schaar,
Singend im Himmel immerdar,
  Hallelujah!

2.

Der für uns sein Leben
In Tod hat gegeben,
Der ist nun unser Osterlamm,
Des wir uns freuen allesammt;
  Hallelujah!

3.

Der am Kreuz gehangen,
Kein'n Trost konnt' erlangen,
Der lebet nun in Herrlichkeit,
Uns zu vertreten stets bereit!
Hallelujah!

4.

Der, so ganz verschwiegen
Zur Hölle gestiegen,
Den wohlgerüst'ten Starken band:
Der wird nur in der Höh' erkannt.
Hallelujah!

5.

Der da lag begraben,
Der ist nun erhaben,
Und sein Tun wird kräftig erweist,
Und in der Christenheit gepreist.
Hallelujah!

6.

Er lässt nun verkünden
Vergebung der Sünden,
Und wie man die durch rechte
Buss'
Nach seiner Ordnung suchen muss.
Hallelujah!

7.

O Christe, Osterlamm,
Speis' uns heut' allesammt!
Nimm weg all' unsre Missetat,
Dass wir dir singen früh und spat:
Hallelujah!

An Easter song, based on I Cor. 5:7, 8 and Rev. 19:6:

> For even Christ our passover suffered for us: therefore let us keep the feast, not with old leaven, neither with the leaven of malice and wickedness; but with the unleavened bread of sincerity and truth.
> Alleluia! for the Lord God omnipotent reigneth.

Weisse's poem is based on "Christ is erstanden von der Martyr alle," the oldest German Easter hynm, found in four versions as early as the 12th century.

Michael Weisse, born at Neisse, Silesia, about 1480, became a priest, and for a time was a monk at Breslau. Influenced by the writings of Luther, he left the monastery to join the Bohemian Brethren, the followers of John Hus, and became their pastor at Landskron and Fulneck, Moravia. Weisse was a man of great influence among the Brethren and was appointed a member of their council. Of a deeply spiritual nature and possessing rare poetic gifts, he translated the old songs of the Bohemian Brethren into German and composed many original poems. He edited the first Brethren hymnbook in German, *Ein Neu Gesengbuchlen*, 1531, in which the present hymn first appeared. The book, proclaimed by Luther as "the work of a good poet," contains 155 hymns, all apparently either translations or originals by Weisse himself.

Our translation is by Catherine Winkworth, with stanza 4 omitted. For comments on Miss Winkworth see Hymn 236.

MUSIC. MACHE DICH, MEIN GEIST, BEREIT is an adaptation of a chorale tune, "Straf mich nicht," published in *Kirch-und Hausbuch*, Dresden, 1694. The composer is not known. Refrains are not commonly used with German chorales. The present setting of the tune and words, with a refrain, was made by the editors especially for the *Hymnary*. It is suitable for children's choirs as well as for congregational use.

545. Lo, the day of days is here   *Frederick L. Hosmer*, 1840-1929

A joyous Easter song in which the springtime awakening in nature symbolizes the newness of spiritual life.

For comments on Frederick L. Hosmer see Hymn 72.

MUSIC. SALZBURG appeared in the 19th edition of Crüger's *Praxis Pietatis Melica*, 1678, a work which contained the main stream of Lutheran hymnody in the middle of the 17th century. The tune was set to the hymn, "Alle Menschen müssen sterben."

The composer, Jacob Hintze, 1622-1702, was born in Bernau, Brandenburg. He became court musician to the Elector of Brandenburg, in Berlin, in 1666, and in the year 1662 succeeded Crüger, upon the latter's death, as editor of the *Praxis*. The present version, slightly altered from the original, is from J. S. Bach's *Choralgesänge*. The tune is also associated with Stopford Brooke's hymn, "Let the whole creation cry." (No. 49.)

WHITSUNTIDE

546. O Holy Spirit, enter in   *Michael Schirmer*, 1606-73
Tr. Catherine Winkworth, 1829-78

1.
O heil'ger Geist, kehr bei uns ein
Und lass uns deine Wohnung sein,
O komm, du Herzenssonne!
Du Himmelslicht, lass deinen
Schein
Bei uns und in uns kräftig sein
Zu steter Freud' und Wonne,
Dass wir in dir
Recht zu leben uns ergeben
Und mit Beten
Oft deshalben vor dich treten.

2.
Gib Kraft und Nachdruck deinem
Wort,
Lass es wie Feuer immerfort
In unsern Herzen brennen,
Dass wir Gott Vater, seinen Sohn,

Dich, beider Geist, in einem
Thron
Für wahren Gott bekennen.
Bleibe, treibe
Und behüte das Gemüte,
Dass wir gläuben
Und im Glauben standhaft bleiben!

3.
Du Quell, draus alle Weisheit
fleusst,
Die sich in fromme Seelen geusst,
Lass deinen Trost uns hören,
Dass wir in Glaubenseinigkeit
Auch können alle Christenheit
Dein wahres Zeugnis lehren!
Höre, lehre,
Herz und Sinnen zu gewinnen,

Dich zu preisen,
Gut's dem Nächsten zu erweisen!
4.
Steh uns stets bei mit deinem Rat
Und führ uns selbst den rechten
Pfad,
Die wir den Weg nicht wissen!
Gib uns Beständigkeit, dass wir
Getreu dir bleiben für und für,
Wenn wir nun leiden müssen!
Schaue, baue,
Was zerrissen und geflissen,
Dir zu trauen
Und auf dich allein zu bauen!
5.
Lass uns dein' edle Balsamkraft
Empfinden und zur Ritterschaft
Dadurch gestärket werden,
Auf dass wir unter deinem Schutz
Begegnen aller Feinde Trutz,
Solang wir sind auf Erden!
Lass dich reichlich
Auf uns nieder, dass wir wieder
Trost empfinden,
Alles Unglück überwinden!
6.
Du starker Fels und Lebenshort,
Lass uns dein himmelsüsses Wort
In unsern Herzen brennen,
Dass wir uns mögen nimmermehr

Von deiner weisheitreichen Lehr'
Und reinen Liebe trennen!
Fliesse, giesse
Deine Güte ins Gemüte,
Dass wir können
Christum unsern Heiland nennen!
7.
Du süsser Himmelstau, lass dich
In unsre Herzen kräftiglich
Und schenk uns deine Liebe,
Dass unser Sinn verbunden sei
Dem Nächsten stets mit Liebes-
treu'
Und sich darinnen übe!
Kein Neid, kein Streit
Dich betrübe, Fried' und Liebe
Müssen schweben;
Fried' und Freude wirst du geben!
8.
Gib, dass in reiner Heiligkeit
Wir führen unsre Lebenszeit,
Sei unsres Geistes Stärke,
Dass uns forthin sei unbewusst
Die Eitelkeit, des Fleisches Lust
Und seine toten Werke!
Rühre, führe
Unser Sinnen und Beginnen
Von der Erden,
Dass wir Himmelserben werden!

This hymn for Whitsuntide, addressed to the Holy Spirit, went through various alterations in German hymnbooks until it finally appeared in 8 stanzas, as here. It is a beautiful New Testament paraphrase of Isa. 11:2:

> And the spirit of the Lord shall rest upon him, the spirit of wisdom and understanding, the spirit of counsel and might, the spirit of knowledge and of the fear of the Lord.

Michael Schirmer, born in Leipzig, received his education at the University of Leipzig, graduating with an M.A. degree in 1630. He was appointed assistant rector of the Greyfriars Gymnasium in Berlin, but on account of ill health was compelled to resign. Besides the hardships of the Thirty Years' War, Schirmer experienced added sorrows in the death of his wife and two children. At times deep melancholy fell upon him, lasting for years at a time. Schirmer was crowned court poet in 1637. His published works include a metrical version of *Ecclesiasticus*,

1655; a scriptural play, *Der verfolgte David*, 1660; and versions of the Songs of the Old and New Testaments, *Biblische Lieder und Lehrsprüche*, 1650. Five of his hymns came into wide use in Germany but only this one passed into English.

The translation is by Catherine Winkworth in her *Chorale Book for England*, 1863. The present hymn is composed of stanzas 1, 4, 6, and 8. For comments on Miss Winkworth see Hymn 236.

MUSIC. NICOLAI, better known as "Wie schön leuchtet der Morgenstern," has long been known as the "Queen of Chorales." (For the "King of Chorales," see Hymn 522.) It is a magnificent tune. In Germany it was set on many city chimes.

For comments on the composer, Philipp Nicolai, see Hymn 522.

547. O Spirit of Life, O Spirit of God

Johann Niedling, 1651
Tr. John C. Mattes, 1876-1948

1.
O heiliger Geist, o heiliger Gott,
Du Tröster wert in aller Not,
Du bist gesandt vom Himmelsthron
Von Gott dem Vater und dem Sohn,
O heiliger Geist, o heiliger Gott.

2.
O heiliger Geist, o heiliger Gott,
Gib uns die Lieb zu deinem Wort,
Zünd an in uns der Liebe Flamm,
Dass wir uns lieben allesamt,
O heiliger Geist, o heiliger Gott.

3.
O heiliger Geist, o heiliger Gott,
Mehr unsern Glauben immerfort,
An Christum niemand glauben kann,
Es sei denn durch dein Hilf getan,
O heiliger Geist, o heiliger Gott.

4.
O heiliger Geist, o heiliger Gott,
Erleucht uns durch dein göttlich Wort,
Lehr uns den Vater kennen schon,
Dazu auch seinen lieben Sohn,
O heiliger Geist, o heiliger Gott.

5.
O heiliger Geist, o heiliger Gott,
Du zeigest uns die Himmelspfort,
Lass uns hier kämpfen ritterlich
Und zu dir kommen seliglich,
O heiliger Geist, o heiliger Gott.

6.
O heiliger Geist, o heiliger Gott,
Verlass uns nicht in Not und Tod;
Wir sagen dir Lob, Ehr und Dank
Jetzund und unser Leben lang,
O heiliger Geist, o heiliger Gott.

The original hymn, in six stanzas, first appeared in Johann Niedling's *Lutherisches-Altenburgisches Handbüchlein*, Naumburg, 1651. Some of the hymns in this collection are original with Niedling, and bear his name. This hymn, however, appears anonymously, leaving doubt as to its authorship. The *Common Service Book* of the United Lutheran Church credits it to Niedling.

The English translation was made especially for the *United Lutheran Hymnal,* in 1913, employing the first four stanzas of the original.

The translator, John Casper Mattes, was born in Easton, Pa. After graduating from Lafayette College and Mt. Airy Theological Seminary, he served as pastor of the Church of the Saviour, Trenton, N. J., 1901-15, and St. John Lutheran Church, Scranton, Pa., 1915-38. From 1939 until his death in 1948 he was a teacher at the Wartburg Theological Seminary, Dubuque, Iowa. Mattes was a frequent contributor to Lutheran publications and served on the United Lutheran Church Common Service Book Committee. He was a member of the Intersynodical Committee on translation of Luther's *Small Catechism,* and is translator of Koberle's *Rechtfertigung und Heiligung.*

MUSIC. O HEILIGER GEIST, O HEILIGER GOTT, also called "O Jesulein Süss," first appears in *Auserlesene Catholische Geistliche Kirchengesäng,* Cologne, 1623, set to the hymn, "Ist das der Leib, Herr Jesu Christ." In *Christliche Seelenharfe,* Halle, 1650, it is set to "Komm heiliger Geist, mit deinen Genad" while in S. Scheidt's *Tabulatur Buch,* Görlitz, 1650, it is used with the hymn, "O Jesulein süss, O Jesulein mild." The melody appears in many later collections, both Catholic and Protestant. Its present form, a variant of Scheidt's, appeared in the *Neu Leipziger Gesangbuch,* Leipzig, 1682, set to the hymn, "O heiliger Geist, O heiliger Gott." It is an attractive tune in triple time, of the type associated with early German carols.

Samuel Scheidt, 1587-1654, the composer, was born at Halle, the son of Conrad Scheidt, overseer of the salt works. He had for his teacher the famous Peter Sweelinck of Amsterdam, and became a noted organist and composer. His *Tabulatura Nova,* 1624, set a new standard in organ playing, by showing how to make it less ostentatious and more meaningful and coherent. His great work, *Tablaturbuch,* is a series of harmonized chorales, published in three parts, 1624-53.

548. Come, O come, Thou quickening Spirit

Heinrich Held, c. 1620-59
Tr. Charles W. Schaeffer, 1813-96

1.

Komm, o komm, du Geist des
   Lebens,
Wahrer Gott von Ewigkeit!
Deine Kraft sei nicht vergebens,
   Sie erfüll' uns jederzeit;
So wird Geist und Licht und
   Schein
In dem dunkeln Herzen sein.

2.

Gib in unser Herz und Sinnen
   Weisheit, Rat, Verstand und
   Zucht,
Dass wir anders nichts beginnen,
   Denn was nur dein Wille sucht!
Dein' Erkenntnis werde gross
Und mach uns von Irrtum los!

3.
Zeige, Herr, die Wohlfahrtsstege!
Das, was wider dich getan,
Räume ferner aus dem Wege;
Schlecht und recht sei um und
an!
Wirke Reu' an Sünden Statt,
Wenn der Fuss gestrauchelt hat!

4.
Lass uns stets dein Zeugnis fühlen,
Dass wir Gottes Kinder sind,
Die auf ihn alleine zielen,
Wenn sich Not und Drangsal
find't;
Denn des Vaters liebe Rut'
Ist uns allewege gut.

5.
Reiz uns, dass wir zu ihm treten
Frei mit aller Freudigkeit;
Seufz auch in uns, wenn wir beten,
Und vertritt uns allezeit!
So wird unsre Bitt' erhört
Und die Zuversicht gemehrt.

6.
Wird auch uns nach Troste bange,
Dass das Herz oft rufen muss:
Ach, mein Gott, mein Gott, wie
lange?

Ei, so mache den Beschluss;
Sprich der Seele tröstlich zu
Und gib Mut, Geduld und Ruh'!

7.
O du Geist der Kraft und Stärke,
Du gewisser, neuer Geist,
Fördre in uns deine Werke,
Wenn der Satan Macht be-
weist;
Schenk uns Waffen in dem Krieg
Und erhalt in uns den Sieg!

8.
Herr, bewahr auch unsern Glau-
ben,
Dass kein Teufel, Tod noch
Spott
Uns denselben möge rauben!
Du bist unser Schutz und Gott.
Sagt das Fleisch gleich immer nein,
Lass dein Wort gewisser sein.

9.
Wenn wir endlich sollen sterben,
So versichre uns je mehr,
Als des Himmelreiches Erben,
Jener Herrlichkeit und Ehr',
Die uns unser Gott erkiest
Und nicht auszusprechen ist.

A fine hymn of invocation to the Holy Spirit, written for Whitsuntide, in 9 stanzas.

The author, Heinrich Held, a lawyer by profession, was born in
Guhrau, Silesia. After receiving his education at the Universities of
Königsberg, Frankfurt a. Oder, and Leyden, he practiced law in his
home town of Guhrau where he lived all his life. He became one of
the best Silesian poets and hymn writers, probably because he was
taught in the school of affliction and suffering, brought about by the
Thirty Years' War.

The translation is by Charles W. Schaeffer, a native of Hagerstown,
Maryland. After graduating from the University of Pennsylvania and
the Theological Seminary at Gettysburg, he held several pastorates and
then became a teacher in the Lutheran Theological Seminary in Philadelphia. Our hymn is a selection of stanzas 1, 2, 7, and 8.

MUSIC. EISENACH, also known as "St. Leonard," and "Komm, O
komm, du Geist des Lebens," is an attractive melody, composed by
Johann Christoph Bach, 1642-1703, an excellent musician, and a first

cousin of the father of the eminent Johann Sebastian Bach. He was organist at Eisenach where he spent most of his life. The name of the tune is derived from Bach's town. Much of the music he composed is extant, mostly in manuscript, but some keyboard and choral music is in print. His motet, *I wrestle and pray*, was published by Novello.

THE CHURCH

549. A Mighty Fortress is our God   *Martin Luther*, 1483-1546
Tr. Frederick H. Hedge, 1805-90

1.

Ein' feste Burg ist unser Gott,
  Ein' gute Wehr und Waffen;
Er hilft uns frei aus aller Not,
  Die uns jetzt hat betroffen.
Der alt' böse Feind,
Mit Ernst er's jetzt meint,
Gross' Macht und viel List
Sein' grausam' Rüstung ist,
  Auf Erd' ist nicht seinsgleichen.

2.

Mit unsrer Macht ist nichts getan,
  Wir sind gar bald verloren;
Es streit't für uns der rechte Mann,
  Den Gott hat selbst erkoren.
Fragst du, wer der ist?
Er heisst Jesus Christ,
Der Herr Zebaoth,
Und ist kein andrer Gott,
  Das Feld muss er behalten.

3.

Und wenn die Welt voll Teufel
  wär'
  Und wollt' uns gar verschlingen,
So fürchten wir uns nicht so sehr,
  Es soll uns doch gelingen.
Der Fürst dieser Welt,
Wie sau'r er sich stellt,
Tut er uns doch nicht,
Das macht, er ist gericht't,
  Ein' Wörtlein kann ihn fällen.

4.

Das Wort sie sollen lassen stahn
  Und kein'n Dank dazu haben;
Er ist bei uns wohl auf dem Plan
  Mit seinem Geist und Gaben.
Nehmen sie den Leib,
Gut, Ehr', Kind und Weib:
Lass fahren dahin,
Sie haben's kein'n Gewinn,
  Das Reich muss uns doch bleiben.

Based on Psalm 46:

God is our refuge and strength,
A very present help in trouble.
Therefore will we not fear, though the earth do change,
And though the mountains be shaken into the heart of the
  seas;
Though the waters thereof roar and be troubled,
Though the mountains tremble with the swelling thereof.
  The Lord of hosts is with us,
  The God of Jacob is our refuge.

James Moffatt names this the "greatest hymn of the greatest man in the greatest period of German history." More than any other, this hymn has transcended all national boundaries and denominational lines, and has become a truly ecumenical church song. It has been translated into nearly two hundred languages. "Ein feste Burg" was sung over Luther's grave at Wittenberg in the Schloss-Kirche, on the door of which some 30 years before, he had nailed his 95 theses against Roman Indulgences. The hymn has been used at many historic occasions and conventions. In 1925, at the meeting of Christians from all parts of the world in Stockholm, the opening hymn was "Ein' feste Burg ist unser Gott." Each delegate sang in his own tongue, but it was the same tune, the same hymn and the same spirit; and the great conference, assembled to consider the life and mission of the church, adopted the hymn as an ecumenical symbol. It was adopted as the Conference hymn for the fourth Mennonite World Conference held at Goshen, Ind., and North Newton, Kan., August 3-10, 1948.

The hymn arose out of the writer's conflict with the evil forces of the world and the corrupt hierarchy of a corrupt church. When Luther was summoned to the Diet of Worms, he was warned by his friends not to go. He ignored their advice, and, standing before that assemblage of emperors and principalities and powers, he spoke these memorable words:

> It is neither safe nor prudent to do aught against conscience. Till such time as either by proof from holy Scripture or by fair reason or argument I have been confuted and convicted, I cannot and will not recant. Here I stand. I cannot do otherwise. God be my help. Amen.

It is against this background of opposition and trouble that the great hymn was penned.

There are more than sixty versions of the hymn in the English language. The translation used here is by Frederick H. Hedge, then Professor of Ecclesiastical History, and later of German Literature, at Harvard. It is the commonly accepted version in America. In England, the translation by Thomas Carlysle is the most widely used.

For ordinary occasions the use of the first two stanzas is sufficient.

MUSIC. EIN' FESTE BURG IST UNSER GOTT, also by Luther, is one of the great chorales destined to be sung to the end of time. It is perfectly adapted to the words and especially effective with large congregations. The musical merits of the tune have been recognized by the great masters. Mendelssohn used the tune in the last movement of his *Reformation Symphony* and Bach used it in several of his cantatas.

Albert Schweitzer writes of this melody:

> "Ein feste Burg" is woven out of Gregorian reminiscences. The recognition of this fact deprives the melody of none of its beauty and Luther of none of the credit for it. It really takes considerable talent to create an organic unity out of fragments.

550. The work is Thine, O Christ our Lord

Stanzas 1 and 2, S. Preiswerk, 1799-1871
Stanza 3, F. Zaremba, 1794-1874
Tr. Julius Henry Horstmann

1.

Die Sach' ist dein, Herr Jesu
    Christ,
Die Sach' an der wir steh'n,
Und weil es deine Sache ist,
Kann sie nicht untergeh'n.
  Allein das Weizenkorn, bevor
  Es fruchtbar sprosst zum Licht
    empor,
Muss sterben in der Erde Schoss
Zuvor vom eig'nen Wesen los.
  Durch Sterben los,
Vom eig'nen Wesen los.

2.

Du gingst, O Jesu, unser Haupt,
Durch Leiden himmelan,
Und führest Jeden, der da glaubt,
Mit dir die gleiche Bahn.
Wohlan, so nimm uns allzugleich
Zum Teil am Leiden und am
    Reich;
Führ uns durch deines Todes Tor
Samt deiner Sach' zum Licht em-
    por,
  Zum Licht empor,
Durch Nacht zum Licht empor!

3.

Du starbest selbst als Weizenkorn
  Und sankest in das Grab;
Belebe denn, o Lebensborn,
  Die Welt, die Gott dir gab.
Send Boten aus in jedes Land,
Dass bald dein Name werd' bekannt,
Dein Name voller Seligkeit;
Auch wir steh'n dir zum Dienst bereit
In Kampf und Streit,
Zum Dienst in Kampf und Streit.

A missionary hymn written at the request of students at the Basel Mission House, Basel, Switzerland. The students wanted a good missionary poem to use with the present tune, then erroneously ascribed to J. Michael Haydn. Preiswerk supplied the first two stanzas. They were first sung June 17, 1829, at an anniversary festival. The third stanza was added by Count Felician von Zaremba, since it was felt that the first two did not have enough emphasis on foreign missions.

The hymn was sung at the laying of the cornerstone of Bethel College and again at the sixtieth anniversary of that event, celebrated October 12, 1948.

Samuel Preiswerk was born in Rümlingen, Switzerland, the son of the pastor of the Reformed Church at that place. He was educated at the Universities of Basel, Tübingen, and Erlangen. After serving in a curacy at Benken and on the staff of the Basel Orphanage, he taught Hebrew at the Basel Mission House, later accepting a pastorate at Muttenz, and a professorship at the Ecole de Théologie in Geneva. In 1840 he was called to the St. Leonhardt Church in Basel, where he became the main pastor in 1843. Finally he was made Antistes or Superintendent of the Reformed Churches in the Basel Area. Preiswerk was one of the editors of the *Baseler Gesangbuch* of 1854 and was otherwise active as a hymnologist.

Felician von Zaremba, author of the third stanza, was born at Zaroy, Poland, and died in Basel. A descendant of an old Polish noble family, he received a good education at the University of Dorpat, excelling in languages. Although he prepared himself for the diplomatic service to Russia, he became greatly interested in the missionary work centering in Basel, and eventually entered the work carried on among the Mohammedans and Nestorians in South Russia and the Caucasus regions. For many years he was an itinerant preacher in Germany and Switzerland.

The translator, Julius Henry Horstmann, was born at Naperville, Ill., and is living in retirement at Maplewood, Mo. He was educated at Northwestern College, Elmhurst College and Eden Theological Seminary. He served churches in Indiana and Texas and from 1906 to 1936 was editor of the *Evangelical Herald*.

MUSIC. DIE SACH' IST DEIN, a popular, effective melody, is of uncertain origin. It was formerly attributed, without evidence, to Haydn.

551. Spread, still spread, thou mighty word

J. F. Bahnmaier, 1774-1841
Tr. Percy Dearmer, 1867-1936

1.
Walte, walte nah und fern,
Allgewaltig Wort des Herrn,
Wo nur seiner Allmacht Ruf
Menschen für den Himmel schuf;
2.
Wort vom Vater, der die Welt
Schuf und in den Armen hält
Und aus seinem Schoss herab
Seinen Sohn zum Heil ihr gab;
3.
Wort von des Erlösers Huld,
Der der Erde schwere Schuld
Durch des heil'gen Todes Tat
Ewig weggenommen hat;

4.
Kräftig Wort von Gottes Geist,
Der den Weg zum Himmel weist
Und durch seine heil'ge Kraft
Wollen und Vollbringen schafft.
5.
Auf zur Ernt' in alle Welt!
Weithin wogt das weisse Feld;
Klein ist noch der Schnitter Zahl,
Viel der Garben überall.
6.
Herr der Ernte, gross und gut,
Wirk zum Werke Lust und Mut;
Lass die Völker allzumal
Schauen deines Lichtes Strahl!

One of the best and most useful hymns for Foreign Missions. It has been rendered into English by such eminent translators as Frances Cox, H. J. Buckoll, and Catherine Winkworth. But in order to make a freer and more modern use of the original, Percy Dearmer made this new translation for *Songs of Praise*, London, 1931, of which he was the editor.

For comments on J. F. Bahnmaier see Hymn 329.

Percy Dearmer was born in London and educated at Oxford. After serving as vicar in the church of St. Mary the Virgin, Primrose Hill, he became Professor of Ecclesiastical Art at King's College, London. He was an authority on hymnology and liturgics, and wrote extensively on these subjects. His works include *The New Reformation, A Short Handbook of Public Worship, The Story of the Prayer Book,* and *Songs of Praise Discussed.*

MUSIC. GOTT SEI DANK appeared in Freylinghausen's *Geistreiches Gesangbuch,* Halle, 1704, where it is set to the hymn, "Gott sei Dank in aller Welt." It is also called "Lübeck," "Berlin," and "Carinthia." The composer is unknown.

THE LORD'S SUPPER

552. Deck thyself, my soul, with gladness

Johann Franck, 1618–77
Tr. Catherine Winkworth, 1829–78

1.

Schmücke dich, o liebe Seele,
Lass die dunkle Sündenhöhle,
Komm ans helle Licht gegangen,
Fange herrlich an zu prangen!
Denn der Herr, voll Heil und Gnaden,
Will dich jetzt zu Gaste laden;
Der den Himmel kann verwalten,
Will jetzt Herberg' in dir halten.

2.

Eile, wie Verlobte pflegen,
Deinem Bräutigam entgegen,
Der da mit dem Gnadenhammer
Klopft an deine Herzenskammer!
Oeffn' ihm bald des Geistes Pforten,
Red ihn an mit schönen Worten:
Komm, mein Liebster, lass dich küssen,
Lass mich deiner nicht mehr missen!

3.

Zwar in Kaufung teurer Waren
Pflegt man sonst kein Geld zu sparen;

Aber du willst für die Gaben
Deiner Huld kein Geld nicht haben,
Weil in allen Bergwerksgründen
Kein solch Kleinod ist zu finden,
Das die blutgefüllten Schalen
Und dies Manna kann bezahlen.

4.

Ach, wie hungert mein Gemüte,
Menschenfreund, nach deiner Güte!
Ach, wie pfleg' ich oft mit Tränen
Mich nach dieser Kost zu sehnen!
Ach, wie pfleget mich zu dürsten
Nach dem Trank des Lebensfürsten!
Wünsche stets, dass mein Gebeine
Sich durch Gott mit Gott vereine.

5.

Beides Lachen und auch Zittern
Lässet sich in mir jetzt wittern;
Das Geheimnis dieser Speise
Und die unerforschte Weise
Machen dass ich früh vermerke,
Herr, die Grösse deiner Werke.

Ist auch wohl ein Mensch zu finden,
Der dein' Allmacht sollt' ergründen?

6.

Nein, Vernunft, die muss hier weichen,
Kann dies Wunder nicht erreichen,
Dass dies Brot nie wird verzehret,
Ob es gleich viel Tausend' nähret,
Und dass mit dem Saft der Reben
Uns wird Christi Blut gegeben.
O der grossen Heimlichkeiten,
Die nur Gottes Geist kann deuten!

7.

Jesu, meines Lebens Sonne,
Jesu, meine Freud' und Wonne,
Jesu, du mein ganz Beginnen,
Lebensquell und Licht der Sinnen,
Hier fall' ich zu deinen Füssen;
Lass mich würdiglich geniessen

Dieser deiner Himmelsspeise
Mir zum Heil und dir zum Preise!

8.

Herr, es hat dein treues Lieben
Dich vom Himmel hergetrieben,
Dass du willig hast dein Leben
In den Tod für uns gegeben
Und dazu ganz unverdrossen,
Herr, dein Blut für uns vergossen,
Das uns jetzt kann kräftig tränken,
Deiner Liebe zu gedenken.

9.

Jesu, wahres Brot des Lebens,
Hilf, dass ich doch nicht vergeben
Oder mir vielleicht zum Schaden
Sei zu deinem Tisch geladen!
Lass mich durch dies Seelenessen
Deine Liebe recht ermessen,
Dass ich auch, wie jetzt auf Erden,
Mög' dein Gast im Himmel werden

The finest of all German communion hymns. It expresses the reverent joy that should accompany the sacrament of the Lord's Supper. The hymn is sung, invariably, in many German churches on communion occasions.

Johann Franck was born at Guben, Brandenburg, the son of a lawyer, and was himself educated for the law. At the University of Königsberg he was greatly influenced by Simon Dach, Professor of Poetry, and, in spite of his law practice and the holding of public offices, he became an important poet and hymn writer of his time, second only to Paul Gerhardt. The dominant theme of his hymns is the mystical union of the soul with the Savior. Franck's hymns had appeared in the works of his friends Weichman and Crüger, and later were published, 110 in all, at Guben, in 1674, in a volume entitled *Geistliches Sion*.

The hymn is a selection of stanzas 1, 2, 7, and 9 of the original.

For comments on the translator, Catherine Winkworth, see Hymn 236.

MUSIC. SCHMÜCKE DICH is a beautifully expressive tune by Johann Crüger, 1598-1662, first published in the composer's *Praxis Pietatis Melica*, 1644. J. S. Bach used the tune for an organ setting which constitutes one of the most beautiful of Bach organ chorales. Upon hearing it played by Mendelssohn, Robert Schumann wrote concerning the chorale:

Round the *cantus firmus* hung golden garlands of leaves, and such blissfulness was breathed from within it, that you yourself avowed that if life was bereft of all hope and faith, this one chorale could renew them for you. I was silent and went away dazed into God's acre, feeling acutely pained that I could lay no flower on his urn.

For comments on Johann Crüger see Hymn 242.

MORNING

553. Light of Light, enlighten me   *Benjamin Schmolck, 1672-1737*
Tr. Catherine Winkworth, 1829-78

1.
Licht vom Licht! erleuchte mich
  Bei dem neuen Tageslichte!
Gnadensonn', enthülle dich
  Segnend meinem Angesichte;
Lass durch deinen hellen Schein
Meinen Sabbath heilig sein!

2.
Brunnquell aller Sussigkeit,
  Lass mir deine Ströme fliessen!
Mache Mund und Herz bereit,
  Dich in Andacht recht zu grüssen.
Streu' das Wort mit Segen ein,
Lass es hundertfältig sein.

3.
Zünde selbst das Opfer an,
  Das auf meinen Lippen lieget.
Sei mir Weisheit, Licht und Bahn,
  Dass kein Irrtum mich betrüget,
Und kein fremdes Feuer brennt,
Welches dein' Altar nicht kennt.

4.
Lass mich heut' und allezeit:
  Heilig, heilig, heilig! singen
Und mich in die Ewigkeit
  Mit des Geistes Flügeln schwingen.
Gib mir einen Vorschmack ein,
Wie es mag im Himmel sein.

5.
Ruh' in mir und ich in dir!
  Bau' ein Paradies im Herzen.
Offenbare dich doch mir,
  Schenke meiner Andacht Kerzen
Oel des Lebens immerzu,
O du Liebesflamme du!

6.
Dieser Tag sei dir geweiht,
  Weg mit allen Eitelkeiten!
Ich will deiner Herrlichkeit
  Einen Tempel zubereiten,
Nichts sonst wollen, nichts sonst tun,
Als in deiner Liebe ruh'n.

7.
Du bist mehr als Salomon,
  Lass mich deine Weisheit hören!
Ich will deinen Gnadenthron
  Mit gebeugten Knieen ehren,
Bis mir deine Sonne lacht,
Und den schönsten Sonntag macht.

A hymn for the Sabbath morning, reflecting the light, joy, and peace that the day of rest brings to the worshipper. It is one of the finest chorales in our collection.

For comments on Benjamin Schmolck see Hymn 505.

The translation is from *Lyra Germanica,* published by Catherine

Winkworth, 1855. Our hymn is a selection of stanzas 1, 2, 4, and 3, in that order, of the original seven stanzas.
For comments on Miss Winkworth see Hymn 236.

MUSIC. LIEBSTER JESU appeared in the *Alterdorfer Gesangbuch,* 1671, set to the words, "Liebster Jesus, wir sind hier," by Tobias Clausnitzer. J. S. Bach made a setting for the tune, used in some hymn books, and also arranged it as a chorale prelude for the organ.

The composer of the tune, Johann Rudolph Ahle, 1625-73, received his education at the Universities of Göttingen and Erfurt. He was elected Cantor of St. Andreas' Church, and director of the music school, at Erfurt. Interested also in civic affairs, he was elected to the town council at Mühlhausen in 1656, and made mayor in 1661. He became one of the most radical reformers of church music, cultivating the simple chorale style and avoiding the polyphonic counterpoint then in use. Ahle wrote over 400 songs, many of which are still in use among the Protestant churches of England and America.

553. Liebster Jesu, wir sind hier   *Tobias Clausnitzer, 1619-84*

1.
Liebster Jesu, wir sind hier,
  Dich und dein Wort anzuhören;
Lenke Sinnen und Begier
  Auf die süssen Himmelslehren,
Dass die Herzen von der Erden
  Ganz zu dir gezogen werden!

2.
Unser Wissen und Verstand
  Ist mit Finsternis umhüllet,
Wo nicht deines Geistes Hand
  Uns mit hellem Licht erfüllet;
Gutes wollen, tun und denken,
  Muss uns deine Gnade schenken.

3.
O du Glanz der Herrlichkeit—
  Licht vom Licht, aus Gott geboren,
Mach uns allesamt bereit,
  Oeffne Herzen, Mund und Ohren!
Unser Bitten, Fleh'n und Singen
Lass, Herr Jesu, wohl gelingen!

Based on Acts 10:33: "Now therefore are we all here present before God, to hear all things that are commanded thee of God." The third stanza is reminiscent of a phrase in the Nicene creed: "God of God, Light of Light, begotten, not made." The hymn, written to be sung by the congregation just before the reading of the Scripture lesson, has had wide use among German speaking churches.

Tobias Clausnitzer was born at Thum, Saxony. He graduated from the University of Leipzig in 1643 and became a chaplain in the Swedish army, for a time, during the Thirty Years' War. In 1649 he became minister at Weiden where he remained until his death.

MUSIC. See 553 above.

554. Come, Thou bright and morning Star

Christian Knorr,
Baron von Rosenroth, 1636-89
Tr. Richard Massie, 1800-87

1.
Morgenglanz der Ewigkeit,
Licht vom unerschöpften Lichte,
Schick uns diese Morgenzeit
Deine Strahlen zu Gesichte
Und vertreib durch deine Macht
Unsre Nacht!

2.
Deiner Güte Morgentau
Fall' auf unser matt Gewissen,
Lass die dürre Lebensau
Lauter süssen Trost geniessen
Und erquick uns, deine Schar,
Immerdar!

3.
Gib, dass deiner Liebe Glut
Unsre kalten Werke töte,
Und erweck uns Herz und Mut
Bei entstandner Morgenröte,
Dass wir, eh' wir gar vergehn,
Recht aufstehn!

4.
Ach du Aufgang aus der Höh',
Gib dass auch am Jüngsten Tage
Unser Leichnam aufersteh'
Und, entfernt von aller Plage,
Sich auf jener Freudenbahn
Freuen kann!

5.
Leucht uns selbst in jene Welt,
Du verklärte Gnadensonne,
Führ uns durch das Tränenfeld
In das Land der ew'gen Wonne,
Wo die Lust, die uns erhöht,
Nie vergeht!

One of the best and most spirited of morning hymns, "as if born from the dew of the sunrise."

The author, Christian Knorr, Baron von Rosenroth, was the son of a Silesian pastor. After years of study and travel, he also settled down to a pastorate in Silesia. He was well versed in philosophy and chemistry, as well as theology, and his memory was so remarkable that he knew nearly the whole Bible by heart. He took special interest in the study of the Jewish Kabbala, the so-called secret wisdom of the rabbis, and his writings on this literature made him world famous. Knorr wrote seventy hymns, the present being the only one now in general use among English speaking people.

The translator, Richard Massie, was the son of the Rev. R. Massie, a minister in the Anglican church. A man of wealth and leisure, he was able to devote himself to literature and gardening. His rock garden, a rare thing in those days, attracted wide attention. Massie and his mother and sisters are remembered for their quiet spirituality and saintliness.

MUSIC. MORGENGLANZ DER EWIGKEIT is an adaptation of an air by Johann Rudolph Ahle. The tune appeared in Freylinghausen's *Gesangbuch*, Halle, 1704, set to this hymn. Its beauty of melody and rhythm is extraordinary. For comments on the composer see Hymn 553.

555. Evening and morning, sunset and dawning

Paul Gerhardt, 1607-76
Tr. Richard Massie, 1800-87

1.

Die güldne Sonne,
Voll Freud' und Wonne,
Bringt unsern Grenzen
Mit ihrem Glänzen
Ein herzerquickendes,
  liebliches Licht.
Mein Haupt und Glieder,
Die lagen danieder;
Aber nun steh' ich,
Bin munter und fröhlich,
Schaue den Himmel mit meinem
  Gesicht.

2.

Mein Auge schauet,
Was Gott gebauet
Zu seinen Ehren,
Und uns zu lehren,
Wie sein Vermögen sei mächtig
  und gross,
Und wo die Frommen
Einst sollen hinkommen,
Wann sie mit Frieden
Von hinnen geschieden
Aus dieser Erde vergänglichem
  Schoss.

3.

Lasset uns singen,
Dem Schöpfer bringen
Güter und Gaben!
Was wir nur haben,
Alles das sei Gott zum Opfer
  gesetzt.
Die besten Güter
Sind unsre Gemüter;
Lieder der Frommen,
Von Herzen gekommen,
Sind Opferrauch, der ihn am
  meisten ergötzt.

4.

Abend und Morgen
Sind seine Sorgen;
Segnen und mehren,
Unglück verwehren,
Sind seine Werke und Taten
  allein.
Wann wir uns legen,
Ist er zugegen;
Wann wir aufstehen,
So lässt er aufgehen
Ueber uns seiner Barmherzigkeit
  Schein.

5.

Ich hab' erhoben
Zu dir hoch droben
All' meine Sinnen:
Lass mein Beginnen
Ohn' allen Anstoss und
  glücklich ergehn!
Laster und Schande,
Lucifers Bande
Fallen und Tücke
Treib' ferne zurücke;
Lass mich auf deinen Geboten
  bestehn!

6.

Lass mich mit Freuden,
Ohn' alles Neiden
Sehen den Segen,
Den du wirst legen
In meines Bruders und Nähesten
  Haus!
Geiziges Brennen,
Unchristlich Rennen
Nach Gut mit Sünde
Das tilge geschwinde
Aus meinem Herzen, und wirf
  es hinaus!

7.

Menschliches Wesen,
Was ist's gewesen!
In einer Stunde
Geht es zu 'Grunde,
Sobald das Lüftlein des Todes
   drein weht;
Alles in Allem
Muss brechen und fallen;
Himmel und Erden,
Die müssen das werden,
Was sie gewesen, eh' Gott sie
   erhöht.

8.

Alles vergehet;
Gott aber stehet
Ohn' alles Wanken;
Seine Gedanken,
Sein Wort und Wille hat
   ewigen Grund.
Sein Heil und Gnaden,
Die nehmen nicht Schaden,
Heilen im Herzen
Die tödtlichen Schmerzen,
Halten uns zeitlich und ewig
   gesund.

9.

Gott, meine Krone,
Vergib und schone!
Lass meine Schulden
In Gnad' und Hulden
Aus deinen Augen sein
   abgewandt.
Sonsten regiere
Mich, lenk' und führe
Wie dir's gefället!
Ich habe gestellet
Alles in deine Beliebung und
   Hand!

10.

Willst du mir geben,
Womit mein Leben
Ich kann ernähren,
So lass mich hören
Allzeit im Herzen dies heilige
   Wort:
"Gott ist das Grösste,
Das Schönste, Beste!
Gott is das Süss'ste,
Das Allergewiss'ste
Von allen Schätzen, der edelste
   Hort!"

11.

Willst du mich kränken,
Mit Galle tränken,
Und soll von Plagen
Ich auch was tragen:
Wohlan denn, so mach' es, wie
   dir es beliebt!
Was gut und tüchtig,
Was schädlich und nichtig
Meinem Gebeine,
Das weisst Du alleine,
Hast niemals einen zu bitter
   betrübt.

12.

Trübsal und Zähren
Nicht ewig währen;
Nach Meeresbrausen
Und Windessausen
Leuchtet der Sonne verklärtes
   Gesicht.
Freude die Fülle,
Und selige Stille
Hab' ich zu warten
Im himmlischen Garten;
Dahin sind meine Gedanken
   gericht't!

"A splendid hymn of our poet, golden as the sun going forth in his beauty, full of force and of blessed peace in the Lord, full of sparkling thoughts of God." (Lauxmann). Our hymn is a selection of stanzas 4, 8, and 12 of the original twelve.

For comments on Paul Gerhardt see Hymn 134.

This excellent translation by Richard Massie has come into general use.

For comments on Massie see Hymn 554.

CHORALES

MUSIC. DIE GÜLDNE SONNE, also called "Franconia," is a beautiful melody by Johann G. Ebeling, 1620-76. A number of his chorales are still in high favor. The name of the tune is derived from the title of Gerhardt's hymn for which it was written.

For comments on Ebeling see Hymn 525.

EVENING

556. The duteous day now closeth

Stanzas 1, 2, Paul Gerhardt, 1607-76
Tr. Robert Bridges, 1844-1930
Stanzas 3, 4, Robert Bridges

1.
Nun ruhen alle Wälder,
Vieh, Menschen, Städt' und Fel-
der,
Es schläft die ganze Welt.
Ihr, aber, meine Sinnen,
Auf, auf! ihr sollt beginnen,
Was eurem Schöpfer wohlgefällt.

2.
Wo bist du, Sonne, blieben?
Die Nacht hat dich vertrieben,
Die Nacht, des Tages Feind.
Fahr hin, ein' andre Sonne,
Mein Jesus, meine Wonne,
Gar hell in meinem Herzen
scheint.

3.
Der Tag ist nun vergangen,
Die güldnen Sterne prangen
Am blauen Himmelssaal.
Also werd ich auch stehen,
Wann mich wird heissen gehen
Mein Gott aus diesem Jammertal.

4.
Der Leib eilt nun zur Ruhe,
Legt Kleider ab und Schuhe,
Das Bild der Sterblichkeit.
Die zieh ich aus; dagegen
Wird Christus mir anlegen
Das Kleid der Ehr' und Herrlich-
keit.

5.
Dast Haupt, die Füss und Hände

Sind froh, dass nun zum Ende
Die Arbeit kommen sei.
Herz, freu dich! du sollst werden
Vom Elend dieser Erden,
Und von der Sünden Arbeit frei.

6.
Nun geht, ihr matten Glieder,
Geht hin und legt euch nieder,
Des Bettleins ihr begehrt.
Es kommen Stund' und Zeiten,
Da man euch wird bereiten
Zu Ruh' ein Bettlein in der Erd'.

7.
Die Augen stehn verdrossen,
Im Nu sind sie geschlossen;
Wo bleibt dann Leib und Seel'?
Nimm sie zu deinen Gnaden,
Sei gut für allen Schaden,
Du Aug' und Wächter Israel!

8.
Breit' aus die Flügel beide,
O Jesu, meine Freude,
Und nimm dein Küchlein ein!
Will mich der Feind verschlingen,
So lass die Engel singen:
"Dies Kind soll unverletzet sein!"

9.
Auch euch, ihr meine Lieben,
Soll heute nicht betrüben
Ein Unfall noch Gefahr;
Gott lass' euch selig schlafen,
Stell' euch die güldnen Waffen
Ums Bett und seiner Engel Schar!

350

Gerhardt's hymn appeared in nine stanzas in Crüger's *Praxis Pietatis Melica*, 3d ed., 1648. The hymn became known everywhere in Germany and was a favorite of the poet Schiller.

For comments on Paul Gerhardt see Hymn 134.

Stanzas 1 and 2 are free translations by Robert Bridges who added stanzas 3 and 4, his own work, for his *Yattendon Hymnal*, 1899.

For comments on Bridges see Hymn 32.

MUSIC. INNSBRUCK is commonly attributed to Heinrich Isaak, *c.* 1460-*c.* 1527, a German or Dutch (it is not certain which) born musician who spent most of his life in Italy, an eminent organist and composer. Isaak was kapellmeister of Lorenzo the Magnificent and later of Maximilian of Vienna. The tune was first published, so far as is known, in Nürnberg, 1539, in a different version, set to the words, "Innsbruck ich muss dich lassen." Later it was adapted to the hymn, "O Welt ich muss dich lassen," and then to Gerhardt's evening hymn, "Nun ruhen alle Wälder." The melody has appeared in many different forms in German collections. The arrangement here is that made by J. S. Bach and used in his *St. Matthew Passion* and elsewhere.

557. Now cheer our hearts this eventide

Nikolaus Selnecker, 1532-92
Tr. Robert Bridges, 1844-1930

1.
Ach bleib' bei uns, Herr Jesu Christ,
Weil es nun Abend worden ist;
Dein göttlich Wort, das helle Licht,
Lass ja bei uns auslöschen nicht!

2.
In dieser letzten, bösen Zeit
Gib uns des Glaubens Beständigkeit,
Dass wir dein Wort und Sakrament
Rein b'halten bis an unser End'.

3.
Herr Jesu, hilf, dein' Kirch' erhalt'!
Wir sind sicher, arg, träg' und kalt;
Gib Glück und Heil zu deinem Wort,
Dass es erschall' an jedem Ort.

4.
Erhalt' uns nur bei deinem Wort,
Und wehr' des Teufels Trug und Mord;
Gib deiner Kirche Gnad' und Huld,
Fried', Einigkeit, Mut und Geduld.

5.
Ach Gott, es geht gar übel zu,
Auf dieser Erd' ist keine Ruh'!
Viel Sekten und viel Schwärmerei
Auf einen Haufen kommt herbei.

6.
Den stolzen Geistern wehre doch,
Die sich mit Macht erheben hoch,
Und bringen stets was Neues her,
Zu fälschen deine rechte Lehr'.

7.
Die Sach' und Ehr', Herr Jesu Christ,
Nicht unser, sondern dein ja ist;

Darum so steh' du denen bei,
Die sich auf dich verlassen frei.

Dass wir nichts Andres suchen
mehr!

8.

9.

Dein Wort ist unsers Herzens
Trutz
Und deiner Kirche wahrer Schutz;
Dabei erhalt' uns, lieber Herr,

Gib, dass wir leben in dem Wort,
Und darauf fahren ferner fort
Von hinnen aus dem Jammertal
Zu dir in deinen Freudensaal!

The author, Nikolaus Selnecker, an ardent Lutheran, was a scholar and accomplished musician. He became church organist when only twelve years old and afterwards, in succession, lecturer at the University of Wittenberg, Professor of Theology at Jena, and pastor of St. Thomas' Church at Leipzig. He wrote Latin verse and composed many German hymns but is chiefly known through this evening hymn. The English rendering of it we owe to Robert Bridges' *Yattendon Hymnal*. It was made to suit Bach's setting of the Proper tune, and freely though finely expands stanzas 1 and 9 of the original.

For comments on Robert Bridges see Hymn 32.

MUSIC. ACH BLEIB BEI UNS, "one of the most famous of German chorales," appeared in *Geistliche Lieder,* Leipzig, 1589, and in other contemporary collections.

The composer, Seth Calvisius, 1556-1615, was the son of poor parents, but succeeeded in obtaining an education at the Universities of Helmstedt and Leipzig. He was an astronomer and chronologer, besides being a musician, and was offered the Chair of Mathematics at Wittenberg in 1611. Calvisius refused the offer in order to devote himself to music. After holding various musical posts in churches in Leipzig and Schulpforta, he became music director at the Thomaskirche in the former city. Calvisius wrote treatises on the theory of music and published several collections of his own and others' music, among them *Hymni Sacri Latini et Germanici,* 1594, in which this tune appears in the alto as a descant to another melody. The present version is from J. S. Bach's *Vierstimmige Choralgesänge,* 1769.

GENERAL

558. Commit thou all thy griefs

Paul Gerhardt, 1607-76
Tr. John Wesley, 1703-91

1.

Befiehl du deine Wege,
Und was dein Herze kränkt,
Der allertreusten Pflege
Des, der den Himmel lenkt!

Der Wolken, Luft und Winden,
Gibt Wege, Lauf und Bahn,
Der wird auch Wege finden,
Da dein Fuss gehen kann.

2.

Dem Herren musst du trauen,
  Wenn dir's soll wohlergehn;
Auf sein Werk musst du schauen,
  Wenn dein Werk soll bestehn.
Mit Sorgen und mit Grämen
  Und mit selbsteigner Pein
Lässt Gott sich gar nichts nehmen,
  Es muss erbeten sein.

3.

Dein' ew'ge Treu' und Gnade,
  O Vater, weiss und sieht,
Was gut sei oder schade
  Dem sterblichen Geblüt;
Und was du dann erlesen,
  Das treibst du, starker Held,
Und bringst zum Stand und We-
  sen,
  Was deinem Rat gefällt.

4.

Weg' hast du allerwegen,
  An Mitteln fehlt dir's nicht;
Dein Tun ist lauter Segen,
  Dein Gang ist lauter Licht,
Dein Werk kann niemand hin-
  dern,
  Dein' Arbeit darf nicht ruhn,
Wenn du, was deinen Kindern
  Erspriesslich ist, willst tun.

5.

Und ob gleich alle Teufel
  Hier wollten widerstehn,
So wird doch ohne Zweifel
  Gott nicht zurückegehn;
Was er sich vorgenommen,
  Und was er haben will,
Das muss doch endlich kommen
  Zu seinem Zweck und Ziel.

6.

Hoff, o du arme Seele,
  Hoff und sei unverzagt!
Gott wird dich aus der Höhle,
  Da dich der Kummer plagt,
Mit grossen Gnaden rücken;
  Erwarte nur die Zeit,
So wirst du schon erblicken
  Die Sohn' der schönsten Freud'.

7.

Auf, auf, gib deinem Schmerze
  Und Sorgen gute Nacht!
Lass fahren, was dein Herze
  Betrübt und traurig macht!
Bist du doch nicht Regente,
  Der alles führen soll;
Gott sitzt im Regimente
  Und führet alles wohl.

8.

Ihn, ihn lass tun und walten,
  Er ist ein weiser Fürst
Und wird sich so verhalten,
  Dass du dich wundern wirst,
Wenn er, wie ihm gebühret,
  Mit wunderbarem Rat
Die Sach' hinausgeführet,
  Die dich bekümmert hat.

9.

Er wird zwar eine Weile
  Mit seinem Trost verziehn
Und tun an seinem Teile,
  Als hätt' in seinem Sinn
Er deiner sich begeben,
  Und sollt'st du für und für
In Angst und Nöten schweben,
  Frag' er doch nichts nach dir.

10.

Wird's aber sich befinden,
  Dass du ihm treu verbleibst,
So wird er dich entbinden,
  Da du's am mind'sten gläubst;
Er wird dein Herze lösen
  Von der so schweren Last,
Die du zu keinem Bösen
  Bisher getragen hast.

11.

Wohl dir, du Kind der Treue!
  Du hast und trägst davon
Mit Ruhm und Dankgeschreie
  Den Sieg und Ehrenkron'.
Gott gibt dir selbst die Palmen
  In deine rechte Hand,
Und du singst Freudenpsalmen
  Dem, der dein Leid gewandt.

12.

Mach End' o Herr, mach Ende	Uns allzeit deiner Pflege
An aller unsrer Not,	Und Treu' empfohlen sein,
Stärk unsre Füss' und Hände	So gehen unsre Wege
Und lass bis in den Tod	Gewiss zum Himmel ein.

This "Hymn of Trust" is Gerhardt's finest lyric. It is based on Psalm 37:5: "Commit thy way unto the Lord; trust also in him; and he shall bring it to pass." The initial words of each stanza form an acrostic of the German version: "Befiehl dem Herrn deine Wege, und hoff auf ihn; er wird es wohlmachen." The hymn first appeared in Crüger's *Praxis,* 1646. It expresses the simple trust in God that supported Gerhardt through the troubles that arose out of the Thirty Years' War, as well as his own personal sorrows.

For comments on Gerhardt see Hymn 134.

Of the many translations of this hymn, this one by John Wesley remains the most popular. It was published in 16 four-line stanzas in his *Hymns and Sacred Poems,* 1739, with the title, "Trust in Providence." Since the hymn was written in Short Meter, the editors of the *Hymnary* had to abridge the third line of each stanza to fit this tune with its 7.6.7.6. meter, a practice which Wesley himself would have heartily condemned. Wesley's unaltered version of his eight stanzas used here are as follows:

1.
Commit thou all thy griefs
And ways into His hands,
To His sure truth and tender care
Who earth and heaven commands.

2.
Who points the clouds their course,
Whom winds and seas obey,
He shall direct thy wandering feet,
He shall prepare thy way.

3.
Thou on the Lord rely,
So safe shalt thou go on;
Fix on His work thy steadfast eye,
So shall thy work be done.

4.
No profit canst thou gain
By self-consuming care;
To Him commend thy cause; His ear
Attends the softest prayer.

5.
Thy everlasting truth,
Father, Thy ceaseless love,
Sees all Thy children's wants, and knows
What best for each will prove.

6.
And whatsoe'er Thou will'st
Thou dost, O King of kings;
What Thy unerring wisdom chose,
Thy power to being brings.

7.
Thou everywhere hast sway,
And all things serve Thy might;
Thy every act pure blessing is,
Thy path unsullied light.

8.
When Thou arisest, Lord,
Who shall Thy work withstand?
When all Thy children want,
Thou giv'st;
Who, who, shall stay Thy hand?

The latter part of the hymn, in Wesley's translation, is found at No. 246.

For comments on John Wesley see Hymn 170.

MUSIC. The tune, BEFIEHL DU DEINE WEGE, appears anonymously in the *Gesangbuch mit Noten*. It is probably of American origin.

559. Abide with us, our Savior

Josua Stegmann, 1588-1632
Tr. Anonymous

1.
Ach bleib mit deiner Gnade
Bei uns, Herr Jesu Christ,
Dass uns hinfort nicht schade
Des bösen Feindes List!

2.
Ach bleib mit deinem Worte
Bei uns, Erlöser wert,
Dass uns beid' hier und dorte
Sei Güt' und Heil beschert!

3.
Ach bleib mit deinem Glanze
Bei uns, du wertes Licht;
Dein' Wahrheit uns umschanze,
Damit wir irren nicht!

4.
Ach bleib mit deinem Segen
Bei uns, du reicher Herr!
Dein' Gnad' und all's Vermögen
In uns reichlich vermehr!

5.
Ach bleib mit deinem Schutze
Bei uns, du starker Held,
Dass uns der Feind nicht trutze,
Noch fäll' die böse Welt!

6.
Ach bleib mit deiner Treue
Bei uns, mein Herr und Gott!
Beständigkeit verleihe,
Hilf uns aus aller Not!

A simple and beautiful hymn, having as its keynote the saying of the two disciples at Emmaus: "Abide with us: for it is toward evening, and the day is far spent" (Lk. 24:29). It originally appeared in the author's *Christliches Gebetsbüchlein*, Rinteln, 1627, and later in his *Erneuerte Hertzen-Seufzer*, 1630, under the title, "For the Blessing and Support of the Ministry," to be used as a closing hymn after the "Prayer for the Preservation of the Doctrine, and of the Church of God."

Our version is a free translation of stanzas 1 to 3 as it appeared, anonymously, in the Dalston Hospital *Hymn Book*, 1848, and as repeated in the Pennsylvania Lutheran *Church Book*, 1868.

Josua Stegmann, son of a Lutheran pastor, was born at Sülzfeld, Germany. He was educated at the Universities of Leipzig and Wittenberg. After holding several positions as teacher and pastor, he became Professor of Theology at Rinteln. With the outbreak of the Thirty Years' War, he was forced to flee but returned after several years. He suffered much at the hands of his Catholic opponents. Benedictine monks claimed to be the rightful professors and demanded the restoration of certain church properties. At one time soldiers were sent into Stegmann's house, demanding a refund of his salary, compelling him to a public disputation, and otherwise subjecting him to humiliation.

MUSIC. ACH BLEIB MIT DEINER GNADE is a simple but lovely tune, permeated with a feeling of deep serenity, fitting the present hymn perfectly. It appeared in the composer's *Ein Schön Geistlich Gesangbuch*, Jena, 1609, set to the hymn, "Christus der ist mein Leben," by which name the tune is also known. J. S. Bach used the melody in his chorale cantata, *Christus, der ist mein Leben.*

The composer, Melchior Vulpius, c. 1560-1616, was precentor at Weimar about 1600. He composed a number of tunes and published them in his *Ein schön geistlich Gesangbuch, &c., durch M.V. Cantorem zu Weymar*. Others of his tunes were published after his death.

560. God is my Light

Johann H. K. Hengstenberg, 1770-1834
Tr. Ernst Wm. Hengstenberg, 1835

1.
Gott ist mein Licht!
Verzage nicht, mein Herz
  In banger, dunkler Zeit!
Die Sonne sinkt,
Die Nacht bringt Furcht und Schmerz,
  Mein Licht strahlt allezeit!
Es schimmert an dem Tag der Freuden;
Es leuchtet durch die Nacht der Leiden:
  Gott ist mein Licht!

2.
Gott ist mein Heil!
O Seele, fürchte nichts!
  Dein Helfer ist getreu.
Er lässt dich nicht,
Sein Vaterwort verspricht's.
  Er steht dir mächtig bei.
Er will mich bis ins Alter tragen,
Kein wahres Gut mir je versagen:
  Gott ist mein Heil!

3.
Sein ist die Kraft!
Er spricht und es geschieht,
  Gebeut und es steht da.
Und wenn mein Blick
Noch keine Hoffnung sieht,
  Ist schon die Rettung nah.
Wo schwache Menschen nichts vermögen,
Do kommt uns stärkend Gott entgegen.
  Sein ist die Kraft!

4.
Sein ist das Reich!
Er herrscht im Weltgebiet
  Mit Weisheit, Huld und Macht.
Die Sterne ziehn;
Der Strom der Zeiten flieht,
  Von seinem Arm bewacht.
Und alles lenket er im stillen
Zum Ziel nach seinem heilgen Willen
  Sein ist das Reich!

5.
Gott ist mein Schild!
Mein Schirm in der Gefahr,
  Die er nur wenden kann.
Er deckt mein Haupt,
Und ohn ihn fällt kein Haar.
  Er nimmt sich aller an.
Ob Tausende, die mit mir wallen,
Zur Rechten oder Linken fallen—
  Er ist mein Schild!

6.
Gott ist mein Lohn!
Drum geh ich unverzagt
  Die Bahn, die er nur zeigt.
Der Gang sei schwer—
Er wird mit Gott gewagt,
  Der dort die Palme reicht.
Froh wird gekämpft, um Sieg gerungen
Voll Mut der Widerstand bezwungen.
  Gott ist mein Lohn!

The hymn was written by Johann Heinrich Karl Hengstenberg, a Lutheran pastor in the town of Wetter in Westphalia. His literary work is *Psalterion* published in Essen, 1825, a collection of his hymns, several of which passed into general use in the Lutheran churches of Germany.

The translator has not been identified.

MUSIC. GOTT IST GETREU is a melody contributed by J. R. Ahle, in his *Geistliche Arien,* 1662, where it is set to the hymn, "Es ist genug," by Franz Burmeister.

For comments on Ahle see Hymn 553.

561. Take Thou my hand, O Father

Julie von Haussmann, 1825-1901
Tr. H. Brueckner

1.
So nimm denn meine Hände
Und führe mich
Bis an mein selig' Ende
Und ewiglich!
Ich kann allein nicht gehen,
Nicht einen Schritt;
Wo du wirst geh'n und stehen,
Da nimm mich mit.

2.
In Deine Gnade hülle
Mein schwaches Herz,
Und mach' es endlich stille
In Freud' und Schmerz;
Lass ruh'n zu deinen Füssen
Dein schwaches Kind,
Es will die Augen schliessen
Und folgen blind.

3.
Wenn ich auch gar nichts fühle
Von deiner Macht,
Du bringst mich doch zum Ziele
Auch durch die Nacht;
So nimm denn meine Hände
Und führe mich
Bis an mein selig' Ende
Und ewiglich!

Julie von Hausemann, born in Mitau, in the province of Kurland, was the second youngest of a family of six daughters. Her father had been a teacher in a Gymnasium at Riga, later moving to Mitau where he held a government position. Julie, never in vigorous health, was a shy, retiring young woman, but keen of intellect. On several occasions she accepted positions as governess in private homes but was always compelled to give up on account of her health. She finally dismissed all thoughts of a career and devoted herself to the care of her father who had become blind, until the latter's death in 1864. The following two years she lived with a married sister in Germany and Switzerland and then accompanied her younger sister to Biarritz in southern France where the latter held a position as organist. In 1870 both went to St. Petersburg to be with two other sisters, one of them employed as Director of St. Annenschule. The family circle was broken in 1896 and 1898 upon the death of the youngest and oldest sister. In 1901 Julie settled with relatives near Wösso in Estonia. In spite of old age and weak eyesight, she was busily engaged, until her death, with charities and literary work. She published a devotional book, *Hausbrot*, and, upon the insistence of a friend, Gustav Knak, her lyrics were published in three volumes, entitled, *Maiblumen, Lieder einer Stillen im Lande.* "So nimm denn mein Hände" appeared in *Maiblumen*, 1862, Vol I. It has been translated into many languages.

For comments on the translator, H. Brueckner, see Hymn 517.

MUSIC. SO NIMM DEINE MEINE HÄNDE first appeared with the present hymn in 1883. The tune was composed by Friedrich Silcher, 1789-1860, a German musician, born at Schnaith, Württemberg. For 43 years Silcher was the director of music and organist at the University of Tübingen. He composed popular songs and hymns, and a cantata.

562. What mercy and divine compassion

Philipp F. Hiller, 1699-1769
Tr. Frieda Kaufman, 1883-1944

1.
Mir ist Erbarmung widerfahren,
Erbarmung, deren ich nicht wert!
Das zähl' ich zu dem Wunderbaren;
Mein stolzes Herz hat's nie begehrt.
Nun weiss ich das, und bin erfreut,
: Und rühme die Barmherzigkeit:

2.
Ich hatte nichts als Zorn verdienet,
Und soll bei Gott in Gnaden sein;
Gott hat mich mit sich selbst versühnet,
Und macht durchs Blut des Sohn's mich rein,
Nicht durch Verdienst der Kreatur,—
: Erbarmung ist's, Erbarmung nur:

3.
Das musz ich dir, mein Gott, bekennen,
Das rühm' ich, wenn ein Mensch mich fragt;

Ich kann es nur Erbarmung nennen,
So ist mein ganzes Herz gesagt;
Ich beuge mich, und bin erfreut,
: Und rühme die Barmherzigkeit :

4.
Dies lass ich kein Geschöpf mir rauben,
Dies soll mein einzig Rühmen sein;
Auf dies Erbarmen will ich glauben
Auf dieses bet' ich auch allein;
Auf dieses duld' ich in der Not;
: Auf dieses hoff' ich noch im Tod :

5.
Gott, der du reich bist an Erbarmen,
Nimm dein Erbarmen nicht von mir,
Und führe durch den Tod mich Armen
Durch meines Heilands Tod zu dir;
Da bin ich ewig hoch erfreut,
: Und rühme die Barmherzigkeit :

Based on I Tim. 1:13: "aber mir ist Barmherzigkeit widerfahren" ("but I obtained mercy").

The hymn appeared first in Hiller's *Geistliches Liederkästlein,* Part II, 1767, with the following note by the author:

> An unconverted person is much too proud to say these words sincerely from the heart; but the converted person confesses them freely before God and man.

For comments on the author, Philipp Friedrich Hiller, see Hymn 524. The hymn is credited, erroneously, to Gerhard Tersteegen, in the *Hymnary.*

A number of Hiller's hymns have been translated but this one apparently had never before been put into English. Our translation, consisting of stanzas 1, 2, 4, and 5, was made especially for the *Hymnary* by Sister Frieda Kaufman who was for many years associated with the Bethel Deaconess Hospital, Newton, Kansas. Sister Frieda was born near Basel, Switzerland; came with her parents to Halstead, Kansas; and attended Bethel College. After graduating from a nursing course in Cincinnati, Ohio, she received her deaconess garb and has since been known as "Sister Frieda." From 1908 to 1943 she served as sister-in-charge of the hospital and during much of that time served also as its superintendent. She had much to do with the planning of the Home for the Aged which is operated in connection with the hospital. To these two institutions she devoted her rare gifts and set for them a high standard of Christian service. Sister Frieda had unusual literary and artistic endowments and translated several German hymns into English.

MUSIC. ERBARMUNG is a popular Swiss melody which appeared anonymously in the *Gesangbuch mit Noten.* It was composed by Johann Gottfried Schicht, 1753-1823, who was born in Zittau. Schicht composed 3 oratorios, church and chamber music, and edited Bach's motets. He became cantor of the Thomasschule in Leipzig in 1810.

563. Strive aright when God doth call thee

Johann J. Winckler, 1670-1722
Tr. Catherine Winkworth, 1829-78

1.
Ringe recht, wenn Gottes Gnade
Dich nun ziehet und bekehrt,
Dass dein Geist sich gantz entlade
Von der Last, die ihn beschwert.

2.
Ringe, denn die Pfort' ist enge,
Und der Lebensweg ist schmal;
Hier bleibt alles im Gedränge,
Was nicht zielt zum Himmelssaal.

3.
Kämpfe bis aufs Blut und Leben,
Dring' hinein in Gottes Reich;
Will der Satan widerstreben,
Werde weder matt noch weich.

4.
Ringe, dass dein Eifer glühe,
Und die erste Liebe dich
Von der ganzen Welt abziehe,
Halbe Liebe hält nicht Stich.

5.

Ringe mit Gebet und Schreien,
Halte damit feurig an;
Lass dich keine Zeit gereuen,
Wär's auch Tag und Nacht getan.

6.

Hast du dann die Perl' errungen,
Denke ja nicht, dass du nun
Alles Böse hast bezwungen,
Das uns Schanden pflegt zu tun.

7.

Nimm mit Furcht ja deiner Seele,
Deines Heils mit Zittern wahr,
Denn in dieser Leibeshöhle
Schwebst du stündlich in Gefahr.

8.

Halt ja deine Krone feste,
Halte männlich, was du hast.
Recht beharren ist dast Beste,
Rückfall wird zur schweren Last.

9.

Lass dein Auge ja nicht gaffen
Nach der schnöden Eitelkeit;
Bleibe Tag und Nacht in Waffen,
Fliehe träge Sicherheit.

10.

Lass dem Fleische nicht den Willen,
Gib der Lust den Zügel nicht;
Willst du die Begierden stillen,
So verlischt das Gnadenlicht.

11.

Fleisches Freiheit macht die Seele
Kalt und sicher, frech und stolz;
Frisst hinweg des Glaubens Oele,
Lässt nichts, als ein faules Holz.

12.

Wahre Treu führt mit der Sünde
Bis ins Grab beständig Krieg,
Richtet sich nach keinem Winde,
Sucht in jedem Kampf den Sieg.

13.

Wahre Treu liebt Christi Wege,
Steht beherzt auf ihrer Hut,
Weiss von keiner Fleischespflege
Hält sich selber nichts zu gut.

14.

Wahre Treu hat viel zu weinen,
Spricht zum Lachen: du bist toll;
Weil es, wenn Gott wird erscheinen,
Lauter Heulen werden soll.

15.

Wahre Treu kommt dem Getümmel
Dieser Welt niemals zu nah;
Denn ihr Schatz ist in dem Himmel,
Drum ist auch ihr Herz allda.

16.

Dies bedenket wohl, ihr Streiter!
Streitet recht und fürchtet euch;
Geht doch alle Tage weiter,
Bis ihr kommt in's Himmelreich,

17.

Denkt bei jedem Augenblicke,
Ob's vielleicht der letzte sei;
Bringt die Lampen in's Geschicke,
Holt stets neues Oel herbei.

18.

Liegt nicht alle Welt in Bösen?
Steht nicht Sodom in der Glut?
Seele, wer soll dich erlösen?
Eilen, eilen ist hier gut.

19.

Eile, wo du dich erretten,
Und nicht mit verderben willst;
Mach dich los von allen Ketten,
Fleuch, als ein gejagtes Wild!

20.

Lauf der Welt doch aus den Händen;
Dring' in's stille Zoar ein;
Eile, dass du mögst vollenden
Mache dich von allem rein.

21.

Lass dir Nichts am Herzen kleben,
Fleuch vor dem verborg'nen Bann,
Such in Gott geheim zu leben,
Dass dich nichts beflecken kann.

22.

Eile, zähle Tag und Stunden,
Bis der Heiland dir erscheint,
Und wenn du nun überwunden,
Ewig sich mit dir vereint!

23.

Eile, lauf' ihm doch entgegen,
Sprich: mein Licht, ich bin bereit
Nun mein Hüttlein abzulegen,
Mich dürst't nach der Ewigkeit.

24.

Mich verlangt bei dir zu wohmen,
Jesu! teurer Gottes Sohn,
Ach führ mich zum Himmels-
    throne,
Setz' mir auf die Lebenskron'.

Based on the following scripture passages: (1) Stanzas 1 to 5, Luke 13:24: "Strive to enter in at the strait gate; for many, I say unto you, shall seek to enter in, and shall not be able;" (2) stanzas 6 to 15, Philippians 2:12: "Work out your own salvation with fear and trembling;" (3) stanzas 16 to 24, Genesis 19:15-22: "Haste thee, escape thither," and the story of Lot's flight from Sodom.

Johann J. Winckler was a Lutheran pastor of the early Pietistic group. After receiving his education in the University of Leipzig, he held important church posts in the city of Magdeburg, climaxed by his appointment as chief preacher at the Cathedral. He made enemies in Magdeburg on several occasions, first, by his stand against theater going, and afterwards, by his well-meant though futile attempt to bring about a closer union between the Lutheran and Reformed Churches in Prussia. But he bore his opposition with Christian patience and fortitude. His hymns, all of them lengthy, are distinguished by a firm faith and earnestness. They represent the better productions of the early Pietistic writers of Germany.

Our version is a translation of stanzas 1, 13, and 16, by Miss Winkworth, from her *Chorale Book for England*, 1863. For comments on Catherine Winkworth see Hymn 236.

MUSIC. RINGE RECHT first appeared in Freylinghausen's *Gesangbuch*, 1714, and later in Johann Thommen's *Musikalischer Christenschatz*, Basel, 1745, set to Winckler's hymn from which it derives its name. The tune appears in a number of hymn books, sometimes with slight adaptations, and given such names at "Batty," "Turnan," and "Invitation." The composer remains anonymous.

564. Jesus, priceless Treasure

Johann Franck, 1618-77
Tr. Catherine Winkworth, 1829-78

1.

Jesu, meine Freude,
Meines Herzens Weide,
    Jesu, meine Zier,
Ach, wie lang, ach lange

Ist dem Herzen bange
    Und verlangt nach dir!
Gotteslamm, mein Bräutigam,
Ausser dir soll mir auf Erden
Nichts sonst Liebers werden!

2.

Unter deinem Schirmen
Bin ich vor den Stürmen
 Aller Feinde frei.
Lass den Satan wittern,
Lass die Welt erschüttern,
 Mir steht Jesus bei.
Ob es jetzt gleich kracht und
 blitzt,
Obgleich Sünd' und Hölle schrek-
 ken,
Jesus will mich decken.

3.

Trotz dem alten Drachen,
Trotz dem Todesrachen,
 Trotz der Furcht dazu!
Tobe, Welt, und springe,
Ich steh' hier und singe
 In gar sicherer Ruh';
Gottes Macht hält mich in acht;
Erd' und Abgrund muss verstum-
 men,
Ob sie noch so brummen.

4.

Weg mit allen Schätzen,
Du bist mein Ergötzen,
 Jesu, meine Lust!
Weg, ihr eitlen Ehren,

Ich mag euch nicht hören,
 Bleibt mir unbewusst!
Elend, Not, Kreuz, Schmach und
 Tod
Soll mich, ob ich viel muss leiden,
Nicht von Jesu scheiden.

5.

Gute Nacht, o Wesen,
Das die Welt erlesen,
 Mir gefällst du nicht!
Gute Nacht, ihr Sünden,
Bleibet weit dahinten,
 Kommt nicht mehr ans Licht!
Gute Nacht, du Stolz und Pracht,
Dir sei ganz, du Lasterleben,
Gute Nacht gegeben!

6.

Weicht, ihr Trauergeister,
Denn mein Freudenmeister,
 Jesus, tritt herein!
Denen, die Gott lieben,
Muss auch ihr Betrüben
 Lauter Zucker sein.
Duld' ich schon hier Spott und
 Hohn,
Dennoch bleibst du auch im
 Leide,
Jesu, meine Freude.

In its depth of spiritual experience, this hymn by Franck resembles Wesley's "Jesus, lover of my soul." It has made a wide appeal and the words have been translated into various tongues. Peter the Great, the irreligious Czar of Russia, of all people, had the hymn done into the Russian language, and it has also been translated into Esthonian.

For comments on the author, Johann Franck, see Hymn 552.

For comments on the translator, Catherine Winkworth, see Hymn 236.

MUSIC. JESU MEINE FREUDE is an adaptation of a traditional melody found in J. Crüger's *Praxis Pietatis Melica,* 1653, where it is set to the present hymn. Our version of the melody and the harmony is by J. S. Bach. It is a superb tune and rates as one of the finest of all German chorales.

For comments on Johann Crüger see Hymn 242.

For comments on J. S. Bach see Hymn 539.

565. I am the Lord, O hear my voice

Johann Scheffler, 1624-77
Tr. Joanna Andres

1.
Mir nach! spricht Christus, unser Held,
Mir nach, ihr Christen alle!
Verleugnet euch, verlasst die Welt,
Folgt meinem Ruf und Schalle,
Nehmt euer Kreuz und Ungemach
Auf euch, folgt meinem Wandel nach!

2.
Ich bin das Licht, ich leucht' euch für
Mit heil'gem Tugendleben.
Wer zu mir kommt und folget mir,
Darf nicht im Finstern schweben.
Ich bin der Weg, ich weise wohl,
Wie man wahrhaftig wandeln soll.

3.
Mein Herz ist voll Demütigkeit,
Voll Liebe meine Seele;
Mein Mund, der fleusst zu jeder Zeit
Von süssem Sanftmutsöle;
Mein Geist, Gemüte, Kraft und Sinn
Ist Gott ergeben, schaut auf ihn.

4.
Ich zeig' euch das, was schädlich ist,
Zu fliehen und zu meiden
Und euer Herz von arger List
Zu rein'gen und zu scheiden.
Ich bin der Seelen Fels und Hort
Und führ' euch zu der Himmelspfort'.

5.
Fällt's euch zu schwer, ich geh' voran,
Ich steh' euch an der Seite;
Ich kämpfe selbst, ich brech' die Bahn
Bin alles in dem Streite.
Ein böser Knecht, der still darf stehn
Sieht er voran den Feldherrn gehn!

6.
Wer seine Seel zu finden meint,
Wird sie ohn' mich verlieren;
Wer sie hier zu verlieren scheint,
Wird sie nach Hause führen.
Wer nicht sein Kreuz nimmt und folgt mir,
Ist mein nicht wert und meiner Zier.

7.
So lasst uns denn dem lieben Herrn
Mit Leib und Seel' nachgehen
Und wohlgemut, getrost und gern
Bei ihm im Leiden stehen!
Denn wer nicht kämpft, trägt auch die Kron'
Des ew'gen Lebens nicht davon.

Based on Matt. 16:24: "If any man will come after me, let him deny himself, and take up his cross and follow me." The hymn has been called a "masterpiece of scriptural didactic poetry." It appeared first in the author's *Heilige Seelenlust*, 1668.

Johann Scheffler, author of the hymn, holds a high place in the first rank of German poets. Born in Breslau, Silesia, the son of Lutheran parents, he studied in the Universities of Strassburg, Leyden, and Padua, graduating with the degrees of Ph.D. and M.D. Early in life he became deeply interested in the famous shoemaker, Jacob Böhme, a mystic and writer of poplar books on the inner life. As a result of his studies in mysticism, Scheffler left the Lutherans and became a priest in the Roman Catholic Church. He then gave up the medical profession to devote himself to writing and the priesthood. Scheffler's hymns, on the whole, are, however, not distinctly Roman Catholic in sentiment, and they became much more popular among the Lutherans and Moravians than among the Catholics. Scheffler wrote under the nom de plume, "Angelus Silesius," "Angelus" being the name of a Spanish mystic who influenced him greatly, to which he added "Silesius" to indicate his native country.

The translation was made especially for the *Hymnary*, by Mrs. Joanna Andres, Newton, Kansas. The hymn is unusual in its use of the personal pronoun "I" in the first three stanzas.

MUSIC. MIR NACH! SPRICHT CHRISTUS UNSER HELD is a popular tune composed by Johann Hermann Schein (misspelled "Rhein" in the *Hymnary* and the *Gesangbuch mit Noten*).

For comments on Schein see Hymn 508.

566. O God, Thou faithful God

Johann Heermann, 1585-1647
Tr. Catherine Winkworth, 1829-78

1.
O Gott, du frommer Gott,
    Du Brunnquell guter Gaben,
Ohn' den nichts ist, was ist,
    Von dem wir alles haben:
Gesunden Leib gib mir,
    Und dass in solchem Leib
Ein' unverletzte Seel'
    Und rein Gewissen bleib'.

2.
Gib, dass ich tu' mit Fleiss,
    Was mir zu tun gebühret,
Wozu mich dein Befehl
    In meinem Stande führet!
Gib, dass ich's tue bald,
    Zu der Zeit, da ich soll,
Und wenn ich's tu', so gib,
    Dass es gerate wohl!

3.
Hilf, dass ich rede stets,
    Womit ich kann bestehen,
Lass kein unnützes Wort
    Aus meinem Munde gehen;

Und wenn in meinem Amt
    Ich reden soll und muss,
So gib den Worten Kraft
    Und Nachdruck ohn' Verdruss!

4.
Find't sich Gefährlichkeit,
    So lass mich nicht verzagen;
Gib einen Heldenmut,
    Das Kreuz hilf selber tragen!
Gib, dass ich meinen Feind
    Mit Sanftmut überwind'
Und, wenn ich Rats bedarf,
    Auch guten Rat erfind'!

5.
Lass mich mit jedermann
    In Fried' und Freundschaft
    leben,
Soweit es christlich ist.
    Willst du mir etwas geben
An Reichtum, Gut und Geld,
    So gib auch dies dabei,
Dass von unrechtem Gut
    Nichts untermenget sei!

6.

Soll ich auf dieser Welt
Mein Leben höher bringen,
Durch manchen sauern Tritt
Hindurch ins Alter dringen,
So gib Geduld. Vor Sünd'
Und Schanden mich bewahr',
Auf dass ich tragen mag
Mit Ehren graues Haar!

7.

Lass mich an meinem End'
Auf Christi Tod abscheiden,
Die Seele nimm zu dir
Hinauf zu deinen Freuden,

Dem Leib ein Räumlein gönn',
Bei frommer Christen Grab,
Auf dass er seine Ruh'
An ihrer Seite hab'.

8.

Wenn du an jenem Tag
Die Toten wirst aufwecken,
So tu auch deine Hand
Zu meinem Grab ausstrecken;
Lass hören deine Stimm'
Und meinen Leib weck auf
Und führ ihn schön verklärt
Zum auserwählten Hauf'!

First published in the author's *Devoti Musica Cordis*, Breslau, 1630, where it was entitled "Daily Prayer." Regarding the hymn, originally appearing in 18 stanzas, Fischer writes in his *Kirchenlieder Lexicon*, 1878:

> It is one of the most widely used and signally blessed hymns and has not unjustly been called his "Master Song." If it is somewhat "home baked" yet it is excellent, nourishing bread. It gives a training in practical Christianity and especially strikes three notes—godly living, patient suffering, and happy dying.

For comments on Johann Heermann see Hymn 534.

For comments on the translator, Miss Winkworth, see Hymn 236.

MUSIC. O GOTT, DU FROMMER GOTT, also known as "Darmstadt," is attributed to Ahasuerus Fritsch, a German poet and composer who lived in the second half of the 17th century. The music appeared in his *Himmels-Lust und Welt Unlust*, Jena, 1679. The present version is from J. S. Bach's *Vierstimmige Choralgesänge*, 1765-9.

567. Whate'er my God ordains is right

Samuel Rodigast, 1649-1708
Tr. Catherine Winkworth, 1829-78

1.

Was Gott tut, das ist wohlgetan!
Es bleibt gerecht sein Wille.
Wie er fängt meine Sachen an,
Will ich ihm halten stille.
Er ist mein Gott, der in der Not
Mich wohl weiss zu erhalten;
Drum lass' ich ihn nur walten.

2.

Was Gott tut, das ist wohlgetan!
Er wird mich nicht betrügen;
Er führet mich auf rechter Bahn,
Drum lass' ich mir genügen
An seiner Huld, und hab Geduld;
Er wird mein Unglück wenden,
Es steht in seinen Händen.

3.

Was Gott tut, das ist wohlgetan,
Er wird mich wohl bedenken;
Mein Arzt, der alles heilen kann,
Wird mich mit Gift nicht tränken.
Er ist getreu, und steht mir bei;
Auf ihn nur will ich bauen,
Und seiner Güte trauen.

4.

Was Gott tut, das ist wohlgetan!
Er ist mein Licht, mein Leben,
Der mir nichts Böses gönnen kann;
Ihm will ich mich ergeben
In Freud und Leid; es kommt die
Zeit,
Da öffentlich erscheinet,
Wie treulich er's gemeinet.

5.

Was Gott tut, das ist wohlgetan!
Muss ich den Kelch gleich schmek-
ken,
Der bitter ist nach meinem Wahn,
Lass' ich mich doch nichts schrek-
ken,
Weil er zuletzt, mich doch ergötzt,
Mit süssem Trost im Herzen;
Da weichen alle Schmerzen.

6.

Was Gott tut, das ist wohlgetan!
Dabei will ich verbleiben;
Es mag mich auf die rauhe Bahn
Not, Tod und Elend treiben:
So wird Gott mich, ganz väterlich,
In seinen Armen halten;
Drum lass' ich ihn nur walten.

Based on Deut. 32:4; "He is the Rock, his work is perfect: for all his ways are judgment; a God of truth and without iniquity, just and right is he."

Samuel Rodigast, Professor of Philosophy at the University of Jena, and later rector of the Greyfriars Gymnasium in Berlin, wrote this hymn for his friend Severus Gastorius, precentor of the church at Jena, when Gastorius was ill. Gastorius in turn composed the tune on his sick bed, requesting that the hymn be sung at his funeral. The condition of his health turned for the better whereupon Gastorius ordered his choir to sing the hymn at the door of his house once each week during the period of his convalescence. The music and words became widely known and are used throughout the whole of German Protestantism. The hymn appeared first in *Hannoversches Gesangbuch,* 1676. The melody appeared in the *Auserlesenes Weimarisches Gesangbuch,* 1681.

The translation, stanzas 1, 2, and 6 of the original, is Miss Winkworth's in her *Chorale Book for England,* 1863.

For comments on Catherine Winkworth see Hymn 236.

568. Lord, Thou hast been Thy people's rest

James Montgomery, 1771-1854

A metrical version of the 90th Psalm.

For comments on James Montgomery see Hymn 62.

MUSIC. ALLEIN GOTT IN DER HÖH' SEI EHR' appeared in *Geistliche Lieder,* Leipzig, 1539, where it is set to the hymn, "Allein Gott in der Höh sei Ehr," by Nikolaus Decius. The tune is of pre-Reformation origin. It is an adaptation from an Easter *Gloria* of anonymous composition, and appears with variants in different collections. Many settings

of the tune have been made by Bach and other great composers, the one
here being by Mendelssohn, used in his oratorio, *St. Paul.*

569. Jehovah, let me now adore Thee

Bartholomäus Crasselius, 1667-1724
Tr. Catherine Winkworth, 1829-78

1.
Dir, dir Jehova, will ich singen,
  Denn wo ist doch ein solcher
  Gott wie du?
Dir will ich meine Lieder bringen,
  Ach gib mir deines Geistes Kraft
  dazu,
Dass ich es tu' im Namen Jesu
  Christ,
So wie es dir durch ihn gefällig ist.

2.
Zeuch mich, o Vater, zu dem
  Sohne,
  Damit dein Sohn mich wieder
  zieh' zu dir;
Dein Geist in meinem Herzen
  wohne
  Und meine Sinne und Verstand
  regier',
Dass ich den Frieden Gottes
  schmeck' und fühl'
Und dir darob im Herzen sing'
  und spiel'.

3.
Verleih mir, Höchster, solche
  Güte,
  So wird gewiss mein Singen
  recht getan,
So klingt es schön in meinem
  Liede,
  Und ich bet' dich im Geist und
  Wahrheit an,
So hebt dein Geist mein Herz zu
  dir empor,
Dass ich dir Psalmen sing' im
  höhern Chor.

4.
Denn der kann mich bei dir vertreten
  Mit Seufzern, die ganz unaus-
  sprechlich sind,

Der lehret mich recht gläubig beten,
  Gibt Zeugnis meinem Geist, dass
  ich dein Kind
Und ein Miterbe Jesu Christi sei,
Daher ich Abba, lieber Vater!
  schrei'.

5.
Wenn dies aus meinem Herzen
  schallet
  Durch deines heil'gen Geistes
  Kraft und Trieb,
So bricht dein Vaterherz und wal-
  let
  Ganz brünstig gegen mich vor
  heisser Lieb',
Dass mir's die Bitte nicht versagen
  kann,
Die ich nach deinem Willen hab'
  getan.

6.
Was mich dein Geist selbst bitten
  lehret,
  Das ist nach deinem Willen
  eingericht't
Und wird gewiss von dir erhöret,
  Weil es im Namen deines Sohns
  geschieht
Durch welchen ich dein Kind und
  Erbe bin
Und nehme von dir Gnad' um
  Gnade hin.

7.
Wohl mir, dass ich dies Zeugnis
  habe,
  Drum bin ich voller Trost und
  Freudigkeit,
Und weiss, dass alle gute Gabe,
  Die ich von dir verlanget je-
  derzeit,

Die gibst du und tust über-
schwenglich mehr,
Als ich verstehe, bitte und
begehr.

8.

Wohl mir, ich bitt in Jesu Namen,
Der mich zu deiner Rechten
selbst vertritt;

In ihm ist alles Ja und Amen,
Was ich von dir im Geist und
Glauben bitt.
Wohl mir, Lob dir jezt und in
Ewigkeit,
Dass du mir schenkest solche
Seligkeit!

A prayer for the spirit of grace rightly to praise and worship God, based on John 16:23-28. The hymn was first published in *Geistreiches Gesangbuch*, Halle, 1697, and appeared again in Freylinghausen's *Gesangbuch*, 1704.

Bartholomäus Crasselius, son of a cooper, was born in Wernsdorf, Saxony. He became an ardent disciple of A. H. Francke, leader of the Pietistic movement at Halle. Crasselius was an aggressive advocate of the new life. As Lutheran pastor at Nidda, and later at Düsseldorf, he was known for his unrestrained testimony against the people and the times. Crasselius was nearly always in conflict with the authorities and at one time was suspended four weeks from his office and punished with fines and imprisonment.

The translation, consisting of stanzas 1 and 2, is somewhat altered from Catherine Winkworth's as it appeared in her *Chorale Book for England*, 1863.

For comments on Catherine Winkworth see Hymn 236.

MUSIC. DIR, DIR JEHOVAH has been coupled with this text since its first publication in 1704 in Freylinghausen's *Gesangbuch*. It is an altered form of a melody set to "Wer nur den lieben Gott lässt walten," published in the *Musikalisches Handbuch*, Hamburg, 1690. The composer is not known. In England the tune was altered to fit the long meter hymn, "Ride on, ride on in majesty," and is called "Winchester New." See Hymn 369.

570. The Spirit of the Lord revealed George W. Briggs, 1875—

A hymn on the Scriptures, setting forth the truth that what the Spirit of God revealed dimly in the Old Testament was fulfilled in the New Testament by the Incarnate Word which is Jesus Christ. George W. Briggs wrote the hymn for *Songs of Praise*, London, 1931.

For comments on Briggs see Hymn 307.

MUSIC. AUS MEINES HERZENS GRUNDE, also known as "Wolder," is a traditional tune of anonymous origin. It is found in D. Wolder's *Neu Catechismus Gesangbüchlein*, Hamburg, 1588, but is doubtless much older than this book. In the *Gesangbuch mit Noten* the tune is set to the words, "Aus meines Herzens Grunde," by J. Matthesius, from which it derives its name.

571. He who would be in God confiding *Georg Neumark, 1621-81*

Tr. J. J. Voth

1.

Wer nur den lieben Gott lässt walten
Und hoffet auf ihn allezeit,
Den wird er wunderlich erhalten
In allem Kreuz und Traurigkeit.
Wer Gott, dem Allerhöchsten, traut,
Der hat auf keinen Sand gebaut.

2.

Was helfen uns die schweren Sorgen?
Was hilft uns unser Weh und Ach?
Was hilft es, dass wir alle Morgen
Beseufzen unser Ungemach?
Wir machen unser Kreuz und Leid
Nur grösser durch die Traurigkeit.

3.

Man halte nur ein wenig stille
Und sei nur in sich selbst vergnügt,
Wie unsers Gottes Gnadenwille,
Wie sein' Allwissenheit es fügt.
Gott, der uns sich hat auserwählt,
Der weiss auch gar wohl, was uns fehlt.

4.

Er kennt die rechten Freudenstunden,
Er weiss wohl, wann es nützlich sei.
Wenn er uns nur hat treu erfunden
Und merket keine Heuchelei,
So kommt Gott, eh' wir's uns versehn,
Und lässet uns viel Gut's geschehn.

5.

Denk nicht in deiner Drangsalshitze,
Dass du von Gott verlassen sei'st,
Und dass der Gott im Schosse sitze,
Der sich mit stetem Glücke speist.
Die Folgezeit verändert viel
Und setzet jeglichem sein Ziel.

6.

Es sind ja Gott sehr leichte Sachen
Und ist dem Höchsten alles gleich,
Den Reichen arm und klein zu machen,
Den Armen aber gross und reich.
Gott ist der rechte Wundermann,
Der bald erhöhn, bald stürzen kann.

7.

Sing, bet und geh auf Gottes Wege
Verricht das Deine nur getreu
Und trau des Himmels reichem Segen,
So wird er bei dir werden neu;
Denn welcher seine Zuversicht
Auf Gott setzt, den verlässt er nicht.

One of the most popular of the German hymns. The heading given it by the author was:

A Song of Comfort. God will care for and help every one in His own time. Cast thy burden on the Lord and He shall sustain thee. Psalm 55:22.

The hymn arose out of the author's personal need and suffering. On his way to Königsberg, to attend the University at that place, Neumark was robbed of his money and stripped of all his possessions except his prayer book and a small amount of cash which he had sewn into his clothing. He was therefore destitute and in despair, with no prospect of going to school or making a living. After many privations, he at last received an appointment as private tutor in the family of a judge at Kiel, "which good fortune, coming suddenly and as if fallen from heaven," he wrote, "greatly rejoiced me, and on that very day I composed to the honour of my beloved Lord the hymn, well known here and there, 'Wer nur der lieben Gott lässt walten,' and had certainly cause enough to thank the Divine compassion for such unlooked-for grace shown to me."

Neumark was now able to enter the University and became a student of law and poetry. After years of hardship, he finally had the good fortune of being appointed court poet, librarian, and registrar to Duke Wilhelm II of Saxe-Weimar, and custodian of the ducal archives. Shortly before his death in 1681 he became blind. The hymns he wrote during his prosperous years were markedly inferior to those written during his earlier years of hardship and privation.

The translation was made by Rev. J. J. Voth, North Newton, Kansas, then a member of the Bethel College staff, and pastor of the Gnadenberg Mennonite Church near Whitewater, Kansas. There is also a fine translation of this hymn, by Catherine Winkworth.

MUSIC. WER NUR DEN LIEBEN GOTT is wrongly attributed in the *Hymnary* to the author of the words. Neumark wrote an extraordinarily fine tune, in the minor mode, for these words, used in many collections, including the Canadian Mennonite *Gesangbuch,* 1942. The present tune is simpler and more popular than Neumark's. The composer is not known.

572. Our Lord, His passion ended   Francis C. Burkitt, 1864—

A hymn for Whitsuntide.

Francis Crawford Burkitt, born in London, is a scholar of wide repute in England, the author of many linguistic and theological works. He holds honorary degrees from the Universities of Edinburgh, Dublin, St. Andrews, and Oxford. Burkitt was, for many years, Professor of Divinity in Cambridge University.

The meter of the hymn is unique in that the second quatrain of each stanza changes from the common Iambic (- —) to the Trochaic (— -).

MUSIC. FORTEM VIRILI PECTORE, of unknown origin, has much of the character of a German folk tune. It appears in various editions of the *Catholisches Gesangbuch,* Strassburg, 1697 and onwards, set to a German version of the words, "Fortem virili pectore."

573. God who madest earth and heaven

Heinrich Albert, 1604-51
Trs. Johann C. Jacobi, 1670-1750
Arthur T. Russell, 1806-74
Catherine Winkworth, 1829-78

1.
Gott des Himmels und der Erden,
Vater, Sohn und Heil'ger Geist,
Der es Tag und Nacht lässt wer-
den,
Sonn' und Mond uns scheinen
heisst,
Dessen starke Hand die Welt
Und was drinnen ist, erhält.

2.
Gott, ich danke dir von Herzen,
Dass du mich in dieser Nacht
Vor Gefahr, Angst, Not und
Schmerzen
Hast behütet und bewacht,
Dass des bösen Feindes List
Mein nicht mächtig worden ist.

3.
Lass die Nacht auch meiner Sün-
den
Jetzt mit dieser Nacht vergehn!
O Herr Jesu, lass mich finden
Deine Wunden offen stehn,
Da alleine Hilf' und Rat
Ist für meine Missetat!

4.
Hilf, dass ich mit diesem Morgen
Geistlich auferstehen mag
Und für meine Seele sorgen,
Dass, wenn nun dein grosser
Tag
Uns erscheint und dein Gericht,
Ich davor erschrecke nicht.

5.
Führe mich, o Herr, und leite
Meinen Gang nach deinem
Wort!
Sei und bleibe du auch heute
Mein Beschützer und mein
Hort!
Nirgends als von dir allein
Kann ich recht bewahret sein.

6.
Meinen Leib und meine Seele
Samt den Sinnen und Verstand,
Grosser Gott, ich dir befehle
Unter deine starke Hand.
Herr, mein Schild, mein' Ehr' und
Ruhm,
Nimm mich auf, dein Eigentum!

7.
Deinen Engel zu mir sende,
Der des bösen Feindes Macht,
List und Anschläg von mir wende,
Und mich halt in guter Acht;
Der auch endlich mich zur Ruh
Trage nach dem Himmel zu.

8.
Da die Auserwählten alle
Dich, Gott Vater, Sohn und
Geist,
Loben mit fröhlichem Schalle,
Gott! der du Zebaoth heisst.
Heil'ger, heil'ger, heil'ger Herr!
Dir gebührt Lob, Preis und
Ehr'.

9.
Höre, Gott! was ich begehre;
Vater, Sohn und heil'ger Geist,
Meine Bitte mir gewähre,
Der du selbst mich bitten heisst;
So will ich dich hier und dort
Herzlich preisen fort und fort.

A morning hymn. Stanzas 2, 3, and 5 were special favorites in Germany, stanza 5 having been adopted by children, by brides, by old and young, as a morning prayer. Concerning this hymn, Dr. Cosack, a Königsberg writer, says:

> For two hundred years it is hardly likely that a single day has greeted the earth that has not, here and there, in German lands, been met with Albert's hymn. Hardly another morning hymn can be compared with it, as far as popularity and intrinsic value are concerned, if simplicity and devotion, purity of doctrine and adaptation to all the circumstances of life are to decide.

The author, Heinrich Albert, was the son of a tax collector at Lobenstein, Voigtland. He began the study of music under his uncle, Heinrich Schütz, Court Kapellmeister at Dresden, but abandoned it, at the desire of his parents, to become a lawyer. The profession of law had, however, little interest for him and he returned to his first love, accepting, in 1631, the position of organist of the Cathedral of Königsberg. Albert wrote several hundred secular and sacred poems and composed in all 78 sacred melodies. Most of the former were published in his *Etliche Arien.*

The hymn has been rendered into English by five or six eminent translators. Johann Christian Jacobi, a native of Germany who was Keeper of the Royal German Chapel, St. James Palace, London, for 42 years, made a translation of this hymn which he included in his *Divine Hymns,* 1720. Our second stanza, slightly altered, is the work of his hand.

Arthur Tozer Russell, an Anglican clergyman and prolific writer, translated many hymns and composed about 140 original hymns besides a large number of chants and hymn tunes. To him belongs the credit for our 3d stanza which is a translation of stanza 6 of the original. Russell's translations, on the whole, are "vigorous and strong, but somewhat ultra-faithful to the original metres."

Catherine Winkworth made a full translation of Albert's hymn for her *Lyra Germanica,* 1st Ser. 1855. Our first verse is taken from this work.

For comments on Miss Winkworth see Hymn 236.

MUSIC. GOTT DES HIMMELS UND DER ERDEN was composed by Albert, author of the words. The tune is known too by the names "Godesberg," and "Waltham." (See Hymn 370). J. S. Bach used the melody in his *Christmas Oratorio.*

574. Jesus, still lead on
Nicolaus L. von Zinzendorf, 1700-60
Tr. Jane L. Borthwick, 1813-97

1.

Jesu, geh voran
Auf der Lebensbahn,
Und wir wollen nicht verweilen,
Dir getreulich nachzueilen.
Führ uns an der Hand
Bis ins Vaterland!

2.

Soll's uns hart ergehn,
Lass uns feste stehn
Und auch in den schwersten
Tagen
Niemals über Lasten klagen;
Denn durch Trübsal hier
Geht der Weg zu dir.

3.

Rühret eigner Schmerz
Irgend unser Herz,
Kümmert uns ein fremdes
Leiden,
O so gib Geduld zu beiden;
Richte unsern Sinn
Auf das Ende hin!

4.

Ordne unsern Gang,
Jesu, lebenslang!
Führst du uns durch rauhe
Wege,
Gib uns auch die nöt'ge Pflege.
Tu uns nach dem Lauf
Deine Türe auf!

Entitled, "Following Christ." The hymn has become a great favorite in Germany, especially as a children's hymn. Stanzas 1, 3 and 4 are from Zinzendorf's "Seelenbräutigam, O du Gotteslamm," a poem of 11 stanzas, written September 1721. The second stanza is from "Glanz der Ewigkeit," a 15-stanza poem, dated Berlin, May 1721.

Nicolaus Ludwig, Graf von Zinzendorf, was born at Dresden of a noble, wealthy and religious family. Early in life he came under the teaching of influential Pietists, having Philipp Spener for his godfather and Augustus Francke for his tutor. From his earliest years he had strong religious impressions. As a child his favorite play was "preaching;" as a boy in school he organized the "Order of the Mustard Seed," the members of which bound themselves in a special manner to the service of Christ, and above all to promote the conversion of the heathen. Upon the insistence of non-pietistic relatives, he attended the University of Wittenberg to study law and to acquire such accomplishments as dancing, fencing, and shooting, but he himself would have preferred the study of theology.

At the age of 21, Zinzendorf bought an estate in Saxony with the view of gathering a number of truly religious persons into a community, which should be a source of new religious life. He invited a group of Moravian exiles, a religious body which sprang from the work of John Hus, to settle on the estate. Thus was formed, in 1722, the Moravian settlement which took the name Herrnhut, "Shelter of the Lord." The colony grew rapidly and attracted to its numbers not only immigrants from Moravia but many others. In 1727 Zinzendorf gave up his post as an official at the Court of the King of Saxony, to join the Moravian

373

colony and superintend the growing community. Accusing him of spreading false doctrines, his opponents secured an edict from the king, banishing Zinzendorf from Saxony. During this exile, which lasted 10 years, he was engaged in unceasing missionary efforts, from St. Petersburg to the West Indies.

In 1741, Zinzendorf came to America to visit the Moravians in Pennsylvania to organize them into congregations and encourage them to do missionary work among both whites and Indians. Under his leadership, the Moravians became a famous missionary group. As early as 1731, two of the Brethren were sent to the West Indies and two to Greenland. And in Zinzendorf's lifetime Moravians were at work in Europe, Asia, Africa, North and South America. In a few years, the little colony at Herrnhut had sent out more missionaries than had gone from all European Protestantism during two centuries. They went to the hardest and most dangerous places and the most unpromising peoples. Everywhere they were strengthened by the joyful, confident faith and loyalty to Christ expressed in Zinzendorf's hymn, "Jesu geh voran."

The Moravians had a powerful influence on hymnology. Zinzendorf himself, all the members of his family, and most of the early leaders wrote hymns. Singing was a prominent part of their worship and they early began publishing hymnbooks. Concerning Zinzendorf's hymns, Catehrine Winkworth says in her *Christian Singers of Germany:*

> His hymns, of which he wrote more than two thousand, are of exceedingly different value; some are fantastic and irreverent, some mere rhymed prose, others again have a real sweetness, fervour, and song in them.

She cites "Jesu geh voran" as one of his best hymns.

For comments on the translator, Jane Borthwick, see Hymn 54.

MUSIC. SEELENBRÄUTIGAM is a tune of a "pleasingly ingenious tinge, very simply constructed." It is found in many English hymnbooks.

The composer, Adam Drese, 1620-1701, was born in Thuringia. He became director of music at the Court of Count Wilhelm IV of Saxe-Weimar; then was appointed kapellmeister in Weimar, and later at Arnstadt, living meanwhile a life of selfish indulgence in the atmosphere of the courts. Upon reading the works of Spener and Luther's *Introduction to the Epistle to the Romans,* Drese experienced a spiritual awakening which led him to aggressive missionary efforts and the organization of prayer meetings in the community. He wrote hymns and tunes which were sung at the meetings of pious persons in his house, before they came into print.

The tune was first published in the *Hasselesches Gesangbuch,* 1695, but it was used in manuscript form as early as 1690, in the composer's home.

374

BOOK V

Metrical Psalms

575. That man hath perfect blessedness   *Psalm I*
                                        Scottish Psalter, 1650

Psalm 1. The Tree and the Chaff.

The psalm embodies a fundamental teaching of the Old Testament, namely, that true happiness is to be found only in knowing and serving God.

MUSIC. DUNFERMLINE is a Scottish tune of unknown origin. The name is that of a town in Scotland. It appeared as one of the twelve "Common Tunes" (tunes not attached to any particular psalms) in *The CL Psalms of David, &*, Edinburgh, 1615. In England the tune was included in Ravencroft's *Whole Book of Psalms*, 1621.

Note on the Scottish Psalter, 1650

The origin of the *Scottish Psalter, 1650*, which is the source of nearly all the metrical psalms in Book Five of the *Hymnary*, may be briefly summarized as follows:

The church in Scotland, at the time of the Reformation, modeled its service after Calvin's in Geneva. No hymns were permitted to be sung; only the words of inspired Scripture were allowed for use in worship. For two hundred years after Luther had inspired a rich treasury of "man-made" poems for use in congregational singing, the Calvinistic churches were still using only psalms and paraphrases of Scripture.

In compiling a Psalter, the Scottish reformers adopted the entire *Anglo-Genevan Psalter* used by John Knox, to which they added selections from the English *Old Version* by Sternhold and Hopkins, and 21 more by Scottish writers. Tunes, over 100 in all, were adopted from the Anglo-Genevan, French, and English Psalters, in each case the melody only being printed. In 1635 an edition was published with the tunes in harmony, the work of Edmund Millar.

In 1643, the House of Commons and the Westminster Assembly, interested in establishing uniformity of worship between the churches of England and Scotland, voted to adopt Francis Rous' version of the psalms for use throughout the kingdom, after extensive revisions of the work. The Scottish church, not satisfied with the Rous' version, appointed a commission of four men to revise it still farther, largely to satisfy the Puritan demand for more literalness to the Hebrew original. The result of this revision was the classic *Scottish Psalter* of 1650, still in use in Scottish Presbyterianism and in American Covenanter Churches. The renderings are quaint and rude in spots but their faithfulness and vigor cannot be denied. It is in this form that millions of people have learned to love the psalms and all attempts to improve or moderinize them have so far failed.

Unfortunately, no tunes were provided with the *Scottish Psalter* of 1650. This limited the singing to such tunes as precentor and people knew by heart, resulting in a long period of decline in church music in the Church of Scotland. Later editions corrected this defect. In 1929, the General Assemblies of the Church of Scotland and the United Free Church of Scotland, then entered into union, published a new edition of the *Scottish Psalter,* with 192 tunes.

576. Lord, Thou shalt early hear my voice

Psalm V
Scottish Psalter, 1650

Psalm 5:3, 4, 7, 11. A Prayer for Divine Aid.

A morning prayer in which the Psalmist confidently looks to God, assured of an answer. He shows a deep concern for ethical purity and sincerity in worship.

MUSIC. For comments on WARWICK see Hymn 20.

577. Within Thy tabernacle, Lord

Psalm XV
Scottish Psalter, 1650

Psalm 15. The Friend of God.

The psalm speaks of the type of life that brings man into the Divine Presence and makes of him a good citizen.

MUSIC. TALLIS' ORDINAL. For comments on this tune see Hymn 326.

578. God's law is perfect, and converts

Psalm XIX
Scottish Psalter, 1650

Psalm 19:7-11. God's Praise in the Moral Universe.

The psalm describes God's revelation to man. God is revealed to us

376

"in the starry heavens above and in the moral law within," (to use the phrase of Immanuel Kant). The hymn, composed of verses 7-11, deals only with the latter, the law in the heart.

MUSIC. ST. ANDREW appeared in *The New Harmony of Sion* by William Tans'ur, in 1764, where it was set to Psalm 150, and inscribed "Barby Tune, composed in four parts, W.T." The initials may mean only that the harmony was by Tans'ur.

For comments on William Tans'ur see Hymn 74.

579. The Lord's my Shepherd, I'll not want
Psalm XXIII
Scottish Psalter, 1650

Psalm 23. The Good Shepherd Psalm. It has probably been translated and paraphrased more frequently than any other piece of literature in the world, yet always carries the same joyous and sure faith in the Good Shepherd. A version by James Montgomery is found at No. 62.

MUSIC. MARTYRDOM. For comments on this tune see Hymn 108.

580. Ye gates, lift up your heads on high
Psalm XXIV
Scottish Psalter, 1650

Psalm 24:7-10. A Marching Chorus and Triumphant Song of Victory.

The procession escorting the ark, symbol of God's presence, has now reached the city gates and Jerusalem is called upon to open wide its gates to its true King. "Raise up your arches, O gates, and open wide your ancient doors, that the King of Glory may enter in." The full glory of God can come into our lives only as we enlarge the receiving facilities of our hearts and minds.

MUSIC. ST. GEORGE'S, EDINBURGH was composed especially for these words by Dr. Andrew Thomson, minister of the church by the above name in Edinburgh. It became the custom in many places in Scotland for the congregation to sing this psalm at Communion while ministers and elders in solemn procession brought the bread and wine into the church before the administration of the sacrament.

Andrew Thomson, 1778-1831, trained in the University of Edinburgh, was an outstanding Scottish Presbyterian preacher and leading public figure in Edinburgh. He had musical gifts and set himself to improve the psalmody of his church and composed a number of tunes. In collaboration with his precentor, R. A. Smith, he compiled several collections of psalms and hymns. He also published books of sermons and lectures and wrote numerous magazine articles. Thomson died suddenly within a few steps of his own door when returning from a

377

Presbytery meeting. His son became professor of music in the University of Edinburgh.

581. Show me thy ways, O Lord

Psalm XXV
Scottish Psalter, 1650

Psalm 25:4-7. A Prayer to God for Guidance and Forgiveness.

MUSIC. ST. BRIDE appeared in *Parochial Harmony; consisting of a collection of Psalm tunes in three and four parts, &,* by William Riley, 1762, where it was set to the new version of Psalm 130 and headed "St. Bridget's Tune by Mr. Sam'l Howard." The tune is in strict psalm-tune style and therefore simple in structure. But it has strength and high quality and is deserving of its wide and continuous use.

Samuel Howard, 1710-82, London musician, was organist of St. Clement Danes and of St. Bride's churches. He was a popular composer of both sacred and secular music.

582. The Lord's my light and saving health

Psalm XXVII
Scottish Psalter, 1650

Psalm 27:1-5. A Song of Assurance.

These verses reflect a confidence that knows no fear in the midst of danger, because of God's protecting care.

MUSIC. ST. MAGNUS, also called "Nottingham," is a "good solid melody, built on familiar lines." It appeared, anonymously, in 1709 in a book called *The Divine Companion: or David's Harp new tuned. Being a choice collection of New and Easy Psalms, Hymns and Anthems.* In 1762 the tune, bearing its present name and assigned to Jeremiah Clark, appeared in W. Riley's *Parochial Harmony.* In Gawthorn's *Harmonia Perfecta,* 1730, it is named "Nottingham."

The composer, Jeremiah Clark, 1670-1707, a Londoner of keen sensibility and gifted musicianship, wrote operatic music, a cantata, numerous songs, and church music—anthems and psalm tunes. In a mood of despondency he took his own life.

583. Through all the changing scenes of life

Psalm XXXIV
New Version, Tate and Brady, 1698

Psalm 34:1-10, 22. The Goodness of God.

A hymn of praise to God for his care and protection in time of great need.

Most of our metrical psalms in the *Hymnary* are from the *Scottish Psalter,* 1650. (See under Hymn 575.) But this one is from the revised edition of 1698, of the *New Version of the Psalms* first published in

378

England in 1696, by the two Irishmen, Tate and Brady. This version partly supplanted in England the older version of Sternhold and Hopkins.

Nahum Tate, 1652-1715, son of an Irish clergyman, was a literary man, playwright, and a poet. Finally, to the surprise of everyone, he became poet laureate, by appointment of William III.

Nicholas Brady, 1659-1726?, received the degree of D.D. from Dublin University and had a varied clerical career in Ireland and England, finally becoming chaplain to King William. Brady and Tate collaborated to produce the *New Version,* a work which received royal endorsement and was officially adopted in England. Though better in smoothness and literary grace than the versions of Sternhold and Hopkins, very little of it remains in modern hymnals. This hymn and "As pants the hart," (586), are among the gems still in use. "While shepherds watched their flocks by night" (73 and 74) a masterly adaptation of the Nativity story, appeared in the supplement of the *New Version,* 1703, and is found today in nearly all hymnals.

MUSIC. WILTSHIRE, known in Scotland as "New St. Ann," appeared first in *Divine Amusement,* by Sir G. Grant, set to Psalm 48. The tune appears with variants in other collections.

The composer, George Thomas Smart, 1776-1867, was an organist and composer and a popular conductor of choral groups in London. He gave lessons in singing and harpsichord and composed anthems, chants and psalm tunes.

584. O children, hither do ye come

Psalm XXXIV
Scottish Psalter, 1650

Psalm 34:11-19. The Goodness of God.

The psalmist here becomes a teacher, instructing his listeners in the right paths of life.

MUSIC. ARNOLD was first published in *The Psalms of David for the Use of Parish Churches. The Music celected, adapted, and composed by Dr. Arnold . . . assisted by J. W. Callcott,"* 1791. The tune was set to Psalm 15, arranged so that the first two lines should be sung as a duet by soprano and alto, repeated as a duet by tenor and bass, and then the third and fourth lines sung in full chorus. The present form of the tune is first found in Scotland in Robert Gilmore's *Psalm Singers Assistant* (undated, but before 1793).

Samuel Arnold, 1740-1802, after ventures and heavy losses in the theater business, received the degree of Mus. Doc. from Oxford and then became organist and composer to the Royal Chapel. Later he became conductor at the Academy of Ancient Music, and in 1789 was appointed organist of Westminster Abbey. He wrote numerous songs, four oratorios and many anthems and edited important musical works, including *The Works of Handel,* in thirty-six volumes, at the request of King George III.

585. I waited for the Lord my God
Psalm XL
Scottish Psalter, 1650

Psalm 40:1-5. A Prayer for Speedy Relief from Trouble.

After long and patient waiting, the psalmist's prayer for relief from trouble has been answered, giving occasion for fresh thanksgiving for His mercy.

MUSIC. BALLERMA. For comments on this tune see Hymn 57.

Robert Simpson, 1790-1832, who adapted this tune from a melody by F. H. Barthélemon (See Hymn 57) was a weaver by trade, but of good education and fine musical taste. He was choir-leader in a Congregational Church in Glasgow, then became precentor and session-clerk of the East Parish church at Greenock, at a salary of forty pounds a year, and from that time onward made music his profession. Of weak constitution, he fell victim of one of the cholera epidemics.

586. As pants the hart for cooling streams
Psalm XLII
New Version, Tate and Brady, 1698

Psalm 42:1, 2, 5, 9, 11. Exiled from the House of God.

The psalmist, alone among taunting heathen strangers, yearns to return to the place of worship where he may again commune with God. His faith is sorely tried but it does not fail him. He recalls the mercy of God and renews his hope in God.

For comments on *New Version,* Tate and Brady, see Hymn 583.

MUSIC. SPOHR is an adaptation from the solo and chorus, "Though all thy friends forsake thee," in *Calvary,* an oratorio by Spohr.

Ludwig Spohr, 1784-1859, a German musician, born at Brunswick, was a composer and noted violinist. He went annually on concert tours throughout Europe, with brilliant success. Few musicians have enjoyed so high a reputation with their contemporaries. Many musicians of his time considered Spohr a greater composer than Beethoven. His reputation, however, did not stand the test of time, partly because his compositions are characterized by a peculiar chromaticism. Most of his numerous works, including operas, oratorios, 34 string quartets, violin concertos, etc., have been forgotten. His oratorios, *Calvary* and *The Last Judgment,* lasted longest.

The tune, "St. Anne," now fittingly sung to "O God our help in ages past," (No. 61), was composed for this psalm, and may be used as an alternative tune. The Psalm has also been set to "Martyrdom" (579).

587. O send Thy light forth and Thy truth   *Psalm XLIII*
Scottish Psalter, 1650

Psalm 43:3-5. Exiled from the House of God (continued).

Psalm 43 is clearly a continuation of Psalm 42. The same spirit, language and situation are to be found in both and each ends with the same refrain. Psalm 42 speaks of God as a fountain of living water; Psalm 43, as a guiding light. These vivid metaphors are combined in Psalm 36:9: "For with Thee is the fountain of life; in Thy light do we see light."

MUSIC. FARRANT is adapted from an air in the anthem, "Lord, for thy tender mercies' sake." usually attributed to the English organist and composer, Richard Farrant, c. 1530-1580, but by some to John Hilton, and by others to William Mundy.

588. God is our refuge and our strength   *Psalm XLVI*
Scottish Psalter, 1650

Psalm 46:1-5. The Mighty God.

Psalm 46 has been a source of strength in time of dire distress, sustaining the spirit of the persecuted and dying, in all ages.

One should compare this version from the *Scottish Psalter* with that of Isaac Watts (No. 257), and of Martin Luther in his classic hymn of the Reformation, "Ein feste Burg ist unser Gott" (No. 549).

MUSIC. WINCHESTER OLD is from *Este's Psalter* which was entitled *"The Whole Booke of Psalmes with their wonted Tunes, as they are song in churches, composed into foure parts .... compiled by sondry authors,* London, Thomas Este, 1592, where it is set to Psalm 84.

Thomas Este, 1540?-1608?, was a London printer and music publisher. He printed an important edition of the psalter in 1592 in which the tunes were harmonized in four parts by ten eminent musicians of the time. In his dedicatory word Este wrote: "In this booke the Church Tunes are carefully corrected, and other short tunes added, which are sung in London and other places of this Realme." The Church Tunes (known also as Proper Tunes), forty-six in all, were attached to their proper psalms and the remaining psalms were set to short, four line tunes, Common Tunes, not attached to any particular psalms. Este's book is the earliest example in which the voice parts are printed on opposite pages—"Cantus and Tenor (i.e. the Melody) on the left-hand page, and the Altus and Bassus on the right"—instead of in separate books as was then the custom. New editions of *Este's Psalter,* with slight changes, were published in 1594, 1604, and 1611. In the 19th century it had the honor of being reprinted by the Musical Antiquarian Society of England.

589. After thy loving-kindness, Lord

Psalm LI
Scottish Psalter, 1650

Psalm 51:1-3, 10, 17. A Prayer for Pardon.

The psalmist prays for pardon and cleansing, confessing the greatness of his sins, and offering the sacrifice of a broken heart. Psalm 51 is the fourth of the seven psalms known from ancient times as the Penitential Psalms. The others are 6, 32, 38, 102, 130, and 143.

MUSIC. DUNDEE, also known as "Windsor," is first found in Damon's *Psalter,* which was entitled, *The Booke of the Musicke of M. William Damon, late one of her maiestes Musitions: conteining all the tunes of David's Psalmes, as they are ordinarily sung in the Church; most excellently by him composed into 4 parts,* 1591. The tune, DUNDEE, is there set to Psalm 116.

Damon's *Psalter* was one of the many private editions through which the *Old Version* of Sternhold and Hopkins went, besides numerous official editions. William Damon, c.1540-c.91, was organist of the Chapel Royal under Queen Elizabeth but is best known for the collection of psalms which he published in four parts. The work is in eight books, the first four of which have the melody in the tenor, and the second four in the soprano. Copies of Damon's *Psalter* are rare. A few are to be found in the British Museum.

590. Praise waits for Thee in Zion, Lord

Psalm LXV
Scottish Psalter, 1650

Psalm 65:1-4. A Liturgy.

A hymn of praise and thanksgiving to God for an exceptionally abundant harvest.

MUSIC. ST. STEPHEN (ABRIDGE).

For comments on this tune see Hymn 266.

591. His name forever shall endure

Psalm LXXII
Scottish Psalter, 1650

Psalm 72:17-19. A Description of the Ideal King.

A universal hymn of praise.

MUSIC. For comments on the tune, DUNFERMLINE, see Hymn 575.

592. How lovely are Thy dwellings fair

Psalm LXXXIV
John Milton, 1608-74

Psalm 84:1-7, 12. The Joy of the Godly.

One of the Songs of the Sanctuary, expressing the joy and happiness of the pilgrim who, coming from afar, has at last arrived at the sanctuary of his God at Jerusalem. The vale of Baca (v. 6), a waterless, barren valley through which he passed on the journey to Jerusalem, became, to the devoted pilgrim, a place of springs and refreshment.

The version here is by John Milton and constitutes an improvement over that in the *Scottish Psalter*.

For comments on Milton see Hymn 64.

MUSIC. SALZBURG. For comments on this tune by J. Haydn see Hymn 167. A different tune by J. Hintze bears the same name (No. 545).

593. The Lord doth reign, and clothed is He

Psalm XCIII
Scottish Psalter, 1650

Psalm 93. The Ruler of the Universe.

A Song of Thanksgiving in which the psalmist celebrates God's sovereignty, not only over Israel, but over the whole world.

MUSIC. IRISH. For comments on this tune see Hymn 268.

594. All people that on earth do dwell

Psalm C
William Kethe, c. 1561
Scottish Psalter, 1650

Psalm 100. The Faithful God.

The Psalm was used as a processional hymn to be chanted by the people as they went up to the temple for worship.

Sclater, in *The Public Worship of God,* discussing opening hymns of adoration, says: "There is none better than that grand old Puritan anthem, the 100th Psalm, set to Louis Bourgeois' noble tune," and adds that "those who are in perplexity to find hymns which precisely fit into various parts of the service might do a great deal worse than take a look at the Scottish Metrical Psalms. They will find them peculiarly rich in the noblest and simplest form of opening adoration."

In verse 4 the printer has omitted the question mark (?) after the word "why," in the early editions of the *Hymnary.*

William Kethe, to whom this version is ascribed, was one of the exiles with John Knox in Geneva during the persecutions of Mary, Queen of the Scots. Little is known of him but his name has been immortalized by this justly renowned paraphrase of Psalm 100.

MUSIC. OLD HUNDREDTH is the most famous of all Psalm tunes. It was adapted from a secular source by L. Bourgeois for Psalm 134 in the *Genevan Psalter* of 1551. In later collections—the Genevan *Fourscore and Seven Psalms of David,* and John Day's *Whole Book of Psalms,* both published in 1561—the tune was attached to Kethe's version of Psalm

100 and has remained associated with this Psalm ever since. The tune is one of 46 known as "Proper" or "Church" tunes which are distinguished by the adjective "Old" prefixed to the number of the psalm to which they were attached. A later form of the melody, introduced about the middle of the 18th century, is widely used with the "Doxology" (No. 618).

For comments on Louis Bourgeois see Hymn 34.

595. Thou shalt arise, and mercy yet
Psalm CII
Scottish Psalter, 1650

Psalm 102:13-22. The Everlasting God.

One of the Penitential Psalms. (See under Hymn 589.)

Zion is in ruins and her people in exile, but God, who is unchangeable, will yet fulfill His promises to His people and make Jerusalem the center of a world-wide worship.

MUSIC. DUKE STREET. For comments on this tune see Hymn 341.

596. O thou my soul, bless God the Lord
Psalm CIII
Scottish Psalter, 1650

Psalm 103:1-5. The Goodness of God.

The psalm sets forth with exquisite beauty and tenderness the enduring goodness and mercy of God. It is a song of thanksgiving to God for his many benefits and blessings.

It was the custom in Scotland to sing the opening verses of this psalm as a song of thanksgiving and praise after the communicants had received the bread and wine of the Lord's Supper. The people poured evangelical content into the words, thinking as they sang, of the great redemption through Jesus Christ: "who doth redeem thy life, etc."

MUSIC. ST. PAUL. The origin of this tune is unknown. It appeared first in *A Collection of Twenty Church Tunes,* 1749, published by James Chalmers, c. 1700-64, Aberdeen, Scotland, who was printer to the Town Council and publisher of *The Aberdeen Journal.* Only one copy of this small book is known to survive.

597. I love the Lord, because my voice
Psalm CXVI
Scottish Psalter, 1650

Psalm 116:1-7. Votive Song of the Worshipper.

A Song of Thanksgiving to God for favors received and an expression of triumphant faith in the Helper of the poor and needy.

MUSIC. ST. ANDREW. For comments on this tune see Hymn 578.

384

598. Unto the hills around do I lift up

Psalm CXXI
John Campbell, 1845-1914

Psalm 121. The Guardian God.

A splendid picture of the fatherly goodness of God and His watchful Providence over His people.

The version is by John Campbell, Duke of Argyll, who married Princess Louise, the daughter of Queen Victoria. At one time he was the Governor-General of Canada and Commander-in-Chief of Prince Edward Island. He was keeper of the seal of Scotland. Though engaged in many and varied activities, he was an earnest Christian and found pleasure in the study of the Psalms and in making them available for use in Christian worship.

MUSIC. SANDON. For comments on this tune see Hymn 163.

599. I joyed when to the house of God

Psalm CXXII
Scottish Psalter, 1650

Psalm 122. A Prayer for Jerusalem.

A song of the pilgrims who, having arrived at the gates of Jerusalem, are filled with admiration for the Holy City. They are moved at its beauty and strength, recall its past stories, and pray for its peace and welfare.

In the church of Scotland it has been the traditional practice to sing verses 3, 4, and 5 of this hymn immediately before the Benediction which closes the General Assembly. Sung to the stately tune of "St. Paul," it leaves an indelible impression on the mind.

MUSIC. ST. PAUL. For comments on this tune see Hymn 596.

600. O Lord, Thou art my God and King

Psalm CXLV
Scottish Psalter, 1650

Psalm 145:1-7. A Festal Anthem.

A praise song celebrating the greatness and goodness of God as manifested in all creation. The praise of God and of His marvelous works shall go on forever. The psalm has been called the *Te Deum* of the Old Testament and this version is worthy of its original.

MUSIC. DUKE STREET. For comments on this tune see Hymn 341.

BOOK VI

Responses

601. Holy, holy, holy, Lord God of hosts

Known as the *Ter Sanctus* or *Trisagion*. It is an anonymous 2d century reproduction of a Jewish synagogue "Doxology," based on Isaiah 6:3:

> And one cried unto another, and said, Holy, holy, holy is the Lord of hosts: the whole earth is full of the glory of God.

It is intended to be sung at the beginning of a worship service.

MUSIC. SANCTUS. The composer of the tune, Alexander Samuel Cooper, was born in London in 1835. The date of his death is not known. He was an organist and composer of anthems, chants, and hymn tunes, and edited *The Parochial Psalter* and *The Parochial Chant Book*, both of which have passed through numerous editions.

602. Holy, holy, holy, Lord God of hosts

For comments on the words see No. 601.

MUSIC. SANCTUS. No information has been found concerning W. A. C. Cruickshank, composer of the tune.

603. The Lord is in His holy temple   *Habakkuk 2:20*

An "Opening Response" or "Invocation Sentence" widely used to introduce services of worship. The words are taken from Habakkuk 2:20.

QUAM DILECTA. For comments on George F. Root, the composer of this tune, see Hymn 418.

387

604. Hear our prayer, O Lord

A response to be sung by choir or congregation or both after public prayer.

George Whelpton, 1847-1930, composer of the tune, was born at Redbourne, England, but came to America with his parents when he was a child of four years. He studied music under H. R. Palmer and with a private teacher in Boston. He became a well-known choir director in Buffalo and served as editor of various publications. He died suddenly at Oxford, Ohio.

605. Thy word have I hid in my heart

A response suitable for use in connection with the reading of the Scriptures. The words are taken from Psalms 119:11, 12.

No biographical information regarding the composer, E. D. Beale, has been ascertained.

606. Gloria Patri

An ancient canticle which is used in the service to give a trinitarian form to Old Testament unitarianism.

The first part, "Glory to the Father, and to the Son, and to the Holy Ghost," was used very early in the apostolic era of the church, as the common doxology. The second part, "As it was in the beginning, is now, and ever shall be, world without end," was added by the Western Church during the second and third centuries when the Arian controversy raised the question as to whether the God of the Old Testament is the same as the God manifested in Christ in the New Testament. The answer, incorporated in the song, was an affirmative. It was always sung after the Psalms to give them a New Testament or Trinitarian ending. This is still the chief use of the Gloria Patri, though it is attached sometimes to some other part of the service. Concerning this point, Dr. Henry Sloan Coffin says: "In view of the origin of the Gloria Patri and its long historical association with the Psalms, it is vandalism to tear it from its proper context, and attach it to something else in the service." (The Public Worship of God, Westminster Press, p. 101).

MUSIC. For comments on Henry Greatorex see Hymn 230.

607. Gloria Patri

For comments on the words see No. 606.

MUSIC. The tune was composed by Charles Meineke, 1782-1850, a German pianist and organist who came to America in 1810. For a time he was organist at St. Paul's Church, Baltimore.

608. Let the words of my mouth

From Psalm 19:14.

Prayer, "uttered or unexpressed," is a spiritual sacrifice. The sentence is used in the Jewish liturgy at the close of silent worship. If sung in a quiet mood, the response is suitable for use by soloist, choir, or congregation, before or after pastoral prayer of the worship service.

MUSIC. The music was composed by Adolph Baumbach, 1830-80, teacher of piano and organ and composer of instrumental and choir music. Baumbach was born in Germany about 1830, came to America in 1855, and lived in Boston and Chicago.

609. Father, O hear us

Anonymous.

Suitable for use as a response after prayer, or before a prayer of special petition, as in the case of Elijah in I Kings 18:37: "hear me, O Lord, hear me, that this people may know that thou art the Lord God."

MUSIC. The tune is attributed to Handel but the work from which it is taken has not been identified.

For comments on George Frederick Handel see Hymn 73.

THE LORD'S PRAYER

610. Our Father, who art in heaven

The Lord's Prayer, as found in Matthew 6:9-13.

The prayer which Christ taught the disciples is in its comprehensiveness a pattern of prayer and may well be used in the prayers of the church.

MUSIC. The musical setting is from a Gregorian Chant. In singing it, the following general directions for chanting may be found useful:

1. Chants consist of two distinct divisions, one portion is recited, the other portion is sung.

2. The words from the beginning of each line up to the accented word, which is printed in italics, are called the Recitation, and should be sung smoothly, without undue haste, and observing stops (,) as in good reading. The Recitation may be of any length. The note on which it is sung is called the Reciting note.

3. On reaching the accented word and beginning with it, sing in strict time. If there is no syllable after that which is accented, as, for example, in "Thy Kingdom *come,*" the accented syllable is held for the time value of one whole measure.

611. Bless Thou the gifts our hands have brought

Samuel Longfellow, 1819-92

An offertory hymn to be sung by the choir or congregation or both.

For comments on the author, Samuel Longfellow, see Hymn 28.

Concerning the place of the collection in the worship service, Henry Sloan Coffin says in his excellent book on public worship:

> Whether the collection be made in the middle of the service or near its conclusion, it should be an act of worship. The gifts of the people should be carried up to the holy table, and received and placed upon it by the minister. While they are brought up, the congregation may stand and sing a dedication, "All things come of Thee, O Lord, and of thine own have we given Thee," or a similar sentence. This may be varied by using Ken's familiar doxology, or a verse from an appropriate hymn, such as Bishop How's "We give Thee but Thine own." When the Offering is for a cause—missions or a hospital or the Bible Society—a stanza from a hymn which fits the purpose may be selected for use as the dedication and be printed on the order of worship in the calendar. A minister may use a prayer in the act of dedication, but it is difficult to find variety in its expression, and the prayer should usually be comprised in a short sentence. Congregations are helped to realize that in this act they are the offerers if they join the choir in singing the dedication. *(The Public Worship of God,* Westminster Press, 1946.) Quoted by permission.

CANONBURY. For comments on this tune see Hymn 296.

612. All things come of Thee, O Lord

From 1 Chron. 29:14.

This is one of the mostly widely used offertory responses, usually sung by a congregation during the consecration of the offering.

The setting of the words is significant in its conception of the spirit of sacrifice and worship. David was assembling the material with which Solomon might build the temple. The people and leaders brought their gifts, all voluntarily, with no mention of a tithe or temple tax. Gratitude for what God had done for them stirred their generosity and they counted it a privilege to give back to God what came to them from His hand.

MUSIC. The tune is an arrangement from Beethoven. The work from which it comes has not been identified.

For comments on Ludwig van Beethoven see Hymn 10.

613. May the grace of Christ our Savior

John Newton, 1725-1807

A metrical version of the apostolic benediction in II Cor. 13:14: "The grace of the Lord Jesus Christ, and the love of God, and the communion of the Holy Spirit, be with you all." The hymn has been translated into several languages. For more than 100 years the weekly meeting of the Presbyterian ministers in New York City closed with the singing of these words.

MUSIC. DORRNANCE first appeared in *The Choral*, 1845, by Isaac B. Woodbury and Benj. F. Baker.

For comments on the composer, Isaac B. Woodbury, see Hymn 261.

614. The Lord bless you and keep you

From the Authorized Version of the Aaronic blessing in Numbers 6:24-26, with order of verses 25 and 26 reversed.

MUSIC. The musical setting, the original of which has an elaborate contrapuntal and sevenfold "Amen," not suitable for congregational use, was written as a farewell to William Smedley, choirmaster at the St. James Protestant Episcopal Church, Chicago. Without Smedley's knowledge the congregation, all kneeling, sang this with great effect, after the benediction, at the service of farewell.

For comments on Peter C. Lutkin see Hymn 390.

DOXOLOGIES

615. Now to the King of heav'n

Isaac Watts, 1674-1748
and Philip Doddridge, 1702-51

This doxology, according to James Moffatt, is made up of lines from a hymn by Doddridge and Watt's paraphrase of Psalm 148.

MUSIC. ST. JOHN. There seems to be no information concerning the composer or source of this tune. It has been traced to the third volume of *The Parish Choir*, 1851, where it appears anonymously. It should be sung with vigor.

616. To God the only wise

Isaac Watts, 1674-1748

A paraphrase of the doxology found in Jude vv. 24, 25.
For comments on Isaac Watts see Hymnal 11.

MUSIC. OLD 134TH (ST. MICHAEL) is one of the greatest of short meter tunes, derived from the tune composed by L. Bourgeois for Psalm 101 in the *Genevan Psalter* of 1551. It has been set to a number of

391

other psalms and hymns and appears at Hymn 128 set to "Ye servants of the Lord" by Doddridge.

For comments on Louis Bourgeois see Hymn 34.

617. Now to Him who loved us, gave us

Samuel Miller Waring, 1792-1827

From the author's *Sacred Melodies,* 1826, where it was followed by a second verse.

Samuel Miller Waring, an Englishman, was brought up in the Society of Friends but left it to unite with the Church of England. He published *Sacred Melodies* in 1826, in which his hymns appear.

MUSIC. TRIUMPH appeared first in *The Church Hymn and Tune Book,* 1852, edited by W. J. Blew and H. J. Gauntlett.

For comments on the composer, Henry J. Gauntlett, see Hymn 412.

618. Praise God from whom all blessings flow

Thomas Ken, 1637-1711

The most famous of all doxologies and the most frequently sung of all hymn stanzas.

Bishop Ken wrote three hymns, for morning, evening, and midnight, (See Nos. 25 and 33), ending each with this stanza. The words are simple enough so a child can sing them with understanding, yet they are so profound that the wisest and most prudent cannot exhaust their meaning.

For comments on Thomas Ken see Hymn 25.

MUSIC. OLD HUNDREDTH. The original form of this tune is found at No. 594.

For comments on Louis Bourgeois see Hymn 34.

AMENS

619. Dresden Amen

A cadence, or ending, much used in ecclesiastical music in the Royal Chapel of Dresden (common also throughout Saxony). Wagner immortalized it in his *Parsifal* and the tune also appears in Mendelssohn's *Reformation Symphony,* Stanford's *Service in B flat,* and elsewhere.

The composer, Johann Gottlieb Naumann (or Giovanni Amadeo), 1741-1801, well-known musician in his day, was born at Blasewitz, near Dresden, the son of peasant parents. He was a successful opera composer in Saxony, Italy, Sweden, and Prussia. Naumann was also a prolific composer of church music: 13 oratorios, 21 masses with *Te Deums,* and smaller church pieces. Some of his compositions are still in use. His best known single work known beyond Dresden is his setting of Klopstock's *Vater unser*.

620. Threefold Amen

The tune is from an unknown Danish source and has wide use in the Lutheran churches of Denmark.

621. Amen Sequence

An effective piece for women's voices, of unknown origin.

622. Fourfold Amen

For comments on the composer, John Stainer, see Hymn 111.

623. Sevenfold Amen

First appeared in *A Choir-book for the Office of Holy Communion,* 1873, edited by Stainer.

For comments on John Stainer see Hymn 111.

NOTE ON THE USE OF "AMEN"

In the Jewish and early Christian Church, the people said "Amen" after prayers were offered. Cf. I Cor. 14:16. In so doing, they gave a deliberate endorsement to what had been said or sung. The "Amen," meaning "so be it," should be sung with conviction, not thoughtlessly or half-heartedly, as if what went before is of doubtful importance.

The settings given here are principally for use by the choir after the pastoral prayer or at the close of a service, in churches where such musical elaboration is practiced.

The use of "Amen" after a hymn is optional. If sung well, it serves as a satisfying concluding formula. Its use is entirely appropriate only with those hymns which are prayer, praise, or otherwise addressed to God.

The first instance of its use at the end of a hymn is in a curious hymn book entitled, *Seven Sobs of a Sorrowful Soul for Sinne,* published in England in 1583. During the last century most editors of hymnals have adopted the custom of adding the "Amen" to all hymns. The *Songs of Praise,* published in England in 1933, is a notable exception.

PRINCIPAL WORKS CONSULTED

General

Benson, Louis F., *Studies of Familiar Hymns*. Series I and II.
Westminster Press, 1903 and 1923.
An authoritative study. One of the best

Breed, David R., *The History and Use of Hymns and Hymn-Tunes*.
Revell, 1903.
Useful but somewhat out of date, especially in its classification of hymns.

Brown, Theron, and Butterworth, Hezekiah., *The Story of the Hymns and Tunes*.
American Tract Society, 1906.
Based on Butterworth's *Story of the Hymns and Story of the Tunes*, with much added material.

Gillman, Frederick John, *The Evolution of the English Hymn*.
Macmillan, 1927.
Well written. Resembles Horder's *Hymn Lover* but brings the material more nearly up to date.

Horder, W. Garrett, *The Hymn Lover*. Curwen, 1889.
An excellent introduction to Christian hymnology.

Julian, John, ed. *A Dictionary of Hymnology*. Murray, 1908.
A comprehensive and invaluable book of reference.

Maitland, J. A. Fuller, ed., *Grove's Dictionary of Music and Musicians*.
Theodore Presser Co.
A famous work in four volumes. 1940 edition by H. C. Colles.

McCutchan, Robert G., *Hymns in the Lives of Men*.
Abingdon-Cokesbury, 1945.
An interesting study of the influence of hymns.

Phillips, Charles S., *Hymnody Past and Present*. S.P.C.K., 1937.
Scholarly. Deals largely with hymnody of the Church of England.

Robinson, Charles S., *Annotations upon Popular Hymns*. Hunt, 1893.
Comments on hymns contained in *Laudes Domine*.

Ryden, Ernest Edwin, *The Story of Our Hymns*.
Augustana Book Concern, 1930.
Popular in style. Part III deals with Scandinavian hymnody. The author is a Lutheran hymnologist.

Schaff, Philip, *Literature and Poetry*. Scribner, 1890.
Contains an informative chapter on St. Bernard as a hymnist.

PRINCIPAL WORKS CONSULTED

English Hymnody

Benson, Louis F., *The English Hymn.*   Doran, 1915.
> Best source of information on the development and use of standard English and American hymns. Scholarly. Unfortunately out of print.

Brawley, Benjamin, *History of the English Hymn.*
       Abingdon Press, 1932.
> Popular in style.

Duffield, Samuel Willoughby, *English Hymns.*
       Funk and Wagnalls, 1886.
> An old standard work giving the origin of hymns to the middle of the 19th century.

Marks, Harvey B., *The Rise and Growth of English Hymnody.*
       Revell, 1937.
> An excellent account.

American Hymnody

Foote, Henry Wilder, *Three Centuries of American Hymnody.*
       Harvard University Press, 1940.
> An authoritative and readable account of American hymnody from the publication of the *Bay Psalm Book*, 1640, to the present day.

Ninde, Edward S., *The Story of the American Hymn.*
       Abingdon Press, 1921.
> Popular stories of hymns. Supplements the more scholarly work by Foote.

Stories of Hymns and Hymn Writers

Butterworth, Hezekiah, *The Story of the Hymns.*
       American Tract Society.
> Deals with nearly one hundred hymns, emphasizing those that resulted from unusual religious experiences.

Cope, Henry F., *One Hundred Hymns You Ought to Know.*
       New York, 1906.

Laufer, Calvin W., *Hymn Lore.*   Westminster Press, 1932.
> Comments on 50 hymns, mostly of American origin.

Price, Carl F., *One Hundred and One Hymn Stories.*   Abingdon.

——————, *More Hymn Stories.*   Abingdon, 1931.
> Popular but authoritative.

Smith, H. Augustine, *Lyric Religion.*   Century, 1931.
> Excellent account of 150 hymns with suggestions for their use at song services.

Stead, W. T., *Hymns That Have Helped.*   Doubleday, 1897.
> Brief notes on 150 popular hymns.

396

PRINCIPAL WORKS CONSULTED

The German Chorales

Bacon and Allen, *The Hymns of Martin Luther.*   London, 1884.
Luther's hymns set to their original melodies. Includes Luther's prefaces to successive hymn books published during his life time and under his supervision.

Collitz, Klara Hechtenberg, *Selections from Classical German Litera-ture.*   Oxford University Press, 1914.
Includes biographical notes.

Knapp, Albert, *Evangelische Liederschatz.*   Stuttgart, 1865.
More than 3,000 of the great hymns of Germany are included in this work, the most comprehensive hymn collection ever published in Germany. But Knapp took undue liberties in revising the hymns of some of the older writers.

Koch, Edward Emil, *Geschichte des Kirchenlied und Kirchengesengs.*
        Stuttgart, 1867.
A standard work.

Schultz, Walter, *Reichsänger.*   P. Ott, Gotha, 1930.
A popular account of hymns used in Germany, including translations from English sources. The author was a pastor in Marburg.

Wilson, A. W., *The Chorales.*   Faith Press, London, 1920.
A 78 page monograph by the then organist of Manchester Cathedral.

Winkworth, Catherine, *Christian Singers of Germany.* London, 1869.

—————————, *Lyria Germanica.*   London, 1881.
England's foremost translator of German chorales gives in these volumes a history of German hymnody and collections of her translations.

Wolff, Dr. Eugen, *Des Deutsche Kirchenlied des 16 und 17 Jahrh.*
        Stuttgart.
Detailed and scholarly account.

The Gospel Songs

Gabriel, Chas. H., *The Singers and Their Songs.*
        The Rodeheaver Co., 1915.

Hall, J. H., *Biography of Gospel Song and Hymn Writers.* Revell, 1914.

Rodeheaver, Homer A., *Hymnal Handbook for Standard Hymns and Gospel Songs.*   The Rodeheaver Co., 1931.

Sankey, Ira D., *My Life and the Story of the Gospel Hymns.*
        Harper and Brothers, 1907.

Showalter, A. J., *The Best Gospel Songs and Their Composers.*
        A. J. Showalter Co., 1904.

Stebbins, George C., *Reminiscences and Gospel Hymn Stories.*
        George H. Doran Co., 1924.

PRINCIPAL WORKS CONSULTED

Handbooks to Hymnals

Covert, W. C., and Laufer, C. W., *Handbook to the Hymnal.*
Presbyterian Board of Christian Education, 1935.
A Handbook to the current Presbyterian hynmal of 1931.

Dearmer, Percy, *Songs of Praise Discussed.*
Oxford University Press, 1933.
Based on Moffatt's *Handbook to the Church Hymnary.* A companion to the popular English collection, *Songs of Praise.*

Hymns Ancient and Modern, Historical Edition.   Clowes, 1909.
Hymns and music of the famous English hymnal, with an account of all the hymns and tunes.

Macmillan, Alexander, *Hymns of the Church.*
United Church Publishing House, Toronto, 1935.
A companion to the *Hymnary* of the United Church of Canada, constructed in the sequence of history.

McCutchan, Robert Guy, *Our Hymnody.*
Methodist Book Concern, 1937.
A manual to the Methodist hymnal. Scholarly and comprehensive.

Moffatt, James, and Patrick, Millar, *Handbook to the Church Hymnary*
with Supplement.   Oxford University Press, 1925.
A companion to the Scottish *Church Hymnary.* One of the best Handbooks published.

Polack, W. G., *Handbook to the Lutheran Hymnal.*
Concordia Publishing Co., 1942.

Practical Hymnology

Ashton, Joseph N., *Music in Worship.*   The Pilgrim Press, 1943.
A manual for ministers, organists, and choir directors.

Clokey, Joseph W., *In Every Corner Sing.*
Morehouse Gorham Co., 1945.
A small, practical book, written for amateurs and laymen, on music for the small church.

Harper, Earl, *Church Music and Worship.*   Abingdon Press.

Lorenz, E. S., *The Singing Church.*   Cokesbury, 1938.
Much practical material. The author makes about as good a case as can be made for the use of Gospel songs.

Pratt, Waldo S., *Musical Ministries of the Church.*   Revell, 1901.

Wolfe, Paul Austin; Dickinson, Helen A., and Clarence, *The Choir Loft and the Pulpit.*   H. W. Gray, 1943.
Includes Services of Worship and lists of choir and organ music used in the Brick Presbyterian Church, New York.

398

PRINCIPAL WORKS CONSULTED
Hymn Tunes and Composers

Dickinson, Edward, *Music in the History of the Western Church.*
Scribners, 1902.
A broad survey. Excellent chapters on Luther and Bach.

Douglas, Winfred, *Church Music in Theory and Practice.*
Scribners, 1937.
Emphasis on liturgical music, written from the point of view of an American Anglo-Catholic.

Lightwood, James T., *Hymn Tunes and Their Story.*
Epworth Press, London, 1923.
A good account of tunes up to the latter part of the 19th century.

Metcalf, Frank J., *Stories of Hymn Tunes.*   Abingdon Press, 1928.
A popular treatment.

Scholes, Percy A., *The Oxford Companion to Music.* 7th Ed. Revised.
Oxford University Press, 1947.
A one volume encyclopedia of music, for both the amateur and professional musician.

Mennonite Hymnody

Bender, H. S., *Two Centuries of American Mennonite Literature.*
Mennonite Historical Society, Goshen, Ind., 1929.
Lists books, hymnbooks, pamphlets, papers and magazines by all branches of Mennonites since the beginning of the 18th century.

Hohmann, Walter H., *Outlines in Hymnology with Emphasis on Mennonite Hymnology.*   Mennonite Publication Office, 1941.
The Outline, for the most part, follows Breed's *History and Use of Hymns and Hymn-Tunes.* Part II consists of a chronological list of Mennonite hymn books.

Mennonitisches Lexikon.   Frankfurt-am-Main und Weierhof.
A comprehensive work begun in 1913 by Hege and Neff, still unfinished.

Smith, C. H., *The Story of the Mennonites.*
Mennonite Book Concern, Berne, Ind., 1941.
By request of the author before his death in 1948, the work is being revised and brought up to date by Dr. C. Krahn.

Index of Scripture Texts

INDEX OF SCRIPTURE TEXTS

Topical Index of the Metrical Psalms

To facilitate the practical usefulness of the Psalms found in Book Five of the *Hymnary*, this brief subject index is given here. The numerals refer to the *number of the Psalm.*

Index of Composers and Sources of Tunes

COMPOSERS AND SOURCES OF TUNES

404

COMPOSERS AND SOURCES OF TUNES

COMPOSERS AND SOURCES OF TUNES

Index of Authors, Translators, and Sources

407

AUTHORS, TRANSLATORS, AND SOURCES

409

AUTHORS, TRANSLATORS, AND SOURCES

411

Index of Tunes

412

INDEX OF TUNES

413

INDEX OF TUNES

414

INDEX OF TUNES

INDEX OF TUNES

416

INDEX OF TUNES

Index of Original First Lines of Translations

ORIGINAL FIRST LINES

Index of First Lines

Capital letters indicate titles of hymns rather than first lines.

419

INDEX OF FIRST LINES

420

INDEX OF FIRST LINES

421

INDEX OF FIRST LINES

422

INDEX OF FIRST LINES

423

INDEX OF FIRST LINES

INDEX OF FIRST LINES

DATE DUE

DATE DUE			
NOV 19 1995			
OCT 0 2 1998			